Cardozo

CARDOZO

Andrew L. Kaufman

HARVARD UNIVERSITY PRESS
Cambridge, Massachusetts
London, England

Copyright © 1998 by the President and Fellows of Harvard College

All rights reserved

Printed in the United States of America

Fifth printing, 2000

First Harvard University Press paperback edition, 2000

Library of Congress Cataloging-in-Publication Data

Kaufman, Andrew L.
   Cardozo / Andrew L. Kaufman.
     p. cm.
   Includes bibliographical references and index.
   ISBN 0-674-09645-2 (cloth)
   ISBN 0-674-00192-3 (pbk.)
   1. Cardozo, Benjamin N. (Benjamin Nathan), 1870–1938. 2. Judges—United
States—Biography. I. Title.
   KF8745.C3K38 1998
   347.73'2634
   [B]—DC21   97-29729

For Linda,
who has shared Cardozo with me these many years

Contents

Doing the Law's Work: 1914–1932

The Supreme Court: 1932–1938

Illustrations follow page 113.

Acknowledgments

This must surely be the last book that owes its beginning to Felix Frankfurter. He and Joseph Rauh, who was Benjamin Cardozo's last law clerk and Frankfurter's first, suggested in the winter of 1957 that I write this book. They gave me their personal Cardozo files as well as regular help and encouragement during their lifetimes. Joe Rauh also read substantial portions of the manuscript in draft. Michael H. Cardozo IV, first cousin twice removed of Benjamin Cardozo, who read most of the manuscript more than once, was a constant source of information, suggestions, and advice during the last fifteen years of the project. I owe Felix Frankfurter, Joe Rauh, and Mike Cardozo deep debts of gratitude. I hope that I have justified their faith.

From the Nathan side of Cardozo's family, I received valuable help from Rosalie Nathan Hendricks, Henry Hendricks, Emily Nathan, and Frederic Nathan. A great many other people assisted by providing their Cardozo correspondence and by giving me interviews. These people are identified in the endnotes to this volume, and I thank them all.

Samuel and Sylvia Kaufman, my parents, and John Kaufman, my brother, encouraged me to undertake the project; and Samuel and John, my law partners at the beginning of the work, made it possible for me to do numerous interviews of people who had known Cardozo.

The Harvard Law School has supported my work with research leaves, sabbaticals, and other forms of assistance for thirty years. Six deans, Erwin Griswold, A. James Casner, Derek Bok, Albert Sacks,

James Vorenberg, and Robert Clark, have helped in many ways. This is the appropriate time and place to record my gratitude to the Harvard Law School and a host of classmates, teachers, students, and colleagues on the faculty and staff who have been my friends since 1951. It has been my privilege to call the Harvard Law School a home since that date.

Any scholar who does research depends on the assistance of devoted librarians who maintain the collections that contain so much of legal history. There is not enough space to mention all the people and places that have contributed to this book, but I should mention the principal ones: the Rare Book and Manuscript Division of Butler Library, Columbia University, which houses the major Cardozo collection; the Columbia Oral History Project; the Manuscript Division of the Library of Congress; the Franklin Delano Roosevelt Library, Hyde Park, New York; the Federal Records Center, Saint Louis, Missouri; the library of the Association of the Bar of the City of New York, which most helpfully made available the briefs and records in cases from Cardozo's practice so that I could work on them in Cambridge; the New York Public Library; the Beinecke and Sterling libraries of Yale University; the American Jewish Archives, Cincinnati, Ohio; the American Jewish Historical Society and the Farber Library of Brandeis University, both in Waltham, Massachusetts; the Barnard College Library; the Herbert Hoover Library, West Branch, Iowa; and Shearith Israel, the Spanish and Portuguese Synagogue, New York, and Susan Tobin, its archivist.

I made endless use of the facilities of various Harvard University libraries—the Schlesinger Library, Widener and Lamont Libraries, and especially the Harvard Law School Library. Erika Chadbourne, Judith Mellins, Morris Cohen, Margaret Moody, Terry Martin, David Warrington, David de Lorenzo, and the entire Special Collections and Reference staffs provided me with an endless flow of materials over many years. Naomi Ronen, senior reference librarian, has been my liaison with the library, and a good friend. She read and commented on a substantial part of the manuscript. I should also acknowledge the special help of Milton Halsey Thomas, curator of the Columbiana Collection at Columbia, where its Cardozo Collection was initially stored. He personally guided me through the materials at the outset of the project and made copies of much of them for my use. The Lexis Division of Elsevier, Inc., provided me with Lexis-Nexis service; it was invaluable in my research.

The New York Court of Appeals gave me access to its collection of confidential reports written by Cardozo to his colleagues. I am grateful to Chief Judge Sol Wachtler, who supported my request in 1990, and to Chief Judge Judith Kaye, who gave me the Court's approval of my use of particular materials. Chief Judge Kaye, who is a member of Cardozo's synagogue and has herself given two lectures about the man and his contributions, read two different versions of the half of the book that makes use of the reports and gave me many useful suggestions. The New York State Archives processed the Cardozo reports so that I might use them, and I am grateful for the personal attention given by James Folts, Head of Research Services, and William Evans.

I have presented portions of this book at workshops at the Harvard Law School, Northeastern University, and the University of Texas, and in lectures at Boston University and before the American Society for Legal History, the Supreme Court Historical Society, and the Jewish Historical Society of Greater Washington. The comments of participants in these events have improved the book.

Many Harvard Law School students helped me during the course of my work. I would not have had the help of any of them if Alan S. Schwartz, '68, had not persuaded me by word and deed that research assistants could give me significant assistance. He was followed, chronologically, by David Berman, Martin Redish, Richard Perlman, Stanley Parzen, Jay Henderson, John Wellington, Lauren Sandler Zurier, Robert Kravitz, William Weinreb, Mark Burnette, Susan Spotts, Gail Levine, and Harry Sandick. I am grateful to all of them for the valuable research and editing tasks that they performed and for their friendship. At the outset of her own career in teaching and scholarship, Mary Bilder, '90, gave a thorough critique of several chapters that was very helpful.

Matthew Seccombe walked into my office in May 1994. A teacher, biographer, and freelance editor, he offered to be my editor. The smartest decision that I made in writing this book was to accept his offer. He made me work harder than I ever had in my whole professional career. His excellent suggestions on everything from content to structure to style turned a group of loosely connected essays into a book. He is responsible for the strength but not the failings of this book.

Aïda Donald, Assistant Director and Editor-in-Chief of the Harvard University Press, has shepherded this book to publication. She read many early drafts and gave me needed encouragement for many long years. Thank you, Aïda. My thanks also to Elizabeth Suttell and Donna Bouvier of the Press for their care in producing the book and to Carolyn Ingalls for expert copyediting.

Several other people read portions of my manuscript, and their suggestions have helped me enormously. They include Judges Richard Posner, Michael Boudin, and Robert Keeton; my colleagues Clark Byse, Charles Donahue, William (Terry) Fisher, Randall Kennedy, and Todd Rakoff; and Aviam Soifer, Zipporah Wiseman, Jay Westbrook, Gary Schwartz, and Nancy Cott. Alan Stone, who several times read the materials dealing with Cardozo's relations with his family, gave me thoughtful suggestions. I have benefited from the advice and friendship of my colleague Bernard Wolfman in so many matters that this seems the appropriate place to acknowledge him. Anne Kaufman, a scholar in her own right, read much of this manuscript critically, and Linda Kaufman did research with me at the beginning, footnotes at the end, and reading in between.

A succession of assistants contributed to the preparation of this book over the years. Sally Littleton was the first, long before the days of the word processor. Virginia Severn and Laurie Raine followed, and then for many years, Kathleen Harrison Eramo typed and retyped successive drafts. Nancy McHose, Mary de Bever, and Joe Guberman computerized the manuscript, and Joe Guberman also commented helpfully on parts of it. Melinda Eakin assisted at the end and then expertly proofread the entire manuscript. Marco Castilla, LL.M. '95, and Cyrus Daftary of Lexis made a last-minute research project possible. Susan Salvato, Co-ordinator of the Word Processing Center at Harvard Law School, and Cheryl Frost produced the final manuscript and parts along the way. Susan Salvato and Ruth Block, Director of Computer and Audio-Visual Services, provided computing advice and rescued me many times when computers crashed or when I destroyed current files. I am indebted to them all.

This is a welcome opportunity to acknowledge my intellectual debt to three teachers who taught me how to think historically and analytically. Professors Myron Gilmore and Oscar Handlin at Harvard College and Professor Benjamin Kaplan at Harvard Law School changed my life, and I have tried hard to live up to their example.

My wife, Linda; my children, Anne, David, and Daniel; my son-in-law, Robert Scott; and my daughter-in-law, Carol Millard, have contributed more than they know to this project. They have made a wonderful place for me in their lives, and their support was essential for the completion of the book. Finally, I want to salute my granddaughter, Sophie Scott Kaufman, who has arrived just in time to get her name in print.

Beginnings: 1870–1891

1

Cardozo's Heritage: The Sephardim and Tammany Hall

Benjamin Nathan Cardozo lived for the law, and the law made him famous. He earned his fame both by his influential judicial opinions and by his lectures and books, which explained the work of judges and defended a creative lawmaking role for them. He enhanced his fame with a memorable literary style and a personal kindness, courtesy, and gentleness that led many to describe him in later life as a saint. Cardozo was no saint, though, for his life included the toughness of his many years as an ambitious lawyer, and his character contained such human failings as vanity and prejudice; however, he was a good man with extraordinary talents. He became one of the most distinguished judges in the history of American law.

Cardozo's life spanned a period of great change in American history. He was born in 1870, just after the Civil War, and died in 1938, near the end of the New Deal. His family, the Cardozos and the Nathans, were rooted in New York's old Sephardic Jewish community, and he took pride in the fact that his ancestors had arrived in America before the Revolution. Cardozo's father had disgraced the family, however, when he engaged in conduct that forced his resignation amid charges of judicial corruption. In the course of time, Benjamin Cardozo's achievements would help redeem the family name. His relationship with his older sister Nellie provided him with support and warmth as she helped raise him in his early years, as they later presided together over their family and their home, and finally as he took care of her during her last, long illness. These experiences helped contribute to his strong personal values of duty, honor, and individual responsibility that were often evident in his judicial opinions. Cardozo's family life and loyalty to his Sephardic heritage also reflected a moral and social conservatism that balanced his progressive, modernizing instincts.

Cardozo was well bred, well educated, and elaborately courteous, and over time he revealed qualities of devotion and serenity. But he was also a self-confident, ambitious, and tough-minded man who looked out for himself and those he loved in a conscientious pursuit of success. For twenty-three years he was a first-rate practitioner in the trial and appellate courts of New York. His skill and his ties in the Sephardic community attracted the notice of influential people who referred cases to him and then helped advance his judicial career at every stage. Cardozo observed the conventions of judicial politics; he did not actively seek the positions that he attained, but he allowed his friends and supporters to work for him.

Cardozo earned a national reputation as an outstanding judge within a few years of his promotion to the New York Court of Appeals in 1914. During the twin eras of progressivism in politics and legal realism in jurisprudence, Cardozo supported the modernization of the law, approved many forms of legislative and executive activism, and practiced and advocated the role of the judge as a creative lawmaker. He did so not only eloquently and persuasively, but also carefully. Cardozo's eighteen years on the New York bench won him a national reputation as an outstanding judge, second only to that of Oliver Wendell Holmes among American judges; and when Holmes retired in 1932, Cardozo succeeded to Holmes's place on the United States Supreme Court. Cardozo spent the last six years of his life arguing out the constitutional issues that divided the country, and finally he became part of the majority that reshaped American constitutional law and set the Supreme Court on the doctrinal path that it has followed ever since.

Cardozo's importance lies in the impact of his judicial opinions and writings in a critical period in American law. During Cardozo's tenure as a judge, the central innovative forces in lawmaking were legislative and, to a lesser degree, executive; but the courts too responded to great changes in society, sometimes negatively. At the end of the nineteenth century an influential method of legal thought called *legal formalism* concealed or even denied the creative role of judges. Cardozo, following Holmes and Roscoe Pound, helped combat that doctrine. As a judge, he reshaped rules in many areas of private and public law, such as refining many elements of negligence law and expanding the boundaries of government's power to regulate the economy in constitutional law. At the same time, in his extrajudicial work of lecturing and writing, he explained and defended judicial lawmaking.

The progressive side of Cardozo's work is well known, but there was also a cautious side to his work as judge and theorist. Cardozo was no revolutionary. What he described was a version of what English and American judges had done for centuries, reaffirmed and adapted for modern use. He believed that the major role in guiding social change in a democracy belonged to the legislature and the executive. Thus, he innovated the most when the step to be taken was modest and when the innovation did not violate the prerogatives of other institutions of government—and ideally when the legislative or executive branch had already pointed the way. Although Cardozo often adapted law to new social conditions, he also often declined to make such adaptations. Fairness was important to him, but he did not believe that judges could simply do whatever they thought was fair or just. Cardozo believed that he had to respect precedent, history, and the powers of other branches of government. He believed that judging involved taking all of those factors into account, methodically and impartially. The example that he set as a common law judge was another element of Cardozo's importance.

Cardozo presented his views to the profession and the public in a powerful and wide-ranging fashion. Even though he led a sheltered personal life, he was adventurous in the world of ideas. From his college years to his death he read widely, and he shared his learning as he tried to educate the legal profession and the public about the role of judges. His theories of judging, like his substantive decisions and his methods of decision-making, were often finely balanced, carefully limited, and subtle. Those theories fused and accommodated contending schools of thought. Cardozo's style, reflecting his personality and education, was elegant but, to modern ears, ambiguous. All these elements have made many of Cardozo's opinions a staple of legal education and a continuing influence in judges' work even sixty years after his death. Cardozo helped to modernize the law and to provide a structure for other judges to modernize it further; he illuminated the tradition and craft of judging; and he practiced that vocation supremely well.

The family into which Benjamin Nathan Cardozo was born on May 24, 1870, was part of a distinct and well-established Jewish community in New York City. It was a Sephardic family, descended from those Jews who had fled from the Iberian peninsula during the Inquisition and had come to America via the Netherlands and England. Both branches of the family (the Cardozos and the Nathans) had arrived in the American colonies before the American Revolution. Albert Cardozo, Benjamin's father, was at the height of his legal career. The family was well-to-do, lived in a fashionable neighborhood just off Fifth Avenue, and had links with the political and mercantile powers of the city. Albert had been a judge for six years, the last two as a Justice of the Supreme Court of New York County, but trouble was brewing in his career. In addition, because Rebecca Nathan Cardozo, Benjamin's mother, had been in delicate mental health for several years, her condition was a matter of considerable concern within the family. Each of these elements—the Sephardic community, the prominent but tainted career of his father, and family duties—would play important roles in the life of Benjamin Cardozo.

Cardozo family tradition holds that their ancestors were Portuguese Marranos—Jews who practiced Judaism secretly after forced conversion to Christianity—who fled the Inquisition in the seventeenth century. They took refuge first in Holland and then in London.[1] Later, members of the family emigrated to the New World. Aaron Cardozo was the first Cardozo to settle in the American colonies, arriving in New York from London in 1752. He lived in Wilton, Connecticut, during the Revolution and later resided in Richmond, Virginia.[2] He married Sarah Nunez, his double first cousin.[3] In the small Sephardic community, marriage of close relations was common.

Two of Aaron and Sarah Cardozo's six children, David and Isaac, lived in Charleston, South Carolina, where there was an active Jewish community.[4] They both served in the Revolutionary War, David as a soldier who participated in the defense of Charleston, Isaac as a seaman. David Cardozo remained in Charleston after the Revolution, where he was a schoolteacher, a lumber measurer, and a prominent member of Congregation Beth Elohim. David's son, Jacob Nunez Cardozo, who later called himself Jacob Newton Cardozo, was well known as a political economist and statistician, an editor and later owner of an influential newspaper, *The Southern Patriot,* and a leading exponent of free trade and an opponent of nullification. Jacob's brother, Isaac, was a weigher in the Charleston customs house and a vice president of the Reformed Society of Israelites. One of the two brothers, apparently Isaac, cohabited with Lydia Williams, a free woman of African American and Native American descent. Their three children are ancestors of the well-known African American branch of the Cardozo family.[5]

The Isaac Cardozo who was Aaron Cardozo's son left Charleston after the Revolutionary War and lived in Philadelphia for a while, where he helped found the Philadelphia Congregation. He married Sarah Hart, also a Sephardic Jew, whose family was among the founders of Easton, Pennsylvania. One of their children, Michael Hart Cardozo, was working in a shoe and clothing store in Richmond, Virginia, in 1819 when he married his first cousin, Ellen Hart.[6] Michael and Ellen Cardozo lived in Richmond for several years and then moved to Philadelphia, where Albert Cardozo, their fourth child and the father of Benjamin Cardozo, was born in 1828. Shortly after Albert's birth, the family moved to New York City and joined the oldest community of American Jews in the colonies.

In the nineteenth century, many Sephardic Jews considered themselves the elite of American Jewry.[7] The Cardozo and Nathan families, which had arrived in the middle of the eighteenth century, shared this sense of superiority. Benjamin Cardozo, a fourth-generation member of this proud community, was influenced by its heritage all his life.

The Sephardic Jews had established their first permanent community in the New World in New York in the seventeenth century. A group of twenty-three refugees from Brazil arrived in New Amsterdam in 1654 after the Portuguese capture of Bahia from the Dutch. This first community of Jews in New York City grew, and in the last years of Dutch rule and the early years of English rule in New York, the community won freedom of religious worship. At first, the members held religious services in their homes; later, in 1730, their congregation, Shearith Israel, to which Cardozo belonged, built their first synagogue. Although its traditions and services remained Spanish-Portuguese Sephardic, Shearith Israel admitted Jews of other backgrounds as members. By the early years of the nineteenth century, the influx of the other main body of Jewish practice, the Ashkenazim, from Central and Northern Europe, transformed the congregation from a Sephardic to a heavily Ashkenazic majority; however, the ritual and Sephardic traditions remained unchanged.[8]

Thus, in the mid-nineteenth century, when all of the other Jewish congregations were quite young, Congregation Shearith Israel was celebrating two hundred years of existence. Whereas the other congregations were composed largely of newcomers to the United States, most of the families of Shearith Israel had deeper roots in the city. Many of the family members had built business and civic relations with the Protestant leaders who controlled the political, social, and economic life of the city. Colonial Jews had entered the trading life of the country in substantial numbers, and many of them became important in business and amassed substantial fortunes.[9] Close family ties were reinforced by intermarriage within the community. Thus, when the numbers of Jews began to swell in the 1830s, 1840s, and 1850s with increased immigration from Western Europe and especially when huge numbers of people came at the end of the century from Eastern and Central Europe, there existed in New York City a small, closely connected group of older Jewish families, many of whom had achieved economic success and even some cultural and political influence.[10] Emma Lazarus, author of the famous poem of welcome to newcomers inscribed on the pedestal of the Statue of Liberty, was one of Benjamin Cardozo's many first cousins. Small wonder that a feeling of pride and achievement existed within the older group and that many felt superior to the struggling newcomers.

That family feeling was evident years later as Maud Nathan, another of Benjamin Cardozo's first cousins, gave a revealing explanation of her resentment about the exclusion of Jews from the Grand Union Hotel in Saratoga in the 1880s: "Proprietors of fashionable resort hotels and of New York apartment houses frankly advertise that they exclude all Jewish patrons, using no discernment between Jewish families who have had generations of culture and refinement and those who lack such a background."[11] Her sister, Annie Nathan Meyer, one of the founders of Barnard College, expressed the same point of view somewhat differently:

We are all Sephardim which is defined in the Jewish Encyclopaedia as those whose "many sufferings, which they had endured for the sake of their faith, had made them more than usually self-conscious; they considered themselves a superior class—the nobility of Jewry." Looking back on it, it seems to me that this intense pride, accompanied by a strong sense of *noblesse oblige* among the Sephardim was the nearest approach to royalty in the United States. The Nathan family possessed this distinguishing trait to a high degree. *Noblesse oblige* is certainly not a bad slogan to live by.[12]

Although Mrs. Meyer was progressive and egalitarian in many respects, she still considered herself as *noblesse*. As we shall see later, there were traces of that attitude in Benjamin Cardozo as well.

———

If the name Cardozo today means Benjamin Cardozo and if it stands for a distinguished model of judging, in the nineteenth century the name Cardozo meant Albert Cardozo, and it stood for the corrupting effect of politics on law. Albert Cardozo's career was thus a chapter in American political history, as well as a chapter in the life of his son Benjamin.

Albert was educated in the New York City public school system. Having decided to become a lawyer, he eventually went to work in the law office of Archibald Hilton. Hilton had a reputation as a fine lawyer, and Albert, known for his hard work and ambition, must have learned much from him. Albert was admitted to the bar in 1849 and apparently declined an opportunity to work in the city government early in his career, devoting himself to building up a "good business as a lawyer" and a "reputation as a skillful politician."[13] He appears to have practiced law with Hilton until the latter's death in 1854. Until this time, Albert had also lived in his parents' home. Then on August 16, 1854, he married Rebecca Washington Nathan, daughter of Seixas and Sara Seixas Nathan, and the couple moved to a house of their own at 23 West 27th Street.[14]

The Nathans were a well-to-do and prominent Sephardic family. Simon Nathan, the first American representative of the family, had come to New York from England between 1746 and 1750. He moved to Philadelphia during the American Revolution and established himself quickly in a "handsome genteel House, Garden and Stables in Arch Street known by the name of Rock Hall."[15] Following the Revolution, he returned to New York, describing himself as a merchant, and served as parnas (president) of Shearith Israel.[16] Simon married Grace Seixas, a member of another prominent Sephardic family.[17] One of Grace's brothers, Gershom, was hazzan (cantor-reader of the service) of Shearith Israel at the time of the Revolution and for a generation thereafter.

Gershom was also the first Jewish trustee of Columbia College and was the last Jew to serve in that position until Benjamin Cardozo.[18] Seixas Nathan, son of Grace and Simon and father of Rebecca Nathan Cardozo, was a member of the original board of the New York Stock Exchange in 1820, an inspector of customs at the Customs House in 1849, and a president of Shearith Israel.[19]

Seixas and Sara Seixas Nathan had fifteen children, all but one of whom survived to adulthood. Rebecca, Albert Cardozo's wife, was born in the middle of this large brood. Many of her brothers and sisters were prominent in the professional and religious life of the Sephardic community in New York City. Her oldest sister, Grace, was married to Jacques Judah Lyons, for thirty-eight years hazzan of Shearith Israel.[20] Her oldest brother, Jonathan, began his legal career in one of the leading law offices in the city, Strong & Griffin, where he was "a favorite law student" of George Washington Strong. Jonathan practiced law for many years; and he too was a president of Shearith Israel.[21]

Rebecca Nathan's next oldest brother, Benjamin, was a well-known figure in New York. Initially an importer, he was later a broker, vice president of the New York Stock Exchange, and, at the time when Albert Cardozo was courting his sister, president of Shearith Israel. Benjamin was also active in Jewish social and philanthropic organizations.[22] Some of the other brothers were also brokers, and one was a bookseller.[23] The city and the Jewish community were still small enough, and the leading Sephardic families had been in the country long enough, for considerable interaction between prominent Jews and non-Jews.[24] Although the Sephardic Jewish community was not part of the socially exclusive "Old New York" that is so well characterized in Edith Wharton's *Age of Innocence*, it nevertheless had numerous connections with members of that group.[25]

Albert Cardozo's alliance with the Nathan family helped bring him into prominence. Benjamin Nathan was an incorporator and secretary of the new Jews' Hospital, now called Mt. Sinai. That participation doubtless accounted for the invitation to Cardozo to speak briefly at the dinner prior to the hospital's dedication a year after his marriage to Nathan's sister.[26]

Two children were born in the first two years of Albert and Rebecca's marriage, but they were either stillborn or died almost immediately after birth. Thereafter, they had three children in less than three years: Albert, Jr., born in 1857, Ellen in 1859, and Grace in 1860.[27] Cardozo's career prospered in the years following his marriage; thus, in 1861 he moved his growing family to a large brownstone house in a fashionable new neighborhood at 12 West 47th Street, just off Fifth Avenue.[28] Six years later, a fourth child, Elizabeth, was born. She had a severe spinal problem and within the family became known as Albert's "special pet."[29]

As Albert Cardozo's legal practice grew, he embarked on a political career in the 1850s.[30] In this undertaking he followed the example of many members of Shearith Israel who took an active role in politics, including leadership positions in Tammany Hall, which was the major force in the Democratic Party in New York City.[31] In the early 1860s, Mayor Fernando Wood, one of the first of the big city machine politicians, fought for control of the local Democratic Party. His organization was known as Mozart Hall, and his major antagonist was the rising political star and chairman of the Board of Supervisors, William Marcy ("Boss") Tweed, who had gained control of Tammany Hall. Originally allied with the Wood partisans, Albert Cardozo joined Tammany Hall and managed to keep a foot in each camp. Consequently, he was in a good position when Tammany Hall and Mozart Hall cooperated in the face of attacks from Republicans during the Civil War.

When the two groups allocated the various nominations in the local elections in 1863, Cardozo was an acceptable choice to both factions, so that they agreed to nominate him for a Court of Common Pleas judgeship. That was an important position, for the Court of Common Pleas conducted trials and heard appeals and was the highest New York City court.[32] The *New York Leader,* a newspaper allied with Tammany Hall, commented, "Albert Cardozo is one of *the* rising men of New York. He is a well read lawyer, and one of the workers in his profession. He is peculiarly gifted as a speaker. His speeches are marked by conciseness of language, closeness of reasoning and practical good sense. He will shine especially at *nisi prius* [the trial level]. He is withal a gentleman of cultivation and elevated social relations."[33] In the November balloting, Albert Cardozo was elected to the Court of Common Pleas over the incumbent, Judge Henry Hilton, brother of his former mentor, Archibald Hilton. He took his seat the following January.

A political man, Albert Cardozo did not put politics behind him when he went on the bench. One example was his handling of a "blue law" case early in his judicial career. In 1866 the state legislature, over the opposition of most Democrats, passed a statute prohibiting the sale of liquor after midnight and on Sundays. In a test case, Holt v. Commissioners of Excise, Cardozo held the statute unconstitutional as a violation of both the Due Process Clause of the New York Constitution and the Contract Clause of the United States Constitution because one provision required old license holders to apply for new licenses at higher fees before the old licenses had expired. Cardozo then held, without discussion, that the effect of that holding was to render the whole act void.[34]

When his fellow judges suggested a procedure for speedy review by a special session of the General Term[35] so that this important public question could be presented to the Court of Appeals, Judge Cardozo reacted strongly. He wrote a long, heated letter objecting to a special session and defending his decision: "I have announced the law, as I believe it to be and while I do not doubt that any other conclusion would have been my political death, I know my own firmness sufficiently to assert that if I had had different convictions of the law, I should have boldly declared them." The liquor law and the judges who had upheld it, he continued, "will assuredly ultimately meet the condemnation which they deserve at the hands of the people, to who[m] I shall also make an appeal in due time."[36] Although Cardozo claimed that political factors did not determine his decision, he was remarkably frank in asserting the appropriateness of keeping the political context of a case in mind when deciding how to cast his judicial vote. For Albert Cardozo, judicial decision-making was part of the democratic political process, subject to approval or condemnation by the electorate. As a judge, he not only followed the election returns but also anticipated them.[37]

Despite Cardozo's conduct in the Excise Law case, there was little public comment about the effect of his political connections on his judicial decisions while he was a member of the Court of Common Pleas.[38] Even his performance in naturalizing an enormous number of new citizens, and hence new voters, before the election of 1866—up to 800 per day—did not attract much notice.[39]

In 1867, the term of a justice of the Supreme Court in the First Department (comprising Manhattan and a small portion of the Bronx) expired. The Supreme Court was the principal trial court in the state and, professionally, a step up from the Court of Common Pleas. Cardozo, who again allied himself with both Boss Tweed and Fernando Wood, secured support from all factions of the Democratic Party in place of the incumbent.[40] In his nominating remarks, Fernando Wood reportedly made quite explicit the necessity of selecting a judge who would decide cases according to correct political principles: "Judges were often called on to decide on political questions, and he was sorry to say the majority of them decided according to their political bias. It was therefore absolutely necessary to look to their candidate's political principles. He would nominate as a fit man for office of Judge of the Supreme Court, Albert Cardozo."[41]

Cardozo's candidacy produced an unusual statement of editorial support from the *World*. It used its formal endorsement of Cardozo to comment on the relationship among judges, the law, and public policy. Moreover, the *World* noted the growing public participation in politics and asserted that the most delicate and difficult task of judges was "the adjusting of old principles to new cases, presented by the rapid transition of the business of men." Although the editorial referred to Cardozo's ability and conscientiousness, it especially emphasized his facility for expressing the popular will by transforming outmoded precepts into new principles of law. The editorial presented a more thoughtful defense of popular election of judges than was usually seen at the time. In an era when even lawyers and judges did not always perceive clearly the role of judges in lawmaking, the *World* obviously understood that a judge was a lawmaker.[42]

On election day, Cardozo participated in the general Democratic sweep, rolling up a margin of fifty-seven thousand votes over his Republican opponent, with 76 percent of the vote.[43] In January 1868, Cardozo took his seat as Justice of the New York Supreme Court.

––––––––

Although Cardozo's performance on the Court of Common Pleas had not drawn a great deal of public notice, his activities on the Supreme Court led to an increasing volume of public criticism. First, there was the manner in which he conducted business. He occasionally heard matters in a room at the courthouse that he had had fitted for his own use: it could be opened from the outside only with a key and had special locks that permitted it to be locked from the inside.[44] Exactly what occurred in that room was a matter of conjecture, and many lawyers readily concluded that such a setting hid a host of irregularities.

Then there was the actual judicial performance itself. Early in his tenure on the Supreme Court, Cardozo came under fire for his handling of the Wood Lease case. This case involved a fraud suit brought by New York City against former Mayor Wood to set aside a lease of property from Wood to the city on the ground that Wood had procured it by fraud or bribery. Cardozo first rejected the city's proposed evidence because he found technical defects in the city's pleadings, and then he directed a verdict for Wood.[45]

Cardozo was also involved in many of the notorious cases in which some of the leading capitalists of the nineteenth century sought to use the courts to further their business schemes. He issued several controversial orders in the later stages of the struggle over the Erie Railroad between the forces of Jay Gould and Jim Fisk, who controlled the railroad and had put Boss Tweed on its board, and those of Commodore Cornelius Vanderbilt and the New York Central, who wanted to gain control. The contest became a public scandal after Charles Francis Adams described it in "A Chapter of Erie" in the *North American Review* in 1869.

The courts became heavily involved when the parties sought to enjoin one another from all sorts of activity relating to the Erie Railroad. There was a bewildering series of injunctions, stays, and counterinjunctions, and many receivers (court-appointed private parties who took custody of specific property) were named almost simultaneously by state and federal judges to take over Erie property. Although the Gould and Fisk forces had obtained most of their orders from Judge George Barnard, late in the struggle they turned to Judge Cardozo for judicial protection. He responded by issuing an order, even before his own term as sitting justice began, setting aside an order of the regular sitting justice in his own district.

In discussing the shift that Gould and Fisk made from Barnard to Cardozo, Adams made this assessment of Cardozo:

> The change spoke well for the discrimination of those who made it, for Judge Cardozo is a different man from Judge Barnard. Courteous but inflexible, subtle, clear headed, and unscrupulous, this magistrate conceals the iron hand beneath the silken glove. Equally versed in the laws of New York and in the mysteries of Tammany, he had earned his place by a partisan decision on the excise law, and was nominated for the bench by Mr. Fernando Wood . . . Nominated as a partisan, a partisan Cardozo has always been, when the occasion demanded.[46]

Adams's charge that Cardozo was unscrupulous was echoed within the bar as well.[47]

Cardozo's appointments of receivers and referees[48] formed the basis for one of the most serious criticisms leveled against him. Cardozo clearly used his appointing power for political and personal patronage purposes. The principal beneficiary of Albert Cardozo's favor was his wife's young nephew, Gratz Nathan. Out of 1,182 references made by Judge Cardozo in the years between 1868 and 1871, 407 were to Gratz Nathan. Cardozo also appointed Nathan a commissioner in lunacy hearings and in city actions to open up new streets. Nathan was often selected as counsel for other receivers appointed by Cardozo.[49] Cardozo also favored other family members and those closely associated with Tammany Hall.[50] Even though such favoritism was common practice in New York and elsewhere, it added to Cardozo's image as an unscrupulous and corrupt partisan.

Critics used his personal appearance to embellish attacks on his professional conduct. Albert Cardozo's appearance and demeanor were notable. His niece, Annie Nathan Meyer, described him as "tall and striking looking—great bushy eyebrows hung low over dark piercing eyes. There was in his lean, nervous face nothing of the repose or the kindliness of his son's [Benjamin]."[51] While commenting on Albert Cardozo's skill, self-possession, and calm, courteous manner, one writer then got carried away by apparent hatred, with a flavor of anti-Semitism: "His features had a slight Hebrew cast; his face was beardless and his complexion almost livid; he wore long, thick curly hair but his eye was his most marked feature. It was black, piercing, and ever alert. A bitter opponent once said that he had the eyes of a serpent looking from the face of a corpse."[52]

The year 1870 was an important one in the life of the Cardozo family. Albert Cardozo was at the height of his career. He received an honorary Doctor of Laws degree from Fordham.[53] On May 24, Rebecca Nathan Cardozo gave birth to twins, Benjamin Nathan and Emily Natalie Cardozo. Benjamin, however, had a difficult start; in his early days of life, he was reported to be in "feeble health."[54] The day after the twins were born, Albert Cardozo was the "orator of the day" at the laying of the cornerstone of a new building at Mt. Sinai Hospital.[55] His brother-in-law, Benjamin Nathan, was an incorporator and secretary of the hospital, and Nathan invited Governor Hoffman and Judge Cardozo to lunch at his home before the dedication.[56]

Shortly after Benjamin's birth, disaster struck the family. Benjamin Nathan, the uncle for whom Benjamin Nathan Cardozo was named, was savagely beaten to death one night in his newly built home on West 23rd Street. The murder created a sensation. It was featured on the front pages of New York newspapers; crowds filled the streets in front of the Nathan home for days; and Mayor Hall offered a reward for discovery of the murderer. Adding to the family distress, Washington Nathan, the victim's handsome and extravagant son, was first mentioned publicly as a suspect. Then, to establish an alibi, he had to admit that he had spent a large part of the evening on which the murder occurred with a lady in a neighborhood bordello. No one was ever prosecuted for the murder. The tragic death of a family leader, together with a whiff of scandal, cast a pall over the whole Nathan-Cardozo family.

At the same time, trouble loomed for Albert Cardozo. Some two hundred lawyers, responding to perceptions of judicial corruption, organized a reform movement. Secret meetings followed, and the result was the creation in 1870 of the Association of the Bar of the City of New York. The bar association began its reform efforts in April 1870 by attempting to persuade Governor John Hoffman to appoint judges from outside the city to the General Term of the Supreme Court that sat in New York City. Boss Tweed, however, persuaded Governor Hoffman to appoint Cardozo and his two New York City Supreme Court colleagues, George Barnard and Daniel Ingraham.[57] With this appointment to the General Term, Albert Cardozo's career reached its peak, but it also was to be the prelude to his fall.

Shortly thereafter, in the summer of 1870, the *New York Times* began a new crusade against the Tweed Ring. At the end of June, suspicion of graft was replaced by firm evidence when members of the Ring gave various city records to the *Times,* which began publishing them. The public clamor that followed resulted in a "nonpartisan" reform movement whose candidates were largely successful in the fall elections of 1871. Following the election, the Association of the Bar forwarded a report to the New York legislature outlining various abuses of power committed by unnamed judges in the city and requesting action. In response, the Judiciary Committee of the Assembly requested the Association to specify charges, and it did so with respect to Judges Cardozo, Barnard, and McCunn. Counsel for the Judiciary Committee and three members of the Association prosecuted the charges against all three judges before the full committee from February 19 through April 11, 1872.[58] The purpose was to enable the Judiciary Committee to decide whether to recommend that the Assembly prefer impeachment charges for trial by the Senate. Conviction would result in the removal of the judges from office.

At the hearings Cardozo faced five specific charges of misbehavior.[59] The first charge related to Cardozo's part in the aftermath of the Gold Conspiracy of 1869 when Jay Gould and James Fisk, having failed in their effort to corner the gold market, sought to employ the legal system to reduce their losses. The second charge involved unlawful release on habeas corpus of convicted clients of the law firm of Howe & Hummel. The third charge alleged that Cardozo failed to specify charges against two women whom he had imprisoned in an effort to force them to reveal the whereabouts of a child whose custody was at issue; the charge also alleged that he had prevented a lawyer from acting on the women's behalf. The fourth charge concerned his refusal to vacate an order that Judge Barnard had issued in a case that Barnard had not himself heard. Cardozo allegedly would not correct the obvious error because Barnard's order had denied alimony to the wife of State Senator Thomas C. Fields, an influential member of Tammany Hall. The fifth charge concerned both Cardozo's alleged nepotism respecting Gratz Nathan and his general political favoritism in the appointment of receivers and referees.

The evidence that was presented by the Bar Association is difficult to assess. Although the significance of some of the evidence was doubtless clear to lawyers familiar with events in New York at the time, now we can but guess at its relevance. Moreover, the committee received much testimony of uncertain reliability that would have been excluded in formal court proceedings. Finally, proof of most of the allegations required evidence that the judicial actions in question had been motivated by corruption rather than by honest misinterpretations of the law. Since there was no proof of bribery, the Bar Association needed to establish either that Cardozo had improper motives for particular decisions or at least that he must have known that there was no possible legal justification for a specific decision. The Bar Association's evidence was aimed at proving both conclusions, but it had a very difficult task.

The Gold Conspiracy charge was the principal focus of the testimony. Albert Cardozo was charged with having entered orders in a receivership proceeding against the Gold Exchange Bank without proof of the necessary facts and with the intent to benefit Jay Gould and James Fisk in violation of the rights of the bank.[60] Although the papers prepared in support of the receivership seem inadequate to support the claim of insolvency, and Cardozo's political connections with Gould and Fisk rendered his conduct suspicious, the Bar Association's evidence appears insufficient to prove guilt.[61] The next three charges leveled against Cardozo typically asserted that a particular order handed down by Cardozo lacked sufficient factual support or that it involved assertion of some rather far-reaching judicial power.[62] The suspected, but unproven, presence of political or personal considerations motivating Cardozo's actions gave bite to the charges. Without that suspicion, Cardozo's conduct would doubtless have been discussed privately among lawyers in the same manner in which they typically complain about the "incompetence" or "arbitrariness" of even the best judges, especially trial judges who have to make decisions without time to reflect on all the issues and alternatives. However, it would probably not have led to misconduct hearings.

The fifth charge, corruption in the appointment of referees, was the one for which the Association's lawyers produced substantial proof. Nepotism, especially in favor of Gratz Nathan, and other political patronage were clearly demonstrated. The evidence also showed that Gratz Nathan split with Albert Cardozo fees that he had received as a result of those appointments.[63] That charge alone would have justified impeachment and conviction.

After the hearings were completed, the committee's report to the legislature was remarkable for its brevity.[64] The report set forth the efforts that went into the inquiry and the procedures that the committee adopted, and then without discussing the evidence at all, it concluded that "the evidence adduced before them contains sufficient to make it proper that [Albert Cardozo] should be placed on trial before the court of impeachment." The committee therefore recommended that the Assembly adopt a resolution "That Albert Cardozo, a justice of the Supreme Court of this State, be, and he hereby is, impeached for mal and corrupt conduct in office, and for high crimes and misdemeanors."[65]

On May 1, 1872, the day that the report of the Committee on the Judiciary was to be presented to the legislature, Assemblyman David Hill read to the legislature a letter from Judge Cardozo resigning his judgeship. Noting that he had "accepted judicial office for the honor and distinction which it conferred, and at pecuniary loss in surrendering a lucrative practice at the Bar," Cardozo attacked the decision of the committee as partisan, but he stated that the proceedings had made it impossible for him to command the public confidence and freedom from suspicion demanded of a judge.[66]

Within the Cardozo-Nathan family the story was told that Albert Cardozo resigned at the urging of his wife, who had become paralytic and said that a trial "would kill her," and that he was "entirely vindicated" when at his death he was found to have left only "a very moderate fortune."[67] That hardly constitutes vindication. The Assembly voted to proceed against Justices Barnard and McCunn, and the Senate subsequently removed both men from office. There is no doubt that Cardozo would have been convicted as well.

After Cardozo's resignation, the Association of the Bar considered whether to take further steps to urge that he be disbarred.[68] His former colleague on the Court of Common Pleas, Judge Charles Daly, noted later that "Judge Brady, at his [Cardozo's] request, induced the Bar committee not to take any steps afterwards, so that he . . . might remain in the City, which he did, and practice his profession until his death."[69] In fact, Cardozo opened an office almost immediately, and he soon appeared in court as counsel for two defendants in a murder case before the Court of General Sessions.[70] But his disgrace had an immediate impact on the family's comfortable lifestyle, and they were forced to move from the large brownstone at 12 West 47th Street to less elegant quarters at 62 East 53rd Street and a year later to 212 West 44th Street.

Albert Cardozo's new law firm was the one that his son Benjamin would join seventeen years later. Albert's partner was Richard S. Newcombe, who also had Tammany connections. The *New York Times,* later commenting unfavorably on Newcombe's political aspirations, stated that he was "known as a 'smart' lawyer, who has no superior in the special field of legal practice to which he is devoted, except, possibly, it be his own partner, ex-Judge Cardozo." The firm's special field was insolvency practice, with some matrimonial law as well.[71] Albert also did some criminal work and had some poor clients, perhaps through his Tammany connections. Cardozo's friends at Tammany Hall did not forget him. In 1878, he was made a member of its General Committee, and later he became one of its sachems. Finally, in what appears to have marked a return to former comfort, the Cardozos moved in 1877 to a substantial home, still standing, at 803 Madison Avenue between 67th and 68th Streets, where they lived for many years next door to Albert Cardozo's partner, Richard Newcombe.[72] Cardozo continued to practice with Newcombe until his death in 1885.

The career of Albert Cardozo permits us a glimpse of the seamier side of the relationships between the legal profession and the new economic and political forces that were emerging in America. But what of Albert Cardozo himself? What was it that drew this hard-working family man into partisan and corrupt conduct on the bench? He was not a new immigrant struggling for survival. He came from a well-established family with deep roots in the country. He married into a family that was even richer and more prominent. His early professional career was promising, and he developed a feel for the nuances of New York City politics. However, his political ambitions and greed led him into trouble. By the end of his career, he had certainly mastered the political game, to his own benefit—and detriment.

The most striking feature of Albert Cardozo was the disparity between the conscientious, temple-going, family man and the public man, the partisan judge motivated by political considerations who took money beneath the table. He got caught up in, and then caught by, the colorful, corrupt world of New York City politics in the latter half of the nineteenth century. Albert Cardozo was a "good family man" who had a weakness in his public character.

The Sephardic community, family devotion, and hard work were also features in the life of Albert's son Benjamin. But the contrast in their professional careers was enormous. Politics was a major feature, and merit but a minor feature in Albert's advancement. The opposite was the case in Benjamin's rise to prominence. As a judge, he decided cases according to a well-considered judicial philosophy. His concept of public policy did not include personal or political favoritism. And there was never a whisper of scandal.

2

Young Cardozo

Benjamin Cardozo grew up in a period of family turbulence. Albert Cardozo resigned from the bench when Ben was two, and he struggled to put his life back together. Rebecca Cardozo, who was already forty-two when Ben and Emily were born, had been chronically ill for some time before their birth.[1] While Rebecca's parents had led busy social lives and her brother, Robert Weeks Nathan, entertained Van Rensselaers, Schuylers, and Remsens, "old" New York society, in his home,[2] Albert and Rebecca Cardozo led private and quiet lives even before Albert's resignation from the bench. They almost never went out in the evening, and Albert could invariably be found working in his library.[3] After he resigned from the bench, Albert persevered in his practice; and even though he did not succeed in restoring the family's good name, he did at least restore its financial security, so that the children grew up in well-to-do circumstances.

Rebecca's mental problems increased, however, and she spent some time in a sanitarium.[4] Later, she had a stroke and was paralyzed for several years before she died in 1879 from another stroke at the age of fifty-one.[5] Ben was only nine. After Rebecca's death and probably for several years before, a substantial amount of Ben's upbringing was left to his oldest sister, Ellen, and perhaps to governesses as well.[6]

Ellen, called Nell or Nellie, was eleven years older than Ben, but their relationship became so close that it occupied her whole life and a very substantial part of his. Grace, a year younger than Nellie, had artistic

21

ability and a caustic wit but was never mentioned as having taken much part in the upbringing of her younger siblings.[7] In the early years, Ben's constant companion was his twin sister, Emily. Their sister Elizabeth, only three years older and suffering from a spinal ailment, probably spent a good deal of time with them. Albert, Jr., "Allie," was nearly thirteen years older than Ben; indeed, by the time that Ben was nine, Allie had a degree from Columbia Law School and was practicing law.

Descriptions and pictures of Ben and Emily suggest a dark-haired, sensitive, shy Ben, or Master Ben, as he was occasionally called, and a voluble, cheerful Emily, who was merry, full of fun, and the "sweetest thing that ever breathed."[8] Another source of companionship was the larger Cardozo-Nathan family group. Ben later in life referred to the hundred first cousins whom he always had to invite to birthday parties, so that he never got to invite anyone else.[9] The number was something of an exaggeration, but family visiting, including the children, was a tradition, as were Sunday open houses featuring large turkey dinners.[10] Family visits contained their own formalities and strains. It was expected in the Cardozo-Nathan clan that, on meeting a relative, one inquired specifically after the health of every other member of the family. "Any deviation, any temporary forgetfulness," said Annie Nathan Meyer, "was set down as a deliberate slight, to be resented as such. In this respect, I am certain that my beloved cousin, Mr. Justice Cardozo, would never be caught napping."[11] Ben mastered the rules at an early age.

The Cardozo home on 47th Street was a favorite with his cousins because it had a "real playroom."[12] The family moved to less splendid quarters in 1873 when Ben was three, but the family visits continued. The atmosphere of the subsequent houses was quite different after Albert's disgrace and Rebecca's illness. Ben's first cousin Ernest, who was nine years younger and lived at 45 East 65th Street, three blocks from the Cardozos' Madison Avenue home, reported that in his family the Albert Cardozo house was known as "the morgue."[13] The Cardozos had a more social existence in their summer headquarters at Long Branch, New Jersey, where they had owned property since 1855. Long Branch had become fashionable after President Grant spent a summer there.[14]

Ben's early schooling remains a mystery. His father, Albert, had been educated in the city's public schools, but there is no firm evidence that Ben ever was. He himself later referred only to a private tutor.[15] Education at home was common in his family's circle,[16] and it is probable that Ben's earliest education was provided by his mother, if her health permitted, or perhaps by a governess. Ben also learned to play the piano, and his piano teacher suggested that he had sufficient talent to pursue music seriously.[17] One literary effort of his early years remains, a poem written by him in an ornate handwriting in his Aunt Adeline's album. Ben was not yet ten when he wrote the following stanzas, which he entitled "The Dream":

> As I slept t'other night in the old arm chair
> A little black spirit to me did appear
> And as he kept hovering over my head
> He spoke a few words and thus to me said
> Come arouse thee get up for by the bright sun
> I sware, you shall write in Ad's album
> There is no use in saying you haven't the time
> For I am here now and will help you to rhyme
> Then out of his pocket he drew forth a pen
> And handing it to me said Sir—now begin
> Seizing hold of the pen, for I never knew fear
> The Subject said he   Sir said I the New Year,
>
> Begin Sir—
>   Each coming year brings new delight
>   What now is that, twas Aunty said good night.
>
> Aunty I wish you had not said good night
> You have arroused me from a worlds delight
> Both spirits & dreams have flown away
> Perhaps to come some other day
> And when they do I promise truly then
> You shall heare more from
>   Master Ben[18]

Ben was raised in the life of Congregation Shearith Israel. Albert Cardozo was a vice-president and trustee of the congregation,[19] and his family followed the customs of the orthodox religious community, neglecting "no detail of ancient ritualistic custom as to prayers, to food, and to special observances of religious holidays."[20] When Albert Cardozo ascended the bench, he even consulted the beth din (the religious court) in London for advice about whether he could hold court on Saturday, as was the custom, in light of the requirement of proper observance of the Sabbath. The beth din advised him that state-required public duties took precedence over this requirement.[21]

We know but few of the details of Ben's religious training, although late in life he referred to "the old days when Passover was a great experience in my life."[22] It is probable that his upbringing was similar to that described by his first cousin Maud Nathan: "We always said our prayers at night at our mother's knee . . . partly in Hebrew and partly in English."[23] Children began going regularly to Sabbath services at Shearith Israel at the age of five. "We were brought up to keep the Sabbath day holy, according to the literal rendering of the Commandments. Therefore, we walked to and fro, in order that no horse should be compelled to work for us." In Shearith Israel, according to orthodox and Sephardic custom, men and boys sat in the main portion of the synagogue, and women and girls sat upstairs in the gallery. At the end of each service, the boys would be blessed by their fathers and by the rabbi (then sometimes called the preacher). Services in Ben's early years were conducted by Hazzan Lyons, who was the husband of Rebecca Cardozo's oldest sister, and thereafter by the rabbi, Dr. Pereira Mendes, who was a leading figure in Jewish religious life in the country.[24]

The congregation also had a religious school, where twice a week children "were taught the history and principles of our religion and were also taught to read Hebrew."[25] No records exist to show whether or not Ben went to the religious school, but he did receive the religious training necessary to prepare him for the Bar Mitzvah ceremony by which a boy, at the age of thirteen, becomes an adult in the eyes of the congregation. Whether in the school or as a result of private instruction, Ben received much of his early religious instruction from Dr. Mendes, and was bar mitzvahed at the Sabbath service on June 2, 1883, where he read the fifth section of the Torah portion for the day.[26] Thereafter, Ben's interest in temple-going waned. Shortly after his Bar Mitzvah, he ceased attending religious services, except those in connection with funerals.[27] Later in life, Cardozo often referred to himself in private correspondence as a "heathen."[28]

Cardozo's break with the practice of religion after his Bar Mitzvah was an early assertion of his individuality and independence. His father and his extended family were mainstays of Shearith Israel, which was a center of their social as well as their religious life. It could not have been an easy matter in that setting for the young Cardozo, still in his teens, to cease regular religious observance. He did so, but he kept his personal and public identity as a Sephardic Jew. He retained his membership at

Congregation Shearith Israel and later participated on rare occasions in congregational affairs.

A new and famous figure came into Ben Cardozo's life when he was thirteen, to tutor him for the entrance examination to Columbia College—Horatio Alger. Cardozo later recounted the basic fact of Alger's tutorship in his usual self-deprecatory fashion: "My education was the work of Horatio Alger. He did not do as successful a job for me as he did with the careers of his newsboy heroes."[29] Alger was a curious figure. He had graduated from Harvard College in 1852, where he was popular and had made lifelong friendships with men like the well-known lawyers Joseph Choate and Addison Brown. He spent his life trying to make his way in the literary world as a journalist, poet, and author of juvenile fiction, first writing the rags-to-riches stories for which he is well known, later turning to more sensational juvenile stories, and still later writing juvenile biographies of famous men. Throughout his whole life, Alger sought the friendship of boys and young men, both as a benefactor of homeless street boys who flocked to his lodgings and as a tutor to the children of the wealthy. He tutored the five sons of the banker Joseph Seligman, living in his house for several years. The Cardozos must have learned of Alger's abilities as a tutor from the Seligmans, their summer neighbors in Long Branch, New Jersey. They hired Alger to tutor Ben and Elizabeth many years after he had finished his employment with the Seligmans.[30]

One incident in Alger's life was not part of his public reputation. After trying to make a living as a teacher and professional writer, Alger had turned to the ministry and accepted a position in 1864 as a Unitarian minister in Brewster, on Cape Cod in Massachusetts. Fifteen months later, a committee of the congregation found that he had sexually abused several boys within the congregation. When confronted privately by the committee, Alger did not deny the charges and hastily departed.[31] The fact that Alger committed pedophilia at the age of thirty-four casts a shadow over his subsequent yearning for relationships with boys and young men, but there is no evidence of any later misconduct.[32]

Alger had two students in the Cardozo household: Ben, whom he was preparing for the entrance examination to Columbia, and Ben's older sister Elizabeth. Alger's course of study with Ben, whom he called "Bennie,"[33] may be surmised from the requirements of Columbia's entrance examinations: applicants for the freshman class were tested in "the

English, Latin, and Greek grammars; in Greek and Latin prosody, and in Greek, Latin and English composition; in ancient geography; in modern geography (Appleton's Higher Geography or equivalent); in ancient history (Rawlinson's Manual of Ancient History or equivalent); in arithmetic, including the metric system of weights and measures; in algebra, on the first five chapters of Peck's Manual of Algebra; in geometry, on the first four books of Davies' Legendre; and in the following books, or their equivalents, in the Latin and Greek languages, viz., five books of Caesar's Commentaries on the Gallic Wars; the Eclogues (entire) and the first six books of Virgil's Aeneid; six orations of Cicero; four books of Xenophon's Anabasis; and three books of Homer's Iliad."[34] Such training in classical culture formed the heart of the education of upper-class Americans throughout the nineteenth century.

Although he "was a lax disciplinarian and more diminutive than his charges" and thus was often the "butt of their boyish pranks,"[35] Alger was a good teacher. E. R. A. Seligman, a distinguished political economist who later taught Cardozo at Columbia, reported his own indebtedness to Alger "for a sense of good literature and a solid grounding in the classical languages."[36] Cardozo developed similar tastes and skills.

Cardozo finished his studies with Alger in the summer of 1884 at Long Branch. During that summer, the future Justice of the Supreme Court met the future Chief Justice, Charles Evans Hughes. Hughes had just finished Columbia Law School and was taking a vacation to restore his somewhat impaired health. Hughes later remembered the incident: "Two of the young ladies at the boarding house at which I was stopping at Long Branch asked me to escort them to a 'hop' at the West End Hotel. I did so, and while we were sitting on the veranda, up came Albert Cardozo, a friend of the young ladies, with his young brother Ben—then a shy lad of fourteen, in knickerbockers—and we spent a large part of the evening together."[37] Since Cardozo was soon to take the Columbia entrance examinations, their conversation was most probably about life at Columbia.

Cardozo took and passed the five-day entrance examinations and was admitted to Columbia. In February 1885, eight months before Ben began his studies there, the Cardozo family suffered a new blow. Ben's sister Grace contracted measles; a bout of pneumonia followed, and she died.[38] The following autumn, Ben began his college career. He was then fifteen, the earliest age at which he was eligible for entry, and the youngest in his class.[39] Ben had grown up in a family that had to deal with the problem of Albert Cardozo's disgrace and temporary financial difficulties, and he then had to endure the loss of his mother and a sister. He had the support that came from membership in the Sephardic community, the large extended Cardozo-Nathan family, an extroverted twin sister with whom he was close, and his older sister, Ellen, who devoted herself to him. He also had an extraordinary intelligence.

––––––––

The Columbia College that Benjamin Cardozo entered in 1885 had a very different student body and educational mission from the cosmopolitan college of today. It offered a classical education to its small, homogeneous student body, which was drawn largely from well-to-do New York families, many of them "old" New York families.[40] The entering class in the School of Arts, as the undergraduate portion of the college was called, numbered sixty-one, of whom only thirty-four eventually obtained degrees.[41] For Cardozo, Columbia was virtually a neighborhood school. He walked, or in bad weather rode a horsecar, the eighteen blocks from his Madison Avenue home to the College's location in the square block bounded by Madison and Fourth (now Park) Avenues, between 49th and 50th streets.

Cardozo was only two months into his freshman year when he interrupted his studies to mourn the death of his father. Albert Cardozo, who had suffered for several years from nephritis, a kidney disease, died of complications from the illness at the age of 56.[42] Later in life, fending off an inquiry from a friend about his father's career, Cardozo responded, "I was born in 1870 and I didn't know anything about what was happening to my father, but he was a fine Dad."[43] The newspaper reports of his father's death reminded Ben's teachers and classmates of the corruption associated with the name Cardozo and reinforced his natural shyness.

The one thing that Ben could do was to earn respect by his intelligence and hard work. He must have realized that he was going to have to make his own way in life and that he might also have to support his sisters in the future. For the moment, however, although Albert Cardozo did not leave his family a proud name, he did leave it well provided for. He left an estate of $100,000, consisting principally of the houses on Madison Avenue and in Long Branch, New Jersey, and a life insurance policy. He had an extensive law library, which he left to Albert, Jr., but Ben was to share it jointly if he became a lawyer. Albert requested his sons to look after their sisters' support.[44] The family continued to live in the Madison Avenue house, and Ben threw himself into his college studies.

Cardozo's freshman course work concentrated on the study of ancient languages. Six of a freshman's nine required first-term courses and four of the seven second-term requirements were in Latin and Greek grammar, prosody, and reading. The other requirements were geometry and algebra; German or French; and an English course consisting of grammar and analysis, the prose of Addison and Thackeray, and composition. The sophomore year followed the same general course of study, adding chemistry and German or French history depending on the language studied in the freshman year. Ten of the prescribed fifteen hours per week of courses in the junior year consisted of required work in Latin, English, history and political economy, and logic and philosophy, leaving room for elective studies amounting to one-third of the program. The curriculum of the senior year was entirely elective.[45]

Cardozo was an undergraduate during the last years of the tenure of President Frederick Barnard and the first years of his successor, Seth Low. Barnard was a man of considerable vision, although when Cardozo arrived, Barnard was in his late seventies and quite deaf. Shortly before Cardozo's arrival, Barnard incorporated modern languages into the undergraduate course of study; also, he introduced public law into the curriculum by bringing John W. Burgess, a distinguished teacher and scholar, from Amherst to teach political science and American and European constitutional history to both undergraduates and graduates.[46] After Barnard's retirement and death in 1888, the trustees and their new president, Seth Low, reorganized the university to raise standards and to make it more cohesive. Some of the changes directly affected Cardozo's education because he became a student both at the new School of Political Science and in the new graduate faculty of Philosophy.[47]

Professor Burgess had a low opinion of the undergraduate student body of Cardozo's day. Upon his arrival, he reported that "there were some men of intelligence among them and one or two earnest students, but almost all of them regarded their college attendance as a joke."[48] One student's view of Columbia between 1884 and 1893 revealed where many students' energies were directed: life at Columbia was characterized by "fights in street, campus, coat-room or corridor . . . Men were wont, after lectures, to gather in the coat-room, thence to pour forth a volume of College songs and Limericks that sent an echo through the whole Arts building. The studious quiet of the halls was often broken by cheers and class yells; in the coat-room groups of men might constantly be found matching nickels and quarters, and in more than one instance, the spirit of lawlessness invaded even the sacred precincts of the class-rooms."[49]

But that was only part of the story. Columbia also produced a number of thoroughly educated men.[50] Nicholas Murray Butler, a leading figure in American education as President of Columbia from 1902 to 1945, studied there from 1878 to 1882 under largely the same faculty that taught Cardozo.[51] Butler viewed the required education in classics in the first two years as being "almost wholly of that dry-as-dust type which has pretty nearly killed classical study in the United States." On the favorable side, Butler admired Burgess's lectures on the constitutional history of Europe and the United States: "He made the story of the development of political and social institutions so vivid and so real that it has never been even dimmed." Butler particularly remembered Burgess's emphasis on the importance of "the distinction between the sphere of government and the sphere of liberty." Summing up his student experience with a flourish, Butler listed "two priceless possessions" that he gained from his undergraduate years: "One was the constant companionship of ideas and ideals and the second was a profound respect for scholarship and for scientific method."[52] Intellectual excitement could indeed be found at Columbia in the 1880s.

———————

Cardozo found both intellectual challenge and excitement. Several hundred pages of lecture and reading notes survive from his years in college and graduate school. Among the papers are materials from courses in ethics, jurisprudence, history of philosophy, social science, English grammar, psychology, comparative constitutional law, political science and economy, and administrative law, as well as a fragment from his law school real estate lectures. The class notes, in addition to giving us a sense of how Columbia's professors taught this student, also give us some understanding of how Cardozo taught himself.[53]

Cardozo's notebooks are quite remarkable. Cardozo took down in his own speed-writing shorthand, virtually everything that each professor said. He then rewrote the notes after class.[54] In the process he transformed each professor's lectures into a book-length essay in what appear to be substantially the professor's own words, stringing the lectures together as he went. Cardozo took his education seriously. Transcription of lecture notes took time, and a student who took that time was likely to have kept up with class assignments on a daily basis as well. Cardozo was doubtless helped in this task by his prodigious, virtually photographic, memory, which his friends remarked on all his life.

Based on these lecture summaries, Cardozo's later observation that his education at Columbia was "superficial" was partially, but not entirely, true.[55] Many of Cardozo's classes were dull. A pattern for those classes emerges from his notes: each lecture topic consisted of a recitation of names, dates, and key ideas presented chronologically without much analysis, following which the teacher moved on to the next topic.

Professor Archibald Alexander's course in the history of Greek philosophy was representative. His lectures marched methodically through the various schools of thought and individual authors with little comparison of the historical periods or philosophical ideas. His discussion of pre-Socratic philosophy identified seven schools of thought, all preoccupied with the question, what is the principle of the universe? Alexander identified the major philosophers within each school and described the key ideas of the schools and their representatives, but never in great detail and not at all analytically.[56] He then moved on to the Sophist, or Socratic, period and repeated the same sort of plodding presentation. Alexander did not question why Greek society cared about the ideas being debated or whether they were still important; nor did he suggest ways of analyzing them. He wanted students to learn about the different schools of thought and their principal ideas. That was not a negligible goal; still, Alexander did not encourage the students to confront any of the issues for themselves.

Although the form of Nicholas Murray Butler's lectures on philosophy resembled those of Alexander, the content was substantially different. Cardozo's notes indicate that Butler's course was as detailed and thorough as a survey course could be and that it was taught by a man of substantial intellect. Butler began with Stoics, Epicureans, Skeptics, Jewish Alexandrians, Neo-Pythagoreans, and Neo-Platonists, and then covered one thousand years of thought from Patristic philosophy through Scholasticism, until he reached what he called the streams of modern philosophy descending from Bacon and Descartes. He contrasted Hobbes, Locke, Berkeley, and Hume first with Spinoza, Leibniz and Wolff, and then with Kant, Schelling, and Hegel, before concluding the course with a discussion of the Scottish School and James and John

Stuart Mill. Not only was Butler's presentation much more thorough than Alexander's, but it was also much more analytical, discussing and comparing ideas of various philosophers and even referring to contemporary political, social, and intellectual events.

For example, Butler used his discussion of Hume to challenge his students to think about causation, a difficult subject that Cardozo would address as a judge when he analyzed issues of liability. Butler taught that Hume "invalidate[d] entirely the doctrine of causation as involving a necessary connection between cause and effect," denying that "we can tell what the ultimate cause of things is." In fact, Butler argued at length, Hume reduced causation "to the position of an empirical inference, and had no certainty about that." Butler argued that the notion of causality was "best expressed in the philosophical axiom that every effect has a cause and, as a necessary corollary, that power necessary to produce the effect is inherent in the cause."[57] When Cardozo later wrote about causality in law, he would treat it as a practical issue: as a matter of policy, what relation between apparent "causes" and their effects was sufficient to justify imposition of liability? Cardozo had to be pragmatic rather than abstract in order to decide cases, but he was philosophical in the way in which he acknowledged uncertainty and recognized that he was making inferences on the basis of experience.

The focus of Cardozo's subsequent ethics course with Butler was substantive, not historical, and addressed three questions: "1st, is there any . . . law [of ethics]? 2nd, in what does it consist, if it exists? 3rd, on what does it rest? What is the principle or basis of that which we call moral obligation?"[58] Butler's teaching of ethics was prescriptive as well as descriptive. He asserted the importance of duty and obligation as he led students to apply the materials of his History of Philosophy course to the solution of the questions that he posed in his Ethics course. He encouraged students to think theoretically and to apply a body of learning to the resolution of an issue. Butler's educational goals were important contributions to Cardozo's education. Butler's emphasis on duty was a value that Cardozo would also stress in his judicial thinking and his personal life.

Another renowned teacher was John W. Burgess. Cardozo's notes from Burgess's course in Political Science and Comparative Constitutional Law indicate that Burgess added a dogmatic and sometimes demagogic element to Cardozo's education. Burgess's subject was the formation and organization of nation-states. He taught that the Greeks and

Slavs had a low order of political genius and achieved a general constitution only when it was imposed by outsiders. The Celts, having organized themselves only at the level of the clan, were even more unpolitical. He maintained that the Latin races, however, showed a high order of political genius, having dictated the organization of the world three times, through the Roman empire, the Catholic church, and civil law. Burgess's highest accolade was reserved for the Teutonic races: they had founded the modern form of political organization, the nation-state, and that construction stamped them as *the* political race. The colonizing spirit of the Teutonic nations exported modern civilization to the rest of the world, which was still in a barbaric state. One requirement for a nation-state was ethnic homogeneity, and it was therefore permissible to deport "ethnically hostile" elements. It was the duty of the nation-state, then, to defend against internal and external disorder and finally to establish individual liberty for its own citizens.[59]

Cardozo's notes reveal that Burgess presented a strong strain of Social Darwinism, as well as what we would today call racism. Such views were certainly not unusual in the late nineteenth-century United States. We do not know whether Cardozo listened sympathetically or critically to this aspect of Burgess's presentation, although we shall see that he was impressed by certain aspects of Social Darwinism. Burgess combined his stereotypes about race with an elitist view of the social and political order. In discussing the role of the judiciary in the United States, Burgess approved very strongly of the power of judicial review. He saw it as creating an "aristocracy of the robe" and spoke of the judiciary's need to preserve its "spiritual power over the masses."[60] These lectures by Burgess, additional comparative constitutional law lectures by Professor A. C. Bernheim, administrative law lectures, and Professor Munroe Smith's lectures on Roman Law were all given in the School of Political Science and constituted Cardozo's formal education in public law.[61]

Cardozo's existing lecture notes cover only a small portion of his college experience, but they indicate that he considered carefully a wide variety of challenging material. Moreover, two pieces of written work that Cardozo saved indicate that at least occasionally he undertook written assignments of substantial scope. One such assignment is a completed essay on "The Moral Element in Matthew Arnold," which appears to come from the middle of Cardozo's college career, and the second was a draft of an essay on George Eliot, which seems to have been written near the end.

Both essays begin with the same thought, indeed with some of the same sentences. The thought is that the works of most authors contain a recurring theme that reveals the inner spirit of the writer. The first essay emphasizes Arnold's concentration on the importance of moral human conduct. Cardozo brought to bear the philosophy he had learned from Butler, comparing Arnold and his emphasis on "perfection" with Plato among the ancients and Leibniz among the modern philosophers and contrasting Arnold to the "prevailing Hedonism" of Bentham, Mill, and Spencer. "The history of the world," Cardozo argued, discloses that the two forces of transcendent power were "Hellenism and Hebraism, the power of beauty and intelligence and the power of right conduct," and in their union lay "the order of the world."[62] The notion of "right conduct," which Cardozo associated with Hebraism and hence implicitly with his own heritage, was another personal value, like duty, that would be important to his later judicial thought.

After that grand beginning, Cardozo's essay then wandered off to discuss briefly a whole series of barely related ideas: the democratizing power of literature; the relation of Arnold's view of ethics to that of Spencer; his contributions to the study of the Greeks; his style; and finally his faults—an occasional stooping to personal invective, his trivializing of the virtues of the United States, and sometimes a primness and daintiness to the point of affectation. Cardozo's discussion of Arnold's style was an early expression of his belief in the power of rhetoric to promote ideas: "Most of our so-called noble thoughts have been at bottom pretty prosy and commonplace sentiments. It is the vitalizing power of style that lends them force and loftiness, and imparts a semblance of novelty to notions as old as man himself."[63] Although the essay is competent and fluent, it is not a sophisticated piece of work. It is largely descriptive, somewhat rambling, and fairly superficial, devoid of serious analysis or of much realization of the complexities of Arnold's work.

Cardozo's essay on George Eliot is a longer, more thoughtful, and more mature piece, probably a product of senior year work. One of its features is a stylistic quirk that would become a hallmark of his judicial writing, the inverted sentence. One sentence, which adds a mixed metaphor, is a particularly awkward example: "Very beautiful is the picture of the first struggling dawn in Marner's mind of the old forces that had been sleeping there so long."[64] The substance of the essay, however, is impressive. Cardozo reviewed, and more importantly he analyzed, a considerable amount of Eliot's work. He compared her various novels with one another and with other writings, especially those of Henry James. He began with an attempt to find a generalizing theme in a notion of "the law of causation," in "the generative power of any, even the smallest act, in its effect both upon the agent himself and upon society at large." Although the attribution was to Eliot, Cardozo indicated his agreement with the message that people must take personal responsibility for their actions and that everything that they do matters.[65]

Cardozo then moved on to Eliot's preoccupation with "the unity and coherence of life"[66] and her analysis of the motivations of her characters. He spent considerable time expounding on the conflict between the sensations of pleasure and gratitude in the character Tito in *Romola*. While he had not made use of existing critical writing about Arnold, Cardozo did some research in literary criticism on Eliot. He used William Dean Howells's criticism of Eliot to demonstrate the novelty of her method of analysis, to portray it as the precursor of the even more analytical school of Henry James, and to distinguish Eliot's concern with ethical purpose from James's concern with artistic purpose.

Cardozo did not rely just on Howells. He went on to argue that Eliot was more concerned with mental phenomena and James with external conduct. The point is not so much the accuracy of Cardozo's perception but the fact that he demonstrated a critical faculty that was so lacking in the Arnold essay. Indeed, he was ready to choose between what he saw as Eliot's concern with internal states and James's concern with external behavior. He showed a decided preference for judging people on the basis of what they did as opposed to their supposed mental states. "Now, that the latter [James's] method of analysis is, theoretically at least, the more correct of the two, can hardly, it seems to me, be open to question. It leaves us to perform for ourselves the inferences from the external to the mental that in life we actually perform. It preserves to the novel the possibility of following the objective method and at the same time of dealing adequately with purely subjective experiences." Cardozo noted the artificiality of Eliot's elaborate preoccupation with her characters' mental processes before every decisive action and as-cribed part of the problem to her eagerness to explain the meaning of the story rather than to let the story tell itself.[67] Then, as later in life, Cardozo was not fond of psychological analysis. He was more interested in words and deeds.

Cardozo did not overgeneralize. He demonstrated how Eliot overcame these limitations in some of her work, most notably in *Silas Marner,* a novel that he admired for its beauty, generous human sympathy, and sense of symmetry and proportion. He contrasted *Silas Marner* with *Middlemarch,* which he criticized for its preoccupation with the inner consciousness of its characters and too many reminders to the reader that the tale was imaginary. In passing, Cardozo confessed that he had "always felt sorry for Casaubon," for although sparsely favored with talents, he put whatever he had to creditable employment.[68]

Cardozo then turned to the ideas that dominated Eliot's work. "Dominant was the obligation of sympathy, but unlike a philosopher, she made no effort to explain the ground of the obligation."[69] "A system that makes our inborn dislike of inflicting pain the motive for right conduct" is not very helpful when aimed at those who do not share that dislike.[70] The essay constantly recurred to Eliot's love of humanity and her faith in the distinction between right and wrong, but concluded that "her ideal was visionary and her faith in mankind was childlike."[71] Cardozo invoked Arnold's vision that "literature should be, in substance, a criticism of life," an approach that he found more powerful and useful. It was "but one phase of the world-wide truth that unless we relate our knowledge and our thoughts to the needs and the hopes of humanity, humanity will not prize the knowledge, and will not ponder the thoughts."[72] Eliot's sentimentalism needed to be sharpened by Arnold's critical thinking. The practical application of ideals was a preoccupation of Cardozo's judicial life, but he was not drawn to Eliot's focus on the inner self. He was usually uncomfortable with expressed emotion, and he often deflected and evaded emotional questions.

The Eliot essay demonstrated a wide learning, a capacity to analyze, to criticize, and to synthesize. Cardozo may have found much that was "superficial" at Columbia, but he also found much that challenged him to mental growth. By the time he wrote the Eliot essay, Cardozo was well educated and had grown up intellectually. He was thinking about ideas, idealism, and the way to translate morality into everyday living—what he would later call "right conduct."

William Speer, who was two years behind Cardozo at Columbia, remembered many animated conversations with him in the library about books, particularly talks about Arnold's essays and Cardozo's partiality for John Ruskin's discussion of the moral element in political economy in *The Political Economy of Art*.[73] But Cardozo left a different impression with some classmates. George Flint Warren, Jr., a lawyer who disclaimed intimate acquaintance, thought that while at college, Cardozo's "outlook on life seemed dry and technical though that idea was a mistaken one we all know now; for one of his chief characteristics [as a judge] was the intensive human grasp he had of the affairs that came before him for adjudication."[74] At Columbia, Cardozo stood apart from the social life of the college, and his understanding of people was in substantial part the product of the years of practice that were yet to come. Other classmates and teachers later remembered him as a "desperately serious" student,[75] who was self-contained and of "modest demeanor,"[76] "the star spirit of our class,"[77] and "intellectually . . . head and shoulders above us all."[78]

Cardozo's hard work and talent were rewarded. Columbia grade records show that in his freshman and sophomore years, he achieved the maximum grade points in Greek, Latin, and German, and very high grades in Mathematics, Rhetoric, and History. Only in Chemistry was there a little slippage; his grade was 128 out of a maximum of 160 (the equivalent of 80 percent).[79] In his final two years, the faculty changed to letter grades and began awarding honors to the two or three outstanding students in each subject. In Cardozo's junior year, he was ranked first on the honors list in Political Economy, Logic and Philosophy, English, and Greek, and second in Latin.[80] In his senior year, Cardozo was ranked first in the honors list in Greek and Political Economy and second in Latin and Philosophy.[81] Although Cardozo did well in his science courses, that was the one area of the curriculum in which he did not achieve honors. Cardozo also earned a string of As in such other courses as History, History of England, Physics, and Psychology.

Columbia awarded prize scholarships, based on competitive examinations, in various subjects. Cardozo tried for and won several—in his freshman year, the $100 prize in Latin; and in his sophomore and junior years, the $100 prize in Greek and an honorable mention in Latin.[82] This was a substantial amount of money in the 1880s, and it covered a large portion of his college expenses. The overall ranking of the top students at graduation ceased with the class of 1888, but from a comparison with the honors achieved by other classmates, Cardozo was at, or very near, the top of his class.

Cardozo worked hard and socialized little. "We were all very fond of him, but he was too young to enjoy our social activities, a fact that he appreciated and regretted in later years," recalled his classmate Remsen Johnson.[83] Too young, and probably also too shy and too devoted to family and work. Whatever regrets Cardozo may have felt for the fun he had missed, he did not change his ways much in later life.

Cardozo did participate in one social tradition, the cane rush, in his freshman and sophomore years. That was a particularly brutal "game" between the freshman and sophomore class in which the winning class was determined by counting the number of hands from each class on the "cane," which could be anything from a broomstick to a curtain pole, at the end of the prescribed period. Virtually any method of pulling an opponent off was tolerated. The rush during Cardozo's freshman year was so violent that one of his classmates was killed. This death led to an official ban, which in reality simply forced the cane rush off campus. Cardozo's hands were among those on the cane at the end of the 1886 rush.[84] Since Cardozo was no athlete, his participation, like that of many of his classmates, probably reflected the social pressure of the student body to join the game. But once he joined, he played it with determination.[85]

In his junior year, Cardozo joined the debating society, Barnard Literary Association, and later, his classmates remembered him as a good debater and moderator.[86] His debating work at Columbia helped develop him into the effective public speaker that characterized his professional career. His participation in the Literary Association and in a club of unknown purpose called the Moustache Club, where he obtained the title of Herald, comprised Cardozo's only known extracurricular activities.[87] He did not join the Shakespeare Society, which was very popular, the Chess Club, the Glee Club, the Orchestra, two Greek letter fraternities, or the various athletic teams. Whereas Cardozo's youth, shyness, and studious habits may partially account for his minimal social life at Columbia, there was an additional reason. His lifelong friend, Frederic Coudert, Jr., who was a year behind him, remembered that there was some "boycotting" of Cardozo on account of his father's blemished career.[88]

Cardozo thus commanded respect at Columbia, but he did not fit in. The *1889 Columbiad,* the school yearbook published in 1888 by Cardozo's class, poked fun at Cardozo's habits:

'Tis he, 'tis Nathan, thanks to the Almighty.
Women and men he strove alike to shun,
And hurried homeward when his tasks were done.[89]

Cardozo also appeared in the "Bets" section of the 1888 *Columbiad*: "Dollars to pennies that Cardozo has been eating snowballs again." That statement was explained fifty years later by E. H. Hornbostel, who was a year behind Cardozo, as referring to Cardozo's "placidity and calmness and poise," that he was cool as a snowball.[90] His classmates also appreciated his intelligence.[91] At the end of his final year, they voted him the "cleverest" and the second "most modest."[92] Although not elected valedictorian by his classmates, he was selected to be one of the speakers at Commencement exercises, and he was elected class vice president at the graduation dinner.[93]

Cardozo recalled his own performance at the graduation exercises when he addressed a graduating class at Columbia in 1915:

> It was the last Commencement of the old type. There were speeches by the students. The program characterized them as orations, and I was one of the orators. The truth of history requires me to say and I do say without feeling, that, at the next Commencement, when the echoes of my oration had scarcely died away, the University decided that it could dispense with speeches by the students, and it never had them again . . . I read the speeches the other day. Mine was . . . called "The Altruist in Politics." What he was doing in politics, I must own that the oration does not make clear, but I think, after all, that I must be credited with some vision in foreseeing that some day there might be found for him a place in politics at all.[94]

But Cardozo's later characterization of his address was misleading. In 1889, he had not foreseen a place in politics for the altruist. His speech attacked the altruist in politics, for he saw the altruist as the preacher of communism:

> Again and again, the altruist has arisen in politics, has bidden us share with others the product of our toil, and has proclaimed the communistic dogma as the panacea for our social ills . . . Instead of the present world, where some at least are well-to-do and happy, the communist holds before us a world where all alike are poor . . . Absorbed, as they are, in the principle of equality, they have forgotten the equality of work in the equality of pay; they have forgotten that reward, to be really

equal, must be proportionate to effort, and they and *all* socialists have forgotten that we cannot make an arithmetic of human thought and feeling . . . perhaps it may serve to lessen cant and open the way for fresh and vigorous thought, if we shall once convince ourselves that altruism *cannot* be the rule of life; that its logical result is the dwarfing of the individual man.[95]

Later he referred to the graduation talk and the senior thesis on which it was based as "schoolboy efforts" that "ought not to be preserved," and he expressed dismay that a prospective biographer was thinking of publishing them. "I fancy I said a good many things . . . that I might wish to disavow." But he was quick to add—this in 1932 just after he had been appointed to the Supreme Court—that "I am not a Communist now any more than I was then."[96] Cardozo was not one of those people who graduated as a radical and became more conservative with passing years. When he graduated in 1889, Social Darwinism had reached its peak of influence in this country, and its assumptions and those of laissez-faire doctrine pervaded much of the education that Cardozo received at Columbia. Cardozo, still untouched by reformist doctrine, spoke in accordance with orthodox premises and the cult of success promoted by his earlier teacher, Horatio Alger. The talk also reflected the personal drive of a young man whose parents had already died, whose father had disgraced the family, and who realized that any success in his life would depend upon his own efforts.

Benjamin Cardozo had already achieved a great deal by the time that he graduated from Columbia. He had borne the burden created for him by his father's career and had won respect by combining his intelligence with hard work. It was a prescription for the rest of his life. He was now an educated young man, and he loved learning. He would continue to educate himself throughout his life. As he left college for law school, he still lived with his family and enjoyed their support, especially that of Nellie, his sister-mother. The next task was to train himself for a career that would provide an income for himself and his sisters and redeem the family honor.

3

Columbia Law School

During his senior year at Columbia College, Cardozo seriously considered pursuing graduate work in political economy at Columbia. One day, according to his professor E. R. A. Seligman, Cardozo declared that he had decided to go into law. He felt that he had to clear up the disgrace to his family name and could do this only as a lawyer.[1] If that story is accurate, it was one of Cardozo's most revealing personal statements. Cardozo generally guarded his privacy carefully. Perhaps he felt that he owed some explanation to Professor Seligman because Seligman was his teacher and a family friend. The story was corroborated after Cardozo's death by Judge Abram Elkus, a friend from practice and briefly a colleague on the Court of Appeals. Elkus remembered that Cardozo once mentioned to him a desire to "work away" his father's disgrace.[2]

Only those brief fragmentary accounts remain to aid speculation about Cardozo's decision. There were other reasons for Cardozo to choose law as a career. His father had practiced law both before and after his service as a judge. His father's office was still in existence, and Benjamin's older brother Albert, who had graduated from Columbia Law School in 1879, was a member of the firm. Although we know almost nothing of the personal relationship between the two brothers, it was apparently strong enough that they practiced together from the time Benjamin left law school until Albert's death eighteen years later. In addition, the two brothers had to help support their three sisters, and

Ben may have thought that law provided more assurance of financial success than an uncertain career as an economist.

His father's disgrace must certainly have been on Cardozo's mind. He never forgot his father's fall and what it had done to the family. Even decades later an oblique reference crept into one of his judicial opinions. A tax case concerned the ability of the agent of a bankrupt company to deduct his payments to company creditors as an "ordinary and necessary" business expense. Looking for "bizarre analogies" in which the door of deductibility would be opened, Cardozo wrote, "One man has a family name that is clouded by thefts committed by an ancestor. To add to his own standing he repays the stolen money, wiping off, it may be, his income for the year."[3] That example was painfully close to Cardozo's own personal situation. Cardozo could not have consciously meant to call attention to his father; yet his father's example still "clouded" his own memory sufficiently that he produced that pointed analogy. By the same analogy, Cardozo needed to clear his family name in the same arena where it had been damaged—in the law.

The Columbia Law School that Cardozo entered in 1889 was a school wracked with dissension. The leadership and the method of teaching were being examined by the trustees. The dominant spirit, virtually *the* law school for many years, was Theodore W. Dwight, then nearing the end of a long career as one of the best-known legal educators that the country has ever produced. Dwight had strong views about the purposes of law, the role of lawyers, and the way they should be taught.

Dwight equated the rise of lawyers with the rise of freedom, seeing the primary function of lawyers in previous centuries as drawing "a satisfactory and permanent line between the power of the State and the freedom of the individual; to prevent man from unjustly warring on his neighbor; and to promote such action by the law-making power, and such interpretation by the courts, as will advance social order and national prosperity." Over the past fifty years, he argued, legal issues regarding liberty and life had been largely resolved. "The great legal questions to-day are those involving property." The task of the lawyer was to "stand like a wall" in defense of "the sacred right of property," which he perceived as a gift of God to man. Dwight held before his students a vision of the lawyer as representing "all that is worth fostering and preserving in the State—the family and individual life," protecting life and property, and standing by the poor man in his cabin and the rich man in his mansion, urging the dispensation of an even-handed justice.[4] Cardozo, as he had shown in his recent commencement address, was a true believer in the Dwight creed as he entered Columbia Law School.

Dwight had developed a philosophy and technique of teaching that became identified as the "Dwight method," which attempted to teach students legal doctrine at a very practical level. It was consciously aimed at the average student, with an emphasis on memorizing general principles of law so that when faced with specific problems, the practicing lawyer would be able to use them as a starting point. Students learned the general principles of existing law from treatises and textbooks, and their teachers explained the materials in lectures. Teachers told the students about cases, but cases were not the staple of teaching. In order to impress the principles expounded in class on the minds of the students, lecture notes for all the classes were published in the *Columbia Law Times,* the monthly journal of the Law School and the School of Political Science.[5]

Dwight's own classroom performance was masterful, and he made a deep impression on a great number of students. He knew the names and abilities of his students, and, unlike many of the most renowned exponents of the case method, he sought to instruct without humiliating or embarrassing the student. He was always available to students to explain lectures and answer questions outside of class. Dwight delighted in his role.[6] He and his followers espoused the virtues of his method of teaching against two rival methods. One was the old tradition of learning law as an apprentice in the office of a mentor. The second was the "case method," which had been developed by Dean Christopher Columbus Langdell at the Harvard Law School and which emphasized a search for the principles that underlay doctrine through Socratic dialogue between teacher and student.

While Dwight and his colleagues recognized that the body of principles that composed the common law had developed over centuries and doubtless also recognized that these principles were not static, they made little or no effort to encourage a student to ascertain why a particular principle had gained acceptance or what values and principles underlay the choice of one rule or another. Students were simply told what the governing principles were. Not that the case system necessarily involved the search for first principles, either. Depending upon the teacher's own frame of reference, the questioning induced by the case method could emphasize logical derivation from previously declared rules; history; or the economic, social, political, and moral bases of various rules. But the case method did stimulate a questioning attitude that was lacking in the Dwight method's heavy emphasis on memorizing basic principles and rules of law.

Benjamin Cardozo entered Columbia Law School with 250 other first-year (called junior) students, less than half of whom held undergraduate degrees, in the fall of 1889.[7] Three professors were scheduled for the entire first-year curriculum, one subject at a time: Theodore Dwight for "elementary law" and contracts, Benjamin Lee for real estate, and Robert Petty for "Redress of Private Wrongs by Courts."[8] The class was divided into two sections that met for ninety minutes a day Monday through Friday either at 11:00 A.M. or at 3:00 P.M.[9] Because Professor Dwight was absent for the opening weeks of the term, Professor George Chase introduced the students to the study of law by plunging them into the law according to William Blackstone, the traditional starting point in the education of American lawyers.[10]

By 1889, however, Blackstone's ponderous compendium of the law of England in the 1760s was hardly an appropriate introduction to the study of law for Americans whose country had experienced vast political, social, and economic changes since Blackstone's time.[11] In recognition of the difficulties, Chase omitted large portions of the original work, especially those relating to the English government and ecclesiastical law. Yet he preserved much that was obsolete because of its historical value, including such topics as the feudal system, ecclesiastical courts, and "benefit of clergy."[12]

Despite the difficulties of beginning a law career in this manner, there were also several advantages for a student, like Cardozo, with a scholarly bent. With Blackstone, Cardozo began the study of law with a discussion of the meaning of "law." Blackstone's firm pronouncements on that subject, complemented in the notes by references to Jeremy Bentham and quotations from John Austin's work on analytical jurisprudence and Henry Maine's *The Early History of Institutions,* focused the student's attention at the outset on very large topics about the meaning and purpose of law. Many years later, Cardozo noted the sharp contrast between this beginning and the rest of his legal education by remarking that in his day, these chapters comprised the entire content of the teaching of jurisprudence and legal philosophy at Columbia Law School.[13] Chase's presentation of Blackstone served not only to summarize the development of the common law but also to underscore the ever-changing nature of law and to provide a counterpoint to Dwight's emphasis on learning only current legal doctrine. Through Blackstone, Cardozo also received at the beginning of his studies a general survey of large areas of the law—moving rapidly through such topics as the rights of individuals (civil and political liberty), various personal relations (husband-wife, master-servant), corporations, personal property, and wills and estates.

After these introductory weeks of studying "Elementary Law," Cardozo took up the study of contracts with Dwight for the next several months. His textbook was the seventh edition of Theophilus Parsons's massive, three-volume *Law of Contracts,* still in use thirty-six years after the first edition had appeared. The course in contracts, like Parsons's treatise, conceived of the subject matter in very broad terms. "The Law of Contracts, in its widest extent, may be regarded as including nearly all the law which regulates the relations of human life. Indeed, it may be looked upon as the basis of human society . . . almost the whole procedure of human life implies, or, rather, is, the continual fulfillment of contracts."[14] Thus, aside from covering the subject matter of the modern law school course on contracts, Dwight used the Parsons book to deal also with the law of agency, partnerships, and corporations; trusts; bills and notes; sales and secured transactions; marriage and divorce; and conflict of laws.[15]

To the modern reader, the Parsons book is about as stimulating as an encyclopedia, which it resembled in format, style, and depth (or lack of depth) of analysis. One student referred to it as a "bulky and sometimes confusing, though ably arranged, compilation of precedents unilluminated by principles."[16] The art of textbook writing had not progressed much beyond the rudimentary level of Blackstone, Kent, and Story, except in the amount of coverage of particular subjects. Discussion of problem areas of the law, detailed analysis and criticism of existing doctrine, and a probing of the political, economic, or social values implicit in the choice of particular doctrine was a later development in the twentieth-century legal textbook.

For Dwight, the Parsons treatise suited nicely. The emphasis on current legal doctrine served to separate law from the political struggles of the day and kept students from learning how different some of the crucial doctrines of contract law had been one hundred years before. The main ingredient that students carried away from Dwight's contracts course was a sense of the rules of contracts at that particular moment in time.

Cardozo remembered years later that "I would no more have dreamed of questioning in word or spirit the rules which he laid down to me as law than I would have questioned the ten commandments."[17]

Cardozo and his classmates then spent the months of February through most of May studying real estate law with Professor Benjamin Lee, using *Washburn on Real Property* as a text. Lee had been a practitioner, specializing in real estate and patent work. He had come to Columbia in 1883, and the year that he taught Cardozo's class was his last year as a regular member of the faculty. The final course offering was by Robert Petty, an 1885 graduate of Columbia Law School who had begun teaching the previous year. He gave a short course at the end of the year on "Redress of Private Wrongs by Courts." The other required work consisted of eighteen weeks of instruction in the writing of briefs. A "Prize Fellow," a recent graduate hired from practice, conducted those sessions for one hour a week on Saturday mornings. A group of prize fellows also gave quiz sessions regularly on Thursday evenings.[18]

Cardozo was not satisfied to pursue just the course in legal studies, which focused so narrowly on private law and current doctrine. He took advantage of the opportunity offered by the School of Political Science to pursue a public law program as well. Professor Munroe Smith had advertised such a joint program by arguing that the best lawyer was "not he who simply knows the positive rules of law as embodied in decisions and statutes, but he who grasps their spirit, who sees that the established rule *is* because it *must* be, and who is therefore able to forecast a rule not yet fixed." The issues of the predictability and "inevitability" of law, largely ignored in the law school, exposed Cardozo quite early in his career to a central question of American jurisprudence with which he would later deal in his own judicial career.[19] Cardozo took Comparative Constitutional Law, History of European Law, and Administrative Law in the School of Political Science during his first year as a law student.[20] Those courses earned him a Master of Arts degree in June of 1890. The following year Cardozo also broadened his education beyond the traditional law school fare. He enrolled as a special student in the Faculty of Philosophy, taking courses in the History of British Philosophy and the History of Education.[21] Although Cardozo had made the decision to become a lawyer and not to pursue an academic career, his interests were greater than law, and during his law training he undertook the wider study that he would continue all his life.

Cardozo's second year at Columbia Law School began in ordinary fashion, but there was trouble on the horizon. The course of study had been expanded from two years to three the year before he entered, but the class ahead of his was dismayed at the expansion and the lack of planning for the third year. Only one-third of that class returned for the third year.[22] Meanwhile, Cardozo and his classmates took the traditional second-year course of study, which followed Dwight's prescription of only one required course at a time:

Oct.	Equity Jurisprudence	Prof. Keener
Nov.	Torts	Prof. Chase
Dec. and Jan.	Evidence	Prof. Chase
Jan., Feb., and Mar.	Code of Civil Procedure	Prof. Chase
or		
Jan. and Feb.	Common Law Pleading	Mr. Reeves
Feb. and Mar.	Equity Pleading	Mr. Reeves
Apr.	Admiralty, Shipping, and Insurance	Prof. Dwight
Apr.	Review of Contracts	Prof. Dwight
May	Review of Real Estate	Mr. Reeves[23]

In addition, the Law School offered optional courses and lectures in criminal law, medical jurisprudence, private corporations, and comparative constitutional law.

The greatest change was the bombshell that exploded with the arrival of Professor William Keener from Harvard Law School. The Dwight method, with its courteous laying out of "the law," was not for him. He was a fierce proponent of the Socratic dialogue associated with the case system, and "his personal manner in the classroom was brutally aggressive." Keener was not interested in whether students could memorize principles from a textbook; he forced his students to reason their way through a problem. His Harvard students remembered that he was neither scholarly nor popular but was "a teaching genius."[24]

Keener taught the course in Equity to Cardozo and his classmates in the fall of 1890. He did attempt to conform somewhat to the Columbia method. He used the standard text, *Bispham on Equity*, and he revised his lecture notes for publication in the *Columbia Law Times* in the usual pedestrian, skimpy form. Yet he "followed so different a course from that usually pursued in the Law School" that he made a vast difference in the classroom.[25] Whereas Dwight sought to furnish the average student with legal rules, Keener sought to train the student to do critical analysis of principles, facts, and their relation to one another. The training was rigorous.[26]

The exposure of Cardozo and his classmates to Keener lasted just a month. It would have required a person who was quick, argumentative, self-confident, and perhaps also bored by the Dwight method, to have appreciated the Keener style. Cardozo did not respond eagerly to Keener; although he certainly had the innate ability to keep up with Keener's teaching, Cardozo was used to a sedate style of teaching at Columbia. A classmate remembered many years later that Cardozo said at the time that he found the change "confusing."[27] Cardozo himself later viewed the response of his class to Keener as "varying from rage to incredulity, and from incredulity to despair." Keener, he thought, was trying to demonstrate that "we had learned nothing in the past, were learning nothing in the present, and were not likely, unless we improved a good deal, to learn anything in the future."[28]

Cardozo's lack of appreciation of Keener's aims seems somewhat surprising in retrospect. Cardozo's work at Columbia College and his other graduate work indicate that he was both analytical and interested in the search for policies and principles. Perhaps a month with Keener was not enough, and perhaps Cardozo felt that Keener's probing, aggressive personality invaded his personal privacy.

After a month with Keener, Cardozo and his classmates turned to the study of torts, the law of civil wrongs, under the familiar teaching of Professor Chase. One month seems a short time to comprehend the law of torts, especially since Chase used Thomas Cooley's comprehensive *Law of Torts,* with its more than eight hundred pages.[29] Moreover, Cooley attempted a broad approach to the subject, beginning with a discussion of the growth and adaptability of the common law, the relation between legislation and judicial decision, and the nature of legal rights. In fact, Cooley's whole discussion of tort law was based on theories about the nature of an individual's rights in society—rights to property and liberty, civil rights, political rights, family rights.[30] Although Cooley's treatment of this aspect of the subject was not extensive or profound, it did, for a perceptive student, relate particular legal topics to broader social issues of rights and duties, including the role that judges were playing when they resolved disputes. A student who pondered this discussion could use it to complement the Dwight presentation, which focused on the present rule in itself rather than as an evolution from former doctrine. Cooley's glorification of the role of the common law in promoting "steady and almost imperceptible change" in the law provided some perspective on and one theory of the nature of the common law.[31]

After the month on torts, Cardozo's class then spent the following six weeks with Chase, studying his edition of James Stephen's *Law of Evidence*. This was probably the most unusual text that students used during their law school career. Based on a draft of an Evidence Act that Stephen had prepared for introduction into Parliament in 1873, this little book was arranged as a compilation of statements of principles of law followed by illustrations, each containing a brief problem and a solution that was not explained except by the statement of principle.[32] Whatever value Stephen's *Law of Evidence* had for the practitioner—and judging from its many editions, it was very popular—it must have been baffling for the student. The subject matter of the law of evidence is so elusive that the use of a text like Stephen's, which contained no discussion or explanatory material at all, was almost a parody of the Dwight method.

The last four months of Cardozo's second year at law school witnessed another upheaval. In January 1891, Professor Dwight announced his retirement, to take effect in July. Since Dwight was sixty-eight, his retirement was expected. Two months later, however, both Professor Chase and Professor Petty unexpectedly announced their resignations, also to take effect in July. The student body was in turmoil. Although no public statement was made by any of the participants, suspicion was immediately voiced that Keener and his new methods of teaching were involved. Various groups of students composed resolutions and petitions, and numerous letters commenting on the affair appeared in the *Columbia Law Times*. The student opposition to the changes in curriculum and personnel centered in Cardozo's class, although his name did not appear as one of its leaders. The class argued that by the end of the year, it would have completed all the work that for thirty-two years had resulted in the conferring of the Bachelor of Laws degree. Since the class had entered the school on the faith of a method of teaching and a known corps of professors and could not have anticipated a complete change in both elements, its members should receive their degree in June 1891 instead of being forced to take a third year with new professors and a new method of instruction.

The class prepared a petition to this end after a mass meeting on

March 9, 1891. The board of trustees rejected the proposal five weeks later, pointing out that the course of study was known to have been three years long when the class of 1892 entered and that in fact this class was the second class to have entered under the new program.[33] This response left the students with the choice either of submission or of departure. Leaving without a degree was not a disaster, because the degree was not a requirement for admission to the bar. The previous year, two-thirds of the class departed after finishing the second year. Cardozo later reported that he had been "anxious to go out into the world and make [his] living." He joined the overwhelming majority of his class and departed after the second year. Of the 202 second-year students enrolled in 1890–1891, only 64 took the third year and received the degree in 1892.[34]

There is no record of Cardozo's performance during his Columbia Law School career. The curriculum organized by Dwight and the faculty required a comprehensive examination at the end of the course of study. Apparently no course marks were given along the way, or at least none that were preserved. Cardozo's departure at the end of his second year meant that he did not take the comprehensive examination and did not get his degree.[35]

Later, Cardozo discussed his legal education quite dismissively: "As ill luck would have it, I went to Columbia Law School in the transition days when the old order was passing into the new, the text book system into the case one . . . For one year I had the old text book system under Prof. Dwight and his associates. For the second year, I had a mixture of the old one and the new. It was neither one thing nor the other. As I look back on it now, it seems as if we didn't have any instruction worthy of the name. We just grew up into lawyers, or rather into members of the bar."[36] Or, as he put it more succinctly in 1924, "The Law School of my time was in effect a business college. It had no thought of a greater mission. It did the day's work decently and honorably, and recked not of the morrow."[37]

But he also indicated that he had come to appreciate the educational value of the new method of instruction that Keener had brought to Columbia Law School while he was a student. "More important even" than new courses was "the introduction of the case method of instruction. No longer did the student learn by rote out of a text book some hasty and imperfect generalization, swallowed whole as it was given him . . . With the cases themselves before him, he analyzed the facts, dissected the reasoning, criticised the conclusion." Law training in his day had not developed the critical insight of students or helped them to develop a philosophy of law. Cardozo had no metaphysical aim in mind, "for by a philosophy of law . . . I mean this and nothing more: the knowledge of what law is, how it grows, and whither it tends, a philosophy of genesis, of growth, of end and aim."[38]

Cardozo's training at Columbia did give him a substantial amount of the education that he needed for practice and for his subsequent judicial career. Requiring students to read treatises instead of casebooks meant that Cardozo, with his prodigious memory, learned a lot of legal doctrine. Some of the treatises dealt at least summarily with the larger issues in law. Although Cardozo complained that the law school's curriculum had been deficient in its offerings, he was nonetheless able to enrich his education by seeking out courses at the School of Political Science. He had developed a love of philosophy in his college studies with Nicholas Murray Butler, and his graduate work in the Philosophy Department exposed him to its broader questions. Cardozo added to the education he received at Columbia College and Columbia Law School during his years as a practicing lawyer and judge and, on his own, he developed what he called a "philosophy of law," an understanding of the life of the law.

In June of 1891, Benjamin Cardozo was twenty-one. He had acquired a good education at Columbia College and had added two years of professional and graduate training thereafter. He had learned a good deal of law at Columbia Law School, despite all its deficiencies. He had prepared himself for his future, and now he was ready to go to work.

Lawyer: 1891–1914

4
Apprenticeship

Cardozo began the practice of law in 1891. During his first five years at the bar, he set a pattern of work and family life that was to last until his sister Nellie's death. He continued to live at home, with his family as the principal part of his social life. He worked hard to learn his craft, but his mentor was the profession. Cardozo was given responsibility immediately. He learned by doing, largely on his own. The young lawyer taught himself well and was a rapid success.

―――――

Cardozo continued to live with his siblings in the family home at 803 Madison Avenue, and he joined his brother in his father's former law firm. The family household then consisted of his older brother and partner Albert, Jr. (Allie); his older sisters Ellen (Nell or Nellie) and Elizabeth (Lizzie); and his twin sister Emily. Allie had been practicing law since his graduation from Columbia Law School in 1879. His outspoken cousin Annie Nathan Meyer felt that Allie had some charm but very little brains. A secretary who worked at the law firm after his death referred to his reputation as being a little "cookoo."[1] Allie and Ben were apparently close enough that it was natural for Ben to join Allie in their father's old firm. They shared the same house and remained partners until Allie's death in 1909. Although Allie may have felt that he was helping his young brother get a start, he soon learned what a help his brother would be to him.

Cardozo applied for admission to the bar on June 26, 1891, a month after reaching the required age of twenty-one. After he had been "duly examined," he was admitted as attorney and counselor-at-law on October 26, 1891.[2] His brother was then practicing with Richard Newcombe, his father's long-time partner, and Charles Donohue, a former judge. Ben's association with Newcombe and Donohue was brief. Newcombe died in July 1891, just as Ben joined the firm. Donohue had joined the firm in 1889 after serving a fourteen-year term as a justice of the Supreme Court of New York. His peculiar judicial conduct destroyed his previous reputation as one of the foremost admiralty practitioners in the city, and he never regained his former large practice.[3] Donohue remained in the new firm until the fall of 1892 before leaving it for unknown reasons. An employee of the firm during Cardozo's early years was Stephen C. Baldwin, a young lawyer who had been admitted to practice in the early 1880s and joined Cardozo & Newcombe in 1887. Baldwin left the firm in 1893. He quickly established himself as one of the leading trial lawyers in the city, sometimes calling on Cardozo to argue an appellate matter.[4] Within two-and-a-half years, with the death of Newcombe and the departure of Donohue and Baldwin, the firm of Cardozo, Newcombe & Donohue became Cardozo Brothers. They kept their office at 96 Broadway until 1898 when they moved to 52 Broadway.[5]

The profession that Cardozo entered in 1891 was in the process of transition. The work of lawyers had long been divided between the office lawyer, who drew wills, contracts, and real estate deeds, and who settled estates, and the litigator, who tried commercial and other common law cases and also handled matters in the equity courts. During the twenty-three years of Cardozo's practice, rapid industrial development affected the work of lawyers. New forms of financing were needed to create the large amounts of capital required by big corporate enterprises. This work fell into the hands of a small number of highly paid, specialized law firms. Another new development was the creation of a class of lawyer-promoters, the forerunners of today's "rainmakers."[6]

Large-scale industry and the beginnings of regulatory reaction from government strained the lawyer's role, especially the tradition of the lawyer as independent professional. This is the period when the image of lawyers changed, at least in the public's view, from persons who were "valuable both to . . . client and to . . . community for [their] independence of . . . thought" to persons who spoke "on every occasion for their clients' interests." The best-known lawyers of the day were the innovators: John G. Johnson and Francis Lynde Stetson, who pioneered new legal forms of corporate organization; Louis Brandeis, who used the machinery of government to regulate the new capitalism; Paul Cravath, William D. Guthrie, and John W. Sterling, who helped develop the large law firm as a resource to make and carry out business policy.[7]

Technological developments also changed the way in which lawyers interacted with one another. The advent of the typewriter and the telephone made lawyers' communications more formal and impersonal. Lawyers visited each other less, gossiped around the courtroom less, and therefore knew one another less well. As the country's population and the bar grew, it was harder for lawyers to be widely known among their colleagues and in the world at large.[8]

The expansion of business activity also affected the work of small firms such as Cardozo Brothers. The surge in real estate investment, stock transactions, and business dealings generally produced increased conflict. Judicial resolution of most litigation was still swift and, in contrast to the profession one hundred years later, ordinary businesspeople and the middle class were able to afford its costs. Their affairs were the staple of Cardozo's practice.

———

One of Ben Cardozo's first assignments as a fledgling lawyer was to make a study, for his firm's use, of a recent multivolume annotated version of the Field Code of Civil Procedure, which regulated the course of litigation in New York courts. Although he had not been asked to learn the statute section by section, he did just that. He had a retentive memory, and his newly acquired encyclopedic knowledge of New York procedure earned him a reputation as a master of that subject quite early in his career.[9]

New York law firms generally assumed that recent law school graduates, although qualified in academic terms, lacked the practical experience to function as effective lawyers.[10] Cardozo, however, did not serve in the traditional assistant's role of the young lawyer who prepared papers for, and worked closely with, older, experienced lawyers. He was thrown into the current litigation of the office as soon as he was admitted to the bar. In his first year at the bar, he argued and won four cases on appeal in New York's intermediate appellate court, the General Term of the Supreme Court. He also won one and lost one case in New York's highest court, the Court of Appeals.[11]

Cardozo obtained practical experience early and largely on his own. That outcome may have been partly due to Newcombe's death and Donohue's departure. Also, his brother may have encouraged, and relied upon, this independence. Indeed, while Allie had been active in court before his younger brother's arrival in the firm, handling a variety of work including some litigation for persons injured by railroads and streetcars, his name does not often appear in the case reports that followed. He let Ben handle the court work, especially the appellate work. Benjamin Cardozo thus began his legal career doing battle with more experienced lawyers. His youth, lack of social maturity, and inexperience could have led to a personal disaster. Cardozo, however, did more than cope. He thrived.

Cardozo's early appellate efforts demonstrate that he possessed good lawyering skills right from the beginning of his career. Frank v. Davis is the first case in which Cardozo's name appears in the reports.[12] This case, which he argued in 1891 less than three weeks after his admission to the bar, was typical of his future practice in two respects. It was a real estate matter. Over the years, Cardozo would become an expert in arguing difficult questions of real estate law. In addition, right from the outset, Cardozo was a resourceful advocate. He was a master of procedural niceties and technical arguments when the case called for that type of argument. Occasionally, therefore, he rescued a lost cause, as in this case. In an earlier proceeding, argued by Albert Cardozo, Jr., the Court of Appeals had affirmed a judgment of foreclosure of a second mortgage held by Julius J. Frank, as assignee, on the property of Cardozo's client.[13] The action had been brought in a court of equity where proceedings were conducted without a jury. While the appeal was pending, however, the first mortgagee foreclosed and its debt was satisfied. Some money was left for Frank, the second mortgagee, from the proceeds of the sale, but its debt was not fully satisfied. Frank therefore made a motion in his action against Cardozo's client and obtained a "deficiency judgment" for the balance in his equity action in the trial court, the Special Term of the Supreme Court.

Cardozo successfully maintained in the General Term, the appellate division of the Supreme Court, that Frank could obtain a deficiency judgment only after a sale of the property and that since a prior party had foreclosed in another action, the jurisdiction of the court of equity was at an end. Frank could proceed against his client only in an action in the law courts where Cardozo's client would have the right to a jury trial.

Cardozo's success was short-lived. The Court of Appeals, the highest court in New York, reversed the judgment that he had won for his client. Chief Judge Robert Earl characterized Cardozo's position as "extremely technical" and invoked a statute to bring mortgage foreclosures within the general rule that permitted a court of equity with original jurisdiction of a suit to render all necessary relief in order to avoid another lawsuit.[14] Cardozo did the best he could, but his case was too weak.

Another early lawsuit, Friedland v. Myers, introduced Cardozo to the difficulties of establishing the boundaries of damages for breach of contract.[15] A landlord leased premises to a druggist who, in anticipation of moving in, purchased fixtures and a supply of drugs, some of which were perishable. The landlord, however, lost a suit to force the current tenant to vacate. The druggist brought suit against the landlord for damages resulting from the landlord's breach of his agreement to lease the premises. The case had probably been tried by Albert Cardozo, who won a verdict for $1,328, representing the loss from forced sale of the fixtures and the perishable drugs. After the landlord appealed, Benjamin Cardozo argued the case at the General Term of the Supreme Court.[16]

Cardozo's argument related primarily to the damages that his client was entitled to recover by reason of the landlord's breach. The general principle of liability had been set forth in the famous English case of Hadley v. Baxendale, which was widely cited in the United States.[17] Damages were those that were the "natural consequence" of the breach, that is, those that were foreseeable. Cardozo's brief discussed the precedents in New York, in other states, and in England, in trying to convince the court that the landlord should have anticipated that the druggist would prepare for moving in by purchasing the necessary fixtures and stock of drugs.

Cardozo succeeded in the General Term but only partially in the Court of Appeals, which held that it was appropriate for the druggist to have purchased the fixtures but not the perishable drugs. Judge Isaac Maynard took a rather strict view of the *Hadley* rule in relying on the fact that there had been no showing that the drugs had to be bought in advance from a distant source. The druggist could have waited until he gained possession of the premises before ordering his supply of drugs. Maynard rejected Cardozo's formulation, or at least his application, of the rule. In declining to hold the landlord liable, he concentrated not on whether it was reasonable for the druggist to try to get as many things as possible done in advance of the start of his lease, but rather on whether he could have gotten his supplies in time if he had waited. In effect, the court was discouraging careful business planning in order to lessen a landlord's liability for breach of contract. The druggist had bought at his own risk. Cardozo's later judicial career would be much concerned with similar problems of foreseeability in dealing with issues of risk and liability, and he sometimes took an approach that resembled the perspective of Judge Maynard.

Other lawyers began to refer cases to Cardozo even in the early period of his practice, and these cases show that he was already a skillful lawyer. In his third year of practice, while representing a creditor in a complicated proceeding, he was asked by several other lawyers, all of whom were many years his senior, to present a brief and argue an appeal on behalf of the joint interests of their respective clients.[18] Cardozo was making an impression in court. Judge Edward Patterson of the New York Supreme Court told of having the reading of the day's calendar answered in one case by someone who seemed to be either the office boy or the junior clerk. When the case was reached, the same "stripling" tried it. "The issue was involved but I have never heard a better or more lucid argument." The "stripling" was Cardozo. Patterson was well regarded, and repetition of the story must have helped Cardozo's career.[19]

After a few years of practice, Ben was called upon for assistance by his first cousins, Edgar Nathan, Sr., and Michael H. Cardozo, who practiced together as the firm of Cardozo & Nathan.[20] They were ten and nearly twenty years Ben's senior respectively and had a large commercial practice, representing many insurance companies and some banks. They also had a reputation as good lawyers and good people.[21] They called on Ben in a real estate matter in which several of their relatives were parties. Nathan had won the case in the lower courts. Ben Cardozo argued and won the case in the Court of Appeals, using a brief written by Nathan.[22] That case marked the beginning of a close professional and personal association between Benjamin Cardozo and Edgar Nathan, who became one of the closest friends Cardozo had outside his own immediate family. After Ben, Nellie, and Allie moved to 16 West 75th Street in 1902, Ben and Edgar would often walk to work together through Central Park to the Elevated Line at 58th Street and 6th Avenue.[23]

Of even more importance to his future career, Cardozo came to the attention of Angel Simpson, who had a sizable real estate and business practice and often represented creditors in insolvency situations.[24] Simpson brought Cardozo in to argue Galle v. Tode for him in the Court of Appeals, although he had won both at the trial level and at the General Term of the Supreme Court.[25] Simpson made a fortunate decision. He had brought a suit on behalf of a group of creditors who had obtained judgments against Tode Brothers. Tode Brothers had previously given other creditors the power to "confess judgments" against them.[26] Those other creditors then entered judgments and seized the Tode Brothers' property. Simpson was successful in having these confessed judgments set aside at trial and in the General Term on the ground that they were fraudulent. The result was that the property was restored to Tode Brothers and became available to satisfy the claims of Simpson's clients. There was no problem with respect to those creditors who had participated in the fraud. Some of the judgments, however, had been confessed to innocent creditors. These too were held fraudulent in the lower court because of the fraudulent intent of Tode Brothers. The innocent creditors then appealed to the Court of Appeals. They asserted that their judgments were valid and were prior in time to the claims of Simpson's clients because of the rule that the date when their rights arose was the date when the debtor gave the creditor the power to confess a judgment, not the date when the judgment was eventually entered or the property of the debtor was seized.

Simpson & Werner had filed a brief in the Court of Appeals seeking to uphold the judgment of the General Term on the grounds asserted by that court's opinion before they had decided to ask Cardozo to argue the appeal. It became clear at the argument that some of the judges were troubled about the ground of the General Term's opinion, fearing that it subjected every confession of judgment to attack on the basis of the debtor's state of mind. Cardozo responded to that fear in a skillful supplemental memorandum that relieved the fear and preserved his client's judgment. Even if the other creditors' judgments were valid, the so-called relation back of the time of the confessed judgments was a legal fiction that ought to yield to the intervening rights of his clients. His position, he argued, "has been announced in all the treatises upon the law of agency; it has been announced in repeated decisions by courts of high repute; and it is in its essence, a just and wise and reasonable limitation upon the fiction."[27] This persuasive statement of an intermediate position struck the right note. The court was unwilling to declare the consent judgments to innocent creditors to be void, but it did agree that they should be subordinated to the rights of Cardozo's clients.

Another referred matter allowed Cardozo to go far beyond the usual course of legal argument in presenting an elaborate discussion of the meaning of "knowledge" in order to preserve a verdict already won by his client at the trial level. He was called into the case of Ladenburg v. Commercial Bank at the appellate level by the law firm of Steinhardt & Goldman.[28] The issue involved the bank's nonpayment of a bill of exchange (for our purposes, a check).[29] The Goldman firm, representing Ladenburg, the holder of the check, had submitted an affidavit to prove his assertion that the bill of exchange had not been paid. The bank claimed that the affidavit was defective because the person making the affidavit was not present when payment was supposed to have been refused and therefore could not swear to the requisite facts of his own personal knowledge.

Cardozo argued forcefully and successfully against a rule that would limit someone submitting an affidavit to swearing only to matters perceived immediately through his own senses. Cardozo used social science writing about the meaning of "knowing" to argue on principle for a practical definition of the knowledge about which one may testify:

Alike in common life and in judicial proceeding we constantly claim a knowledge of facts where our knowledge in ultimate analysis is the product of association, of comparison, of inference and of belief. Courts of justice in dealing with such matters must be governed, not by metaphysical distinctions between knowledge and opinion, but by the conceptions and distinctions of the common understanding. All knowledge, save the barest residuum, is, when finally analyzed, the product of association; the result, not of immediate perception, but of a series of inferences and judgments which are merged in the conclusion to which they lead . . . If there can be no legal knowledge save knowledge which is derived through the medium of the senses, if all convictions based upon inference are to be classified as opinion or belief, if the legal definition of knowledge is to be governed not by the standards of the average intelligence, but by the standards of analytical psychology, it should not be forgotten that there is hardly an imaginable event in the experience of the human race that comes to us as an immediate perception, and not as the result and conclusion of a long association of ideas . . .

With such metaphysical subtleties courts of justice have no concern. The knowledge which they may rightly recognize as sufficient is the knowledge which is recognized as sufficient by the average intelligence of men.[30]

Cardozo's argument had intellectual force, and it represented his own practical approach to life. It combined legal principle and precedent with some philosophical learning obtained from Nicholas Murray Butler's course on moral philosophy and his own reading to rebut the metaphysical definition—in which true knowledge was virtually unobtainable—in favor of a commonsense definition that ought to be recognized in a court. Having made the argument from principle, he then went on to show that it comported with the few cases that had considered the problem. The court agreed, stating that the person submitting the affidavit had sufficient knowledge, for purposes of the governing statute, if he had documentary evidence showing that the bills of exchange had been "protested" for nonpayment.

Cardozo did not employ many such imaginative sorties outside the usual boundaries of legal argument, because he was an advocate and because the right situation for such a flight of fancy did not often present itself. But this episode shows that early in his professional career, he had an expressive streak. Part of it was a capacity to relate legal problems to other aspects of life. Part of it was erudition. And part of it was showmanship. This talent would help make Cardozo famous when he went to the bench. His sophisticated style served practical purposes. He argued against metaphysical subtleties, not for them. The basic common-sense, common-understanding approach that he relied on in both these cases was the hallmark of his approach to judging and to law generally.

Cardozo was clearly an early success in the business of lawyering, particularly in his appellate practice. During his first five years of practice, he argued at least twenty-four distinct matters on appeal, some in more than one appellate tribunal.[31] Eight of these appearances were in the Court of Appeals. Cardozo's early practice illustrates an interesting feature of the business of New York courts. The New York reports for this period are filled with cases involving piecemeal appeals of procedural matters, most of which were decided summarily, with the court announcing the result without writing an opinion.[32] Nearly half of the appeals that Cardozo handled involved procedural maneuverings undertaken before reaching the substance of the litigation—the sufficiency of a bill of particulars filed by a plaintiff to fill out the details of a complaint, the sufficiency of the affidavit required to validate an attachment (seizure) of property, the appropriateness of referring a case to a special master (private parties appointed by the court to conduct hearings and to report their conclusions to the court), and the like.

The nonprocedural appellate work handled by Cardozo in this period consisted primarily of private, commercial matters of relatively modest character. Many of these cases involved real estate in one way or other, either mortgage foreclosures or contracts to purchase real estate or questions of the validity of title. Most of the remainder involved a variety of claims arising out of commercial contracts.

We know that Cardozo's appellate practice continued to develop but, without the firm's office records, we cannot obtain a full picture of the rest of his practice. We do know that Cardozo Brothers had a good deal of trial work. For example, the calendar of the Supreme Court of New York, Trial Term for December 26, 1895, listed eleven cases in which the firm represented a party, and indeed the party was the plaintiff in every case.[33] At the same time, Cardozo Brothers turned up in the legal notices as attorneys for the assignee for the benefit of the creditors of a business partnership, that is, the attorneys represented the person to whom an insolvent firm had conveyed its property so that it could be divided among its creditors.[34] With only the two brothers as partners in the firm, Benjamin Cardozo must have handled some of this trial work and the general office work of the firm. But his appellate work was becoming the major part of his practice. His achievements began to make his reputation and to bring him more business.

––––––––

One mark of Cardozo's early success was an invitation when he was just twenty-four years old to contribute an article to a treatise on legal medicine.[35] The editors asked him to discuss two related subjects: proof of an individual's identity, and property rights following a common disaster, that is, when a husband and wife died at the same time under circumstances that made it difficult or impossible to know the order of death.

Cardozo began his exposition, intended for doctors and lawyers, with a discussion of the development of the importance of individual identity as opposed to clan identity. Using such diverse legal sources as Bracton's *On the Laws and Customs of England,* Maine's *Ancient Law,* Jhering's

The Struggle for Law, and Holmes's *The Common Law,* he traced quickly the law's purposes in attempting to pick out individuals to punish for commission of crimes and its development into a system where rational logic, not arbitrary presumptions, predominated.

Turning to the specifics of proof of identity, he set forth several different classifications of evidence that should be considered: general appearance, physical peculiarities (physical marks, teeth, hair, size and stature, voice, dress), mental traits, history and experiences, and incriminating circumstances. Under each heading, Cardozo discussed a number of situations drawn from cases or treatises in which a particular item was crucial in proving or disproving identity. Because of the unique, even bizarre, nature of the available illustrations, the article was anecdotal. Whether by design or not, Cardozo held the reader's interest by the examples, and not because the subject presented any fascinating legal problems. The most interesting discussion, similar to some of his appellate arguments, was his disparagement of the distinction between "direct" and "circumstantial" proof:

> From the standpoint of psychology, the distinction is of doubtful validity at best. So little of our knowledge is directly given us by our senses, so little of it but is the product of association and comparison working upon the raw material which the senses supply, so much that seems to us immediate and direct is, in reality, mediate and indirect, that from a philosophical standpoint almost all evidence is the evidence of a fact, not directly, but indirectly perceived . . . Every now and then a case arises which puts the problem in its true light; and the knowledge that seems to us immediate is seen to be the result of a long process of reasoning—an elaborate train of thought.[36]

This point about the contingency of knowledge is the one he later put to the use of his client in the *Ladenburg* appeal that was discussed earlier. But Cardozo did not contribute any new insight useful to the law of evidence. The article was designed to be descriptive.

The second part of the article, concerning survivorship when husband and wife die in a common disaster, was an exercise in legal analysis that adhered closely to traditional legal doctrine. However, Cardozo also surveyed other systems of law, from "mahometan" law in India, to Roman law, and to the Code Napoleon, in order to compare systems that operate on the basis of fixed, formal presumptions with those that require proof of what actually happened. The most interesting part of his discussion was his general attitude toward deciding upon a rule: "I can never believe that it is wise to place the doctrines of the law out of relation either to the teachings of experience or to the promptings of reason; and it seems to me that courts of justice, by frankly admitting their inability to solve a problem which in its nature is insoluble, will better promote the ends of their existence than by the forced assumption of a knowledge which it is not given them to have."[37] Here quite early in his career is a brief expression of the importance for him of the notion that rules of law had constantly to be responsive to reason and common experience. Cardozo was reflecting on the purposes of law in a way that few lawyers ever did, or do, in their entire careers.

By 1896, Cardozo had completed his first five years of practice with an impressive record of appearances in the trial and appellate courts. Although only twenty-six, his successes had made him known and respected at the bar. His career was ready to expand and flourish.

Benjamin's life outside the office during these years remained centered around the family's Madison Avenue home. There were some strains in the family. Allie and Lizzie did not get along. Lizzie spoke of Allie "with contempt," and he reciprocated those feelings, later referring to her home in Long Island as Matteawan (the state home for the criminally insane).[38] Lizzie's health problems were of considerable concern to her other siblings. She was still living at home when Ben began his career. From infancy she had had a spinal ailment that caused her considerable pain, and she subsequently developed mental problems.[39] She suffered from obsessions, such as wishing to retrace her route in a carriage to assure herself that the carriage had not run over a child, and constantly washed her hands to rid herself of germs.[40] She studied painting at the Art Students League in New York and then with Kenneth Hayes Miller, a well-known Realist painter. Miller has left us an acute description. Lizzie was "very thin," "ascetic," "pleasant," but "extremely neurotic," looking like "the end of a long line of aristocrats," with "dark and intense" eyes, and an "aquiline, aristocratic nose," resembling a "feminine edition of Dante."[41] Lizzie spent her time painting and writing poetry. She stayed in touch with Horatio Alger after finishing her studies with him and later sent him some of her poetry with a request for his opinion.[42] Eventually she published a small book of poems entitled *Salvage*.

Lizzie was good-hearted. She admired and loved Ben and had special feelings toward Nellie, her "mother-sister," to whom she directed one of her poems. It spoke of Nellie's role in raising her and helping her in her illness, and of the "tie that was forged of those shed tears" for the members of their family who had died.[43] At about the time Ben left Columbia, Kate Tracy, a young Irish nurse, was hired as nurse-companion for Lizzie. Miss Tracy's job was to last forty-six years, for after Lizzie's death in 1917, she stayed on as family nurse, manager of the house, and friend, through Nellie's illness and death until Ben's death in 1938.[44] Soon after Miss Tracy joined the family circle, she and Lizzie moved to the country, first to a farmhouse in Amityville, Long Island, and later to a cottage at Shippan Point, Connecticut. Country living was a standard prescription for the mentally ill at that time.[45] Lizzie does not appear to have cut herself off completely from either her family or the outside world, but her situation was a source of constant worry for Nellie and Ben.

During the early years after his graduation, Ben's twin Emily also lived in the Madison Avenue home. She was the extrovert of the family— cheerful, lovable, and loving. On occasion, her outspokenness shocked the more staid of the family friends.[46] She often teased Ben that he had gotten all the brains when they were born. Her sharp-tongued, perceptive first cousin, Annie Nathan Meyer, considered Emily the least intellectual of the Cardozo children.[47] Emily had an active social life, which she did not restrict to the Sephardic community, and must have found life at home fairly gloomy.

Emily was the only one of the six brothers and sisters to marry; thus, the Albert-Rebecca branch of the Cardozo family died out when Emily and her husband, Frank Bent, had no children. Emily's marriage doubtless caused distress for some of the family because Frank Bent was not Jewish. Frank worked in a real estate office at 769 Madison Avenue, near the Cardozo home, and later held clerical jobs.[48] The couple struggled to make ends meet. Ben helped out, especially when Emily developed a chronic illness many years before her death in 1922 at the age of 52.[49] All this contributed to some strain between Frank and the Cardozo clan. Ben, however, got along with his brother-in-law and spoke of remaining "companions as in youth" with Emily and of being "greatly attached to her."[50]

After Emily's death, Ben wrote some revealing notes for Rabbi Stephen Wise's use in conducting Emily's funeral service at the Woodlawn Cemetery in the Bronx.[51] They not only described Emily but also revealed something of his own feeling and personality:

> Emily C. Bent was my twin sister.
>
> I am going to ask you to believe, on the faith of my word, that she had traits of character which were very distinctive and very beautiful.
>
> First, perhaps, I would place warmth and cheerfulness and cordiality of disposition which made her love everyone, and which in turn made every one love her. I do not know any one else who was able to elicit such friendships almost overnight. You will see it at her funeral. Her friends *loved* her—not in the loose sense in which we often use that word, but truly and deeply. Of course, she did not receive without giving. She loved her friends in return. They were all precious to her. People who seemed tiresome or flat or commonplace or even a bit vulgar to Nellie and me, were all dear to her. She saw the essential human traits, and what we often thought her blindness was truer than our wisdom.
>
> But . . . there is another trait which I must mention, and which moves me very deeply,—that is her generosity, her unselfishness. She did not have many worldly goods. She saw others about her—her brother and sister—who had much more. Never in all her life did I note even a passing shadow of jealousy or envy, never did she seem to wish that they might have a little less and she a little more, never was there anything but happiness and joy in every success and blessing that came to them, and gratitude, far beyond their deserts, for every little kindness that they bestowed and every trifling help that they might offer.
>
> She loved her husband with the utmost devotion. She often said she did not wish to survive him. She said the same, indeed, of Nellie and me. Her last illness was greatly soothed by his loving care, and by that of his brother who made his home with them, and who tended her with a devotion which has won my gratitude and affection.
>
> I have spoken of her traits as distinctive, but I suppose that this is wrong. After all, they are the fundamental traits which redeem and transfigure our weak humanity, the fundamental traits which place saints and angels in every home, the great and eternal virtues of gentleness and charity which shine for each of us in the faces and the conduct of those we love and cherish.[52]

Ben's notes were not the vague words of one who is casting around for something nice to say. He described not just her good deeds but also the nature of her personality and emotions. And he made clear that these were feelings that mattered to him as well. The "fundamental traits" were embodied in his own devotion to Nellie when she became ill. Ben's mention of Emily's excessive gratitude for trifling kindness might also have been applied to himself. Profuse thanks for service—whether a glass of water from Kate Tracy or a useful precedent from a law clerk—characterized his dealings with others.[53] Cardozo's praise of Emily also contained a comparison of her reaction to people with that of Nellie and himself that recognized his own impatient, judgmental, and elitist streak. Although he may have included himself along with Nellie in the comparison with Emily to avoid seeming to be critical of Nellie, he too made judgments about people, and the privacy of his home was the likely outlet for expressing them.[54]

As suggested earlier, the closest relationship in Benjamin Cardozo's life was with his sister Nellie. When their mother died in 1879, Nellie was twenty and Ben was nine. The oldest sister had assumed the maternal responsibilities of taking care of the younger children and running the household. A story was told in later years that Nellie had given up the opportunity to get married in order to help bring up the family.[55] By the time that Ben left Columbia Law School, he was twenty-one and was capable of taking care of himself as he entered on his professional career. Nellie was thirty-one, still a relatively young woman. With the arrival of Kate Tracy to look after Lizzie, Nellie could have led a more active life in society. The pattern, however, had already been set. Her secluded life was to continue. Much later in life Nellie would say that she had never dined anywhere but in her own home.[56] That statement, even if exaggerated, reflects the quality of her life. Absorbed in the life of her family, she had her happiest moments at family dinners where she would say "I love you" to each of her siblings.[57] Ben later copied down this description of the character Aunt Ann from Galsworthy's *Forsyte Saga:*

> It was her world, this family, and she knew no other, had never perhaps known any other. All their little secrets, illnesses, engagements, and marriages, how they were getting on, and whether they were making money—all this was her property, her delight, her life; beyond this only a vague, shadowy mist of facts and persons of no real significance.[58]

Ben surely had Nellie in mind as he recorded those words.

Ben's own proclivities fit in with Nellie's life. With but little interest in socializing, he was ready to continue living in a household run by Nellie. He worked hard at his law practice, and doubtless much of his time at home was spent writing memoranda and briefs or preparing a case for trial. Once in a while he went out with Nellie's close friend, Louise Waterman, who married Rabbi Stephen Wise in 1899.[59] One summer at least, he went to Lake Saranac for a while and stayed in the Hotel Ampersand with his friend Theodore Herrmann. Herrmann was there to visit his future wife, Lillian Siesfeld, who was staying nearby, and Cardozo joined in outings with them and Lillian's sister Ethel.[60] Emily and his cousin Adeline Cardozo tried to get Ben to join their social activities. They generally failed, though, finally commenting, "You've got all the brains and we've got all the fun."[61] Instead, Ben's life revolved increasingly around Nellie. Both parents and one sister were already dead, and Lizzie was an invalid. Only two of the family, Ben and Nellie, would reach the age of sixty, and they shared the responsibility and worry for the well-being of Lizzie and Emily.[62] Ben and Nellie (we do not know about Allie) spent their free time together at home.

Although there were frequent visits from other members of the Cardozo-Nathan clan and from a few friends, such as the Wises, Ben and Nellie were one another's best friends. During these years, the relationship between Nellie and Ben lost its maternal overtones and became a strong, vital relationship between a brother and a sister who enjoyed each other's company and were devoted to one another. Ben shared the details of his day with her, and they played chess and the piano together.[63] Nellie was intelligent, well read, and "had a sharp and at times caustic wit." She was an iconoclast who did not suffer fools easily. "No person except Ben and no idea was sacred to her."[64] She was aristocratic in her speech and disliked mingling with people in streetcars.[65] On the other hand, when she got to know people, like the shopkeepers with whom she dealt at the family summer home in Allenhurst, New Jersey, she came to like them and was well-liked in return.[66]

This was an intense relationship, but there is no evidence at all to suggest that there was anything romantic or sexual in it. Learned Hand, who knew something about human nature and sexuality and was Cardozo's friend, thought that sex "not just in the carnal sense alone but all that goes with it . . . was as nearly absent from his [life] as it is from anybody I ever knew that wasn't gaited the other way." Continuing his reference to "gaited the other way," Hand added, "He [had] no trace of homosexuality anyway."[67] Although one cannot be absolutely certain, it seems highly likely that Cardozo lived a celibate life.

————————

During this early period of his career, Cardozo demonstrated that although he had ceased to attend religious services, he had been born a Sephardic Jew and he remained one. Even though on occasion he might poke fun at the airs of Sephardic Jews, he had his own airs, one of which was his great pride in the length of his family's ancestry in this country.[68] He and Nellie refused to serve shellfish and pork products in their home. It was somehow disrespectful to their ancestors and their upbringing. Even after he lost belief in the religious tenets of Judaism, he saw no hypocrisy in respecting traditions that might impinge a small amount on his pleasure but not on his intellectual honesty. Ben retained his formal ties to his synagogue to the end of his life. He paid his dues and kept his seat for services, albeit it was his relatives and not he who used it.[69] He retained his hereditary voting status as an elector of the congregation.[70] In the end, he would bury his siblings, except for his twin sister Emily, in the family plot in the congregation's cemetery. The synagogue was not merely a house of religion. It was also a symbol of the heritage of the Cardozo-Nathan family and of his membership in the Sephardic community.

Cardozo did more than retain his seat in the synagogue. He returned to take part in a controversy at a critical moment in the history of the congregation. The efforts of German Reform Judaism throughout much of the nineteenth century to "modernize" Jewish religious traditions and practices had been increasingly successful in the United States and indeed had come close to inducing some changes in Shearith Israel in 1878, in Benjamin Cardozo's youth. The Reform effort was renewed in 1893–1895. One proposal, associated with the move of the synagogue from 19th Street to its current location on Central Park West, was to end the practice of seating men and women separately. Cardozo took an active role in organizing a group of women to oppose the proposal. He got all the women of the Cardozo family to sign a petition, which eventually secured one hundred signatures from women, objecting to any change.[71]

A meeting of the electors of the congregation was called on June 5, 1895. A motion to end segregated seating was made by Gratz Nathan— the same Gratz Nathan with whom the elder Albert Cardozo had split fees—and seconded by Harmon Hendricks. Both men were Ben's first cousins. The other two speakers supporting the motion were Jonathan Nathan, Ben's uncle, and Henry Allen, his cousin. The minutes of the meeting record matter-of-factly that four speeches in support of the motion were made and that Dr. Mendes, rabbi of the congregation, and Adolphus Solomons, a respected philanthropist,[72] spoke in opposition. The minutes then report a third speech in opposition by twenty-five-year-old Benjamin Cardozo, "making a long address, impressive in ability and eloquence." Cardozo put his debating skills to good use. He pointed out that the Constitution of Shearith Israel forbade any boy from going into the women's gallery. He argued that the principle of separation of the sexes was embodied in the fundamental document of organization and that the electors could not violate the Constitution of Shearith Israel. He then warned the group that the law was on the side of the opponents of the motion and that if they were outvoted, there were laws outside to which the opponents could turn.[73] After Cardozo's speech, the electors took a vote and rejected the motion seventy-three to seven.[74]

It took a strong sense of self, indeed some substantial chutzpah, for a young man to put himself in the problematic position of defending a tradition in which he had chosen not to join. His participation in the meeting also demonstrates that although Cardozo had ceased to take part in the practice of Judaism, he had not fled his Jewish heritage. He thought of himself as a Jew and returned to his congregation in a moment of crisis, not to pray but to uphold a major feature of its religious practice.

The substance of Cardozo's position may also surprise those who are aware only of his progressive judicial reputation. Cardozo's personal values in family matters were traditional and old-fashioned. That attitude carried over to the religious tradition of separate seating, which was based substantially on the need for the members of the congregation to avoid distractions during their prayers, and it overcame the arguments for togetherness and against gender discrimination that were raised by the proponents of change. Cardozo's performance demonstrates that the youth who had been a shy college student had become a self-confident man with a strong public presence.

5

Developing a Practice

The first five years of Cardozo's practice up to 1896 had been an impressive beginning. During the next ten years, he established himself as an expert practitioner with a regular network of lawyers who sent him a constant stream of business. He also joined a new firm, wrote his first book, and settled into the pattern of his personal life.

Cardozo's successful handling of Galle v. Tode, the first case referred to him by Simpson & Werner, brought him considerable business from that firm. During the seven years thereafter he handled twenty-two different appeals for them.[1] Many of these appeals involved personal representation of the partners with respect to their private affairs or their professional conduct. One was a defense of Louis Werner on a contract of guaranty he had signed.[2] Another, which involved a charge of improper conduct against Angel Simpson, sought his removal as an assignee for the benefit of creditors. Cardozo was successful in defeating the charges and received a fee of $250 for his services on appeal.[3] Further proceedings in the same case involved additional charges of misconduct against Simpson, this time for having hired his partner, Louis Werner, as counsel to the receiver. The court condemned the practice of receivers hiring their law partners as their counsel but upheld it as not illegal when, as in this case, Simpson was not to share in Werner's fee.[4]

Another case, Wagstaff v. Marcy, also involved representation of

Simpson and Werner as clients, this time in their capacity as executors of a will.[5] The case demonstrated Cardozo's ability and willingness to attack hostile witnesses. The litigation was a classic family struggle, which occurred after the death of a father, between the children of his first wife and the child of a second wife who was the sole beneficiary of her father's $7,000 estate. Cardozo Brothers sought to uphold the will. The children of the first wife attacked the will on the ground that Mr. Parsons, the father, had been incompetent when he signed it. They introduced testimony from a variety of people, including the doctors who treated him as he was dying and some acquaintances who testified to a number of "peculiar" incidents. The dispute was bitter, but the will was upheld at trial on a verdict directed by the judge. The plaintiffs appealed.

Cardozo entered the case at this stage, wrote the brief, and argued the appeal. To uphold the directed verdict, Cardozo had to demonstrate that there was no evidence to warrant a jury finding of incompetence by reason of insanity or undue influence. Cardozo attacked with gusto the testimony of the plaintiffs' witnesses. He disposed of one doctor simply by noting that the doctor had testified "based on the patient's condition [in March 1897] and on hospital experience of a year and a half, that Mr. Parsons was irrational in December, 1896,"[6] and then, upon being shown letters written by Mr. Parsons after 1896, had completely reversed his conclusion. Cardozo dismissed the testimony of another doctor with the remark that this doctor's opinion carried "the weight that is born of a short term of experience in a hospital where there is no ward for the insane."[7] That doctor had also retreated in the face of Mr. Parsons's letters. Two other medical witnesses received similar sharp treatment in Cardozo's brief. "So it was that the evidence of plaintiffs' expert witnesses dissolved away. They had gone on the stand as witnesses for the plaintiffs. They had left it as witnesses for the defendants."[8]

Cardozo treated the testimony of the rest of the plaintiffs' witnesses with similar disdain. "Such trivialities, such arid and meaningless proof—the idle gossip, the careless banter, the rumors and the prattle of the village grocery and the servant's table, have seldom been submitted to influence the judgment of a court of justice on a grave and weighty issue."[9] Cardozo then demonstrated the irrelevance of the testimony of a whole series of witnesses: the servant girl who testified to conversations that she heard through the keyhole; the blacksmith who testified about a fainting spell; the gardener who testified that Mr. Parsons gave in to his beneficiary daughter in the matter of how the grapes should be trimmed; and the schoolteacher who testified that in 1886 Mr. Parsons did not want his daughter to read novels but then gave her some. As Cardozo put it with sarcastic humor, "The germs of mental decay and irresolution were clearly visible. The step was a short one between humoring a taste for novels and yielding upon vital issues like the trimming of a vine."[10] And so Cardozo proceeded through the record, destroying the testimony of the plaintiffs' witnesses and demonstrating that the deceased father had been well able to manage his affairs. The Appellate Division affirmed the judgment for Cardozo's clients without writing an opinion.

Wagstaff demonstrates that Cardozo was adept not only at arguing questions of law but also at marshaling testimonial evidence when the issue was almost wholly one of fact. He did not hesitate to be harsh with witnesses. Cardozo, who normally shrank from speaking ill of anyone, was ready with words of scorn when the case demanded.

Cardozo's performance in *Wagstaff* was not unique. Whenever he believed that the opposition, either the parties or their counsel, was trying to take advantage of his client or his firm, he fought back. Another instance was the lengthy litigation in Dickinson v. Earle.[11] The setting was an assignment for the benefit of creditors. In *Dickinson*, Cardozo represented an owner of summer resort hotels who had transferred the hotels to an assignee who was to manage them for the benefit of the owner's creditors. The owner subsequently settled with his creditors but then got involved in bitter litigation with the assignee over the assignee's compensation and operation of the hotels. The court finally removed the assignee and appointed the owner to run the hotels until the matter was settled. Instead of appealing that order, the assignee sought twice before different judges to have the order vacated. In the affidavits, the assignee and the owner accused one another of fraud and overreaching. The assignee's motions were denied, and he finally appealed the second denial. Cardozo made a powerful attack on the conduct of the assignee, arguing that the court should not hear the appeal because the assignee had failed to appeal the original order and that there were no new facts that would justify overturning the original order:

> The assignee who secretly left the country in October, 1898, who abandoned the property till June, 1899, who delayed the accounting by his absence for the greater part of a year, has the temerity to claim

that the defendants have been dilatory in the litigation of this cause . . .
At every stage, he has hampered and harassed the defendants by technical and captious opposition . . . At every stage he has sought to make
good his original threat to fight this case from Court to Court, and to
coerce the assignor into submission to his demands . . . The orderly
administration of justice requires that this guerrilla warfare, these harassing assaults, should end. They are an abuse of legal remedies and of
the privilege of counsel.[12]

This counterattack against the assignee was also an assault on the
assignee's counsel for serving as the instrument of harassment. As advocated by Cardozo, the Appellate Division affirmed the lower court's
order in favor of the hotel owner. That opinion did not end the litigation,
and Cardozo argued four more appeals in which he strongly castigated
the assignee's conduct before he finally succeeded in getting his client's
property back for him.[13]

In another case, Lamprecht v. Mohr, Cardozo directly attacked the
conduct of the opposing counsel, Franklin Bien. Bien was representing
plaintiffs in their attempt to revive a suit for breach of contract that had
lain dormant for nine years. In the interim, the defendant, his lawyer,
and the associate in charge of the case had all died.[14] The executors of
the original defendant's estate defended the suit by asserting that they
knew nothing of the matter and had settled his estate long since. Bien
filed an affidavit stating that the suit had not been pressed because the
original defendant's lawyer, Abram Kling, kept suggesting settlement.
The motion to revive the suit was denied, but the plaintiff appealed.
Cardozo was called in by Angel Simpson to argue the appeal on behalf
of the defendant's executors.

Cardozo dealt first with the case law relating to the executors' defense
that the plaintiffs were guilty of "laches" (undue delay). He then turned
to Mr. Bien's affidavit. Cardozo and Bien were not strangers. They had
worked together in litigation and Cardozo had been Bien's lawyer once
when Bien was a trustee.[15] The circumstances of the case required an
attack on Bien's affidavit, and Cardozo did not hesitate. Nor did he limit
himself to a suggestion that Bien was mistaken or had forgotten:

It is true that Mr. Bien says that if his recollection serves him aright,
one of the executors was in Mr. Kling's office when a settlement was
discussed . . . but the executor shows that Mr. Bien's recollection does

not serve him aright, and that in reality he had never been in Mr. Kling's office, or consulted with him at all.

It is, of course, impossible at this date to overcome by direct proof the allegation that Mr. Kling kept suggesting settlements in behalf of the estate. Mr. Kling is dead. His clerk, Mr. O'Connor, who had the case in charge, is also dead. But as neither of these gentlemen represented the estate and as neither of them had ever consulted with the executors about the action, it is probable that here again Mr. Bien's recollection has failed to serve him aright.[16]

Cardozo's strategy was to use the doubt he had cast on one portion of Bien's affidavit to discredit another portion of the affidavit where he had no contrary evidence to present. This method of argument is proper, although many lawyers would hesitate to press an attack against the word of an attorney to such lengths. Cardozo's willingness to go all out demonstrates his zeal as an advocate. He was tough.

That ability was an asset in dealing with his most troublesome opponent, Samuel Webber Parker, a businessman who used every known technique to forestall his creditors. Before Cardozo was admitted to practice, his brother Allie had handled a suit for a client who had a dispute with Parker and his Altonwood Stock Farm. Parker had agreed to settle the case in 1890 by paying $10,000 to Allie Cardozo's client. Parker had not paid, and Cardozo's client began an action to recover under the settlement. When the case was called for trial, Parker's witnesses were absent, and a default judgment was entered for the plaintiff. When Parker moved to reopen the case in 1893, Benjamin Cardozo then entered the litigation to oppose the motion, using affidavits that asserted Parker's financial irresponsibility and attacked Parker's veracity. The trial judge expressed doubts about Parker's good faith but allowed the motion on condition that Parker's company pay the plaintiff's expenses in the event of further delay. Parker's company appealed the conditions imposed by the order. Benjamin Cardozo wrote a brief referring to Parker's excuses as palpably false, and the conditions were upheld.[17]

Although there were no further reported proceedings in that Altonwood case, Benjamin Cardozo was not finished with Mr. Parker. Cardozo & Nathan represented the American Exchange National Bank, which had been trying to collect a $217,000 debt from Parker and Altonwood Park Company for over thirteen years. By 1905, after further loans and numerous transactions relating to real estate held by the bank as collateral, Cardozo & Nathan started a foreclosure proceeding on behalf of the bank to collect its debt, which it then calculated at $697,000. Parker and Altonwood Park Company asserted a variety of defenses and a counterclaim for $1,350,000 at the trial, which was handled by Michael Cardozo. The parties filed a stipulation reciting a $600,000 debt owed by Parker and Altonwood Park, the invalidity of their counterclaims, and the right of the bank to foreclose, but withholding entry of a judgment for $600,000 for three months to give the Parker family time to redeem, i.e., to retain their ownership of the property by paying off the debt.

The Parker family did not pay the debt and began what Benjamin Cardozo later described as a "long series of elusive and harassing proceedings to nullify or evade the judgment of the court . . . [that were] revolting in their hypocrisy."[18] Altonwood obtained four adjournments of the foreclosure sale. Eventually, however, the sale took place, the property was bid in by the bank, and the sale was confirmed. Thereafter, Altonwood moved to set aside the foreclosure, largely on the ground that the original stipulations had not been authorized by the company. Mrs. Parker filed an affidavit to that effect, adding that her husband had no authority to hire lawyers for Altonwood on his own. She also began a stockholder's suit to set aside the judgment and sale on the ground that the corporation had not been served with a summons. Michael Cardozo, who had been handling these matters, was nominated to run for the Supreme Court of New York and then suddenly died.[19] Edgar Nathan took over the suits, and he called in Benjamin Cardozo.

The *Parker* case was a cause célèbre in both Edgar Nathan's firm and Benjamin Cardozo's firm. In a letter to a vacationing Edgar Nathan in 1907, Cardozo commented, "I hope that you are loading yourself up with strength and health at Atlantic City so that you may cope with the Parker demons and the other powers of darkness."[20] Later that year, in a letter written while he was vacationing in Europe, Cardozo expressed the hope that "the . . . insignificant atom, Samuel Webber Parker, has done no mischief, and brought no other suits."[21]

Shortly after Cardozo returned from Europe, however, he was again embroiled with the Parkers. The Altonwood Park Company made an assignment of its assets to an assignee who was to pay off its creditors. The assignee brought suit to have the foreclosure and sale that had been conducted by Nathan's bank client overturned. After a three-day trial, the trial court denied any relief, and the assignee appealed. Cardozo argued that the judgment in the foreclosure proceeding could not be attacked except for fraud, which had not been shown, and the Appellate Division decided for his client on that ground.[22]

Parker's assignee appealed to the Court of Appeals. Benjamin Cardozo and Edgar Nathan filed a fiery brief. They castigated Parker for seeking refuge first behind his "wife's skirts," then behind the Altonwood Park Company, and then behind an assignee: "The orderly administration of justice, the sanctity of judicial decrees, the imperative need that litigants shall not be suffered to play the game of litigation with something hidden up their sleeves . . . all these fundamental considerations of public policy require that there be an end to the harassing attacks by the plaintiff and those behind him."[23] The Court of Appeals affirmed in 1911 on the basis of the opinion of the Appellate Division. That apparently ended Samuel Webber Parker's efforts to forestall the victory obtained by Cardozo's clients.[24]

In trying to wear down Cardozo in court, Parker had underestimated his adversary. Cardozo was not only a good legal craftsman. He knew how to argue a case; he gave no quarter when antagonized; and he fought tenaciously.

––––––––––

Cardozo had an opportunity to fight for a principle that he would later establish as a judge in a case referred to him by Simpson & Werner in 1897. The case was Hastings v. Consolidated Dental Manufacturing Company. The principle was the high standard of fiduciary conduct required of people engaged in business together.[25] Cardozo's clients (Hastings) lost out to Consolidated in their attempt to purchase the dental gold manufacturing portion of a business from the estate of its former owner. Dr. Frantz, president of Consolidated, had started out negotiating for Hastings and submitted an offer on their behalf for the portion of the business that they wanted. Dr. Frantz then learned that the entire business was available, and he purchased it for Consolidated. Cardozo contended that Dr. Frantz was legally the plaintiffs' agent; but in seeking a preliminary injunction from the trial court against Consolidated's operation of the manufacturing business, he argued that his clients should prevail even if Dr. Frantz had only been a volunteer.

The case showed Cardozo at his best. Dr. Frantz had submitted a lengthy affidavit asserting that he had voluntarily tried to help the plaintiffs out, but that of course the interests of his own company came first. Cardozo used that affidavit as the basis for his legal argument in a very persuasive way. He reviewed the Frantz affidavit fact by fact and then summarized it effectively: "It is proved . . . by the defendant's own admissions, that Frantz undertook to purchase this property for the plaintiffs . . . that he diverted them from negotiating for themselves, and that, surreptitiously and without warning, and while he was holding out to them the promise of success, he abandoned their interests and purchased the property himself."

Cardozo used this factual conclusion to support his legal argument that his clients were entitled to an injunction against Continental's operation of the business that it had purchased.

> The great principle of the courts of equity that an agent or trustee or one who occupies a fiduciary relation may not purchase, either for himself or for anyone with whom his interests are united, the property which he has undertaken to purchase for his principal . . . is as broad and comprehensive as the dictates of morality which called it into life . . . It simply asks whether the relation between the parties is such that it is against equity and conscience that the property should be retained, and when that question has been answered in the affirmative it acts upon the parties and the property through the theory of a constructive trust. No legal contract of agency need be proven; no contract that would be enforceable at law need be shown to exist; it is enough that good conscience demands the restoration of the property, and that its retention by the defendant should shock the sense of right.[26]

The *Hastings* case demonstrates that Cardozo knew how to make a powerful appeal to equity, justice, and morality when the facts and the law permitted. It would be tempting, but dangerous, to assume that all such arguments derived from his own personal sense of morality. As an advocate, Cardozo argued for a variety of positions that he would later regard unsympathetically when he became a judge. His *Hastings* argument, however, did reflect his personal view of duties and obligations, and he would later move legal doctrine in that direction.

But his argument in *Hastings* failed. In a two-sentence opinion, the lower court denied the motion for a preliminary injunction on the ground that no agency had been shown. The Appellate Division also refused preliminary relief, because in its view the affidavits did not establish a fiduciary relationship. The court left the plaintiffs to attempt to prove the fiduciary relationship at trial. The ultimate fate of the case is not recorded.

During this period, Cardozo met a lawyer who would play an important role in his professional future. That man was Louis Marshall, an able, well-known attorney with wide interests outside the law—in Jewish affairs, civil rights, conservation, and New York politics.[27] Cardozo was first associated with Marshall in a major case referred to him in 1899 by Simpson & Werner. In Mahoney v. Bernhard, Cardozo and Marshall each represented groups of stockholders of a failed bank seeking to avoid statutory liability for the debts of the bank.[28] They each made similar, and unsuccessful, technical arguments in the Appellate Division denying the right of creditors of the insolvent bank to enforce stockholder liability. On the appeal to the Court of Appeals, Marshall's brief repeated his earlier arguments. Cardozo, however, completely rethought the case and argued that the legislature did not mean to impose liability retroactively on persons who had been stockholders prior to the effective date of the law. He backed up his statutory interpretation with the argument that retroactive imposition of liability would violate the Contract Clause of the federal Constitution.[29] The Court of Appeals was not impressed, and it affirmed the judgment without writing any opinion at all. Quite possibly that court was not willing to consider the important arguments Cardozo raised when they had not been raised at the trial level and in the Appellate Division.

Louis Marshall's experience working with the twenty-nine year old Benjamin Cardozo in *Mahoney* and against him in another matter at the same time left him with a favorable impression.[30] He called Cardozo in to assist his firm in litigation that constituted a skirmish in a larger war between two giants in the American copper mining industry.[31] Marshall's clients, Lewisohn Brothers, were sales agents for the Boston & Montana Company, one of the large copper companies, and also stockholders in the Anaconda Company. They sought to obtain an injunction against an Anaconda stockholders' meeting that had been called to approve the sale of a mining claim to the Montana Company, controlled by F. A. Heinze. The Boston & Montana Company was offering Anaconda more money for the claim and asserted that the Montana Company's purchase contract with Anaconda was not binding. Heinze was the enfant terrible of the copper industry. A former engineer for the Boston & Montana Company, he had parlayed mining knowledge, audacity, and ruthlessness into an empire.[32]

Leading New York counsel, Alexander & Green, Esek Cowen, and Everett Masten, senior partner of Masten & Nichols, represented Anaconda and Heinze. Marshall's decision to call in Cardozo indicates his regard for Cardozo's ability. The New York injunction suit, which failed in the lower courts, was not pursued further.[33] The main litigation between the copper companies took place in the Montana courts, and Marshall and Cardozo were not involved.

Still not thirty, Cardozo's practice was more and more that of a lawyer's lawyer, an attorney whom other attorneys called in to help with difficult matters. Sometimes that involved rescuing other lawyers from their mistakes. One such effort involved a reference from his cousins in the Lyons firm in connection with an agreement that had been badly drawn by Alfred Lyons.[34] The Lyons firm represented the State Bank, a small New York bank, in connection with many of its real estate transactions.[35] The State Bank held a mortgage on property of Mr. and Mrs. Petschaft that was in default. After the bank foreclosed its mortgage, the Petschafts wished to get their property back, "redeem" it in legal terms. Alfred Lyons drafted an agreement that appeared to permit the Petschafts' prospective son-in-law to redeem by payment of the price paid at the foreclosure sale without any provision for full payment of the Petschafts' original debt to the bank, which was greater than the sale price. The Petschafts' son-in-law sued the bank to force it to carry out the agreement as written, allowing him to redeem by paying just the foreclosure sale price.

The Lyons firm called in Cardozo at the trial level to handle the proceedings before a referee who had been appointed by the court to hear the testimony. Cardozo's crucial task was to force the Petschafts to elaborate the basis of the agreement as it was written. The purpose was to demonstrate how utterly improbable their explanation was so that the court would credit the testimony of his client and "reform" the contract, that is, enforce it in accordance with the parties' actual oral agreement instead of as written. Cardozo pressed Mr. Petschaft and his prospective son-in-law very hard on cross-examination, so that they came forth with different, and remarkable, stories to explain why they believed the bank would enter into a contract that would involve a windfall for them and a loss to the bank. Cardozo also demonstrated that the prospective son-in-law was unable to understand the agreement that he had signed. Cardozo's cross-examination was sufficiently successful that the referee concluded that he could not give "full credit" to Mr.

Petschaft's testimony.[36] The referee, however, was not willing to "reform" the contract because, applying a reasonable doubt standard, he was not certain that both parties had made a mistake. He did conclude that there was a mistake on the bank's part and on that basis held that it would be inequitable to order the written agreement enforced. When the son-in-law appealed, the Appellate Division affirmed the decision, adding that on the testimony, reformation might have been granted.[37] The case demonstrates that Cardozo was not just a good appellate lawyer but that he was equally skilled at the trial level.[38]

Cardozo's work in this intermediate portion of his practice was largely in the fields of business and personal finance. His clients were usually middle-class business and professional people. His success in financial litigation brought him a good deal of work in the stock brokerage field. Many of these cases involved collection of customers' accounts on behalf of a brokerage house.

One case, Douglas v. Carpenter in 1897, had far-reaching significance because Cardozo attacked the general custom of brokers who used their customers' securities as collateral to secure the loans that they regularly needed to conduct their business.[39] Cardozo's clients had bought stock through a stockbroker on "margin," that is, they paid only a small portion of the purchase price, expecting to pay the balance by selling when the price rose. They were sued by the brokers for a balance due in the margin account. Cardozo Brothers defended the suit with an innovative argument. They claimed that the brokers had made improper use of the stock that their clients had purchased on margin, in legal parlance, that the brokers had "converted" it and were liable to their customers for its value. The brokers had followed a common practice of borrowing money themselves, using the stock of Cardozo's clients and other customers as collateral to secure an operating loan that was larger than the customers' indebtedness. Cardozo's clients had offered to prove that the brokers' loan left the brokers without sufficient unpledged stock to give customers who paid off their loans immediate possession of their stock. The case was heard by a referee at the trial level, and he gave a judgment for the brokers for the balance due. The customers then appealed to the Appellate Division, and Benjamin Cardozo wrote the brief and argued the case.

Cardozo's argument threatened the universal "custom of the street." Indeed, since margin customers typically paid only a small percentage of the purchase price of their own stock and since banks were willing to finance these transactions by making a small number of large loans to stockbrokers but not a large number of small loans to their customers, the brokers' pledges of the underlying stock were essential to the continuation of margin business.[40]

Cardozo, who understood the practicalities of the securities markets, argued that a conclusion that the brokers had "converted" his clients' stock would not have a negative impact on the brokerage business. Brokers could get their customers' consent to repledging their stock to secure broker loans. Stockbrokers, however, were reluctant to seek such consent because it would emphasize to margin customers that they were taking an additional risk beside the known risk of having to put up a greater percentage of the purchase price of their own stock if the price of the stock fell. They also ran the risk of losing their stock if a broker was unable to pay off its own loan against which the customer's stock was pledged.

The Appellate Division reversed the judgment for the brokers. It accepted Cardozo's argument that there was a conversion if the brokers did not have enough unpledged stock to return to customers who repaid their loans. Henceforth, careful brokers and their lawyers would have to weigh the risk of not getting their customers' consent to use their stock as collateral for the brokers' loans against the possibility that a subsequent dispute with a customer might produce a claim of conversion against them. Douglas v. Carpenter produced a stir "on the street" and thereby brought Cardozo's name to the fore in financial circles as a powerful and innovative advocate.[41]

Cardozo's practice also expanded geographically beyond the bounds of the state court system's First Department (Manhattan and a portion of the Bronx) where his office was located. He tried In re Simpson in Saratoga Springs, north of Albany, and argued the appeal of that case three times in the Third Department (the Albany area) in the years 1897–1899.[42] Cardozo Brothers also represented Catherine Ann Cornell, widow of banking, railroad, and real estate magnate Thomas Cornell, and later her estate.[43] There were several proceedings upstate in Ulster County involving the Cornell estate in which the trustee's bond and the right to income from the sale of a steamboat company were at issue. Allie Cardozo handled some of the early motions before the Surrogate (the judicial officer in probate matters), but Benjamin Cardozo appeared in the Appellate Division and the Court of Appeals.[44]

Cardozo also appeared several times in litigation in the Second Department, comprising Brooklyn and the rest of Long Island.[45] An important case was People ex rel. Linton v. The Brooklyn Heights Railroad Company, decided in 1902.[46] The railroad had obtained control of all elevated railroad service in Brooklyn. It thereupon terminated some through service to the Cypress Hills terminus and required passengers to change from elevated trains to surface transportation in order to reach that terminal during non–rush hour times. A passenger brought suit seeking a writ of mandamus, a court order compelling the performance of a duty, in this case the operation of service to the Cypress Hills terminal as it had been operated prior to the defendant's lease. Stephen Baldwin, who had once worked for Cardozo, Newcombe & Donohue and subsequently became a well-known trial lawyer, handled the case for the plaintiff at the trial level. The jury found that public necessity required the defendant to operate its service as before, and it issued a writ of mandamus to compel it to do so.

Baldwin brought Cardozo in to help with the brief when the railroad appealed, although Baldwin argued the case both in the Appellate Division and in the Court of Appeals. The great problem in upholding the writ was the general rule that a court would not issue a writ of mandamus to compel the exercise of a discretionary act. Railroad law gave the company's board of directors power to regulate its service, and there was no legal requirement regarding the manner of carrying passengers between terminals. In addition, there was an administrative agency, the Board of Railroad Commissioners, to whom complaints about service could be taken, and so there was no need for the extraordinary interference represented by a writ of mandamus.

Cardozo and Baldwin filed good briefs in both appellate courts even though they failed to convince the courts to uphold the order of mandamus. They attempted to encourage the courts to exercise some control over the exercise of discretion of corporate managers, at least where a public franchise was involved. They sought to overcome the difficult point that courts would not enforce a discretionary duty when there was no clear statutory requirement, by raising the question involved to a more generalized one of principle. They argued that the withdrawal of elevated service for long hours every day and for whole days on weekends and holidays amounted to a virtual abandonment of the elevated service. The court should therefore issue the writ of mandamus to compel the railroad to continue the previous service because of the monopoly that had been given to it.

Baldwin and Cardozo attempted to use the facts in such a way as to come within existing legal doctrine justifying the use of mandamus to compel the railroad to take action. But they were really asking the court to accept their public policy arguments and to exert judicial power to ensure the continuation of service to the public. That argument sought to capitalize on the current political controversy about misuse of corporate privilege, but it failed.[47] Both the Appellate Division, one judge dissenting, and the Court of Appeals rejected their argument. The courts regarded the case as involving only the regulation of hours of service, and the Court of Appeals held that the Board of Railroad Commissioners, whose powers had recently been increased by statute, was the proper forum for complaint about abuse of discretion.

After having served as an adjunct of Simpson & Werner for so long, Cardozo Brothers merged with them in 1903. The new firm of Simpson, Werner & Cardozo maintained its office at 52 Broadway, where both firms had previously had separate offices.[48] The merger did not change the nature of Cardozo's practice. He continued the same busy schedule of trying cases and arguing appeals. During this period, Cardozo also made his first appearance in United States Supreme Court matters, once in 1902 and twice in 1905. The fact of his appearance was notable, but the cases were not. In one case, he assisted in defending a judgment obtained by the receiver of an insolvent steamship company against the suit of a supplier who claimed a lien on the company's boats. The Supreme Court refused to hear the claim of the supplier.[49] In another case, the Supreme Court upheld Cardozo's argument on behalf of the receiver of a bankrupt brokerage house that the Court had no jurisdiction to hear an appeal by a member of the firm from an order of the district court that he sell his Stock Exchange seat as an asset of the house.[50] In the third, the Court agreed with Cardozo's argument that the service of a summons by a plaintiff on a foreign corporation was defective and that the trial court therefore had no jurisdiction.[51] These decisions were all based on written submissions by the parties. Cardozo did not make a personal appearance before the Court.

This ten-year period between his mid-twenties and mid-thirties confirmed the pattern of Cardozo's personal life. These were the years in which many of his contemporaries were marrying and beginning to raise families. Cardozo, though, did not marry. He continued his life with

Nellie in the Madison Avenue home and then in the home at 16 West 75th Street to which they moved in 1902.[52] Ben's cousin Annie Nathan Meyer had sharp views about Ben's relationship with Nellie. Annie was an intelligent, spirited, and competitive woman, a doer for whom Nellie's quiet life carried no appeal. Believing that Nellie's love for Ben was too possessive, Annie blamed her for his never having married.[53]

A number of people have linked Ben's name to various women, and others have stated that he would have married but could not bear to leave Nellie.[54] A dinner companion reportedly asked Cardozo whether he had ever been in love and said that Cardozo replied "once." Cardozo also told a cousin who asked whether he would consider marrying that he could "never put Nell in second place."[55] Nellie told her friend Louise Wise that she would die if Ben married. She even expressed some displeasure when Ben was not home in the evenings.[56] Some of these comments may relate to later years, after Nellie was ill and totally dependent on him for attention and care. Ben's response about being in love "once" could conceivably have referred to Nellie, if made after her death. A remarkable handwritten note addressed "To whom it may Concern" stated simply, "This is to certify that I love my Nunnie better than all the rest of the world combined. Dated, N.Y., Aug. 20, 1898. B.N.C."[57] Nunnie is not otherwise identified, but it seems plausible that it had been Ben's best effort at saying the name Nellie when he was a baby and that the name remained a private joke. This surmise is fortified by the letter's location in Cardozo's desk when he died. He may have reclaimed it after Nellie died and kept it as a memento when he destroyed his other correspondence.

The various stories of Cardozo's near-marriage are difficult to credit. None mention a long-lasting courtship. Ethel Siesfeld, to whom he has been linked, stated much later that her only acquaintance with Cardozo was one summer meeting at Lake Saranac.[58] Blanche Content, who had been a friend of both Emily and Ben and was a gregarious woman who loved to go to parties, stated later in her life that Ben had wanted to marry her.[59] Other than her assertion, there is no evidence to support the story. Ben's cousin Addie Cardozo, who had joined Emily in trying to include Ben in their social lives, agreed with the Annie Nathan Meyer view of Nellie's influence. Addie did not credit the stories linking Ben with various women. She did "not believe that he was ever in love or thought of marriage. He was too much absorbed, and also owned, by . . . Nellie."[60]

Benjamin Cardozo's bachelor status was not unusual in the Sephardic community and especially in the Cardozo-Nathan family. Half of Ben's first cousins who lived to adulthood never married.[61] If many of this group were looking to marry within the Sephardic community, and such marriages were indeed common, then the small size of the community hindered the search. Although his twin sister Emily did marry someone who was not Jewish, Ben was proud of his heritage, believed in tradition, and may well have believed that he ought not to marry outside his community.

There were additional obstacles for Ben. Although we know nothing at all about the force of his sexual drive, it seems apparent that he lived a chaste life. Even in his later years, when he had a few friendships with some women, mostly married women, and displayed a courtly attitude toward women generally, he was still noticeably shy and ill at ease until he knew them well. The women whom he knew best were members of his family and the women who worked in his household. Work and family obligations consumed nearly all of his time.

But it was neither Nellie nor these social obstacles that prevented Cardozo from getting married; that circumstance was a result of his own choices. Ben had a strong will and knew how to achieve the results that he set his mind to, whether as a student, lawyer, or judge. Young, successful, and reasonably handsome, he would have been an eligible suitor and a good prospect had he wanted to marry. But he stayed, single, in the family home. His work habits and his shyness around women suggest that it would have taken either an unusual stroke of fortune or a push, perhaps from Nellie herself, to engage him in the kind of activities that would have led to marriage. Apparently, Ben simply did not want to get married.

That decision did not leave him unfulfilled. He had performed spectacularly well at Columbia and had achieved recognition from his peers and his teachers. He also received admiration at home, especially from Nellie. She must have been as proud of his achievements as any parent. Indeed, after the family's earlier disgrace, she must have seen Ben as the redeemer of the family name.

Work dominated Ben's daytime activities. Nellie occupied a large part of the rest of his life. She filled the need for close human companionship, and their closeness was a salvation for him. From 1891, when Ben began his professional career, until 1929, when Nellie died, she was always home when he came home. Except for the last years, when she was ill, she was there to share intelligent conversation, books, chess, the piano, gossip, humor, worries, and the intimacies of family life.

————

Cardozo engaged in a few Jewish communal activities during this period. He sometimes attended the Sabbath afternoon gatherings at Shearith Israel on honorific occasions.[62] He also joined an elite club of New York Jewish professionals, the Judaeans. The club, a social and cultural association "designed to gather together a body of cultured Jewish gentlemen . . . to advance the intellectual and spiritual aspirations of the Jews," was formed in New York City in 1897.[63] The founders were all prominent men, and the society was a Jewish version of another exclusive New York institution, the Century Club.[64] The club held dinner meetings several times a year and listened to papers presented by their members and invited guests on topics of interest to Jews. There is no list of the original members, and Cardozo was likely too young in 1897 to have been asked to be a founder. Sometime between 1897 and 1913, as his reputation grew, he was asked to join. He remained a member during all his years in New York.[65]

In 1898, when Cardozo was in his late twenties, he addressed the subject of his Judaism, indirectly but clearly enough, in an evening talk—possibly at Shearith Israel—on Benjamin Disraeli.[66] Like Cardozo, Disraeli had been a Sephardic Jew who ceased to believe in the religious tenets of Judaism as a youth. But unlike Cardozo, who kept his ties to the synagogue, Disraeli broke his ties. At the age of thirteen, he turned from studying for his Bar Mitzvah to be baptized a Christian. Even though Cardozo forgave Disraeli the renunciation of his faith, he could not forgive the cutting of ties with the community, with his ancestors, that was implied by Disraeli's conversion to Christianity. Cardozo reminded his audience of the "playful" irony that Disraeli was still known and remembered as a Jew.[67] Cardozo did not, however, disown Disraeli completely. Cardozo honored him for his devotion to Jews, for preaching to the world the dignity, the merit of Jews. But Cardozo deplored Disraeli's "disloyalty to the faith" in attempting to justify his own path by claiming that Christianity was the perfection of Judaism.[68]

Cardozo then addressed the issue of Disraeli as a public man, and Albert Cardozo's public career could not have been far from his mind. Cardozo saw Disraeli as a man with a consuming ambition who took a stand on the wrong side of many important issues, supporting protectionism, monarchy, slavery, and jingoism in his favoring Turkey against Russia. Although Cardozo credited Disraeli with a vision of promoting the greatness of his country, he whisked his praise away by concluding that "[i]t was, I think, in his conception of glory that difficulty lay. His oriental nature, his passion for display, for gorgeous richness which manifested itself in dress, in speech, in writing, too often made him disposed to identifying the true glory of nations with the splendor and show of imperial supremacy."[69]

In the end Cardozo could not come to terms with his subject. Disraeli was sometimes partisan, but in his best moments a statesman, sometimes eloquent, sometimes turgid, sometimes brilliant, sometimes arid, sometimes hinting at philosophy, sometimes cynical and sarcastic, sometimes a magnificent success, sometimes a magnificent failure. But withal he was a "splendid Titan" who in the end "affected [Jews] for good. He taught us to think worthily of ourselves."[70] Although he should have stood for higher things, he helped raise the self-consciousness of Jews. Hertzl and Zionists worked on soil tilled by Disraeli, and for that he should be honored.

Cardozo's tribute to Disraeli was painfully measured. The modern publisher of Cardozo's essay, Michael Selzer, contrasted Disraeli's enthusiastic view of his Jewishness with Cardozo's tentative relation to his Judaism, always looking over his shoulder, always concerned as an assimilationist with how others regarded him. Selzer traced this attitude to Albert Cardozo's disgrace, which led Benjamin to lead his life with an "immense and impregnable, perhaps even an excessive, propriety."[71] But Selzer's comparison of Cardozo and Disraeli as Jews fails. It simply neglects the fact that whatever Disraeli did for Jews, he did as a practicing Christian. As for Cardozo, his cautious manner covered a strong character, including a strong identification of himself as a Jew. Cardozo showed something of himself in his reaction to the life of Disraeli. He disparaged the public man who was consumed by desire for glory. More importantly, he was critical of the Jew turned Christian. This was a criticism of Disraeli's fractured identity, not his beliefs. Cardozo did not say one word extolling the religious beliefs of Judaism. But his ties to the Sephardic community and thereby to his ancestors were fundamental elements in Benjamin Cardozo's life.

Cardozo made ambitious use of his spare time in these years and produced his first book, *The Jurisdiction of the Court of Appeals of the State of New York,* published in 1903. Cardozo stated that recent amendments to the state constitution and to a portion of the statutes governing the jurisdiction of the Court of Appeals had motivated him to write the book. He wanted to set forth the jurisdiction of the court as an aid to lawyers, especially since failure to comprehend that jurisdiction had "resulted, on many occasions, in a denial of justice."[72]

Cardozo wrote the book before securing a publisher. Once the text was completed, Cardozo turned to Louis Marshall, who had widespread connections, for assistance. Marshall was obliging. He read the manuscript, albeit "hastily," and praised it. More importantly, he enclosed a letter of introduction to A. Bleecker Banks, an Albany law book publisher. Marshall also wrote to Banks commenting on the confusing nature of the subject and commending Cardozo for the "clearness of thought and expression and intelligent appreciation of the Judiciary Article—and of the decisions which have interpreted and applied it or which bear upon its interpretation."[73] Banks undertook to publish the manuscript, and Marshall became negotiator and middleman between Cardozo and Banks. All matters, including suggestions for changes and even transmission of proofs, went through Marshall's hands.

In form, Cardozo's book presented legal principles in much the same way that Theodore Dwight might have done. Cardozo broke his subject matter into 134 topics in which he set forth the basic legal doctrine under each heading with citations to, and quotations from, the relevant court decisions. Cardozo wanted the book to be both technical and practical. He accepted the jurisdiction of the Court of Appeals in the court system as it was and sought to help lawyers understand it. But he also delved into the complexities of the court's jurisdiction, especially those created by the constitutional restriction of its jurisdiction, except in death penalty cases, to questions of law as opposed to questions of fact. The prohibition against reviewing facts had produced an intricate and important body of legal doctrine. Cardozo went to great pains to discuss it in detail.

While Cardozo reported legal doctrine in the narrow areas of law that he covered, he also often analyzed the cases and the distinctions they drew among various situations quite critically with respect to internal consistency and achievement of the purpose of the statutory and consti-

tutional provisions. But he made no effort to deal with larger aspects of
the topics—no effort to trace the historical development of the Court's
jurisdiction as a response to perceptions of its role in the judicial system
and of the judicial system in society, and no systematic effort to judge
how well the system met the needs of the times.[74]

Cardozo's statement of the role of the Court of Appeals was "classic."[75] He began by identifying the function of the court as "not of
declaring justice between man and man, but of settling the law." He did
not intend to sever the concept of law from the concept of justice. His
point was that the court must keep in mind that its job was to determine
principles of justice that would apply across the board and that it should
not focus just on a particular case. Later, as a judge, he would find that
that was a complicated task and that often it was preferable to limit the
announcement of a principle to the facts of the particular case.

The core of the book was Cardozo's discussion of the myriad ramifications of the restriction of the court's jurisdiction to questions of law.
What constituted a question of law? Could the Court of Appeals look
beyond the order of the Appellate Division to its opinion in order to
determine the basis for that court's judgment? When should an order
state that it was based on questions of fact or law? What was the Court's
power to review the Appellate Division's reversal of a jury verdict? How
far might the Court consider facts not embodied in a judgment in order
to reverse, or to affirm, a judgment? What was its power to review a
discretionary order of the Appellate Division?

The Court of Appeals had discussed these issues in numerous opinions, and so a great deal of Cardozo's discussion consisted of an orderly
explanation of the precedents. When the rule was not wholly clear,
Cardozo said so, and he did not hesitate to criticize the Court's decisions.
Under the guise of criticizing the constitutional command restricting the
Court of Appeals to questions of law, he criticized the Court of Appeals'
decision in a recent major case without naming it at that point.[76] The
issue in National Harrow Company v. Bement & Sons related to the
Court's review of a judgment entered in the so-called "short form,"
without elaborate findings of fact and conclusions of law. When the
Appellate Division had unanimously affirmed a judgment, the Court of
Appeals had held that all allegations of the complaint were presumed to
have been found in the plaintiff's favor and that all issues arising upon
defenses pleaded in the answer were presumed to have been found
against the defendant. Cardozo argued that under the rule "actions may

conceivably be decided contrary to the real truth and justice of the case, in obedience to an elaborate system of artificial presumptions." In fact, if a trial court found against a defendant and entered a judgment in "the short form" on a legal issue in a case in which the facts were agreed upon, the Court's rule, in cases of unanimous affirmance by the Appellate Division, presumed that the trial judge had found against the defendant on the facts as well as the law. "Thus by two fictions,—one the fiction that the trial judge negatived the existence of uncontroverted facts, and the other the fiction that there was evidence to sustain him in so doing," the Court must inevitably affirm the judgment of the Appellate Division—even if it agreed with the appellant on the legal issue. "A question, in its origin one of law, Do certain admitted facts constitute a defense? becomes by the legerdemain of an appeal and unanimous affirmance transformed into a question of fact. No doubt the purpose of the Constitution was to restrict the Court of Appeals to questions of law, but under the rule which the Constitution lays down, the court in many an instance never reaches the real questions of law which underlie the case. Its progress is inexorably barred by fictions and presumptions."[77]

This commentary by Cardozo, which was the sharpest in the book, was courageous criticism of a decision that, as Louis Marshall reported, had "surprised a considerable portion of the Bar."[78] But Cardozo's original criticism had been even stronger. Cardozo had used the opinion to discuss the source of the jurisdiction of the Court of Appeals and of the power of the legislature to restrict it. After noting the almost unlimited restrictive power of the legislature, Cardozo had added, in language reminiscent of Chief Justice John Marshall's comment on the asserted power of the states to tax a national bank, that "the power to restrict jurisdiction involves the power to destroy it and thus to leave the Court the form of existence only and not the substance of authority."[79] From this Cardozo drew the conclusion that "this unchecked power of limitation stamps the Court as a statutory rather than a constitutional body."[80]

This conclusion, demeaning to the Court of Appeals, was too much for "Judge Parker" to whom Banks had sent the manuscript for comment. There were two eminent Judge Parkers in New York, and Louis Marshall's correspondence does not identify which Judge Parker received the manuscript. It was most likely Chief Judge Alton Parker of the Court of Appeals, author of the opinion in *National Harrow,* but possibly it might have been Presiding Judge Charles Parker of the Appellate Division, Third Department.[81] At all events, "Judge Parker" was critical of Cardozo's treatment of National Harrow Company v. Bement & Sons. On the basis of Judge Parker's criticism, Banks asked Cardozo to delete the comments that relegated the Court of Appeals to a "statutory" body and "[a]fter some discussion," Marshall induced Cardozo to do so. The strength of Judge Parker's objection may be judged by the fact that Marshall felt compelled to tell Banks that Cardozo "did not in anything that he said intend the slightest disrespect to the Court."[82]

Cardozo was not alone in his criticism. While his book was at the press, the legislature abolished the short form of decision, thus limiting the effect of *National Harrow.* The following year, the legislature overrode the decision by restoring the right of litigants to submit proposed findings of fact and requiring the trial court to rule on them.[83] Thus, the main reform of procedure urged by Cardozo was met by the legislature.

Cardozo's book filled a need in New York practice and brought him to the attention of the entire bar of the state.[84] It proved useful to lawyers involved in appellate work. In 1909, the publishers brought out a second edition, which was a reprint of the first with the addition of a supplement commenting on various sections of the original work in light of recent developments.

At the end of this intermediate period of Cardozo's practice, he had established himself in the profession. He was known throughout the state by his frequent appearances in the appellate courts and by his book. In just fifteen years of practice, he had achieved the rare status of a "lawyer's lawyer," that small group of lawyers to whom other lawyers regularly turned for help.

6

Lawyer's Lawyer

At the beginning of 1906, Benjamin Cardozo was thirty-five years old. As successful as he had already been, his career now took a notable leap forward. His Court of Appeals caseload quadrupled.[1] His circle of forwarding lawyers expanded. He handled more varied and interesting cases. His reputation increased, and Attorney General Wickersham offered him an appointment as a federal district judge.

———

The usual run of cases that Cardozo had handled prior to 1906 involved contract interpretation and commercial debt collection litigation. Rawson v. Leggett, which Cardozo argued in 1906, is an example of the new kinds of cases that Cardozo argued in the last third of his career as a practicing lawyer.[2] *Rawson* was a "torts" case, a field in which Cardozo would make a major contribution when he became a judge. Such cases deal with those rights and duties of individuals toward one another that are not created by an explicit agreement. An employee of a wholesale grocery company misappropriated money, and when caught, he implicated Byron Rawson in his confession. At the instigation of the grocers, indictments for grand larceny were filed against Rawson but were later dismissed. Morris Hirsch, an able lawyer who was to become a good friend of Cardozo, filed a complaint for malicious prosecution on behalf of Rawson against the grocers and won a jury verdict for

$25,000, a large sum at the time, for Rawson. The grocers appealed, arguing that the jury's verdict should be overturned because there was not sufficient evidence to support the jury's finding that the grocers lacked "probable cause" for instituting criminal proceedings.

Hirsch brought Cardozo in to assist on the brief, but Hirsch argued the appeal himself successfully in the Appellate Division.[3] When the case was appealed to the Court of Appeals, there was another change of counsel. Cardozo argued the case for Rawson, and the grocers hired Alton Parker. Parker had been Chief Judge of the Court of Appeals and the Democratic presidential candidate in 1904. Cardozo was now litigating in the major leagues. The large verdict and the finding that they had invoked the criminal law maliciously obviously made the matter an important one for the grocers. Rawson's case was buttressed by the affirmance in the Appellate Division and by a persuasive brief that combed the record to set forth every scrap of evidence that cast doubt on the defendant's good faith in instituting the criminal proceedings. Nevertheless, the Court of Appeals reversed, 4–3, finding that the grocers had had probable cause as a matter of law to instigate the criminal charges.

Cardozo argued a more typical torts case, a personal injury case, at the same time as *Rawson*. In Carpenter v. The City of New York, Cardozo argued unsuccessfully to sustain a verdict for Robert Carpenter, a bystander injured by an explosion of dynamite stored unlawfully on a public street during construction of a subway in New York City.[4] Carpenter's verdict had been based on a trial judge's instruction to the jury that the city would be liable if the dynamite had been stored unlawfully for a long enough time for the city safety officials to have discovered it by exercising reasonable diligence.

The city appealed, urging that the legislature had authorized the building of the subway under the supervision of the Board of Railroad Commissioners and that the city had no power to intervene. Cardozo made an innovative policy-oriented argument in favor of spreading of loss from public development through an expansion of public liability, that is, that the damages from the injury should be spread among the city's taxpayers rather than borne solely by Carpenter. Although the argument was good for Cardozo's client, it did not reflect Cardozo's personal views on tort law, for later when he was a judge, he would be quite reluctant to expand governmental liability. The Appellate Division, voting 3–2, accepted the city's argument and reversed Carpenter's judgment. There was no further appeal.

Cardozo's next tort case, Devine v. Alphons Custodis Company, presented a negligence issue that was even closer to the major tort decisions in which Cardozo made notable contributions as a judge.[5] The defendant, Alphons Custodis, was a contractor that was building a brick chimney for a power house. It used handcars on rails to move the needed bricks to the construction site. Once there, the bricks were hoisted through a chute more than one hundred feet to the top of the chimney. Over the course of a three-month period preceding the accident, bricks fell down the chute and twice hit the rail. Once a workman had suggested to the superintendent that the rail be moved. After these incidents Patrick Devine, the plaintiff, was loading bricks into a bucket near the bottom of the chute when a brick fell down the chute, hit the rail, and then hit Devine on the head.

Devine sued the employer for failure to provide a reasonably safe place to work. He obtained a jury verdict, which was affirmed by the Appellate Division. When Alphons Custodis appealed to the Court of Appeals, Devine's lawyer called Cardozo in to write the brief. New York law at the time was not clear on the precise formulation for determining liability for negligence. The term "proximate cause" was used to provide a link between a defendant's carelessness and its liability—that is, the defendant's acts of negligence had to be the "proximate cause" of a plaintiff's injuries for liability to follow. The term concealed many issues of public policy within a formulation that sounded quite factual.[6] The proximate cause issue in *Devine* was whether the employer's failure to move the track was sufficiently related to Devine's injury that it should be liable to him. Cardozo could not have argued that the contractor was liable for the negligence of its employee who dropped the brick because of New York law that held that an employee could not recover for negligent acts of a "fellow servant."

Cardozo did not seize the opportunity to argue the public policy issues involved in the Court of Appeals' many formulations of "proximate cause." Nor did he argue the favorable precedents, especially those emphasizing respect for the jury's verdict, forcefully. He simply argued that a jury was justified in concluding that the employer's failure to move the track after the earlier incidents with falling bricks was negligence and the "proximate cause" of the accident. Cardozo's brief was as perfunctory and pedestrian a brief as he ever filed in the Court of Appeals.

The Court was not impressed with his argument. It held that as a matter of law, the "occurrence . . . was too remote to be reasonably apprehended . . . It was not, reasonably, to be demanded of the defendant that it should guard against the erratic trajectory of a brick rebounding from impact with a hard substance."[7] In using the concept of foreseeability of injury as a touchstone for determining whether the employer had fulfilled its duty of care, and in applying its own judgment of what was reasonably to be anticipated, the Court of Appeals presaged Cardozo's later use of that concept in his important torts opinions.

During the last period of his practice years, Cardozo treated himself to a vacation. In 1907, he took a long trip of seven-and-a-half weeks to Europe, apparently with his law partner Angel Simpson.[8] He described his trip in two letters to Edgar Nathan. He first wrote from the ship *Kaiser Wilhem Der Grosse* on the way abroad:

> Dear Edgar,
> It was not till after the pilot had waved good-bye to us that a steward handed me "The Common Lot." Surely it is not the Common Lot to be treated by one's friends with so much consideration & thoughtfulness. I thank you heartily for the book, which I have just finished, and which I read with great pleasure. It helped to while away the intolerable tedium of a sea voyage, for the prison life on shipboard has no charms for me. The ocean has been very well-behaved, and has probably meant to do the best it could, which is about all I can say for it. Whatever its intentions may have been, the relation between it and me was far from harmonious at the beginning. I don't think I felt right when I started (that is what people always say; no one admits that under normal circumstances, he would ever be seasick); but whether or not I was right when I started, I certainly was not right before I had gone very far. Over the happenings of the second day out, I will draw the veil of secrecy & silence. You shall never even guess what occurred. I have emerged serene & triumphant, though I still eye with some suspicion each approaching wave. By Tuesday morning the 6th, we hope to reach Plymouth, & Bremen the day after. Our itinerary is subject to change. We expect, however, to go at once to

Cologne, & then up the Rhine, stopping at the chief places, & through the Black Forest to Switzerland. From Switzerland, we shall work up, via Munich & Dresden & Berlin, to Bremen and our ship. If all goes well, I should be back by Sept. 24 . . .

> Yours always,
> Ben[9]

The Common Lot was a serious novel by Robert Herrick, with a moral as well as a political message. Surprisingly, Cardozo did not react to the substance of the story about an architect who designed a building that was dangerous in order to make a quick dollar and about the effect on his life of the death of all the tenants when the building burned.[10] Perhaps Cardozo's lack of reaction was part of his general view, expressed later in life, that a conversation, not a letter, was the best place for serious exchange of ideas.

Cardozo wrote Nathan four weeks later, having changed his planned itinerary. Rather than traveling north from Switzerland to the Baltic, he headed south to Italy.

My Dear Edgar,

I understand that you are still a practicing lawyer in New York. It is a great mistake. You should follow me, and become a tramp. I have been wandering all over Europe, first to Cologne, then up the Rhine, then to Frankfurt and its neighboring summer resorts, then through Switzerland, at Zurich, Lucerne, Interlaken, Geneva & Zermatt, with the snow fields & glaciers as neighbors, and finally from the cold of the Matterhorn to the sunny cities of Italy. I cannot let the trip pass without sending you a line from amid the enchantments of Venice. It is deliriously beautiful; and I am sorry that you are not at hand to share the delirium. I used up my stock of superlatives in Switzerland, and have no longer any words left with which to express my emotions. We float about the canals in the gondolas, amid ancient palaces, and through all sorts of curious by-streets; and Samuel Webber Parker assumes his true proportions as an insignificant atom, and nothing is of any importance whatever except the peace and beauty of the scene.

Tomorrow we are leaving for Munich, with a long and tiresome ride of thirteen hours before us—Nuremberg, Dresden & Berlin will about fill up our time till Sept. 17, when we set sail for home & work. I shall have to get my Blackstone out, and begin over again.

I haven't thought of a law point or a law case since I set sail
from N.Y. . . .

> Always affectionately yours,
> B.N.C.[11]

Cardozo took a typical "grand tour" of Germany, Switzerland, and
Italy, and he obviously enjoyed it enormously.[12] His language about the
places he visited was as extravagant as it ever got. The references to his
seasickness and to Samuel Webber Parker give some inkling of the sense
of humor that marked his private conversation.[13] His humor was not
boisterous or rollicking, but gentle, subdued, laconic, and wry.

———

The seven-week interlude over, Cardozo returned to his practice. It was
an extraordinarily busy practice, and Cardozo was in court on average
considerably more than one day a week.[14] Cardozo's successes enhanced
his reputation, which spread beyond the city. The circle of forwarding
lawyers that had comprised family members and Simpson & Werner in
the earlier years now included a large group of able lawyers, among
whom were Louis Marshall, Alton Parker, Cardozo's Columbia classmate James Watson Gerard, Nathan Ottinger, Morris Hirsch, Herbert
Limburg, William Klein, Julius Goldman, Moses Esberg, Sol Stroock and
Moses Stroock, and Malcolm Sundheimer. The forwarding group was
composed largely of Jewish lawyers who brought Cardozo their most
difficult commercial work. Many of them had first encountered him as
an adversary. Cardozo also appeared against many of the best-known
New York lawyers—Alton Parker, Edwin Countryman (an Albany law-
yer who argued many cases in the Court of Appeals for other lawyers),
Louis Marshall, Max Steuer, Harlan Fiske Stone, John Milburn, Charles
Tuttle, Charles Whitman, Peter B. Olney, Bronson Winthrop, Joseph M.
Hartfield, and Arthur Garfield Hays.

Cardozo occupied a special niche in the hierarchy of legal practice.
The staple of his practice involved the ordinary business and personal
affairs of middle-class New York, not the litigation or the financing of
large corporations. Although he did not count the richest corporations
as his clients and did not often handle the most important litigation in
New York, as measured by the issues or the money at stake, he was
sought after by an ever-widening circle of lawyers to handle difficult

litigation. He appeared in the Court of Appeals more often than most of the better-known lawyers. His career did not contain the public-service aspects of the careers of Charles Evans Hughes or Louis Brandeis—no investigations of the evils of the life insurance industry or of corruption in government.[15] Nor did his career resemble those of Jewish lawyers like Morris Hillquit or Julius Henry Cohen, who were deeply involved with new immigrant groups, unionism, the use of arbitration in industrial disputes, and public service as counsel to various administrative agencies.[16] But Cardozo was a first-rate litigator, especially in the appellate courts. When their clients were in trouble, New York lawyers knew they could turn to Cardozo.

Cardozo's practice grew to include some newer and more important kinds of commercial litigation. In one case shortly after his return from Europe, an old friend, former Judge William Cohen,[17] sought his assistance in halting a merger between two banks represented by two leading Wall Street firms, Cravath, DeGersdorff & Henderson, and Alexander & Green.[18] Cardozo contributed to the memoranda and briefs that were filed. A second case of importance to the financial community was Zimmermann v. Timmermann.[19] Zimmermann and the other plaintiffs (Zimmermann) were bankers and brokers, as were Timmermann and the other defendants (Timmermann). Zimmermann agreed to purchase $100,000 of railroad bonds from Timmermann "when, as and if issued." At a time when $3.5 million of the total $20 million in bonds had been issued, Zimmermann demanded that Timmermann sell him the bonds as agreed. Timmermann refused, and Zimmermann sued for damages for breach of contract. Louis Werner was Zimmermann's lawyer, and even with Cardozo available to handle the matter, Werner brought in Alton Parker to assist in trying the case.

The damages sought were $12,000, then a large but not an enormous amount. Zimmermann, however, had been suspended by the Stock Exchange in connection with another aspect of this transaction, a damaging fact that raised the need for a "big name" as counsel. Parker and Cardozo tried the case together at the trial level, with Cardozo presenting Zimmermann's case and he and Parker sharing the cross-examination. The jury found for Zimmermann. Parker argued both appeals, losing in the Appellate Division but prevailing, 5 2, in the Court of Appeals.

Two aspects of the litigation provide an insight into Cardozo's professional resourcefulness. Even though the prior action by the Stock Exchange was not legally relevant, Cardozo and Parker evidently feared that it might cast a shadow of wrongdoing over their client. In their brief in the Court of Appeals, they therefore portrayed the Stock Exchange as a biased tribunal of privilege:

> The defendants [Timmermann] have had their day before [the Stock Exchange], where the accused [Zimmermann] was without the benefit of counsel, where there was no compulsory process to secure the attendance of witnesses, where the rules of evidence were unheeded, where power and wealth and influence were arrayed on the side of the complainants. The plaintiffs are now to have their day in the calm atmosphere of the courts. They submit their case with the consciousness that they have done no wrong,—unless it be a wrong to have brought the wealth and power of the Stock Exchange before the ordinary tribunals of justice, to be judged not by the favor of friends and associates, but by the law of the land.[20]

This attack was not an anticapitalist statement by crusading lawyers. Cardozo's uncle, Benjamin Nathan, had been a vice-president of the Stock Exchange, and Parker had been the presidential nominee of the conservative wing of the Democratic Party. The disparaging of the Stock Exchange was simply a piece of legal strategy designed to defuse the effect of the Stock Exchange's suspension of their client.

A second noteworthy aspect of this litigation is that some evidence indicated that Zimmermann may have been involved in fictitious sales of bonds of the railroad at prices that would have permitted Zimmermann to claim larger damages. Cardozo and Parker realized that this was a problem and refused to use those sales to increase the claim of damages. Judge Willard Bartlett pointedly acknowledged in his opinion that Zimmermann's counsel had disavowed any claim based on these sales.[21] Cardozo and Parker concluded quite rightly that their professional obligation to their client permitted them to attack the New York Stock Exchange but did not permit an argument for a remedy based on a fictitious claim.

Cardozo's growing prominence was recognized with an attractive offer. In 1908 or 1909, United States Attorney General George Wickersham had Charles C. Burlingham ask Cardozo if he would accept a judgeship on the United States District Court for the Southern District of New York.[22] Cardozo refused, saying that he had two sisters to support and that the salary of $6,000 was too low.[23] $6,000 toward the beginning of the century roughly equals $100,000 in mid-1990s dollars.[24] (The base salary of a federal district judge in 1995 was $133,600.) But Cardozo was supporting an expensive household. It is true that an offer of a federal judgeship to a politically connected lawyer would not necessarily demonstrate the lawyer's professional achievement, but Cardozo had taken no part in political life. He came to the attention of men like Wickersham and Burlingham solely through his professional accomplishments.

Cardozo's last years of practice introduced him to the legal aspects of the theater world, especially the various enterprises of the Shubert brothers. In one breach of contract case, Perley v. Shubert, Cardozo handled a trial, three appeals to the Appellate Division, and one appeal to the Court of Appeals.[25] Perley was a producer of plays, and Lee Shubert had agreed to provide Perley with six good routes covering Shubert theaters in different cities for production of Perley's plays. Perley claimed that Shubert had failed to provide the routes and won a large verdict, exceeding $25,000, against Shubert. Shubert's regular attorney, William Klein, turned to Cardozo to argue Shubert's appeal. Cardozo urged a number of points on appeal and secured a favorable opinion from the Appellate Division, which held that Shubert had not broken his contract.

Perley exercised his right under New York law to have a second trial. This time Cardozo tried the case and demonstrated his skill as a trial lawyer. Part of Shubert's defense was that Perley had not acted in good faith because he had tried to induce the Shuberts to commit a technical breach of contract so that Perley could sue for the damages specified in the contract. In cross-examining Perley, Cardozo laid the groundwork for proving that defense and at the same time refused to allow Perley to answer more than he was asked. Cardozo (Q.) elicited the following testimony from Perley (A.):

Q. Now when you got that letter [from Mr. Shubert stating that the routes had been ready for four weeks] did you send any answer to Mr. Shubert?

A. No, sir; because it was absolutely false.

Q. Not "because." You did not do it. When you received that letter did you go to see Mr. Shubert?

A. No, sir. What he said was untrue there.

Q. That is all, Mr. Perley, you have answered. How long after receiving this letter did you bring your action?
A. I don't remember exactly.

The record indicated that the answer to that question was two days, and Cardozo had made the point that Perley was not interested in getting the routes but rather in setting up a lawsuit. Cardozo obtained a judgment in this trial court and defended it successfully in the Appellate Division and the Court of Appeals.

Cardozo was quick to take advantage of this evidence in his briefs on appeal. He used it not only to support his substantive legal argument but also to make an additional point: "It shocks the sense of justice that a man assuming such an attitude should recover a judgment for $25,000."[26] The "sense of justice" was an important weapon in Cardozo's arsenal of legal arguments. When he tried a case, he marshaled evidence to allow him to argue that point, and when he had not tried the case, he sifted the record for every scrap of evidence to allow him to make the appeal to fairness and justice whenever he could. Later, as judge, he was more discriminating about the situations in which he would recognize the merit of "justice" arguments.

Cardozo also represented another leading figure in the theatrical world, Flo Ziegfeld, at the behest of William Klein. The defendant was the equally well-known actress, Nora Bayes. While under contract with Ziegfeld, Bayes appeared in a play produced by a rival. Klein had already obtained an injunction forbidding Bayes from performing on stage except under Ziegfeld's management during the term of her contract with him. He called Cardozo into the case to press contempt charges against her for violating that injunction. Cardozo's effort to have her held in contempt failed. Bayes had the better case on the law. Although Ziegfeld had obtained an injunction against Bayes, he had agreed to a consent order that vacated the injunction unless he put her to work in his own play and paid her. Cardozo had the better case on the facts because the court found that the actress had acted in bad faith in obtaining the modifying order and had failed to attend rehearsals of Ziegfeld's play. But Cardozo was unable to persuade the Appellate Division that justice required a holding of contempt. That court was unwilling to find contempt without violation of a clear order of the court. Its original injunction order had been modified, and Ziegfeld and Klein had not had the injunction reinstated after Bayes violated the modified order.[27]

The final years of Cardozo's career as a practicing lawyer saw many changes in his law firm. In 1909, his brother Allie died of congestive heart failure at the age of fifty-one.[28] Shortly thereafter, the firm moved its offices from 52 Broadway to the Trinity Building at 111 Broadway. By now, Cardozo was handling virtually all the courtroom work of the firm. Simpson's practice had become largely a business practice, with a good deal of real estate work. Werner spent much of his time recruiting business, but in 1911 he withdrew from the partnership. He had apparently gotten the firm into some kind of trouble, the details of which went discreetly unrecorded.[29] The firm name then changed to Simpson & Cardozo. George Engelhard joined the firm, and he became a partner in 1912. When Angel Simpson retired from practice in 1913, the firm name became Cardozo and Engelhard.[30]

The office of Simpson, Werner & Cardozo and its successors was an eight-room suite occupying half of the 16th floor of the Trinity Building and overlooking the Trinity Church courtyard. The staff included a bookkeeper, a telephone operator-receptionist, two office boys, and three secretaries. In the last years of Cardozo's practice, there were also two younger lawyers just beginning their legal careers. One was Raymond Sarfaty, nephew of Leah Simpson, Angel Simpson's wife, and the other was Walter Pollak, who later became a well-known lawyer and handled a number of important civil rights cases. Pollak often worked with Cardozo and thought him a very good cross-examiner of witnesses. Pollak remembered that Cardozo once brought a real estate expert to the edge of tears as a result of an effective cross-examination.[31] One of the secretaries, Miss Miller, worked exclusively for Cardozo for many years. Indeed, she became extremely upset if he gave work to anyone else. Nevertheless, he occasionally had to do so and once in a while even had one of the other secretaries come to his house on a Sunday so as not to upset Miss Miller. Cardozo sometimes dictated his briefs. When he did so, he would pace up and down the room, hands clasped behind his back. When he dictated at home, Nellie sat on the sofa knitting and watching him as he worked. Although Cardozo was a hard worker who gave the staff plenty to do, he had a nice touch in his personal relations with them. They all adored him.[32]

In his final years of practice, Cardozo did his first important criminal work. One case concerned a civil rights issue. Civil rights was not then a major field of litigation, and there is nothing to indicate that Cardozo had any particular interest in those issues, either as an advocate or as a private citizen. His work in the theatrical field, however, brought the segregation issue to him in 1913 in People v. Levy.[33]

Louis Baldwin, a black real estate investor and post office employee, bought two tickets in the orchestra for a performance at The Lyric, a Shubert theater. He testified that when he arrived at the performance, he was denied admission to the orchestra and offered "equally as good seats" in the balcony. He objected, and Harry Levy, assistant treasurer of the theater, told him that no first-class theater would seat "colored people" in the orchestra because it would hurt its business. Mr. Baldwin complained to the District Attorney's office, which prosecuted Mr. Levy for violation of New York's Civil Rights Law providing that "[a] person who . . . [e]xcludes a citizen, by reason of race, color, or previous condition of servitude, from the equal enjoyment of any accommodation, facility, or privilege furnished by . . . owners, managers, or lessees of theaters . . . is guilty of a misdemeanor."[34]

William Klein defended Levy in the Court of Special Sessions. The testimony as to what happened at the theater, including the theater's seating policy, was in sharp conflict. The court believed Baldwin's version and found the defendant guilty. The presiding judge, noting that he knew of no previous prosecutions of this sort, imposed a minimum sentence of $50 or ten days in jail to preserve a right of appeal so that the appellate courts could settle the legal issues.

Klein called on Cardozo to argue the appeal. At that moment, Cardozo had a choice to make. If he had had a strong opinion against segregation, he could have declined the matter. He was under no professional obligation to represent a hateful cause because of the party's inability to get other counsel. The Shuberts would not have had trouble getting a lawyer; they had a lawyer already. But Cardozo accepted the case. Klein was a regular forwarder of business to Cardozo, and Cardozo had represented the Shuberts previously. He tried to make the best arguments he could to overturn Levy's conviction. Clearly, he had no strong opinion that segregation was an evil.

Since the trial court had not believed Levy's version of what had happened at the theater, the only issues left for Cardozo to argue were issues of law. He produced a number of them for the consideration of the Appellate Division. His first argument was that the evidence did not establish a violation of the statute. Relying heavily on the "equal enjoyment" language of the statute, he argued that the issue was not whether a particular seat had been denied to Mr. Baldwin but whether equal accommodations had been denied to him. There was no proof of such a violation of the statute. Indeed, Cardozo asserted, the evidence was to the contrary. The court could not say as a matter of law that balcony seats were inferior to orchestra seats. It was common knowledge that many people thought that front balcony seats were the best in the house.

That line of argument was supported by a recent decision of the Fourth Department of the Appellate Division, which affirmed a lower court that had taken precisely this ground.[35] Cardozo reached back to Shakespeare to add historical support to his empirical argument:

> Indeed, we know from the literature of the theatre that only in recent times has the orchestra become in any degree the abode of wealth and fashion, and that formerly it was set aside for "the groundlings" under the comprehensive description of "the pit." If Shakespeare was right in asserting that the "groundlings, for the most part are capable of understanding nothing but inexplicable dumb shows and noise" (Hamlet, Act III, Scene II) we may justly infer that to have been put in the balcony in those times would have been a mark of distinction rather than the contrary.[36]

Thus Cardozo not only evaded the point that white patrons were given a choice that was denied to black patrons but also ignored his own language indicating that the orchestra had become the preferred seating for "wealth and fashion."

Cardozo's main effort to support his restrictive interpretation of the state statute involved an argument similar to the one that the United States Supreme Court had adopted in holding the federal Civil Rights Act of 1875 unconstitutional in the *Civil Rights Cases*.[37] Cardozo argued as follows:

> The law does not seek to secure to colored men equality of social recognition. It merely seeks to secure them equal—not identical, but equal accommodations. Discrimination within those limits is not illegal, even if we assume it to be ungenerous or narrow. If substantial

equality of accommodations is secured, discrimination on the ground of color by the separation of the races is not, under the decisions, to be deemed a badge of inferiority . . . Probably if the rule of the house had assigned the balcony to whites and the orchestra to colored folk, the complainant would have been equally resentful. What he really resents is the social stigma put upon him, as he contends, by the enforced separation. The redress of such wrongs, however, if wrongs they be, is not to be gained through resort to law, but by cultivation of the spirit of larger tolerance and wider brotherhood.[38]

Cardozo thus perceived and was willing to state exactly what the issue was: that the theater's policy enforced a social stigma against African Americans. By calling the stigma "social," however, Cardozo sought to protect his client by invoking those earlier Supreme Court cases that had drawn distinctions between "political" and "social" rights, holding that the Fourteenth Amendment prohibited only state action that violated political rights. Cardozo quoted heavily from Plessy v. Ferguson, the 1896 case upholding the constitutionality of "separate but equal" public facilities.[39]

Cardozo argued that the *Plessy* doctrine should be stretched further than the Supreme Court had extended it. The Supreme Court cases dealt only with how far the Thirteenth and Fourteenth Amendments themselves outlawed discrimination and how far Congress could prohibit discriminatory conduct. The Court never indicated that a state could not itself prohibit discrimination or provide for greater equality of "social" rights.[40] Cardozo's statement of the issue argued that it was beyond a state's power to pass laws that had social equality as their goal: "redress . . . is not to be gained through resort to law."[41]

Later in the brief he made this argument quite explicit. Noting the current doctrine that the legislature might regulate only those private businesses "affected with a public interest," Cardozo conceded that theaters had a "public aspect." But he urged that they were mainly private and that legislatures could regulate them only with respect to that portion of their business that in fact touched the public interest. "Equality of social recognition is something which the law does not attempt to regulate. In so far as that aspect of the theatrical business is concerned the business is strictly private."[42]

A strong answering brief was filed by the District Attorney, Charles Whitman, whose career would later intersect with Cardozo's several times. The brief distinguished the Fourteenth Amendment cases as not preventing states from passing public accommodations laws and took an expansive view, akin to that which eventually prevailed in the Supreme Court in 1937, of the power of the legislature to pass laws regulating social and economic affairs. Whitman also relied on a second Fourth Department opinion, Joyner v. Moore-Wiggins Company, which upheld the application of the New York statute to conduct like that of Mr. Levy.[43]

Cardozo's reply brief again demonstrated his technical skill at distinguishing a damaging precedent. He argued that there were differences between *Joyner* and *Levy* that prevented *Joyner* from controlling the result: The *Joyner* case involved a civil action under provisions of the Civil Rights Law providing for "full" enjoyment of places of public accommodation, whereas the *Levy* case involved criminal prosecution under the provision of the Penal Law punishing the violation of "equal" enjoyment of that right. Cardozo argued that even though in a civil suit the flouting of a contract right to a particular seat might be a denial of "full" enjoyment of a place of public accommodation, the refusal to honor Baldwin's orchestra ticket did not, for purposes of a criminal statute, involve denial of "equal" enjoyment. In fact, he went on to assert that the statute would be unconstitutional if breach of contract were made a crime. Cardozo's failure to elaborate his constitutional arguments, either in his main brief or in his reply brief, suggests that he probably did not put much faith in them.[44] The conclusion of People v. Levy was an anticlimax. The Appellate Division affirmed Levy's conviction, 3–2, in a brief order without writing an opinion. Levy did not appeal, and his minimal sentence stood.

Once Cardozo had agreed to handle Levy's appeal, he was professionally obligated to do his best to secure a reversal of his conviction. That obligation required him to defend the Shuberts' policy of segregated seating. In so doing, he exerted his ingenuity to think of every argument, however technical or rhetorical, to obtain that result. Fourteen months after the decision in *Levy*, Cardozo, then sitting as a judge in the Court of Appeals, expressed his judgment on the *Joyner* result by joining a unanimous court in affirming the judgment in that case.[45] Cardozo believed that New York had the power to provide a private cause of action to the victims of segregation in public accommodations against the perpetrators.

Although Cardozo was willing to defend a segregation policy in the courtroom, he gave quite different advice outside the courtroom. His firm had a sizable $10,000 per year retainer (worth at least $150,000 in late twentieth-century dollars) from Gimbel Brothers department store. The store sought Cardozo's advice about how to prevent a black woman from visiting its beauty parlor every week. Cardozo advised that he knew of no law that would allow the store to exclude her.[46] Even though Cardozo was advising on the law and not stating his own personal view of Gimbel's aims, he was not influenced by the large retainer to try to help the client segregate its beauty parlor.

A second notable criminal case involved Cardozo in an effort to overturn the conviction of a brewery president, Charles Katz, for conspiring to steal $100,000 worth of mining stock in a scam operation.[47] After the Appellate Division had affirmed Mr. Katz's conviction in December 1912, Cardozo came into the case at the request of John F. McIntyre, a former assistant district attorney with a large criminal defense practice, to replace Morgan O'Brien, who had argued the case in the Appellate Division. O'Brien had been assisted at the Appellate Division level by Samuel S. Koenig, the Manhattan Republican party leader. Cardozo did not ask Koenig to assist him on the Court of Appeals brief, an omission that probably helped make Koenig a political opponent later that year.

Judge Werner, writing the majority opinion in the Court of Appeals, described the case as "one of unusual interest, both in respect of the novel scheme . . . by means of which the crime is said to have been perpetrated, and the number, variety, and importance of the questions we are asked to decide."[48] The appeal showcased Cardozo's ability to make a powerful factual presentation. He portrayed his client, "a prosperous and respected citizen," as "the innocent tool of evil associates, who required a man of respectability and standing in order to effect their purpose." He demonstrated that the crime was certain to be detected because the victim was bound to discover that the people to whom he had entrusted his stock, Katz's alleged coconspirators, had sold it and divided the proceeds among themselves. Therefore, "only men of settled criminal purpose, reckless and abandoned men, who had neither property nor reputation nor settled homes nor anything else to lose, the derelicts and outcasts of society, would have ventured to commit it." He concluded his factual statement with an appeal to the apparent injustice of the proceeding: "Every one [of the alleged conspirators] except the defendant—even those whose guilt is not questioned—has thus far escaped punishment. Justice has singled out for its single victim the man whose guilt is denied."[49]

This talent for stating facts persuasively would later be a feature of Cardozo's judicial opinions. He sought to raise sufficient doubts in the judges' minds about the correctness of the jury's verdict to induce them to examine carefully all his claims of error. Cardozo's brief raised fifteen serious claims of error, many of which had not been argued in the Appellate Division, in an all-out attack on every aspect of the trial. The court took the claims seriously, but Cardozo's argument fell just short as the court, 4–3, affirmed the conviction.

Big money and eminent domain were the issues in Cardozo's representation of the Ontario Knitting Company against the state of New York.[50] Ontario claimed over a million dollars from the state in an eminent domain proceeding. The state's Special Deputy State Engineer had certified a map that showed that all of Ontario's property had been taken by the state in connection with planned improvements to the Oswego Canal. The claimant had opposed the taking, but after the map was filed, it shut down its business because it believed its arguments had been definitively rejected. Subsequently, however, the canal board moved the route of the canal, so that no part of the claimant's land was used. Ontario claimed that the earlier actions of the state had constituted a taking of its property and sued the state for compensation.

The case raised important issues of state power. In particular, the courts had to decide what action in the planning process constituted a "taking" and which state officers or bodies had ultimate power to commit the state financially to acquisition of property. The case also involved a great deal of money. Cardozo was brought in by Ontario's lawyers to assist at the trial level and to argue the appeals after they lost 3–0 in the Court of Claims, the court established to try eminent domain claims against the state. The state had a strong interest in avoiding payment for lands it had not used and further in not being held responsible for decisions made at a low level in the bureaucracy. Cardozo made an elaborate argument based on the statute authorizing the taking of private property for canal building but he eventually lost 3–2 in the Appellate Division and 5–2 in the Court of Appeals.

Cardozo does not appear to have had a substantial practice in the federal courts, for there are few cases with published opinions in which his name appears.[51] But during his last few years at the bar, Cardozo had a few cases in the United States Supreme Court. Like his earlier cases, they were handled summarily by the Court without an opinion on the merits of the underlying controversy and without any oral argument before the Court.[52] While Cardozo's growing experience and reputation had brought him both high-stakes cases and litigation in new areas of the law, at the end of his lawyering career he was still handling many cases that were like those that had occupied him earlier in his practice. Thus, in Howell v. Christlieb in 1912, he lashed out at Franklin Bien once again for filing a frivolous appeal.[53] Cardozo had been brought into the case by his regular forwarding attorneys, Morris Hirsch and Herbert Limburg, to argue against a motion to vacate a judgment previously won by their client. Cardozo prevailed in the Appellate Division. When Bien filed an appeal in the Court of Appeals, Cardozo filed a short brief that clearly expressed his annoyance with the tactics of the moving parties and their counsel. "On the face of the moving papers, the objections which they urge are quickly perceived to be barren even of technical merit; but when the full narrative of their harassing and obstructive tactics is spread forth, the baseless character of their motion becomes still more clearly apparent."[54] The Court of Appeals agreed, dismissing the appeal without writing any opinion.

One final case that Cardozo handled during this period was the only matter that we know of that he handled pro bono, that is, without fee. Cardozo had a reputation for charging modest fees, and it may well be that there were other situations in which he charged either a reduced fee or no fee at all.[55] A committee had collected a fund to assist the survivors of a pogrom against a Jewish community in Russia. Apparently, more money had been collected than was needed, raising the question of the disposition of the remaining proceeds. Cardozo was asked by Louis Marshall, President of the American Jewish Committee, to seek to have the money paid over to the Committee. Cardozo worked on the case for two years, and finally, in 1913, the court granted his petition.[56] Referee Larremore's opinion noted that the issue had been "argued with very unusual ability and with exhaustive citation of authorities" by Cardozo for the fund's trustee and Louis Marshall for the American Jewish Committee. He noted specifically that since Cardozo's client was seeking the instructions of the court, Cardozo had shown "great propriety" in presenting both the affirmative and the negative arguments for the request.[57]

During this final period of his practice, Cardozo showed growing interest in professional matters beyond his own cases. In 1908, a group of two dozen lawyers and judges, chaired by Dean George Kirchwey of the Columbia Law School, formed an informal group to consider problems of professional ethics. Cardozo was invited to join the group, which also included Learned Hand, then still a practicing lawyer. He missed the first meeting, but the schedule for the following year lists an assignment for him to prepare a paper dealing with "Problems arising out of Special Defenses, such as the Statute of Limitations, the Statute of Frauds, Usury, and the Plea of Infancy."[58]

Cardozo did not join the leading local professional organization, the Association of the Bar of the City of New York, perhaps because of its role in conducting impeachment proceedings against his father.[59] Once the New York County Lawyers Association was formed in 1908, he immediately joined it and became active in the organization. In 1911, he was a member of its committee on legislation. In 1912 and 1913, he was a member of the finance committee and was one of three vice presidents.[60] Cardozo also belonged to the New York Law Institute. That organization had been founded with lofty aims by Chancellor James Kent in 1828, but its primary activity was the maintenance of a downtown law library.[61] Cardozo played a small role in its affairs, serving as a member of its auditing committee in 1908.[62]

These modest activities represent the sum total of Cardozo's recorded professional services while he was a practicing lawyer. But lawyers do not become vice presidents even of newly organized bar associations unless they are active in seeking office or unless others seek them out. The nature of Cardozo's practice—handling cases for other lawyers—suggests that he probably achieved office through the efforts of the lawyers with whom he worked. It seems likely that lawyers who thought well enough of him to keep sending him business also thought well enough of him to select him for bar association offices.

The year 1913 marked the end of Cardozo's twenty-three year career as a practicing lawyer. There was a resurgence of reformist politics in New York City at that time, and a Fusion ticket combining disparate anti-Tammany elements was put together to combat the dominance of Tammany Hall. As we shall see in the next chapter, Cardozo was named to a judicial slot on that ticket and was elected to his first judgeship. He never returned to private practice and spent the next twenty-five years of his professional life as a judge.

When Cardozo entered his father's old law office in 1891, he had been just twenty-one years old. His life up to that point had been sheltered at home and solitary at school. He had endured the experience of being young and shy among his Columbia classmates and of being the son of a disgraced father. Certainly, he had been bright and strong-minded. Even so, his early success as a lawyer was remarkable. The young Cardozo matured rapidly into an able and determined lawyer. He was a prodigious worker and a persuasive advocate. He wrote powerful briefs, tailoring them to the needs of the case. He argued the facts when they were helpful to his cause, and he argued the law when precedent or principle favored his client. If he could appeal to moral justice, he did so in eloquent fashion. If a technical argument was his only salvation, he would turn in that direction. He never got distracted from the client's goal. His briefs bore the mark of considerable effort spent thinking about the best way to present his client's cause. Finally, he did not shrink from personal attack on the opposition or its counsel if the needs of the case called for it.

Cardozo the advocate was not the saintly man that others have associated with the older Cardozo, Cardozo the judge. Later chapters will argue that *saintly* is the wrong adjective even for that period. The qualities of the "gentle scholar" that have been applied to his practice years are also off the mark.[63] The scholarship in his briefs was always a means to an end. Frequently, he rejected academic abstraction in favor of "common sense" analysis or arguments based on the "justice" or "fairness" of the situation. Cardozo was above all a forceful advocate who put his ability to the service of his clients' interests. Cardozo's portrait, a photograph taken at about the time that he ended his career as a practicing lawyer, is the picture of a self-confident man in the prime of a successful life. The photograph, reproduced in the section of photos following this chapter, reminds us that Cardozo was a human being and not a bloodless, idealized essence. It exudes power and, perhaps, even a bit of arrogance.

Twenty-three years of practice had a major impact in preparing Cardozo for his judicial career. His college and law school education furnished a substantial amount of intellectual capital and the habits of reading and study that lasted his whole life. His work matured him socially, and his colleagues soon discovered not only his ability but also the strength of his character and personality. Having lived a sheltered personal life, he used his work as his window on the world. A good litigator gets to understand people, both their strengths and their weaknesses. His work gave him firsthand experience with the human condition, with human frailty, trickery and deceit. A good litigator also learns a great deal about the subject matter of his cases. Cardozo read widely and was more familiar with new ideas than most practicing lawyers, but he came to the bench with a view of the judge's role as a resolver of disputes, not as a dispenser of legal theory. Even though his experience as a judge would enlarge his view of the judicial role, Cardozo never lost his lawyer's touch.

Rebecca Nathan Cardozo as a young woman. (Rare Book and Manuscript Library, Columbia University)

Ben and Emily with their mother. (Rare Book and Manuscript Library, Columbia University)

Ben and Emily. (Rare Book and Manuscript Library, Columbia University)

Ben at twelve. (Rare Book and Manuscript Library, Columbia University)

Ben at twenty-four. (Rare Book and Manuscript Library, Columbia University)

Benjamin Cardozo when he first ran for justice of the New York Supreme Court in 1913. (Courtesy of Hon. Louis H. Pollak, Federal District Judge, Eastern District of Pennsylvania)

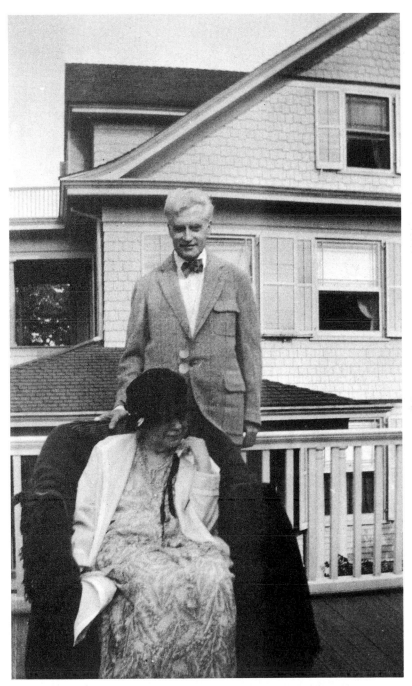

Ben and Nellie in the summer at Allenhurst. (Courtesy of Rosalie Nathan Hendricks)

The New York State Court of Appeals in the mid-1920s. Sitting: Chief Judge
Frank Hiscock. Standing (from left to right): Judges William Andrews, Chester
McLaughlin, Cardozo, Cuthbert Pound, Frederick Crane, and Irving Lehman.
(Rare Book and Manuscript Library, Columbia University)

Chief Judge Cardozo with his colleagues on the bench in Court of Appeals Hall
seated under portraits of their predecessors. (Courtesy of Hon. Judith S. Kaye,
Chief Judge, New York Court of Appeals)

Judge: 1914–1932

7

New York Supreme Court

In 1913, Benjamin Cardozo was forty-three years old. He was a successful lawyer, but he had not been involved in political life, and his extracurricular professional life had been limited. Barring extraordinary chance, little change in career was in order. But extraordinary chance, in the form of New York politics, intervened.

The year 1913 was the time for another of the periodic campaigns to overthrow Tammany Hall—the same sort of political coalition that had worked to oust the Tweed machine (and Albert Cardozo) in the early 1870s, that had elected Mayor William Strong in 1895 and Mayor Seth Low in 1901, and that would later elect Fiorello LaGuardia in 1932.[1] Meetings were begun in December 1912 that led to a conference of anti-Tammany Democrats, Republicans, and Progressives and to the formation in April 1913 of a 107-member Citizens' Municipal Committee charged with organizing a slate of candidates from among the various groups that comprised the Fusion movement.[2]

The most important decision was the choice of a candidate for mayor, and there was an understanding that if the nomination went to one of the major parties, the other parties would gain more places on the rest of the ticket. After the executive committee of the Fusion movement failed to agree on a candidate, the full committee met at the Fifth Avenue Hotel on July 31. There were three major candidates: the independent

Manhattan Borough President George McAneny; the Republican Manhattan District Attorney (and later Governor) Charles Whitman, who had just been Cardozo's adversary in the *Levy* case; and the candidate of the Democrats and Progressives, the Democrat John Purroy Mitchel, former president of the Board of Aldermen, whom Woodrow Wilson had appointed Collector of the Port of New York. After McAneny was eliminated, the balance of power was in the hands of a small group of reform-minded independents, Charles C. Burlingham, Henry DeForest Baldwin, and Cardozo's Columbia friend, Frederic Coudert. As Burlingham explained, "As btw. M. & W. it was a toss up . . . We three voted for Mitchel first in order to eliminate McA. & next to hold back Whitman a bit & satisfy the Radicals (!) that their candidate was having a square deal. We were all willing to switch to W. if W. proved stronger, i.e., gained as the voting went on, but he didn't & there's an end on't (Dr. Johnson)."[3]

Before the nomination of Mitchel, Joseph Price, chairman of the executive committee and also chairman of the committee on candidates, had appointed a subcommittee to consider nominations for judicial positions on the Fusion ticket.[4] Burlingham was chairman of the five-member subcommittee, which also included Henry Stimson, the distinguished lawyer and public servant who had just finished a stint as Secretary of War.[5] The subcommittee held a great many meetings and publicly solicited suggestions for potential nominees. Many names surfaced as possibilities in the newspapers, but Cardozo's name was not among them.[6] There were two judgeships to be filled in the Supreme Court, the major trial court in New York. The subcommittee decided to support one of the incumbents, the Democrat Eugene Philbin, but not the other, Bartow Weeks, who had been appointed by Governor Henry Sulzer to fill a vacancy. The subcommittee then decided to select a Jew for that position to balance the ticket religiously.[7] One day Robert Grier Monroe, who was involved in the Fusion effort, mentioned to Abraham Tulin, New York lawyer and important Zionist leader, that "they were looking for a very high class Jew to nominate to the Supreme Court" and asked for suggestions. Tulin replied, "Benjamin Nathan Cardozo."[8]

Despite Tulin's recommendation, the subcommittee's first choice was Julius J. Frank, a lawyer against whom Cardozo had argued one of his first cases. Burlingham reported this decision to Henry Moskowitz, who had been temporary chairman of the Committee of 107 before Norman Hapgood was selected. Moskowitz came to civic affairs from work in settlement houses and the labor movement. He was also a Reform Jew and active in Felix Adler's Ethical Culture movement, but he told Burlingham that Frank was the wrong person to nominate: "You haven't got the right kind of Jew. Frank is a Felix Adler Jew, a Modernist. The man you want to get is a *real* Jew. I'll tell you the man, Cardozo. He is [in] the Portuguese Synagogue."[9] Cardozo's future thus turned on the Sephardic heritage whose religious tenets he had long since discarded.

Burlingham accepted Moskowitz's judgment and used Cardozo's name as the touchstone to test other proposals.[10] Just eight days after Mitchel's nomination, Burlingham wrote to Learned Hand, "I'm going to nominate Carl Nott & Benj. Cardozo if I can, throwing them [the Republicans] Wadhams for City Court & Wasservogel for the other Gen'l Sessns place—both decent men."[11] Burlingham viewed the Republicans' reluctance to endorse the Fusion coalition after the defeat of Whitman in the convention as a power play to get more places on the rest of the ticket. In particular, the Republicans wanted the Supreme Court and not the General Sessions nomination for their candidate, William Wadhams, because there was patronage attached to the former position, but not the latter. Burlingham opposed those wishes. "They won't get [those] places sans [except] over my dead body," he declared in somewhat fractured French.[12] Burlingham then went to see Cardozo and offered him the nomination. Cardozo, a Democrat who had once turned Burlingham down on a judgeship offer, accepted this time, although he said that he did not think that he would be elected.[13]

There was a personal aspect to Cardozo's nomination that must have been extraordinarily important to him. He had grown up in the shadow of his father's disgrace. He came to grips with the past by challenging it. When the time came, Cardozo chose the law, and indeed he chose his father's law firm. By 1913, the name Cardozo at the bar was associated with the son and not the father. Now he had a chance to join the very court from which his father had resigned in disgrace forty-one years before.[14] Election would be redemption.

Cardozo's acceptance of Burlingham's offer did not end the controversy among the Fusion leadership. Although the Progressive convention endorsed Cardozo unanimously after he had been nominated by Stanley Isaacs, the Republicans were still angry about the ticket, especially the Cardozo nomination. Samuel Koenig, the Manhattan Republican leader whom Cardozo had recently replaced in the *Katz* case, wanted a Republican instead of Cardozo in the Supreme Court slot and made no secret of his views.[15] Finally, Otto Bannard, who had been the Republican mayoral candidate at the preceding election, suggested that Burlingham invite him and Koenig to lunch.[16] Burlingham did and Koenig said, "I don't want your friend Cardozo." Burlingham responded that he had only met Cardozo once before offering him the nomination. Then, taking the offensive, Burlingham said he was not so pure that he couldn't talk with politicians and that Koenig should have complained earlier if he had objections. Since Cardozo had not sought the job, Burlingham did not see how he could ask him to withdraw. Koenig replied that Burlingham was a good politician and finally agreed to Cardozo's nomination.[17]

The Fusion ticket, however, encountered a serious problem. Tammany Hall nominated former Judge Edward McCall for mayor, denying renomination to Mayor William Gaynor, who was generally thought to be able and honest. Gaynor became the rallying point for anti-Mitchel Fusionists and other anti-Tammany groups, who persuaded him to run as an Independent. There was talk that the Independence League, which had been formed several years before to support the candidacy of William Randolph Hearst for mayor and was believed to be controlled by him still, would join a Gaynor ticket. Meanwhile, Charles Whitman, who had accepted Fusion's nomination for District Attorney, also accepted a Tammany nomination for the same position. Many of the supporting organizations named their own candidates instead of the Fusion nominees for particular positions. Fusion seemed to be falling apart.[18]

At this critical juncture, the Fusion ticket received unexpected assistance. Mayor Gaynor, who had been ill for some time, died suddenly on September 11, 1913, while sailing to Europe for a vacation. That event immediately ended talk of a third major mayoral candidate, and a large number of Gaynor supporters decided to back Mitchel and the Fusion ticket.[19] The second major event was the impeachment and conviction of Governor Henry Sulzer. Sulzer, who had been elected with the aid and support of Tammany, had apparently worked closely with it for a while. Subsequently, however, he had defied Charles Murphy, the Tammany leader, in connection with some appointments. In apparent retaliation, the legislature began to investigate allegations of improper reporting of campaign contributions by Sulzer. A legislative committee voted articles of impeachment in August, and the Court of Impeachment, which comprised the Senate and judges of the Court of Appeals, convicted Sulzer and removed him from office on October 17. One result was that the

Lieutenant Governor, Martin Glynn, became Governor, and the president pro tem of the state Senate, Robert Wagner, became Lieutenant Governor and President of the Senate. Both men would later play roles in Cardozo's career.

The Sulzer conviction had more immediate consequences. Although many were willing to believe that Sulzer had in fact violated the campaign fund law, his impeachment and conviction were widely viewed as the product of Tammany Hall's revenge. Sulzer fought back. In mid-October, Sulzer and John Hennessy, the special investigator whom he had appointed while governor, began making revelations about Tammany corruption. Every day the newspapers were filled with sensational charges of improper conduct by high-ranking political figures, including Charles Murphy and Edward McCall. The charges were specific. Names, dates, and places were detailed. Although some of the accused issued denials, others, including Tammany chief Murphy, temporized or refused comment.[20] Sulzer himself drew huge crowds wherever he went. He was even nominated for the Assembly by the Progressives and won the election.

Tammany's loss was Fusion's gain. The 1913 campaign centered largely around the election of the mayor and the Board of Estimate. The judicial contests went almost unnoticed. This lack of attention was not unusual. The tradition, in New York as elsewhere in most of the country, was that judges ought not to campaign actively for office and should not take stands on issues about which they might later have to render an impartial judgment.[21]

Cardozo followed the general pattern of a low-key campaign. After enlisting Walter Meyer, a New York lawyer, as his campaign manager, he left the public part of his campaign largely to his friends.[22] As the election drew near, several of them took energetic steps to promote his candidacy. Walter Pollak, who was from his office, and William Cohen, who was his old friend, circularized the bar and compiled a list of some 130 endorsements, including Joseph Choate, Henry Taft, Harlan Stone, Henry Stimson, William Travers Jerome, and Elihu Root, Jr. Although Cardozo did not permit the list to be published, he did allow his friends to circulate it among lawyers, and the *New York Times* mentioned the list and some of the names in a news story.[23] Near the end of the campaign, John Mitchel spoke publicly in favor of Cardozo's election, referring to his nomination as "the finest made by any party. Every lawyer recognizes his splendid qualifications, his sterling character, and his entire independence from any unworthy influence."[24] Mitchel endorsed all the judicial nominees on the Fusion ticket; however, he singled out Cardozo's presence on the ticket as special, testifying to the reputation that Cardozo had earned at the bar.

Cardozo's friends also attempted to obtain newspaper support. At the suggestion of Henry Moskowitz, Walter Meyer enlisted the help of Cardozo's old mentor, Louis Marshall, in seeking endorsements from the Jewish newspapers.[25] Marshall wrote lengthy letters that were published in the *Jewish Morning Journal, Jewish Daily News,* and the *Warheit,* urging a vote for Cardozo. Marshall wrote in glowing terms of Cardozo's "extraordinary capacity," "preeminent ability," and "sterling character," and then moved on to the whole point of writing the letter to a Jewish newspaper. He eschewed the notion that Jews should vote for a Jew on that basis alone. "In this case, however, because of Cardozo's qualifications, if elected, he would shed luster upon the Jewish name."[26]

Newspaper support was important. William Randolph Hearst's newspapers, the *Morning Journal and Advertiser* and the *Evening Journal,* naturally supported the Independence League ticket.[27] Hearst's Independence League gave only qualified support to the Fusion ticket. Although it supported Mitchel and several other Fusion candidates, it did not nominate McAneny and Prendergast. It also nominated Bartow Weeks instead of Cardozo for a Supreme Court judgeship.[28] Most of the other major newspapers supported Cardozo, including the *Times,* the *Tribune,* and the *Herald.* The *Sun,* which was widely read by well-off people likely to be ticket-splitters, remained noncommittal. Walter Pollak knew John Garver, the law partner of James Beck, who was counsel for the *Sun.* Pollak urged Garver to persuade the *Sun* to endorse Cardozo. Garver had become acquainted with Cardozo because of the latter's work on libel cases for the *Globe,* and he agreed to see what he could do. Shortly before the election, the *Sun* endorsed Cardozo.[29]

Weeks's supporters sought to counter some of this activity and obtained the assistance of N. Taylor Phillips. Phillips, who was Cardozo's second cousin, was prominent in both Shearith Israel and Tammany Hall.[30] He was a partner of Robert F. Wagner (the future United States Senator), a former state legislator, and he had been mentioned as a possible nominee for comptroller on the Tammany ticket. Phillips sought to cut into Cardozo's Jewish vote by obtaining the support of prominent Jews for Weeks. He called the prominent clothing manufacturer Joseph

H. Cohen, and the real estate developer and philanthropist Harry Fischel, and asked them to join him in a Yiddish circular supporting Weeks to be distributed among Jewish voters. They agreed.[31]

When the circular came to Louis Marshall, he fought back. Marshall sent a letter to Phillips, Cohen, and Fischel expressing surprise that they "should array [themselves] in opposition to such a man as Benjamin Cardozo." After referring to Cardozo's sterling qualities, Marshall then made a delicate reference both to the past that Cardozo had overcome and to Jewish pride. "There are sentimental reasons which should appeal to you for putting him on the bench, reasons which would appeal to those who know the history of Mr. Cardozo and the magnificent victory which he had gained, not only for himself, but for the Jewish people, in attaining the high position that he now occupies in the profession." Marshall closed with the hope that they would try to repair the damage done by their circular.[32]

Fischel and Cohen were both crestfallen. The former called Marshall to express his regrets, saying that he had done business with Judge Weeks and had not realized that support for him would affect Cardozo. Cohen wrote that he agreed to the use of his name without even knowing that the opposing candidate was Cardozo. Both stated that they intended to write letters of support for Cardozo to their personal friends.[33] Cardozo thanked Marshall for coming to his defense. He then went on to demonstrate that he was not above the political fray and was indeed interested in promoting his own candidacy. He suggested a stronger remedy than had already been undertaken: "Do you think Fischel would write a letter to some of the East Side papers? To do so might counteract the effect of his circular."[34]

Marshall had no success with Phillips. Phillips agreed with Marshall that the judiciary should not be treated in a political fashion, but he argued that capable judges should be retained on the bench by consent of all parties and not thrown into political contests. He could not understand why the Fusion campaign had applied that principle to Judge Philbin, but not to his lifelong friend, Judge Weeks. Phillips then discussed Cardozo in a way that, behind the expressions of friendship and respect, revealed the feelings of a longtime leader of Shearith Israel about a nonparticipating member:

> You certainly do not have to argue with me the merits of Mr. Cardozo. He is my kinsman and I have known him since childhood as our

ancestors have known each other for generations. His ability is of course unquestioned and my . . . personal affection for him and his family is very deep. While it is but the truth to say that he has never been a Jew in any sense but that of having been born one, nor has ever taken the slightest interest in any of our people, still I think I understand the reasons why in your opinion his election would be beneficial to us.[35]

Phillips did not agree with the Fusion leaders who selected Cardozo because he was a "real Jew." Phillips regarded a Jew, as one who believed Jewish doctrine and observed Jewish rituals. Although Cardozo did not fit Phillips's description, he identified himself personally as a Jew, and, as Phillips knew, Cardozo had taken part in the affairs of Shearith Israel on at least one notable occasion.[36] Phillips maintained his support for Judge Weeks over Cardozo; at the same time, Phillips did Cardozo an important courtesy by keeping his personal views about him quiet.

Among the byzantine maneuvers of New York's borough politics, events in the Bronx proved crucial for Cardozo's candidacy. The Supreme Court judgeship that Cardozo was seeking, the First Judicial District, covered thirty and one-half Assembly districts in Manhattan and four and one-half Assembly Districts in the Bronx. Previously, the Bronx and Manhattan were all part of one county, New York County, but new legislation, to be effective in 1914, would turn Bronx Borough into a separate county. New county officials were to be chosen at the November 1913 election. Several Bronx Democratic leaders split from Tammany Hall and formed two opposition organizations: the larger Bronx County Jeffersonian Union led by Eugene McGuire and James Donnelly, and the Anti-Tammany Jeffersonian Alliance, led by former Congressman Steven Ayres. The Jeffersonian Union obtained the whole-hearted support of the only Bronx newspaper, the *Bronx Home News,* and fielded a joint ticket with the Bronx Republicans. Although the Jeffersonian Union at first intended to avoid involvement in the citywide contests, later it supported Mayor Gaynor's candidacy and after his death, it supported Mitchel. More critically, it decided to support Cardozo over Bartow Weeks.[37]

The Anti-Tammany Jeffersonian Alliance meanwhile cooperated with the Progressives, and both those groups also supported Cardozo over Weeks. The endorsements of the two Bronx anti-Tammany groups were crucial in the Cardozo–Weeks race for the Supreme Court judgeship, although the Bronx districts were only a small part of the First Judicial

District. Voters who did not know the men or much care about the office tended to follow the party endorsement, and Cardozo enjoyed some local Democratic, as well as Fusion, support.

Election day finally arrived on November 4. The change in Fusion fortunes that began with Mayor Gaynor's death and continued with the Sulzer removal and the following sensational revelations culminated in an enormous backlash against Tammany Hall. Mitchel swept to victory with a citywide plurality of over 120,000, carrying the entire citywide ticket with him. Even in Manhattan, stronghold of Tammany Hall, Fusion was successful in the major races. Further down the ticket, however, Tammany was stronger, and its candidate for the Supreme Court, the incumbent Bartow Weeks, was one of the strongest. Cardozo lost Manhattan to Weeks by a narrow margin: 118,374 votes for Weeks, and 115,481 for Cardozo. However, Cardozo carried the Bronx districts with 38,156 votes to 32,999 and won the election by 2,264 votes.[38]

Cardozo later claimed that he "would never have been elected had I not received the support of a group of Italian-Americans who voted for me on the supposition that since my named ended in 'o' I was one of their race."[39] With a margin of less than 2,300 out of approximately 300,000 votes, there were doubtless a number of "causes" for his success. Mistaken identity, however, was probably not a major factor. Voting and census returns indicate that in both Manhattan and the Bronx, Cardozo lost the districts with the heaviest percentage of Italian-Americans and that his greatest margins of victory were in districts with the smallest percentage of Italian-Americans.[40]

A major factor in Cardozo's election was the unexpected support of the largely Irish-American Democrats in the Bronx who bolted Tammany to form the Jeffersonian Union and the Anti-Tammany Jeffersonian Alliance. Cardozo polled approximately 8,500 of his 38,156 Bronx votes on the Union and Alliance lines on the ballot.[41] These votes, a by-product of internal Bronx politics, were crucial to Cardozo's election when combined with the base of support provided by the whole Fusion ticket.

One month after his election, Cardozo wrote Agnes Goldman, the daughter of his friend Julius Goldman, that "I am not sure precisely what I am. I am not a judge, for that transformation is postponed until the arrival of the New Year. I am no longer a lawyer, for my friends all greet me as judge, most of them with a semi-idiotic grin as if they thought it a joke. As I respond to their greeting with a like grin and a like feeling, the situation has not yet become oppressively serious." He then commented more seriously upon the responsibility that he was about to undertake, in response, apparently, to a comment from Agnes Goldman about appreciating democracy from the vantage point of a traveler abroad: "Even if my own election has its humorous side for me, I can appreciate all that you say in your letter about your feeling toward democracy. I think I have some of it here, while I am with our own people [i.e., in the United States], and I should have it more, I am sure, if I were away for any length of time. But it is a fine thing to feel that even in a small way and in a modest sphere one has been given the right in office to help to vindicate the great experiment."[42]

Cardozo was accurate to view the scope of his initial judicial position as "modest." He would be one of twenty-nine Supreme Court justices in the First Judicial District, the New York state trial court with the broadest jurisdiction. The typical rulings of those judges meant something to the parties but were not of lasting importance because significant decisions were usually reviewed in the appellate courts. But New York's trial courts provided ordinary people with relatively open access to seek justice at a fairly rapid pace. Cardozo's response to Agnes Goldman showed that he understood the important role that judges played in a democratic society. The importance of his particular role would increase rapidly.

In the few weeks before he took office, Cardozo wound up his law practice and responded to the congratulations of his colleagues at the bar. After Cardozo sent a letter of thanks to Louis Marshall, Marshall recommended that Cardozo hire Abraham Paley of Marshall's office as "attendant and confidential stenographer." Cardozo promised to consider Paley and eventually hired him.[43]

Cardozo brought his intelligence and his substantial abilities as a practicing lawyer to the bench. His record, solid as it was, gave little hint of the performance that would follow: elected justice of the New York Supreme Court in 1913; designated within five weeks to sit on the New York Court of Appeals; appointed and then elected as a regular member of the Court of Appeals in 1917; elected chief judge of that Court in 1925; and appointed to the Supreme Court of the United States in 1932. The list of positions is impressive, but it was his performance in those roles that counts. It was distinguished. He demonstrated that a judge could creatively modernize law while maintaining a genuine respect for history and precedent that embodied the notion of the rule of law.

Cardozo took his seat as a justice of the New York Supreme Court on January 5, 1914, forty-two years after his father had resigned from the very same court. John B. Stanchfield, one of the leading trial lawyers of the day, spoke for the bar. He ventured "the prophecy that [your new career] will measure up to your professional reputation, your personal integrity and probity." That was one of the few tributes to a new judge that turned out to have been understated. Cardozo's response that "I will do the best I can in the performance of the common task in which we are all engaged—the great and sacred task—the administration of justice" was an accurate representation of his effort and his view of his job throughout his judicial career.[44]

Cardozo's first assignment was to hear nonjury cases and decide motions (requests that the court enter ancillary orders of a procedural or substantive nature in pending cases). The Supreme Court, which was the major trial court of the State of New York, handled all kinds of civil cases. During the five weeks that Cardozo sat in the Supreme Court, he rendered opinions in five cases—three commercial, one trust, and one matrimonial.[45] He also presided over one jury trial of a negligence action involving a passenger thrown from a street railway car.[46] This was just a taste of the life of a trial judge.

While Cardozo was gaining this brief experience, Governor Martin Glynn was trying to decide which Supreme Court justice he should designate to sit in the Court of Appeals, the highest court in New York, to assist in clearing up that court's backlog.[47] There was a vacancy in the designated judges because Justice Frank Hiscock had been elected to a regular seat on the Court of Appeals in the November 1913 election. Glynn eventually chose Cardozo, but the full story was complicated. The judges of the New York Court of Appeals traditionally played a role in the designation by making a recommendation to the governor.[48] In this instance they twice requested that Glynn designate Cardozo. The judges appreciated his ability because of his regular appearances before them as a practicing lawyer. Glynn did not immediately honor their request.[49]

Glynn first offered the designation to Justice Samuel Greenbaum, who turned him down for financial reasons. Surprisingly, a Supreme Court justice in the First Department (Manhattan and the Bronx) was paid more than a judge of the Court of Appeals, $17,500 as compared with $13,700 (roughly $290,000 as compared with $228,000 in mid-1990s dollars). With the extra expense of living in Albany during court sessions as well, Greenbaum thought he could not afford to accept the offer.[50] He thereupon recommended Cardozo.

But Glynn was also considering Samuel Seabury, another of Cardozo's colleagues. A month before naming Cardozo, Glynn first told one, then the other, to clear his desk for the job.[51] Apparently several judges of the Court of Appeals opposed Seabury's nomination because Seabury had publicly branded that court as reactionary for its decision in the *Ives* case, which held New York's workers' compensation law unconstitutional.[52] Finally, after several weeks of indecision, at the end of January Glynn authorized Justice Greenbaum to approach Cardozo to see whether he would accept a designation. Cardozo thought very highly of Greenbaum as a judge and a human being.[53] Greenbaum's son recalled the meeting between the two men:

> I remember well the night that Cardozo was at the house; my father urged him to take the job, telling him he was just the person needed for that bench, that he had the ability to do it, and that he would make a fine judge. Then Father added that no Jew had ever been on the Court of Appeals and that he hoped Cardozo would be the first. Cardozo, who was unmarried and lived with his sister, had reasons for not accepting, but money was not one of them. Cardozo felt that he did not have the qualifications or experience: he had served as a judge only for a very short time; he would be frightfully embarrassed with his new associates on the highest court, as well as with the members of the Supreme Court, where he was then sitting. However, at my father's insistence, he agreed to think it over and give his answer the next week. When he came back, he told us that Father's arguments had persuaded him. As I recall, his words were something like this: "All right, Judge, because you want me to, I'll do it. I'll try to be a good judge and a good Jew, and I'll live at the North Pole [Albany] and cut my pay in two."[54]

Armed with that vintage Cardozo epigram, Greenbaum then told Glynn that Cardozo would accept, and Glynn announced his designation on February 2, 1914.[55] Glynn later told Judge Irving Lehman that "he was prouder of that designation than of any other act of his career."[56] The *New York Law Journal*, commenting enthusiastically on Cardozo's designation, recognized that "he has qualities of legal scholarship, analytical thought and literary felicity especially adapting him for the work of the court of last resort."[57]

Cardozo also received a formal resolution of congratulations from the trustees of Shearith Israel. They noted proudly that "the first Israelite" to be a member of the Court of Appeals had come from the earliest Congregation in North America and that he was "one whose ancestors have been faithful officers and members for two centuries and himself an Elector."[58] Cardozo's response reflected the nature of his tie to the Congregation. "I am deeply sensible of the fine impulse of friendship and of brotherhood disclosed in your generous words of greeting and good-will. The friendship, I am glad to believe, is personal, but the brotherhood is something larger and more vital for it is the tie that binds this historic Congregation to all the members of our race. I know that your tribute comes to me in this two-fold spirit; and I accept it as the offering of friends and brothers."[59] Cardozo saw his membership as part of his tie of "brotherhood" with the Congregation and with all Jewry. It reflected an identity—that he was a Sephardic Jew—rather than a participation in a common ritual and shared convictions. Cardozo was careful not to mention religion, wishing neither to offend nor to pretend.

Cardozo's designation to the Court of Appeals caused him one problem. He had presided over the case of Drucklieb v. Harris, a stockholder's action to impress a trust in favor of the company on property in the hands of the company's president. He had already written an opinion in favor of the plaintiff but had not entered a final order. The attorney for the defendant argued that he no longer had power to enter the final order as a trial court judge because of his designation to sit on the Court of Appeals. Cardozo called in the attorney for the plaintiff to discuss the issue. He also apparently spoke to judges of the Court of Appeals, who differed as to what his status was after being designated but before taking the oath.[60] The defendant offered to pay the amount of judgment, which could have ended the case and provided the way out for Cardozo, but the situation was not resolved in time. Cardozo filed a memorandum on February 9 that he had no power to enter a judgment.[61] Two days earlier, on February 7, 1914, Cardozo had taken the oath of office as a Court of Appeals judge and embarked on a career that would make him the outstanding state court judge in the country.

8

The Job of a Judge

Cardozo joined a controversial Court of Appeals. It had been excoriated as reactionary for its 1911 decision in the *Ives* case, which held the New York workers' compensation law unconstitutional. Election of its members had been caught up in the political turmoil that accompanied the progressive movement. Two of its members had run against one another for the chief judgeship. But change was in the air. Of the ten judges who were sitting on the Court of Appeals in November 1913 when Cardozo was elected to the bench, five would retire by the end of 1916, and all but Judge Emory Chase and Chief Judge Frank Hiscock would be gone by the end of 1923.

The Court of Appeals during Cardozo's years became one of the outstanding courts in the country. The state's large population and economic power gave the Court of Appeals a head start in prominence. But the caliber of the personnel was the principal reason for the court's new fame. Cuthbert Pound, who sat with Cardozo during most of his tenure, was a creative and thoughtful judge.[1] Pound, who was a cousin of Dean Roscoe Pound of Harvard Law School, was a classicist from Lockport in upstate New York and a former Cornell Law School professor. William Andrews and Irving Lehman joined Cardozo on the court in 1917 and 1923 respectively. Andrews was the son of Charles Andrews, who had been judge of the Court of Appeals and briefly Chief Judge in the 1880s. The younger Andrews, who is best remembered for his dissent in the *Palsgraf* case, was an able, scholarly judge.[2] Lehman came from the well-known German-Jewish family that founded Lehman Brothers, the banking and investment firm. He was Cardozo's closest friend on the court, and the friendship expanded to include Irving Lehman's wife Sissie, a powerful woman whose father, Oscar Straus, had been a member of Theodore Roosevelt's cabinet. Lehman was a vigorous, intelligent man who occasionally wrote very intricate opinions. Frederick Collin and Frank Hiscock, Cardozo's predecessor as chief judge, had considerable ability as well.[3] It was a vigorous, able, and strong-minded group of men, by and large, with whom Cardozo worked during his eighteen years on the Court of Appeals.

The court met in the Court of Appeals building, which looked diagonally uphill across a green square to the Capitol. Court of Appeals Hall is a massive Greek-style building with large pillars supporting a portico with a rounded dome on top. The building, the former State Hall, was remodeled in 1916 to allow the Court of Appeals to move from the third floor of the Capitol to its own home. The old courtroom, which had been much admired, was substantially duplicated, and, indeed, parts of it were simply transferred.[4] It is an elaborate, striking room with its red marble floor, huge double fireplace, paneled walls, high windows with red velvet curtains, and chandeliers hanging from an elaborately carved ceiling. The courtroom is filled with portraits of former judges of the court. Behind the judges' bench and over the chief judge's chair was a large portrait of John Jay with portraits of Chancellor James Kent and Judge Greene C. Bronson beneath.

The business of the Court of Appeals was deciding civil and criminal cases appealed from decisions of the lower courts, primarily from the Appellate Division, the intermediate appellate court. Parties could not appeal every decision of a lower court to the Court of Appeals, and the scope of that court's reviewing power involved complex legal issues. Simply put, under the New York Constitution between 1895 and 1925, the Court of Appeals could usually review only questions of law (for example, was it negligent to drive faster than the speed limit?) and not questions of fact (was the driver exceeding the speed limit?). The Court of Appeals could not even review the issue whether there was evidence to support a finding of fact if the Appellate Division had decided that question unanimously. In 1925, in the middle of Cardozo's tenure on the court, the New York Constitution was amended to permit the Court of Appeals to review all questions of law and also questions of fact in certain situations when the Appellate Division had reversed a judgment because the evidence did not support the lower court's conclusion on the facts.[5] Thus, for a large portion of Cardozo's career, the court operated under severe constraints in its ability to review the factual conclusions of the Appellate Division.

When cases were reviewed by the Court of Appeals, the lawyers for the parties filed written briefs for the judges to read before the case was argued orally. Each side was allotted an hour for argument, except in special circumstances.[6] While the court was behind in its work, as it was until 1923, the judges did not ask the lawyers many questions during oral argument. Hiscock used to say that judges should listen, and interrupt only when they needed information. Each case was randomly assigned to a judge before argument, and that judge would make an oral report at the court's postargument conference, which was called the "consultation."[7] If a tentative decision was reached to decide the case without a written opinion, the judge to whom the case was assigned would often follow up his oral report with a written report setting forth the facts and discussing the applicable legal principles. This report was for the judges' use only. The court's written order stated only that the decision of the court below was affirmed or reversed, sometimes with a sentence of explanation or the citation of a controlling precedent.[8]

If the court decided that the case warranted a written opinion, the judge with responsibility for the case did not circulate a written report. If in the majority, the judge would prepare and circulate a draft opinion for the comments of his colleagues. If not, one of the majority judges would prepare the opinion. When the majority opinion was completed and any dissents or concurring opinions had been prepared, the decision would be released to the parties and the public. On average, Cardozo wrote thirty majority opinions, one concurring opinion, and one dissenting opinion each year.[9] Part of the court's work also involved consideration of motions filed by parties: for example, a motion for leave to appeal to the Court of Appeals in those cases where permission of the court was required or a motion to amend the judgment entered after a decision by the Court of Appeals (the remittitur). The judges also reported to the consultation, often by written report, in these instances. Justice was swift in the Court of Appeals, especially after the court was caught up in its work. In most cases, the court handed down an opinion within two months of the argument.

————

The following section of this book, "Doing the Law's Work," will consider the substance of Cardozo's opinions, but two early Cardozo opinions will give some idea of the workings of the court system and of Cardozo's approach in deciding cases and writing opinions.

Howard v. City of Buffalo was a suit by farmers to require the city of Buffalo and a number of railroads to undo extensive construction work that resulted in regular flooding of their farm.[10] Beginning in about 1888, a number of railroads closed up openings in approaches to railroad bridges and filled in culverts under various embankments. The city of Buffalo also changed the grade of a road in the same area. The result was that annual spring and fall floods of the Buffalo River and Cazenovia Creek, which had formerly flowed in flood channels to Lake Erie, now regularly flooded the plaintiffs' farm. In 1906, they brought suit against the city and the railroads and sought both damages and an injunction to require the railroads to reopen their embankments and take other action to restore the flood channel and to require the city to regrade the road to the same end. The course of proceedings took a long time before a judgment was finally entered by the trial court in 1910. The plaintiffs were victorious. They obtained damages and an injunction requiring restoration of the flood channel. The defendants appealed to the Appellate Division. In 1912, that court, with one judge dissenting, affirmed the decision of the trial court, although portions of the injunction were suspended to see whether other mandated action cured the problem. The defendants appealed to the Court of Appeals.

That court heard argument on April 12, 1914, and handed down its decision in an opinion by Cardozo less than a month later. (Cardozo was a rapid opinion-writer from the very start of his career.) Cardozo's opinion reversed the judgment of the lower courts almost entirely. He found not only that the plaintiffs had failed to prove the existence and location of the prior flood channel but also that they could not even trace a present channel. Moreover, the city had the right to lower a highway grade that it had previously raised so long as it did not lower the grade below that of the adjacent land. Those conclusions were sufficient to justify reversal.

Rather than stopping there, Cardozo went on to include lengthy dicta, that is, statements that were unnecessary to support the precise holding of the court but that he included to explain his views on larger issues. He noted that the whole area surrounding the river had been built up with factories and homes. This construction contributed to the change in flow of the river at flood times. If the defendants could be compelled to undo their changes in the flood plain, everyone else could be compelled to do so as well. Moreover, removal of the defendants' alterations would lead to flooding of some of these newly developed areas. He recoiled from the consequences of upholding the plaintiffs' claims:

> The rules applicable to the obstruction of streams in an unsettled or rural region cannot be rigidly applied where an urban population has planted its factories and homes. The law of water rights is not an inflexible body of precedent. It takes heed of the varying wants of varying localities . . . No court would presume by mandatory injunction to compel the destruction of a great section of a city because in building it the limit of some ancient flood channel were obstructed . . . An absurdity, of course, it would be [to destroy the improvements along the riverbanks], for the decrees of a court of equity are framed in reason and justice.[11]

The only remedy for the plaintiffs' troubles was legislative, a state program to deepen and widen the riverbed. The legislature had already provided for that work, and it was even then going forward.

Cardozo's opinion in *Howard* exhibited many characteristics of his judicial work. Emphasis on the facts had characterized his briefs as a practicing lawyer, and he carried that empirical approach to the bench. Cardozo himself took note of this quality in a characteristic simile designed to draw a smile: "This opinion in its review of the facts may seem, like the floods of which it treats, to have swollen to extravagant size."[12] Cardozo was also willing to look beyond the alleged wrongful acts of the defendants to the entire picture of events as presented by the evidence in order to establish that more was at stake than just the plaintiffs' farm. His extensive look at the facts indicated that urban development was threatened by the trial court's order, and he was ready to adapt the legal rule to modern conditions.

Another theme in Cardozo's opinion was the traditional reliance on "reason and justice" as one basis for considering a request for an injunction, which was a form of equitable relief.[13] As he looked at the case in its larger context, the balance of equitable considerations, of "justice," lay with the defendants and the urban development that they represented. Yet another theme was Cardozo's understanding that the courts were not the only source of help in society. Indeed, sometimes they were not an available source of help at all, and an aggrieved party had to look to the legislature.

Focus on the facts, adaptation of doctrine to social conditions, emphasis on reason and a sense of justice, respect for the role of the legislature in lawmaking, and the occasional rhetorical flourish were all notable elements in *Howard*. They would be hallmarks of Cardozo's judicial style.

The excerpt quoted from the opinion also contained another hallmark of Cardozo's style, the inverted sentence. ("An absurdity, of course, it would be . . .") The inverted sentence had turned up in his college writing, and he found it useful in his brief-writing.[14] It is no surprise that he brought it with him to the bench. Many years later Thomas Reed Powell sought to tease Cardozo out of his fondness for inversions: "Some day I may suggest the reading of Fowler's title on Inversion. Glad would I be if your predicates more often lagged behind their subject, though once did I discover a place where you failed to commit inversion when it would have added fiber instead of taking it away."[15] Cardozo responded with grace and humor, and without inversions: "Ungrateful man. You told me about two years ago that I used inversion too often, and I have shunned them ever since like the plague! May one never live down one's early sins!"[16] A little earlier, when his friend Charles Burlingham made the same criticism, Cardozo defended himself: "I think inversion is often very helpful—partly for emphasis and partly for the avoidance of a uniformity of construction unpleasant to the ear. I gladly follow brother Fowler when he discourses upon words, but not so slavishly when he discourses upon style."[17]

Cardozo exhibited his ability to see a serious principle in a trivial encounter in another early case, Morningstar v. The Lafayette Hotel Company.[18] William Morningstar asked the dining room of the Lafayette Hotel in Buffalo, where he was staying, to prepare some food that he had bought. He refused to pay what he considered an excessive service charge of $1 (equivalent to roughly $15 in the mid-1990s). At a later meal, he was told publicly, in the hearing of other guests, that he would not be served. He sued the hotel for damages arising from the public humiliation caused by the hotel's wrongful refusal to serve him. The trial judge instructed the jury to find for the hotel if it concluded that the service charge was not excessive, and it returned a verdict in favor of the hotel. Morningstar appealed to the Appellate Division, which affirmed the judgment without writing an opinion in 1912. Morningstar then appealed to the Court of Appeals, arguing that the instruction to the jury was wrong and that the hotel had an obligation to serve him so long as he was still a guest. He also contended that it was an error for the trial judge to have permitted testimony of other hotel proprietors that he was a chronic fault-finder.

Cardozo, writing for a unanimous court, reversed the judgment for the hotel and ordered a new trial. This was a dispute that the court could easily have brushed aside as frivolous, but Cardozo treated it with the utmost seriousness. He agreed with the Appellate Division that the instruction to the jury was correct; a hotel had no obligation to serve a guest who refused to pay a legitimate charge, and whether the charge was excessive was a matter for the jury to decide. But Cardozo held that the trial judge had committed error in permitting the hotel to introduce evidence that Morningstar was a complainer. That other hotel owners considered him undesirable was irrelevant to the issue whether he had wrongfully been refused service.

The case involved two important principles, the right of a human being to be treated with dignity and the duty of the law to respond to a violation of rights. Rebutting the argument that no substantial issue was at stake, Cardozo stated that it was "no concern of ours that the controversy at the root of this lawsuit may seem to be trivial." Arguing that enforcement of one's rights "is never a legal wrong, and may often be a moral duty," he called on the insight of the philosopher von Jhering that the development of law owes much to individual resistance in cases like this.[19] Cardozo the practical lawyer might have used von Jhering's comment pragmatically to support a client's cause. Cardozo the judge used it to support his instinct that this little case involved a big principle.

———————

Cardozo had a routine for the court sessions. In the early years, until 1923, when the court was trying to clear its backlog of cases, sessions were five or six weeks long with one- or two-week recesses. In those years, when there were the three additional Supreme Court judges designated to sit with the seven judges of the Court of Appeals, three of the ten judges would be off every session. After the court was caught up in its work, its sessions generally lasted three weeks, followed by three-week recesses. Sometimes the sessions lasted only two weeks, with four-week recesses between them. The judges used the recesses to write opinions, to review colleagues' opinions in cases that had been argued in recent sessions, and to prepare for upcoming arguments.[20]

When Cardozo was not sitting in a session, he worked in his New York City office. When he was scheduled for a court session, Cardozo took a Monday morning train to Albany. There, especially in the later years, Andrew Lynch, confidential assistant to the court, met him at the train to help carry his huge load of briefs and records to the hotel. The hotel was the Ten Eyck, where all the judges stayed. Cardozo always had the same room, number 852, overlooking State Street. His distant view was the Mohawk River, while in the foreground was the National Savings Bank and a burlesque theater. The room was very simple—a double bed, a desk, a few chairs, and a bathroom. Hotel employees remembered him as a quiet guest who never asked for much in the way of service. He never asked, for example, for liquor as others did during the years of prohibition.[21]

The court followed a regular routine during an argument week. On Monday the judges would arrive by the late morning, have lunch, and hear arguments from 2:00 to 6:00 P.M. On Tuesdays, Wednesdays, and Thursdays, they spent from 9:30 A.M. to 1:00 P.M. in "consultation," discussing the cases heard the previous day and other court business. These meetings were private, but the court's card clerk recorded the proceedings.[22] After lunch, they heard arguments from 2:00 to 6:00 and worked for another hour before going to dinner. Cardozo, at least, also worked after dinner until 10:30 or 11:00. There were no arguments on Friday. The judges conferred until 12:30 P.M. or so, and then Cardozo took the 1:00 or 2:00 o'clock train to New York. At some point in this period, at least by 1921, the Friday consultation was shifted to the afternoon, and then Cardozo would arrive home in the evening.[23]

In Cardozo's later years on the court, Herbert Cone, the law assistant to the Chief Judge, often drove Cardozo to the Albany train station in what Cardozo called the "death car" because of Cone's propensity to look around when driving. Lynch packed a meal for Cardozo to take on the train, and Cardozo ate at his Pullman chair while working.[24] Once, returning from Albany, Cardozo was jostled while leaving the subway carrying his bag in one hand and an umbrella in the other. Later, he discovered that his "pocket-book" was missing from his inside jacket pocket, and still later, he figured out that his pocket had been picked. He was angry that he had been "such an easy mark."[25]

The judges spent most of their time in Albany with one another. The circumstance that the court sat only in Albany, where none of the judges lived, enforced a camaraderie that carried over into the court's work. The judges ate most meals together, sitting in the same places (Cardozo between Henry Kellogg and Frank Hiscock) at their own round table in the main dining room of the Ten Eyck, served by the same waiter, Charlie Schubert, every day. Cardozo and Hiscock would generally arrive first in the morning, around seven o'clock. Cardozo's breakfast was invariably orange juice, cereal (oatmeal or Wheatena), and coffee. After breakfast the two of them would take a short walk before going to court. Lunch also was very simple—a cup of soup, rye toast, and milk. In the early years, the judges ate lunch together at the Ten Eyck, although later Cardozo took to eating his lunch in chambers. Dinner was a regular meat, potatoes, and vegetable meal. When the maître d'hôtel, Chris Bogiages, would sometimes suggest that a salad would be good for him, Cardozo would reply, "you're just like my sister." Once, when Judge Kellogg made a sarcastic comment to Bogiages, Cardozo calmed the waters. He instantly turned to Kellogg and said, "Now Judge, suppose you were Chris and someone said that to you." Kellogg apologized.[26]

The judges made up a companionable group, bringing a variety of experiences from the worlds of law, politics, and business with them to the court. Cardozo enjoyed and joined the camaraderie and humor that held the group together. He appreciated amusing stories, which he preserved for future use in his commonplace book.[27] A sample of the stories and sayings that he thought worth recording indicates Cardozo's taste and sense of humor:

"Judge John M. Woolsey in his address to the Columbia Law Alumni . . . told of a Federal Judge in Georgia who was said to be 'the only man who could strut sitting down.'"[28]

"George IV is said to have at last believed that he was at the battle of Waterloo, because he had so often said that he was."[29]

"We are reminded of the answer given by the devil when somebody—I suppose a disciple of Herbert Spencer—had explained to him that under the beneficent working of the law of evolution social equilibrium would presently be attained and his reign come to an end. 'You forget,' said the devil, 'that I, too, am evolving.'"[30]

"The golden mean has been recommended chiefly, not because it was golden, but because it was safe."[31]

"At a dinner in honor of George Curzon (later Lord Curzon, Viceroy of India) Lord Houghton was present. Lord Houghton had got very drowsy . . . and woke up just as the hero of the evening, now in the middle of a suave and polished oration, was assuring his admirers that any success that had come to him was entirely due to his having made it a rule of his life only to associate with his intellectual superiors. This was a very apt and pretty compliment to everybody present, and they gently preened themselves on being his associates. But Lord Houghton saw it in another light. 'By God,' he exclaimed, 'that wouldn't be difficult.'"[32]

"Chesterton says of Shaw that he was 'a man always ready to get into hot water, especially by throwing cold water.'"[33]

"If you must tell me your opinions," said Goethe, "tell me what you believe in. I have plenty of doubts of my own!"[34]

"Gladstone said of Kinglake's History of the Crimean War: 'His book is too bad to live, and too good to die.'" (To which Cardozo added a reminder to himself: "Say this of my own book.")[35]

Cardozo enjoyed good stories, bons mots, and puns, especially when told with style. Most of the stories that he recorded also had a point, often a point about human folly, pride, or some other failing. With his photographic memory, Cardozo could draw on this stock of sayings for dinner-table conversation just as he did in his public talks and lectures.

Once in a while Cardozo did a little socializing away from the Ten Eyck. Judge and Mrs. Kellogg were very close to Mary Hun, daughter of Marcus Hun, the reporter for the Court of Appeals, and the Kelloggs took Cardozo to dinner at her house on occasional Thursdays, which was "judges' night out." Cardozo, like the other judges, rarely went to dinner parties or other social functions during the week when the court was in session because, as Cardozo put it, a judge "will fall behind in his work if he does." Evenings were for preparing for the next day's work.[36]

The judges lived together as a little club during the Albany session. Whatever professional and personal disagreements they had, they treated one another with courtesy and respect. They were not only colleagues but also friends.

Cardozo's reports to the consultation in motions and in cases in which no opinion was to be written provide a good insight into the thoughtfulness and conscientiousness with which the court pursued its job. The reports served the important purpose of assuring the judges that they had dealt with all the issues and that their decision not to write an opinion was justified. The usual reason for not publishing an opinion was that the decision of the lower court was correct and the legal principles were settled. Sometimes, when the issues were doubtful, the judges decided not to write an opinion because the record was too meager or the presentation had been so bad that the court was unsure of the factual setting or even the contentions that were being made. "There is great danger," Cardozo wrote in one such case, "when such questions are discussed with reference to the facts of a particular and meagre record, that conclusions based upon that record will be interpreted by the bar too broadly, and lead to confusion in the future."[37] Sometimes, the court believed that a previous opinion made it so clear that the lower court's conclusion was wrong that no opinion was necessary.

Cardozo treated the preparation of reports quite seriously. His memoranda all contain a full statement of the facts and appear to respond, however briefly, to every argument made by the losing party, both in cases that had been argued and in the various motions addressed to the court. His memoranda were usually a few pages long, but sometimes they were much longer. Even though he presented his views more informally than in an opinion, he wrote in a format that made it easy for him to turn the report into an opinion if the court decided that an opinion was called for. At consultation, as several transcripts show, he presented his views forcefully and acknowledged and met contrary arguments in a manner that reflected his thorough knowledge of the precedents, in New York and elsewhere.[38]

Since the reports described cases in which a tentative judgment had already been reached to decide a case or a motion without an opinion, Cardozo generally presented the issues as indicating a clear outcome. "The only question is whether the evidence sustains a verdict that [the homicide] was deliberate and premeditated. I have no doubt that it does, and the case seems to me to be a clear one." (Recommending that the court affirm a first degree murder conviction.)[39] "The motion is made in total disregard of the limitations on our jurisdiction resulting from the unanimous affirmance." (Recommending that the court deny a motion for leave to appeal because the state Constitution foreclosed a reconsideration of the evidence after a unanimous affirmance in the Appellate Division.)[40]

But Cardozo was candid with his colleagues when he felt doubt. Indeed, Cardozo occasionally expressed uncertainty even after studying a matter for some time. "This little case growing out of a controversy about $3 has caused me an amount of trouble quite disproportionate to its importance . . . I do not know whether the majority of the court will agree with my conclusion, which I have reached with a good deal of doubt and hesitation."[41] "I am in doubt what to recommend in this case."[42] "I incline to the belief, though with some hesitation, for I am always at sea in the discussion of mechanical problems, that there is evidence, not only of faulty construction, but of a causal relation between defect and accident . . . I shall be glad to reconsider the case, if my associates are of the opinion that I have misinterpreted the evidence."[43]

Cardozo was open-minded. He changed his mind in many cases after further study or after listening to his colleagues. "At consultation, all of us agreed with Judge Collin that the defendant's appeal must fail. Some of us were inclined to think, however, that the judgment ought to be reversed to the extent that it was appealed from by the plaintiff. That was my own impression, and I took the case to develop that view. After further thought, I am led to the conclusion that Judge Collin was right in recommending that there be an affirmance as to both parties."[44] "This case was assigned to me that I might write an opinion for reversal. I have written one, but have not distributed it, for reflection has made me doubtful of the correctness of my conclusion. I should like to submit to you this point which has not yet been considered."[45] "[M]y report at consultation was in favor of reversal, but some of my associates disagreed, the votes of those who concurred were tentative, and I expressed a good deal of doubt myself. Subsequent reflection has led me to believe that justice will be done if we affirm without opinion."[46] "This case has been entered in the register as affirmed without opinion, and I concurred in the vote. I felt doubtful about it, however, and took the record home with me for further consideration. Reflection leads me to the conclusion that the judgment is erroneous."[47] "I have come to the conclusion that I have been on the wrong tack in this case. I therefore withdraw my opinion in its several revisions, and come around, at least in result, to Judge Lehman's dissent."[48]

Cardozo also occasionally circulated memoranda to persuade his colleagues to change their views or to remain steadfast when there was disagreement. "It was the view of a majority of the court at consultation that no useful purpose would be served by an opinion for affirmance. In the fear that Judge Kellogg may succeed in winning over another vote for reversal, I am sending this memorandum to remind you of some of our decisions which he may have overlooked."[49] Sometimes he was successful.[50] If not, he often simply noted a dissent without filing a dissenting memorandum.[51] The records do not indicate why he chose to remain silent. Sometimes it may have been collegiality. Sometimes it may have been that he thought the case not important enough to warrant a published statement of reasons, especially if his views were sufficiently reflected in an opinion in a lower court. And sometimes he may have wished to avoid magnifying what he viewed as the court's error by calling attention to it or to avoid a polarization that might lead the majority to state a more dogmatic or even a more extreme position.

The informality of the reports allows insights into Cardozo's response when faced with cases in which the governing legal principles clashed with his sympathies concerning the people or facts of the case. "This is a hard case, but I see no escape from an affirmance of the judgment . . . it illustrates again . . . the necessity of legislation which will give the court some power of amendment in furtherance of justice."[52] "The result seems to me to be unfortunate, but I think the statute makes it unavoidable."[53] "I think the ruling is very harsh and technical, and though we may have to sustain it, I feel satisfied that we ought not to do so without fuller consideration."[54] "I have a feeling that very possibly the plaintiffs have been swindled. If so, I think the fault is chiefly due to the failure of their own lawyers to protect them adequately."[55] Cardozo did not flinch. He voted against his sympathies when he concluded that the governing legal principles required him to do so.

And finally, there was an occasional plea for institutional candor, to correct an error in an opinion. Cardozo agreed with the position taken in one motion for reargument that there was a misstatement of fact in the original decision. Although he thought that the decision was still correct and that the motion for reargument should be denied, he did not take the easy way out by simply recommending that the motion be denied without saying anything. Fairness to the parties and the honor of the court required more. "I think we shall perhaps seem to be lacking in candor if we do not say why the error is unimportant."[56] The error, even though unimportant, should be admitted.

The picture from Cardozo's memoranda is one of a conscientious and collegial court. The judges were respectful as they sought to persuade one another in contested matters. Part of the respect consisted of their formal courtesy toward one another. Judges always addressed or referred to their colleagues as Judge X and Judge Y, never by first name. Even when they disagreed, they did not do so in a polarizing way. They worked together to make the court work. Part of the collegiality of the court was that no judge or group of judges dominated it. But Cardozo was one of the judges who had substantial influence in that setting, an influence that grew with seniority and with his eventual elevation to the chief judgeship.

———

Cardozo's working life outside the Albany sessions was simple and routine. He worked at his own office in New York City. Initially, he had offices downtown at 51 Chambers Street. In 1922, he moved his offices midtown to Room 701 of the new City Bar Building, at 36 West 44th Street. There he had easy access to the bar association's library where he did a great deal of his research.[57] Despite the availability of a library staff to retrieve books, Cardozo always got his own books, even climbing the book stack ladders all over the reading room. That bit of informality reflected his notion of doing his own research, analysis, and writing. In other matters, Cardozo was very formal. Even if the thermometer hit 100 degrees, Cardozo would work in the library, wearing his coat, tie, and stiff shirt with a high linen collar.[58]

If the weather was nice, Cardozo would walk to his office at the Bar Building with Judge Nathan Bijur of the New York Supreme Court. Although Bijur was not an intimate friend, as was Cardozo's earlier walking companion, Edgar Nathan, Cardozo respected and liked him. He wrote that Bijur had gone on the bench "with good, though not an extraordinary equipment, but by force of sheer devotion to his work, he made himself an accomplished judge. Withal he was a most lovable man."[59] Much of the conversation between the two men was about Bijur's cases. Judge Bijur once induced Cardozo to express, reluctantly, a view about a pending matter.[60] Bijur adopted Cardozo's view, but the Court of Appeals later reversed his decision, with Cardozo writing the opinion. When Bijur burst into Cardozo's office, expostulating, Cardozo responded that Bijur had omitted a fact that the court viewed as critical.[61]

Cardozo did all his own work—opinions, books, speeches—in long-hand with little contribution from his clerk. He read and wrote very rapidly and had a photographic memory, often startling people with his ability to support his views not merely with the precedents but with their citations. He performed this feat not only in private conversations but also in the consultations of the Court of Appeals. The most telling tribute was Judge Kellogg's when Cardozo recalled the volume number of a relevant case: "By God, he's forgotten the page!"[62] In those days, when the position of the law clerk was very new, Cardozo did not make much use of his clerk for important legal work. He had only three law clerks in his New York judicial career: Charles Evans Hughes, Jr., son of the future Chief Justice, for the brief month Cardozo spent in the Supreme Court; Abraham Paley for four years; and then, after the death of Abraham, Abraham's brother Joseph Paley, for the remaining fourteen years on the Court of Appeals and for a few months in Washington.[63] Sometimes Joseph Paley would do research on a specific point, or would write memoranda on undecided cases, or would add something to the draft of an opinion, but that was the extent of the legal work.[64]

Joseph Paley functioned more as secretary, messenger, and errand boy than as a modern law clerk, and, in fact, the title of the position was "secretary." The relationship began in 1918 when Paley's brother, the prior secretary, died quite suddenly, and Cardozo, in response to Joseph Paley's application, appointed him secretary at a salary of $2,000. Neither of the Paleys was a lawyer when hired; both earned their degrees while working for Cardozo.[65] Joseph Paley typed and circulated various kinds of memoranda and opinions and typed the lectures that Cardozo prepared.[66] Cardozo often made numerous revisions, many of them minor, and Paley was kept busy retyping corrected versions.[67] Occasionally, Cardozo had him look for very particular legal information—cases from other jurisdictions, specific kinds of language, or holdings that fit a particular thought.[68] But Joseph Paley also spent a great deal of time buying railroad tickets, stamps, pads of paper, and books; investigating various aspects of Cardozo's insurance policies; and handling other personal matters.[69] He made Cardozo's life easier by performing all these tasks, but he did not have a serious professional function. Cardozo's intellectual companions were his colleagues on the court.

When Cardozo was designated to sit in the Court of Appeals to help that court catch up on its work, the court acquired an ideal judge. Cardozo's work habits filled the court's need, and he fit into its collegial atmosphere. He was courteous and considerate, and his store of humorous quips and stories, derived primarily from his reading, added to the life of the group. His personality, character, and ability won the admiration and affection of his colleagues. He gradually came to be lionized by the bench, the bar, and academia, and his judicial life was a pleasure.

9

Private Life and Private Views

The bedrock of Cardozo's life was his daily companionship with Nellie at home. His twin sister, Emily, married Frank Bent and lived on Long Island, in Flushing. His other sister, Elizabeth, lived at Shippan Point, Connecticut, with Kate Tracy. After Elizabeth died in 1917, Kate Tracy joined the family at 16 West 75th Street. Ben and Nellie were able to afford a good deal of help in running the house. In addition to Kate Tracy, there were Mary Walsh, who was first a maid and later the cook, her sister Catherine, who became the maid in the mid-1920s, and a chauffeur.

Their home was a substantial four-story brownstone, with a flight of stairs from the street to the front door. One flight down was a kitchen and a sitting room for the servants. The main floor contained a parlor filled with large, old family furniture. Next to the parlor was a dining room with a great deal of family silver sitting on the sideboards. The pantry was just off the dining room. The second floor had a bedroom each for Nellie and Ben, with a washroom in between. Ben's room included a desk. A large library was on the third floor in the front over Nellie's room, and Miss Tracy's room was in the back. Finally, the top floor had a room for Mary and Catherine Walsh in back and a spare bedroom in front. There was also a large dumbwaiter, which, after Nellie was ill and had difficulty walking, she sometimes rode downstairs in order to go outside.[1]

By the time Ben became a judge, Nellie had begun to have serious health problems, and Ben became more and more the caretaker. Nellie developed a nervous twitch of the head and high blood pressure, which was probably associated with the hyperthyroid problem called Graves Disease (people noticed her bulging eyes), and she may have already suffered the first of many heart attacks.[2] Nellie's health was a continuous preoccupation for Ben, and he fussed over her a great deal. Sometimes he would treat his devotion lightly, as when he referred to himself as "Nellie's doggie."[3]

When Ben went to Albany for court sessions, he would return to New York to be with Nellie over the weekends. While in Albany, he talked with her every day by telephone. When Nellie became quite ill, Kate Tracy wrote him in the morning and evening to report on her condition, and Cardozo would call Miss Tracy at night to get another report. Evidently, Ben also wrote Nellie every day.[4]

Only one of those letters survives, and it is like no other in Cardozo's papers.[5] Written in 1916 from the train on the way to Albany, it was filled with concern for her health. Ben referred to Nellie as "Dear darling" or "Dear dearest" five times during the course of three paragraphs, said that he would not want to keep living if anything happened to her, spoke of his inability to thank her enough for all she did for him, and regretted being unable to be better to her. There was a light touch in his reference to still being able to beat her at chess and an odd reference to her dear "neb" ways cutting him to the heart. If "neb" stood for the Yiddish expression nebbish, meaning a nothing, a nobody, it was an unlikely thing for Cardozo to say to his sister. Yiddish was not part of Cardozo's Sephardic heritage, but perhaps it was a private joke between them. The tone of the letter was warm and loving. It was written by a devoted brother to an ailing sister whose life depended on him. He knew that she doted on him, and he wrote what he believed she wanted and needed to hear. But he did not write hypocritically, just extravagantly, even more extravagantly than the praise he heaped on his friends.[6]

Ben and Nellie were private people who left little evidence regarding their relationship, and their few close friends also protected their privacy. One of the few intimates outside the immediate family was Louise Waterman Wise. Her friendship with Nellie and Ben, especially with Nellie, went well back into the nineteenth century. She and her husband Stephen would visit Nellie and Ben on the weekends, once or twice a month, and Louise visited Nellie regularly.[7] Louise was one of the few friends with whom Ben corresponded on a first-name basis.[8] Justine Wise Polier, Louise and Stephen Wise's daughter, shared in her parents' relationship with Cardozo. She characterized his relationship with Nellie as going beyond that of a devoted brother and an ill sister. He was devoted to Nellie in an intense fashion that was in sharp contrast to his dispassionate relations with everyone else. In response to a question about the letter from Ben to Nellie, she said that he had a great capacity to understand people and a nineteenth-century chivalrous attitude toward women, and that he wrote what he thought Nellie needed to read.[9] That assessment of Ben's feeling seems entirely accurate.

Even though Ben's home life revolved around Nellie, he did get out occasionally for professional and social activities. His judicial position required him to show up at bar meetings, and he delivered a number of talks every year at such meetings and elsewhere. Likewise, he attended dinners of the discussion groups to which he belonged. He met frequently with a group, which he had nicknamed The Philosophers, who met regularly for thirty years at the house of his friend Frederic Coudert, where the group talked about everything "from the amoeba to the immortality of the soul." The members were an interesting collection of intellects. The Nobel Prize winners, Alexis Carrel, biologist and surgeon, and Henri Bergson, philosopher, were regulars, as were Father Cornelius Clifford, philologist, Boris Bakhmeteff, a former Russian diplomat who taught engineering at Columbia, and Alfred Noyes, the poet. Others joined them from time to time.[10]

Cardozo lunched with friends on Saturdays and occasionally during the week at the Lawyers Club, the Century Club, or the Columbia University Club across the street from his office.[11] Friends and family—for example, Felix Frankfurter and Marion Denman—called on him two or three times a year to perform civil marriages.[12] Occasionally, he would dine out with a cousin, old friends, or a new friend like Judge Learned Hand, who sat on the federal Court of Appeals in New York.[13] Cardozo went to the theater once in a while. His friends Walter and Hortense Hirsch took him to see a Bea Lillie review, and another time he went with Lafayette and Aline Goldstone to a Galsworthy play.[14] Often when Cardozo ate out, he would slip quietly away around a quarter to ten, explaining that he had to get home to read to Nellie, something he did in the evening from eleven to midnight.[15]

One regular outing was a Sunday morning walk with his cousin Edgar Nathan, Sr. Nathan would come over to Cardozo's house from his home nearby on West 76th Street, and they would stroll along the park side of Central Park West for an hour or an hour and a half. Sometimes Edgar's young daughter Emily would accompany them, although all the Nathan children understood that "this was their father's friend who was not to be pestered."[16] This routine ended in 1923 when the Nathans moved away from the neighborhood.

During the summer recess, Ben and Nellie rented a small home on Cedar Avenue in Allenhurst, New Jersey, where Ben read and worked on the various lecture series that he gave throughout the 1920s. In the early years in Allenhurst, Nellie was able to get around and do the shopping in town. Her heart attacks in the spring of 1919 and the fall of 1923 restricted her activities.[17]

One occasional summer outing for Ben at the New Jersey shore was a round of golf at the Norwood Country Club, where he was a member. At the urging of friends and his doctor, who thought he needed exercise, he played golf once or sometimes twice a week.[18] Judge Elkus and Judge Lehman were his golfing companions, and often they spent as much time talking as playing. Cardozo was a terrible golfer and appears to have enjoyed talking about how bad he was more than he enjoyed playing.[19] Except for the walks he took with Edgar Nathan and Judge Bijur and the occasional "forced" outings on the golf course, Cardozo avoided all forms of strenuous exercise. Once, he was assigned to report to his colleagues on a case that required the court to decide whether using dynamite to blast rock could constitute "recreation" under the terms of an insurance policy. Cardozo commented as follows on various forms of exercise: "The statesman chopping trees is a familiar illustration. Many of us would probably stand aghast at the strenuous diversions of Mr. [Theodore] Roosevelt. I know a judge of the Supreme Court who shovels snow and puts in coal for pleasure. I know another who is an expert carpenter . . . I should not enjoy such things myself."[20]

What he did enjoy was talking with friends and with Nellie and playing chess and occasionally duets on the piano with her. Cardozo's home life during the years he was a Court of Appeals judge was private, but not reclusive. He probably was out of the house in the evening several times a month, as often as many other professionals with demanding jobs. The difference was in the quality of his home life. He and Nellie rarely had guests to dinner.[21] Since there were no children in the house, Cardozo had no experience, after his own childhood, of the noise and the problems that accompany raising children. Although he made efforts to get to know the children of his cousins and of a few friends like the Wises and the William Cohens, he saw them from a distance, and his correspondence indicates that his real relationships with children formed only as they grew up. His home life was his life with Nellie.

Ben and Nellie enjoyed a comfortable existence. Even though he and his siblings had inherited a house and a moderate amount of money from their father, it was his earnings from practice and from his judicial salary that helped support that home, a rental home in the summer months, and a household of servants. He also helped support his sisters, including Elizabeth's art schooling and her separate home with Kate Tracy.

Ben did not spend all his income. He saved some and invested it in the most prudent investments of the times, government bonds and real estate. He purchased the house next door at 18 West 75th Street and leased it to tenants. When he died in 1938, his estate was valued at $362,000, a substantial sum during the Depression. He owned United States Treasury and other federal bonds in the amount of $145,000. He also owned twenty-seven mortgages on single and multifamily private homes in New York City, although several of these were in default. These mortgages, which were valued at some $162,000, were the largest asset in his estate. There were also three parcels of real estate that had been acquired in foreclosure proceedings on mortgages that he had owned. Cardozo lived well all his life, and when he died, he was worth, in late-twentieth-century terms, over two million dollars.[22]

Cardozo was meticulous in overseeing his personal affairs. William Freese, who had run the administrative side of Cardozo's former law firm, managed his funds and prepared his tax returns. He represented Cardozo in the sale of the property at 18 West 75th Street in 1919. He handled the investments in real estate mortgages on two- and three-family homes in New York City. Freese discussed with Cardozo how to handle missed payments by debtors on his mortgage investments. On occasion, especially during the Depression, Cardozo instructed Freese to extend the time of the homeowners' payments in the face of claims by the Bond Guarantee and Mortgage Company, which insured the mortgages, that Cardozo's generosity would release it from all legal obligations under its guarantee. Cardozo did not press hard on homeowners in financial distress.[23]

Cardozo watched his income and expenses and monitored Freese's handling of his money. When a mortgage payment due him was three days late, he noticed it.[24] He often used Joseph Paley as a messenger to

Freese. When he sold the house at 18 West 75th Street, Paley did some of the legwork involved in dealing with the tenant.[25] When Cardozo was out of town in Albany, or in New Jersey during the summer, he had Paley deposit and cash checks for him.[26] He also had Paley deposit some of the checks that represented periodic payments from the mortgagors.[27] He asked Paley to let him know when receipts arrived for payments of his own debts so that he would know that his own check had been received.[28] Indeed, Cardozo often sent Paley reminders to make sure that Paley had followed his instructions about a whole variety of matters, some quite trifling. He took for granted Paley's de facto status as a part-time messenger and clerk.

Cardozo was careful not to abuse his official position. He would not seek special treatment, for example, when obtaining books at a library. He waited in line like everyone else.[29] But he did not hesitate to exercise his rights when he thought that the improper activities of others impinged on them. A neighbor on 75th Street informed him that another neighbor was using the basement of 20 West 75th Street for a business, complete with signs advertising "tailoring" and "fur remodeling." Cardozo asked Paley to get the appropriate city department to investigate and, if there was a violation, to put a stop to it "before it spreads and destroys the street." Cardozo added, "I am not anxious to have my name used by the Dep't any more than is necessary. Probably they will not need to mention me to the occupant. But, of course, you may tell the Dep't whom you are representing."[30] As a resident and property owner, Cardozo was concerned enough about protecting his interests to take action. At the same time, he avoided the unpleasant task of going to the relevant city department himself and hoped to conceal his identity as the complaining party. He was willing to have his name used—discreetly, of course—as long as he did not have to make the complaint himself. Certainly, he felt no compunction about using Paley to do unpleasant or menial tasks.

One major activity for Cardozo was correspondence with family and friends. Cardozo had three major kinds of correspondents. First, there were acquaintances with whom he corresponded for specific purposes. Next, there were family members with whom he corresponded informally, but generally only to express appreciation for a greeting or a present, to respond to inquiries about Nellie's health and to inquire about the health of others, or to make meeting arrangements. He also corresponded with a large number of family members on a regular basis because he handled the funds raised in the family to help support his first cousins Rosalie Boyd and Gertrude Kari.[31] Finally, there were other relatives and friends with whom he engaged in fairly regular correspondence about a variety of matters, often relating to things that he had read. The family correspondence of any substance that remains consists primarily of letters to his cousins Edgar and Sallie Nathan and their daughter Rosalie Hendricks, and to his cousins Maud Nathan and Annie Nathan Meyer. The Cardozo-Nathan family was centered in New York, and it was therefore only when one member was away or when the occasion called for a note of appreciation that there was need to write. Cardozo did not often write lengthy letters on serious topics, and when the subject came up, he expressed surprise at the notion that family letters would discuss ideas.[32] His correspondence does disclose that he kept in touch with, and saw, many family members and their children fairly regularly.

Much of Cardozo's correspondence was therefore quite brief, often repeating what he had written to someone else. Moreover, with the exception of phrases of praise to others or thanks in return for praise by others, his letters were usually stylistically quite plain. Cardozo did not lavish the same energy and attention on letters that he did on his opinions and lectures. Yet the letters do reveal some notable characteristics. One is that he dispensed praise in large doses. To Dean Roscoe Pound of the Harvard Law School: "I do not know where else to look for so extraordinary a fusion of learning at the service of wisdom, and of wisdom illumined by learning."[33] To his Columbia friend, Frederic Coudert: "I can't tell you what a help it is to get now and then an encouraging word from those who know. In the list of that elect class, your name has always had in my thoughts a high and honored place."[34]

Occasionally, giving or receiving praise was mixed with another characteristic, self-deprecation. Here is a comment to Felix Frankfurter about Supreme Court Justice Oliver Wendell Holmes, whom he often referred to as "the Master" and who was the object of Cardozo's most effusive remarks: "I gnash my teeth with mingled feelings of admiration, jealousy and despair. What is the use of toiling and struggling, painfully giving birth to some commonplace statement of the obvious, which neither uplifts nor enlightens, when this man is able in a flash and without any bother or fuss to say something that lifts you up, at the summit, bathed in eternal light."[35] Again to Frankfurter: "I am grateful to you for what you say about my little book [*The Nature of the Judicial Process*]. I have felt like burning it up, and what you tell me induces me to withhold the match."[36] To Learned Hand, after reading Hand's review of *The Nature of the Judicial Process* in the *Harvard Law Review*: "I have seen the sword of justice above my head, and yet the head is still there, not severed, but swollen with human pride and vanity. I am grateful for what you say of me. What one is, counts for more than what one says; and I am willing to be wrong in everything that I have ever said, if I am even a small part of what you fancy me to be."[37] And again to Learned Hand, who had sent congratulations when Cardozo received an honorary LL.D. from Harvard: "Of course I like praise and honors—more I fear than I ought—but my predominating emotion is a sort of puzzled wonder as to what the fuss is all about . . . There are times, all the same, when praise is felt to be an ultimate good, as solid and satisfying as if one had deserved it utterly. So I feel when I get such a letter as yours. To have won such a friendship is really a finer distinction than a conventional LL.D."[38] Cardozo was right in confessing to pride and vanity. He worked on self-deprecating humility to balance them, and at times it was a little obvious.

Another major feature of Cardozo's correspondence was that he was discreet, rarely venturing an opinion about a person or a controversial subject. Moreover, in a letter to Learned Hand, he put out warning signals about the ideas he did express:

[Y]ou came sharply to my mind while I was reading "Autobiographies" by William Butler Yeats. He speaks of a friend as one accustomed to "the gay exaggeration of the talk of equals" . . . One mustn't try in talk to express definite convictions, or rather one mustn't always be interpreted as doing so. One is giving a glimpse of a passing mood, a phase of truth, but a very partial one . . . The trouble is that convictions are few and far between while the play instinct on the other hand is universal and imperative. So we talk to our equals, or those whom we like to think that we equal, with "gay exaggeration."[39]

The Yeats reference fell right in with the natural Cardozo caution. Cardozo's vivacious friends—Learned Hand, Felix Frankfurter, C. C. Burlingham—sometimes drew Cardozo out to the point of "gay exaggeration," for Hand observed that Cardozo could be "at times a little naughty."[40] Cardozo took advantage of his correspondence to remind Hand not to take his talk too seriously. In the course of his little discourse, he also let fall his notion that his convictions were few and far between, and that description fit the observations of others that Cardozo was not a man of passionate convictions, or at least he did not let those that he had show very often.

But Cardozo did engage in substantive correspondence with his cousins, the sisters Annie Nathan Meyer and Maud Nathan. They were both active in community affairs in an era when such activity was not the norm for women.[41] Some of Ben's friends were surprised that he was friendlier with Annie, who was seen as aggressive, than with Maud, who was perceived as sweet and generous. It is apparent from the correspondence, though, that Ben saw Annie as an intellectual companion, and he enjoyed exchanging ideas with her.[42] Years later the novelist Robert Nathan, nephew of Annie and Maud, commented on the Nathan family after reading the memoirs of Frances Nathan Wolff, daughter of Benjamin Nathan: "How the Nathan-voice, the family-voice—which is really the voice of its women—comes through: upright, virtuous, self-satisfied, invincibly innocent . . . obsessed with trifles, unforgiving."[43] Benjamin Cardozo possessed those qualities, except the last, in varying measure.

One of the most revealing insights about Cardozo in his correspondence is contained in a 1924 letter to Annie Nathan Meyer about a play that she had just completed. It was entitled "Black Souls," and it involved the rape of a black woman by a white politician, a love affair between that politician's daughter and his victim's brother, a lynching, and revenge on the white politician. These themes were novel for 1924 when the play was written and for 1932 when it was published. The play dealt explicitly with sexual relationships between blacks and whites, the situation of blacks in American society generally and in the South specifically, and the different approaches of blacks—patience or militancy—toward remedying their situation. It also reversed one stereotype in having a white woman pursue a black man. None of these issues were in the forefront of the consciousness of white Americans, including most liberals.

When Annie completed the play, she sent it to Ben, who sent her his comments at once. He first praised the "vivid, moving, eloquent" literary style. He then turned "to the practical" and noted the "debit side" in terms indicating a combination of racial and sexual prejudices:

I find it hard to believe that an American audience will be in sympathy with the theme. The love of a white woman for a black man has in it something so revolting that many—I fear most—will not wish to hear of it. I know that you will say such things exist in life. So do many sex perversions that it is unpleasant to think of, and still more to discuss. Then too the average listener will think of the play as an attack upon womankind generally and an attempt to prove that the black man is rarely the pursuer. I appreciate your answer that this is a foolish misconception. I know that the literary artist in selecting one phase of life as the subject of his drama does not commit himself to universality of the truth which it embodies. I am thinking of the crowd, not of the judgment of the elect; and I fear that I do not misread the reaction of the multitude.

I see no reason why this should daunt you. One of the weaknesses of the drama is that even more than other forms of literary expression it needs applause to make its way. But those who care for art must not let themselves bother too much about such repulses and disappointments.[44]

He underlined the personal nature of his reaction many years later when Annie sent him a copy of *Black Souls* after it had been published. He speculated that the hostile reaction of the critics might be explained by the fact that "perhaps there is something repellent and unpleasant in the theme of black and white love which prevents such a play from being popular."[45]

Cardozo's difficulties with his cousin's play were not due solely to his fears about the reactions of others, nor even to his own squeamishness about sex. Cardozo phrased his critique in class-conscious terms, foreseeing the hostility of "the multitude," not of "the elect." Although he clearly did not place himself in "the multitude," in fact his own reaction was the same. His language was uncharacteristically harsh. "Repellent" and "revolting" were not typical Cardozo words. They were not attached to his attribution of views to "the multitude." They were his personal reaction, as was his comparison of interracial love to "sex perversions."

Cardozo rarely expressed himself in passionate language about anything. But here his prejudices in matters of race, gender, and sexuality came together in one outburst that was marked also by the hypocritical comment that the elect were less prejudiced. While it is true that Cardozo's observations were made long before the revolution in race relations in this country raised the level of consciousness of white America about the issue of racial justice, nevertheless Cardozo followed the multitude and not his cousin when he wrote that the love of a white woman for a black man was "revolting."

Cardozo held those views without any personal acquaintance with black America. He did have a brief correspondence with one black leader from whom he could have learned a great deal. Something led the civil rights lawyer James Weldon Johnson to send two of his own books plus one by W. E. B. Du Bois, the well-known black activist, to Cardozo in 1929.[46] Although Cardozo did not enter excerpts from any of the three books into his commonplace books, he was sufficiently impressed with one of Johnson's volumes to send a copy to Justice Holmes. "I am not sure that this little volume of negro sermons will interest you," he wrote, but "[i]f you had heard 'Go down Death' recited by its author with all the fervor and exaltation of his race, you would be able to supply something that the printed page may lack."[47] Cardozo had heard that "sermon" recited, and he was moved by it, albeit in terms that sound like a patronizing stereotype. Holmes responded warmly to Cardozo, who paid Johnson the compliment of sending him a copy of Holmes's letter.[48] But that was the end of Cardozo's efforts.

Cardozo was aware, in a general way, of the discrimination against African Americans in the United States. In commenting in 1933 about Hitler's actions during the first year after he came to power, Cardozo added, "Well, the United States has its own record of brutalities, as the poor negroes know, but nothing quite so bad as this."[49] But he never expressed any passionate concern for a cure. The only black person Cardozo ever knew before he went to Washington, so far as the evidence discloses, was a chauffeur whom he employed for a time in the late 1920s and early 1930s.[50] In Washington, his experience was much the same. He had a black messenger, Elmer Jones, who had been Chief Justice Taft's messenger, but apparently no other black acquaintances.[51] Annie Nathan Meyer lived in a similar social and professional group, but she overcame its limitations. Ben did not. Although Cardozo was proud of belonging to a social and intellectual elite and educated himself on many subjects, in this area he shared the prejudices of most of the country.

This side of Cardozo also appeared in the occasional ethnic slur in his private correspondence. Over the course of many summers, he attempted to learn to read Italian, and in writing to Learned Hand, he punctuated a prosaic letter with an exclamation: "Such a beautiful language! I take off my hat to every Dago that I meet."[52] Even though such terms are still common in private conversation and were more common in Cardozo's day, it is striking that such a courteous and respectful man used that term in 1929, especially in a letter. That was not his only lapse, either. In 1932, after reading a memorial from the Japanese government, Cardozo commented on Japan's aggressive conduct: "I find myself casting furtive glances here and there, wondering when and where the Japs will be upon us."[53] By themselves these instances would not be worth significant attention, but for Cardozo they indicate a failure to live up to his own standards of conduct.

A more positive note in Cardozo's correspondence was his interest in good government, especially in his home city. One such occasion concerned the Democratic primary election for mayor in 1925. Although a Democrat, Cardozo had never before voted in a Democratic primary, perhaps because he did not view himself as a party person. That election raised issues similar to those of the Fusion campaign of 1913. An odor of corruption surrounded Mayor Jack Hylan, who was running for reelection. Cardozo, responding to the challenge, voted for State Senator James J. Walker, the candidate of both Governor Smith and Tammany Hall. "I felt," he wrote, "if I didn't vote this time, I should forfeit the privilege of swearing at Hylan and his crew if perchance they were returned to power. They are down in the dust, and the fickle public has its new idol."[54] The reform issue aroused his sense of responsibility although he could not resist a skeptical comment about "the fickle public." A few years later, after the election of Fiorello La Guardia as mayor, Cardozo commented to C. C. Burlingham that his "appointments have been superb. No such a thing has been seen in our civic life during all the years that I have watched it."[55]

One of Cardozo's favorite occupations was reading. His range was extraordinary. He consumed books on religion, including the Bible; philosophy and political theory (Aristotle, Plato, Charles Peirce, Bertrand Russell, Will Durant, Alfred North Whitehead, Arthur Schopenhauer, Irwin Edman, John Dewey, Morris Cohen, and George Santayana); literature (Homer's *The Odyssey*, the *Rubaiyat of Omar Khayam*, Chaucer, Dante, Shakespeare's plays, John Milton, Joseph Addison, Richard Steele, Desmond McCarthy, Vernon L. Parrington, Oliver Goldsmith, Victor Hugo, James N. Barrie, Robert Browning, Yeats's essays,

John Galsworthy, Robert Louis Stevenson, and Thornton Wilder); science (Arthur S. Eddington, Cassius J. Keyser, Bertrand Russell); biography and autobiography (lives of Henry VII, Henry VIII, John Stuart Mill, Viscount Haldane, Benjamin Franklin, Edward Marshall Hall, Daniel Webster, Abraham Lincoln, Theodore Roosevelt, Richard Wagner, Herbert Asquith, Charles W. Eliot, Thomas Aquinas, Heinrich Heine); and history (Alfred Zimmern's *Greek Commonwealth,* the *Cambridge Medieval History,* George Trevelyan's *History of England,* Mark Sullivan's *Our Times,* Denis Brogan's *Government of the People,* Charles and Mary Beard's *Rise of American Civilization*); as well as a large number of books relating to legal topics.[56]

The sheer volume of the reading is astounding, especially for a man who spent his normal work day reading and writing. The total just of those that contained something worth noting in his commonplace books was over two hundred seventy-five volumes for the thirteen years that they cover. Cardozo's taste was almost universal. The most notable omission was modern fiction, with a few exceptions like Galsworthy's *Forsyte Saga,* and anything light, like mystery stories. He does not appear to have needed to rest his mind with such fare after the intellectual exertion of his daily work. He was forever asking his friends for recommended reading, and he gave lists of books to Carrie Bijur of the Beacon Bookshop on East 45th Street in New York so that friends could give him birthday presents from those lists.[57] With his friends' help, Cardozo kept himself surprisingly abreast of new ideas in the rapidly changing intellectual world of the first third of the twentieth century.

In addition to the experience that Cardozo brought from his legal practice, his reading was the other source that informed his judicial career. His education did not stop with his departure from Columbia Law School. He made use of what he read, both by way of self-education and, in a practical sense, by way of obtaining material for use in his own writings and talks. Reading was one of the great pleasures in his life, and there were not many others. It was, in fact, integral to his life. The commonplace books recount a conversation in 1931 with Moses Hadas, the noted classicist, who "used the term polymath—a man who knows many things." Cardozo appended his own comment, "That's what I admire."[58]

The commonplace books indicate that Cardozo set out to be a polymath himself, but with a pragmatic purpose. A quotation from Alfred North Whitehead expressed Cardozo's view that learning should be put to use, in his own case that he bring to decision-making a broad familiarity with the best insights into the society in which he lived. "Culture is activity of thought and receptiveness to beauty and humane feeling. Scraps of information have nothing to do with it. A merely well informed man is the most useless bore on God's Earth."[59] Cardozo's experiences in life and his reading left him skeptical about abstract and theoretical ideas. He wanted his knowledge to be useful.

When Cardozo recorded an author's ideas in the commonplace books, he usually did not note whether he agreed or disagreed.[60] Sometimes he reacted to his reading in his correspondence. Although he first commented to Annie Nathan Meyer that Charles and Mary Beard's *History of American Civilization* was "very fine, though I think a trifle cynical," he later expressed a stronger view about its emphasis on economic causation in a letter to Learned Hand: "Beard's history is very fine, though it leaves me with a bad taste in my mouth, which makes me think that something is wrong with the diet that brings the taste about. Are we all so sordid? If it can be proved that I was glad to have my salary as judge made more than it ought to be, does that prove that I hold my job for the salary alone? See what comes of telling the worst about every one."[61] In the same letter to Hand, he also complained about "dreary tomes on sociology" that he had read "from a sense of duty."[62]

Cardozo tried to understand what was going on in science. Einstein's theory of relativity had upset several centuries of certainty. Combined with new thinking in mathematics, it had opened the possibility for new ways of thinking about social science and indeed about all human reasoning. These new ideas had begun to enter the popular consciousness.[63] Cardozo had trouble comprehending the new science. "I don't feel altogether at home with scientists. I am oppressed by my own lack of knowledge about the things that concern . . . the students of natural science . . . I have just finished Haldane's Reign of Relativity, and its description of Einstein's discoveries and theories has left me chastened, if unenlightened. I have a great curiosity to know more about all these things, but life is too short, and I must be satisfied with my little vineyard."[64] Cardozo persevered but confessed defeat a few years later in his attempt to comprehend Arthur Eddington, a leading explicator of Einstein's theories. "I think Eddington would suit me . . . if only I could understand him; and even the mere attempt to understand him has something of the joy of combat. But he is too much for me, and I capitulate."[65] Cardozo reproduced Holmes's comment that "he saw no reason for believing this is a rational universe" and paired it with an excerpt from Bertrand Russell: "I see no reason to believe that the world must be convenient for the man of science. It may be that all the law and order that we seem to perceive in the world is due to our own selective apperception."[66] He was taken with the idea that the universe might not be orderly. He understood that important and complex new ideas were being generated, but he was frustrated with his inability to grasp them.

Cardozo also had some acquaintance with the world of contemporary art. Alfred Stieglitz, the noted photographer and patron of avant-garde art, sent him the artist John Marin's *Letters*. Cardozo probably was introduced to Stieglitz and his wife, the painter Georgia O'Keeffe, by his law partner George Engelhard, who was married to Stieglitz's sister. Cardozo came to know Stieglitz and O'Keeffe well enough to refer to them as "old friends," and he was quite familiar with the Stieglitz gallery, An American Place.[67]

————

Cardozo's life changed in the mid-1920s as Nellie became more of an invalid. She had a stroke in 1924 or early 1925 that affected her ability to walk, and thereafter she did not often get out of the house. In the spring of 1925, she had another heart attack that delayed their summer departure to Allenhurst for several weeks. Nellie's condition had a serious impact on Ben. Worry filled his letters: "I have been so upset and worried that I have had time and mind and heart for little beyond the sick room."[68]

In January 1926, Cardozo had a serious health problem of his own, a "dangerous" staphylococcus infection in his face that kept him away from court for over a month, for his doctors sent him to Atlantic City to rest for ten days after they released him from the hospital. Immediately upon his return, he suffered another attack, somewhat less serious than the first, when the infection lodged in his kidney and he had to be carried from the courtroom on a stretcher.[69] He made a fairly rapid recovery, but his doctors told him to confine his activities to his judicial work "for the next few months."[70] Those orders did not stop him from attending the meetings of the American Law Institute in April 1926 in Washington, where he went with Justice Stone to pay a visit to Justice Holmes.[71] He also visited the Lincoln Memorial for the first time and reported that "it almost took my breath away. French, the sculptor, has put into the figure and face of Lincoln more than one could suppose that sculpture could express, and the statue is housed in a temple that is worthy of it."[72]

When the Court of Appeals finished its work in mid-June, Ben and Nellie went to Allenhurst for the summer. Ben was still under doctors' orders to rest, and he had therefore refrained from accepting any commitments to write lectures.[73] But Nellie's condition deteriorated, and Cardozo turned to work for solace. "With so much illness and the house so quiet, there is need of occupying one's thoughts in some way."[74] The lectures thus begun were the Carpentier Lectures that he would finally deliver as "The Paradoxes of Legal Science" at Columbia in November 1927. Toward the end of the summer of 1926, Nellie improved a little, and they returned to New York for the beginning of the fall term of court. Ben had recovered from the winter's illness but was under the considerable stress of Nellie's deteriorating health. Ben and Nellie continued to be the center of one another's lives.

Cardozo's private life while he was on the Court of Appeals was his life with his family, especially his life with Nellie. He was a hard-working man who lived well and was a little obsessive in his personal life. He had saintly manners and was saintly toward Nellie, but he was no saint. He was simply a good man, with ordinary human failings that included some prejudices. His life centered on self, family, and work. As time went on, his home life was largely determined by Nellie's worsening health. His major interest outside the law was the world of ideas. The richness of Cardozo's knowledge made him unusual among judges and contributed both to his judicial work and to the standing that he achieved during his career on the Court of Appeals.

10

A Judge's Service

Cardozo justified the applause that greeted his arrival on the bench with early opinions like *Morningstar*, the case of the hotel guest who was refused service, and *Howard*, the case of the flooded farm. Columbia, his alma mater, recognized his growing prominence by conferring the first of his many honorary degrees upon him at its commencement exercises in June 1915, just eighteen months after he went on the bench. It must have been a special pleasure for Cardozo to receive the award from Nicholas Murray Butler, Columbia's president and his former teacher.

In the following year, when Cardozo was still sitting on the Court of Appeals only by designation, he drew wide attention when he addressed an issue of national importance. In MacPherson v. The Buick Company, a tort case that will be discussed at length in Chapter 14, Cardozo interpreted New York law to permit a car buyer, injured because of a defective wheel, to sue the manufacturer for its negligent failure to discover the defect.[1] Previously, in most jurisdictions and in most circumstances, buyers of a product had not been permitted to sue a manufacturer for negligence if they had bought the product from a dealer or retailer rather than directly from the manufacturer. *MacPherson* represented a substantial advance in consumers' rights and manufacturers' responsibilities. It also made Cardozo well known in the legal profession, in the law schools, and throughout the country. Henceforth, professionals began to take note when Cardozo wrote.

Shortly after the *MacPherson* decision, the elections of 1916 began a series of events that was crucial for Cardozo's career. Nationally, Charles Evans Hughes resigned from the Supreme Court of the United States to run on the Republican ticket against Woodrow Wilson, the incumbent Democrat. Cardozo, a Democrat all his life, voted for his party's leader "though it cost me many a pang to turn against Hughes, who is—in spite of some limitations—a fine and noble man. I believe he never did a thing in his public life that was not dictated by a high sense of right and duty."[2] But the aftermath of New York's state elections affected Cardozo, and his caution about electoral politics nearly cost him his opportunity for advancement. Although Justice Samuel Seabury had lost out to Cardozo in the designation process in 1914, he had been elected to a regular seat on the Court of Appeals later that year. In 1916, however, Seabury resigned his seat to run for governor against the Republican incumbent, Charles Whitman. After Governor Whitman was reelected, he had to fill the Seabury vacancy as well as another created by the election of Associate Judge Frank Hiscock to the chief judgeship. In New York, the governor's appointments to the Court of Appeals were temporary, and the appointees then had to run at the next regular election.

Governor Whitman offered the Seabury vacancy on the Court of Appeals to Cardozo in late 1916 or early 1917. It is unclear how Republican Governor Whitman came to offer the appointment to the Democrat Cardozo. One unlikely theory appeared in a book about a famous New York murder trial. The author, Andy Logan, noted in two consecutive sentences Whitman's choice of Cardozo and the fact that Cardozo had previously voted with the majority of the Court of Appeals to uphold the conviction of Police Lieutenant Charles Becker for the killing of a notorious gambler, Herman Rosenthal.[3] The prosecution of Becker by the then District Attorney Whitman helped Whitman's election as governor in 1914. Logan argued that Becker was innocent and that both his conviction and its affirmance were tainted. Logan's implication of a connection between Cardozo's vote and his subsequent appointment is not supported by any evidence, at least insofar as Cardozo was concerned. There is certainly no evidence to suggest that Benjamin Cardozo emulated his father in allowing political or career ambitions to influence a vote. To the contrary, in many cases Cardozo rejected arguments of lawyers like Louis Marshall and George Ingraham, who had been instrumental in advancing his career.

Indeed, Cardozo did not even welcome Whitman's offer. According to Whitman, Cardozo rejected it and refused to reconsider. The problem was that he would have to resign his Supreme Court judgeship, which still had eleven years to run, in order to accept a temporary Court of Appeals appointment that would require him to run for election that November. The promotion might prove to be temporary. Cardozo liked being a judge and did not want to run the risk of losing his position in the election. Whitman reported Cardozo's reaction and the consequent necessity to make another choice to George Ingraham, a good friend of the governor who had recently retired as Presiding Judge of the First Department of the Appellate Division. Ingraham, who had returned to private practice, was at that time president of the Association of the Bar of the City of New York. He asked Whitman to wait while he consulted with Republican and Democratic leaders about the possibility of joint nominations of Cardozo and Judge Chester McLaughlin for the two Court of Appeals vacancies to be filled in the November elections.[4]

Ingraham and other bar leaders were successful in getting the Republican and Democratic party leaders to agree on a joint designation of McLaughlin, a Republican, and Cardozo, a Democrat. Since neither candidate would face opposition, their election would be assured. Ingraham, Henry Gildersleeve, the President of the New York County Lawyers Association, Charles Evans Hughes, the President of the New York State Bar Association, along with the judiciary committees of their associations, then urged Cardozo and McLaughlin to accept the appointments.[5]

Cardozo told Learned Hand that he "was very reluctant to accept the new appointment, for, from any personal point of view, I did not gain enough to compensate for resigning the office which I held, and taking the chance and bother of re-election," but he added that "requests from the bar and from my associates made it impossible to refuse."[6] As he put it in a letter to the bar associations, "your request is a call to duty which cannot be ignored."[7] Cardozo and McLaughlin accepted Whitman's offer of temporary appointments, and both were subsequently elected to full fourteen-year terms in the November 1917 election.

———

Right from the beginning of his career, Cardozo was highly regarded by his fellow judges, and his influence grew with time. The assessments of his judicial work after his death by some of his colleagues and others knowledgeable about the Court of Appeals, even allowing for the tendency of eulogies to embroider the subject's contributions, were particular and persuasive. Judge Seabury, who was his colleague in his first two years of service, noted some of the characteristics that accounted for Cardozo's influence even in his early years:

> He was a man of deep learning and great gentleness of character, with a charming literary style which added much to the great reputation he attained. I do not think his convictions were strong, or if they were his inherent tact led him to be very cautious in discussing them. He was indefatigable in his industry. The cautious manner in which he expressed his views, especially in the early days of his service in the court, aroused no antagonism. He was . . . very tactful in his arguments and discussions, and in consultation, rarely taking an uncompromising position on any subject.[8]

Seabury summarized most of the major elements of Cardozo's influence within the court: learning, industry, a persuasive literary style, tact, and an undogmatic, collegial approach to the process of decision-making. Seabury was on the mark in describing Cardozo's tact in discussion, but Seabury's doubts about the strength of Cardozo's convictions were probably influenced by his own more combative method of argument. Once Cardozo made up his mind about the disposition of a case, he was firm. Cardozo's demeanor could also change sharply after he mulled over a problem and then made up his mind. As Learned Hand noted, "At times to those of us who knew him, the anguish which had preceded decision, was apparent . . . and he wrote his opinion with his very blood . . . But when once his mind came to rest he was as inflexible as he had been uncertain before. No man ever gave more copiously of himself to all aspects of his problem, but he knew that it was a judge's job to decide, not to debate, and the loser who asked him to reopen a decision once made, found a cold welcome."[9] Later, on the Supreme Court, Cardozo put his view about a petition for rehearing sardonically, saying "I will give it my most biased consideration."[10]

Seabury's emphasis on Cardozo's collegiality was confirmed by others. Irving Lehman recalled two cases in which Cardozo, who had written majority draft opinions, changed the result when he came to agree with dissents written by Lehman. In one of those cases, Cardozo insisted that Lehman write the majority opinion, even though Lehman stated that he

would use most of Cardozo's written opinion with just a new conclusion.[11] The harmony within the Court of Appeals was not just a platitude
invoked on ceremonial occasions.[12] The Court of Appeals in Cardozo's
years enjoyed a collegiality that was nurtured first by Hiscock and then
by Cardozo. This quality was noted by insiders and outsiders alike.
When Cuthbert Pound paid tribute to Cardozo on his elevation to the
Supreme Court of the United States, Pound referred to the "sweet serenity of your Albany life," and to the harmony of the court and the "tender
relations" among the judges.[13]

The handling of dissents was an indication of the harmony within the
court. Most of the judges wrote dissenting opinions only when they
thought an important issue was at stake, and as we shall see, sometimes
not even then. In eighteen years of service on the Court of Appeals,
Cardozo considered 8,415 cases (not including motions seeking leave to
appeal or various forms of relief while a case was pending). Of these,
2,822 were decided with full opinions, and 5,593 were memoranda
decisions, that is, decisions issued without an opinion or with only a
short explanation. Cardozo wrote for the court in 566 of the full-opinion
cases. He noted a dissent from a majority opinion 133 times but wrote
only 16 dissenting opinions. Once in a while he joined someone else's
dissenting opinion. Sometimes he added, or joined someone else's, one-
or two-sentence explanation of the disagreement with the majority.
More often, he dissented without any explanation. Once in a while he
wrote a brief concurring opinion or concurred, without explanation, in
the result reached by the majority. He followed a similar procedure with
respect to the memoranda opinions. He dissented 198 times from memoranda opinions of the court, more often than not silently, but sometimes
adding an explanatory phrase or sentence.[14]

Cardozo was not unusual in his habit of seldom writing separate
opinions. In the years that they served with Cardozo, Kellogg and Andrews each wrote 11 dissenting opinions in seven and nine years respectively; Lehman 22 in nine years; Pound 32 in seventeen years; and
Hiscock only 5 in the thirteen years. The most prolific dissenter was
McLaughlin, who wrote 49 dissents in ten years. The practice of writing
few dissenting opinions lessened contention among the judges.

Cardozo liked and respected his colleagues, and they liked and admired him. Many observers noted this phenomenon: "Everybody in the
Court adored him."[15] "No one received the adulation of fellow judges
like Cardozo. Even Pound was an idolater."[16] Cardozo "had a wonderful

time in the Court of Appeals."[17] "He had been very happy in the Court here."[18] "The nature of the man, the social intimacies, plus the nature of the issues all combined to make a happy family, plus [the other judges'] sense of almost deference to him as a spirit."[19]

Cardozo stood out among his peers, but not over them. It was not a one-man court, nor a group of disciples under a master. The court as a whole was a strong one, with strong personalities. Occasionally, some testiness appeared, even in public. Cardozo and McLaughlin engaged in two exchanges in 1920 and 1921 that suggested some personal tension over the disposition of a case.[20] In 1925, Cardozo jousted twice with Chief Judge Hiscock. In the first case, a majority of the Court held in Ader v. Blau that a suit against the owner of a defective picket fence that caused injury to a boy could not be united in one complaint with a cause of action against the doctor whose negligent treatment of the injured boy caused his death.[21] Cardozo's proposed dissent led Chief Judge Hiscock to write to his colleagues: "My brother Cardozo is evidently spending some time in training his artillery on my opinion . . . I think that his second shot misses its aim just as much as the first one did." After explaining why he disagreed with Cardozo's view, he added, showing some sensitivity about recent criticism from Walter Cook of Yale Law School, "I assume that if my views should prevail our friend, Professor Cook, will again feel compelled to point out the lack of intelligence afflicting most of the members of the Court, but even in the presence of that dire possibility I am going to stick."[22] The rest of the Court went with Hiscock, and Cardozo dissented by himself in a short memorandum.

At about the same time, Hiscock circulated a memorandum in another case stating that if three members of the well-known Flonzaley String Quartet had wrongfully excluded the fourth member (the plaintiff) from participation in the quartet, the excluded member would be entitled to enjoin the other three from playing under that name. Cardozo circulated a memorandum stating that "If that is so, a name which has become precious to music lovers, must be abandoned for ever."[23] Hiscock replied that he had no sympathy with the plaintiff's claims and did not believe that the plaintiff would ever be able to establish them. He thought, however, that his statement would be correct if the plaintiff did prove his case. Quoting Cardozo's sentence, he added, "That seems to be an argument based on sentiment rather than upon the allegations of the complaint."[24] Hiscock then smoothed the waters by stating that he would eliminate the offending sentence from the opinion if the majority thought it best. The sentence was omitted, and Cardozo joined Hiscock's unanimous opinion. Although persuasive, Cardozo did not always persuade.

———

Cardozo's life changed in some notable ways when he became a judge. His work was performed on a larger, more public stage. His daily working life, especially in his New York City office, was more solitary. Instead of interacting with firm members and staff, clients, other lawyers, and occasionally judges, he now worked largely alone, interrupted or relieved only by conversations with his law secretary and brief visits from judges or lawyers. But the change for Cardozo was probably not so great as for many judges, who often had to give up the lunches, dinners, parties, recreational activities, and directorships that were related to obtaining and holding legal business. Cardozo had done little, if any, of that type of socializing. Angel Simpson had been the major business-getter. Although Cardozo had a substantial referral practice, he had obtained it because other lawyers sought him out. He spent most of his evenings at home, with Nellie or working. After he went on the bench, his evenings were spent the same way.

The regular three-week sessions in Albany made a major change in his life. Ironically, the effect on him was the opposite of the effect on most of his colleagues. Unlike the other judges, who gave up their busy family and social lives at home, Cardozo was thrust into a club-like existence in Albany. Over the years, this small group became more and more important to him. It provided both a social life and a certain intimacy with colleagues that he had not previously enjoyed.

Another change came about more gradually. Cardozo had entered into a larger arena, which enlarged the circle of his professional relationships. In his legal practice, there had been his brother, his partners, especially Angel Simpson and George Engelhard, his cousins Edgar Nathan, Sr., and Michael Cardozo, and the circle of lawyers with whom he did business on a regular basis—men like Judge William Cohen, Morris Hirsch, Louis Marshall, and William Klein. That circle was relatively small—composed primarily of Jewish lawyers with well-established business clienteles. After Cardozo became a judge, he became much better known among the leading New York lawyers and judges, and as time went on, his reputation became nationwide. His relationships with C. C. Burlingham, Learned Hand, and Felix Frankfurter developed into friendships.

Cardozo's closeness to Burlingham led him to make one controversial decision. The Century Club was an elite male dining club in New York whose admissions requirements focused on intellectual attainment. There were some Jews in the Club, but none had been elected for a while, and anti-Semitism in the membership was a problem.[25] In 1925, Burlingham wanted to propose Cardozo, but Cardozo was reluctant. As Burlingham told a friend, Cardozo felt that "it might be embarrassing to him and to us [Burlingham and his friends]" if his nomination met with opposition.[26]

Cardozo eventually told Burlingham to do as he wished. Although Cardozo was always nonconfrontational in his personal relationships, there is something problematic about his willingness to be left in the dark while Burlingham and others maneuvered his membership past potential anti-Semitic opposition. Burlingham first sought to have Cardozo proposed by the president of the Century Club, Elihu Root, who had been Secretary of War, Secretary of State, and United States Senator. Root, fearing that he would have to resign as president if Cardozo was rejected, declined to propose but agreed to second. Burlingham then arranged for a highly regarded lawyer, John Milburn, to propose Cardozo, saying, "This is rather high-handed business on my part, is it not?"[27] The list of supporters, orchestrated at least in part by Burlingham, included Justice Harlan Stone, Augustus and Learned Hand, Frederic Coudert, Henry Stimson, Chief Justice William Howard Taft, former Attorney General George Wickersham, Max Farrand, George W. Murray, John Finley, and Burlingham's partner, Van Vechten Veeder.[28] Indeed, there were so many supporters that many years later John Brooks stated that "the space opposite his name looks like embroidery."[29] Cardozo was duly elected and thanked Burlingham with warm appreciation for his efforts in orchestrating the election:

> Your friendship and your energy are alike without limits.
> Of course, I remembered our talk, but I fancied that you had found it prudent to let the matter drop. I ought to have known that you never give up—at least when by keeping on you can be helpful to a friend.
> I shall prize the honor of membership in the Century Association.

Even more, however, I shall prize the memory of the fact that such men became my sponsors. To one and all of them and to you, I send my grateful acknowledgments.[30]

Many years later, Frankfurter, who was an admirer of Cardozo, questioned his decision to join the Century. Frankfurter reported that when he himself was on the Supreme Court, he had turned Burlingham down when Burlingham wanted him to join the Century because the problem of anti-Semitism had persisted. Frankfurter questioned Cardozo's motives in joining such a club:

> [T]hat's subject to interpretation, and there's a wholly innocent interpretation, namely, he was devoted to Mr. Burlingham and . . . was almost in some ways guided in minor matters . . . by Burlingham. Why not? On the other hand . . . it may have pleased him to have been elected to the Century Club. You know, a club that doesn't admit people indiscriminately and also there were members in it . . . who were great friends of his. But from my point of view a little stiffer austerity would have been in order.[31]

There was more to Cardozo's decision than just acceding to the wishes of Charles Burlingham, for Cardozo knew how to say "no" when he wanted to. He may have thought that anti-Semites should not be permitted to have their way. He also looked forward to the company of distinguished men and good friends. But there was another feature to Cardozo's decision. Joining the Century fit with Cardozo's view of his social position. He was not social-climbing. Despite his father's disgrace, his upbringing in the Cardozo-Nathan family and the Sephardic elite had given him the social graces that enabled him to fit in with elite New York society. Cardozo cherished his new non-Jewish friends, and he used the Century often to meet them for lunch. At the same time, he did not neglect his old Jewish friends and his Jewish connections. He continued to maintain close ties with George Engelhard, Morris Hirsch, William Cohen, and Nathan Bijur, among others, including his many relatives.

Even though Cardozo chose to ignore the anti-Semites in the Century Club and did not act or speak publicly against anti-Semitism, he did comment privately, sometimes satirically. For example, a community at Spring Lake on the New Jersey shore was well known for excluding Jews. Cardozo took note of the colony in a 1923 letter to Edgar Nathan:

"I rode in the car all the way to Bay Head this morning, ostensibly to visit Dr. Meyer and Annie who have a bungalow there for the summer, but really to discover an anti-Semite to be converted by [Louis] Marshall's letter. There is a little colony of them at Spring Lake, but the poor things are in danger of being inundated any moment by Jews to the right and to the left, so I left them to themselves till the floods carry them away."[32]

Although Cardozo sometimes poked a little fun at Louis Marshall's obsessive campaign against anti-Semitism in whatever form it appeared, he appreciated what Marshall did. He commended Marshall for his legal defense of an Iowa newspaper editor who had been held in contempt by an Iowa judge, in part for his attack on an opinion of the judge that commented on Jews in quite scurrilous fashion:

> I have read with great interest and satisfaction the brief in Harris v. Hume which you were good enough to send to me. One finds it almost inconceivable that any man occupying a judicial position could be so lost to all sense of decency as to write the opinions by which Judge Hume has disgraced his court. Your brief flames with a just indignation, and its argument is crushing and convincing. I thank you for the generous words in which you have referred to me and to my work . . . While I am on the subject of your championship of the Jews, I must tell you how much I admired the telling retort which you made to Judge Clearwater at the last meeting of the State Bar Association.[33]

Cardozo's growing prominence as a judge expanded his friendships beyond the largely Jewish group that had comprised his social and professional circle. However, he did not turn his back on the Jewish community and in fact increased his involvement in its public affairs.

———

Cardozo's extracurricular activities expanded considerably after he became a judge. He engaged in the usual run of appearances at bar associations, law schools, and other institutions where he was expected to give little talks. Cardozo also delivered more substantial lectures that he prepared during the summers. The first of these were the 1921 Storrs Lectures, which will be the subject of Chapter 12. They were enormously successful, and, published as *The Nature of the Judicial Process*, they made him a national figure in the legal world.

Cardozo's growing prominence was reflected in his selection in 1920 as a member of Harvard University's Board of Overseers' Committee to Visit the Law School, essentially an oversight committee.[34] The following year, Cardozo and the Committee were called upon when a group of Harvard alumni under the leadership of Austen Fox, with the covert assistance of some Department of Justice lawyers, filed an accusation with the Board of Overseers against Professor Zechariah Chafee. In an article in the *Harvard Law Review*,[35] Chafee accused Judge Henry Clayton, the trial judge in a famous World War I espionage case, United States v. Abrams, of improper conduct in the course of the trial.[36] Fox charged that the article was inaccurate, that Chafee failed to publish corrections, and that the errors were perpetuated in an amnesty petition for Abrams signed by Chafee, Dean Pound, Professor Frankfurter, and two others. The Overseers responded by referring the charges to the Committee to Visit the Law School, which met on May 22, 1921, to investigate. The meeting, which became known as the Trial at the Harvard Club, was the occasion for Professor Chafee's well-known remark that "I want my side to fight fair."[37]

The visiting committee was chaired by Judge Francis Swayze of the New Jersey Court of Errors and Appeals, and included Cardozo, Judge Augustus Hand of the federal district court in New York, Judge Julian Mack of the Court of Appeals for the Second Circuit, and many other well-known lawyers and judges. Harvard's president Abbott Lawrence Lowell attended and strongly defended Chafee on the merits and on the grounds of academic freedom. The debate between Chafee and his accusers was ardent. The visiting committee finally determined unanimously that Chafee had made no statements that were "consciously erroneous"; moreover, it rejected, by a close vote of 6–5, the complaint that Chafee should have corrected statements that were erroneous. The majority concluded that Chafee "made no statements that were culpably negligent and so far as any material statements of law or fact may have been erroneous, the errors, if any, were in matters of opinion only."[38] The committee recommended that no further action be taken by the Board of Overseers, and the Board adopted the committee's report. President Lowell later cryptically referred to the majority as "being determined by Judge Cardozo."[39]

Cardozo was sufficiently well known by 1922 that his name surfaced briefly as a possible nominee to the Supreme Court of the United States when Justice William Day retired. Judge Charles Hough, a highly regarded judge of the Court of Appeals in the Second Circuit, paid Cardozo a high compliment. When Hough, who had also been mentioned as a nominee, learned that Cardozo was being talked about, Hough told his own supporters to stop pushing him for the vacancy. When asked why, he said that Cardozo was a better man and that he wanted Cardozo to get the appointment. But Cardozo was not seriously considered by President Harding, and eventually Pierce Butler was appointed.[40]

Cardozo's opinions, lectures, and reputation made him a natural choice for inclusion in the group that created the American Law Institute. The Institute became his major nonjudicial professional activity, aside from his writing, between 1923 and 1932. Cardozo was drafted to play a role in its creation.[41] The Association of American Law Schools (the AALS) had considered for many years a number of plans for the formation of a national center to systematize American law. The issue came to a head at the annual AALS meeting in 1921.

The majority of a divided committee, chaired by Joseph Beale of Harvard, proposed a new center dedicated to law reform. The dissenter, Dean James Parker Hall of Chicago, the incoming president of the AALS, argued for a more limited project. On the floor, Beale scrapped the committee's report in favor of an oral report that stressed the items of consensus: the need for creation of a national law reform center, the extent of whose work would be left for the future once the job of law reform—of organizing, clarifying, and modernizing the vast outpouring of American case law—had begun.

Arthur Corbin of Yale, the outgoing AALS president, had arranged to have the AALS pay Cardozo's expenses to come to the 1921 meeting to discuss the law reform project.[42] After Beale's presentation, Corbin, who was supportive of the reformist features of the original majority report, called on Cardozo before giving Dean Hall the opportunity to present any opposing views. Cardozo did a masterful job in defusing Hall's opposition. Stressing the common ground shared by Hall and the rest of the committee, Cardozo tactfully praised the work of Hall at the Commonwealth Fund in putting together a group of lawyers and academics to investigate fields of law in which reform was needed. Having identified Hall's own work as a model, Cardozo then advised that the work could now be carried on with greater prestige and authority by an organization sponsored by the AALS. Cardozo's skill at accommodating different views carried the day. When Dean Hall finally got the floor, he simply stated that he "entirely concurred" in "the chaste and eloquent language in which the report is now reformed."[43] The proposal to appoint a committee to meet with other groups in the profession to organize a law institute was adopted unanimously.[44] The Committee on the Establishment of a Permanent Organization for the Improvement of the Law was created in 1922 as the direct result of the 1921 AALS meeting. Cardozo was a member of the committee and helped produce a report that led to the establishment of the American Law Institute in April 1923.

The Institute's major initial work was its attempt to organize the myriad decisions in numerous fields of law into a series of statements of governing principles with examples and commentary. The purpose was to "restate" the law in those fields for the benefit of the bench, the bar, and the public. As Professor N. E. H. Hull has pointed out, the "restatements" were intended to be reformist and progressive in nature, expressive of the "better" decisions, and not just an exposition of existing law.[45] From the outset Cardozo was a member of the Institute's governing council and executive committee and was also a vice president. Although he resigned as vice president when he was appointed to the United States Supreme Court in 1932, he continued as a member of the council until 1937.[46] Twice he was the principal speaker at annual dinners of the Institute.

Although a leading proponent of the common law approach to adjudication, Cardozo was also a strong supporter of the "Restatement" concept. He defended it in vivid, metaphorical language against charges that restatements would stultify growth in law: "Things dimly seen before, floating vaguely before minds that have felt them rather than perceived them, the protoplasmic beginnings of new norms of right and justice, will fall into their framework and their setting, and be revealed to us thereafter, not as novelties or anomalies at all, but as part of the ancient order, needing only their Linnaeus, to classify and sift them, to expose the ties of kinship, to give them rank and standing."[47] In other words, Cardozo saw the Institute as continuing his own work as a common law judge: to show that new decisions that modernized law had their roots in ancient notions of the purpose of law to accomplish justice through an ongoing reformulation of the governing rules.

Cardozo also contributed to the substantive work of the Institute, especially the work on the Restatements of Torts and Conflict of Laws. Although he had his name removed from the official list of advisory committee members on those restatements, he attended numerous conferences and took an active role in the discussions and review of working drafts.[48] Judge Herbert Goodrich, a later director of the American Law Institute, echoed the testimony of Cardozo's colleagues about his persuasiveness, stating that Cardozo's "comment upon any legal question carried such weight that an expressed doubt by him was a source of danger to the acceptance of any proposition, no matter how plausibly urged."[49]

Cardozo's work with the ALI brought him into close and continuing contact with a large group of influential lawyers and academics throughout the country. The impression that he made in these meetings enhanced the reputation that he had gained by his opinions and extrajudicial writings. This work also encouraged him to think in a systematic way about legal doctrine, especially in the field of torts where a stream of cases came to his court.[50]

Cardozo also began to do some Jewish communal work once he became a judge. When the time came to be counted with respect to Jewish affairs, Cardozo spoke out—softly. During World War I, when Jews all over the world were split by the Zionist question, Justice Louis Brandeis sought his support for the Zionist movement. Cardozo had earlier been quite negative regarding Zionism, responding to a plea for support from Abraham Tulin in 1916 with an offhand and self-centered remark that he did not "see how it would help me walking up Fifth Avenue in New York if there were a Jewish state in Palestine."[51] One year later Brandeis, who had met Cardozo through Stephen and Louise Wise, got a different response from Cardozo.[52] Brandeis put to his ally Jacob de Haas, publisher of the *Jewish Advocate,* the rhetorical question, "Is not this the time for Dr. Wise to remind Judge Cardozo of Zionism?"[53] Consequently, Rabbi Wise and Judge Julian Mack[54] discussed the issue with Cardozo and finally sent him an application to join the Zionist Organization of America. Cardozo responded, "You do me too much honor. I have signed the application with some misgiving, for I have confessed to you that I am not yet an enthusiast. But to-day, the line seems to be forming between those who are for the cause and those who are against it, with little room for a third camp. I am not willing to join those who are against, so I go over to the others."[55]

Cardozo later gave permission to use his name and his letter for support, remarking to Rabbi Wise that the "sentence which you quote [regarding the third camp] does not sound to me like a bugle call, but perhaps it will fit the mood of some other laggards like myself."[56] Cardozo did nothing more than lend his name to the Zionist cause. He followed its course, sometimes sympathetically, sometimes doubtfully. A few years later, he commented to his cousin Elvira Solis about the Zionist effort to create a Jewish state in Palestine: "Alas! poor Palestine! So much brains and energy given to it, and such disheartening results."[57] Later he observed to Felix Frankfurter, "Sometimes I have misgivings about the whole Palestinian project," although he added that he had "none as to England's duty to keep the faith."[58]

Although Brandeis had urged Cardozo in 1917 to get involved in the Zionist cause, by 1927 he had a different view of Cardozo's participation in Jewish affairs. He wrote to Frankfurter expressing his hope that Frankfurter would "protect Cardozo from all this Jewish pressure—local, national & international. He will serve the Jewish people best by conserving his health and calmness of spirit in order to do his judicial job as well as he can do it. With his frail health and unfamiliarity with tribal warfare, this course seems imperative."[59] Brandeis had seen that Cardozo was not by nature a public warrior.

But Cardozo continued his modest participation in Jewish organizations. At some time in the 1920s, Cardozo was induced to become a member of the General Committee of the American Jewish Committee. He contributed some of his time to its activities, even during the course of the Court's term. He described one day-long meeting as "interesting in a way, but exasperating like all committee meetings, because of the waste of time."[60] In 1929, Herbert Lehman, Felix Warburg, and he were elected together to the executive committee.[61] Although he occupied an important position with the American Jewish Committee, he seems, as in his other Jewish affiliations, to have held a position without being a leader. Cardozo was not deeply involved in its work, and he did not even understand that the organization was controversial within the Jewish community for its moderate stance on civil liberties issues and for its allegedly elitist membership. Eventually, he confessed his naïveté in a letter to Stephen Wise, noting that he had been wrong in thinking that it was "one of the few organizations that had the approval of all Jewry."[62]

Cardozo also accepted membership in a number of other Jewish organizations after he went on the bench. He joined the board of governors of the American Friends of Hebrew University in Jerusalem and the executive committee of the Jewish Welfare Board. When he became a trustee of Columbia, he was a member of the Committee on the Advisor to Jewish students at Columbia.[63] Although he was nowhere near so active as his prominent Jewish contemporaries, Louis Brandeis, Rabbi Stephen Wise, Felix Frankfurter, and Louis Marshall, when his professional prominence brought him opportunities for serving the Jewish community, he served. And except for his service as trustee of his alma mater, Columbia, he accepted positions for nonprofessional service only with Jewish organizations during his judicial career. Cardozo was probably responding to a sense of obligation to Jewish friends who had supported him and to the Jewish community as a whole, and it is also likely that he felt some pleasure at the honor these affiliations brought to the Cardozo name. Even if his active service was modest, Cardozo identified himself proudly and publicly as a Jew, and he gave Jewish causes the benefit of his growing personal prestige.

Cardozo's judicial service from 1914 to the middle 1920s featured remarkable growth. Right from the start he wrote notable opinions. His modest demeanor, collegial approach to judging, and strong intellect gave him enormous influence within the Court of Appeals. His colleagues liked and admired him enormously. Outside the Court, his lectures made him a national figure within the profession, known to members of the bar and academics. His work in the American Law Institute solidified his reputation. His outside activities also engaged him with other people and other issues, and diverted him from constant preoccupation with Nellie's sickness. The combination of judicial and extrajudicial activities made Cardozo, as he reached his mid-fifties, the best-known judge on the Court of Appeals and a national figure in the profession.

As 1925 drew to a close, Cardozo still had six years to serve of the fourteen-year term to which he had been elected. But because Chief Judge Hiscock was nearing the mandatory retirement age of seventy, a replacement would have to be elected at the fall elections. The chief judgeship would be the next step in Cardozo's career.

11

Chief Judge

Cardozo's last seven years on the Court of Appeals were very satisfying in his professional life but very sad in his personal life. He had already achieved a position of intellectual leadership on the court as well as a national reputation. Now he became the court's leader in every respect. But he would lose his intimate relative, Edgar Nathan, and then suffer the crushing blow of the death of Nellie. His life as chief judge was marked by both success and loneliness.

A large issue threatened the collegiality of the Court of Appeals in the mid-1920s. Chief Judge Hiscock, who was nearing the mandatory retirement age of seventy, would be replaced at the November 1926 general elections. The leading candidates for nomination by the respective parties were Benjamin Cardozo, a Democrat, and Cuthbert Pound, a Republican. Both wanted the job.

The maneuvering began over a year ahead of the election date. One issue related to the question of seniority among the associate judges of the Court of Appeals. In 1913, there had been a contest for chief judge between two sitting associate judges, Willard Bartlett and William Werner. That contest had been divisive within the court and disturbing to many lawyers. Leaders of the bar reportedly engineered a "gentleman's agreement" among Democratic and Republican leaders to nominate jointly the senior associate judge for any future vacancy in the chief judgeship.[1] If there was such an agreement, the Democrats did not abide by it in the very next election for chief judge in 1916. They nominated Almet Jenks to run against Frank Hiscock, the senior associate judge, who had been nominated by the Republicans. Hiscock won that election. Nevertheless, political leaders in both parties and bar leaders assumed that seniority was important when Hiscock had to be replaced.

Both Cardozo and Pound had claims to seniority. Cardozo had been designated as a Supreme Court justice to sit on the Court of Appeals in 1914, appointed a Court of Appeals judge in January 1917, and first elected to a term in November 1917. Pound was designated as a Supreme Court justice to sit on the Court of Appeals in August 1915, and he became a Court of Appeals judge by election in November 1916. Cardozo's claim to seniority was based on longer service on the Court of Appeals, and Pound's claim was based on becoming a regular Court of Appeals judge first.

In November and December 1925, Cardozo's friend Judge Abram Elkus, who had served briefly as a Court of Appeals judge in 1919–1920, wrote letters to prominent members of the bar in various parts of the state urging Cardozo's selection. Enthusiastic support came from Adelbert Moot, a prominent Buffalo lawyer, Samuel Seabury, and Adolph Ochs, publisher of the *New York Times*. Cardozo's friends even tried to lobby Charles Evans Hughes, the former governor and former United States Supreme Court Justice. Hughes was noncommittal, pleading ignorance of the issues and indicating some annoyance at being importuned so early and so often. William D. Guthrie, president of the Association of the Bar of the City of New York, did not want to commit himself to any candidate before the judiciary committee of the Association had acted. But he reminded Elkus of the previous success in linking Cardozo's election to the Court of Appeals with that of a Republican, and suggested a meeting to discuss strategy.[2]

Elkus was not so cautious. He wrote Governor Alfred T. Smith, urging him to support Cardozo's nomination. Smith replied that he was "strong with you for Judge Cardozo" and added that "No promise was made or implied at the time of the nomination of Judge Lehman," doubtless meaning that no promise had been made to the Republicans at the time of Lehman's nomination to the Court of Appeals about nominating a Republican as chief judge. Smith noted that the "matter has quite some time to stand in abeyance," and he was looking forward to a personal talk about it.[3]

Judge Elkus must have sent Cardozo copies of his correspondence with Governor Smith, for Cardozo responded warmly, "The Governor is a brick and so are you."[4] Shortly thereafter Cardozo contracted the serious staphylococcus infection that put him in the hospital twice during the winter of 1926. He was considerably preoccupied with his health problems for several months.[5] In June, Cardozo wrote to Felix Frankfurter that he thought it "very likely that the Chief-Judgeship will go to Pound. As you know, I like and admire him greatly, and he will make a strong leader for the court."[6]

At the same time, Charles Burlingham reported that Governor Smith was also under some pressure from Tammany Hall to nominate a Catholic, since there was no Catholic member of the Court. Tammany's candidate was Supreme Court Justice John McAvoy. Burlingham reported as "the latest graveyard gossip" that the Catholic Smith did not want another Catholic on the ticket with him in the fall elections.[7] One maneuver being suggested was that if Cardozo became the joint nominee for chief judge, he should resign his Court of Appeals judgeship, effective as of January 1, 1927, so that his vacancy could also be filled in the November 1926 elections. Cardozo's friend Nathan Bijur reported to Burlingham that Cardozo would do that at the request of "the bar" but not at the request of politicians. Burlingham, who had promoted Cardozo's original selection for the bench, was not active in supporting Cardozo at this point. His major objective was to achieve the two parties' agreement on a joint ticket, and he did not think it made "an awful lot of difference" whether Pound or Cardozo became chief judge.[8]

During the summer, although Cardozo's own health had recovered, he was preoccupied with the deterioration of Nellie's health.[9] Responding to an inquiry from Learned Hand at the end of the summer, he wrote philosophically,

You ask about the chief-judgeship. I haven't hear[d] a word. The last thing I read was a statement that there had been some agreement to take Pound, which was very likely premature, though I think it will turn out that way. It would be a pretty decoration, and I should be pleased at getting it—pleased in the act of getting it, I should say. How I should feel afterwards I don't know. I fancy a chief-judge is bothered more than others with a duty to make speeches and all that sort of thing, which I hate. So very likely I'll be happier as associate. In any event I shall accept the verdict with equanimity. Pound is a splendid man—really better in many ways than I am, though I am glad you don't think so.[10]

Despite the tone of that letter, Cardozo was following the matter closely. He wanted the position. Shortly before the nominating conventions in the fall of 1926, he was clearer about his feelings. "The World yesterday had an editorial as fine as that of the Times. All the same, I believe the politicians will beat me. The report today is not encouraging."[11] The circumstance that changed the earlier predictions that Cardozo would be selected is that Governor Smith had gotten the mistaken impression that Pound was unquestionably the senior judge and had indicated to the Republican leader, Senator James Wadsworth, that he had no objection to a joint nomination of Pound as chief judge so long as the Republicans agreed to a joint nomination of a Democrat to replace Pound as associate judge.[12]

Joseph Paley, Cardozo's law secretary, remembered that during the time when the Republicans had Governor Smith's assurance of support for Pound, Pound had written Cardozo a letter stating that he had both the Republican nomination and the tacit acquiescence of Smith regarding the Democratic nomination. Pound added that he was very happy at the turn of events. He hoped that he and Cardozo would continue to be good friends and that Cardozo would be his first lieutenant as Cardozo had been Hiscock's first lieutenant. According to Paley, Cardozo was very upset, not so much because he wanted to be chief judge, but because he thought that the position ought to be his because of seniority. Paley reported that Cardozo said that he would serve out his term and then retire.[13] That was an extraordinary statement for Cardozo, assuming that Paley recalled it accurately, for it revealed a passion that Cardozo did not often exhibit.

When Cardozo's supporters discovered that Smith had made some commitment to Pound, they mounted a strong campaign in the fall of 1926 to persuade Smith to change his mind and to obtain an agreement among leaders of both parties to name Cardozo for the chief judgeship and a Republican as associate judge. While Rabbi Wise harangued the governor, Louis Marshall and others organized political support for Cardozo. Marshall persuaded Adolph Ochs, owner of the *New York Times,* to publish an editorial supporting Cardozo's nomination.[14] Marshall and some bar association leaders met with Governor Smith to urge nonpartisan joint selection of candidates for the two vacancies by the two parties. Governor Smith told them that he had been willing to support Pound because he thought that Pound was senior; when he learned that Cardozo had served on the Court of Appeals eighteen months longer than Pound, Smith did not see how he could pass over Cardozo, who was senior and "an outstanding figure in the judicial history of the state." Smith concluded that the Republicans should nominate the associate judge, and the consensus of the group was that that person should be Judge Henry Kellogg. Marshall, who was a Republican, wrote to Charles Hilles, Republican National Committeeman from New York, pointing out the political advantage to the Republicans of the proposed arrangement and urging him to support the joint nomination of Cardozo and Kellogg.[15]

Other Cardozo supporters were also at work. Burlingham, becoming more active, sought to enlist the support of Franklin Roosevelt and Nicholas Murray Butler for Cardozo, and Burlingham believed that Joseph Proskauer had been influential on Cardozo's behalf.[16] The deal outlined in the meeting between the bar leaders and Governor Smith was finally struck just before the nominating conventions in late September 1926. Cardozo was elected chief judge and Henry Kellogg associate judge in the November elections on joint nominations of both parties.

The Benjamin Cardozo who became chief judge of the New York Court of Appeals on January 1, 1927, was an imposing figure in the legal profession. His opinions and his writings, which we shall study in detail in the "Doing the Law's Work" part of this book, were the source of his reputation, but his personality contributed to his acclaim. It made an impact in small groups, like the consultations of the Court of Appeals, and on large audiences as well.

Cardozo had a unique charisma. By the time he became chief judge, his features had softened. The self-confident, almost arrogant look of the man who had joined the Court of Appeals in 1914 had been gradually replaced by a reflective, dignified expression. He was not imposing physically. He was of medium height, about 5 feet, 9 or 10 inches tall, with a slight stoop, a raised shoulder, bushy eyebrows, and a complete head of silvery white hair of which he was proud. His quiet demeanor disappeared in public speech. He was a commanding speaker, who projected his thoughtfulness and judiciousness in a remarkable fashion in his public appearances. He delivered his lectures and speeches in a distinctive, literate, and forceful manner that struck responsive chords in his audience. One listener described his presentations as "extraordinary." There was the "slightest tremor in his voice," which was "charged with feeling." His "whole being went into the delivery."[17] A recording of his voice confirms that description. Although soft-spoken in private conversation, he had developed a fluent, emotional, oratorical style of public speaking that, combined with the content of what he had to say, explains why he was such an effective lawyer and public speaker.[18]

Cardozo also made a powerful personal impact on many of his colleagues and friends. "Christ must have been like that," was one expression.[19] Many others, including some of his colleagues, referred to him as "a saint" or talked of his "quiet, priest-like" qualities.[20] John F. O'Brien, who sat on the Court of Appeals during Cardozo's last five years there, said that "[o]utside of my family there was no one for whom I had such affection. He was a genius and a saint."[21]

Obviously, Cardozo was not a saint in the religious sense. The term was doubtless meant more casually to denote a gentle, considerate person who did not take or give offense. Cardozo made that impression on many people, both within and without his private circle. He was a hero to those who worked for him because he was constantly appreciative of their efforts on his behalf and because he took care to talk with them at their level of interests and conversation. Also, he was understanding when things went wrong. When the cook sought to help out by ironing Cardozo's favorite suit and then ruined it, Cardozo simply said that he was about to throw the suit out anyhow.[22] Cardozo was "saintly" where Nellie was concerned. His devotion and care, especially at the end of Nellie's life, was extraordinary, combining gentleness, kindness, and self-sacrifice, for he gave up many things to be with her. Kate Tracy, who knew him for forty-six years and had both wit and iron in her soul, was absolutely devoted to him. "He was the most unique and lovable soul I have ever known, more like a Heavenly Being than a human."[23] Judge Richard Posner has reminded us, however, that "No saint has ever been a successful trial lawyer."[24] Nor has any saint ever been a judge, at least not in any American court of law. We would not want someone who had not a single human vice to be a judge.

As noted earlier, Cardozo was no saint. We have seen a strain of aristocratic elitism, some arrogance, and some prejudices that were part of his character. Cardozo also had his share of petty foibles. As he was generous in his praise of others, he greatly liked to receive praise in return, and he was hurt by criticism. Indeed, he sometimes sought to ward it off. In a letter to Thomas Reed Powell, a constitutional scholar and a biting critic, Cardozo commented on his "cruel lampoons" of an unidentified author and then remarked, "Dear wicked man, I am willing to think anything you say I should if you will promise in return to keep that lambent wit of yours at such a distance from my person that I shall only feel its glow and not feel its blistering heat."[25] Cardozo's implicit message to Powell was, please don't lampoon me.

In addition, Cardozo had a strain of vanity, which showed in the great care he devoted to combing his hair just right. Addie Cardozo, an older cousin who knew him from childhood, delighted in teasing him that "there's a hair out of place." In his later years, Cardozo's barber came every Friday to Cardozo's home to groom his "famous tousled hair." He owned fifteen identical black suits, custom made to hide a bit of a hump on his back.[26] He also cared about pictures of himself. When he had several proofs, he would ask a variety of people their opinions so that he could be sure to pick the best one.[27]

Cardozo was not averse to playing a little at the game of politics in order to advance his career. He also enjoyed receiving honors, such as his admission to the Century Club and the many honorary degrees that came his way. Moreover, as the incident, cited earlier, concerning his neighbor with the tailoring business indicates, he could look out for his own interests by asking, in a most unsaintly way, that someone else do the dirty work.

His correspondence and his speech were full of self-deprecation, although occasionally he would admit that he "did really accomplish something [on the Court of Appeals] that gave a new direction to the law."[28] His admirers acquit him of "false" modesty, but it is hard to know how to treat his practice of putting himself down.[29] Perhaps it was a stylized courtesy, in order to put others at ease. Perhaps it was simply a habit that was as much a part of him as was his habit of inverting his sentences. But in a literal sense at least, it was false modesty, for he understood his own abilities.

Cardozo's family, friends, and colleagues understood that these frailties existed in a predominantly good and kind man, and they overlooked or forgave them. During his years as a judge, Cardozo generated a feeling of genuine affection from those who got to know him. As far as his public persona was concerned, Cardozo's personal qualities added to his stature and image. Indeed, these qualities may have helped shield him from substantial professional criticism during his whole judicial career.

When Cardozo became chief judge, the court's practice changed under his leadership. Now that the court was up-to-date with its caseload, the judges engaged in more dialogue with lawyers who appeared before them. Cardozo was always well prepared. He was one of the few judges who invariably read all the briefs in advance, and he was known for asking incisive questions in a soft, musical voice.[30] Occasionally, he would even tell a lawyer not to argue a specific point because the court had made up its mind or because the point was irrelevant or not properly in issue.[31] Yet Cardozo was attentive, respectful, and considerate to counsel during argument. He would help a lawyer who was having difficulty and would occasionally ask, "Do you mean thus and so," going on to make the argument that the lawyer should have made.[32]

But Cardozo did not hesitate to exercise his authority as chief judge when he thought it was necessary. On one occasion during argument, he tapped a blotter on the bench and told a lawyer who interrupted him that "When the court and counsel wish to speak at the same time, it does seem to me that the court should have precedence."[33] Another time, he expressed some anger when a lawyer kept on with an argument after being informed that his time was up.[34] And he could be quite brusque in handling requests for reargument.[35]

Cardozo was a strong chief judge. Felix Frankfurter attributed a great deal of Cardozo's influence within the court to personal qualities—his silken voice, his ability to listen, his quiet, courteous, emollient nature, the gentleness of his gestures, and the little stoop in his posture.[36] Courtesy and effectiveness were the marks of his dealings with his colleagues. On one occasion, even though Cardozo was in dissent, he was able to convince a colleague to correct some misstatements of law in a majority opinion after Lehman had failed in the same mission.[37] On another occasion, according to Irving Lehman, a new Court of Appeals judge (whom he did not name) had prepared himself carefully to discuss at consultation the first case that had been assigned to him. After he cited many precedents to support the result that he had reached, Cardozo, then chief judge, responded that he had reached the opposite result but declared himself "much shaken" by the new judge's views. Cardozo then expressed "with some hesitation" the views that he had formed so that all sides of the case would be before the court. According to the new judge, "Cardozo then proceeded to state his own views with a force and persuasiveness that left me in no doubt that he was right, and all I could do was to bow my head and admit my error."[38] Part of Cardozo's leadership style was his ability to treat the efforts of a colleague, especially a new one, with kindness. His personal qualities combined with his analytical and intellectual ability to make him a persuasive, powerful, much admired, and beloved leader of the Court of Appeals.

Cardozo's years as chief judge were busy. His position brought invitations and honors. One year after becoming chief judge, Cardozo resisted another judicial offer that came his way. In the summer of 1927, Charles Evans Hughes, acting on behalf of President Coolidge, asked Cardozo to accept a part-time assignment as an American member of the Permanent Court of Arbitration at The Hague. Cardozo declined the appointment. His major reason was that acceptance might raise the question whether he was violating the provision in the New York state constitution that prohibited a state official from holding any other office or public trust. He did not believe that in fact there would be a constitutional violation but feared that others would disagree, and he was unwilling to injure the reputation of the Court of Appeals. Cardozo's sensitivity may have reflected his memory of the disgrace that his father had brought on the New York judiciary and his desire to avoid controversy about an issue of propriety. In stating his reason, he expressed pride in his court and his role. "The post of chief judge of the Court of Appeals is in my opinion one of the great official positions in the land."[39]

Cardozo was careful in other ways to observe the proprieties regarding his judicial role. He would not sign a certificate for admission to the New York bar for a friend of Louis Marshall without meeting the lawyer first, even if that meant that the lawyer had to make a special trip to New York City.[40] He also declined to give a recommendation to a lawyer for a position because he did not know the applicant well enough.[41] When Augustus Tack painted his portrait for the Court of Appeals, Cardozo presented it to the court himself because he did not want anyone to contribute to its purchase.[42] And a little later when Cardozo was on the United States Supreme Court, Moses Grossman, a New York lawyer, made him a present of an old English deed. Cardozo returned it with a deft touch: "It was a graceful and friendly thing for you to do. But . . . I am going to send it back to you. I am fussy about receiving gifts. You'll forgive me, won't you? Anyhow I had the fun of looking at the document, which is almost as good as owning it." Chief Justice

Charles Evans Hughes and Justices Louis Brandeis and Harlan Fiske Stone kept similar gifts from Grossman, but Cardozo wanted to avoid any appearance that he was profiting by his position or was susceptible to influence.[43]

Coolidge's offer of membership on the Hague Tribunal did not tempt Cardozo, but an invitation from his former teacher did. In 1928, Nicholas Murray Butler, president of Columbia, invited Cardozo to be a member of the board of trustees of Columbia University. When he accepted, he became the second Jew to be named to that position; the first had been his great granduncle, Gershom Mendes Seixas, nearly a hundred and fifty years before. Cardozo served four years before he had to resign when he was appointed to the United States Supreme Court.[44] The board of trustees did most of its work through committees; Cardozo was a member of the committee on honors and of the committee on legal affairs. The work did not occupy a great deal of his time.

Butler also arranged for Cardozo to join the Round Table, a group of men who met once a month at the Knickerbocker Club for general conversation. Butler, who was a member of the nominating committee, had recommended Cardozo strongly: "He is plainly one of the most remarkable and one of the most attractive personalities of our generation. He is an omnivorous reader, a real philosopher and has a most subtle and supple mind."[45] There he spent evenings with a variety of people like Learned Hand, Cass Gilbert, the architect of the Capitol, Thomas Lamont, the international financier, and Brander Matthews, the Columbia professor of dramatic literature. For a year and a half before he left New York to go to Washington, Cardozo belonged to a group of lawyers and judges organized by C. C. Burlingham as the Dinner Party, which met occasionally at the University Club.[46] He also belonged to the Century Club, the Lawyers Club, the Columbia University Club, the Manhattan Club, the City Club in New York City, and the Fort Orange Club in Albany. The Century Club seems to have been the place he used most often.[47] In 1928, Cardozo even allowed himself to be made an honorary member of the Association of the Bar of the City of New York.[48] Once he became chief judge, he doubtless felt some pressure to join the older local organization.

While chief judge, Cardozo kept up his interest in local and national affairs. He believed that political views, his own included, contained something of the instinctive, that they were "somehow or other, matters of inward, almost indefinable feeling rather than reasoned conviction."[49]

His political instinct was Democratic, and he remained a member of the Democratic Party.[50] He had strong views about the election of 1928 and its meaning for him as a Jew. He attempted to convince Aline Goldstone to support Al Smith for President with a passion that rarely appears in his writing: "In the opposite camp will be found all the narrow minded bigots, all the Jew haters, all those who would make of the United States an exclusively Protestant government. I do not mean, of course, that only those will be found there, but I mean that the defeat of Smith will be acclaimed as a great victory by that narrow-minded group, and will hearten them and the friends of obscurantism generally." His next letter pursued this line of argument: "I cannot believe, however, that dislike of the Jews, whether otherwise well founded or not, can excuse their indiscriminate exclusion [by Republicans] from posts of responsibility and honor."[51] Cardozo's views about anti-Semitic forces in the Republican Party reinforced his lifelong leaning toward the Democratic Party, which he found more welcoming to him in terms of his Jewish identity.

Cardozo favored Smith and opposed Hoover on general political principles as well. He expounded his view to Felix Frankfurter, whom he knew as an ardent Smith supporter: "The worst of it is that every bigoted and reactionary group will hail [Smith's] defeat—if defeated he is—as the downfall of liberalism and the triumph of reaction. The extent of the misfortune will not be capable of measurement by the personal qualities and policies of Hoover, whatever they may be. The battalions of darkness have chosen to enlist under his banner."[52]

These strong words indicate how far Cardozo had come since he delivered "The Altruist in Politics" at his Columbia commencement in 1889. The Social Darwinism that infused that address had completely disappeared. No evidence exists to mark the time or the precise cause of the change. Given his identification with Woodrow Wilson, the change appears to have occurred by the time he went on the bench.[53] But it was not his clientele that changed his views, for his clients were mostly from the field of business.

More likely, it was the rise of the progressive movement in reaction to the perceived excesses of late-nineteenth-century capitalism that influenced him as it had so many others. His contemporary, the noted Kansas editor William Allen White, spoke of the "quickening sense of the inequities, injustices, and fundamental wrongs of the political and economic overlays on our democracy" that had driven White himself out of his earlier conservatism.[54] Although Cardozo grew up with different experiences in a very different part of the country, he felt the same political winds, and they changed him into a moderately liberal Democrat who subscribed to the liberal *New Republic* and *Nation*.[55] The irony of Cardozo's prediction about the enthronement of the forces of bigotry under Hoover is that it was Hoover who, three-and-a-half years later, appointed Cardozo to the United States Supreme Court.

While chief judge, Cardozo reflected about the meaning of religion and spiritual values on several public occasions. In 1927, he responded to a call from Shearith Israel. Cardozo spoke at the dinner honoring Dr. Pereira Mendes for his seventy-fifth birthday and fifty years of service to Shearith Israel. Dr. Mendes was the rabbi of Cardozo's youth, and during his talk, Cardozo gave a glimpse into his own view of the meaning of life. Speaking of his lifelong friendship with Dr. Mendes, he recalled the simple and unadorned exterior of the old synagogue that proclaimed "the eternal message that within [the individual] and not without are the values that endure." The talk was filled with literary references, as was Cardozo's wont in such talks; and all the authors, Sainte Beuve, Matthew Arnold, Charles Francis Adams, and William Lecky, were not Jewish. But he used Sainte Beuve's commentary on Pascal's belief in God to say something of his own view of Judaism: "Pascal's outlook on life was essentially Hebraic. He made conduct, in Arnold's phrase, four-fifths of life . . . Indeed, if I had to choose, I should have to say that there is matter for religion in any and every activity that has relation to the good life in all its fullness and perfection."[56]

Good conduct rather than religious doctrine was Cardozo's view of the essence of human existence, and his sources were the Hebrew prophets. In characterizing Dr. Mendes's life, he turned first to the words of the prophet Micah: "What doth the Lord require of thee but to do justice and to love mercy and to walk humbly with thy God"; and then to the prophet Samuel: "'And I will raise me up a faithful priest,' said the Lord, 'that shall do according to that which is in mine heart and in my mind and I will build him a sure house, and he shall walk before mine anointed forever.'"[57] The choice of biblical texts—doing justice, loving mercy, walking humbly, and being faithful—was appropriate to the occasion and to Cardozo's sense of his relation to Judaism and to the home of Sephardic Jewry in New York City, Shearith Israel. It also provided a standard of good conduct for life and for his work in his own calling.

He sounded the same theme at a dinner the same year in honor of his friend Rabbi Stephen Wise. "Religion is worthless if it is not translated into conduct. Creeds are snares and hypocrisies if they are not adapted to the needs of life. Dr. Wise has known this from the beginning and . . . has interpreted religion in no cramped and narrow sense. Has there been some social wrong, some oppression of the people, some grinding of the poor? That is a matter for religion. Has there been cruelty to Jews abroad or to colored men at home; has there been obscurantism in Russia or Roumania, or in Georgia or Tennessee? That is a matter for religion. Has the sacred name of liberty, which should stand for equal opportunity for all, been made a pretext and a cover for special privileges for a few? That is a matter for religion."[58] Cardozo could not understand or approve a morality that regarded membership in the religion as more important than leading a good life.[59] But religion posed more personal issues too, and as Nellie's condition worsened, Cardozo opened up a little bit to his old friend Louise Wise: "I think a good deal these days about religion, wondering what it is and whether I have any. As the human relationships which make life what it is for us begin to break up, we search more and more for others that transcend them."[60] But he stopped far short of revealing any conclusion.

Cardozo delivered a talk in 1931 in which he expanded on his vision of the meaning of religion. Persuaded by Rabbi Wise to deliver the commencement address at the Jewish Institute of Religion, Cardozo used Alfred Noyes's poem, "The Watchers of the Sky," as the centerpiece of a little talk entitled "Values."[61] Cardozo had earlier summarized the poem in his own notebook: the poem "tells of Tycho Brahe the astronomer and of his long, long years to mark and register the stars and of the mockery of the crowd, who asked him to what end . . . The answer that Tycho Brahe made is the answer that everyone must make, everyone who in his own small way, needs before him the eternal light of a standard of perfection which he will not soil or mar."[62] Cardozo translated his notion of the poem's meaning for his audience. "The submergence of self in the pursuit of an ideal, the readiness to spend oneself without measure, prodigally, almost ecstatically, for something intuitively apprehended as great and noble, spend oneself one knows not why—some of us like to believe that is what religion means."[63] Submergence, in the sense of total immersion, of the self in the pursuit of an ideal—his view of his duty as a brother and as a judge—is a good description of Cardozo's personal choices in his own family and professional life.

Cardozo himself did not often engage in public good conduct by engaging in activities that addressed the evils of the world. As a practicing lawyer, he had devoted himself wholly to his professional work and to the heavy burden of responsibility that he bore at home. He had not made time for public activities. He also seems to have felt that he lacked the emotional and intangible gifts that made for natural public leaders. As a judge, his ability to do such work was circumscribed by his position, but he did some public work within those bounds. He admired his friends who were active in social causes, and he saw their work as involving the "good conduct" that he associated with the real work of religion. And he knew that his own instincts were different. He was committed to good conduct in his own sphere—the duties to his family and work—but not outside it. Regarding the world at large, Cardozo was an observer, a thinker rather than a doer, a reader and an intellectual. He sought to understand issues but was profoundly skeptical about claims that sounded dogmatic or extreme to him. He was a man whose convictions about ultimate values were "few and far between."[64] We shall see in later chapters that in the law, he was essentially eclectic, seeking what seemed sensible in divergent approaches and theories.

Cardozo's notion of spiritual conduct included personal qualities as well as public activity. Behind the calm exterior and behind the life of the mind lay a core of sentiment that Cardozo revealed on special occasions. When Sarah Lyons, his older first cousin and a matriarch of the family, died, Cardozo wrote a warmly appreciative, honest little portrait: "her going leaves a great gap in the family life. She was a fundamentalist in her beliefs but fundamentalism does not often present itself in a garb of such simplicity and gentleness. For those she liked her affection was unbounded, though she was not sparing in her hates. The union of those qualities marks a mind that does its own thinking." Ben Cardozo was one of those whom she liked, and he reciprocated her feelings.[65] Simplicity, gentleness, and love were qualities of right conduct, too, and he spoke of them with feeling.

Personal qualities were those that Cardozo emphasized when he spoke of the death of friends. At the funeral of his friend Morris Hirsch, Cardozo referred only briefly to "the wise counsellor, the sagacious lawyer, the graceful and ready speaker . . . the writer of countless letters bristling with quips and repartee. We are thinking of other things, the great fundamental virtues of tenderness and gentleness and charity. These are the things that last."[66] At times, his words carried even more emotion, as at the funeral of Sarah Goldman, wife of his friend and colleague, Julius Goldman: "I have spoken of her gayety. Gayety is of kin to tenderness, and tenderness to love. Those who were privileged to claim her friendship—it was mine for close to forty years—have seen and felt her tenderness . . . and here in this family of husband, children, and grand-children, here in this dear united family, was the very presence of love incarnate."

Cardozo had known sustaining tenderness and love in his own family, as well as among his friends. No doubt he gave his audience tears, but he offered them comfort too as he reflected on the components of a good life in his farewell to Sarah:

> And so, dear friend, good-bye. It is a word one finds it hard to say, for all the moralizing of the sages who bid us not to mourn. I seem to find a ray of comfort in the message of Santayana's latest book. "That the end of life," he writes "should be death may sound sad; yet what other end can anything have? The end of an evening is to go to bed; but its use is to gather congenial people together, that they may pass the time pleasantly." So it is with this strange sociable of life when death puts out the lights. For a time there has been gayety and gentleness and kindness and good cheer. Then, in the darkness, the gracious guest slips out. Ah, but it was good to see her and to know her when the lights were burning bright![67]

Cardozo was preoccupied with matters of sickness and death as Nellie's health continued to worsen during his service as chief judge. Although Nellie was able to walk, she spent much of her time in bed. She took dinner in bed, and Ben would sit by her, eating his dinner on a tray. They kept up their normal routines as much as possible and continued to rent a house in Allenhurst every summer. Alec Heisman, the chauffeur, took Nellie for drives in the country in the family Franklin. Nellie tried hard to be cheerful. Even near the end of her life, until she lost her speech, she was still able to appreciate humor and could laugh so heartily that tears would come. Family and a few friends, like Louise Waterman Wise, would call. Nonetheless, Nellie's life, which had never been very active, became more and more restricted.[68]

In February 1928, she suffered a stroke that greatly affected her speech.[69] Thereafter her health deteriorated further.[70] Although Ben did manage to get her to Allenhurst in the summers of both 1928 and 1929, she remained under the care of day and night nurses. Ben took her decline hard. He could do little for Nellie except to be with her. Once all the court work was done in the middle of July 1928, he found time "rather heavy" on his hands. He worked on some talks and spent much of the rest of his time reading. He received few visitors and "hardly left the house."[71]

The year 1929 was sad for Cardozo. In June, Edgar Nathan, Ben's cousin and closest friend, died. Then on November 23, Nellie finally died, leaving Ben as the last of the children of Albert and Rebecca Cardozo. Ben buried Nellie with their parents and all their deceased siblings except Emily in the family plot at Shearith Israel's cemetery in Cypress Hills, Long Island.[72]

One week after Nellie's death, Ben reflected in a letter to Learned Hand on what life with Nellie had meant to him.

> When the end comes, we generally reproach ourselves for this failing or that, saying to ourselves that we might have done a little better here or shown ourselves a little kinder there.
>
> It is simple truth to say that I have no such reproaches now. I could not do it any better if I were to do it again. The credit is not mine. My sister's nature was so beautiful that to be good and kind to her was to be good and kind to myself, and praise would be no more due for the one than for the other. Often during her life she said to me that if anything befell her, I was to remember of our life together that it had been perfect. So I think it was.[73]

Nearly thirty years later, Hand remembered how powerful the letter was: "[W]hen she died . . . I had a letter from him which was unique in my experience with him. It was almost like a lover's letter . . . I didn't realize that there lay beneath his very . . . unmoved exterior, deep passion. I fancy that . . . everything he had lost elsewhere centered in her."[74]

Cardozo had lost his companion, confidante, and mainstay. For fifty years, Nellie had been Cardozo's family life, first as sister-mother, then as partner in caring for the rest of the family, and finally as his dependent. The shock was enormous. "I feel very strange. I do not owe a duty to any one in the world. So many years of taking care of family, and then suddenly to be alone."[75]

Duty was replaced by loneliness. Although his work and visits from relatives and friends kept him occupied and although there was a household, run by Kate Tracy, to take care of him, the heart and soul of his daily life had been Nellie. No one else even came close to filling her place in his life. The first year was especially difficult. Cardozo was depressed for a long time. He took to eating by himself on a tray upstairs either in Nellie's room or in the upstairs sitting room. He tried not to let his feelings show, but when he smiled a friendly good-bye to visitors, his face would immediately fall back into sadness.[76] In February 1930, he confessed to Felix Frankfurter how difficult a time he was having: "I haven't recovered yet from the shock of my bereavement, and going on seems very flat and stale. I must wait for Time to do its work."[77] Things had not changed a month later when he wrote Learned Hand, "I haven't stirred from the house a single evening since I have been in town."[78]

Kate Tracy expected that Ben would not want to stay in the West 75th St. home and she raised the issue of the household's future with him. He replied that he was going to remain and added, "You don't suppose I'd let those two women downstairs [Mary and Catherine Walsh] go."[79] Loyalty to Kate Tracy and the Walsh sisters was one factor in his decision. It also seems likely that he did not wish to upset his own settled routine any further, to lose the companionship of those with whom he had shared his life with Nellie, or indeed to leave the house where he and Nellie had lived so many years together.

His appreciation for those who had taken care of Nellie extended beyond the household employees. Mrs. Alice Williams, who had been the night nurse for the two years preceding Nellie's death, became ill and had to stop nursing. Cardozo gave her $15 a month to help with hospital bills. (Fifteen dollars went further and hospital bills were considerably smaller in the 1930s than at the end of the century.) Mrs. Williams wanted to open a newsstand along the line of the new Eighth Avenue subway, and she therefore turned to Cardozo for help. He set Joseph Paley to work to get the necessary application and to find out who had the power to issue a permit. No records exist to show what more Cardozo or Paley did to secure the permit, but Mrs. Williams did get one for a good location at Eighth Avenue and Forty-Second Street.

Cardozo gave her $100 to build the stand and continued to provide an allowance. During the last year of his life, even after he became ill, he sent her a series of $25 to $50 checks regularly from Washington.[80]

Cardozo's relatives and friends, especially Irving and Sissie Lehman, were constant in their attention, and after a while his spirits began to recover, although the memory of Nellie was never far away.[81] Responding to a letter from Rabbi Wise that must have praised his work, Cardozo responded, "Praise is precious even now—such is the vanity of human nature—though I ask myself in wonderment why I should value it, now that the one who would have shared it with me so fully has gone from me for ever."[82]

The long years of caring for Nellie and watching her decline took a toll on Cardozo. They wore him down both physically and mentally. The effect is quite noticeable in successive pictures of him over the years. The supremely self-confident expression of the lawyer in his early forties was gradually replaced by the gentler, and wearier, demeanor of the Court of Appeals judge and Supreme Court justice. Cardozo suffered the beginning of his heart problems shortly after Nellie's death, with an angina attack on the street in Albany in June 1930. His regular physician, Dr. John Keating, and several specialists treated him. That attack must have been mild, for his activities were only restricted for a week.[83] Nevertheless, his heart had sufficiently weakened that Dr. Alfred Cohn, one of the specialists who examined him the following year, later said that Cardozo had lived longer than was reasonably to have been expected at that time.[84]

Court work kept him in New York the entire summer of 1930. He began to pick up his life again. His colleague Frederick Crane took him off to the Metropolitan Museum of Art to see the Havemeyer Collection. Then he went by train to Boston, spent a night at a hotel, and was driven by Felix Frankfurter to spend a day with Justice Holmes in Beverly Farms "in response to an 'entreaty,' which from him has the force of a command."[85] One Sunday, he spent a day in Mamaroneck, on the shore of Long Island Sound, with Rosalie and Henry Hendricks, the daughter and son-in-law of Edgar and Sallie Nathan. He joined them for an afternoon of sailing on Long Island Sound, although he did not know how to swim.[86] At home, he sat for a bust commissioned for Columbia Law School. He then had the painters in to renovate some of the rooms in his house and had his library moved down from the third floor to the second.[87]

Finally, a year after Nellie's death, he summed up his feelings: "Irreparable the loss to me has been, and yet I have survived it, and now a year has passed, and I am going through the paces—the daily routine of life and work—with a dumb wonder at myself that with so much that has been changed the change has been so little. Even so, there is hardly a vacant moment when I do not think of her with love and gratitude."[88]

Cardozo helped himself survive by keeping busy beyond the daily routine of life. He wrote a little talk that he would give at a dinner in his honor in December 1930 at the New York County Lawyers Association.[89] He worked on an article for the *Harvard Law Review*'s special issue to honor Justice Holmes on his ninetieth birthday.[90] He also worked on his talk on "Values." In the summer of 1931, he began a remarkable address on jurisprudence, which is discussed in Chapter 23, for delivery at a meeting of the New York State Bar Association the following January.

By the fall of 1931, the wounds from Nellie's loss had healed sufficiently that Cardozo was able to reflect publicly on the meaning of life, death, and love. He agreed to perform the marriage ceremony between his relative Dorothy Harwood and Alan Herbert. Cardozo worked hard to produce a thought worthy of the occasion, and he did so beautifully: "Three great mysteries there are in the lives of mortal beings: the mystery of birth at the beginning; the mystery of death at the end; &, greater than either, the mystery of love. Everything that is most precious in life is a form of love. Art is a form of love, if it be noble; labor is a form of love, if it be worthy; thought is a form of love, if it be inspired; and marriage is love incarnate. So may it be for you throughout all the years to come."[91] He was clearly thinking of his own great loves—Nellie and his life's work—as he prepared his remarks for the young couple.

Cardozo's career during the Court of Appeals years was a combination of professional triumph and personal tragedy. As his professional star rose, his personal life, so bound up in his family and especially Nellie, waned. By the end of the 1920s he had lost Nellie, the centerpiece of his life. But he had earned a reputation as one of the three outstanding judges in the country—the others were Oliver Wendell Holmes and Learned Hand. The substance of that achievement, Cardozo's contribution to law, is the subject of the next section.

Doing the Law's Work: 1914–1932

12

The Nature of the Judicial Process

The previous section dealt with Cardozo's life during his years on the Court of Appeals. It also described how cases came to that court and how the court operated. This section deals with Cardozo's contributions to law during his years on the Court of Appeals in his extrajudicial writings and in his opinions. This chapter sets out the process of decision-making as Cardozo presented it in his public lectures. The succeeding chapters discuss his actual performance as a judge. The cases are grouped by subject matter to trace the development of his ideas and his contributions to legal doctrine in each area. Some students of Cardozo's opinions have found them dominantly pragmatic and utilitarian.[1] Others believe that Cardozo's decisions represented moral choices and occasionally a reaching for perfectionism.[2] In fact, we shall see that Cardozo was guided by all these impulses.

Cardozo's enduring importance arises out of his approach to judging. He was the first modern judge to tell us how he decided cases, how he made law, and, by implication, how others should do so. He declared his views in *The Nature of the Judicial Process,* a group of lectures delivered and published in 1921, and exemplified them in his judicial opinions.[3] Both his views and his example influenced other judges. He gave us a model for judging that emphasized both its creative possibilities and its limits. His description of those possibilities and limits remains influential and controversial today. Even though contemporary society, which forms a modern judge's frame of reference, has changed from Cardozo's day, and even though many judges now give less heed to institutional considerations than Cardozo gave, most judges still go about the job of deciding cases within the framework that Cardozo described.[4]

The proper role of the judge has been the subject of a continuous debate that has renewed itself in every generation because judicial law-making both reflects and affects American institutions, politics, and society. In the late nineteenth and early twentieth centuries, debate focused on whether judges "found" or "made" law. The "find law" view saw judges as ascertaining a law that already existed in prior precedents, in customary practices, or in immutable "natural law." The "make law" view saw law as a matter of prophecy. It never "was"; it was always about to be. Adherents of the "find law" view denied that judges had a policy-making, quasi-legislative role. Adherents of the "make law" view asserted that role as a truism of judicial decision-making. Some extreme adherents of the "make law" school have gone on to imply that legal doctrine is so manipulable that it is essentially indeterminate. Judges decide cases any way they wish and then dress up the result in traditional legal language. In that view, what judges do is not much different from what legislators do. It is all politics.[5] Judges and scholars have ranged themselves along a spectrum between the extremes of these two definitions.

Although recognizing restraints on judges, Cardozo weighed in on the side of those who argued that there was more to judging than "finding" law. Indeed, the "find law" view was subjected to ridicule by several generations of scholars and judges beginning with Oliver Wendell Holmes and Roscoe Pound. Cardozo joined the fray. In time, the "make law" view that he championed, that judges had a creative function subject to various constraints, became orthodox. This school was in the ascendancy for most of the twentieth century, but the debate has now resurfaced. The new form of the "find law" argument is the assertion of the primacy of "original intent" in interpreting the language of the Constitution and statutes.[6] These are the same issues, stated in new terms, that Cardozo faced. Cardozo's notion of the way in which judges decide cases contains a core of practical and theoretical sense that is useful to both sides of the modern argument.

Cardozo's views on the role of judges were influenced by three powerful voices, Oliver Wendell Holmes, John Chipman Gray, and Roscoe Pound. Pound was a contemporary of Cardozo, and Holmes and Gray were a generation older. Like Cardozo, all had been practicing lawyers for a substantial period and brought this experience to their writing about law. All three addressed the issue of judge-made law and defended the necessity of judicial modernization of common law.

Of the three, Holmes was the most philosophical, and the publication of his *The Common Law* in 1881 was a landmark in intellectual history. Its opening salvo—"The life of the law has not been logic: it has been experience"—was the clarion call for the next generation of legal thinkers. Cardozo called it "the text to be unfolded. All that is to come will be development and commentary."[7] Holmes was elliptical, but he espoused a creative role for judges. In "The Path of the Law," written in 1897, Holmes stated his central thought clearly: "Behind the logical form lies a judgment as to the relative worth and importance of competing legislative grounds, often an inarticulate and unconscious judgment, it is true, and yet the very root and nerve of the whole proceeding . . . I think that the judges themselves have failed adequately to recognize their duty of weighing considerations of social advantage."[8] Cardozo would later make this insight about the interrelation of social benefit and logical extension of precedent one of the major themes of his *Nature of the Judicial Process*.

John Chipman Gray went at the problem of judge-made law from a different aspect. Founder of the Boston law firm Ropes & Gray, which still bears his name, he combined a career in practice with teaching at the Harvard Law School from 1863 to 1913. He was a master of feudal property law and the author of two of the leading property treatises of the day.[9] His interest in comparative law and in jurisprudence, the philosophy of the law, led him to deliver a series of lectures that he published in 1909 as *The Nature and Sources of the Law*. But he was not a system-builder. His jurisprudence was practical, and that aspect was the basis of his influence on Cardozo.

Gray anticipated Cardozo and the "legal realists" in more than one respect. He shared with them not only an awareness of the role of policy-making in judges' decisions but also a strong appreciation of the importance of "facts" for lawyers and the law. Gray disagreed with the notion that the law found by judges already existed in the common consciousness of the people, and he argued strongly that courts are in the business of making law. Gray set forth three ways of approaching

legal decision-making: the historical; the systematic, analytic, or dogmatic; and what he called deontological, or ethical, law as it ought to
be. Gray examined five sources from which courts draw the rules that
make up the law: statutes of the legislature (the clearest source); judicial
precedents; opinions of experts; customs; and principles of morality
(including public policy).[10] He argued that judges should follow their
own notions of right and wrong when they found no statute, no judicial
precedent, no consensus of judges or of jurists, and no actual practice
of the community against their own notions, even if there was a prevalent, perhaps universal, opinion in the community against them.

The third major influence on Cardozo's legal thought was Roscoe
Pound. Pound, like Cardozo, was born in 1870. He too was the son of
a lawyer and judge, with ancestors who had been in the country since
before the Revolutionary War. Pound's parents, however, came from
Protestant rural stock in upper New York state who moved to Nebraska
in frontier days. Roscoe Pound entered the University of Nebraska at
the age of 14, and like Cardozo pursued a classical course, mastering
Greek and Latin literature. Unlike Cardozo, Pound was much taken with
science, and following graduation from college, he studied botany and
law virtually at the same time. In 1889, he went to Harvard Law School
for a year and then returned to practice law in Nebraska. Pound was
active in Republican politics and served as a member of the Nebraska
Supreme Court Commission, a temporary body appointed to help the
Court clear up its docket.[11]

In 1903, Pound was selected dean of the Nebraska College of Law.
From that position and thereafter from the law faculties at Northwest-
ern, Chicago, and Harvard, Pound attacked the legal structure of the
day, especially the prevalent forms of judicial reasoning, which he labeled
mechanical jurisprudence. Like Holmes, he saw law as having reached
one of those stages where concepts had become too rigid; principles were
no longer examined; everything was reduced to simple deduction from
them; and law had become simply a body of rules. Pound argued for "a
jurisprudence of results," focused on how rules actually worked in
application. Unlike so much professional writing that was hostile to
legislation, he saw legislation, when the product of a thorough study of
conditions, as the salvation of the legal system.

Pound argued that American law had become sterile, as reflected in
its failure to respond to modern economic and social developments. This
sterility included the failure of federal common law to develop a uniform

commercial law, the failure of the courts to remedy discrimination by public service companies, and the failure to promote and enforce fiduciary and corporate responsibility. He compared these examples with prior judicial achievements, "Lord Mansfield's development of mercantile law by judicial decision . . . Kent's working out of equity for America from a handful of English decisions, [and] Marshall's work in giving us a living constitution by judicial interpretation."[12] Pound's skepticism about some aspects of the realist movement and his opposition to some of the legislative and administrative activity of the New Deal later tarnished his image as a legal innovator. But among progressive elements in the profession in the 1910s and 1920s, including Cardozo, Pound was an energetic leader in the effort to modernize law so as to deal with the vast social and economic changes in the country and to encourage pragmatism in the law through "sociological jurisprudence."[13] Cardozo would echo Pound's call for a sociological jurisprudence and later wrote Pound that "[t]houghts that seem fairly obvious today have become part of the common stock of ideas for American lawyers and judges as a result, in large measure, of your efforts."[14]

Holmes, Gray, and Pound attacked what they saw as the "formalist" style of reasoning that characterized much of late nineteenth-century judicial decision-making. By that they meant an overreliance on deducing rules from prior precedent with insufficient attention paid to the policy implications of the rules. Holmes and Pound also criticized the results reached by that style of reasoning, especially those that held legislative reform efforts unconstitutional. All three men influenced a large group of legal scholars who advanced their ideas more systematically after World War I in a loose intellectual grouping that became known as Legal Realism.[15] Throughout his career, Cardozo paid tribute to their influence on his own thinking.

In the winter of 1920, when Cardozo was forty-nine and had been on the bench for six years, he was invited by Dean Thomas Swan of the Yale Law School to deliver the Storrs Lectures. Cardozo declined at first, saying he had "no message to deliver." But he was pleased to be asked, and he made an appointment to meet the dean and faculty. After Cardozo repeated his refusal, a faculty member had a suggestion: "'Judge Cardozo, could you not explain to our students the process by which you arrive at the decision of a case, with the sources to which you go for assistance?' With a bird-like movement of the head, and a mere moment of hesitation, he replied: 'I believe I *could* do that.'"[16]

Cardozo worked on the lectures for a year and delivered them on February 15, 16, 17, and 18, 1921.[17] No record exists to indicate whether he showed them to friends in advance or discussed the ideas with anyone as he went along. Professor Arthur Corbin of the Yale Law School faculty described the delivery of the first lecture in a hall that held 250 people:

> Standing on the platform at the lectern, his mobile countenance, his dark eyes, his white hair, and his brilliant smile, all well lighted before us, he read the lecture, winding it up at 6 o'clock. He bowed and sat down. The entire audience rose to their feet, with a burst of applause that would not cease. Cardozo rose and bowed, with a smile at once pleased and deprecatory, and again sat down. Not a man moved from his tracks; and the applause increased. In a sort of confusion Cardozo saw that he must be the first to move. He came down the steps and left, with the faculty, through a side door, with the applause still in his ears.

The hall was so jammed at the next lecture that it had to be moved to another room twice as large, and Cardozo delivered the final three lectures to capacity crowds. He captivated his audience, including Professor Corbin, who described the powerful effect of both the substance and the style of Cardozo's words. "Never again have I had a like experience," Corbin wrote. "Both what he had said and his manner of saying it had held us spell-bound on four successive days."[18]

Corbin and other faculty members pressed Cardozo to let them have the manuscript for publication by the Yale University Press. He said that he did not "dare to have it published," adding that "[i]f it were published, I would be impeached."[19] But he quickly yielded, and the lectures, published as *The Nature of the Judicial Process,* helped make Cardozo well known to lawyers throughout the country and to generations of lawyers and scholars who have followed. The book's vitality has endured; its sales between 1960 and 1994 totalled 156,637 copies, far in excess of the 24,805 copies sold between 1921 and 1960.[20]

Just as Cardozo is often paired with Holmes among famous American judges, so too *The Nature of the Judicial Process* is often paired with *The Common Law* among famous American law books. It was, however, a different sort of book. *The Common Law* was a historical and comparative study of major fields of private law. Cardozo's work sought to describe how a judge decides cases. The lectures quickly became famous, in part because they addressed a growing interest in the subject of judging. In this area, Cardozo was first: no other judge had undertaken such an endeavor.

––––––––

Cardozo's aim in the lectures was to give a practical answer to the question, "What is it that I do when I decide a case?"[21] Cardozo saw the judge's task as twofold. "[H]e must first extract from the precedents the underlying principle [of law] . . . he must then determine the path or direction along which the principle is to move and develop, if it is not to wither and die."[22] The idea was that the judge needed to understand the reason why particular prior cases were decided as they were and then to decide whether the principles that governed earlier situations should still apply.

Cardozo presented the first task as the one that was then more consciously addressed by judges and jurists, although the second task most interested those who cared about judging and law. In most cases, in his view, a judge was not often faced with the second task, for it was apparent how the governing rules applied to the current case. He explained, in a much-quoted statement, that "of the cases that come before the court in which I sit, a majority, I think, could not, with semblance of reason, be decided in any way but one."[23] That was an eminently accurate statement, at least for his day. Cardozo heard a great many cases that involved no real dispute about the governing principles of law. They turned on the judges' perception of the facts or their interpretation of a document. Others were cases in which the jurisdiction of the court was quite limited and the court was not at liberty to reverse the lower court's judgment unless an egregious error had been made. Still others involved the applicability of a technical legal rule. There remained a percentage of cases, however, "not large indeed, and yet not so small as to be negligible, where a decision one way or the other, will count for the future, will advance or retard, sometimes much, sometimes little, the development of the law. These are the cases where the creative element in the judicial process finds its opportunity and power."[24]

The cases with potential for judicial creativity were a major focus of Cardozo's lectures. But he set those cases in the context of his declared subject—how he decided cases. He began by identifying what he saw as the four methods of decision-making available to judges. "The directive force of a principle may be exerted along the line of logical progression; this I will call the rule of analogy or the method of philosophy; along the line of historical development; this I will call the method of evolution; along the line of the customs of the community; this I will call the method of tradition; along the lines of justice, morals and social welfare, the *mores* of the day; and this I will call the method of sociology."[25]

The lectures elaborated each method of decision-making. Cardozo started first with logic, deciding by analogy from principles already established, not because it was most important, but "because it has, I think, a certain presumption in its favor."[26] The presumption was based on the idea that like cases should be decided alike. But logic should not be pushed too far. Cardozo described and rejected a type of logical reasoning that in its most stylized form is sometimes labeled, pejoratively, "formalism."[27] "The common law does not work from pre-established truths of universal and inflexible validity to conclusions derived from them deductively." Nevertheless, Cardozo gave logic a substantial place in decision-making. "Given a mass of particulars . . . the principle that unifies and rationalizes them has a tendency, and a legitimate one, to project and extend itself to new cases within the limits of its capacity to unify and rationalize."[28] Recalling Holmes's aphorism that "The life of the law has not been logic: it has been experience," Cardozo pointed out that "Holmes did not tell us that logic is to be ignored when experience is silent."[29] Cardozo argued that logic should remain the default method for decision-making.

Cardozo saw logic as a key to the very idea of law. Absent another relevant test, "the method of philosophy must remain the organon [i.e., the instrument] of the courts if chance and favor are to be excluded, and the affairs of men are to be governed with the serene and impartial uniformity which is of the essence of the idea of law."[30] Only a strong argument based on history, tradition, or justice should overcome the presumption in favor of logic as the governing method of decision-making. In defending the method of logic, Cardozo also clarified his goal. Judges needed to use disciplined methods in order to avoid tainting justice with "chance and favor" and in order to achieve a "serene and impartial uniformity." Thus, at the outset, before relating legal doctrine to political, social, and economic experience, Cardozo postulated the importance of the rule of law—which to him meant the neutrality and uniformity of its judicial process—for a society in which law was a vital force.

Having postulated the "firstness" of logic, Cardozo ended the first lecture on a tantalizing note. Sometimes, he conceded, logical elaboration of principle goes just so far, or having gone a certain way, competing logical principles appear and a choice must be made. At such a time, "[h]istory or custom or social utility or some compelling sentiment of justice or sometimes perhaps a semi-intuitive apprehension of the pervading spirit of our law, must come to the rescue of the anxious judge, and tell him where to go."[31] Thus, the first lecture left Cardozo's listeners with a general statement of the sources of judicial decision-making. It also left them, no doubt, with the hope that subsequent lectures would explain those sources with greater specificity. This was a rare opportunity for students who had never heard a judge explain his work, and the reputation that Cardozo had brought to the occasion was enhanced by the oratorical persuasiveness of his delivery.

Lecture Two was entitled "The Methods of History, Tradition and Sociology." It began with a comparison of the method of logic and the method of history, the former seen as an effort of pure reason, the latter involving an investigation of origins. Using the law of real property, especially the land tenure system as an example, he demonstrated that sometimes it was impossible to understand a legal principle without knowledge of history. In general, however, the method of history prevailed over other methods only in those cases that turned on "concepts of the law [that] have been in a peculiar sense historical growths."[32] History was a useful source, but not a dominant factor.

Cardozo then turned briefly to custom or tradition as an aid in fixing the direction of a principle, but he did not find custom, especially in modern times, to be a very useful source of assistance. To be sure, the customary degree of care exercised in certain circumstances by persons of ordinary prudence may be consulted in order to elaborate the meaning of due care. So too in the world of commerce new practices that develop from business necessity are recognized as customs in the law. But in general, "We look to custom, not so much for the creation of new rules, but for the tests and standards that are to determine how established rules shall be applied."[33] At this point Cardozo referred quite casually and briefly to the important topic of the relation of judges to legislators. "When custom seeks to do more than [supply the tests and standards for established rules], there is a growing tendency in the law to leave development to legislation."[34] In other words, customs that supported well-established rules were useful reference points for judges, but otherwise customs could not be treated as having the force of law unless they had been embodied in legislation.

Having discussed logic, history, and custom, Cardozo had set the stage for the role of public policy considerations in judicial decision-making. He spent a major portion of his lectures on that topic, "the force which in our day and generation is becoming the greatest of them all, the power of social justice which finds its outlet and expression in the method of sociology."[35] Cardozo noted that this method, like the others, had a traditional element. The sense of social justice was often a reflection of custom: "A slight extension of custom identifies it with customary morality, the prevailing standard of right conduct, the *mores* of the time."[36] But he pointed out that unlike the other methods of decision-making, which found the proper direction of the law's growth by extension from its pedigree, the method of sociology focused on normative aspects of the law, derived from contemporary values. This method looked forward, not backward. Cardozo was quite explicit about his aim: "Not the origin, but the goal, is the main thing. There can be no wisdom in the choice of a path unless we know where it will lead."[37] The method of sociology made the ultimate test of a rule its value for society. "Logic and history and custom have their place. We will shape the law to conform to them when we may; but only within bounds. The end which the law serves will dominate them all."[38]

Thus, when judges were "called upon to say how far existing rules are to be extended or restricted, they must let the welfare of society fix the path, its direction and its distance."[39] Although Cardozo used the term "social welfare" loosely, at one point he elaborated its meaning:

Social welfare is a broad term. I use it to cover many concepts more or less allied. It may mean what is commonly spoken of as public policy, the good of the collective body. In such cases, its demands are often those of mere expedience or prudence. It may mean on the other hand the social gain that is wrought by adherence to the standards of right conduct, which find expression in the *mores* of the community. In such cases, its demands are those of religion or of ethics or of the social sense of justice, whether formulated in creed or system, or immanent in the common mind.[40]

This was a key point in Cardozo's idea of making law. Sometimes judges made law on a pragmatic basis, but sometimes the situation called for the use of different values, call them religious or moral or simply a sense of justice. However, they were society's values, not the judge's individual values.

Having stated a potentially wide-ranging role for judges in implementing social policy, Cardozo moved quickly to put limits on that possibility. He pointed out that the welfare of society was seldom advanced by abandoning existing rules or directions. "One of the most fundamental social interests," he said, "is that law shall be uniform and impartial."[41] This meant that "adherence to precedent should be the rule and not the exception."[42] Similarly, because society valued certainty, order, and coherence, judges normally should permit laws born of logic, history, or custom to develop along the lines of their birth—but not too far. A judge must never confuse the social value of continuity with "the demon of formalism [that] tempts the intellect with the lure of scientific order."[43] Cardozo clearly understood this issue as one of balancing competing values rather than declaring postulates. When orderly development of the law led to an oppressive result, "[t]he social interest served by symmetry or certainty must then be balanced against the social interest served by equity and fairness or other elements of social welfare. These may enjoin upon the judge the duty of drawing the line at another angle . . . of marking a new point of departure from which others who come after . . . will set out upon their journey."[44] That sort of creativity was part of the tradition of judging.

Cardozo discussed situations in which the method of sociology held primacy over the virtues of logic, coherence, and consistency. Foremost among these was the whole field of constitutional law, especially questions touching on the meaning of liberty and property. Cardozo noted that liberty was once conceived of as something "static and absolute" in the same way that nineteenth-century legal theory, as Roscoe Pound put it, sought to apply "eternal legal conceptions" with pure logic to find "an exact rule for every case."[45] Cardozo set forth approvingly the emerging view, championed by Holmes, that emphasized the changeability of constitutional values and gave great weight to the legislature's vision of the needs of society. Thus, while once property could be regulated only if "affected with a public use," jurists increasingly recognized that "property, like every other social institution, has a social function to fulfill."[46] Cardozo saw these developments as emblematic of the desirable adaptation of the method of sociology to constitutional law. Although the Constitution put limits on legislation, these limits were sufficiently flexible to permit the law to adapt to social change.

Cardozo's discussion of the Constitution led him to the ever-present question of the wisdom of allowing courts to have the power to declare statutes unconstitutional. He supported judicial review in brief, but eloquent, compass. Without worrying about any antidemocratic implications, he supported it as a given part of our form of government, whatever it might be labeled.

> The utility of an external power restraining the legislative judgment is not to be measured by counting the occasions of its exercise. The great ideals of liberty and equality are preserved against the assaults of opportunism, the expediency of the passing hour, the erosion of small encroachments, the scorn and derision of those who have no patience with general principles, by enshrining them in constitutions, and consecrating to the task of their protection a body of defenders. By conscious or subconscious influence, the presence of this restraining power, aloof in the background, but none the less always in reserve, tends to stabilize and rationalize the legislative judgment, to infuse it with the glow of principle, to hold the standard aloft and visible for those who must run the race and keep the faith.[47]

This rhapsodic defense of judicial review included a Statue of Liberty metaphor that would have pleased Cardozo's cousin Emma Lazarus. The judges held aloft the beacon for all those charged with the duty to respect the constitutional rights of the people.

Cardozo's final two lectures discussed the policy-making function of the judge, the sources that informed that role, and the differences between the policy-making roles of the judge and of the legislator. Although Cardozo conceded that judges had no special competence as lawmakers, he considered the legitimacy of judicial lawmaking unproblematic. The power of "interpretation" had to be lodged somewhere, and the "custom of the constitution" put it in the judiciary.[48] "I take judge-made law as one of the existing realities of life."[49] Three years later, in a series of follow-up lectures, Cardozo explained why judges were better at the task than legislators would be:

> If legislation is to take the place of the creative action of the courts, a legislative committee must stand back of us at every session, a sort of

supercourt itself. No guarantee is given us that a choice thus made will be wiser than our own, yet its form will give it a rigidity that will make retreat or compromise impossible. We shall be exchanging a process of trial and error at the hands of judges who make it the business of their lives for a process of trial and error at the hands of a legislative committee who will give it such spare moments as they can find amid multifarious demands.[50]

The argument was essentially practical. Judges had more time than legislators and were much more focused on application of principles to differing combinations of circumstances. They could therefore better adapt the law case by case to the changing circumstances of society. Indeed, he wrote, almost belligerently, "The adaptation of rule or principle to changing combinations of events demands the creative action of the judge. You may praise our work or criticize it. You may leave us with the name we have, or tag us with some other label, arbitrators or assessors. The process is here to stay."[51]

Since the judicial role was a fact of life and not a troubling one for Cardozo, he quickly turned in his 1921 lectures to the question of how judges should exercise it—how judges actually decide cases. Cardozo emphasized and elaborated the importance of respecting "customary morality, the prevailing standard of right conduct, the *mores* of the time."[52] Judges' notions of right and wrong were to be guided by community, not personal, standards. With typical qualification, Cardozo quickly added that judges had the power to raise the level of prevailing conduct by appealing to the more considered judgment of the community—as, for instance, when assessing the conduct demanded of trustees and other fiduciaries. But social mores did not "automatically shape rules which, full grown and ready made, are handed to the judge."[53] The judge had to be conscious of these mores and use them carefully in shaping rules of law for the community. Cardozo espoused the dominance of community standards, both as actually practiced and in their normative or ideal sense, without advertising the problem that these two standards, actual and normative values, might often conflict with one another.

Cardozo believed that there was no one decision making "formula" to follow when the methods of decision pointed in different directions. He quoted the constitutional law critic Thomas Reed Powell, who preached that we must "spread the gospel that there is no gospel that will save us from the pain of choosing at every step."[54] Cardozo's ultimate answer was quite general and abstract: "Which of these forces shall dominate in any case, must depend largely upon the comparative importance or value of the social interests that will be thereby promoted or impaired . . . If you ask how [the judge] is to know when one interest outweighs another, I can only answer that he must get his knowledge just as the legislator gets it, from experience and study and reflection; in brief, from life itself."[55]

In itself, that answer seems almost a useless truism, but Cardozo's general line of argument gave it force. If he could not tell judges how to decide particular cases, he was nevertheless telling them to think carefully about the methods of decision-making, to weigh them against one another within the factual context in each case, and to bring to bear conscientiously their experience, study, and reflection. The lesson was not how to decide but how to do the job.

The notion that life and experience help the judge weigh competing interests was a familiar theme in Cardozo's opinions too. He also believed that the different life experiences of different judges complemented one another and contributed to the collegial conclusions of an appellate court. That was, at least, his experience with his court.

Although Cardozo never explicitly addressed the question whether difficult cases had only one right answer—that became a matter of jurisprudential interest later—he did give an implicit answer. If life and experience helped provide the answer, then an individual judge could figure out a good answer to a difficult question while acknowledging that another judge might reasonably reach a different conclusion. Years later, Brandeis would comment to one of Cardozo's law clerks, "The trouble with your Judge is that he thinks he has to be one hundred percent right. He doesn't realize that it is enough to be fifty-one percent right." Cardozo did not really disagree with Brandeis's conclusion that a judge often was left with some doubts, but his response was typically ironic: "The trouble with that is that when you [think you] are fifty-one percent right, it may [really only] be forty-nine percent."[56] In fact, Cardozo the judge listened carefully to all arguments, but he knew how to make up his mind with confidence when decision-making time came.

Having contrasted nineteenth-century and modern legal thought rather sharply, Cardozo then tempered the contrast by placing both views in the context of an older, ongoing tradition:

There is in truth nothing revolutionary or even novel in this view of the judicial function. It is the way that courts have gone about their business for centuries in the development of the common law. The difference from age to age is not so much in the recognition of the need that law shall conform itself to an end. It is rather in the nature of the end to which there has been need to conform. There have been periods when uniformity, even rigidity, the elimination of the personal element, were felt to be the paramount needs. By a sort of paradox, the end was best served by disregarding it and thinking only of the means. Gradually the need of a more flexible system asserted itself.[57]

Cardozo was right to disclaim novelty in his description of the judicial process. There were times, though, when the creative function was submerged by a more formal approach, and he emphasized that the law was emerging from one of those periods. It was therefore necessary to justify and defend the policy-oriented and moral ends of law.

Cardozo was not satisfied simply to place judicial lawmaking in its rightful place on the scale. He wished to place all the elements in their appropriate places. The need for judicial creativity was one major theme; another was the limits on that creativity. First, there were the limits imposed by the restricted sphere of judicial action. He asserted, paraphrasing Holmes without quoting him, that the judge's power of innovation is "[i]nsignificant . . . when compared with the bulk and pressure of the rules that hedge him on every side." A judge, Cardozo maintained, "legislates only between gaps. He fills the open spaces in the law. How far he may go without traveling beyond the walls of the interstices cannot be staked out for him upon a chart . . . [R]estrictions . . . are established by the traditions of the centuries, by the example of other judges, his predecessors and his colleagues, by the collective judgment of the profession, and by the duty of adherence to the pervading spirit of the law."[58] This was a critical feature in Cardozo's belief in judicial lawmaking and the rule of law.

Second, there were the limits imposed on responsible decision-making in individual cases, for a judge must respect "the bounds set to judicial innovation by precedent and custom."[59] Every judge had the duty, "within the limits of his power of innovation, to maintain a relation between law and morals, between the precepts of jurisprudence and those of reason and good conscience."[60] But a judge had no license to shape the law according to "the [judge's] individual sense of justice. . . . That might result in a benevolent despotism if the judges were benevolent men. It would put an end to the reign of law."[61] This statement explains the significance for Cardozo of "customary morality." By combining morality and custom in a single phrase, Cardozo expressed his dual commitment to social justice and justice according to law.

Respect for social custom did not mean that judges were powerless to improve on what they found. "In one field or another of activity," Cardozo asserted, "practices in opposition to the sentiments and standards of the age may grow up and threaten to intrench themselves if not dislodged . . . In such cases, one of the highest functions of the judge is to establish the true relation between conduct and profession."[62] The judge was to seek accepted norms in "the customary morality of right-minded men and women."[63] Or, as he would elaborate in a later series of lectures, "The law . . . will follow, or strive to follow, the principle and practice of the men and women of the community whom the social mind would rank as intelligent and virtuous."[64]

Cardozo provided an example of this phenomenon. There were "ancient precedents" that lawful conduct that harmed one's neighbor was not made unlawful by a bad motive. Recent decisions had cut back on that principle and taken bad motive into account. Cardozo associated the new law with the growth of democracy, bringing with it a "growing altruism, or if not this, a growing sense of social interdependence." No statute had been required to transform this new outlook into law. It was "left in the air where the pressure was more effective because felt by all alike. At last, the message became law."[65]

The phrase "customary morality of right-minded men and women" was, perhaps, an unhappy choice of words. It left Cardozo open to three charges: that he gave no clear guide to ascertaining customary morality, that he was being elitist, and that the morality of "right-minded men and women" was just a euphemism for the judge's own values. As to the first charge, the problem of ascertaining the content of customary morality and the identity of "right-minded" people is obvious. Cardozo did not address this issue in these lectures.[66] Nor did he address the tension between the democratic notion of enforcing community values and the aristocratic notion of enforcing the values of "right-minded" people. Aristocratic ideals fit comfortably in a man who took pride in his heritage and in his own talents, and Cardozo was an elitist. But as a judge he saw the legislature as the expounder of community values and gave great deference to its choices if it had spoken. If it had not, judges had to do their best.

As for the charge of subjectivism, Cardozo saw respect for customary morality as a way to avoid subjective decision-making. A judge "would err if he were to impose upon the community as a rule of life his own idiosyncrasies of conduct or belief."[67] But he viewed the debate about an objective or subjective standard for the norms of right conduct and social welfare as unimportant. "At times, the controversy has seemed to turn upon the use of words and little more."[68] Later, he debated the issue with Learned Hand. Commenting on a talk given by Hand that contained a confession of the subjectivity of judging, Cardozo retorted, "Why can't you say that when I am doing my will, I am interpreting the common will, a process ever so much more respectable? I have always professed to be doing this, and now you tell me it was a sham, and maybe it was, though somehow or other there are times when I do feel that I am expressing thoughts and convictions not found in the books and yet not totally my own."[69] Cardozo's inability to pin down this sensibility precisely did not prevent him from acting on it. As a judge he was more concerned with deciding a case than with justifying his method philosophically. He intended his lectures to explain his work in a way that would be useful to others, not to establish absolute proof of a theory.

Cardozo's recognition of the mixture of objectivity and subjectivity in judicial decision-making included recognition that human factors played a role. "[I]nherited instincts, traditional beliefs, acquired convictions" combine to produce "an outlook on life, a conception of social needs . . . which, when reasons are nicely balanced, must determine where choice shall fall."[70] Cardozo observed that discussions of this theme, if they occurred at all, typically lacked candor. He quoted, as close to the truth, the words of Theodore Roosevelt: "The decisions of the courts on economic and social questions depend upon their economic and social philosophy." Responding to the critics who said that "The business of the judge . . . was to discover objective truth," Cardozo stated, "My duty as judge may be to objectify in law, not my own aspirations and convictions and philosophies, but the aspirations and convictions and philosophies of the men and women of my time."[71] Cardozo recognized and accepted the inescapable relation between the truth without us and the truth within. The spirit of the age, as it is revealed to each of us, is too often only the spirit of the group in which the accidents of birth or education or occupation or fellowship have given us a place. No effort or revolution of the mind will overthrow utterly and at all times the empire of these subconscious loyalties . . . The training of the judge, if coupled with what is styled the judicial temperament, will help in some degree to emancipate him from the suggestive power of individual dislikes and prepossessions. It will help to broaden the group to which his subconscious loyalties are due. Never will these loyalties be utterly extinguished while human nature is what it is.[72]

Subjectivism thrust out the front door, returned through the back door. But Cardozo presented a chastened subjectivism, made more manageable by being acknowledged and observed. He warned judges to temper it as much as possible by searching for values outside their own inclinations.

Subjectivity and objectivity were "more or less" qualities, matters of degree, and the attempt at objectivity was essential for the good judge. Cardozo's insight that group loyalty affects judges' thinking did not lead him to further speculation about the overall composition of the bench. He could not have been so complacent about the diversity of the bench if he had considered the numerous elements of class, gender, race, and nationality that were not represented on the bench at all. He represented the "average value" of his own group in not mentioning, or perhaps not even noticing, their absence. Cardozo limited his discussion to the diversity of temperaments and approaches that he assumed would be on the bench: "The eccentricities of judges balance one another. One judge looks at problems from the point of view of history, another from that of philosophy, another from that of social utility, one is a formalist, another a latitudinarian, one is timorous of change, another dissatisfied with the present; out of the attrition of diverse minds there is beaten something which has a constancy and uniformity and average value greater than its component elements." And there is this final note of hope about the work of these judges: "What is good in it endures. What is erroneous is pretty sure to perish."[73]

Cardozo shared the optimism that characterized the political philosophy of progressives like Theodore Roosevelt, and his attitude was related to what became known later as the consensus view of American history: What unites Americans as a people is more important than what divides them; society's dominant interest groups accepted a broad common framework of social and economic values.[74] Cardozo's optimistic view of law depended on his belief that good judges, with a common purpose, would in the long run achieve consistent, good results. His experience on the Court of Appeals made him hopeful. Many of his realist contemporaries and even more of the subsequent generations of academics and the public in general have been more skeptical about American judges, especially Supreme Court justices.[75]

Vague and general as Cardozo's precepts now seem to be, they were not too vague for Cardozo and for most judges of his generation. The greatest testament to Cardozo's lectures may be that decades of subsequent discussion have not produced anything that is much more helpful, perhaps because the task does not lend itself to greater specificity. If Cardozo's argument lacked the definitive clarity of logical extremes, it was clear enough as a pragmatic and moderate approach to the work of judging. Cardozo's endorsement of the "method of sociology," with its argument for innovation, was a revolt against the doctrinal rigidity of the preceding generation, and it aligned him with at least part of the progressive or "legal realist" agenda. Cardozo's insight was to see the possibility of strengthening judge-made law while respecting the various restrictions on judicial discretion required by "the rule of law."

––––––––––

The applause that followed each of Cardozo's lectures at Yale was echoed in the reviews of the published work. The major reviews by Learned Hand, Judge Charles Hough, and Dean (later Chief Justice of the United States) Harlan Fiske Stone of Columbia Law School praised Cardozo's justification for the lawmaking function of judges. Learned Hand saw Cardozo's public declaration as a "portent" even though he believed that Cardozo's judicial conduct was much the same as that of his predecessors. Hand understood that many did not see or wish to see lawmaking as part of the judicial function, and he noted that there would be "excellent people who cannot help feeling that the voice of this book is in a way the voice of heresy."[76] Hand's comment was echoed by Stone, who stated that those still caught up in Blackstonian thought might find that the book exhibited "radical tendencies."[77] Judge Hough also recognized that Cardozo's arguments were part of a bitter controversy about judicial lawmaking but saw his views as "so gently put that one rather misses the underlying bitterness,—until the cases cited remind one of the war out of doors."[78] Felix Frankfurter later described the book as "a little classic."[79] The reviewers did not comment on Cardozo's insistence that history, precedent, and logical deduction placed important limits on judicial creativity. That was not news in the judicial wars of the day.

Some later reviewers were critical of Cardozo's philosophy, or lack of it. In a major study of Cardozo's "philosophic" thought, Professor Edwin Patterson of Columbia Law School noted that Cardozo was not a philosopher and had not attempted a systematic statement of a philosophy of law.[80] Patterson was nonetheless critical of what he called Cardozo's excessive concern with judges' lawmaking and his consequent neglect of lawmaking by other bodies and with his lack of interest in more theoretical problems of legal philosophy. Many years later, Grant Gilmore commented in a similar vein that Cardozo's lectures had "almost no intellectual content."[81]

The criticism leveled by Patterson and Gilmore was that Cardozo was not the legal philosopher that Holmes had been. The criticism is accurate—and beside the point. Cardozo had a different purpose in mind. Although *The Nature of the Judicial Process* and Cardozo's later lectures occasionally dealt with topics that philosophers of law also addressed, and although he was familiar with American, English, and European jurisprudence and referred often to the leading writers, Cardozo was not interested in setting forth a systematic theory of legal philosophy. He used philosophy to shed light on the art of judging. Judging was his daily job, and he tried to explain how he did it.

Judge Richard Posner in several recent works has characterized Cardozo as the quintessential pragmatic judge and *The Nature of the Judicial Process* as a leading statement of the jurisprudence of pragmatism. Posner defined pragmatism as a philosophy that distrusted "metaphysical entities" such as truth or nature, that insisted that "propositions be tested by their consequences," and that evaluated legal reasoning by its "conformity to social or other human needs" rather than by "objective" criteria. As such, pragmatism earned the description of "progressive" because it embodied a forward-looking, practical approach to resolving conflict, although pragmatism did not necessarily correlate with a "left" or "liberal" political agenda.[82]

Cardozo was indeed a pragmatic judge, although *The Nature of the Judicial Process* was more an example than an exposition of pragmatism. Cardozo's pragmatism supplied a method of approach, not an ideology, for the resolution of problems. But, as we shall see in succeeding chapters, there were practical, moral, and institutional values that influenced his judicial thinking and decisions.

The publication of the book also called forth commentary on Cardozo the judge. The most stirring tribute came from Learned Hand. He observed that the excellent people who were disturbed by Cardozo's views on judicial creativity would be especially upset that the argument came "from a judge who by the common consent of the bench and bar of his state has no equal within its borders; from one who by the gentleness and purity of his character, the acuteness and suppleness of his mind, by his learning, his moderation, and his sympathetic understanding of his time, has won an unrivaled esteem wherever else he is known."[83] Cardozo had earned that tribute after just eight years on the bench.

––––––––

Cardozo gave three other major lectures or series of lectures after delivering *The Nature of the Judicial Process.* Two of them simply expanded upon and clarified points he had made in *The Nature of the Judicial Process.* The third was an unusual event because Cardozo thrust himself into the middle of an intellectual controversy involving legal realism. He delivered this lecture in 1932 when he was under consideration for appointment to the Supreme Court of the United States. It will be discussed in Chapter 23, which relates the story of the appointment.

Cardozo returned to Yale in December 1923 to deliver a series of three lectures that pursued the topic of judicial decision-making.[84] Cardozo called the lectures "The Science and Philosophy of Law" but considered that name too pretentious for the published version, which he titled *The Growth of the Law.*[85] This second set of lectures, which Cardozo considered "a very feeble echo of the first series," added little to Cardozo's views about judicial decision-making.[86] One new topic was the "Restatement" project of the American Law Institute that was just getting under way. Cardozo expressed optimism that the restatements would achieve a formulation of the principles of the common law that would both avoid setting them in concrete and at the same time "bring certainty and order out of the wilderness of precedent."[87]

Four years later, in the fall of 1927, Cardozo made a final effort to spell out his views of law, especially judicial lawmaking, in *The Paradoxes of Legal Science,* which he delivered as the Carpentier Lectures at Columbia.[88] The relative simplicity of *The Nature of the Judicial Process* disappeared as Cardozo sought to put his own views in a more scholarly form. The structure was more elaborate, and his style and his references to the writings of others were more complex and allusive. The titles that he gave his individual lectures indicated the change:

Lecture I: Introduction—Rest and Motion—Stability and Progress.
Lecture II: The Meaning of Justice—The Science of Values.
Lecture III: The Equilibration of Interests—Cause and Effect—The Individual and Society—Liberty and Government.
Lecture IV: Liberty and Government—Conclusion.

The lectures were filled with references and analogies to new ideas in science and to the thought of philosophers and political scientists.

Although *The Paradoxes of Legal Science* was more sophisticated than the earlier lectures, the message remained the same: the importance, difficulty, and subtlety of the judicial job, which was to shape and reshape, as society changed over time, the common law principles that guided the daily lives of ordinary citizens. Cardozo's statement of the problems facing the working judge was more emphatic than before:

We fancy ourselves to be dealing with some ultra-modern controversy, the product of the clash of interests in an industrial society. The problem is laid bare, and at its core are the ancient mysteries crying out for understanding—rest and motion, the one and the many, the self and the not-self, freedom and necessity, reality and appearance, the absolute and the relative. We have the claims of stability to be harmonized with those of progress. We are to reconcile liberty with equality, and both of them with order. The property rights of the individual we are to respect, yet we are not to press them to the point at which they threaten the welfare or the security of the many. We must preserve to justice its universal quality, and yet leave to it the capacity to be individual and particular. The precedent or the statute, though harsh, is to be obeyed, yet obeyed also, at the sacrifice not seldom of the written word, are to be the meliorating precepts of equity and conscience. Events are to be traced to causes, yet since causes are infinite in number, there must be a process of selection by which the cause to be assigned as operative will vary with the end in view.[89]

Even though Cardozo tried too hard to intellectualize the subject by employing the abstract rhetoric of other disciplines ("rest and motion," "the self and the not-self"), his perception of the clash of interests that underlay judicial doctrine was wholly modern. Indeed, in a few short phrases he identified most of the problems of modern American law. The notable omission was his failure to mention the overriding problem of racial discrimination in the category of equality. But Cardozo's phrasing of the judge's problem indicates the accommodationist nature of his approach—these competing goals were somehow to be harmonized in the judge's work. He quoted René Demogue's remark that the "goal of juridical effort is not logical synthesis, but compromise."[90] That was the view of a working judge rather than a philosopher.

Cardozo also addressed the problem of reconciling the interests of the individual and the group. His examples were recent constitutional law decisions of the United States Supreme Court. Cardozo had much more sympathy with the Court's decisions striking down statutes that encroached upon First Amendment values than with those striking down economic legislation, relegating the latter to "a plane less exalted than these decisions that deal with the liberty of the spirit."[91] Here, without much discussion, was an early formulation, later given voice by Justice Harlan Stone, of the notion of a double standard in applying the Due Process Clauses—much less deference to governmental action when it touched on personal instead of economic liberty.[92]

Cardozo drew a generalization from three personal liberty cases—two striking down laws forbidding the teaching of foreign languages in private schools and colleges and one invalidating a law that required attendance at public school until the eighth grade—that the Supreme Court itself would not declare for another forty-five years.[93] "Restraints such as these [laws]," he said, "are encroachments upon the free development of personality in a society that is organized on the basis of the family."[94] The Supreme Court enunciated a similar principle in justifying the series of cases, culminating in the *Abortion Cases,* that protected a variety of intimate associations.[95]

The final lecture in *The Paradoxes of Legal Science* dealt with the subject of liberty and government. There was, however, no concluding synthesis, only disappointing generality. Cardozo did reflect a strong personal value in declaring that "At the root of all liberty is the liberty to know."[96] Also, he dealt briefly with the supposed conflict between equality and liberty by agreeing with those who contended that the former was the "necessary condition" of the latter.[97] He also set forth at some length a modern doctrine of "natural" rights as evolutionary, the product of the custom and expectations of a given time. But he then concluded by reiterating his accommodationist stance, noting that restraints on change always exist and that compromise between the old and the new, the individual and the group, was the usual outcome.

In his several series of lectures, Cardozo tried to describe and defend what he did as a judge. His lectures were unique, the first attempt by an American judge to pull back the curtain to explain what judges did. The lectures engrossed Cardozo's audiences, and the published texts, eminently readable, were widely read and respected. Intending neither an abstract analysis of philosophic concepts nor a mechanical formula for resolving all cases, he succeeded in what he did intend: a valuable explanation of what judging was all about.

13

Equity, Individual Justice, and the Punctilio of Honor

Cardozo's opinions demonstrated his understanding that deciding cases was a complex business. The jurisdiction of the Court of Appeals limited it primarily to reviewing questions of law and not of facts, although Cardozo's opinions demonstrate that his vision of the events as revealed in the trial record sometimes influenced the way he developed and applied legal rules. There was a pattern to the way Cardozo resolved questions of justice in difficult cases. If he was convinced that justice demanded a change in a rule, he was likely to do so wholesale, to reformulate doctrines that applied to whole classes of cases. Sometimes his reformulation limited the new doctrine to quite specific fact situations, leaving to the future whether that doctrine would apply to somewhat different situations. But that was as far as Cardozo would go. He would not manipulate doctrines, for example the foreseeability doctrine in negligence law, in order to reach a fair result in a particular case. He thought that the harsh application of a generally fair rule was the price that we paid for a system of law.

There was one area of law, however, where Cardozo did work to achieve individualized justice, and it was the area where law traditionally demanded such consideration. Equity is an ancient branch of law that developed in England to provide remedies when there were none at common law and to mitigate the sometimes severe results of following common law rules precisely. In time, various fields of law (domestic relations, estates and trusts where the fiduciary concept predominates, insanity, insolvency) and various types of proceedings (actions for injunctions, accountings, and specific performance of agreements) came to be the exclusive province of equity courts. These featured the discretionary power of the equity judge, operating with the guidance of many abstract and flexible principles, instead of the rules of the common law courts administered by judge and jury. Many equitable principles were captured in maxims stating general notions of fairness: he who seeks equity must do equity; equality is equity; and equity will not suffer a wrong without a remedy. In the early nineteenth century, Chancellor James Kent was instrumental in incorporating and adapting the principles of equity as a vital feature of New York law. Although the law and equity courts were merged in New York in the middle of the nineteenth century, equitable doctrines survived.[1] Cardozo's opinions drew heavily on equitable principles in the traditional areas in which they operated.

Cardozo often addressed those principles when a party requested a specific equitable remedy. The following pair of closely related cases illustrates the considerations that influenced Cardozo's judgment in exercising his discretion in an equity case. The first was Valz v. Sheepshead Bay Bungalow Corporation, a mortgage foreclosure case decided in 1928.[2] Sheepshead Bay, the mortgagee, had obtained a court order allowing it to serve its summons and complaint on nonresident defendants by publication in two named newspapers as well as by mailing copies of the summons and complaints to the nonresidents. By inadvertence, publication was not made in one of the two named newspapers but rather in a different newspaper with a slightly larger circulation. The nonresident defendants received the mailed notice of the suit and chose not to attend the foreclosure sale. After the foreclosure, the property was subdivided, improvements were made, and the value of the land increased enormously. Eight years after the sale, Sheepshead Bay obtained an order amending the court's original order and substituting the name of the newspaper in which publication was actually made. The nonresidents then brought an action to redeem their property, claiming that the failure to comply with the original court order deprived them of legal notice, that the defect left the court without jurisdiction of the suit and hence without power to enter the order of foreclosure, and that they therefore had been deprived of their property without due process. The lower courts held that the failure was a correctable irregularity and ruled for Sheepshead Bay.

The Court of Appeals split 4–3 in upholding the validity of the original foreclosure sale. Judge Lehman wrote a long majority opinion that followed a typical Cardozo line. Lehman demonstrated that the statutory purpose of notice had been fulfilled and that the statutory requirements for jurisdiction had substantially been met. Since the error was inadvertent, the defendants received actual notice, and publication occurred in a newspaper that might lawfully have been selected originally, the error did not deprive the court of jurisdiction, and it therefore had discretion to cure the defect. The opinion followed a classic equity mode.

Cardozo, with Pound and Kellogg, dissented. They wrote no opinion but noted their position that "the defect in service of summons was jurisdictional," and hence the court had no power to entertain the original suit.[3] This was a formal view that would have had the harsh consequence of upsetting a foreclosure that was eight years old.[4] Whether Cardozo's view was inspired by his early immersion in the technicalities of jurisdiction in his book on the Court of Appeals, or whether he thought the principles of jurisdiction required more stringent application because of their constitutional basis, or whether he had some other reason, Cardozo was not willing to be flexible where jurisdiction was concerned. Jurisdictional requirements were exacting.

Cardozo took a different view in the second case, *Graf v. Hope Building Corporation,* two years later.[5] Hope Corporation had given Mr. Graf a mortgage on its property in which it was required to make quarterly payments of interest. Hope's bookkeeper discovered that by mistake, she had sent a check for a quarterly interest payment that was some $400 too little. She notified Graf that the error would be corrected when Hope's president, the only authorized check signer, returned from Europe. On his return, she neglected to tell him of the mistake. Seventeen days later, one day after the grace period expired, Graf brought suit to foreclose the mortgage, a traditional equitable remedy when a mortgagor fails to make scheduled payments. Hope tendered the overdue amount immediately, but Graf rejected the payment because it was late. Graf prevailed in both the trial court and the Appellate Division, and Hope appealed to the Court of Appeals.

That court, in a 4–3 decision, affirmed the judgment of foreclosure. Judge O'Brien for the majority concluded that Graf was not acting unconscionably and that a court applying equitable principles could not compel generosity. "We feel that the interests of certainty and security in real estate transactions forbid us, in the absence of fraud, bad faith or unconscionable conduct, to recede from the doctrine that is so deeply imbedded in equity."[6]

Cardozo, writing for himself, Lehman, and Kellogg, began his dissent by noting that equity will not always enforce the covenants of a mortgage, "unmoved by an appeal *ad misericordiam*," that is, to compassion.[7] He listed some instances of nonenforcement and noted the importance of the general rule enforcing covenants that permit acceleration of a debt when a debtor fails to pay an installment when due. But he stated that since equity recognized the power of courts to create an exception, the question was the definition of the hardship that would justify its exercise. Finally, he probed the majority's characterization of Graf's conduct. "It is not unconscionable generally to insist that payment shall be made according to the letter of a contract. It may be unconscionable to insist upon adherence to the letter where the default is limited to a trifling balance, where the failure to pay the balance is the product of mistake, and where the mortgagee indicates by his conduct that he appreciates the mistake and has attempted by silence and inaction to turn it to his own advantage."[8]

Cardozo came quite close to suggesting that Graf had done something bad. In fact, the case was close to the paradigm case for enforcement of the mortgagee's rights, the situation in which the mortgagee simply waited until the grace period for payment expired and then brought suit. The one additional fact was that Graf had received a letter saying that a mistake had been made and would be corrected. Cardozo made it appear that the receipt of the letter plus immediate suit was something special. It was not. Telling Graf about the original mistake would not seem to improve the equity of Hope's situation when there was still plenty of time to correct the mistake, and Hope failed to do so.

Cardozo was unwilling in the end to call the defendant's conduct unconscionable. "There is not a technical estoppel" (that is, there was no conduct on the part of Graf that would justify refusing to enforce the contract as a matter of legal doctrine).[9] The enforcement of the covenant "is seen to approach in hardship the oppression of a penalty."[10] It approached, but did not equal, oppressive conduct. Cardozo would have resolved the case in Hope's favor by assessing the character of the mistake, the conduct of Graf, and the lack of damage to him. Cardozo concluded that his court as a court of equity had discretion to decline to aid Graf to accomplish an unfair result even when his conduct did not reach the level of unconscionability. A court of equity could refuse to enforce technical legal rules in order to "do justice," even if the suit involved real estate where the rules had long been strictest.[11] Cardozo acted in the long tradition associated with the great English chancellors, Ellesmere, Hardwicke, and Eldon, who developed the flexible powers emphasizing individual justice that characterized the courts of equity.[12] *Graf* represented the limit to which Cardozo would go to relieve mortgagors of the consequences of nonpayment.

A different kind of question of power defeated a claim based on justice in Schaefer v. New York City. The city had granted temporary permits to a company to operate bus routes without complying with the statutory conditions. A taxpayer's lawsuit that sought an injunction, an equitable remedy, to restrain the operation of the routes had been successful in the lower courts. A previous decision of the Court of Appeals had denied the power of a city to operate bus routes itself, and Cardozo, reporting on a motion for leave to appeal, thought that the previous case decided this present one against the city.[13]

He did state that in an extraordinary situation—such as "pestilence, invasion, or the like"—an equity court would not forbid the city from allowing buses to operate in the streets even though the act might be unlawful. But this was not such a situation. Here it was simply a situation of inadequate service that had existed for many years, arising apparently from the city's inability to find a responsible bidder, and the legislature had not responded by enlarging the city's power. While noting that there were "public aspects to the case which may lead my associates to a different view,"—people on those routes were going to lose their buses—Cardozo himself was not moved to provide even temporary relief. "I doubt whether we should prolong the agony. The situation will have to be faced sooner or later, and it might as well be now."[14] There were limits to doing justice in an equitable action. One of them was that the court would not help the city evade the law. Cardozo also implied that if the city was forced to obey the law, it was more likely to address the problem directly and to find or create a legal solution.

Cardozo also enforced more mundane technical requirements against the claims of justice. For example, in one case (not an equity case), where Cardozo was clear that the lower court was wrong on the merits, he recommended denial of a motion for leave to appeal because the required papers had not been filed on time.[15] Cardozo believed that it was important to force lawyers to follow the rules of the legal system even at the expense of the vindication of their clients' rights. The court was more generous, however, for it took the case and reversed unanimously.

One more commercial case should be noted. It was not an equity case, but the ability of the defendant to have sought an equitable remedy defeated its defense. The case was Jewel Carmen v. Fox Film Corp., and Cardozo wrote a report to the consultation recommending denial of Fox Film's appeal, although he thought that Carmen, the winning party below, had behaved dishonorably. Cardozo could have made his point in a one-page memorandum. Instead he wrote his report to his fellow judges in the form of a sustained metaphor. Perhaps it was meant as harmless entertainment for the consultation, and it was certainly an indulgence of his own literary fancy: "Plaintiff [Jewel Carmen] is a star of the first magnitude in the heaven of moving pictures. She is, however, a youthful star, whose light began but recently to shine on things terrestrial. While the value of her effulgence was as yet imperfectly understood, she made contracts with the defendants [Fox Film] . . . The star was then a minor. After making these contracts and entering on performance, she decided to do better."

She could "do better" because, as a minor, she had a right to repudiate her contract. Therefore, while still a minor, Ms. Carmen also contracted to perform with the Frank A. Keeney Pictures Corporation. She ratified the Keeney contracts when she came of age four months later and then gave notice of repudiation to Fox Film. Cardozo continued,

> The defendants were greatly incensed at the star whose beams had been thus withdrawn from them, and directed somewhere else. They gave notice to the Keeney Corporation that the star was their peculiar property, that they would sue out an injunction to restrain the display of any pictures to which the star had contributed the glamor of her light, that the new employer, in a word, would go forward at its peril. The Keeney Corporation succumbed. It preferred to bask in the sunshine of the defendants' favor, for the defendants are powers in the moving picture world, rather than retain the doubtful satisfaction of exploiting a new star among the myriads that a managerial telescope can readily discover.

When Fox Film promised to indemnify Keeney against any loss from a suit by Carmen, Keeney renounced its contract with her. "The star had lost a job and gained a lawsuit."[16] She sued Fox Film in federal court, seeking the equitable remedy of an injunction restraining Fox from enforcing its contract with her.[17] She eventually lost because she could not meet the traditional requirement that a plaintiff in equity must show that she "had clean hands." The federal court concluded that her repudiation of the contract left her with "unclean hands."

Carmen then sued Fox Film in a New York state court tort action for wrongful disruption of her employment relation with Keeney. Fox Film claimed that California law applied and that under that law Carmen had not been a minor when she signed with Fox. Its pressure on Keeney was therefore in lawful protection of its own prior contract. Carmen prevailed in the lower courts, and Fox sought leave to appeal to the Court of Appeals. Cardozo first upheld the trial court's conclusion that New York law applied. He then concluded that Fox could not rely on its honest belief as a defense to the tort action. It had followed the wrong path of seeking recourse by coercing Keeney, thus taking the law into its own hands. It should have gone to court to seek the equitable remedy of an injunction against Carmen to restrain her from performing for Keeney. In effect, Fox tried to issue its own injunction by inducing Keeney to cancel its contract. If Fox had sought equitable relief, it would have lost because Carmen was a minor when she signed the contract, but it would not have left itself open to a tort suit. Cardozo did not let his disapproval of Carmen's manipulative conduct interfere with his recognition of her legal right to repudiate her contract and to recover damages for Fox's interference with that right: "I have little sympathy with the plaintiff's claim. She repudiated contracts intelligently and deliberately made upon the plea that she had made them a few months before majority. If, however, the law gives an infant [a minor] a privilege to disaffirm such a contract . . . I am unable to see how the exercise of the privilege can be deemed a legal wrong." Perhaps Cardozo's satire was his way of giving vent privately to his belief that Carmen had acted dishonorably. The consultation agreed with his recommendation and did not allow an appeal.

This group of cases indicates that Cardozo was willing to exercise equitable discretion on occasion to "do justice" but that he did so in a carefully controlled fashion, examining all the consequences that might ensue. He did not believe that a court of equity enjoyed a license to do "Robin Hood" justice.

————

Cardozo also addressed problems of individual justice in several marital relations cases featuring a personal and social value that was important to Cardozo—honor. Mirizio v. Mirizio, written in 1928, was one such case.[18] Fannie and Cosmo Mirizio, both Catholics, had married in a civil ceremony on the understanding that there would be a religious ceremony thereafter. Cosmo then refused to join in a religious ceremony. The couple never lived together, and Cosmo brought a number of actions for an annulment, which failed. Fannie then sued for separation on the ground of nonsupport. Cosmo defended on the ground that Fannie refused to live with him as his wife. He prevailed all the way up through the Court of Appeals, which upheld his position, 4–2, with Cardozo not sitting on the appeal.[19] Fannie then wrote to Cosmo, offering to live with him "as a wife," but he responded that the passage of five years had extinguished his love. She then filed a second suit for separate maintenance. The trial judge granted her separate maintenance, holding that her refusal to cohabit had been a temporary abandonment pending adjudication of her legal rights. The Appellate Division dismissed her suit, but the Court of Appeals, 5–2, reinstated the judgment of the trial judge.

Cardozo, writing for the majority, considered the relative "fault" of the parties. The first question was whether Fannie had initially refused to live with Cosmo at all without a religious ceremony or whether she was willing to live with him but not to have sexual intercourse until they were married in a religious ceremony. Although Fannie seemed to have taken the former position in her first lawsuit and in the complaint she filed in the second suit, she tried to switch to the latter position, stating that her lawyer had made her testify as she did in the first suit.[20] Cardozo upheld the trial court's decision to hold her to the language in her complaint that she had initially refused to live with him, rejecting her later testimony on ground that an offer to live with Cosmo without having sexual intercourse would not have been a bona fide offer.[21] "For people in their social station, dwelling in one or two rooms, such an offer, if made, would have the aspect of a subterfuge."[22]

The interesting part of the passage is not whether there was a subterfuge, but that Cardozo went out of his way to speculate and pass judgment on what a couple would do "in their social station." It is true that the trial record disclosed that Cosmo earned about $30 a week working as an auto mechanic and that there had been some talk about getting rooms.[23] But Cardozo did not simply refer to the practical problems of two people living at such close quarters. He thought the "social station" of the parties was relevant to their ability to live together without engaging in sexual intercourse. A married couple of lower social station, Cardozo apparently believed, would not be able to stand the sexual temptation and deprivation. Cardozo's gratuitous remark says something about the times, that judges were not sensitive about commenting on and drawing moral inferences from the social status of a party. It also suggests considerable lack of knowledge on Cardozo's part about the sexual proclivities of people of his own social station. It was an elitist attitude and, considering that Cardozo was, as far as we know, a celibate bachelor, one based on ignorance.

The doctrinal importance of *Mirizio* was Cardozo's treatment of the issue whether Fannie's refusal to cohabit constituted a definitive abandonment. Her conduct was to be measured by "tests of right dealing and humanity."[24] Cardozo noted that the close division in the Court of Appeals in the first suit indicated that she had probable cause for following the advice of counsel. She turned out to have been wrong as a matter of law, but once the case was decided, she was ready to follow its command. By breaking his agreement to join in a religious ceremony, Cosmo had treated her with "wanton disregard of his solemn word of honor." Five-and-a-half years was a long time for Cosmo to have to wait for Fannie to join him, but there was never "a day in all these years when he might not have had the plaintiff as his own if he had done what a man of honor and a gentleman should have been prompt and glad to do," namely, to keep his promise and join in a religious ceremony.[25] Fannie was therefore entitled to support.

Although bound by the former judgment of the Court of Appeals that Fannie had committed misconduct by refusing to live with Cosmo, Cardozo narrowed that holding as much as possible. He was clearly moved by the fact that Cosmo had broken an important promise. The religious nature of the promise did not matter much one way or the other; Cardozo emphasized that "a man of honor and a gentleman" would have kept his word. Cardozo's sense of justice was that once Fannie was willing to comply with the court's earlier holding, then it was quite relevant to take Cosmo's conduct into account in assessing whether her conduct should be considered a permanent abandonment. Cardozo's sympathy with Fannie was so strong that although he disbelieved her trial testimony about her initial willingness to live with Cosmo, he did not even question the sincerity of her offer to live with him after five years of court battles and unpleasant personal exchanges. The most important consideration was Cosmo's failure to keep his promise.[26]

Cardozo's old-fashioned views about women coexisted uneasily with his general desire to comprehend modern ideas in politics as well as the law. When women's suffrage came up for a vote in New York, Cardozo listened to the differing views of two of his two closest cousins. Maud Nathan was an ardent supporter of women's suffrage. Her sister, Annie Nathan Meyer, was opposed. Cardozo split the difference. In the words of Maud Nathan, Cardozo "voted in favor of the [New York state suffrage] amendment because he could not conscientiously vote against it. Obviously it was common justice that women should have the vote, but he was sorry we had won as he had sore doubts as to the result of the experiment."[27] That position sounds like Cardozo. His sense of justice and social progress would lead him to vote for women's suffrage, while his traditionalism, including his support for separate seating for men and women in his synagogue and his opposition to interracial romance, suggest that he would fear that undesirable consequences might follow. He had his regrets and doubts, but he did vote for common justice.

Cardozo's traditionalist views about women sometimes emerged in his judicial perceptions. In Proctor v. Proctor, Cardozo reported to the consultation that the trial judge had denied a wife's petition for a judicial separation, finding that the couple's disputes were due largely to the influence of the husband's mother. The trial judge had concluded that it was safe for the wife to live with the husband and that there was insufficient reason for her to leave him. Cardozo recommended denial of the woman's motion for leave to appeal because of the unanimous affirmance by the Appellate Division on a fact issue. He could not resist an additional comment: "I take it that the term 'disputes' was meant by the judge as a euphemistic synonym for a trifling physical encounter, hardly more in his opinion than one of the usual amenities to be expected of a spouse when the influence of a mother-in-law is aggressive and disturbing."[28]

Cardozo put the thought in the trial judge's mind, but the words were his. Cardozo presented the picture of Mr. Proctor's aggressive mother egging him on so that he slapped his wife in the face. Thus Mrs. Proctor's injury—dismissed as a trifling encounter—was not even Mr. Proctor's fault. Another woman, her mother-in-law, was responsible. Cardozo may well have been correct that there were insufficient legal grounds for a judicial separation, but that courtly man and practical judge gave an insensitive rendering of the facts. Perhaps his courtliness, so far removed from domestic conflict, contributed to his attitude. His practice had not involved much contact with domestic relations problems, and Cardozo did not know the realities of domestic abuse. In any event, he did not express the slightest sympathy for Mrs. Proctor's plight.

Proctor was not the only time that Cardozo used stereotypes about women. In re McKenna involved a lawyer's motion for leave to appeal from a decision by the Appellate Division disbarring him for misusing the money of his client, Mrs. Biedler.[29] Cardozo recommended that the court deny the lawyer's motion, but he concluded with a general remark about women: "It is possible that this attorney is the victim of the typical woman client, who leaves everything to her lawyer, and then forgets her own acts or misconceives their significance."[30] We do not know what experiences in practice produced this attitude, but Cardozo brought to the bench a sense that the typical woman client was difficult. Cardozo was most courtly to women who were not involved with the legal system.

Mirizio illustrates Cardozo the equity judge, weighing the various considerations, with a dose of moralism, to find a fair result. Sometimes Cardozo weighed the equities and ended up enforcing the rules strictly. Evangelical Lutheran Church v. Sahlem was one such case.[31] A homeowner had bought land in a subdivision covered by twenty-year restrictive covenants that limited use of the tract to single-family houses. Evangelical Lutheran, wanting to build a church and parish house directly across the street from the homeowner, bought a parcel within the tract after securing consent from all the lot-owners except the defendant. The church drew up building plans, started construction of the parish house, and then stopped and brought suit against the homeowner for a declaratory judgment, asking the court to rule that the restrictive covenants were no longer effective. The trial court and Appellate Division found the restrictive covenants valid but held that the homeowner could obtain only damages, not an injunction that would prevent the church from building on the lot. They reasoned that the damage to the homeowner from building a church would be slight compared with the loss to the church if the use were denied.

The Court of Appeals divided 5–1 in reversing the Appellate Division, Cardozo writing the majority opinion. He recognized that there might be situations in which an injunction might be denied to a homeowner even though the restrictive covenant had been violated. An example would be a situation in which the purpose of the restriction had already been frustrated, such as by changes in the neighborhood or by good faith completion of a building when the covenant was about to expire. "Few formulas are so absolute as not to bend before the blast of extraordinary circumstances."[32] This was not one of those cases. The homeowner had done nothing to diminish his rights, and the church had been perfectly aware of the restriction and of the homeowner's position when it bought the land and began construction. The church was a wrongdoer and suffered no irreparable hardship. The fact that it was a religious corporation gave it no right to nullify a valid covenant. For Cardozo the point was quite the opposite: "Indeed, if in such matters there can be degrees of obligation, one would suppose that a more sensitive adherence to the demands of plighted faith might be expected of [religious corporations] than would be looked for in the world at large."[33] With that language, Cardozo implicitly linked the case with the promise in *Mirizio*. The church should have obeyed the covenant. Honorable behavior counted with Cardozo.

But Cardozo would not let his views about propriety in family life and the rules of law reflecting such propriety stand in the way of common sense. An ancient legal principle was that a child born to a married couple was presumed to be their legitimate offspring. Cardozo refused to give that principle legal effect in In re Findlay.[34] Ann Brooks had fled her husband and children in England with her "paramour," James Findlay. The child whose parentage was at issue (William) was born eleven years later. Ann and James subsequently raised a family, lived together in the United States until their deaths, and always acknowledged William as their child. One of Ann's earlier children, Albert Brooks, came to the United States, lived with his mother and her paramour for a time, and changed his name to John Findlay. When John Findlay died, William obtained letters of administration to manage John's estate. Alfred Brooks, another of the earlier children, sought to have them revoked on the ground that William was not John's brother.

William's claim was that since the original marriage was never dissolved, he was conclusively presumed to be the legitimate son of that marriage and hence the full brother of the decedent. He could therefore be appointed to manage the estate and could claim a share of the estate as an heir. Cardozo noted that the presumption of legitimacy was "one of the strongest and most persuasive known to the law," but that its conclusiveness had been eroded in a number of cases in England and the United States:

A formula so inexorable has yielded with the years to one more natural and supple . . . the courts are generally agreed that countervailing evidence may shatter the presumption though the possibility of access [by the husband to his wife] is not susceptible of exclusion to the point of utter demonstration. Issue will not be bastardized as the outcome of a choice between nicely balanced probabilities . . . They will [also] not be held legitimate by a sacrifice of probabilities in a futile quest for certainty . . . [T]he presumption will not fail unless common sense and reason are outraged by a holding that it abides.[35]

The case allowed Cardozo to write one of his favorite styles of opinion—to review the case law, to find that an ancient doctrine, sometimes stated in absolute form, had already been eroded, and to reformulate the rule to preserve its original function while allowing for exceptions when common sense suggested their need—all stated in the vivid rhetoric of "shattering" presumptions and "outraged" common sense. In the end, Cardozo concluded that William must be found to be illegitimate and hence disqualified under the governing statute to administer the estate. Cardozo was unwilling to use a presumption in a way that offended his common sense, even to achieve the sympathetic result of legitimizing William and his siblings.

Cardozo's sensibilities about family life surfaced again in Coler v. Corn Exchange Bank, upholding a statute whose provisions embodied equitable doctrine. A law empowered the Commissioner of Public Welfare to seize the bank account of a delinquent husband or father who had left a wife or child likely to become public charges and to apply to have the seized property used for the benefit of the wife or child.[36] The commissioner sought to seize a bank account pursuant to the statute, but the bank refused payment. It argued that the statute denied due process under both the state and federal constitutions because it permitted seizure of the account without notice to the absconding father or husband. Cardozo wrote to Felix Frankfurter that "[i]t was easier to have a feeling that the statute was right [that is, constitutional] than to say just why."[37] However, his opinion tried hard to say why. Cardozo traced the statute to an English statute of 1718 and a New York law of

1773 and relied on the fact that they had gone unchallenged all that time. As he put it, with his usual flair, "Not lightly vacated is the verdict of quiescent years."[38] Cardozo rejected the argument that the lack of actual notice to the husband was a fatal defect. The husband had a matrimonial domicile in New York. The statute required proof that the statutory conditions had been met before seizure, and judicial confirmation afterward to reduce the risk of error. In the circumstances of the situation, the absconding husband had received enough notice. The protective purpose of the statute justified the slight risk of error inherent in seizing the husband's bank account without personal service upon him. Cardozo emphasized the point vividly: "The law does not stand upon punctilios if there is a starving wife at home."[39]

———————

One of Cardozo's major contributions to the development of law involved increasing the accountability of fiduciaries, that is, defining the duties attached to special positions or obligations that people have undertaken. An early case dealt with this problem in a family setting. In Sinclair v. Purdy, a brother, who was a court clerk, had transferred his only property to his sister to avoid being importuned to post bail for various defendants.[40] After the death of both the brother and the sister, litigation ensued in which it was important to determine whether the brother had retained an interest in the property or whether the sister owned it all. The trial judge instructed the jury that the brother had divested himself of all title and the Appellate Division affirmed the resulting verdict.

Reversing both lower courts, Cardozo first held that a letter from the sister, which stated that her brother was as much "interested in the houses" as she, had been erroneously excluded as evidence. He also held that even if the letter were insufficient, a jury should have been permitted to decide whether there was sufficient evidence of a confidential relationship between brother and sister with respect to the property to warrant imposition of a trust in favor of the brother.[41] Although he put the point formally in terms of what a jury might have found, Cardozo left no doubt of his views. Noting that the brother had trusted to his sister's "sense of honor," he stated quite plainly, so that there should be no mistake on retrial, that "We think a confidential relation was the procuring cause of the conveyance."[42] Therefore, the brother's interest was preserved. As in *Mirizio,* Cardozo used an equitable proceeding to enforce his notion of generally accepted honorable behavior.

Cardozo's interest in promoting a sense of fiduciary responsibility was applied most notably in business matters, and he constantly raised the issue in his reports to his colleagues. Falk v. Hoffman in 1925 involved a suit by a minority shareholder for an accounting when the dominant shareholders bought the minority's shares without telling them that an opportunity had arisen for all of them to sell the stock of the company at a profit. The majority shareholders then sold at a great profit both their stock and the stock that they had thus acquired. Cardozo suggested that the plaintiff's motion for leave to appeal from an adverse judgment should be granted. "Perhaps there was only a moral rather than a legal duty, but there are cases that suggest the possibility of a different holding." While he was "not at all certain" that the court would interfere with the lower court's judgment, "the amount involved is large, the findings are involved, and the defendants' conduct, even if not condemned by law, was grasping, artful and ungenerous." Therefore the motion should not be denied on the "rather hasty consideration inevitable upon a motion of this kind."[43] The court granted the motion to allow an appeal but ended up affirming the judgment unanimously without writing an opinion.[44]

The following year, in Klaw v. Erlanger, Cardozo once again raised the problem of fiduciary responsibilities in a business setting. Klaw and Erlanger were equal stockholders in a company that held a favorable real estate lease, which was, however, subject to cancellation on sale of the property. When the property was put up for sale, Klaw chose to do nothing, not even to participate in Erlanger's successful negotiations to purchase the property. As part of the sale, the sellers insisted on canceling the lease. Klaw sued Erlanger, claiming not a half interest in the property, which had been offered to him, but instead to be put in the position of half owner of the lease for its unexpired term. In the trial court, Judge Joseph Proskauer issued an order that Klaw could become half owner of Erlanger's purchase but that otherwise, judgment was to be for Erlanger. Judge Proskauer found that Erlanger had fulfilled his fiduciary obligation by giving full notice and by offering Klaw an opportunity to participate. The Appellate Division affirmed without opinion.[45]

Cardozo reported to the Court, recommending that Klaw's motion for leave to appeal be granted. He noted all the factors relied on by Judge

Proskauer in his "excellent" opinion and stated that "[i]f I had to vote at once, I should incline to say that the decision is right, and yet the question is arguable, and important too." Since he viewed the relation between Erlanger and Klaw as trustee and beneficiary, he saw several questions raised by Erlanger's conduct. The first was how imminent the cancellation of the lease had to be before the trustee could sacrifice the trust to save himself. Another was whether it was enough for Erlanger to offer Klaw a half share in the new arrangement if Klaw did not have sufficient funds to contribute. Cardozo concluded that "these questions are so intimately connected with fundamental problems in the law of trusts" that they deserved more careful consideration.[46] The Court granted the motion but again unanimously affirmed the judgment without opinion.[47]

That same year, Cardozo had the opportunity in another case to begin to spell out publicly his views on fiduciary responsibility. In Wendt v. Fischer, he held that a real estate broker who effected a sale of property violated his fiduciary duty to the seller, whose agent he was, when he failed to disclose to the seller his relationship with the buyer. A member of his brokerage firm was the president and manager of the buyer, and that member's fiancée was the beneficial owner of the buyer.[48] Cardozo refused even to consider the fairness of the terms of the transaction because the disclosure was insufficient. Relying on prior authority, he held that the buyer was accountable for the profits realized on resale of the property and that the brokers were liable for their commissions. "Only by this uncompromising rigidity has the rule of undivided loyalty been maintained against disintegrating erosion."[49]

Finally, in 1928, in Meinhard v. Salmon, one of his most famous opinions, Cardozo made a substantial contribution to the law of fiduciary responsibility.[50] Walter Salmon had taken a lease on a hotel for twenty years, with an obligation to convert the property to stores and offices. Morton Meinhard agreed to put up half the funds needed for reconstruction and was to receive 40 percent of the profits for the first five years and half thereafter during the term of the lease. Losses were to be borne equally, but Salmon was to be the sole managing partner. Near the end of the twenty-year period, a new owner of the property, who also owned adjoining land, wanted to tear down the existing buildings in order to construct a larger building. Eventually, to accomplish this project, he negotiated with a company that was controlled by

Salmon. A new building costing $3,000,000 was to be erected. The new rental would range from $350,000 to $475,000, as compared with the original $55,000. Salmon personally guaranteed the covenants of the new lease. Meinhard was not informed of the project until after the new lease had been signed.

Meinhard brought suit against Salmon, claiming that he was deprived of the chance to participate in the new opportunity that arose out of the original venture and asserting his right to a share of the new lease. He prevailed both before a referee and in the Appellate Division. The original judgment limited Meinhard's interest to half the value of the original lease site. The Appellate Division gave judgment for half the new lease, conditioned on corresponding assumption of the obligations under the lease. The Court of Appeals, 4–3, affirmed with a slight modification in the judgment. Salmon was given the option of substituting for a trust attaching to the lease, a trust attaching to the stock of the lessee, with half the stock less one share to be allocated to Meinhard so that Salmon's control would be maintained. Cardozo wrote the majority opinion, Andrews the dissent.

Cardozo's opinion treated the case as presenting a major issue of fiduciary conduct. Salmon and Meinhard were coadventurers, and Salmon had exclusive power of control over the venture. At the very least, that arrangement imposed on Salmon the duty to disclose to Meinhard the project that had been proposed. Joint adventurers, like copartners, owe to one another "the duty of the finest loyalty" while the enterprise continues.[51] Cardozo departed from his usual practice of limiting statements of principle to particular factual settings in order to state a rule that would apply to many fiduciary situations. Fiduciary obligations were to be strictly enforced. "Honor" was featured once more.

Many forms of conduct permissible in a workaday world for those acting at arm's length, are forbidden to those bound by fiduciary ties. A trustee is held to something stricter than the morals of the market place. Not honesty alone, but the punctilio of an honor the most sensitive, is then the standard of behavior. As to this there has developed a tradition that is unbending and inveterate. Uncompromising rigidity has been the attitude of courts of equity when petitioned to undermine the rule of undivided loyalty by the "disintegrating erosion" of particular exceptions . . . Only thus has the level of conduct for fiduciaries been kept at a level higher than that trodden by the crowd. It will not consciously be lowered by any judgment of this court.[52]

There was more to *Meinhard* than the statement of a principle in eloquent, even quaintly eloquent, terms. Although Cardozo relied on his own language from Wendt v. Fischer for the general proposition of a duty of loyalty, the holding of *Meinhard* went far beyond that of *Wendt*. Cardozo broke new ground in finding a fiduciary duty with respect to the proposed new project; moreover, he stated the duty in an unqualified fashion. Neither counsel nor Cardozo could find a case precisely in point, and Cardozo did not contend that the case was controlled by prior decisions. Indeed, he disparaged the effort. "Little profit will come from a dissection of the precedents."[53] He then proceeded to dissect the precedents in order to find their animating principle in the equitable notion that required an "undivided and unselfish" loyalty from a managing coadventurer.[54] It did not matter that a new project, not a renewal of the original lease, was proposed. The second lease was not a new subject matter; it was "an extension and enlargement of the subject matter of the old."[55]

Judge Andrews's dissent demonstrated that another view, grounded more precisely in the facts, was a plausible alternative. Indeed, the generality of Cardozo's formulation and the particularity of Andrews's formulation have been used to illustrate the choice that sometimes exists in framing legal rules.[56] Andrews concluded that the transaction was not an appropriate one for application of strict fiduciary liability. Rather, the inquiry should focus on the conduct of the fiduciary: was there any "actual fraud, dishonesty, unfairness . . . in the transaction"?[57] Focusing on the facts of the transaction, Andrews saw a joint venture as establishing a much more limited business relation than a partnership. The majority opinion would be correct if there had been a partnership between the two men, but there was no general duty of loyalty of the venturers to one another. The duty arose out of the venture, which was for a limited purpose for a limited time. The nub of Andrews's argument was that Salmon brought Meinhard in to help with the financing of a twenty-year lease and that Salmon fully performed his agreement under that original deal. The end of the twenty-year period ended any equitable interest of Meinhard in the lease and any obligation of Salmon to Meinhard.

Reviewing developments in the law of liability for breach of trust nearly fifty years later, Dean Russell Niles saw Meinhard v. Salmon as "the most important modern decision on fiduciary responsibility" because of its "timing and its quotability." Niles concluded that Cardozo had exhibited "prophetic insight." Even though "Salmon had not violated the code that formerly existed in the business community, . . . the commercial ethics of the 19th century would not suffice for the 20th." Indeed, Cardozo had "helped to make the prophecy come true by the ethical force of his argument and by the felicity of his language."[58] Judge Richard Posner also stressed the importance of Cardozo's eloquence to the influence of the opinion. Referring to *Meinhard* as the "most famous" of Cardozo's "moralistic opinions," Posner stated that although the fiduciary's role could have been defined more informatively, no judge has ever come up with "a better formula" for stating the fiduciary's duty. Pointing out how often the case has been cited (653 times as of 1990), Posner noted, quite accurately, that "they are memorable words, and they set a tone. They make the difference between an arm's length relationship and a fiduciary relationship vivid, unforgettable."[59]

Cardozo's language in *Meinhard* did not go unnoticed in its own day. Cardozo commented on the fact, somewhat humorlessly, or perhaps somewhat disingenuously, in a letter to Felix Frankfurter: "Meinhard v. Salmon is one of the cases in which some of my colleagues think that my poetry is better than my law. I think its law is better than its poetry (which indeed I cannot discover)."[60] *Meinhard* was a culmination of Cardozo's efforts to implant a sense of honorable conduct into law. These cases on fiduciaries demonstrate that in dealing with fiduciary duty at least, Cardozo did not apply a consensus or lowest common denominator notion of conduct. He meant what he said about standards in his extrajudicial writing. He applied the standards of "right-minded men and women," that is, people sensitive to the requirements of duty.

Cardozo would take his views of fiduciary obligation with him to the United States Supreme Court, whose caseload included many cases like those that he would leave behind in Albany. In McCandless v. Furlaud, for example, Cardozo wrote for a majority of five that permitted the court-appointed equity receiver of an insolvent corporation to repudiate whatever consent had been given by the corporation to the fraud of its promoters and to compel the promoters to turn over the profits from sale of securities to the public on the basis of overvalued assets. "What is here is a tort growing out of the fraudulent depletion of the assets by men chargeable as trustees if they have failed to act with honor."[61]

Cardozo was a student of equitable doctrine. He understood that equitable principles and equitable remedies had been created to do justice in individual cases and therefore focused heavily on the particular facts in equity matters. He emphasized personal obligation, which meant promise-keeping in family situations and duty and honorable conduct in fiduciary roles. But he did not use equitable powers simply to dispense with legal rules, whether they were rules of jurisdiction, rules regarding legitimacy, or rules allowing minors to repudiate contracts. The reason for the legal rule was also part of the calculus of justice.

14

The Law of Negligence: Duty to Strangers

The focus of Cardozo's interest and the tone of his opinions changed considerably when he moved away from equity, where considerations of fiduciary duty and fairness in individual cases predominated, to the more rule-oriented traditional fields of the common law—torts, contracts, and property. His most famous opinions were in the field of torts, more specifically, negligent injuries to persons and their property. His contribution was a rationalization and some modernization of received doctrine and a judicious application of the rules.

The central task of negligence law that Cardozo and his colleagues and successors have faced is to decide when party A is liable to party B for injuries to B's person or property that are in some sense caused by A's careless action or failure to act. One key question has been whether some kind of "fault" on the part of A is a condition of liability to B. Another way to state the issue is to ask whether A had any legally enforceable "duty" to B, or, on the other hand, whether A had some legal "right" to act the way that A did. Yet another issue has been to resolve the nature of the "causation" between A's actions and B's injuries that must exist to impose liability on A.

With respect to causation, there are easy cases in which most people will agree that the decision is clear. B is in a pedestrian crosswalk with the lawful right of way and is knocked down by A's car because A was speeding and did not stop the car in time. We have no trouble in agreeing that A has caused B's injury. The problem, however, is that almost everything that occurs has multiple causes. For example, if B was a police officer who had been ordered by police chief C to stand in that spot although C knew that in the past, many police officers had been injured there by speeding cars, did C also cause the accident? How about the car builder D, who built the car that would go that fast or that could not stop more quickly? Thus, one of the problems for courts is to define the kind of causation—courts use the term *proximate cause*—that results in liability, or at least in liability unless there is some defense that A, C, or D could assert on the basis of the activity or nonactivity of B. For example, what if B had decided not to move even though he saw the car approaching?

The issues of duty, right, and fault have their complexities as well. B becomes ill because A's nearby food-processing plant emits strong, foul odors. Everyone may agree that the relationship between the smell and B's illness is proven. The argument with respect to liability raises the question of social policy whether or not A ought to have a right to use this particular piece of property as it does even if the use makes B ill and even if A is as careful as modern technology allows in suppressing the smell. The issue may also be put in terms of B's right to be free of the smell. Or the issue may be put in terms of A's duty to act in such a way as not to cause illness to B. Courts and commentators have not always been consistent in choosing and identifying the approach that they use.

These questions may be approached by looking at the facts and circumstances surrounding the parties involved in a particular accident. Attention will then focus on the culpability of the individual actors. Or the issues may be approached in more global fashion, by asking whether some types of parties are better able to bear the costs of inevitable accidents (for example, businesses that can pay the damages and raise the prices of goods or services, thus spreading the costs), or are better able to insure against the risks of accidental injury, or are better placed to reduce injuries by prudent conduct.

Another issue is whether fault should be a requisite of liability at all. We also must ask what we mean when we use the word *fault*. Fault could have the moral connotation of subjective failure to behave in a responsible fashion, as in the deliberate decision not to give a window-washer a safety belt even though one is aware that the job is risky. Fault could also mean failure to live up to an objective standard of responsible, careful conduct (the usual definition today of negligence), as in the decision to drive at the speed limit on an icy road. Or fault could be defined as including even the most careful conduct so long as the operator knows (or ought to know) that the conduct inevitably will (or is likely to) lead to some injuries. For example, sawmill operators know that even though they take every known safety precaution, there will be accidents at the sawmill. If liability is imposed in this situation, modern tort doctrine calls it strict liability, as opposed to fault liability, because the conduct of the operator is not understood to be careless. And even within the realm of strict liability, one can divide up responsibility for accidents on the basis of whether they were foreseeable or not.

In the course of his eighteen years on the Court of Appeals, Cardozo addressed all these issues. Tort law had been completely unsystematized at the beginning of the nineteenth century. The contribution of nineteenth-century law was the creation of an independent law of torts, freed from common law procedural constraints and dominated by the negligence principle. Cardozo's opinions drew very heavily on those developments. A landmark New York case establishing a general requirement of negligence or fault for tort liability was Judge Robert Earl's opinion in 1873 in Losee v. Buchanan.[1] Earl rejected the claim that the superintendents of a company whose boiler exploded and went through the plaintiff's buildings were liable without proof of negligence. He held in lengthy and much quoted language that the needs of a developing industrial civilization demanded a rule based on fault. Encouraging the growth of new industries by protecting them from liability when they were not at fault was an important, but not an exclusive, theme in the second half of the century.

Although Holmes and many later commentators have characterized this period of American legal thought as dominated by "formalist" thinking, *Losee* was not alone in discussing the policy bases for particular rules in the second half of the nineteenth century. The problem for the commentators was often the content of the policies enunciated rather than the form of reasoning employed. The doctrine was clear: the negligence principle meant that liability usually arose only if a person failed to behave according to an objective standard of reasonable, careful conduct.

With the growth of the industrial economy came an increasing number of accidents and a rapid development of negligence doctrine.[2] The themes of the story are the combat between policies protecting industrial development and principles looking to recompense those injured by that development; the efforts, partly successful, to systematize the principles of tort law, and especially of negligence law; the development of the legal doctrines, which we shall examine shortly, of proximate causation, contributory negligence, assumption of risk, and the fellow servant rule; and, finally, an interaction between emerging doctrine and public policies that produced continuing change in the law.[3] By the opening of the twentieth century, the new conceptual structure of liability based almost entirely on fault was coming under attack from the progressive movement, which responded to the problems caused by industrialization. There was substantial public interest about the principles of negligence law because they came to be seen as having important public consequences. For example, dissatisfaction with judge-made negligence law pertaining to workplace injuries led to the passage of workers' compensation laws, which created a wholly new system of compensation that operated largely outside of the courts.

The New York Court of Appeals that Cardozo joined in 1914 was a court under fire from progressive political forces in New York and indeed throughout the country. A major reason was the Court's decision in Ives v. South Buffalo Railway Company, holding New York's workers' compensation law unconstitutional.[4] But the Court's decisions prior to 1914 contained conflicting themes. While the Court had followed general nationwide trends in developing a body of tort law based on fault, the details of the rules that it enunciated were not always favorable to business. In addition, dissatisfaction with the judicially created system had led to legislative tinkering, resulting in modification or elimination of portions of the structure. Although a structure of tort law existed, there was still considerable room for judicial creativity.

Two major issues remained unsettled in 1914. The first issue involved the role of fault in the law of unintentional injuries. Small enclaves of liability without fault had persisted despite the dominance of the fault principle. For example, ultrahazardous activities like blasting, destruction caused by animals, liability of an employer for negligence of an employee toward a stranger, and nuisance law were all areas in which the courts had continued to apply older cases that had found liability without fault or on a rather attenuated notion of fault. At the beginning of the twentieth century, courts had to decide whether these small pockets of no-fault liability should be eliminated to make all tort law consistent with the fault principle or whether the concept of liability without fault should expand into additional areas.[5] Cardozo did not contribute much toward a solution of this particular problem.

The second issue, and by far the more important one during Cardozo's tenure on the court, involved the definition and application of certain concepts used to determine liability within the fault standard. The major concepts that engaged his attention were duty and proximate cause. Although courts had established them as crucial elements in liability, there was a good deal of confusion about their definition and application. The elaboration of these principles was important because they affected the outcomes of many cases, especially those resulting from industrial accidents or product defects. The consequences of those decisions had an impact on all—businesses, workers, and consumers.

As a judge, Cardozo gradually developed a general approach to these issues, which he handled with a distinctive judicial craft. His negligence decisions were marked by three noticeable features. The first feature was the way that he used the methods of decision—logic, history, custom, and public policy—that he outlined in *The Nature of the Judicial Process*. His lectures discussed what a judge should do when the various methods pointed in different directions, but his prescription of turning to the experiences of life was vague. His decisions in negligence cases, however, reveal some specific factors that influenced his decision-making: deference to legislative (and executive) power, reluctance to impose new costs on government, reluctance to impose a new and indeterminate liability on a party, and willingness to impose new liability when the risk of harm to the injured party ought to have been anticipated. It is critical to remember that Cardozo accepted the general framework of nineteenth-century tort law. Whatever he thought about the dominance of the negligence principle, he regarded that issue as having been settled. Thus, in those cases in which we see his policy-oriented "method of sociology" at work, it operated mostly at the edges of doctrine or to aid in reorganizing an aspect of negligence doctrine.

The second feature of Cardozo's approach to negligence law was the balance he struck between creativity and continuity. In his own day, he was known as a progressive judge, one who helped to modernize judicial thought by his advocacy of the creative function and to modernize legal doctrine by his willingness to jettison outmoded doctrine.[6] Recently, however, many academics have emphasized a crafty, manipulative side to Cardozo, describing him as a judge who changed legal doctrine by pretending that his new formulation was an old and accepted rule or by making a narrow exception to a rule and then turning the exception into a new doctrine by dropping the qualifications that he had used to justify the exception.[7] Neither the initial reputation nor the later criticism is entirely accurate.

Cardozo was not such a thoroughgoing progressive as his reputation suggests. He was, and only aimed to be, a modest innovator. He was most willing to modernize law when social conditions had already changed in the same direction or when the doctrinal step to be taken was relatively small and the effect on other parts of government was also relatively small. He had a strong respect for the roles of other agencies of government and was reluctant to make large changes in doctrines that involved issues that were best sifted by other branches of government, especially the legislature. He was more ready to innovate when the legislature had already taken some action to point the way.

A case in which Cardozo concluded that the legislature had pointed the way was the "landmark case" of Altz v. Leiberson in 1922 in which he created a right of action for tenants by inference from a statutory requirement that property be kept in good repair.[8] Housing code legislation modifying the traditional property rules governing the relation between landlords and tenants was a major development in the 1920s. *Altz* involved the scope of New York's Tenement House Law. A tenant was injured in her room by a falling ceiling that the landlord had failed to repair after receiving notice of its defective condition. A verdict for the tenant had been affirmed without opinion by the Appellate Division.[9] Writing for the majority in the Court of Appeals, Cardozo held that the common law rule that a landlord had no duty to repair leased premises had been swept away by the Tenement House Law's requirement that all tenement houses be kept in good repair. Although the statute said nothing about which party bore the obligation and provided criminal rather than civil liability, he swept those objections aside. The command of the statute was directed "plainly" toward the owner, and it was clearly designed to protect "the dwellings of the poor."

> We may be sure that the framers of this statute, when regulating tenement life, had uppermost in thought the care of those who are unable to care for themselves. The legislature must have known that unless repairs in the rooms of the poor were made by the landlord, they would not be made by any one. The duty imposed became commensurate with the need. The right to seek redress is not limited to the city

or its officers. The right extends to all whom there was a purpose to protect.[10]

Following the lead given by the legislature, Cardozo did not hesitate to extend the protection of the statute as far as its purposes logically permitted. Although Cardozo usually did not give weight to the circumstances of the parties—for most purposes legal doctrine was not supposed to regard either wealth or poverty—he did so in this case because that was the purpose of the law. *Altz* was an early example of judicial creation of a private party's right of action for damages resulting from violation of a legislatively imposed duty. With increasing governmental regulation, that precedent would become very important later in the century.

When there was no statute, Cardozo took a different view of the court's power to impose new liabilities. In Cullings v. Goetz, a car owner tried to open a garage door so that he could drive his car into the garage.[11] The door fell on him, and he sued both the owner and the lessee of the garage for negligence because of the unsafe condition of the door. Writing for the court, Cardozo held the car owner's sole remedy was against the tenant who had invited him to use the garage. The owner's agreement to repair the property was insufficient to charge him with tort liability to a third party, since the lessee had complete possession and control over the property. Cardozo noted that a minority of states had taken an opposite view and that the Restatement of Torts had accepted that view. Nonetheless, he followed settled New York law on the ground that the doctrine, "wise or unwise in its origin, has worked itself by common acquiescence into the tissues of our law. It is too deeply imbedded to be superseded or ignored."[12] We shall shortly consider Cardozo's willingness to use the concept of foreseeability of harm to erode the exemption from liability of a remote negligent seller of a defective product to the buyer in MacPherson v. The Buick Company.[13] Even after *MacPherson*, however, he was unwilling to erode a lessor's exemption from liability on the same basis. Perhaps it was because the erosion had already proceeded a long way in the *MacPherson* situation. Perhaps it was because real property was involved in *Cullings*, and courts were least willing to tinker with real property rules. But Cardozo gave his sense of the community's reliance, by which he doubtless meant principally the property owners' reliance, on settled rules the largest weight in resolving the issue.

Although Cardozo was one of those legal thinkers who defended judicial lawmaking, and hence helped establish modern assumptions about American law, he was no radical in this regard. He often discussed the limitations on judicial creativity, and his judicial performance made it clear that this discussion was not a sham. It was a self-conscious attempt to balance essential components of judicial decision-making.

The third consistent feature of Cardozo's negligence opinions was his sense of craft. He had been a first-class lawyer, and he also mastered the different craft of a judge. Rather than arguing for a client's position, a judge decides between two parties' positions, then writes an opinion stating the governing facts and the reasons for reaching a particular conclusion. The judge also writes under the time pressures of clearing a docket and the necessity of satisfying colleagues when writing an opinion that others will join. Although Cardozo occasionally faltered, he was on the whole an excellent judicial craftsman. He was smart; he brought to a controversy the good lawyer's appreciation of the importance of the facts; he was a conscientious student of the law and brought an historical awareness to bear on his judgment; and he had an idea of fairness that comprehended respect for the other branches of government. Moreover, Cardozo's distinctive literary style ensured the longevity of many of his opinions. As he was human, sometimes his sense of the case, or of the institutional necessities, or even of fairness failed. No saint as a person, he was no paragon as a judge. But just as he was a good person despite his human failings, so too, despite occasional professional errors, he was an excellent judge.

The remainder of this chapter and the following two chapters explore Cardozo's judicial approach in the torts cases that were a large share of his court's docket. Most of his opinions, as well as his fame as a torts innovator, involved questions of negligence. The issue of strict liability was less of a problem for the court, and Cardozo's few opinions on the subject were fairly orthodox in approach.

The choice between strict liability and fault as the basis of liability for nonintentional injuries was often discussed in torts literature throughout Cardozo's tenure on the court. *Strict liability* is the term used when defendants are held liable for causing harm even if they have acted carefully. The theory is that accidents are an inevitable part of doing business, and business should figure the cost of compensation into the price of the product, just like any other cost. There was substantial academic debate about expanding the areas in which parties would be held strictly liable, but the controversy was barely reflected in Cardozo's tort opinions. In one case in which the issue was involved, McFarlane v. Niagara Falls, he contributed an important opinion highlighting the importance of the fault principle in nuisance law.[14] A pedestrian sued for injuries caused by a fall when she caught her heel on a projection on a sidewalk that she had seen on other occasions. Claiming that the defective sidewalk constituted a nuisance, she won a verdict after the trial judge refused to charge the jury that any contributory negligence on her part was a defense.

After the Appellate Division affirmed the judgment, Cardozo wrote for a unanimous court that reversed the pedestrian's verdict. He held that although contributory negligence was not a defense in those nuisance suits in which the action of the defendant was taken at its own peril, it was a defense in those cases, like *McFarlane,* where the complaint was that the city had negligently maintained a sidewalk that it had lawfully constructed. Cardozo raised and left open the possibility that contributory negligence might also be relevant in at least some cases of nuisance not based on negligence. On retrial, a jury verdict for the plaintiff was affirmed unanimously by the Appellate Division. Cardozo's report recommended denial of a motion for leave to appeal, reminding his colleagues that "we were doubtful [in the appeal of the original case] whether the chance of a finding of contributory negligence was substantial enough to justify another trial; and we decided as we did chiefly to clarify the law."[15] Cardozo's clarification of nuisance law made it clear that he was not looking for a way of finding the city liable without fault.

Cardozo also considered the problem of liability without fault in the context of issues of vicarious liability. Vicarious liability involves making party A, who is not at fault, liable when the negligence of party B injures party C. The typical situation is the liability of an employer for the torts of an employee. Cardozo rejected attempts to establish or to extend the principle of vicarious liability in many cases. In one case, an employee had been driving his employer's truck and veered off his assigned route to visit his mother. He then gave a ride to a group of boys who were going to a carnival.[16] The driver stopped at a poolroom, returned to the truck, and started back to the employer's garage with the boys still on the truck. A new boy, attracted by the "merrymakers," had climbed onto the truck but fell off and was hurt when the truck started moving. A

general rule of vicarious liability exempted an employer from liability
for the employee's negligence when the employee had "deviated" from
the employer's business. Noting that the driver had broken his connection with the employer's business, Cardozo concluded that the driver
had not resumed his duty to his employer by beginning to return to the
assigned route. In order to find the employer liable, the "dominant
purpose must be proved to be the performance of the master's business."[17] Cardozo could have written an opinion narrowing the employer's exemption to produce liability once the driver had begun to
return to the employer's garage. But he accepted the rule and the "dominant purpose" test and enforced it broadly to exempt the employer from
liability. The breadth of the exemption reflects the breadth of his notion
of not imposing liability for situations beyond the defendant's responsibility.[18]

This refusal to alter rules that exempted employers from liability
appeared also in Cardozo's opinions in Schloendorff v. The Society of
New York Hospital[19] and Hamburger v. Cornell University.[20] Not only
did he accept and extend the immunity of a charitable hospital from
liability for the negligence of physicians and nurses using its facilities,
but he also extended the immunity to cover negligence of the hospital's
teaching staff. Cardozo followed the same course in a municipal liability
case, applying the general rule of nonliability of a municipality for acts
of its employees when acting in a governmental capacity to the case of
a plaintiff injured by a New York City ambulance that was carrying
nurses to a training class. He refused to limit the extent of the exemption,
concluding that the purpose of the transportation pertained to the general purposes of the municipality. He applied this doctrine of immunity
for charities and municipalities firmly, although he disapproved of it.
"The whole doctrine is foolish, antiquated, unjust, and ought to be
abolished. But I suppose we shall have to leave the change to the clumsy
process of legislation."[21] Liability in such circumstances threatened to
impose a significant financial burden on municipalities. Cardozo was
usually unwilling to modify outmoded doctrine when faced with those
consequences. That was a matter for the legislature. He also declined to
hold a parent company liable for the negligence of a subsidiary merely
because there was some control.[22]

Liability without fault was one major area of tort law in which
Cardozo showed absolutely no innovative tendency. He did not attempt
to move doctrine even incrementally in the direction of liability without

fault because he regarded strict liability not as a reform but as an archaic survival. Near the end of his tenure on the Court of Appeals, he referred to liability without fault cases as involving "rare exceptions, survivals for the most part of ancient forms of liability, where conduct is held to be at the peril of the actor."[23] The notion that fault of some sort should be attributable to a defendant before liability was imposed accorded with Cardozo's general sense of the moral element in law. He did not wish to impose liability without irresponsible behavior.

––––––––––

Much of Cardozo's reputation in the field of torts derives from his approach to analyzing the connection that must exist between the careless conduct of A and injury to B in order to establish liability based on negligence. Did A owe B any duty of care in the first place? Did A's carelessness cause, in a legal sense, B's injury? Before examining Cardozo's approach to those complex questions, we should look at his general attitude toward proof of negligent behavior.

As we have already seen, until 1925, the Court of Appeals operated under severe constitutional constraints in reviewing factual conclusions of the Appellate Division.[24] Cardozo nevertheless scrutinized trial records carefully and very often reached factual conclusions favorable to negligence plaintiffs. He wrote opinions for the court in a number of cases disagreeing with decisions of the Appellate Division that had either affirmed judgments for defendants or reversed verdicts for plaintiffs in negligence suits.[25] In these cases, he did not have to decide the ultimate question of the existence of negligence. If he found enough evidence of negligence that the cases should have been left to the jury to decide, his opinion reinstated a verdict for the plaintiff or ordered a new trial. In another group of cases, more than twenty, where injured plaintiffs had won in the lower courts, Cardozo recommended affirmance of jury verdicts or reinstatement of overturned verdicts because he concluded that there had been sufficient evidence to go to the jury.[26] Although he sometimes thought it "a pity that we should be burdened with these trifling controversies," he was willing to carry that burden, and he worked through the records assiduously to find evidence that would preserve jury findings of negligence in favor of injured parties.[27] Just as he resisted imposing liability without a showing of fault, he was inclined to uphold a jury's conclusion that a defendant had been at fault.

Cardozo discussed the public policy considerations embodied in the

formulation of negligence principles in his lectures entitled "The Paradoxes of Legal Science" in 1927:

> The measure of care imputed to that standardized being, the reasonable
> man, is one dependent upon the value of the interests involved . . . The
> law measures the risks that a man may legitimately take by measuring
> the value of the interests furthered by his conduct. I may accumulate
> explosives for the purpose of doing some work of construction that is
> important for mankind when I should be culpably reckless in accumu-
> lating them for pleasure or caprice . . . Inquiries that seem at the first
> glance the most simple and unitary—was this or that conduct negligent
> or the opposite?—turn out in the end to be multiple and complex. Back
> of the answers is a measurement of interests, a balancing of values, an
> appeal to the experience and sentiments and moral and economic
> judgments of the community, the group, the trade. Of course, some of
> these valuations become standardized with the lapse of years, and thus
> instantaneous or, as it were, intuitive. We know at once that it is
> negligence to drive at breakneck pace through a crowded street, with
> children playing in the centre, at least where the motive of the drive is
> the mere pleasure of the race. On the other hand, a judgment even so
> obvious as this yields quickly to the pressure of new facts with new
> social implications. We assign a different value to the movement of the
> fire engine or the ambulance. Constant and inevitable, even when half
> concealed, is the relation between the legality of the act and its value
> to society. We are balancing and compromising and adjusting every
> moment that we judge.[28]

Having accepted the basic doctrines of negligence law, he understood
that fundamental principles of individual duties and responsibilities were
involved. He also understood that at the margins of doctrine he was
supervising line-drawing by juries and engaging in line-drawing of his
own. He was acutely aware that the application of the rules of negligence
law was based on experience and a balancing of social and economic
judgments.

While Cardozo had a strong respect for the work of the judge and
jury of the trial court, he brought from his own legal practice a
confidence in his own ability to grasp particular factual settings, and he
applied that skill to the interpretation of statutes and case records. In
Kettell v. Erie Railroad Company, for example, a negligent railroad
claimed that a statute provided it with an absolute defense to a suit by

an injured passenger.[29] The outcome turned on the proper interpretation of a New Jersey statute disallowing recovery to a passenger injured on the entry platform of a moving car if the railroad had posted a sign forbidding passengers from going onto the platform. The passenger had gone onto the platform of the car after his station had been announced and after the train had slowed as it entered the station. He was injured when he fell from the platform as a result of a sudden jerk just before the train stopped. The trial judge entered judgment for the railroad on the basis of the statute because the railroad had posted a sign prohibiting entry to the car's platform until the train had stopped. The Appellate Division affirmed, 3–2, with lengthy opinions reviewing all the authorities.

The Court of Appeals had determined at consultation, unanimously, to affirm a judgment for the railroad without opinion. Cardozo then circulated a memorandum announcing that he had changed his mind and was going to vote for reversal. Without rehearsing all the precedents, he addressed the key issue—whether the statute and the sign should be read literally to preclude recovery—and concluded that they should not.

> I cannot for a moment bring myself to believe that the legislature meant passengers to keep in their seats until the train was literally at a standstill. Such rules in their practical operation are not enforced that way. The passenger who doesn't "step lively" will be carried beyond his goal. The railroad employees, the brakemen, and the guards, do not keep the doors closed, or warn passengers away. To let a mute sign trap them is to make the statute a medium of oppression and injustice.[30]

Cardozo's memorandum to the consultation did not persuade any of his colleagues, and he merely noted a dissent without writing an opinion. This was a rather personal effort to interpret the law in light of realistic social practice. He was a frequent train traveler in New Jersey, where he and his family had long spent their summers, as well as in New York. Even though he was a strong believer in following legislative directives, he knew by experience that the posted sign did not reflect the way that trains were actually operated, and he therefore interpreted the statute in light of that fact, rather than literally.

Although Cardozo was assiduous in protecting the role of the jury, he did not hesitate to take an issue away from the jury when his reading of a record convinced him that the factual issue should be decided only one way. Caruso v. Steamship Terminal Operating Company was such a case.[31] A longshoreman engaged to remove canned goods from a ship was told by his foreman to move two bags of wool that were in the way. In carrying the bags, the longshoreman held the wool against his skin. Allegedly, anthrax germs entered his body through a cut and caused his death. The trial court dismissed the estate's suit, and the Appellate Division affirmed the judgment for the defendant. When the plaintiff sought leave to appeal to the Court of Appeals, Cardozo recommended that the motion be denied. He saw no evidence of negligence, and there was therefore nothing to submit to the jury. His sense of the situation was that the danger of disease from moving bales of wool was too remote to require a health lecture to longshoremen who knew all about the dangers of anthrax: "I think it would be going too far to say that a foreman, requesting a stevedore to place two bales on the floor, was under a duty to give him a lecture as to wool and germ diseases, or that the employer should have imposed such a duty by the declaration of a rule."[32]

Cardozo also concluded that the realities of social interaction favored the defendant in Greene v. Sibley, Lindsay, and Curr Company.[33] A department store customer, paying for some merchandise, saw a mechanic standing next to her while he was examining a broken cash register. She turned the other way to pick up her change and then turned back, intending to go around the worker. In the meantime, however, the mechanic had dropped to his knees to examine the machine further, and the customer then was injured when she fell over his outstretched legs. The customer won a judgment both at trial and in the Appellate Division. Although Cardozo's report to the consultation stated that "he was uncertain" about his proposed opinion for reversal, it carried a majority.[34]

His opinion recreated the incident, concluding that the mechanic's conduct was normal and the shopper's was careless.

The merest glance would have told her that instead of standing there erect, he was down upon his knees . . . Looking back on the mishap with the wisdom born of the event, we can see that the mechanic would have done better if he had given warning of the change of pose. Extraordinary prevision might have whispered to him at the moment that the warning would be helpful. What the law exacted of him, however, was only the ordinary prevision to be looked for in a busy world. He was doing a common and simple act in the plain sight of those around him.[35]

Cardozo was not sympathetic to the injured customer and was unmoved by the fact that a jury had reached a contrary conclusion. For him, the case did not involve the responsibility of the store to its customers, but rather the responsibility of two people standing next to one another. Cardozo's view of reasonable behavior did not put a responsibility on actors to foresee every possibility of danger in every situation. He placed a measure of responsibility on actors to do some looking out for themselves. His strong personal sense of how people generally—the standardized "reasonable person"—ought to conduct themselves left no ambiguity for the jury to resolve in this case. The customer should simply have looked where she was going. Cardozo's occasional unwillingness to leave a matter to the judgment of a jury may be seen as elitist, but he saw it as part of the business of judging to keep a jury from being swayed by sympathy when the record indicated that there was no factual issue that ought to be submitted to it.

Whether formalism, understood as the tendency to regard principles as fixed and as capable of yielding solutions in new circumstances through logical analysis, had in fact dominated legal thought and judging in the late nineteenth and early twentieth centuries is a matter of some dispute, but formalism did not dominate Cardozo's thinking. His general approach to negligence cases assumed that such inquiries were "multiple and complex" and that the legislature and the jury had roles to play. Within the judicial system, the judges defined the role of the jury, and Cardozo was confident in his ability to read case records and decide when a factual issue was sufficiently clear that it should be decided by the court and not by a jury. He recognized the potential danger of substituting his judgment for that of the jury: "If courts are to resist the present tendency to substitute administrative agencies for the common law tribunals, they must be ready to accredit to the triers of the facts a reasonable equipment of common sense and conscience."[36] But he did overturn jury verdicts in a moderate number of cases. He saw that as his job.

Cardozo's attitude toward negligence defenses followed his tendency to accept the general structure of negligence law. A negligence defense arises when A injures B by negligent action, but A resists liability because of some action or nonaction by B. Cardozo addressed some of the most important defenses—assumption of risk, the fellow-servant rule, and contributory negligence. Although a good deal of dissatisfaction with the fairness of many of these defenses had been expressed by the time that he arrived on the Court of Appeals, he accepted the major precedents supporting each doctrine.

Assumption of risk provided a defense when an injured party was seen as having consented to risks created by another person's conduct.[37] During the second half of the nineteenth century it was applied to a wide variety of situations in which the voluntariness of the consent was extremely questionable. The doctrine often denied recovery to workers who continued working after they had perceived the danger created by the employer's negligence. Even after England, the home of the doctrine, had come to recognize that the conditions of employment generally precluded free choice, American courts continued to apply the concept. Cardozo's friend Professor Francis Bohlen explained the difference by referring to the easier ability of competent American workmen to find other jobs, and the "known tendency of American workmen to take desperate chances touching their safety."[38]

The New York Court of Appeals, for example, applied the rule to an employee who continued to work when she knew that the employer had failed to comply with a statute requiring a cog wheel to be guarded. Even when the legislature passed worker safety legislation on the theory that employees were not in a position to protect themselves, the Court refused to alter the doctrine for a long time because doing so would "deprive [laborers] of their free agency and the right to manage their own affairs."[39] The Court began to ameliorate this harsh application of nineteenth-century doctrine before Cardozo's appointment. By 1912, it had "largely qualified, if not overruled," the idea that employees had assumed the risk if they were aware that an employer had not complied with a safety statute.[40] Outside the workplace, the Court increasingly focused on the facts of individual cases in deciding whether the assumption of risk rule was applicable.[41]

Cardozo, however, stood by the assumption of risk defense. He believed that life was risky and that risks had to be accepted. He wrote two opinions, one in a worker case, Dougherty v. Pratt Institute,[42] and one in a nonworker case, Murphy v. Steeplechase Amusement Company, Inc.,[43] that applied the doctrine in all its rigor. In *Dougherty*, his opinion for a unanimous court reversed a verdict for the estate of a window-washer killed when he fell off the ledge of a school building while washing windows that had no safety hooks. Cardozo concluded that as a matter of law, the window-washer had assumed the risk of falling. Because a statute that required hooks on windows did not apply to schools, the question was whether there was recovery against the Pratt Institute, a private institution, under general principles of negligence law.

Cardozo simply followed the rule that denied recovery when the risk was obvious without any consideration whatsoever of the economic pressures that might cause a worker to take a chance with his own life. If he had been interested in addressing the practicalities that led workers to tolerate dangerous conditions, he could have found support in English cases, some American cases, and academic writing for limiting the defense.[44] Cardozo, however, chose to follow the New York cases that applied the doctrine rigorously.

It may have been that Cardozo was unwilling to consider whether social policy suggested a change in the common law rule because the legislature had passed a statute on this very subject and had not included schools among the organizations for which it mandated the safeguards that were lacking here. While he did not advance this reason specifically, he did point out the lack of coverage in the statute at the point in his opinion where he concluded that the common law rule prevented recovery. If indeed he thought that the statutory omission had a preclusive effect on a common law recovery, a more explicit statement would have been informative. Another likely explanation is that he concluded that the common law rules should not be altered to help people who went into such "obvious" danger with their eyes open.[45] Furthermore, Cardozo had no personal experience that would have taught him how workers often had to accept dangerous conditions in order to make a living. While he was willing to protect train passengers like himself who were in a hurry to leave the train, he had never had a job like washing windows.[46]

Cardozo's lack of sympathy for injured people who had been aware of possible danger appears more reasonable in *Murphy*, a case that has contributed to his fame among generations of law students. An amusement park customer was injured by a fall on a ride known as The Flopper, which was a moving belt that ran upward on an inclined plane. Writing for a unanimous court in overturning a jury verdict for the customer that had been affirmed by the Appellate Division, Cardozo concluded that as a matter of law, the customer had assumed the risk of injury. The risk was open and obvious, and the customer had watched others jumping and falling before deciding to get on the belt. Cardozo rejected the argument that the ride was inherently dangerous by stating that there was no history of serious injuries that would suggest that the ride was too dangerous to be allowed to continue—or, as he put it more memorably, The Flopper was not "a trap for the unwary, too perilous to be endured."[47]

Although the amusement park owner had an economic incentive to cause the dangerous conditions and was in a better position to spread losses arising from that danger, those arguments were neither made nor considered in *Murphy*. Cardozo gave short shrift to the customer's testimony that the belt jerked and hence was defective:

> One who steps upon a moving belt and finds his heels above his head is in no position to discriminate with nicety between the successive stages of the shock, between the jerk which is a cause and the jerk, accompanying the fall, as an instantaneous effect. There is evidence for the defendant that power was transmitted smoothly, and could not be transmitted otherwise. If the movement was spasmodic, it was an unexplained and, it seems, an inexplicable departure from the normal workings of the mechanism. An aberration so extraordinary, if it is to lay the basis for a verdict, should rest on something firmer than a mere descriptive epithet, a summary of the sensations of a tense and crowded moment.[48]

He refused to allow the testimony about a jerk in the movement of the belt to serve as the bit of evidence necessary to get the case to the jury. He emphasized that the risk lay not in the jerk but in the fall and that "[t]his was the very hazard that was invited and foreseen."[49]

Cardozo's opinion in *Murphy* derived from one method of decision-making that he highlighted in his extrajudicial writing and from another that he did not highlight. First, logic, the method of philosophy, determined his result. He had written in *The Nature of the Judicial Process* that a judge should not "mar the symmetry of the legal structure by the introduction of inconsistencies and irrelevancies and artificial exceptions unless for some sufficient reason, which will commonly be some consideration of history or custom or policy or justice."[50] He applied the governing rules of assumption of risk because he saw no reason to conclude that they were outmoded.

A second basis for Cardozo's opinion was his judgment that the factual situation was consistent with the accepted doctrine. His vision of the facts was crucial to the result, and it was clear and confident: *Murphy* was simply a case of a person, one who "was not seeking a retreat for meditation," entering into a game knowing that it involved people falling down, and then falling down and getting hurt. The customer had more or less gotten what he asked for. Cardozo concluded by noting that those who wanted to avoid the risk of injury had an alternative: "The timorous may stay at home."[51] He was not disparaging "the timorous." He doubtless put himself in that category.

Cardozo also decided a number of cases addressing other negligence defenses. The fellow-servant rule barred employees from recovering damages from employers for injuries caused by the negligence of a fellow employee. The doctrine's initial justification rested on the assumption that the wage bargain between employer and employee incorporated the potential negligence of fellow employees.[52] Later, courts and commentators sought to justify the fellow-servant rule on the grounds that it induced workers to take greater care and that it promoted commercial development by avoiding the imposition of crushing liability.[53] The New York Court of Appeals expressly adopted the doctrine in 1851 without stating any reasons, in a case in which the issue had not been argued.[54] Within a few years, however, the New York courts began to cut back on the doctrine by announcing the vice-principal rule. Under this rule, an employee to whom the master's duties of superintendence had been delegated was not a fellow-servant, but a vice principal, whose negligence did not bar employee recovery.[55] Under New York law, the application of the rule depended on the nature of the duty being performed—whether it was "superintendence" or "operational"—and not on the rank of the employee. Thus, low-ranking employees performing superintendence functions could be vice principals. Closely divided New York courts decided similar cases in different ways, leading even proponents of the vice-principal rule to confess that "it is hardly possible to say what is the law."[56] Nevertheless, until the passage of workers' compensation acts removed the fellow-servant defense in most situations, the New York courts did provide some relief to workers from the rigors of the absolute bar of the fellow-servant rule.[57]

The earlier New York decisions reflecting efforts to ease the fellow-servant rule's bar to employee recovery survived into the Cardozo era in a few cases in which the statutory amendment of the rule did not apply. In an early opinion that involved workers injured by other workers' negligence, he accepted the applicability of the fellow-servant rule. When the plaintiff did not argue the vice-principal rule, Cardozo did not mention it either, even though the trial record suggested the possibility of such an argument to support the verdict for the plaintiff.[58] Since the case was being sent back for a new trial, Cardozo could have suggested the possible application of the vice-principal rule if he had been sympathetic to it. He made such suggestions in other areas of the law on other occasions.[59] But in this area, just as in vicarious liability and assumption of risk cases, he was content to let New York law drift back into the mainstream of common law rules without any discussion of the reasons for the special rules lowering some of the barriers to worker recovery that had been developed in New York.

Cardozo exhibited a similar attitude toward the general rules of negligence defenses in contributory negligence cases. The contributory negligence doctrine was also a creature of the nineteenth century, with the first English case decided in 1809 and the first American case decided in 1824.[60] The general rule, in New York as elsewhere in the United States, was that an injured plaintiff was completely barred from recovering from a negligent defendant if the plaintiff had also been sufficiently careless to be found negligent.[61] New York also applied a harsh rule followed by a minority of states that placed the burden of proof on plaintiffs to show that they were free of contributory negligence instead of placing the burden on defendants to prove that the plaintiffs were contributorily negligent.[62]

Cardozo accepted New York's rule without question in McCabe v. Rosoff Haulage Company.[63] A worker, hit by a truck on a pier while crossing a passageway between buildings, won a verdict at trial, and it was affirmed in the Appellate Division. Cardozo recommended reversal on the ground that the worker's failure to look both ways when he crossed the passageway demonstrated as a matter of law that he had not established his lack of contributory negligence. As in the application of assumption of risk doctrine in the workplace, Cardozo did not consider whether New York should follow the rule of a majority of states, which gave the plaintiff the same presumption of ordinary care that the defendant enjoyed.[64] Even though he would agree to a new trial, his recommendation was that "we shall do better to end the litigation."

When Cardozo got to the United States Supreme Court, he wrote an opinion in another contributory negligence case in which his sense of the practicalities of the situation led him to be more understanding of the failure of an injured person to take maximum precautions. In so doing, he limited a prior decision by Oliver Wendell Holmes. In Pokora v. Wabash Railway Company, a truck driver was hit at a railroad crossing by a train that had failed to blow its horn as required by statute.[65] The truck driver, who was denied recovery in the lower courts, was held to have been contributorily negligent as a matter of law because he went forward across the tracks although his vision was obstructed. The lower courts had followed Holmes's dictum in Baltimore & Ohio Railroad Company v. Goodman that a driver had the obligation to get out and look if his view was obstructed.[66] Cardozo, following prior Supreme Court law that placed the burden of proof on the railroad to prove the driver's contributory negligence, drew on his own personal experience as an automobile passenger and limited *Goodman* to its facts, holding that the existence of contributory negligence in this case was for the jury to decide.

> Standards of prudent conduct are declared at times by courts, but they are taken over from the facts of life. To get out of a vehicle and reconnoitre is an uncommon precaution, as everyday experience informs us. Besides being uncommon, it is very likely to be futile, and sometimes even dangerous . . . [There is] need for caution in framing standards of behavior that amount to rules of law . . . Extraordinary situations may not wisely or fairly be subjected to tests or regulations that are fitting for the common-place or normal.[67]

Although Cardozo himself had elevated standards of conduct into rules of law, he rejected Holmes's standard of conduct for drivers because he believed that it had been overtaken by the facts of daily life.

An ongoing problem in the study of Cardozo's opinions is to identify the factors that helped him to decide contested cases. One notable feature revealed by the opinions described in this chapter is a method of approach. Cardozo understood that every case had two elements, the law and the facts. He was a practical judge, who had spent a good part of his career putting the facts of cases before juries and judges, and he brought his experience to the bench. He had confidence in his ability to discern the essential facts of a controversy from the welter of testimony in the trial record of a case. Moreover, he did not flinch at concluding that the facts were sufficiently clear that a reasonable jury could find them only one way. Sometimes, as in the train rider case, his judgment was informed by his own personal experience in life. Sometimes, as in the window-washer case, his lack of experience may have led him astray. But a secure vision of what had happened often pointed toward a solution to the controversy.

More difficult to identify are specific considerations that guided his choice between precedent and logic on the one hand and public policy on the other in the difficult cases when there were persuasive arguments to be made for both methods. He suggested in his lectures that he made the choice on an ad hoc pragmatic basis. But the opinions described in this chapter suggest that there were some specific factors that helped him to make up his mind. Cardozo's general attitude toward the law of accidents derived from his acceptance of the central fault-based principles of negligence doctrine. That acceptance took him a long way toward the decision of most negligence cases, for he did not constantly have to revisit first principles. Within the negligence framework, his opinions indicate that he was neither plaintiff-oriented nor defendant-oriented. He sought to apply doctrine impartially, in line with its purposes. One influential consideration was that he sought to be faithful to the goal of the legislature when it passed laws that changed the common law. Another theme was that he was reluctant to change or modify doctrine, even if change seemed appropriate, if it involved a substantial financial impact on the state. That was a matter for legislative choice. In the succeeding chapters, we shall see other explanations of why Cardozo sometimes was ready to innovate and sometimes was not.

15

Liability and Duty: MacPherson v. Buick

A major theme of Cardozo's negligence decisions was his effort to develop a coherent explanation of two troublesome concepts, duty of care and proximate cause, that helped define the extent of a defendant's liability to an injured party. Cardozo took a firm position that the negligence that led to liability required careless conduct that foreseeably threatened the injured party. Conduct that posed a risk to someone else did not create liability to an unthreatened person who was injured in an unexpected fashion. The distinction was one of Cardozo's most significant contributions to negligence law.

The dominant conception of negligence in 1914 was that it involved a defendant's breach of a duty of care owed to the plaintiff. It was also agreed that before the defendant could be held liable for its negligence, there had to be an injury that was caused, or in the jargon of the day, that was proximately caused or legally caused by the defendant. There was disagreement, however, whether it was enough to show that the defendant had acted carelessly or whether the plaintiff had to show also that the action was careless because the defendant broke a duty owed specifically to the plaintiff. Another way to put the question was whether the defendant should have foreseen that its carelessness would injure someone, or whether the plaintiff had to show that the defendant should have foreseen that its carelessness would injure the plaintiff in particular.

265

Moreover, commentators disputed the necessary relation that had to exist between the breach and the injury in order to find liability, that is, what made particular acts the proximate cause of the injury. "Causation in fact," that is, the accident would not have happened but for plaintiff's negligence, would have made liability endless, for in a "philosophical sense, the consequences of an act go forward to eternity, and the causes of an event go back to the dawn of human events, and beyond."[1] A useful definition of causation was needed, but not easily achieved. Thus, the concepts of duty and proximate cause were confusing, and their elements were often interchanged. What was at stake was not just a nice question of legal theory. The resolution of the question would determine who would bear the loss, at least in the first instance, in more unusual accident cases—the injured party or the careless defendant.

Courts and writers used gallons of ink to attempt to define proximate cause, which included a combination of a factual inquiry and questions of policy. Ever since the time of Lord Chancellor Francis Bacon in the seventeenth century, proximate cause had meant that a fairly close connection had to be shown between the defendant's negligence and the plaintiff's injury.[2] In the mid-nineteenth century, the term was defined as requiring that the injury be a "natural and necessary" or a "necessary and probable" consequence of the defendant's negligence. This formulation allowed enormous flexibility. As cases and factual variations multiplied with new activities in the industrial economy, courts sought to find a way to apply the proximate cause requirement, or to instruct a jury to apply it, with moderate consistency.

Major difficulties arose in cases in which it could not have been easily anticipated that lack of care by the defendant would injure the plaintiff, although it might injure someone else, or that even if it might injure the plaintiff in some other way, it would not injure the plaintiff in the way that it actually did. Courts and academics struggled to decide whether the causation of the injury that occurred "in fact" was sufficient to impose liability on the defendant. Rather than decide that issue doctrinally, the New York Court of Appeals usually responded by selecting a doctrinal exposition of proximate cause that suited the facts of the particular case. Occasionally, it enunciated an interpretive policy based on public policy concerns that were related to the economic or social consequences of particular formulations.

A series of cases after the middle of the nineteenth century set the stage for Cardozo. One of the earliest New York negligence cases to consider the proximate cause problem was Thomas v. Winchester in 1852.[3] Winchester, a seller of drugs, labeled some extract of belladonna, which is a dangerous poison, as extract of dandelion, which is harmless. The drug passed through several intermediate dealers before being sold to the husband of Mary Thomas for her use. She became extremely ill after using the drug. Winchester contended that he owed no duty of care to Mrs. Thomas because there was no "privity" between them, that is, he had had no dealings with her. The Court of Appeals recognized the existence of a general rule of nonliability, expressed in the well-known English case, Winterbottom v. Wright, that liability for failure to perform a contract is limited to a party to the contract.[4] Nevertheless, the Court found Winchester liable to the ultimate user of the medicine, even though unknown, because the act of negligence was imminently dangerous to the user. Winchester was therefore "justly responsible for the probable consequences" of his negligence.[5]

While the Court of Appeals sometimes limited the *Thomas* result to cases in which a dangerous instrument was involved,[6] it continued to follow *Thomas* and began to focus more on the danger to noncontracting third parties than on the inherent dangerousness of the product itself. Thus liability to a noncontracting third party was recognized in two cases of defective scaffolds, a purchaser of a bottle of aerated water that exploded, and a purchaser of a large coffee urn that also exploded.[7]

Torts scholars have argued that historically there were two competing theories of proximate cause. One theory used the language of "natural and probable consequences." It emphasized the foreseeability of the risks or the harm of negligent conduct. The other used the language of "natural and necessary" or "natural and proximate" results. It emphasized the closeness in time or proximity of the negligent conduct to the harm suffered.[8] New York courts, however, used the language of both theories imprecisely, and the choice of wording did not portend any particular outcome. After *Thomas*, Judge (later United States Supreme Court Justice) Ward Hunt gave perhaps the most restrictive and controversial nineteenth-century application of proximate cause in Ryan v. New York Central Railroad Company.[9] The court stated that when an owner's negligence set its woodshed on fire, the owner was not liable for the destruction of a nearby house to which the fire spread. Destruction of the shed, on which sparks first fell, could have been anticipated; but the spread of the fire to other property was not a "necessary or an usual result," even though it was "possible" and "not unfrequent." The chance that the fire would spread was "remote" and depended upon "accidental and varying circumstances" over which the owner had no control. Imposing liability would require that a landowner guarantee the complete security of all his neighbors and would "create a liability which would be the destruction of all civilized society."[10]

Thomas and *Ryan* demonstrate the courts' ability to use rather similar formulations of the general doctrine of liability for negligence to respond to different policy considerations in order to reach different results in cases in which the damage that occurred would seem, to a lay observer, a foreseeable consequence of the defendant's negligent conduct. Much of the history of New York tort law may be understood as an attempt to accommodate the tension between *Thomas*'s expansion of liability on the basis of the foreseeability of the risk and *Ryan*'s limitation of potentially indeterminate liability despite the foreseeability of risk. That tension reappears in the contrast between Cardozo's famous opinions in MacPherson v. The Buick Company and Palsgraf v. Long Island Railroad Company.[11]

After *Thomas* and *Ryan,* the Court of Appeals had difficulty maintaining consistency either in doctrine or in results in cases involving proximate causation, and doctrinal confusion over proximate cause continued through Cardozo's arrival on the Court of Appeals in 1914.[12] The Court expressed no clear theory of legal cause, mingling language and ideas of prior cases as they seemed appropriate to deal with particular cases. Not until Cardozo's opinions in *MacPherson*—and especially in *Palsgraf*—was there any full-fledged discussion of proximate cause or of the related issue of duty in the Court of Appeals.

————

The question of duty first arose in the context of the duties of landlords to persons hurt on their property. The general rule had been that an owner was not liable for injuries on premises that he had leased to another because the tenant had the rights and duties of possession under the lease.[13] New York had created an exception for property that had been leased for use by members of the public. The original explanation for the public use exception had been phrased in terms of a duty of care to invitees, that is, since the owner knew that the public would use the property, the owner had impliedly invited the public to the property and hence was liable for its own negligence. In 1915, Cardozo reformulated the reasons for the exception. In Junkermann v. Tilyou Realty Company, a leased boardwalk in an amusement park had collapsed during a baby parade, injuring a small boy, the plaintiff. The Appellate Division had reversed a verdict in his favor against the man who had leased the boardwalk to the company that operated it. Cardozo wrote for a unanimous court that reversed the Appellate Division.[14] He first summarized the precedents as imposing a duty of care toward unknown third persons not only when a lessor knew of a dangerous condition but also when he "ought in the exercise of reasonable diligence to have known." In other words, he placed a duty of reasonable inspection on the lessor. The duty was derived "more simply, and perhaps more wisely," not from the "fiction of invitation" but rather from the nature of the use of the property.[15] Since a boardwalk was a public place, it was foreseeable that the public would use it and could be hurt by defects. The lessor consequently had a duty to keep it in repair.[16]

In *Junkermann*, Cardozo moved toward a vision of duty based on foreseeability of risk, which would provide the analytical underpinning for one of his major contributions to tort law. In that same year, his opinion in People's Trust Company v. Smith developed another.[17] An uncle who held a bond and mortgage from a third party left it for safekeeping with a lawyer nephew who had the same name as his own. The nephew broke his fiduciary duty by pledging the bond and mortgage in order to borrow money for himself. The bank sought to defeat the uncle's claim to his property by asserting that he was negligent in leaving the property with someone of the same name. The court rejected the argument. Cardozo's opinion exhibits his ever-present concern with standards of behavior. "Faith in the honesty of trusted friends and relatives is seldom negligence."[18] Moreover, it would not be enough to show that the uncle was negligent with regard to his own interests or in carrying out a duty to some third party other than the plaintiff bank. Instead, "[h]e must have been careless in respect of some duty owing to the plaintiff or the public."[19] This identification of the concept of negligence not merely with carelessness but with breach of duty to particular persons would later become one of Cardozo's chief contributions to the law of torts.

Just two years after he went on the bench, these early explorations of the duty concept culminated in MacPherson v. Buick Motor Company, one of Cardozo's most famous opinions.[20] The pre-1914 Court of Appeals had dealt extensively with the problem of the duty of care owed

by manufacturers and suppliers of products and services to third parties
with whom they had no contractual relations and whom they did not
know. *MacPherson* raised this issue once again, and Cardozo's opinion
helped make him famous in the legal world. Cardozo stated the facts
concisely:

> The defendant is a manufacturer of automobiles. It sold an automobile
> to a retail dealer. The retail dealer resold it to the plaintiff [Donald
> MacPherson]. While the plaintiff was in the car, it suddenly collapsed.
> He was thrown out and injured. One of the wheels was made of
> defective wood, and its spokes crumbled into fragments. The wheel was
> not made by the defendant; it was bought from another manufacturer.
> There is evidence, however, that its defects could have been discovered
> [by Buick] by reasonable inspection, and that inspection was omitted
> . . . The question to be determined is whether the defendant owed a
> duty of care and vigilance to any one but the immediate purchaser [that
> is, to any one but the dealer].[21]

Buick realized that MacPherson's suit was important to its business.
It sent a lawyer from Detroit to try the case in Saratoga Springs, New
York. A director from a testing laboratory at Purdue University and
representatives of leading auto and wheel makers from all over the
country testified as experts for Buick. Whether Buick really believed, as
it argued, that "liability would seriously interfere with the commerce of
the world and restrict business," it presented the case as if it expected
those consequences for the automobile industry if it were found liable.[22]
The jury brought in a verdict of $5,025 for MacPherson, and the Ap-
pellate Division affirmed that judgment. Since there was evidence of
Buick's negligence to support the verdict, Cardozo saw the case as
presenting the pure legal issue of the duty owed by Buick to MacPherson.
Cardozo presented the facts in antiseptic fashion so as not to color that
issue. He did not even mention that MacPherson suffered his injury while
driving a sick neighbor to the hospital.

Judge Kellogg's opinion in the Appellate Division had not discussed
the history of the law of manufacturer liability to a third party.[23] By
1916, however, courts and academics were stating confidently that the
general rule for such cases was that a manufacturer was not liable for
injuries resulting from the use of a defective product by a third party

with whom it had no contractual relationship unless certain conditions were met. The relevant conditions were quite narrow: the product must have been imminently dangerous to life and involved in the preservation or destruction of life or that the seller must have known that the article was imminently dangerous and failed to give notice of the danger to the buyer.[24] However, in New York the *Thomas* line of cases had broadened the exception for dangerous articles to the point where it seemed about to swallow the general rule of nonliability.

Cardozo's opinion in *MacPherson* virtually completed the process. The New York Court of Appeals had a choice. It could have pointed to the text writers and to numerous cases in the United States for the proposition that unless the plaintiff fit one of the exceptions, the court would apply the general rule of nonliability of a negligent manufacturer to a third party with whom it had no contractual relations (or, in lawyer's technical language, no "privity"). Of the three generally recognized exceptions, only the one that encompassed sales of inherently or imminently dangerous articles was relevant. Disregarding that exception would have been easy. The court could simply have written, as Chief Judge Willard Bartlett did write in dissent, that "the defective wheel on an automobile moving only eight miles an hour was not any more dangerous to the occupants of the car than a similarly defective wheel would be to the occupants of a carriage drawn by a horse at the same speed." Bartlett pointed out that there would be no liability in the carriage case and indeed that such a case was one of the illustrations of nonliability used by the court in *Thomas.*[25]

The court, with Cardozo writing for the six-judge majority, chose not to follow the so-called general rule. Cardozo's opinion proceeded from the opinion in *Thomas,* the later New York precedents, and his own recent opinion in *Junkermann,* not from broad propositions of negligence law. Thus, he began his review of the precedents not with the "general rule" of Winterbottom v. Wright but with the "general rule" of Thomas v. Winchester, which he viewed as standing for the principle that an injured third party may recover from a seller whose negligence put human life in imminent danger. All subsequent New York decisions had followed this principle.[26] For Cardozo, the *Thomas* rule did not require that a product must be inherently dangerous, like a poison or an explosive. It was enough that the product be imminently dangerous if imperfectly constructed. He relied on *Devlin, Statler,* and *Torgeson* (the defective scaffold and exploding products cases) for that proposition, arguing that even if those cases were viewed as having extended the *Thomas* rule, the court was "committed to the extension."[27]

Turning to English law, Cardozo quoted extensively not from *Winterbottom* but from Lord Esher's opinion in Heaven v. Pender, which placed a broad duty of care on a seller of goods to those likely to be harmed if the goods were defectively made and were likely to be used before a reasonable opportunity arose to discover the defect.[28] Cardozo recognized that Esher's opinion had been criticized and indeed had not been the opinion of the majority of the English Court of Appeal.[29] Yet, relying on the series of New York cases beginning with *Thomas* and perhaps looking to the future statement of a general rule, he accepted Lord Esher's statement as the standard for liability, although he conceded that qualifications might be called for in certain circumstances.

After discussing developments since the original decision in *Thomas*, Cardozo restated the scope of its rule as extending to all articles "reasonably certain" to be dangerous when negligently made. The manufacturer would be liable if it knew that the article would be used without new tests by persons other than the dealer. At this point, Cardozo was willing to throw a few crumbs to the former general rule. Recognizing that anything can be used in a dangerous way, he stated that the required knowledge must be of probable, not just possible, danger. He also concluded that there was no need for the court to consider whether the *MacPherson* principle applied to manufacturers of component parts. Cardozo was then ready to apply his new rule to the particular case, which involved injury to the person who purchased the Buick from the car dealer. Cardozo pointed out the weakness of Buick's position—it recognized a legal duty only to the dealer, the person least likely to use the car—and held that the sale of an automobile fit within the protection of his stated rule. The verdict for MacPherson was affirmed.

Cardozo studiously avoided discussing the broad ramifications of the case. His opinion simply analyzed established principles of negligence law, in particular the duty of a seller of goods to strangers. There was no explicit or implicit consideration of other factors, such as the relative economic position of manufacturers and consumers, the ability to spread costs, the needs of industry to avoid potentially crushing liability, or the relevance of insurance. The issue was conceived of and discussed solely in terms of duty and the persons to whom sellers of products owed duties.

Cardozo gave only glancing intimations that any policy consideration affected his views of the proper outcome in *MacPherson*. Although he recognized that precedents must be adapted to changes in society, he did not state what new conditions or needs of life justified the decision. He seemed concerned only with changed factual circumstances, not with any new social or legal theory. There was absolutely no hint that he was creating any more extensive liability than familiar negligence theory warranted. On the face of it, Cardozo concluded that Buick had a duty to those persons who were likely victims of a negligently made car. The duty was found in general tort law, as expounded in a string of New York decisions. In *MacPherson*, Cardozo used the concept of foreseeability to impose a liability on a manufacturer in a situation in which it had not previously been thought to exist. But foreseeability was not necessarily a liability-increasing notion. Cardozo used it to deny liability as well.

Cardozo's opinion in *MacPherson* did not acknowledge that any important principle was at stake. He disposed of the contrary authorities either by reconciling them on the ground of the remoteness of the negligence in those cases or by viewing them as merely different applications of the same principle. Thus, Cardozo presented the new rule in the most modest terms. This style of argument would become typical of Cardozo's writing—the attempt to narrow differences of principle or to turn apparent differences of principle into differences of application. Although the New York precedents supported his argument, the new rule did represent a break with other jurisdictions. As Chief Judge Bartlett pointed out in his dissent, some of the contrary authorities from other jurisdictions represented differences of principle and not just differences of application.

Cardozo ignored the state of the law in other jurisdictions. Instead, his opinion assembled the analysis and the factual situations in the prior New York cases to enunciate a general New York rule. In New York, prior case law made the innovation less striking than it would have been elsewhere, although this additional change in degree replaced an old rule (which the court had gradually modified) with a different new rule that incorporated the cumulative effect of those modifications.[30] Cardozo made the shift with a characteristic rhetorical flourish: "Precedents drawn from the days of travel by stage coach do not fit the conditions of travel to-day. The principle that the danger must be imminent does not change, but the things subject to the principle do change. They are whatever the needs of life in a developing situation requires them to be."[31] In the national context, *MacPherson* was a major innovation. Cardozo's opinion turned out to be very influential because its careful reasoning attacked the basis of the general rule of nonliability.

Cardozo's innovation also had limits. In his opinion Cardozo allowed for the possibility that manufacturers would not be held liable in all circumstances. Although he mentioned that the provision of extra seats in a car indicated that passengers were within the manufacturer's duty of care, he did not say whether protection extended to an injured pedestrian or to the owner of property damaged by a defective car.[32] He also reserved the case of the manufacturers of component parts for future decision.[33] Finally, he noted that the basis of Buick's liability was in the law of torts and not in the contract between Buick and the dealer to whom it sold the car so that it was uncertain whether anyone other than the dealer could take advantage of warranties made by Buick. The cautions were typical of Cardozo's reasoning process. Rather than suddenly establishing a general, unqualified principle, he tried to preserve flexibility for unforeseen future applications of the rule.

Although Professors Seavey and Prosser later argued that the exceptions were formulated in a way that would allow them to be sloughed off later, Cardozo took the exceptions seriously.[34] Indeed, he later joined Judge McLaughlin's opinion in Chysky v. Drake Brothers Company, holding that a waitress who was injured when she bit into a nail embedded in a piece of cake that had been given to her by her employer could not recover from the producer of the cake in a suit based on contractual breach of warranty. There was no privity, no contract, between the waitress and the cake maker.[35] The court relied on Cardozo's statement in *MacPherson* that the basis of liability in that case was in tort, not contract. If there was to be contractual liability, there had to be privity between the parties. If the exceptions expressed in *MacPherson* had been a smokescreen for the basic principle that a producer of a defective product would be liable to anyone who might be expected to use it, Cardozo would have applied the *MacPherson* principles to permit the waitress to recover regardless of her choice not to sue in tort.[36] Yet Cardozo joined the majority that ruled against the waitress, not Judge Hogan's silent dissent.

Courts and writers generally accepted *MacPherson,* and Professor Prosser was able to report forty years later that it had become "all but universal law in the United States."[37] Professor Lawrence Friedman, after remarking the wide acceptance of *MacPherson,* argued that other courts "cited" rather than "followed" Cardozo. Instead of changing minds by the power of persuasion or eloquence, Cardozo's opinion "eloquently summed up a state of mind which would have made its way on any account. The 20th century was bound to accept the basic idea of products liability, that is, that manufacturers ought to be responsible to ultimate consumers."[38] Whether events are as inevitable as that sentence makes them sound, Cardozo would have been pleased by the comment. A major premise of his later writing about the judicial process was that the essence of common law judging, especially in changing times, was to perceive the "state of mind which would have made its way on any account."

In *The Nature of the Judicial Process,* Cardozo called this the method of sociology—bringing the law up to date by a commonsense rethinking of prior precedents and by a contextual analysis of the facts of the particular case. The New York Court of Appeals was already close to the *MacPherson* result, and Cardozo was most ready to innovate when the distance he had to travel from established law was small. Cardozo did not invent the doctrine that imposed liability on Buick. Analogy powered by public policy considerations—his perception that the exceptions to the original rule were more generally applicable than the rule itself—convinced him to reformulate and improve the governing doctrine. Cardozo's opinion is justly famous as the well-written opinion of an influential court that quickly led other jurisdictions to reach similar conclusions.[39]

Although Cardozo's opinion in *MacPherson* expanded the liability of manufacturers to consumers based on the foreseeability of harm from negligence, it did not use that concept to expand the liability of all defendants or even to formulate a rule for analysis of all negligence cases in terms of duty. Almost immediately after *MacPherson,* the Court of Appeals decided another case in which it used the language of proximate cause to deny liability. In Perry v. Rochester Lime Company, the defendant company stored nitroglycerine caps in tin boxes marked "Blasting caps, handle with care."[40] The tin boxes were placed in wooden boxes in a storage chest on public property along the Erie Canal in Rochester. The storage was done without a permit and in violation of law. Although the company usually kept the chest locked, one night the chest was left unlocked and open. Two boys took one of the wooden boxes and hid it in a neighboring barn. The next day the two boys set out with the box accompanied by an eight-year-old boy. A few minutes later the caps exploded, killing all three boys.

The lawsuit against the company was only for the death of the third boy, who had not been involved in the theft. The trial judge had dismissed the suit, and the Appellate Division affirmed. Cardozo affirmed the lower courts in a unanimous opinion. If he had meant *MacPherson* to state a principle of broad-ranging defendant liability, he could easily have reversed in *Perry* by concluding that the company had stored dangerous material negligently, in violation of law, and that the death of the boy was a foreseeable consequence of its negligence. Cardozo, however, did not even mention *MacPherson* or frame the issue in terms of whether the company owed the boy any duty. Instead, Cardozo began by positing the wrongfulness of the company's conduct in its violation of the statute and framed the issue in terms of the company's responsibility "for the proximate consequences of the wrong . . . for those consequences that ought to have been foreseen by a reasonably prudent man." Cardozo concluded that as a matter of law, there was nothing for the jury to decide: the open chest was not the proximate cause of the boy's death. It was "possible" but not "probable" that the contents would be stolen. The company had not provoked the theft. Although the chest was open, the caps were hidden inside in the tin boxes. The theft and subsequent events culminating in the boy's death were "new and unexpected" intervening causes.[41]

Although Cardozo employed the language of foreseeability of injury that had led to the conclusion of liability in *MacPherson*, *Perry* turned away from the spirit of *MacPherson*. Cardozo focused on the geographic and temporal considerations associated with proximate causation and on the concept of intervening cause. Cardozo's unwillingness to let the case go to a jury is strong evidence that his emphasis on the notion of foreseeability did not carry any ulterior notion of an expansion of defendant liability. *Perry* demonstrated Cardozo's self-confidence in reaching a judgment about what reasonable people ought to regard as foreseeable or not. Injury from the defendant's conduct was clearly foreseeable to Cardozo in *MacPherson* and just as clearly not foreseeable to him in *Perry*.[42]

Cardozo's willingness to deny liability as a matter of law continued when he returned shortly after *Perry* to a more duty-oriented analysis.

In O'Connor v. Webber, butcher shop owners were exonerated from liability to an employee as a matter of law on the basis of a lack of duty to guard against unusual accidents.[43] O'Connor, the employee, had his fingers cut off by an electric chopping machine when the stick used to push the meat into the machine hit the revolving screw and the shock caused the employee's hand to slip into the machine. Cardozo brushed aside the argument that a guard or a different shaped stick was necessary. The owners had fulfilled their duty by furnishing the only machine available on the market: "They were not running a factory, where machinery is the principal thing, the very life of the business . . . If they were charged with a duty to become inventors of improved devices, and that too in an attempt to guard against remote and doubtful dangers, the same duty must attach to every one who uses a standard machine of any kind in his office or his home."[44] Cardozo relied on the remoteness of the danger and on economic and social conditions—the position of the shopkeepers as a small business—to help define the limited duty owed by the butcher shop owners to their employees.[45]

Cardozo's opinions in *O'Connor* and *Perry* indicate that he was prepared to use either of the New York courts' formulations of "proximate cause"—foreseeability of harm or geographic and temporal notions of causation—as seemed appropriate. *Perry* was not an aberration. For example, in a case that involved not torts but an insurance contract, Bird v. St. Paul Fire & Marine Insurance Company, Cardozo linked coverage to geographic considerations by using the language of proximate cause.[46] Damage to a boat resulted when a fire broke out beneath some freight cars loaded with ammunition in the Black Tom railroad yards in New York harbor during World War I. The cars blew up, causing a second fire, which then caused an even more violent munitions explosion. The second explosion caused a shock wave that damaged Bird's boat a thousand feet away. The question was whether the damage to the boat fell within the scope of an insurance policy that quaintly referred to the "Adventures and perils which the said [insurance] Company are content to bear" as those "of the Sounds, Harbors, Bays, Rivers, Canals and Fires, that shall come to the damage of the said boat."[47] As Cardozo noted, there was no express exception in the policy for damage from explosion, although policies commonly contained such exceptions.[48]

Cardozo, writing for a unanimous court, nevertheless overturned a judgment for the boat owner. Cardozo's analysis was interesting but baffling. The parties and the court treated the insurance policy as a fire policy, which required Bird to demonstrate that the damage had been caused by fire. Although New York insurance cases assumed that there was liability if a fire in a building caused an explosion that damaged a neighboring building, Cardozo did not follow those cases and implicitly limited them. In deciding whether the fire caused the damage to Bird's boat, Cardozo stated the guiding principle as "the reasonable expectation and purpose of the ordinary business man when making an ordinary business contract." What was critical was the belief of "the average owner whose boat or building is damaged by the concussion of a distant explosion, let us say a mile away."[49] Such an owner would not expect indemnity. (Bird's boat, of course, was less than one-fifth of a mile away.) Cardozo concluded that if the fire was "near at hand," the boat would be in the danger zone of "normal apprehension" and the owner would be covered under the policy. But when the fire was "remote" and "extraordinary conditions" caused "indirect peril," then the case was out of the realm of probable expectation. The damage to Bird's boat occurred by explosion, not fire, and it occurred over a remote distance and was "twice removed" from the initial cause. The verdict for Bird was therefore reversed.

Cardozo's opinion was heavily influenced by torts concepts. He emphasized the expectations of the average owner—a reasonable person analysis—and the importance of the spatial connection in the definition of causation, a familiar element of proximate cause analysis. Cardozo, in fact, specifically referred to torts cases to support his reliance on spatial proximity in establishing causation. "This [recognition] is true even in the law of torts where there is a tendency to go farther back in the search for cause than there is in the law of contracts."[50]

Bird represented an important step in Cardozo's thinking about causation. It is quite clear that he understood the public policy implications of deciding the nature of the elements of proximate cause. Like the other cases following *MacPherson*, *Bird* established that foreseeability and duty were not, in Cardozo's mind, devices for automatic expansion of defendant liability for careless conduct. Rather than being rhetorical devices that presumed liability, they were standards or tests that needed to be carefully analyzed and applied according to the facts of the case.[51]

Sometimes Cardozo's restrictive application of the notion of foreseeability worked to a plaintiff's benefit. In reversing a judgment that had dismissed a complaint in Lewis v. Ocean Accident & Guarantee Corporation, Cardozo found liability under an insurance policy for injury "effected solely through accidental means," when the opening of an infected pimple by a doctor caused the infection to spread and the patient to die.[52] "To the scientist who traces the origin of disease, there may seem to be no accident" in what occurred. Under that view, the death would not be covered by the policy. But "our point of view in fixing the meaning of this contract . . . must be that of the average man." And to Cardozo the average man would say that "the dire result, so tragically out of proportion to its trivial cause, was something unforeseen, unexpected, extraordinary, an unlooked-for mishap, and so an accident."[53]

Cardozo returned to problems of duty in two 1921 cases, Hynes v. New York Central Railroad Company and Wagner v. International Railway Company.[54] He had just delivered his lectures on *The Nature of the Judicial Process,* and the ideas developed in them must have been much on his mind. In *Hynes,* the court had to choose between two possible duties owed by a landowner: the duty to trespassers not to injure them by willful or wanton conduct and the duty to persons on adjacent public land to use reasonable care that the landowner's property not cause them injury.[55] A sixteen-year-old boy, Harvey Hynes, was swimming in the Harlem River adjacent to a railroad's right of way. A plank, projecting over the river but fixed to the railroad's bulkhead, was used by neighborhood children as a diving board, without the railroad's objection. Hynes climbed from the river to the bank and then onto the plank. While he was poised to dive, high tension wires from one of the railroad's poles fell, striking him and flinging him into the river to his death. The lower courts unanimously viewed Hynes as a trespasser on the railroad's land (the plank) and, applying the trespasser rule of limited duty, denied recovery to his estate because the railway had not willfully harmed him. The Court of Appeals, 4–3, reversed and granted a new trial.

Cardozo's opinion for the majority assumed the existence of a rule of limited duty owed to trespassers but never referred to it explicitly. He refused to view the situation as simply as the lower courts had done. He rejected the notion that the case could be decided by calling Hynes a trespasser because he was standing on a plank that protruded from the railroad's land. Cardozo adopted a more philosophic tone than he had used in earlier opinions. "This case is a striking instance of the dangers of 'a jurisprudence of conceptions' (Pound, Mechanical Jurisprudence,

8 Columbia Law Review 605, 608, 610), the extension of a maxim or
definition with relentless disregard of consequences to 'a dryly logical
extreme.' The approximate and relative become the definite and absolute."[56] "Rights and duties in systems of living law are not built upon
such quicksands."[57] Although Cardozo made a major rhetorical attack
on a mechanical approach to rule-making, it was in the cause of a small
achievement. Cardozo may have thought he needed to go all out with
his colleagues because the vote was so close.

Cardozo emphasized the nature of the boy's activity as a bather in the
public water, the intrusion of the plank into the area of public ownership
(the air and water surrounding it), and the fortuity that the boy stood
on the plank instead of below it or leaning against it where he would
have been in equal danger from the falling wires. In the collision of rules,
one of them being "highly technical and artificial," the more realistic
rule was that "he is still on public waters in the exercise of public
rights."[58]

Hynes demonstrated Cardozo's practice of the technique of decision-
making that he had preached in his recent lectures. His words in *Hynes*
echoed the lectures: "We think that considerations of analogy, of convenience, of policy, and of justice, exclude him from the field of the
defendant's immunity and exemption, and place him in the field of
liability and duty."[59] "Analogy" consisted of Cardozo's allusions to the
undoubted liability that would have resulted had the decedent been
below or leaning against, instead of standing on, the springboard. "Convenience," "policy," and "justice" seemed to refer to the need for flexibility in applying the rule relating to categories of land users and the
protection of the right to use the public waters for public purposes.[60]

Hynes was a strong example of Cardozo's pragmatic and progressive
modernization of legal doctrine.[61] Still, it was a limited ruling, however
boldly phrased, with limited results. Cardozo was vague about the governing considerations of policy and justice, and he did not even suggest
a general rule that the railroad was liable whenever its negligently maintained high tension wires caused injury to a trespasser. Cardozo was not
ready for such a big step. He simply redefined the boy's status from that
of a trespasser to that of a bather in public waters, thus enabling him to
apply the protections accorded such persons. His normative sense of the
railroad's appropriate duty in this factual situation led him to conclude
that a step onto private property in the course of using public property
ought not to extinguish the railroad's duty of care. He was willing to

extend the duty of the railroad a little bit at the geographic boundary of the railroad's property without any suggestion that he wanted to undermine the general rule of nonliability to trespassers. Cases like *Murphy, Perry, Gaines, O'Connor,* and *Martin* suggest that if the boy in *Hynes* had been cutting across the defendant's land to go swimming, Cardozo would not have strayed from the traditional category of trespasser to find liability. Clearly, Cardozo was not making the railroad an insurer of injury caused by its wires.[62] In Adams v. Bullock, he wrote for a unanimous court in taking a verdict away from a twelve-year-old boy who was injured by electricity when an eight-foot wire that he was swinging off the edge of a bridge hit a trolley wire that ran underneath.[63]

Richard Weisberg, who has written admiringly of Cardozo the judge and Cardozo the literary stylist, has used *Hynes* as an example of Cardozo's "overlooking precedents and challenging accepted norms on no more authority than that afforded by his formidable value system alone."[64] Put another way, he has interpreted *Hynes* as an example of Cardozo's bending the rules to do justice in an individual case. If so, it was not a typical Cardozo opinion. We have already seen a few cases in which Cardozo ignored sympathetic circumstances in applying what he regarded as governing legal doctrine, and we shall see many more. Cardozo did not usually bend a rule for one case. Either he changed rules in a defined class of cases, or else he upheld them and reached what he sometimes characterized as a harsh result. Only in one class of situations did he generally decide cases on the individual equities. That was, as we have seen, the class of cases governed by equitable principles.

Rather than manipulating the old rule to do justice in this case by, say, finding that Hynes had not committed a trespass, Cardozo applied a new rule that the landowner's duty of care would apply to a person committing a brief, technical trespass at the boundary of public and private property when the trespasser's primary activity was to exercise his legal right to use the public waters. Using the test of foreseeability, Cardozo declared, "Landowners *are* bound to regulate their conduct in contemplation of the presence of travelers upon the adjacent public ways."[65] Cardozo changed the general rule, but not much, in accord with his view of what an informed public would view as a sensible accommodation in situations like this one.

Cardozo's emphasis on a vision of the facts, his preference for duty analysis, and his catchy rhetoric also characterized his second major 1921 opinion, Wagner v. International Railway Company. Arthur Wagner's cousin Herbert fell from a train whose doors had been left open. Arthur Wagner walked back four hundred feet along a trestle at night looking for Herbert, who had fallen to his death, and was himself injured when he fell off the trestle. Arthur sued the railroad, alleging that his injuries were caused by the negligence of the railroad in causing Herbert to fall from the train. The trial judge instructed the jury that the railroad would be liable only if its conductor had invited Arthur to leave the train to search for his cousin and had followed Arthur with a light, thus taking responsibility for his safety. The conductor had not in fact done so. The jury therefore found for the railroad, and the Appellate Division affirmed.

The Court of Appeals reversed, holding that the instructions were erroneous and that a new trial had to be held to determine whether Herbert's fall was due to the railroad's negligence and whether Arthur had also been negligent and thus contributed to his own injury. On the appeal, the railroad had argued that recovery for injuries from an attempt to rescue someone endangered by its negligence required a finding that the rescue effort had been "spontaneous and impulsive." It claimed that Arthur Wagner's walk along the trestle was his own choice and an intervening cause that broke the causal sequence between any railroad negligence and Arthur's injury.

After stating the facts, Cardozo punctured the company's argument in three words: "Danger invites rescue."[66] Cardozo relied on several prior Court of Appeals opinions in characterizing Arthur Wagner's reaction as "natural and probable" and concluding that the "wrong that imperils life is a wrong to the imperilled victim; it is a wrong also to his rescuer."[67] In those two statements, Cardozo called upon both the older "natural and probable" formulations and the relatively more recent duty-risk analysis. It did not bother him, if he even noticed, that he was using two different formulations of proximate cause analysis. So much the better, if both supported his reasoning. Indeed, in rejecting the distinction between impulsive and deliberate conduct, he used yet a third form of analysis—which rested on foreseeability—in stating simply that it was enough that the act "is the child of the occasion" and that even if the railroad did not foresee the rescue attempt, it should have.[68] Cardozo generally liked to use all available arguments to bolster an opinion. Professor Seavey saw Cardozo's opinions in *Wagner* and *MacPherson* as critical in the development of a new theory of negligence that focused analysis "upon the risk of harm and not upon the manner by which it is caused or the number of events intervening between the defendant's act and the catastrophe."[69] But Cardozo's language in *Wagner* shows that he had not yet focused on the theoretical distinctions among the various formulations of negligence liability. Although *Wagner* is one of Cardozo's better-known opinions, its fame is due less to its innovative or analytical quality than to the force of Cardozo's language.

A third major torts case decided in 1921 was Drobner v. Peters, in which Judge Pound concluded, for a six-judge majority, that it would be too much of a wrench in negligence law to permit a child to sue for prenatal injuries caused by negligence.[70] Cardozo dissented alone. As he wrote Professor Frankfurter, he felt "pretty sure" that he was "right," but he did not write an opinion. "The general line of argument was indicated in Judge Merrell's opinion in the Appellate Division. That being so, I did not feel that it was worth while to write a dissenting opinion, especially as I stood alone."[71] The policy of collegiality won out over the opportunity to write an important opinion recognizing a new cause of action.

In the mid-1920s, Cardozo was working on the problem of merging the geographic and temporal aspects of the causation issue into the concept of duty through the analytical device of foreseeability, that is, those aspects were treated as part of the primary task of deciding whether the dangers of a particular action or lack of action were to be anticipated. In other words, the literal causes of an injury were relevant to, but did not conclude, the larger end of deciding whether the injury was a foreseeable harm that the defendant should have a duty to prevent. Moore v. Van Beuren involved a suit brought by a plaintiff whose lumber was destroyed after a trash fire that was started by the defendant's employees got out of control and burned across several intervening lots before reaching the plaintiff's property. The jury's verdict for the plaintiff was reversed by the Appellate Division and his complaint dismissed on the authority of *Ryan* and the other fire cases referred to earlier in this chapter that had limited recovery to damage on the adjoining property.[72] The Court of Appeals affirmed the judgment of the Appellate Division, with Cardozo, Crane, and Lehman dissenting. No opinions were written.[73] Cardozo had written a report to the consultation urging that the jury's verdict for the plaintiff be reinstated. In this case, Cardozo argued that the court was "not bound to extend . . . the arbitrary rule" of the fire cases because the fire was started intentionally and "the range of prevision is correspondingly enlarged." Those who set the fire saw the "surrounding conditions of vegetation and of atmosphere" and "must be held to such prevision of the consequences as would be imputed in such circumstances to a reasonable man."[74]

Cardozo recognized the arbitrary nature of the limitation of liability contained in the *Ryan* fire rule and found a way to "distinguish," that is, to differentiate, the cases applying it. Indeed, *Ryan* had mentioned the possibility of such a distinction itself. Although *Moore* could have been viewed as involving a negligent and not an intentional tort because the defendant had no intent to burn the plaintiff's property, Cardozo blurred the categories. Seeking to overcome the problem that the fire had burned across several properties before reaching the plaintiff's lot, which would have eliminated liability under *Ryan*, he demonstrated the flexibility of the foreseeability concept. He characterized the defendant's conduct as knowing and willful in order to argue that the range of damage to be anticipated was increased when one started a fire deliberately in an area with combustible material.

This was one instance in which Cardozo's respect for precedent and his wariness about rules that permitted the imposition of enormous liability to a multiplicity of potential plaintiffs took second place to his dislike for an arbitrary rule that was out of harmony with tort law throughout the country. Cardozo probably would have preferred eliminating the presumption of nonforeseeability adopted by *Ryan* in favor of a foreseeability rule to be applied to the facts of each individual fire case. Cardozo's sense of what was foreseeable as a matter of common sense in *Moore* is of a piece with his approach in *MacPherson* to the same subject. He might therefore have been tending toward a conclusion that the known unpredictability of fires, rather than being a reason for limiting liability, was a fact that called for a high duty of care, with a corresponding liability for negligence.

Thus, Cardozo's opinions up to 1928 indicate that, like the rest of the Court, his views on the doctrinal limits of liability for negligence were in a process of evolution. His path-breaking *MacPherson* opinion and many others utilized an analysis that focused on breach of duty to particular plaintiffs, with foreseeability as the key element in determining duty. But other opinions spoke in terms of older formulations of proximate cause, particularly when the case involved the physical aspects of causation or the issue of the geographic closeness of the location of the injury and the defendant's conduct. There was therefore some doctrinal confusion and an ad hoc quality to Cardozo's torts opinions through the mid-1920s, but he was focusing more and more on the notion of duty as central to his analysis.

16

Fireworks and Foreseeability: Palsgraf

On August 24, 1924, a late-arriving passenger at the East New York station of the Long Island Railroad, fighting his way onto a crowded car, dropped a package beneath the train. The doors closed, the train pulled away, and its wheels went over the package. The package contained fireworks. "There was a terrific roar, followed by several milder explosions, and a short-lived pyrotechnic display. The car nearest the explosion rocked and the windows crashed. Pieces of the big salute bomb shot up to the platform and hit persons nearby. The force of the detonation also ripped away some of the platform and overthrew a penny weighing machine more than ten feet away. Its glass was smashed and its mechanism wrecked."[1]

One of the companions of the man who had dropped the package also dropped a package when they fled the station. The police examined it and found several "bombs" about sixteen inches long and several inches in diameter and some smaller firecrackers and other fireworks. The police investigation concluded that the men had been part of a group bound for an Italian festival on Long Island where "fireworks and bombs were to play an important role."[2]

Among the thirteen people injured was Mrs. Helen Palsgraf, who was waiting for a train to take her and her daughters, Lillian and Elizabeth, to the beach. When the weighing machine overturned, it fell on her. Mrs. Palsgraf brought suit against the railroad in October 1924, alleging a

286

variety of negligent actions and omissions and seeking damages for her injuries, principally a stuttering condition induced by the accident.[3] Nearly four years later, Cardozo wrote an opinion in Palsgraf v. The Long Island Railroad Company that made the case "[p]erhaps the most celebrated of all torts cases" and one of the best-known American common law cases of all time.[4]

Mrs. Palsgraf's case was tried in May 1927, nearly three years after the event. At the trial, witnesses testified that the man who dropped the package onto the tracks had jumped onto the train as it was already moving and that a guard, who had held the train door open, helped him on while another guard on the platform pushed him into the car. This maneuvering caused the passenger to drop the package onto the track and under the train's wheels. The explosion followed. Mrs. Palsgraf's evidence did not establish how close she was to the train.[5] The railroad presented no witnesses, and its motion to dismiss the case was denied. The trial judge asked the jury to consider only whether the guards acted as ordinarily prudent and careful trainmen would; and if the guards were negligent, whether Mrs. Palsgraf's injuries resulted from such careless acts.[6] The trial took two days, and a jury returned a verdict for $6,000 in Mrs. Palsgraf's favor. Pursuant to statute, she was also permitted to recover certain costs of trial in the amount of $142. The trial judge denied the railroad's motion for a new trial. The railroad filed a notice of appeal on July 21, 1927, and the appeal was argued in the Appellate Division on October 21, 1927.

Just after the case was argued in that court, Cardozo participated in the last day of an important meeting of the group that was involved in drafting the American Law Institute's Restatement of Torts. The meeting took place from October 20 to 23, 1927. Also present for at least part of the conference were William Draper Lewis, director of the American Law Institute, Professor Francis Bohlen, who was the reporter, or chief drafter, for the Torts Restatement, and Bohlen's "Advisers," Chief Justice George Wheeler of the Supreme Court of Errors of Connecticut, Judge Learned Hand of the United States Court of Appeals for the Second Circuit, Dean James Hall of the University of Chicago Law School, Robert Dechert, a Philadelphia lawyer who taught part-time at the Pennsylvania Law School, Professors Edward Thurston and Leon Green of Yale Law School, and Professor Warren Seavey of Harvard Law School. Harry Shulman, a recent Harvard Law School graduate assisting in the Restatement project, also attended. Cardozo, who participated actively in the Torts project but did not want the title of Adviser, attended just the last day's session, by which time Lewis, Wheeler, Green, Hall, and Dechert had left.[7]

At the October 23 meeting, Tentative Draft No. 18-R on "Negligence" was the subject of discussion. The draft contained language stating that there would be no liability of a careless defendant to an unforeseeable plaintiff. That is, C, whose conduct was negligent because harm to B could have been foreseen, would not be liable for causing harm to A when such harm could not have been foreseen. In a Note to Advisers, Bohlen explained that the proposed draft represented the theories of Professors Terry and Green and followed classical doctrine. Bohlen then pointed out that Professor Terry even further narrowed a defendant's liability: "The interest of the plaintiff which is injured must be the same as, or at least of the same sort as, that which the defendant should have realized was imperilled by his conduct."[8] That issue, Bohlen suggested, needed to be resolved in the Restatement. The *Palsgraf* case offered the opportunity to discuss both issues.

For nearly three-quarters of a century, the New York Court of Appeals and other courts had been resolving questions of the scope of liability under the headings of "proximate cause" and "duty" in an ad hoc fashion. Theorists had attempted to rationalize the results and to formulate statements of the underlying principles to guide juries and courts in particular cases.[9] There were efforts to apply logical and scientific rules and to find a unifying theme in principles of "justice," as well as the less grandiose approach of simply asking whether the negligent conduct was a substantial factor in producing the harm. Sometimes, the discussion was framed in terms of the duty owed by a defendant to a particular plaintiff. At other times, the question addressed was whether the harm that had befallen a particular plaintiff fell within the scope of the risk created by the defendant's conduct. By the 1920s, these attempts to rationalize torts doctrine helped shape the discussions in the American Law Institute's restatement project.

Cardozo was not present at the first three days of the four-day meeting of the torts advisers. But he attended on October 23, and we have a full record of his active participation in discussing some of the basic elements of liability for negligent conduct. Bohlen began by propounding a hypothetical case:

A man leaves a loaded gun in a hall. A child picks it up and drops it on the foot of B, injuring B's foot. The shock of the fall of the gun against the foot discharges it, shooting C. Can both recover?

Cardozo responded,

I should think there would be liability in either case, the child having got hold of the dangerous weapon, you wouldn't have to conceive of the way in which it would be negligence. A principle is followed by the courts that it is not necessary that you should foresee the particular damage that did ensue but that you should see the possibility that some kind of damage will ensue. If you leave a weapon you know that is a dangerous thing. The negligence is that the leaving of a gun is dangerous in all ways. I think that negligence should be put upon him for any injury caused thereby.[10]

Cardozo was moved by the dangerousness of leaving a loaded weapon lying about to find negligence and liability to both B and C, notwithstanding the unusual nature of the accident. At least in those circumstances, Cardozo answered privately the issue raised by Professor Terry whether the interest of the victim who was actually harmed must be the one that was threatened by the negligent conduct. In *Palsgraf,* Cardozo would decline to answer the question.[11] The final version of the Restatement disagreed with his view. It answered the hypothetical case by concluding that there was liability to C but not to B.[12]

Further discussion on the relation between duty, causation, and liability then ensued. Cardozo, Learned Hand, and several others argued their way through the problems that Cardozo would shortly address in *Palsgraf.* Bohlen focused the discussion around a hypothetical that was eerily close to *Palsgraf*—an accident involving hidden explosives. The hypothetical raised the issue whether it was enough for a person whose property was injured to show that the defendant had been careless or whether the plaintiff also had to show that the defendant's carelessness foreseeably threatened an interest of hers or, even more, whether the plaintiff had to show that the carelessness foreseeably threatened her property as opposed to her person. Hand pushed Cardozo hard, and Cardozo pushed back.

CARDOZO: I think if you throw a stone into a house you should recognize that some injury will result, whether it is great or small is immaterial.

HAND: I disagree. It shocks me very deeply. It seems to me that to attribute to an act every consequence which is likely to result is monstrous.

BOHLEN: I am driving along a driveway and see a box which looks to me not like an ordinary paper box but a package wrapped up, obviously a thing of value. Certainly I would be bound to use care not to injure my friend's property. It does in fact contain some high explosive which he is having brought to him for blasting purposes and the resulting explosion wrecks his house and does injury to him. There is a case in which the act was likely to affect only the property interest . . .

HAND: Why should there be a distinction? We all agree that if you are going to hold him for every consequence you have got to extend it to the Chicago fire [that is, the story about Mrs. O'Leary's cow, which kicked over a lantern, thus setting fire to the barn and eventually to the whole city].

CARDOZO: A man drops something while he is standing on a ladder and it falls upon some high explosive and destroys the building. He had no reason to believe that the explosive was there. The very ground which makes him so that he is not responsible to another person is exactly the ground by which you limit the extent of the liability to the person whose interest he has invaded . . . If I run down something on a private road which is not abandoned, I know that is something I ought not to do. It is negligent conduct toward the owner for me to do it just as though I threw a stone into his house. Therefore it turns out it was a highly dangerous thing for me to do it. Now it wrecks his house. You say that because I didn't think it would cause such injury relieves me from liability? The mere fact that the box belongs to someone else other than the owner [of the house] makes no difference. You should not run down something on the owner's property.

HAND: In negligence are you approaching it on the theory that the law sets up a series of duties? I had always supposed that the better view was that you are responsible for the consequences of your act but there was a limitation based upon the degree you are bound to apprehend them.

THURSTON: Is there any reason why a defendant being responsible for unusual harm to A because there was a chance of doing some harm to A; should not also be responsible for harm done to X?

CARDOZO: I didn't suppose I owed a duty to X not to run down a thing belonging to A. Where the wrong is intended you are responsible.

HAND: How fictitious it is to make the ownership the test of the consequences of the act. I have never liked the way of treating negligence as a series of duties on the defendant. The question is whether his act produces damage. Certainly he is responsible for such, if a person of his make-up would be responsible for his act. There is a limitation in the consequences which the law imposes for his safety. You need not ruin a man for a momentary dereliction; when it gets beyond what a man could expect, it is treated as one of those things which are regarded as inevitable.

CARDOZO: It is a question of whether it is a negligent act to destroy the thing at all.

HAND: You want to attribute a cause. There is a fault there. A box is on a drive. Certainly you are not entitled to think that the box is of any value.

CARDOZO: If I run down the box the only interest invaded is the ownership in that box. I run the risk of causing any damage to that box which may happen, no matter how valuable in that respect; the consequences are attributed to me. But I have not been negligent towards any other interest, that is, to the adjoining property. There is no reason to believe that there is any relation to that property. The error I think I started with was assuming that when I destroyed the box I invaded the interest of the ownership of the house. But I think that the general statement that it must be negligent with respect to the interest invaded covers it all. There may be some explanation to show what you mean by the interest invaded.

HAND: It is true but it doesn't conform to practice.

THURSTON: There are three things. There is the interest invaded, the interest imperilled and the particular type of harm.

CARDOZO: That word "interest" has come into the law recently but it seems to me a rather indefinite sort.

HAND: I think that it is a pretty good word.

CARDOZO: I don't think you can get anything better, but I think it necessary to keep in mind its limitations.

BOHLEN: The term "interest" should be defined. We can say in what sense we use it.

CARDOZO: If I destroy a box in your private road in the absence of some warning, I have not the slightest reason to think it threatens undue injury to the building or any other property. If I throw a stone in a building negligently, I certainly cannot avoid the consequence of forecasting that it might hit a lamp. I have invaded the property in that building. Would there be any difference between a lamp and some explosive? Or something the owner has left in the building or someone else?

HAND: The rule ought to make you liable for all the consequences of your act. The theory of the whole thing is that you should be attentive. I admit that it won't work out. Every consequence which in the course of another falls upon your act is in fact caused by your act. The only stopping [point?] for it is that although you are at fault we are not going to ruin you for a momentary fault. I don't think you will get a formula.

Cardozo ended the discussion with a puzzling throwaway line, apparently referring to the amount of damages, not the parties damaged, "I think you should abandon the notion of foreseeable consequences."[13]

One thing that is clear is that by the end of the discussion, months before *Palsgraf* arrived in his court, Cardozo had taken the doctrinal position that he would write into his opinion. His final view was that the driver who carelessly ran over a box on private property was liable for the destruction of its contents but was not liable for the building that was destroyed by the unforeseeable explosion of dynamite in the box. The driver was careless with respect to whatever was in the box but not with respect to the building. That was the logic of the *Palsgraf* conclusion.

Cardozo did not clearly answer the hypothetical whether the person who carelessly threw a stone into a building was liable for the consequences if the stone detonated some explosives. But his comment about abandoning "the notion of foreseeable consequences" may well imply a view that the particular consequences do not have to be foreseeable for liability to ensue if the defendant was careless in the fashion described, because the defendant had no idea what was in the house and threw the stone anyhow.

Cardozo addressed one more hypothetical case, probably prior to *Palsgraf,* that supports this explanation of his views about the requirement that consequences be foreseeable. A memorandum prepared by Professor Seavey reported the reaction of the same group that attended the October 23, 1927, meeting plus Professor Green to the following hypothetical:[14]

(1) "A" negligently drives on the street to the danger of persons on the street, including B. He strikes (unexpectedly and without reason to know what it contains) a box containing dynamite. It explodes; a piece of debris strikes a person washing windows ten stories above the pavement. He falls, injuring B. Is A liable to B?

CARDOZO: Yes. (Hunch)
DECHERT: No. Too extraordinary to be just.
GREEN: No. Not one of the risks within the scope of the duty which A violated.
BOHLEN: Doubtful which way (1) [that is, question 1] would go. Inclines toward saying no liability because extraordinary.
SEAVEY: Yes.

Cardozo's response was consistent with his belief, expressed at the October 23, 1927, meeting, that if the defendant's conduct posed a foreseeable risk of personal injury to the plaintiff, then the defendant was liable when his negligent conduct injured the plaintiff, no matter how unusual the causation link was. This hypothetical was similar in that regard to the loaded gun hypothetical when the person within the risk was injured by the gun's falling on his foot. Cardozo supported a broad notion of liability once negligence to an individual was established.

———————

In December 1927, less than two months after Cardozo's participation in the October advisers conference, the Appellate Division handed down its judgment in the Long Island Railroad's appeal of the verdict for Mrs. Palsgraf. It affirmed the trial court judgment, 3–2. It also awarded Mrs. Palsgraf further costs of $100. The majority explicitly referred to the high degree of duty that the railroad owed Mrs. Palsgraf as a passenger. It concluded that the verdict of negligence was supported by the evidence and that the railroad's negligence caused the accident. That was sufficient for liability. The lack of notice that the bundle contained explosives was no defense. The dissenters concluded that the railroad's negligence was not the proximate cause of Mrs. Palsgraf's injuries. The negligence of the package-carrying passenger intervened, and the explosion was not a reasonably probable consequence of the railroad's negligence, which was too remote for liability.[15] The railroad then appealed to the Court of Appeals.

It is apparent that the discussions of the Restatement of Torts advisers in which Cardozo participated focused his mind on the theoretical and doctrinal problems that he would address in *Palsgraf*. But one story alleges that Cardozo's preparation for dealing with the issues in *Palsgraf* went even further. Twenty-five years after the decision, Professor William Prosser wrote that after the Appellate Division's decision but before *Palsgraf* was argued in the Court of Appeals, Professor Bohlen prepared a draft of a section stating that a defendant had no duty to an unforeseeable plaintiff and added a statement of the facts of *Palsgraf* to his explanatory notes. He then presented the draft to his advisers at a meeting that Cardozo attended. Cardozo "concluded that there would be no impropriety in his presence at the meeting, although he took no part in the discussion, and did not vote. He sat therefore as audience, to a long and lively debate, ranging over nearly all of the questions which since have surrounded *Palsgraf*."[16] Prosser reported that he had been told the story by Dean Young B. Smith of the Columbia Law School before he died. Prosser asserted that Smith "was present as one of the advisers."[17] Prosser's story suggested a previously unknown influence on Cardozo's thinking with respect to his *Palsgraf* opinion, and it raised a question of impropriety in Cardozo's listening to a discussion of a case that he might be called upon to review.

The Prosser story appears to be inaccurate. The discussion he reports did not take place, at least not before the appearance of the Court of Appeals' opinion in *Palsgraf*. Professor Laurence Eldredge, who later became an adviser to the Restatement of Torts, researched the chronology of the events. He lamented the destruction of the minutes of the torts advisers meetings by the American Law Institute but was able to reach some conclusions from its remaining records. Eldredge noted that the only conference of the advisers between the time of the decision of the Appellate Division on Friday, December 9, 1927, and the decision of the Court of Appeals on May 29, 1928, took place on Monday and Tuesday, December 12 and 13, 1927. Eldredge concluded that it would have taken "a lot of doing" for Bohlen to have learned about and presented the case to the advisers over the weekend.[18]

Since the appearance of Professor Eldredge's article, the missing minutes have surfaced. Although their coverage of the December meetings is sketchy, they do disclose that while Young B. Smith was at the December 12 meeting, Cardozo was not, and indeed did not attend that conference at all. And for good reason. The conference met in New York City, while Cardozo was hearing arguments all that week in Albany.[19] Therefore, it was only at the previous October 20–23, 1927, meeting of the advisers that *Palsgraf* could conceivably have been discussed in Cardozo's presence. Those minutes are very complete. *Palsgraf* was not mentioned. Nor were there any railroad hypotheticals. Nor was Young B. Smith at any of those meetings. Nor was it likely that anyone, including Cardozo, would have known about a minor accident case that had just been argued in the Appellate Division. Nor did Bohlen include any railroad accident hypothetical like *Palsgraf* in any draft document until the draft for the meeting in September 1928, months after the Court of Appeals' decision in *Palsgraf*.[20]

Palsgraf probably was discussed at the conference that occurred on June 19–22, 1928. That was three weeks after the Court of Appeals handed down its opinions, and there would have been no impropriety in Cardozo's hearing a discussion of the case at that time. In fact, Professor Thurston wrote on the cover of his copy of Preliminary Draft No. 20, which was the subject of that meeting, "Palsgraf v. LIRy, Cardozo and Andrews decided May 29, 1928 Prox. Causa—N.Y. Law Journal June 11."[21] That sounds very much like the notation of someone who has learned about a case for the first time. At all events, the existing evidence suggests that either Dean Smith made a mistake or that Prosser misunderstood what Smith told him.

Although the *Palsgraf* case probably reached the Court of Appeals unembarrassed by a prior ex parte discussion at a torts advisers meeting with Cardozo present, Cardozo had been exposed to the work of the drafters for several years. The October 23, 1927, meeting appears to have been the first that he attended, but he had received the materials from previous meetings. Unlike his judicial work, which involved deciding particular cases, the task of the drafters of the Restatement was the fashioning of rules for the whole body of torts doctrine. Thus, when *Palsgraf* reached his court in the winter of 1928, Cardozo was prepared to see it as more than a bizarre accident that had injured Helen Palsgraf.

Palsgraf was argued in the Court of Appeals on February 24, 1928, and decided on May 29. The judges split 4–3, with Cardozo writing for the majority and Andrews writing the dissent.[22] The court, reversing the judgment for Mrs. Palsgraf, directed that her complaint be dismissed. Cardozo's opinion made the case legal history. Viewing Mrs. Palsgraf as the prototype unforeseeable plaintiff, he used the case to organize the concept of negligence around the notions of duty and foreseeability. He saw the cause of action for negligence as requiring Mrs. Palsgraf to show that the conduct of the guards broke a duty of care owed to her, and he decided that she had failed to do so. Jostling a package-carrying passenger "was not a wrong in relation to the plaintiff, standing far away . . . Life will have to be made over, and humans transformed, before prevision so extravagant can be accepted as the norm of conduct, the customary standard to which behavior must conform."[23]

The doctrinal heart of Cardozo's view of negligence as relational was expressed in one sentence: "The risk reasonably to be perceived defines the duty to be obeyed . . . it is a risk to another or to others within the range of apprehension."[24] Thus, Cardozo focused on the duty of care of the railroad and defined its duty in terms of foreseeable risk. His legal theory, combined with his mental picture of the factual setting, ended the case. The conduct of the guard involved "no hazard [to Mrs. Palsgraf that] was apparent to the eye of ordinary vigilance." It was "an act innocent and harmless, at least to outward seeming, with reference to her."[25] The fact that the guard's action led to Mrs. Palsgraf's injury made no difference.

Cardozo's opinion used his methods of history and philosophy to demonstrate what he portrayed as a fairly obvious point. He relied on historical themes that he did not feel called upon to prove; he offered merely a citation to William Holdsworth's *History of English Law* and a few other sources. Likewise, he did not lay out the development and complexities of case law; he provided only some relevant citations and analogies. And rather than refuting Andrews's dissent point-by-point, Cardozo dealt with them just inferentially.

Andrews rejected Cardozo's theory that a defendant owed a duty of care only to foreseeable plaintiffs. Andrews began from the premise that a person's duty to act reasonably was owed to society at large, not simply to particular persons. All persons injured by negligent conduct were wronged, not just those as to whom harm was foreseeable. The crucial question for Andrews involved the causation issue that Cardozo thought the court did not have to face. Andrews understood that legal doctrine did not impose liability for all injuries that were "caused" by a defendant's negligence in the sense that they would not have occurred "but for" that conduct. He had to deal with the limiting concept that the injury must have been proximately caused by that conduct. Andrews argued that the term *proximate cause* meant that "because of convenience, of public policy, of a rough sense of justice, the law arbitrarily declines to trace a series of events beyond a certain point."[26] There was no magic formula to determine responsibility for careless conduct.

Prior New York case law justified Andrews's argument that public policy considerations had often been determinative. Andrews did not mean broad political or economic considerations—for example, enterprise liability, loss spreading, fairness to consumers, or economic policy considerations. His "public policy" referred to practical considerations of everyday social life that had long been recognized as relevant to the issue of liability: Could the injury have been foreseen by a prudent person? Was there a "continuous sequence between cause and effect . . . without too many intervening causes?" Was the injury too remote in time and space from the conduct?[27] Because the jury had not been asked to consider the proximate cause issue as a question of fact, the question for the court, in Andrews's view, was whether to take away Mrs. Palsgraf's verdict because the negligence did not, as a matter of law, proximately cause her injury. Andrews concluded that the court should not do so.

Cardozo also did not refer to large-scale public policy considerations. His policy considerations were similar to those that influenced Andrews, although he used them in determining whether there was negligence at all without ever getting to the causation issue. There were two problematic features of Cardozo's opinion in *Palsgraf,* his view of the facts and his view of the law. His statement of the legal principle required him to decide as a matter of fact whether Mrs. Palsgraf was within the range of expectable risk of injury by the guard who pushed a package-carrying passenger onto a moving train. He concluded that a reasonable jury could not so conclude because she was "standing far away" from that incident, that she was "at the other end of the platform, many feet away."[28]

Even though Mrs. Palsgraf's distance from the incident was critical, Cardozo characterized the testimony in just half a sentence when the evidence would have justified a paragraph or two. Cardozo was allergic to lengthy statements of the record. As he later stated in a lecture, "There is an accuracy that defeats itself by the over-emphasis of details . . . one must permit oneself, and that quite advisedly and deliberately, a certain margin of misstatement." Cardozo did not mean deliberate misstatement of the facts, but rather that he deliberately chose to leave out details in an opinion to avoid the problem that "the sentence may be so overloaded with all its possible qualifications that it will tumble down of its own weight."[29]

Cardozo's characterization of Mrs. Palsgraf's location did have a basis in the record. Helen Palsgraf's twelve-year-old daughter Lillian, who was at the newsstand, was close enough to the incident to enable her to see the bundle fall. Lillian testified that the newsstand "was quite a distance; it was *at the other end of the platform* (emphasis added)" from where her mother was.[30] That testimony would seem to justify Cardozo's statement about the location of the scales. But if Cardozo meant to suggest that "far away" and "at the other end of the platform" connoted a great distance, say, 150 to 300 feet, the record did not support him. Other testimony, including testimony from Lillian, suggested that Judge Andrews was not far off in estimating the distance of Mrs. Palsgraf from the spot where the guard pushed the passenger at approximately 25 to 30 feet.[31] The record, however, was not clear about the precise location of Mrs. Palsgraf. The failure by Mrs. Palsgraf's trial counsel to produce clear evidence of the crucial distance led to the ambiguity of Cardozo's description.

In any case, Cardozo believed that the exact distance did not matter because the result would differ only if Mrs. Palsgraf had been within the zone of risk, that is, standing right next to where the negligent conduct occurred, and she was clearly not that close. In that sense she was "far away." The court made that clear in a one-sentence response, probably written by Cardozo, in denying a motion for reargument: "If we assume that the plaintiff was nearer the scene of the explosion than the prevailing opinion would suggest, she was not so near that injury from a falling package, not known to contain explosives, would be within the range of reasonable prevision."[32] The key to Cardozo's conclusion in *Palsgraf* is not just his difference with Andrews on the statement of legal principles. It lies also in his vision of the factual setting, that the sole foreseeable risk of injury from the guards' negligence was to the package-carrying passenger and to other persons who were in the immediate vicinity of the pushing and shoving. That category did not include Mrs. Palsgraf. As in *Perry*[33] (the dynamite box on the Erie Canal), *Bird*[34] (the boat damaged by the Black Tom explosion), and *Greene*[35] (the shopper who fell over the mechanic), Cardozo came away from reading the record with such a confident vision of the facts that he concluded that there was nothing to submit to a jury.

If Cardozo's vision of the facts decided the *Palsgraf* case, its fame arose from his effort to use the case to make New York tort law rational. The division between Cardozo's duty-oriented opinion and Andrews's causation-focused dissent highlighted the intense debate over negligence theory that was occurring at the very moment of decision. Cardozo approached the case with a duty analysis. His factual conclusion, that there existed a limited spatial zone in which injury to others could be foreseen and in which a duty of care therefore arose, led him to decide the case without regard to the issue of proximate causation. According to Cardozo, questions of causation related only to the scope of liability once negligence had been shown, and negligence was a matter of duty. The first question was whether the railroad owed Mrs. Palsgraf any duty at all when its guard was assisting the package-carrying passenger onto the train. The answer was "no" because no risk of harm to her was to be anticipated; therefore, the railroad's carelessness was not negligence toward her.[36]

Using the foreseeability-risk-duty analysis to ask whether there was any negligence at all, rather than asking whether the harm to Mrs. Palsgraf was proximately caused by the careless conduct of the guard, had two consequences. In the first place, phrasing the issue in terms of duty instead of causation made it easier for a judge to view the issue as one for the court instead of for a jury. Although Cardozo overrode a jury's verdict in *Palsgraf,* he rejected the notion that that conclusion was a necessary consequence of his formulation. "The range of reasonable apprehension is at times a question for the court, and at times, if varying inferences are possible, a question for the jury."[37] Cardozo was confident—overly confident—that no "varying inferences" could be drawn with respect to Helen Palsgraf, who seems to have been no more than ten yards away from the negligent conduct.

Second, Cardozo's theory raised the question whether a defendant was liable for unforeseeable consequences of negligent conduct toward a foreseeable victim. Even though it could not be liable to a plaintiff to whom it owed no duty of care, what of a case in which the defendant owed a duty of care to a particular plaintiff because some harm was expectable but in which the harm that actually occurred was extraordinary? Cardozo stated that he assumed, without deciding, that liability would follow in such circumstances for all consequences, "however novel or extraordinary."[38] At this point, he cited the 1884 New York decision in Ehrgott v. Mayor. That decision had upheld a recovery for all damages suffered by a passenger whose injuries in an accident on the street were aggravated by subsequent exposure to the weather in getting home.[39] Cardozo added, however, that there was "room for argument" for nonliability when conduct that was negligent because it threatened insignificant property interests of an individual turned out to cause significant, but unforeseeable, personal injury to that person.[40]

William Powers has argued that Cardozo's doctrinal analysis was "tricky" and "sleight of hand par excellence" because his opinion really overruled *Ehrgott* without saying so.[41] Powers contended that Cardozo's distinction of *Ehrgott* in *Palsgraf* did not make any sense: There was no reason for using foreseeability to determine whether a person was within the scope of liability, as in *Palsgraf,* and then to eschew it, as *Ehrgott* did, to determine whether the injury to that person was within the scope of liability. But it did not follow for Cardozo that using foreseeability to create the duty of care required him to use it to measure liability. Cardozo's treatment of *Ehrgott* merely reflected the position that he had taken at the American Law Institute meeting during the previous October, that the two situations were distinguishable. *Ehrgott* was like the hypothetical of the loaded gun that fell on the plaintiff's foot or perhaps like the stone, which when thrown into the house, detonated some dynamite. Cardozo's position may be questionable, especially once he began to distinguish between threats to different kinds of interest of a given individual. For one holding Cardozo's views, however, it made sense not to address the *Ehrgott* issue directly when he did not have to, and his opinion therefore was not doctrinally tricky.

Palsgraf represented a culmination in Cardozo's thinking about the problem of duty and proximate cause. Various issues that had appeared in earlier cases from *MacPherson* onward were given coherence in *Palsgraf*: an analysis of duty and a clear separation of duty analysis from proximate cause analysis. Where policy issues had been discussed under either heading or under both at the same time, mixing strands of the older formulations of proximate cause, Cardozo now separated them out. Duty analysis became fundamental to measuring the existence of the negligence toward plaintiffs. Proximate cause issues would arise to measure the extent of liability only after a breach of duty resulting in injury had been established. Cardozo agreed with Andrews's estimate of the difficulties of those issues. Earlier the same year, he had written in *The Paradoxes of Legal Science* that there "is nothing absolute in the legal estimate of causation. Proximity and remoteness are relative and changing concepts."[42]

For Cardozo, the choice between his formulation and Andrews's formulation had little to do with the scope of eventual liability. That would still be decided case by case according to the facts of the situation. The factors listed by Andrews as relevant to the proximate cause decision were the same factors relevant to Cardozo in reaching a decision on foreseeability of risk. For all the controversy that *Palsgraf* stirred, it preserved the then current policy considerations underlying negligence law. What had changed was the analytical approach. New ideas—strict liability, enterprise liability, the best cost spreader—that would expand business liability had not yet taken hold. *Palsgraf* was simply Cardozo's attempt to clarify basic negligence doctrines.

Cardozo's formulation was consistent with his general view that liability for negligence was premised on a failure to live up to a standard of conduct. His sense of both logic and fairness dictated that liability to a person should be premised on failure to live up to a duty owed to that person, not on failure to live up to a duty owed to someone else or to the world at large. Conversely, the burden of injuries suffered by someone outside that range of duty had to be accepted by that person as part of the risks of life, acceptance of risk being another key Cardozo principle. From *MacPherson* to *Palsgraf,* Cardozo had consistently showed a preference for addressing negligence questions in terms of duty. Only when geographic considerations seemed central to the case had he lapsed into the language of proximate cause; thus, in *Palsgraf* he found a way to incorporate the geographic considerations into his duty analysis by means of his zone of danger formulation.

Why Cardozo preferred a duty to a causation analysis cannot be decisively determined. He simply asserted its value and demonstrated that it could be applied effectively. His preference accorded with the vision of the world that underlay his equity opinions. Whether he talked of honor in the equity cases or duty in the torts cases, Cardozo focused on the conduct and responsibilities of individuals to other individuals. Even when the conduct was attributable to large corporate business, his focus in negligence cases was on the individual actors. He did not socialize the issue into broader protection. Such large-scale change, like that embodied in worker compensation laws, presumably was for the legislature.

In the end, Cardozo turned a routine case that might have been handled as a simple affirmance on the facts without an opinion into a major cause célèbre in American legal history. His legal triumph was not without cost. Helen Palsgraf had sustained an injury, but she had no valid claim against anyone, except perhaps the unknown passenger who dropped the explosives. Moreover, the Court of Appeals routinely ordered her to pay the railroad's costs—filing fees and so forth, estimated at some $350—in all courts.[43]

Palsgraf has remained controversial. Its holding was adopted almost immediately in the Restatement of Torts, and it has been widely cited in all kinds of cases, although the adoption of its principles was not particularly crucial to the result in many cases in which it has been relied upon.[44] As theorists and courts began to focus more on social and economic factors, such as the inevitability of accidents, the "deep pockets" of the business units likely to be the defendants in accident cases, and their ability to spread the losses from accidents, the Andrews approach has gained in popularity. Although Andrews had not mentioned it, his argument permitted consideration of a wide variety of factors—including the probability that defendants might have better access to insurance and the existence of other mechanisms, such as prices and taxes, to spread costs throughout society. Some commentators have used this theme to criticize Cardozo's opinion.[45]

More recently, other commentators have viewed *Palsgraf* as marking a watershed in American tort law. In their view, the idea of objective causation, which was the centerpiece of prerealist tort doctrine, had failed and was replaced in the mid-twentieth century by the realist notion represented in the Andrews opinion that conceptions of proximate cause reflected issues of practical policy.[46] But the New York tort cases after the middle of the nineteenth century do not demonstrate that any such clear centerpiece had existed. They indicate that New York judges, including Cardozo himself, had used a variety of policies and doctrines aimed more at deciding specific cases than at stating a larger theory. In addition, they indicate that the idea of infusing tort law with public policy considerations was also a nineteenth-century phenomenon. In any event, *Palsgraf* did not represent a radical shift from traditional negligence doctrine. It was traditional doctrine, newly formulated.

Professor G. Edward White has pointed out that Cardozo's emphasis on anticipation of risks as the analytic focus of negligence law invited courts "to ask cost-benefit questions, considering the degree of difficulty in anticipating and preventing certain types of risks and the social desirability of various enterprises, such as railroads." Cardozo's emphasis also asked potential defendants to do this as they planned their operations: to use foresight and act accordingly. These questions prepared the way for additional new questions—for example, "which segments of society were best suited to bear the costs of risky enterprises"—and for "attacks on the negligence calculus itself."[47] But these new questions were not on Cardozo's mind when he wrote his *Palsgraf* opinion. He did not often think about negligence issues in such broad fashion, and those social issues were not much discussed in Cardozo's day. Cardozo was more focused on the relationship between the party alleged to be negligent and the person injured. As for legal doctrine, the spate of cases and articles dealing with duty and proximate cause before and after *Palsgraf* demonstrated that no one rule covered a myriad of factual situations. Proximate cause doctrine continued to survive because it had caused little difficulty in the run-of-the-mill case. Its difficulties arose only in the relatively few unusual cases, and in the bizarre hypotheticals of law professors.

Cardozo's majority opinion might have been treated simply as one attempt among many to refine an aspect of traditional negligence theory around a duty-oriented analysis. But it made a big impact in the legal world. The bizarre facts, Cardozo's spin on the legal issue, the case's timing in relation to the Restatement project, its adaptability for law-school teaching, the policy-oriented dissent by Andrews, Cardozo's rhetoric, and Cardozo's name—all these factors combined to make *Palsgraf* a legal landmark.

One more fact remained to be added to the extraordinary events that linked Helen Palsgraf and Benjamin Cardozo. On August 10, 1991, in Hamburg, New York, Lisa Newell, who is the first cousin four times removed of Benjamin Cardozo, married J. Scott Garvey. Mr. Garvey is the great-grandson of Helen Palsgraf.

Although *Palsgraf* was important for its doctrinal implications, Cardozo wrote other tort opinions in his remaining years on the Court of Appeals that had more immediate practical importance because they involved greater potential liability in situations that were more likely to occur. H. R. Moch Company, Inc. v. Rensselaer Water Company, also decided in 1928, was an important case involving both the tort and the contract obligations of a water company. The Moch Company alleged that its warehouse had been destroyed by fire because the Rensselaer Water Company had broken its contract with the city of Rochester to supply adequate water at sufficient pressure at specific hydrants. The Appellate Division dismissed Moch's complaint for failure to state a good cause of action, and the Court of Appeals affirmed the dismissal unanimously in an opinion by Cardozo.[48]

Cardozo's opinion rejected the plaintiff's three theories of liability—contract, tort, and statutory duty—one by one. Cardozo refused to construe the water company's contract with the city as intended for the benefit of individual members of the public.[49] He was concerned that inferring such a benefit in this situation would expand defendants' liability "beyond reasonable limits."[50] The person who catches a cold when fuel is delivered late to a public building; the merchant who loses a bargain when a mail carrier under government contract makes a late delivery; and the person whose house is destroyed when the fire hose manufacturer makes a late delivery were all examples of people who would recover for a defendant's breach of a contract with another under the plaintiff's theory. Cardozo relied on the example of New York's fire rule in refusing to impose such a "crushing burden."[51]

Cardozo disposed of the tort claim on similar policy grounds of the dangers of indefinite expansion of liability to an indefinite number of beneficiaries. He tried to buttress this conclusion with a confusing distinction between action and inaction, between the denial of a benefit, which created no liability, and the commission of a wrong, which did create a liability. "The query always is whether the putative wrongdoer has advanced to such a point as to have launched a force or instrument of harm, or has stopped where inaction is at most a refusal to become an instrument for good."[52] But the effective reason for rejecting the tort cause of action was the same potential for crushing liability as that which controlled the denial of recovery under the water company's contract with the city.[53] Cardozo also quickly disposed of the claim of breach of the company's statutory duty to supply water at reasonable rates. The statute did not enlarge the tort and contract liability of the company, whose failure to supply water to the fire department could therefore not be made the basis of a cause of action on behalf of a third party. Again, the immensity of potential liability doubtless dissuaded him from following the precedent of his prior opinion for Altz v. Leiberson, which inferred a right of action for an injured tenant against a landlord who failed to comply with the Tenement House Law.[54]

Critics have argued that Cardozo missed the real point of the case, that both the city and the private householders had relied on the water company to perform its contract and had therefore not made other arrangements for protection.[55] Indeed, *Moch* is like *MacPherson* in that the purpose of supplying the fire department with water at hydrants, like the purpose of supplying dealers with cars, was for the ultimate benefit of third parties—the property owner threatened by fire or the retail purchaser of the car. What moved Cardozo in *MacPherson* was that the potential claimant was known. What moved Cardozo in *Moch* was the infiniteness of the potential claimants. Moreover, any decision about compensating property owners for losses had financial implications for the city and its relations with the publicly regulated water companies. Cardozo was generally reluctant to recognize new liabilities that created financial consequences for the state, believing that to be the province of the legislature.[56]

––––––––––––

Cardozo decided one other series of tort cases that raised the issue he had faced in *MacPherson* and *Moch*—the liability of a defendant to a third party for negligent performance of a duty that it had contracted to perform for another. These cases involved misrepresentations made by a party in the course of its business that caused loss to a third party. The general rule at the time was that third parties had no claim if they had no contractual relation with the person making the negligent misrepresentation and if the misrepresentation caused them only pecuniary loss. There were a few limited exceptions.[57] Cardozo used the *MacPherson* principle of foreseeability of harm to justify the imposition of liability in some misrepresentation cases. However, in typical fashion, he recognized the strength of arguments against expansive liability to unknown persons with widely disparate interests and found limits to the new principle.

Cardozo's first confrontation with negligent misrepresentation arose in 1922 in Glanzer v. Shepard.[58] A contract for sale of beans called for the buyer to pay the sellers in accordance with a certificate of weight prepared by the defendants, who operated a public weighing business. The sellers requested the defendants to weigh the shipment and provide the buyers with a certificate. The weighers did so, and the buyers made payment on that basis. When the buyers later learned that the true weight of the beans was substantially less than what had been certified to them, they sued the weighers, not the sellers. The buyers prevailed on the basis of *MacPherson* in the Appellate Division. The Court of Appeals affirmed.

Cardozo described the facts in *Glanzer* so that *Glanzer* appeared an even stronger case for recovery than *MacPherson*. While the Buick Motor Company in *MacPherson* had known that there would be an ultimate purchaser for their car, in *Glanzer* the weighers, who were engaged in a public calling, not only knew that there would be a buyer but also knew who the buyers actually were and sent them a copy of their certificate "for the very purpose of inducing action."[59] Cardozo concluded that there was "nothing new here in principle. If there is novelty, it is in the instance only."[60]

There was novelty in the instance, however, for only a minority of courts had recognized liability for economic loss in this type of situation.[61] Cardozo rejected the limitation of liability to physical harm and gave warning of the implications of the broader duty he was recognizing in breathtakingly swift fashion. After stating the ancient doctrine recognizing the liability of those engaged in public callings to third parties in various instances, he continued, "The most common examples of such a duty are cases where action is directed toward the person of another or his property . . . A like principle applies, however, where action is directed toward the governance of conduct. The controlling circumstance is not the character of the consequence [i.e., not whether there was physical injury or economic loss], but its proximity or remoteness in the thought and purpose of the actor."[62] Foreseeability of injury was the key, and Cardozo saw no purpose in drawing a line between physical and financial harm to a third party once he had concluded that the negligent actor owed the third party a duty of care. The same formula that would work against Mrs. Palsgraf worked for the injured party here. The plaintiff, who had not contracted with the defendant, was nevertheless within the range of its duty.

The cases that immediately followed *Glanzer* demonstrated, in opinions by other Court of Appeals judges, that the new principles established in *Glanzer* were not all-encompassing and instead were to be closely confined.[63] Almost ten years later, Cardozo confirmed this view when he returned to the topic in Ultramares Corporation v. Touche.[64] A firm of accountants had certified a balance sheet for a company and provided it with thirty-two copies for exhibition to suppliers and lenders for a variety of purposes, including the obtaining of credit. Although the company was shown to have a net worth of over one million dollars, its assets had been falsified, and it was in fact insolvent. The plaintiff, the Ultramares Corporation, had extended credit to the company in reliance on the certified report. Ultramares brought suit for negligence and fraud against the accountants.

The trial judge dismissed the fraud count. After the jury brought in a verdict of $187,000 for the plaintiff on the negligence count, the trial judge dismissed that count too. The Appellate Division affirmed a dismissal of the fraud cause of action but reinstated the verdict based on negligence. A unanimous Court of Appeals reversed both of those rulings, finding no cause of action for negligence but sending the case back for trial on the fraud count. Cardozo's opinion demonstrated his ability to set limits on the logical extension of prior doctrine, including his own. The theories of *MacPherson* and *Glanzer* could have justified an affirmance of the negligence verdict. As in those cases, the action of the accountants could easily have been said, as it was in *Glanzer,* to have been "directed toward the governance of [the plaintiff's] conduct."[65] The accountants knew that the purpose of their work was to permit others to rely on it. The class of those who would rely on it, the lenders and suppliers of the company, was equally well known.

For Cardozo, however, the question was not whether the *MacPherson-Glanzer* principle could logically be applied to *Ultramares;* it was whether it should be. Doctrinal distinctions and policy reasons suggested to Cardozo that it should not. First, he sought to establish a distinction between *Glanzer* and *Ultramares* in the "fact" that the service in *Glanzer* was rendered primarily for the benefit of the third party, whereas in *Ultramares* it was primarily for the benefit of the company. In fact, the services were intended in both cases for the benefit of both the companies and third parties.[66]

Cardozo was on stronger ground when he referred to policy distinctions between a case like *Glanzer,* which was a very specific transaction whose ramifications were understood by all parties, and *Ultramares,* which involved potential liability "in an indeterminate amount for an indeterminate time to an indeterminate class."[67] Concern about indeterminate liability had also been a feature of Cardozo's earlier opinions in *Moch* and *Palsgraf*. Furthermore, liability for negligent statements to an amorphous class of persons beyond the parties to the contract would apply not only to accountants but also to lawyers and title companies. Cardozo and the court understood that expanding the duty beyond that recognized in *Glanzer* involved the possibility of a large increase in liability that had not been recognized anywhere else. The court was unwilling to do that on its own. "A change so revolutionary, if expedient, must be wrought by legislation."[68]

Having slammed the door to recovery in negligence, Cardozo quickly reopened it to the possibility of recovery for fraud and sent the case back for retrial on that ground. Distinguishing "honest blunder" from "reckless misstatement" and "insincere profession of an opinion," Cardozo pointed out that if the accountants falsely certified as a fact that the balance sheet was in accordance with the books of account, they would not be exonerated merely if they believed it to be true. If a jury were to find, as it might reasonably do so in this case, that the certification was made without testing the correspondence between the balance sheet and the books, especially in the context of suspicious circumstances, an inference of fraud would be warranted—and so the case was sent back for a new trial on the issue of fraud.

That result was odd. In holding that these facts could support a finding of fraud and in noting that gross negligence could support an inference of fraud, Cardozo was encouraging the development of an area of liability for accountants (and lawyers and title companies) via the harsh route of fraud, with its greater stigma and the possibility of punitive damages, loss of professional licenses, and even criminal punishment. Thus, Cardozo opened up the possibility of "indeterminate liability" in many situations, albeit with a somewhat higher standard of proof, "for an indeterminate time to an indeterminate class" that he sought to avoid by limiting the cause of action for negligence. No wonder *Ultramares* has been controversial.[69]

Indeed, Cardozo's wariness about reformulating doctrine so as to increase a person's duty toward others, especially unknown others, when the result might be to impose crushing liability raises again the problem of *MacPherson*. Why did Cardozo not conclude that the possibility of imposing crushing liability on the manufacturer meant that the matter should be left to the legislature? Although *MacPherson* was decided at the beginning of his New York court career and the restrictive liability cases—*Palsgraf, Moch,* and *Ultramares*—were decided near the end, this was not a matter of changing sides over time. Cardozo intermixed liability-expanding and liability-restricting opinions throughout his career. Perhaps Cardozo did not, in 1916, regard *MacPherson* as involving a vast potential increase in liability for the manufacturer. After all, before *MacPherson,* there was a possibility that the manufacturer might ultimately have been held liable through a chain of lawsuits from buyer to dealer to manufacturer.[70] The negligent representation cases are another example of the fact that when Cardozo innovated with qualifications, the qualifications were real, not just window-dressing.

March 3, 1932, was the last day that Cardozo sat on the Court of Appeals. On that day, the court handed down its opinion in Homac Corporation v. Sun Oil Company, raising once again the question of the applicability of the *Ryan* limitation of liability for fire.[71] Gasoline in the storage tanks of Sun Oil exploded and set several buildings on Homac's property on fire, destroying them all. Homac's property did not adjoin Sun Oil, and in fact nothing on the intervening street was destroyed. A jury verdict for Homac had been affirmed by the Appellate Division. The Court of Appeals affirmed unanimously in a technical opinion by Judge Kellogg that focused solely on legal doctrine and not on the policies embodied in it. Kellogg explained the basis of the fire rule's limitation of recovery to an adjoining property owner: there was no liability if intervening property burned before the fire reached the plaintiff's property because the negligent defendant had no control over the condition of the intervening property, whose burning was the immediate cause of the fire's spread to the plaintiff's property. But where the intervening property did not burn, it was in no sense the cause of the damage to the plaintiff's property, and the defendant's negligence was the sole cause. Cardozo joined that opinion silently. He did not like the absoluteness of the fire rule's premises about foreseeability and cause and had previously sought to persuade the court to modify it.[72] At the same time, he had relied in a number of analogous situations on its underlying public policy argument against the imposition of heavy liability to a multitude of plaintiffs. Cardozo was doubtless pleased on his last day on the Court of Appeals to see his court make a small dent in the absoluteness of the fire rule while respecting its underlying purpose.

Cardozo approached negligence law with a fundamental acceptance of its central premises, even when some of its principal features, including the dominance of the fault principle over strict liability and the persistence of some of the defenses to the negligence action, were coming under strong attack. He viewed the negligence cause of action as one between two parties with the issue being whether one party was responsible for the injuries of another. In that setting, fault was crucial. The larger public issue—who should bear the costs of inevitable accidents in an industrial society—was to be addressed by statute in a legislative setting where all interest groups could be represented. In some instances, he refused to consider whether public policy considerations warranted a modification of an existing rule because the legislature had already modified the rule in part and left the remainder intact.

Cardozo considered the difficult legal issues at the intersection of his method of philosophy, emphasizing logical reasoning, and his method of sociology, emphasizing public policy, on an ad hoc basis that focused on the reasons for particular rules in the context of the facts of each case. In reaching his decisions, Cardozo was not moved by sympathy for parties, like Donald MacPherson or Helen Palsgraf, based on their economic or social status. Unlike equity cases, in which justice was to be done on an individual basis, justice in these cases was done by crafting a just rule, applying it impartially to the relevant facts, and accepting the results, whether seemingly harsh or not.

Cardozo was willing to modernize rules that restricted liability, but often with conditions that gave weight to the reasons for the original rule. This qualified innovation resulted in matched pairs of cases. Thus, after he applied the concept of foreseeability to update an anachronistic privity rule in *MacPherson,* he demonstrated the limits on that concept in *Perry* and on his willingness to abolish privity in *Chysky.* Likewise, his readiness to create a remedy for a tenant against a landlord in *Altz* disappeared in the absence of a relevant statute in *Cummings.* He was willing to modernize land law a bit in *Hynes* to impose on railroad companies the consequences of their lack of care, but he was not willing to impose special precautions on trolley companies in *Adams.* Likewise, the doctrinal advance in *Glanzer* had its limit in *Ultramares.* And he was ready to chip away at aspects of the rigid fire rule of *Ryan* but not to dispense with its restriction of the potential for enormous liability.

From the middle of the nineteenth century, the history of tort law was marked by a conflict between respect for precedent and arguments for change, and a tension between the liability-increasing and liability-restricting nineteenth-century precedents of Thomas v. Winchester and Ryan v. New York Central Railroad. Cardozo's opinions reveal a number of considerations that influenced his accommodation of the contending principles and doctrines: a need to reorient rules to meet modern conditions, reluctance to establish the potential for crushing liability, respect for the special role of the jury, deference to the constitutional authority of the legislature and governor, especially when they had already taken some action, and, finally, confidence in his own ability to read a case record and make up his mind about the relation between the parties and the effect of their conduct.

Foreseeability, not as an abstract notion but in the context of a factual setting, was crucial to Cardozo's idea of the duty of care that underlay liability for negligence. Foreseeability guided or should guide the conduct of all parties. It informed business managers with respect to the risks they needed to avoid, minimize, or insure against. It also informed ordinary people, like the woman who fell over the man repairing the cash register and like the man who rode the Flopper, that life was risky and that everyone had to exercise prudence in their daily lives. But foreseeability was not the only determinant of liability. It was limited by the notion that liability was not to be extended in indeterminate amounts to indeterminate numbers of people or in new situations whose complexity suggested that the legislature or an agency was a better forum for reaching a solution.

There is no formula for explaining why Cardozo viewed some of the considerations more strongly in some cases than in others. It is misleading to try to find a chronological pattern of more adventurous opinions like *MacPherson* in his earlier years and more cautious opinions, like *Palsgraf, Moch,* or *Ultramares* in his later years. The fraud portion of *Ultramares* was creative, and there were many innovative opinions in his later years on the Court of Appeals and on the Supreme Court, as well as some cautious opinions in his early years as a judge.

Cardozo's conclusions in individual cases were based on his judgment about the importance of the relevant guides to decision in each particular factual setting. He understood that his job was to weigh the relevant considerations, including public policy considerations, and to make a pragmatic choice among them in order to decide a case. He did that work conscientiously as long as he was on the court. He was not the first judge to introduce new public policy considerations into the calculus of tort law. Nonetheless, at a time when the use of policy considerations had become obscured, perhaps even to many judges, he trumpeted their relevance. Readers, especially readers of a later day, will not always agree either with the public policy considerations that he espoused or with his ultimate conclusion in a given case. But Cardozo's use and defense of a pragmatic methodology in judging helped pave the way for the changes in tort law that followed after him.

17

Contracts and Promises

Negligence law involves the duties imposed on people by law to govern their interactions with one another; contract law, on the other hand, involves the duties people impose on themselves as a result of promises that they make to one another. Cardozo made important contributions to contract law by considering promises in the context in which they were made, and not abstractly, before deciding whether they should be enforced. As in the tort cases, Cardozo's approach was complex. He took many factors into account in each case. Claims of certainty, especially in the business context, claims of justice, and the wider effect of a rule beyond the particular promise at issue were all important to him. When he was done, he had clarified and changed New York contract law in small but important ways.

The major issues in Cardozo's contracts opinions involved deciding whether to infer a promise from the context of parties' dealings with one another when there was no explicit agreement and whether a person's promise should be enforced. Usually, a promise was not enforced unless the person receiving it had given something of value, by word or deed, in return. That something was called "consideration," and spelling out the contours of the concept was the subject of endless court decisions and academic articles. What was at stake in all the cases in which these issues were involved was which of two parties who had dealt with one another was going to wind up obtaining or losing money as the result of an unkept promise.

Common law courts had been deciding contracts cases for hundreds of years, and a great body of law, much of it quite technical, had developed. The field had been systematized in the nineteenth century in the lengthy textbook of Cardozo's student days, *Parsons on Contracts,* and updated in the early twentieth century by Samuel Williston in a massive treatise that emphasized the technicalities of contract doctrine.[1] During Cardozo's tenure on the bench, challenges began to be issued to the Williston conceptual approach—sometimes called the Williston-Langdell approach because at the end of the nineteenth century Dean Christopher Langdell of Harvard had advocated a "scientific" approach to classifying the principles of contract doctrine from a few generative opinions. One of the leading challengers was Arthur Corbin, an early proponent of a realist approach to law. He sought to adjust doctrine to the practicalities of particular types of contracts.[2] On the face of it, Cardozo used Williston's doctrinal structure, but he did so with the practical, functional approach of Corbin.

A larger issue, with important consequences, that was beginning to emerge in Cardozo's day involved the essence of contract doctrine. Should the law of contract focus attention on the promise that had been made by the promising party? Or should it focus on the reliance by the party to whom the promise had been made? Some scholars applaud the emphasis on the conduct of the promisor for its concern with the moral element of keeping promises in contract law. Others argue that a growing emphasis on the reliance of the promisee directs attention to the fairness aspects of the transaction and hence generalized notions of what fairness requires. This latter group of scholars views a concern with fairness as calling attention to the public aspects of contract law and hence as narrowing the doctrinal distinctions between tort and contract law.[3]

Cardozo was not doctrinaire, and his accommodationist tendencies led him to adopt and adapt insights from a variety of theories. He began with a general acceptance of the contract doctrine that had been put in place over the past centuries. Where the law was unsettled, his inclination, as in his equity and torts opinions, that law should encourage people to behave honorably and act responsibly disposed him to enforce promises, both because they had been made and because of the reliance they induced. Moreover, he recognized that special considerations of public policy favored enforcement in business and some nonbusiness transactions.

———

Although Cardozo's contract opinions can be analyzed most easily when organized along doctrinal lines, such as implied promises, consideration, conditions, remedies, statute of frauds and the parol evidence rule, Cardozo approached his task with a different perspective. He viewed his task more as resolving particular disputes between litigating parties than as resolving arguments among contract theorists or giving guidance to drafters of contracts. Lower court judgments were to be reversed or affirmed. Contract doctrines were just tools used to make decisions. That approach accounts for some of the frustration of contract law teachers with Cardozo's opinions. In conversations with contracts teachers, I have heard references to "ambiguity" and "cryptic hints," and the use of adjectives like "subtle, evasive, hesitant" used over and over again to characterize those opinions.[4] Cardozo's style of judicial reasoning laid out only general directions. He avoided absolute rules that might inhibit the flexibility and creativity of those who needed to make contracts and live by them.

If we look for directions instead of rules, we find that there was one strong pattern in Cardozo's contract cases. His own twenty-three year legal practice had been primarily commercial. He understood business arrangements. His judicial opinions reflected his ability to interpret commercial contracts in accordance with business usage. As a result, he often found that a contract existed even if the technicalities required to make a contract seemed at first glance not to have been met. He accomplished this result by inferring from the parties' conduct the terms that were necessary to complete a contract. In so doing, he was fond of quoting the striking expression of Judge Francis Scott of the Appellate Division that the arrangement in question was "instinct with an obligation."[5]

Moran v. Standard Oil Company was one such case.[6] A paint salesman had agreed to sell the defendant's paint for a five-year period, and the defendant had agreed to pay him commissions on sales. Cardozo interpreted the agreement to require the defendant to employ the salesman for that period and not to permit termination at will. The use of the term "agreement" and the salesman's promise to sell for five years implied a reciprocal obligation to employ for that period. Similarly, in Varney v. Ditmars, Cardozo disagreed with the majority's conclusion that a promise by an architect to a professional employee to pay him "a fair share" of the profits for the year in addition to his salary if he stayed on and helped the business through difficult times was too vague to be enforceable. Cardozo would have enforced the promise if only the plain-tiff had supplied evidence, whether through custom or in some other way, of what a "fair share" of profits would be.[7]

The best known of Cardozo's "instinct with an obligation" opinions is Wood v. Lucy, Lady Duff Gordon.[8] The flair of Cardozo's opening sentences contributed to its inclusion in almost all American contracts casebooks published since 1917: "The defendant styles herself 'a creator of fashions.' Her favor helps a sale."[9] Otis Wood was Lady Duff Gor-don's manager. They had signed an agreement in which she gave him the exclusive right to market her designs and to place her endorsements on designs of others. He was to receive half of the revenues of sales that he might make. When she then gave an endorsement on her own, Wood sued her for breach of contract. She sought a dismissal of the suit on the pleadings, without any trial, arguing that there was no effective contract. Contract law required that for a contract to be enforceable, the parties had to give one another "consideration." Traditional consideration doc-trine required that there had to be a bargain in which something of value was given or promised by the other side in return for the party's prom-ise.[10] There is usually no problem in finding consideration in business contracts because each party usually promises to do something for the other, and mutual promises constitute consideration. But sometimes there is no explicit promise, or the promise is incomplete. Wood was such a case.

Lady Duff Gordon argued that Wood had neither given nor promised anything in the agreement. Since there was no consideration for her promise, Wood could not enforce it. The trial judge ruled that a valid contract existed and denied her motion. The Appellate Division reversed and ordered judgment for Lady Duff Gordon. The Court of Appeals reinstated the trial court's judgment, three judges dissenting without writing an opinion.

Cardozo's opinion for the majority in Wood was typical of his ap-proach. For all his interest in doctrine, Cardozo never lost the focus on the individual case at hand and usually used everything he could find in it to support a judgment. That was the style of the lawyer turned judge (as opposed to the theorist turned judge, or judge turned theorist). Cardozo marshaled every fact, every relevant provision of the arrange-ment in order to support his argument that Lady Duff Gordon's promise was enforceable.

Cardozo carefully orchestrated the court's conclusion that a promise by Wood to use reasonable efforts to make sales was to be inferred from the total circumstances. First came a statement that looked both to history and to a proper method of statutory construction. "The law has outgrown its primitive stage of formalism when the precise word was the sovereign talisman, and every slip was fatal. It takes a broader view today." He was alluding to the days when the old common law forms of action ruled and procedural formalities had to be precisely met or the party would be out of court, but he felt no need to specify which rules had been outgrown. Having used history loosely to set the stage, Cardozo then laid the basis for inferring the necessary promise by Wood to support the promise of Lady Duff Gordon by invoking the formulation that he found so compelling. "A promise may be lacking, and yet the whole writing may be 'instinct with an obligation,' imperfectly expressed . . . If that is so, there is a contract."[11] And he found that it was so.

Cardozo analyzed the written agreement to point out every shred of language that suggested a promise by Wood. Lady Duff Gordon had given an exclusive privilege to Wood to sell her designs. The agreement could not reasonably be interpreted to leave Lady Duff Gordon at Wood's mercy, and his acceptance of an exclusive agency therefore required him to accept the duty to sell. But Cardozo did not stop with that provision, although he might have. He pointed to the provision in the agreement that stated that Wood possessed an organization adapted to securing endorsements for Lady Duff Gordon. It implied that the organization was to be used for those purposes. More importantly, Wood's compensation, half of the profits resulting from his efforts, was linked to those efforts and was backed up by an obligation to account monthly to Lady Duff Gordon for all profits. These provisions helped enforce the conclusion that Wood had a contractual obligation to Lady Duff Gordon, which Cardozo defined as the duty "to use reasonable efforts to bring profits and revenues into existence."[12] There was therefore an enforceable contract, which Lady Duff Gordon had broken, and the judgment in favor of Wood was reinstated.[13]

Contracts teachers like to press the Cardozo reasoning by asking whether a promise would have been inferred if the original suit had been by Lady Duff Gordon against Wood for failing to work hard enough.[14] The logic of Cardozo's opinion, which took no account of the identity of the plaintiff, suggests that the answer for him would have been yes. The point of the question seems to be that sympathy for the worker made it easier for Cardozo to infer a promise on behalf of a salesman against an employer rather than the other way around. But that is precisely the kind of circumstance that would not have influenced Cardozo at all. The judge who took verdicts away from children in *Perry* and *Adams* and from a poor widow in *Palsgraf* would not have been troubled about holding a salesman to his contract.

Another point made by contracts teachers is that the Lady Duff Gordon defense was also a practical business interpretation of the arrangement: that Wood wanted complete freedom and got it because the employer was willing—without a promise on either side—to trust to the salesman's self-interest in promoting Lady Duff Gordon's fashions. Cardozo rejected that argument. For him, fair business practice suggested that Wood's receipt of an exclusive dealing privilege imposed some obligation on him.

We may also ask whether Cardozo's approach imposed the bargain he wanted the parties to have made. Cardozo did not pretend that the identity of the judge was irrelevant to decision, but his aim was to focus on the facts of each case in order to understand the transaction from the viewpoint of the parties. Most of the time, as in *Wood*, he succeeded.

Two cases that followed *Wood* tested the durability of Cardozo's opinion. Cardozo did not sit in the first one, Oscar Schlegel Manufacturing Company v. Peter Cooper's Glue Factory, but he would have to deal with its consequences.[15] *Schlegel* involved a so-called requirements contract. The seller, a glue manufacturer, agreed to fulfill all the buyer's glue requirements for one year at nine cents per pound. When the retail price rose sharply during the year, the buyer escalated its requirements to the point where the seller ceased delivering. The seller was not simply losing profits because of a rising market; it was facing higher manufacturing costs as a result of shortages in raw materials during World War I.[16] The issue, when the case got to the Court of Appeals, was whether the contract was enforceable.

Judge McLaughlin, writing for a unanimous court, held the contract invalid for lack of consideration. Although the seller had given value to the buyer by promising to sell it glue, the buyer had not promised anything of value to the seller. The buyer was a jobber, a dealer in a variety of products, and it was not in any business that required the use of glue. Consequently, its requirements might have been zero. Nor did the contract mention any other standard—such as the typical requirements of a particular glue-consuming business—by which the quantity of glue to be bought could reasonably be forecast. McLaughlin distinguished *Wood* as a case in which the seller had given the agent an exclusive privilege, obliging him to make reasonable efforts to drum up sales. The buyer's privilege in *Schlegel* was not exclusive, and hence no comparable duty could be inferred.

Cardozo dealt with a somewhat similar problem in Cohen & Sons v. Lurie Woolen Company just months after *Schlegel*.[17] The plaintiff in *Lurie Woolen* agreed to buy two hundred pieces of tricotine cloth at a certain price, with an option to purchase all that the seller could obtain. Upon delivery of the two hundred pieces, the buyer demanded in addition all that the seller could obtain. The seller claimed, falsely, that it had only sixteen pieces and withheld an additional five hundred pieces. The buyer sued for breach of contract. It won in the trial court but lost in the Appellate Division.

Cardozo, writing for the six judge majority, reversed the Appellate Division. He rejected the seller's argument that the contract was fatally vague as to the buyer's obligation and therefore that consideration was lacking. Cardozo found consideration in the promise to buy a fixed amount. "This option was drawn by merchants. We are persuaded that merchants reading it would not be doubtful of its meaning. It was meant to accomplish something. We find no such elements of vagueness as to justify the conclusion that in reality it accomplished nothing." Cardozo read the contract in its commercial context as sufficiently stating the quantity, the time for exercise of the option, and the price. The contract gave the buyer the privilege to obtain more than the fixed amount "if [the seller] can get more . . . We think the implication plain that the buyer is to fix the quantity, subject only to the proviso that quantity shall be limited by ability to supply."[18] Thus, there was a valid contract.

Karl Llewellyn, leading realist theorist and commercial law scholar, complimented Cardozo's effort. This was "as strong a statement of the commercial attitude as can be located in the books."[19] But he did so in the context of asserting first that *Schlegel* was wrong and then that Cardozo had covered up Judge McLaughlin's error when he wrote his own opinion in *Lurie Woolen*. The anomalous result in *Schlegel* was simply evidence for Llewellyn that Cardozo's fellow judges could "be led by a Cardozo into a commercial reading" but could not yet do a commercial reading for themselves."[20] In emphasizing Cardozo's strong performance, Llewellyn slighted Cardozo's colleagues. *Schlegel* presented a difficult problem, and its resolution by a unanimous court that included some very good judges, Cuthbert Pound and William Andrews among them, represented a valid "commercial reading" of the situation.[21]

Llewellyn's critique also slighted Cardozo. How, Llewellyn wondered, could the court find a contract in *Lurie* without overruling *Schlegel?* Cardozo distinguished the cases on the basis of the *Lurie* buyer's promise to buy a minimum of two hundred pieces of cloth, whereas in *Schlegel* the "option stood alone."[22] Llewellyn argued that the option in *Schlegel* stood alone by reason of the court's faulty interpretation and not "by force of the raw facts as they came." Llewellyn concluded that Cardozo, "who within the limits of possibility came close to making a fetish of judicial candor then did as technically pretty and as intellectually dishonest a job of face-saving for his brother McLaughlin as you can discover in the books."[23] But Llewellyn misstated the situation. The question in *Lurie*, and the real grounds for comparison with *Schlegel*, was the definiteness of the amount that the buyer could order, i.e., the existence of a limiting standard. The issue for the *Schlegel* court had been whether the court was going to read the contract to allow the buyer to buy an indefinite amount at a fixed price in a rising market even if the seller were bankrupted as a result. In *Lurie*, there was contract language (the buyer can confirm a larger amount, but only if the seller "can get more") that supplied sufficient definiteness in amount to make the contract valid, and the buyer was just claiming goods that the seller had already obtained. On those facts, whatever one thinks of the result in *Schlegel*, *Lurie* was a different case.

The different results in this sequence of contract cases reflected the differences in the facts of the cases more than any gap between Cardozo and his fellow judges. Although Cardozo was not so manipulative as Llewellyn portrayed him, his opinions did justify Llewellyn's high regard for his ability to interpret documents in their commercial context to make sense of the parties' dealings.

Having applied a commercial analysis in order to discover a contract implied in the ambiguous agreement between Wood and Lady Duff Gordon, Cardozo was also willing to apply it to reach a contrary result in another, more complicated business context. In Sun Printing and Publishing Association v. Remington Paper and Power Company, Inc., a buyer of paper had contracted to purchase a specified amount of paper per month over a sixteen-month period.[24] The price was fixed for the first four months. Thereafter, the price and length of time that price was to apply were to be agreed upon, "said price in no event to be higher than the contract price for newsprint charged by the Canadian Export Paper Company to the large consumers."[25] After the four-month period, the seller refused to sell more paper although the buyer tendered payment to the seller at the Canadian Export Paper Company's price for several months. The buyer then sued the seller for breach of contract.

Cardozo, for the majority, again wrote an opinion reflecting his understanding of the commercial background, but this time he refused to enforce the agreement. He intimated that the uncertainty as to price was curable. The contract could be viewed as giving the buyer an option to buy at the Canadian Export price to large consumers. But the uncertainty as to time was not curable. Without the parties' agreement, there was no way to ascertain whether the price prevailing at the end of the four-month period would apply for the remainder of the contract. Because the contract did not indicate that the price would fluctuate during the term if the Canadian Export price fluctuated, it was necessary to have an agreement as to time. Cardozo rejected the various suggestions offered in Judge Crane's dissent of provisions that might be inferred to make the agreement enforceable. Cardozo analyzed the commercial situation concisely, but in depth:

> The argument is made that there was no need of an agreement as to time unless the price to be paid was lower than the maximum. We find no evidence of this intention in the language of the contract. The result would then be that the defendant would never know where it stood. The plaintiff was under no duty to accept the Canadian standard. It does not assert that it was. What it asserts is that the contract amounted to the concession of an option. Without an agreement as to time, however, there would be not one option, but a dozen. The Canadian price to-day might be less than the Canadian price to-morrow. Election by the buyer to proceed with performance at the price prevailing in one month would not bind it to proceed at the price prevailing in another. Successive options to be exercised every month would thus be read into the contract. Nothing in the wording discloses the intention of the seller to place itself to that extent at the mercy of the buyer. Even if, however, we were to interpolate the restriction that the option, if exercised at all, must be exercised only once, and for the entire quantity permitted, the difficulty would not be ended. Market prices in 1920 happened to rise. The importance of the time element becomes apparent when we ask

ourselves what the seller's position would be if they had happened to fall. Without an agreement as to time, the maximum would be lowered from one shipment to another with every reduction of the standard. With such an agreement, on the other hand, there would be stability and certainty. The parties attempted to guard against the contingency of failing to come together as to price. They did not guard against the contingency of failing to come together as to time. Very likely they thought the latter contingency so remote that it could safely be disregarded. In any event, whether through design or through inadvertence, they left the gap unfilled. The result was nothing more than "an agreement to agree."[26]

Such a contract was not enforceable.

Sun Printing has intrigued leading commercial law writers because Cardozo, who was inclined to find binding obligations when business people dealt with one another, refused to do so here.[27] Corbin described Cardozo as having decided the case "somewhat surprisingly" and asked whether he was "less moved to cure defects in the work of the well-paid lawyers of two rich corporations?"[28] Cardozo did not exhibit any such bias in his opinions. His position was quite straightforward. There was an important gap in the terms of the agreement. The plaintiff had produced no evidence of business usage that would fill the gap, and the defect was fatal.

Cardozo put the case in a more theoretical posture some years later:

Here was a case where advantage had been taken of the strict letter of a contract [by the defendant] to avoid an onerous engagement. Not inconceivably a sensitive conscience would have rejected such an outlet of escape. We thought this immaterial. The court subordinated the equity of a particular situation to the overmastering need of certainty in the transactions of commercial life. The end to be attained in the development of the law of contract is the supremacy, not of some hypothetical, imaginary will, apart from external manifestations, but of will outwardly revealed in the spoken or the written word. The loss to business would in the long run be greater than the gain if judges were clothed with power to revise as well as to interpret. Perhaps, with a higher conception of business and its needs, the time will come when even revision will be permitted if it is revision in consonance with established standards of fair dealing, but the time is not yet. In this department of activity, the current axiology still places stability and certainty in the forefront of the virtues.[29]

Cardozo certainly believed in creative interpretation of the language of business contracts to comport with the commercial background. He was not willing, though, to push interpretation to the point where it appeared to him to be revision of a contract that was invalid as written. He would not manipulate the rules of contract interpretation to do justice on an individual case basis.

Cardozo had one more chance in this case to see whether his instinct to uphold commercial contracts could be accommodated within the rules. On remand of the case to the lower court, the plaintiff sought to meet Cardozo's objections by amending his complaint to assert that the price alleged to be the maximum was set, not for the year remaining in the contract, but rather for quarterly periods. The lower court, finding that the original defect persisted, dismissed the complaint. The Appellate Division affirmed the lower court.[30] Cardozo was sympathetic to the plaintiff. "The amount involved is very large, over a million, five hundred thousand dollars. The defendant is trying to squirm out of a contract on very technical grounds. We sustained its position, though with avowed reluctance. If there is any reasonable way of holding this complaint good, I am sure we shall be glad to take advantage of it." After he had recommended the granting of a motion for leave to appeal, the defendant's brief arrived. Cardozo then concluded that the chances for reversal were "so negligible" that he added a note to his report recommending denial of the motion, and the court agreed.[31]

Cardozo's bottom line in *Sun Printing* was that there were areas of commercial dealing where the parties either by design or accident did not reach binding agreements, and in those areas they took their chances. Cardozo's instinct has received a practical confirmation. Stewart Macaulay has reported the habits of the paper trade: "The standard contract used by manufacturers of paper to sell to magazine publishers has a pricing clause which is probably sufficiently vague to make the contract legally unenforceable. The house counsel of one of the largest paper producers . . . said that everyone in the industry is aware of this because of a leading New York case concerning the contract, but that no one cares."[32] Buyers and sellers in that industry have apparently decided to gain flexibility by leaving some uncertainty in their dealings, even with the warning of that leading New York case. Cardozo had not been fanciful in concluding that commercial contracts were not always meant to be legally enforceable. Businesses live with risks.

Cardozo's opinion thus reflected one of his major instincts—that life,

particularly life in modern industrial society, was risky, and that acceptance of a large measure of risk was a necessary cost attending the
rewards. In contracts, as in torts, the law offered some protection, but
only so much. There were times when people and businesses had to look
out for themselves.

———

The consideration issue was important outside the commercial context,
and Cardozo wrote important opinions treating the problem in personal
relationship and charitable subscription cases as well. He often enforced
promises in situations in which it was difficult to find the necessary
consideration. Indeed, Professor Gilmore described Cardozo as a judge
who "could, when he was so inclined, find consideration anywhere."[33]
But Cardozo was not always so inclined, for he saw the idea of consideration as expressing a policy that, in general, promises to make gifts
were not enforceable.

Dougherty v. Salt is an example of Cardozo's holding fast to traditional doctrine.[34] Hellena Dougherty had given a note, a written promise
to pay money, for $3,000 to Charles Dougherty, her eight-year-old
nephew, on a form that stated it was given for "value received." When
the aunt died, Charles's guardian sought payment of the note from her
estate. The executrix of the estate claimed that there was no consideration for the promise. Charles's guardian testified that the aunt had loved
her nephew, wanted to take care of him, and gave him the note with the
comment, "You have always done for me and I have signed this note for
you." Despite the formality of the note with its explicit reference to
"value received" and the possibility that the aunt's remark indicated that
Charles had given her something of value, Cardozo refused to find
consideration in this case. Overturning a jury verdict for the plaintiff,
Cardozo, for a unanimous court, declared that the guardian's testimony
established that the note represented not a debt but a "voluntary and
unenforcible promise of an executory [future] gift."[35] If the distinction
between a promise to make a gift and a contractual promise was to be
maintained, there could be no recovery in this case. An exception here
would mean that all gratuitous promises formalized in a writing would
be enforceable. Cardozo was not ready for a change of that magnitude,
and all Cardozo's consideration opinions have to be understood against
the background of his refusal to find consideration in Dougherty.

Cardozo considered the problem of consideration in an unusual case of a personal promise in De Cicco v. Schweizer, decided in 1917.[36] When Count Gulinelli became engaged to marry Blanche, the daughter of Mr. and Mrs. Schweizer, the Schweizers and the Count entered into a contract. Reciting the engagement and coming marriage, the Schweizers promised to pay Blanche $2,500 per year for as long as she and either parent lived. Mr. Schweizer also promised not to change a provision in his will for the benefit of Blanche and any children. He made payments annually from 1902, the date of the marriage, until 1912. De Cicco, a third party to whom Blanche and the Count had assigned their interest in the 1912 payment, brought suit for nonpayment of that installment. The Schweizers alleged that their promise was unenforceable because it lacked consideration. Since Blanche and the Count were already engaged, their promise to the Schweizers was a promise to do what they were already legally obliged to do. De Cicco prevailed at trial, in the Appellate Division, and in the Court of Appeals.

Prior law favored enforcement of marriage settlements as a corollary of its support for the institution of marriage generally.[37] Notwithstanding this policy and the unanimity of the courts that heard the case, there was a serious doctrinal obstacle to enforcing the promise. There was a general principle of contract law that when B and C (Blanche and the Count) had already contracted with one another, an additional promise by B to induce C to perform the contract was unenforceable for lack of consideration. C was already bound. Great controversy existed regarding the proper result when the additional promise was made to C by S (the Schweizers), a stranger to the original contract, and a wide variety of possible results had been urged by one scholar or another.[38] Under general contract law, De Cicco could not prevail unless the Count and Blanche could prevail. He stood in their shoes.

Cardozo began his discussion of this issue with a concession. "The courts of this state are committed to the view that a promise by A to B to induce him not to *break* his contract with C is void," that is, if Mr. Schweizer had promised money to the Count to induce him not to break his engagement to Blanche, that would not have been enforceable.[39] Cardozo cited four New York cases for that view. Interestingly enough, those cases do not appear to stand conclusively for that proposition, and so it was open to Cardozo to have considered that basic controversial question afresh.[40] Indeed, had he done so, he could have made use of an earlier, well-known New York case and an English case that both pointed in the direction he wished to go.[41] But Cardozo relied on *Shad-*

well, the English case, only as suggesting a point of departure and a method of approach.

Cardozo avoided the four earlier New York cases by regarding the Schweizers' promise as having been made to both the Count and Blanche. "We have never held, however, that a like infirmity [of lack of consideration] attaches to a promise by A, not merely to B, but to B and C jointly, to induce them not to *rescind* or *modify* a contract which they are free to abandon."[42] Cardozo then squeezed the facts of *De Cicco* into this hypothetical situation. Blanche, although a beneficiary of the contract, was not a party to it. Cardozo inferred that Blanche knew of the contract and acted in reliance on it, and he concluded that that reliance put her in the same position as if she had been a promisee.[43] Like all couples, the Count and Blanche were free to terminate their agreement to marry. Consequently, if they forbore from breaking their engagement in reliance on the Schweizers' promise, and if the Schweizers meant for them to rely on the promise, the Schweizers could not retract it. The forbearance by Blanche and the Count constituted consideration, and that made the promise enforceable.

Cardozo concluded that it was not necessary for Blanche and the Count to prove why they went ahead with the marriage. Adopting a traditional tort wording of cause and effect, Cardozo explained that "the natural tendency and the probable result" of the Schweizers' promise was to put "pressure" on the engaged couple to marry.[44] "If the tendency of the promise is to induce them to persevere, reliance and detriment may be inferred from the mere fact of performance. The springs of conduct are subtle and varied. One who meddles with them must not insist upon too nice a measure of proof that the spring which he released was effective to the exclusion of all others."[45] Aside from that much quoted second sentence, Cardozo recognized the importance of reliance by Blanche and the Count as an element in deciding whether to enforce the Schweizers' promise. But Cardozo was generous in presuming the existence of reliance from the fact of the Schweizers' promise.[46] Finally, Cardozo rebutted the suggestion that the Schweizers intended only a gift, with their daughter's engagement simply being the occasion for making it. The formality of the agreement and the covenant language were enough to refute the argument that only a gift was intended.

After going through this lengthy doctrinal analysis to find consideration and thus uphold the Schweizers' promise to make annual payments to their daughter, Cardozo finally adverted to the key policy reason for enforcing the Schweizers' promise: "The law favors marriage settlements, and seeks to uphold them . . . It has enforced them at times when consideration, if present at all, has been dependent upon doubtful inference . . . It strains, if need be, to the uttermost the interpretation of equivocal words and conduct in the effort to hold men to the honorable fulfilment of engagements designed to influence in their deepest relations the lives of others."[47] Precedents encouraging marriage settlements, the parents' "honorable" duty, and the fact that the parties dealt with one another in an elaborate, formal document were the critical factual elements in Cardozo's conclusion.

Arthur Corbin gently but firmly criticized Cardozo's analysis, although not his conclusion, in an article in the *Yale Law Journal*.[48] Corbin doubted very much that Blanche should be regarded as a promisee. She looked more like the incidental beneficiary of a contract between two other people, a "donee beneficiary." Even if she were a promisee, Corbin did not see how a joint offer to the Count and Blanche changed the fact that each was already obligated to perform his or her promise to the other. The case then was just like the case of a promise made by the Schweizers to the Count alone in order to induce him to perform his contract with Blanche. That would be the promise that Cardozo said was unenforceable in New York.

Corbin's solution to *De Cicco* was quite straightforward. In his view, it was likely that the marriage of the Count and Blanche induced the Schweizers' promise. The performance by the Count and Blanche of their duties to one another fulfilled the usual requirements of consideration for that promise. There was benefit to the Schweizers in seeing their daughter married and legal detriment to the Count and Blanche in the extinguishment of the ability of each to offer a rescission, an end of the contractual engagement, to the other. Corbin also addressed the public policy arguments that enforcement of the Schweizers' promise would encourage extortion by an engaged couple against wealthy parents by pointing out that such conduct was much less likely when the promise had been made by the Schweizers, a third party, instead of by one of the engaged parties to the other. Although Corbin thought that these were firmer doctrinal grounds than the one Cardozo had chosen, Corbin also thought that ultimately the issue was not whether there was consideration but whether, as a matter of public policy, promises like this should be enforced. He agreed with Cardozo that they should.

Cardozo responded to Corbin's critique by letter:

I cannot avoid the belief that there is more importance than you seem to discover in the distinction between a promise made to induce *A* not to *break* his contract and a promise to induce *A* and *B* not to *rescind* by joint consent. If Count Gulinelli on the morning of the wedding, as the wedding party was entering the church, had told his future father-in-law that unless he got $100,000 he would humiliate the daughter by making a hasty exit, I think we should all be looking for some way to nullify a promise thus extorted. We should then have what you yourself call a blackmail contract, using the word, of course, in a popular or loose sense. Between such a contract and a contract not to rescind, I find a wide difference. It is important, however, not to treat the mere form of the promise as controlling. Otherwise, the blackmailer could attain his end through ready means of evasion. We must look to the substance of the transaction. In determining what the substance was, I think it is an important consideration that the promise was for the benefit not of one party, but of both. There is nothing in the case in question to suggest the probability that the Count had threatened to break his promise. The implication rather is that the father appreciated the fact that husband and wife would need some aid in the battle of life, and that he promised this aid to them to induce them to proceed.

Cardozo then put his factual vision of the case in passionate terms: "It seems a monstrous thing to say that at such a crisis in the lives of others, one [Mr. Schweizer] may throw dust in their eyes [the eyes of Blanche and the Count], may blind their vision of the future, and their insight into its difficulties and dangers, and yet be heard to say thereafter that the inducement [to marriage] must count for nothing."[49] It is uncertain why Cardozo, with no personal experience of marrying or married life, used such overwrought rhetoric. Perhaps he thought it helped him to defend his opinion.

Unlike Corbin, Cardozo could not, or would not, deal with *De Cicco* on public policy grounds alone. Such policy grounds came in, at the very end of his opinion, to support his doctrinal views. For centuries courts had embodied public policy notions in their definition and redefinition of "consideration." It was unlikely that any judge, and particularly Cardozo, would discard centuries of precedent or start anew by saying that the issue in this case was not whether there was consideration but whether as a matter of public policy the court should enforce this contract. The whole movement of contract law had been to develop a structural framework for narrowing the underlying public policy issues into manageable smaller pieces, and consideration was one of those pieces.[50] Cardozo would doubtless have agreed with Holmes's comment that "A common-law judge could not say I think the doctrine of consideration a bit of historical nonsense and shall not enforce it in my court."[51] Cardozo was not ready to do away with the concept of consideration. He found a theory that respected the legal doctrine and carried out the policy of encouraging the keeping of promises that induced marriage.[52] The strain was to fit the facts within the theory, and he did so, somewhat unrealistically, by including Blanche as a promisee even though she had not been a party to the contract.

Cardozo considered the problem of consideration three times in another area where the decision to enforce a promise had public policy implications, the law of charitable subscriptions. The issue was whether a promise to give money to a charity constituted an unenforceable gift or an enforceable contract. His first encounter with the problem in the case of In re Slocum in 1923 was fairly straightforward. Mrs. Russell Sage, a well-known philanthropist, provided in her will that gifts prior to her death of more than $10,000 to charities mentioned in her will should be regarded as advances on account of the legacies. In her lifetime, she had offered $500,000 to the American Bible Society on the fulfillment of certain conditions, including matching contributions from others. These were eventually met, and the payment was made. Later, the Society contended that the $500,000 should not be deducted from a gift by Mrs. Sage to the Society in her will. The Society argued that the $500,000 it had earlier received was not "a gift" because Mrs. Sage had been contractually obligated to pay it; the legacy in the will should therefore be paid in full. The Surrogate (the name given by New York to the judge handling probate matters) concluded that the $500,000 should be deducted from the legacy, and the Appellate Division affirmed.[53]

In reporting to the consultation on the Society's application for reargument of the court's denial of its earlier motion for leave to appeal, Cardozo brushed aside its argument. For purposes of construing Mrs. Sage's will, the $500,000 payment was a gift pure and simple:

> If A., B., and C. sign a promise to contribute sums of money to a college or a hospital, they would be surprised to be informed by the recipient

of their bounty that the form of the subscription had taken away from the payment the quality of a gift . . . The purpose was benefaction. The Society gave nothing in return. The consideration, if there was any, was technical and artificial, and arose from the fact that like promises were made by others. I cannot doubt for a moment that Mrs. Sage thought she had made a gift. Her thought is controlling, since it is her will that is to be construed.[54]

Cardozo had not yet written on the problem of what constituted a contract in the charitable subscription setting. But the question in *Slocum* was not whether Mrs. Sage should be held to a promise to contribute. Rather, the question was whether a previous contribution should be counted as part of the total gift, and her intention was controlling on that issue. Cardozo's commonsense view was that she would have regarded the payments as a gift, and that was enough to construe the language of her will.[55]

Cardozo's understanding and common sense was tested a few years later, in 1927, by a fact situation that at first glance looked like the hypothetical case of A, B, and C that he had discussed in his *Slocum* report. Cardozo's decision to enforce the charitable subscription in Allegheny College v. National Chautauqua Bank, treating it as a contract rather than as a gift, produced another famous opinion.[56] In response to Allegheny College's capital fund drive in 1921, Mary Johnston pledged $5,000, to be paid out of her estate. The form pledge card recited that her promise was based on her "interest in Christian Education" and was "in consideration of others subscribing." The college undertook to add the money to endowment or to spend it in accordance with written instructions on the reverse side of the pledge. On the reverse, Mary Johnston wrote: "In loving memory this gift shall be known as the Mary Yates Johnston Memorial Fund, the proceeds from which shall be used to educate students preparing for the Ministry, either in the United States or in the Foreign Field."[57] Although the pledge was not due until after her death, she paid $1,000 in December 1923, and the college set the money aside as a scholarship fund for students preparing for the ministry.

In July 1924, Mary Johnston's lawyer notified the college that she was cancelling her pledge. After her death in December 1924, the college brought suit against her estate for the balance. The executor, a bank, hired a distinguished local trial lawyer, Robert Jackson—later Attorney

General and Justice of the Supreme Court of the United States—to defend the lawsuit. Jackson presented a factual picture of an aggressive charity taking advantage of an elderly donor and suggested a legal framework for construing the pledge as revocable. He argued that the ordinary understanding is that a person can revoke a promise to make a gift, including a gift to a charity. Put in legal terms, Jackson argued that Johnston's promise was not supported by consideration and hence was not enforceable. The bank prevailed in trial court and the Appellate Division, but the college won, 5–2, in the Court of Appeals, with Cardozo writing for the majority and Kellogg for the dissent.

Cardozo's previous opinion in Dougherty v. Salt demonstrates that he was prepared to follow the general contract doctrine that lack of consideration is a defense against enforcement of a promise to make a gift. Here, on the face of it, all that had happened was that Mary Johnston had promised to give money to the college and later changed her mind. The college had promised nothing and had apparently done nothing for her, and so there was no obvious consideration. Cardozo began his opinion with a discussion of the precedents. He noted that some New York courts had refused to enforce promises to make gifts to charities if the promises were made without consideration and that other courts had found consideration in situations where general contract law would not support the finding. He discussed an earlier case, Hamer v. Sidway, in which the Court of Appeals had enforced an uncle's promise to pay $5,000 to his nephew if the nephew refrained from smoking, drinking, swearing, and playing cards or billiards for money until he was twenty-one.[58] The court found consideration for the uncle's promise in the bargained-for abstention by the nephew—contract law referred to it as a "detriment"—from undertaking lawful activities. But Cardozo, referring to all the complexities of consideration law, stated that the *Hamer* formula, which was helpful to the route he wished to follow, was only a "half truth."[59] He suggested that perhaps *Hamer* had to be understood with the supplemental gloss of more conventional consideration doctrine, which required that promise and consideration must purport to be the inducement, at least in part, for one another, as they were in that case. It was not enough that the nephew sustained a detriment. It had to have been bargained for by the uncle.

Cardozo's understanding of *Hamer*, which followed a similar implication in *De Cicco*, confounded some Cardozo admirers. Corbin, for one, rejected it, even while approving the result in *Allegheny*.[60] If Gilmore was correct that Cardozo had so broadened the definition of consideration as to make it "meaningless," why would he accept the restrictive, "reciprocal conventional inducement" theory that had been advanced by Holmes?[61] Cardozo's acceptance of a rigid formulation did not mask a deft move to a completely opposite conclusion. Dougherty v. Salt and his struggle in *De Cicco* demonstrate that Cardozo did not believe that the doctrine of consideration was meaningless. Moreover, there was no need to call *Hamer's* statement of doctrine into question unless he really believed that it was questionable. He could have said that it didn't apply to these facts. Cardozo was doubtful that consideration could be found solely from the fact that the promisee had experienced some detriment in reliance on the promise. In other words, Cardozo accepted much of orthodox contract doctrine about consideration even as he searched to uphold promises in some special situations involving marriage settlements and charitable subscriptions.

After stating that *Hamer* did not resolve the *Allegheny* facts, Cardozo might have turned to the complexities of consideration law as applied in charitable subscription cases. Instead, right in the middle of a paragraph, he began to discuss the growth of "promissory estoppel" as a substitute for, exception to, or qualification of the consideration requirement for the enforcement of contracts. Promissory estoppel is a doctrine that makes promises enforceable without any consideration. The promise must be one "which the promisor should reasonably expect to induce action or forbearance of a definite and substantial character on the part of the promisee and which does induce such action or forbearance . . . [and when] injustice can be avoided only by enforcement of the promise."[62]

Cardozo's treatment of the controversial promissory estoppel doctrine was remarkable. After referring to De Cicco v. Schweizer and another case as possible signposts on the road to acceptance of the doctrine as a modification of the general law of consideration in New York, he stated quite unequivocally that the doctrine was good law in New York: "Certain, at least, it is that we have adopted the doctrine of promissory estoppel as the equivalent of consideration in connection with our law of charitable subscriptions."[63] He cited charitable subscription cases as far back as 1854 for this proposition, and he noted others in which consideration doctrine had been expanded. But the cases he cited were ones in which the donee had done something quite substantial, like building a church, in reliance on the promise and the donor had been involved in the planning.[64] Cardozo may well have been justified in regarding the courts' reference to the donee's reliance on the promise as pointing the way toward promissory estoppel. But Cardozo did not say that the court had adopted promissory estoppel as the equivalent of consideration in all charitable subscription cases.

Cardozo was not ready to enforce Mary Johnston's promise on the basis of promissory estoppel, probably because the college had not done much in reliance on her promise. But he used the decisions that implied acceptance of the doctrine to reframe the issue of the existence of consideration: "So long as those decisions stand, the question is not merely whether the enforcement of a charitable subscription can be squared with the doctrine of consideration in all its ancient rigor. The question may also be whether it can be squared with the doctrine of consideration as qualified by the doctrine of promissory estoppel."[65] Cardozo therefore turned back to the issue of the existence of consideration for Mary Johnston's promise. "The concept survives as one of the distinctive features of our legal system. We have no thought to suggest that it is obsolete or on the way to be abandoned. As in the case of other concepts, however, the pressure of exceptions has led to irregularities of form."[66] He declared that his discussion of precedent had been mere background to "an understanding of the implications inherent in subscription and acceptance," and proceeded to demonstrate how the case could be fitted within the traditional view of consideration without recourse to "the innovation of promissory estoppel."[67]

The words written by Mary Johnston suggested to Cardozo that she wanted a memorial to perpetuate her name. As soon as she tendered and the college accepted a partial payment of $1,000, the college entered into a bilateral agreement with her and undertook the "duty to do whatever acts were customarily or reasonably necessary to maintain the memorial fairly and justly in the spirit of its creation."[68] The college, having received the payment, was held to have undertaken to couple the name of the donor with the scholarship in its circulars and in other customary ways. Thus there were mutual promises, and those promises furnished traditional consideration. That done, it was unnecessary to decide whether the promissory estoppel doctrine was applicable.

Cardozo did not say whether the general public policy in favor of enforcing charitable subscriptions would have led him to enforce a simple pledge without any action or reliance by the college. His treatment of the hypothetical case of A, B, and C in his *Slocum* report suggested that he was not yet ready to enforce such a pledge. The fact that he strained so hard to find consideration in *Allegheny* suggests that he still was not ready to enforce a pure pledge. Cardozo's method reminds us of his performance in *MacPherson*. Prior case law had found consideration in charitable subscription cases, based on public policy favoring the enforcement of such promises, when the charity had undertaken to act in reliance on the promise. Cardozo found consideration in *Allegheny* by inferring a promise by the college to act in reliance on the pledge.

Kellogg, dissenting with Andrews, presented a different picture.[69] Noting that Mary Johnston's handwritten indorsement on the pledge card referred to the pledge as a "gift," he argued that it should be treated as such since she requested no action by the college. Even if she had made an offer, it was an offer in exchange for an act yet to be performed, the naming of the gift as the Mary Yates Johnston Memorial Fund. The fund was never so named, and therefore the offer was terminated by her letter.[70] Kellogg saw no new consideration doctrine in the charitable subscription cases that Cardozo cited. In those cases, either there was consideration because the promisee charity actually performed the requested act, or perhaps there was a promissory estoppel, which, Kellogg agreed, was nothing new.

The real puzzle in *Allegheny* is why Cardozo wanted to enforce Mary Johnston's promise. In the ordinary charitable subscription case, the donor has died and a representative of the estate believes that fiduciary duty to the beneficiary requires a refusal to pay the subscription. But in *Allegheny,* the donor, having made a partial payment, had changed her mind before she died and had so notified the college. Moreover, the college had not undertaken any project in reliance on the Johnston pledge. Cardozo was not persuaded by the argument that this was a poor case for enforcing a charitable subscription. He was impressed by the college's action in setting up the fund as a memorial. In finding an obligation on the part of the college to do so, he provided a hypothetical example that had personal meaning for him. "A parallel situation might arise upon the endowment of a chair or a fellowship in a university . . . with the condition that it should commemorate the name of the founder or that of a member of his family. The university would fail to live up to the fair meaning of its promise if it were to publish in its circulars of information and elsewhere the existence of a chair . . . in the prescribed subject, and omit the benefactor's name."[71]

The personal meaning is reflected in Cardozo's own will, in which there were two provisions relevant to personal memorials. One provision gave $7,500 to Mt. Sinai Hospital for the endowment of a bed to be "maintained and dedicated in perpetuity to the sacred memory of my sister Ellen Ida Cardozo." The second left the residue of his estate to Columbia University with a wish and hope, although not a mandatory direction, that the gift be used to found or maintain a chair of jurisprudence in the Law School "to be associated with my name, and to perpetuate the scientific study of a subject which has been one of my chief interests in life."[72] Cardozo clearly felt that the desire to perpetuate a family name was a serious matter. It might explain why he sought to link the public policy reasons for enforcing such gifts with correlative obligations on the part of charities to make sure that the terms were carried out. In finding consideration, Cardozo was seeking to highlight the obligations of the charity in the future, when no one would be looking over its shoulder.

Cardozo's opinion in *Allegheny* has been severely criticized by the commentators either on the basis that a reader cannot tell whether it is based on consideration or promissory estoppel, or on the basis that the facts do not support his result, or both.[73] Cardozo's opinion is certainly exasperating, especially for a contracts teacher. But Cardozo did make reasonably clear, at least at the end of the opinion, the basis on which the case was decided. It was decided on a consideration theory, not on a promissory estoppel theory. The college had not urged a decision on the basis of a promissory estoppel, and Cardozo probably concluded that it was difficult to find the necessary detrimental reliance by the college. It was no less strain, however, to fashion a bilateral contract out of the facts of the case.[74] Given the prior New York cases that had found consideration in many charitable subscription settings, Cardozo's contribution to contract law in *Allegheny*, like that in *Wood*, was in inferring an obligation on the part of the college that would constitute consideration. He also sent a message to charities about the necessity of honoring their obligation to donors.

Cardozo revisited charitable subscriptions once more, in 1931, just before he left the Court of Appeals. First Methodist Episcopal Church v. Howard again involved a question of the binding effect of a charitable subscription after the death of the donor. George Howard had signed a subscription promise for $5,000 toward the construction of a church's war memorial building. He wrote on the subscription form that he made the gift "as a memorial for my wife Joanna." The subscription had not been paid when he died, and his executor refused to pay it. When the church brought suit, the Surrogate followed *Allegheny College,* holding that "there was an implied obligation on the part of the church to use the fund as a memorial to the testator's wife." The Appellate Division affirmed on the ground that the promise became binding when the church expended money on the faith of the promise.[75]

Cardozo recommended denial of the estate's motion for leave to appeal, but he expressed doubt about the ground chosen by the Surrogate. He considered the words of the subscription in light of his own general knowledge. "We find the like again and again in subscriptions to relief funds published in the newspapers." They represented "merely a sentimental tribute . . . to the memory of loved ones" and not "a reciprocal promise on the part of the donee to record the memorial in perpetuity." Howard had not been so specific as Mary Johnston in his designation of the subscription, and so Cardozo declined to find a duty of the charity similar to the one he had found in *Allegheny.* When he provided a memorial for Nellie in his own will, he was careful to heed his judicial prescription.

Cardozo was more impressed with the ground chosen by the Appellate Division. Relying on the earlier New York cases cited in *Allegheny College,* he regarded the church's expenditures before Howard's death as crucial. There were some payments for stationery and an expenditure of $928.62 for a bronze memorial tablet. Cardozo did not think that the size of the payments was critical so long as they were not negligible. The church had spent the money in reliance on the subscription. Howard knew that the project was going forward, and that knowledge was sufficient to bind him within the meaning of the prior cases. Apparently, the moment when consideration arose was when the charity moved from fund-raising to implementing the purpose of the solicitation and when Howard had some general idea that that stage had been reached. Since it was reasonable to infer general knowledge from Howard's close association with the church and its pastor, the estate was bound to fulfill the promise. Cardozo then advised his colleagues that although the "problem presented by these subscriptions is always confusing," and although he was ready to hear the case if anyone wanted to, he tentatively recommended denial of the estate's motion. The court followed his recommendation.[76]

This trilogy of Cardozo responses to charitable contribution cases indicates that he was sympathetic to the public policy argument favoring enforcement of "gifts" to charities; enforcement meant the accomplishment of charitable works. The law of charitable subscriptions was in flux, and Cardozo's response was a pragmatic eclecticism. He tried hard to uphold the gifts, but he had his limits. He was not willing to abolish the test of consideration entirely, and he was ready to reject a claim if one of the recognized events that would turn a gift into a contract had not occurred. Those events included both the promise of action by the charity in response to the charitable subscription and some action by the charity in reliance on the subscription. Cardozo's desire to fit charitable subscriptions within conventional consideration doctrine led him to strain to infer an obligation on the part of the charity in *Allegheny*. The resulting contribution to the law of charitable subscription was not a triumph of simplicity or clarity. His vision of the facts, his vision of existing case law, and his vision of the appropriate direction of the law all provoked controversy. In the end, his general instinct for enforcement of charitable subscriptions has prevailed, with the growing recognition that they should usually be enforced as a matter of public policy, even without a showing of consideration.[77]

Cardozo wrote opinions in a large number of contract cases in which the issue was the enforceability of a promise, and the critical problem was whether the promisee had promised or done anything that should count as consideration for the promise. Cardozo was at his best in the commercial context, where he had long experience as a lawyer. There his touch was deft, and he succeeded in bringing the law relating to enforcement of promises into greater conformity with commercial expectations and practice. His emphasis on practical usage and reality as opposed to abstract rules of law has become the generally accepted mode of legal analysis and is embedded in the Uniform Commercial Code, which has been adopted in nearly all jurisdictions as a codification of American commercial law. The cases involving personal obligations outside the business context were more individual; there was less customary expectation to guide him. Cardozo struggled with some of these cases, with the result that these opinions were more labored and convoluted. But his opinions became both precedents and teaching tools that future courts and academics used as the basis for generating new legal doctrine.

18

Moral Obligation and Damages

Cardozo wrote major contract opinions that dealt with other aspects of law besides the formation of contracts. One important group of cases dealt with the promises and contracts of government. His opinions in these cases indicate that the same considerations of deference to the authority of the legislative and executive branches of government and concern for governmental finances that affected other Cardozo opinions were at work in his contract opinions. A second group of cases dealt with the interpretation of contract provisions in situations in which literal enforcement would cause hardship. The problem is to figure out why Cardozo sometimes enforced such provisions and sometimes did not.

Cardozo addressed the issue of the enforceability of the promises of government in four important cases that pitted two of Cardozo's themes against one another—the desire to enforce promises where the ordinary citizen would expect such enforcement and the desire not to impose extra costs on government without the approval of the legislature.

The first case, People v. Westchester National Bank, in 1921, was very much in the public eye, for it involved the constitutionality of the state's issuance of bonds to pay a bonus to veterans of World War I.[1] The statute authorizing the bonds had been approved, according to its terms, by a statewide referendum. Judge Andrews, for the majority, held the statute

338

unconstitutional as a contravention of Article 7, section 1, of the New York Constitution, which stated that the "credit of the state shall not in any manner be given or loaned to or in aid of any individual, association or corporation." Since the proceeds of the bonds, representing the credit of the state, were to be used only to pay the bonus, the question for the majority was whether the payment represented a "gift" to the recipient. The court acknowledged the existence of prior cases holding that payments in recognition of a moral or equitable obligation of the state did not constitute a gift but held that in all those cases either a benefit was received by the state or an injury was suffered by the claimant in circumstances in which it was fair to ask the state to respond. In the veterans' case, the court held, there was no claim based upon a moral obligation owed by the state of New York because the veterans served in the nation's army, not a state army. Thus, no payment of a claim was involved; there was only a gift, and the New York Constitution foreclosed a payment on that basis.

There were two dissents, one by Pound and one by Cardozo. Pound's dissent was quite technical. In his view, the Constitution had not been violated because the credit of the state had not been given or loaned to the recipients of the bonus. It was sold to the purchasers of the bonds, and the money received became the property of the state. That money could then be given to individuals so long as no other constitutional provision was violated, and in his view, none was.

Cardozo's dissent met the majority opinion head on. He saw the purpose of the constitutional prohibition, as demonstrated by its history, to be the prohibition of public financing of private enterprise. Thus, in determining what was a gift for purposes of the prohibition, he, rather like the majority, saw the issue as requiring him to decide whether the purpose of the bonus was "benefaction" or "requital." He compared the wage paid to soldiers and sailors with that of civilians and concluded that it was reasonable for the legislature and the voters to have decided that wartime service deserved more than had previously been paid. It was not just the courts that were concerned with equity and honor. The legislature was too, and the courts should respect its judgment. "Equity and honor are the same as in olden days. The Constitution does not define them, nor seek to circumscribe their content."[2]

Cardozo was impatient with the argument that distinguished between the moral obligation of the nation and that of the state. Veterans had rendered service to both. He reviewed at great length the cases that had permitted the state to make voluntary payments based on honor, equity, morality, and justice, and then he reviewed at even greater length the relation between the service rendered, the sacrifice endured, and the payment of a bonus in order to refute the "pure gift" conclusion of the majority. He was also impatient with the argument that upholding this statute might lead to abuse and hence to emasculation of the constitutional provision: "the existence of a power is not refuted by demonstrating the opportunity for its abuse. The abuse must be dealt with when it arises."[3]

Cardozo cared about this opinion. The issue was important and much in the public eye. The voters had approved the bond issue by more than a two-to-one margin. Cardozo reported privately that he was opposed to the bonus statute and had voted against it.[4] Nevertheless, he wrote strongly in favor of upholding it against constitutional attack. His opinion was eloquent. It demonstrated that although he was reluctant to impose financial obligations on government, especially when a relevant constitutional provision forbade gifts of public money, he was not doctrinaire in such matters. The legislature and the voters had both approved the expenditure, and he respected their right to make that decision.

Of course, in the age-old dispute about what judges actually do, Cardozo could be accused of imposing his own patriotic sensibilities on the apparent conflict between legislative enactment and constitutional provision. But Cardozo did not make his decision in that fashion. As a judge, Cardozo had to determine whether the payment was based upon some sense of "moral obligation"; however, he did not decide that question on the basis of his own opinion, which was opposed to the bonus. The issue for him was the public's basis for the payment, as expressed through the referendum: "I am persuaded that hundreds of thousands of earnest men and women believe that justice and equity demand the payment of this bonus."[5] The views of those "right-minded men and women" were enough to establish the moral obligation on which the constitutionality of the referendum depended.

Cardozo would not enforce the government's promises in two cases where it had undertaken to pay contractors more than the amount provided by their contracts. The first case, Gordon v. State, in 1922, involved a New York statute that permitted contractors to recover additional compensation by suit in the state Court of Claims in situations in which large increases in prices because of World War I had increased greatly the cost of performing state contracts.[6] The plaintiff contractor sought such a judgment, but the Court of Claims held the statute unconstitutional. The Appellate Division reversed and held the statute constitutional in certain situations. In an opinion by Judge Hogan, the Court of Appeals reversed the Appellate Division. It decided first that there was no basis in contract law to justify the payment of extra compensation for what the contractor was already bound to do. The state had no moral obligation that might serve as consideration. The contractor knew that there were war-related economic risks and that the state was not responsible for the extra costs of completion. Furthermore, the statute violated the constitutional provision that "the legislature shall not . . . grant any extra compensation to any . . . contractor."[7] Cardozo concurred separately in the result solely on the ground of violation of the constitution; he did not pass on the contract law question whether one could find a moral obligation that would serve as consideration in a case such as this.

In the second case, McGovern v. City of New York, Cardozo addressed the contract issue directly in his opinion for the court.[8] The plaintiffs were under contract to build a subway in New York City in 1916. Although they had a contract with the labor union until the completion of the subway contract, the workers repeatedly threatened to strike for wage increases, and the contractors yielded to the union's demands. They were assured by the public service commission that the city would reimburse them. These promises were never fulfilled, and the contractors sued the city for breach of contract.

Cardozo, writing for a unanimous court, concluded that payment was forbidden by the constitutional provision that forbade payment of extra compensation. He interpreted that provision as compelling the protection of the public treasury. First, he rejected the notion that there was any consideration for the city's promise to reimburse the contractor for increased costs. The contractor did not give up any "right" when it paid extra wages on the faith of the city's promise to reimburse. The contractor was legally bound to do what was necessary to complete the contract. "Millions were promised by the city in return for an unreal surrender. Either there was no consideration at all, or the shred of value, if any, is so grossly disproportionate to the return that to uphold it as sufficient would be to nullify the Constitution by subterfuge and fiction."[9]

After refusing to find consideration, Cardozo went further. Even if there was enough consideration to enforce a private promise, there was not enough to enforce this promise by a public body contrary to a constitutional command: "We are dealing here with a restraint imposed by the Constitution itself upon the agencies of government. Its prohibitions are to be interpreted, not narrowly and grudgingly like those of a penal statute . . . but broadly and liberally to promote the policy behind them."[10] The plaintiffs had also relied on two statutes, but Cardozo dealt with them quickly. One, giving a cause of action to contractors who fulfilled their contracts in reliance on the state's promise to compensate them, was brushed off with the comment that a statute cannot make an unconstitutional promise valid. A second statute giving the city a privilege to cancel and remake a contract on new terms required that contractors who took advantage of the statute complete the project at cost without profit. Whether that statute was constitutional or not, the contractors did not comply with it.

Cardozo rejected an alternative approach that was followed by other states dealing with the same factual situation and similar constitutional restrictions. Those courts noted, as Cardozo had done in the veterans' bonus case, that this was not the kind of situation at which the constitutional prohibition was aimed. The contractors were not purposely delaying in order to squeeze more money out of the government, and public officials were not throwing money away. The threat of war and then the war itself caused prices and wages to leap enormously. Strikes were threatened. The workforce might simply have evaporated, and the subway would not have been completed. Faced with such an emergency, the city importuned the contractor to yield to the workers' demand, promising reimbursement. A master of consideration doctrine could have found consideration in those emergency conditions. Indeed, right next door in Connecticut, another excellent judge, William Maltbie, reached that conclusion in the face of a constitutional prohibition that was similar to the one in New York. Maltbie focused on the unforeseen conditions, the harshness of holding the contractor to its old promise, the real benefit to the government from its new promise in getting a contractor to complete a project on time, and the fairness of holding the government to that promise.[11]

By contrast, Cardozo stressed the obligation of the contractor to fulfill its original promise, the failure of the contractor to give up anything or the government to gain anything in connection with its new promise, and the saving of public money. There was a reference in Cardozo's opinion to the greed of the contractors not only in exacting recompense for increased costs of labor and material but also in preserving their profit, but that does not seem crucial to Cardozo's conclusion. Preserving the state's money was crucial. For Maltbie, the most sensible construction of the constitutional prohibition was one that deterred waste and corruption but allowed for extra spending to get important projects completed in times of crisis. For Cardozo, the most sensible construction was the strict one, since the constitution explicitly forbade extra compensation without making any exception directly for the needs of the state.

Cardozo did not address the argument that was later made by Maltbie. If he had, he might well have said that Maltbie's approach would require a balancing of benefits and detriments to the state and to the contractor with the unforeseeability of the intervening conditions in every case. To engage in such ad hoc exercises repeatedly would erode the constitutional protection accorded the public treasury. *McGovern* was therefore a case in which Cardozo refused to enforce a promise in a commercial context for lack of consideration. The public policy concerns that led him to find consideration in the marriage settlement and charitable subscription cases pointed in the opposite direction, but the combination of the explicit wording of the constitutional prohibition and Cardozo's strong concern to protect the finances of the state outweighed the practical arguments of the contractor.

In contrast, a "shred of value" might be enough consideration to support a promise when the recipient of the promise was an agency of the state. The Walton Water Company promised the village of Walton free water for fire-fighting purposes at its hydrants, which had been installed by the company but paid for by the village.[12] The village therefore had title to the hydrants, but it agreed that the company would control their use. It further agreed that it would not detach the hydrants from the main pipes without company consent. After a tax dispute, the company began to charge the village for water supplied for fire fighting and sued when the village refused to pay. The company won in both the trial court and the Appellate Division on the ground that the village had given no consideration for the company's promise to supply free water.

Cardozo found consideration for the promise of free water in the control of the hydrants that had been given by the village to the company. The company used them to flush mains and to sell water both to the village and to private owners. Even if the village could limit or destroy that right, the presence of the hydrants in the streets "gave the company the advantage of economic opportunity."[13] Likewise, there was detriment to the village in having yielded control of the hydrants to the company. Whether the essence of consideration was benefit to the promisor or detriment to the promisee, or both, was a highly controversial issue among the academicians, but Cardozo did not like to deal with doctrinal issues for their own sake. Because he found both benefit and detriment, he thus dispensed with the need for deciding the doctrinal issue of which finding was crucial.

Cardozo then cited arguments that the test of consideration was that it not be fortuitous but must have been regarded as consideration by the parties. Since Cardozo viewed that test as easily met in this case, he did not lay down any hard and fast rules. "These principles may be conceded," he wrote, reserving for a later day any qualifications that would have to be made.[14] Such measured decision-making was characteristic of his approach.

Cardozo saw that the real problem in *Walton* related to the adequacy of consideration, whether control of the hydrants could serve as consideration for free water. In *McGovern,* Cardozo had concluded that "a shred of value" was not enough consideration in the face of a constitutional prohibition against giving extra compensation. In *Walton,* Cardozo relied on the text writers and precedent to support the proposition that, in the absence of a constitutional prohibition, the amount of consideration was not a concern for the court. The parties had bargained about this issue, and the courts should not interfere with their bargain. The company was not entitled to charge the village for water for fire fighting. Cardozo was not about to make any exception to his normal inclination to enforce commercial promises when the public was the beneficiary of a good bargain.

This group of cases reflected Cardozo's method as well as his doctrinal stance. At issue in *Gordon, McGovern, Westchester National Bank,* and *Walton* was the existence of consideration to support the payment of money or other items of value by the state or to the state. In the three public payment cases, Cardozo voted to uphold the state payment against the various constitutional prohibitions only in the veterans' bonus case. Cardozo's dissent in the bonus case combined his view of the history of the constitutional prohibition as designed to prevent aid to private enterprise with his sense of the public view of military service to conclude that the moral obligation owed to the veterans of World War I was of a greater order than that owed to the contractors in *Gordon* and

McGovern. "There is a difference, not to be ignored, between profit and indemnity. If the soldiers had not suffered, and the sole purpose of the bonus were to reward them above others, the reward might be said to have no basis except gratitude, a free offer of thanksgiving, untouched by the admixture of any sentiment of justice. Their service has been coupled with sacrifice, and from the union of the two there is born the equity that prompts to reparation."[15] Accordingly, there was consideration in such measure as to overcome the constitutional prohibition of gifts in the veterans' bonus case but not in the contractors' profit cases.

Deference to the legislature and governor, which was important in Cardozo's torts opinions, was also important in his contracts opinions. Imperator Realty Company, Inc. v. Tull is a good example.[16] It involved interpretation of New York's Statute of Frauds, a generic statute that typically makes an oral contract unenforceable in the following situations: contracts for the sale of land; contracts not to be performed within one year; contracts in consideration of marriage; and indemnity contracts.[17] The policy behind the statutory requirement of a writing is that it provides reliable proof of the terms of the agreement. In *Imperator,* the plaintiff and defendant had agreed to exchange parcels of land pursuant to a written contract under seal—at that time, special rules applied to contracts to which a seal had formally been applied. The defendant refused to proceed with the arrangement on the closing date because various notices of violation of law had not been remedied by the plaintiff, as required under their contract. The plaintiff alleged, and a jury found, that there had been an oral arrangement that a deposit of cash sufficient to remedy the violations could be made in place of actually remedying them. The defendant argued that according to settled law, a written contract under seal could not be changed orally. Judge Emory Chase's majority opinion in the Court of Appeals first intimated that the oral agreement might not have violated the Statute of Frauds because it did not change the written contract. Chase went on to hold that even if there was a violation, the defendant was prohibited—the technical term is "estopped"—from taking advantage of the violation because his own consent had induced it. Therefore, the judgment in favor of the plaintiff was reinstated.

Cardozo wrote a separate opinion concurring in the result. He agreed that as a matter of equity the defendant should not be allowed to trick the plaintiff into breaking the contract. But he took the somewhat unusual step of writing separately in order to state his view that the Statute of Frauds applied to this situation. He began by stating the well-settled proposition that when the Statute of Frauds applied, the parties could abrogate a contract, but could not alter its obligations by an oral agreement. He rejected the distinction drawn by some courts between the formation of a contract, which could not be varied orally, and regulation of its performance, which could. "I do not know where the line of division is to be drawn between variations of the substance and variations of the method of fulfillment. I think it is inadequate to say that oral changes are effective if they are slight, and ineffective if they are important. Such tests are too vague to supply a scientific basis of distinction."[18] Coming from Cardozo, that argument against asking courts to draw distinctions of degree sounds a little hollow. Common law judges did that all the time. Cardozo's next point carried more force. "The field is one where the law should hold fast to fundamental conceptions of contract and of duty, and follow them with loyalty to logical conclusions."[19] The Statute of Frauds expressed a public policy requiring contracts for the sale of real property to be written, and he saw no reason to create an exception. Even if enforcing an oral portion of the arrangement involved only an insubstantial variation from the written document, it would violate a fundamental conception expressed in the statute that the certainty of promises made in writing was an important part of real estate law. For Cardozo, that was binding.

The importance of legislative policy to the result in *Imperator* is underlined by the fact that previously Cardozo had permitted parties to waive a provision in a contract orally when they themselves had originally agreed that no provision could be waived without written consent. "Those who make a contract may unmake it. The clause which forbids a change, may be changed like any other."[20] His point was clear. Although the parties might orally rescind their own requirement that modifications be in writing, they could not change a statutory mandate that modifications be in writing.

Cardozo was even tougher in Burns v. McCormick, holding to an exacting view of compliance with the Statute of Frauds in refusing to follow a less stringent interpretation that had been adopted in other jurisdictions to avoid results that seemed harsh.[21] The plaintiffs in *Burns* said that they had given up their business to take care of a widower in reliance on his promise to leave his house and lot to them when he died.

When he did not do so on his death, the plaintiffs argued that their performance satisfied the Statute of Frauds. Cardozo rejected the argument. The policy of the statute required the certainty of a writing because oral testimony might lead to what Cardozo called "the peril of perjury and error." Part performance provided some assurance that the contract had been made, but Cardozo, writing for a unanimous court, held fast to the requirement that the performance had to refer "unequivocally" to the alleged agreement. "A power of [equitable] dispensation, departing from the letter in supposed adherence to the spirit, involves an assumption of jurisdiction easily abused, and justified only within the limits imposed by history and precedent. The power is not exercised unless the policy of the law is saved."[22] Since the actions of the plaintiffs in moving into the plaintiff's house and taking care of him did not imply anything with respect to future ownership of the property, the alleged agreement would not be enforced. The plaintiffs were left with a suit to recover the value of their services.

Cardozo's most explicit statement about the limitations on changing law by judicial action came in a leading contracts damage case, Kerr Steamship Company, Inc. v. Radio Corporation of America.[23] In 1922, Kerr gave a coded message to RCA's telegraph service for transmission to Kerr's shipping agent in Manila, but RCA failed to send it. As a result, a cargo was not loaded on Kerr's ship, and Kerr lost some $6,600. Kerr sued RCA, claiming that loss of business as damages. RCA asserted that its liability was limited to the $26.78 in telegram charges paid by Kerr because the message form limited liability to the tolls and because the use of a code concealed the nature of the business transaction from RCA. Kerr asserted that the limitation did not apply when the message was not transmitted at all and, moreover, that it was unreasonable. Kerr prevailed in both the trial court and the Appellate Division, and RCA appealed to the Court of Appeals.

Writing for a unanimous court, Cardozo reversed Kerr's judgment. The issue involved the applicability of the leading English case on liability for damages, Hadley v. Baxendale.[24] The plaintiffs in *Hadley*, owners of a mill, were forced to close it when a carrier delayed delivery of a broken crankshaft for repair. The court held that damages from breach of contract were limited to those that arise naturally from the breach or may reasonably be supposed to have been contemplated by the parties. In the absence of special notice to the defendant regarding the importance of the crankshaft to the plaintiff's business, the forced closing of the mill could not have been foreseen, and hence the carrier was not liable for the loss of profits caused by the business shutdown. Cardozo applied this rule in *Kerr* and held, without relying on the damage limitation provision of the message form, that the message communicated to RCA gave no hint of the nature of the transaction, so that Kerr was entitled only to recovery of the charges it had paid.

Cardozo made his job somewhat easier by failing to mention that Kerr's message was written in Scott's code, which was a public code used for economy rather than secrecy, and that a copy of Scott's code was on RCA's message desk.[25] The actual message delivered to RCA began "AKJEDUDAHT AKFREICTOJ KINGHORN URGPOOPGWO SAN-CARLOS THEREFORE GIVE BLOSSOM UTSCAICRUF" and continued in that vein. The translation, in part, was "15 Received 10 Agree Kinghorn 1000 tons minimum San Carlos. Therefore give Blossom utmost additional cargo Stop Telegraph immediately estimated sailing date Blossom . . . as must decide whether Suez Canal or Panama Canal."[26] Cardozo indicated that he did not consider the public nature of the code significant when he made the oblique but accurate comment that even when translated into plain English, the message "remains at best obscure, though some inkling of the transaction may be conveyed to an ingenious mind."[27]

Cardozo also understood that the whole notice discussion had an "air of unreality" because none of RCA's employees were supposed to pay any attention to the content of the messages they were transmitting. Although he may have had some sympathy for Kerr, which suffered a large loss because of RCA's error, Cardozo concluded that it would not be appropriate for the court to change a rule that had existed so long that it had become "tantamount to a rule of property."[28] The rate structure of the industry was built on it. The telegraph company had therefore not insured against the risks, and the potential liability was "crushing."

Cardozo then turned to affirmative reasons for retaining the rule. The senders of messages, who knew what was involved, were in a better position to insure against mishaps than were the telegraph companies, who did not. Placing liability on the telegraph companies would raise rates for all to protect against loss for a few. Finally, Cardozo expounded the difference between the usual recovery of "general" damages, which in a contract for delivery of a telegram was the cost of sending it, and additional "special" or "consequential" damage, which was based on notice to the carrier of the nature of the transaction that depended on delivery of the telegram. The requirement of notice, similar to the concept of foreseeability in torts, was potentially quite elastic, and Cardozo required rather particularized showings in both cases. Cardozo explained the nature of RCA's liability in the language of causation. "The key to *Hadley v. Baxendale,*" he wrote, "is lost if we fail to keep in mind the relativity of causation as a concept of the law."[29] It is clear that the causation he was talking about was not factual causation but "legal causation," the conclusory notion defining the amount of actual injury for which the defendant would be held liable.

Just as Cardozo did not interpret foreseeability in a way that included everything that occurred as foreseeable, so he rejected the broad-ranging argument that the notice necessary for imposing consequential damages could be found in the knowledge that the message to be transmitted concerned business of some sort. Notice about the particular nature of the business involved was essential. Cardozo's references to torts writings about legal cause emphasize the similarity that he saw between the two doctrinal fields. The considerations that underlay the outcome in *Kerr* resemble some of the factors that would later be important in *Moch,* the water for the fire-fighting case, and the negligence portion of *Ultramares,* the accountants' liability case.[30] In those cases, as here, Cardozo thought that threatened "crushing" liability for relatively small transactions was relevant.[31] There, as here, Cardozo viewed any change effected by an expansion of doctrine as so great that it would have to be the product of legislative action.

Whether Kerr's argument outweighed the policy reasons for retaining the rule or not, Cardozo decided that the courts should not alter the existing rule: "We are not concerned to balance the considerations of policy that give support to the existing rule against others that weigh against it. Enough for present purposes that there are weights in either scale. Telegraph companies in interstate and foreign commerce are subject to the power of Congress . . . If the rule of damages long recognized by State and Federal decision is to give way to another, the change should come through legislation."[32] Given the long-established rule and the complexities involved in creating a new rule, and given the legislative role in regulating telegraph companies, this was an area where courts should stay their hand. If there was a problem, any change in the rule needed to come from the legislature or an administrative agency, not the judiciary. For the present, since Kerr knew the risks if the message miscarried, it should have acted accordingly.

————

In business cases, Cardozo often faced a choice between the need for certainty in rules governing commercial conduct and his desire to achieve a fair result in a particular case. Except when the case involved an equitable remedy, Cardozo did not bend the rules in favor of justice in the individual case. The element of fairness, as he said of *Sun Printing,* was "immaterial" to the task, whereas the demand for certainty was "overmastering." Occasionally, however, he concluded that a more flexible, albeit less certain, rule was needed to do justice across a whole spectrum of cases, thus making it possible to do justice on an individual basis.

Cardozo explicitly achieved such a result in one of his most famous and, as characterized by Corbin, one of his "most enlightening" opinions, Jacob & Youngs, Incorporated v. Kent.[33] Jacob & Youngs, a contractor, built a country house for George Kent, a lawyer. The crucial facts were stated succinctly by Cardozo, for the court:

> The plaintiff built a country residence for the defendant at a cost of upwards of $77,000, and now sues to recover a balance of $3,483.46, remaining unpaid. The work of construction ceased in June, 1914, and the defendant then began to occupy the dwelling. There was no complaint of defective performance until March, 1915. One of the specifications for the plumbing work provides that "all wrought iron pipe must be well galvanized, lap welded pipe of the grade known as 'standard pipe' of Reading manufacture." The defendant learned in March, 1915, that some of the pipe, instead of being made in Reading, was the product of other factories. The plaintiff was accordingly directed by the architect to do the work anew. The plumbing was then encased within the walls except in a few places where it had to be exposed. Obedience to the order meant more than the substitution of other pipe. It meant the demolition at great expense of substantial parts of the completed structure. The plaintiff left the work untouched, and asked for a certificate that the final payment was due. Refusal of the certificate was followed by this suit.[34]

The statement was well designed to produce sympathy for the builder at the expense of the wealthy owner. This was a "country residence" whose $77,000 cost in 1914 equaled roughly $1,150,000 in mid-1990s dollars. The owner moved into his new home but then nearly a year later ordered the reconstruction of a substantial part of it, at the builder's expense, for reasons that appear captious, if not vindictive.[35]

The trial court, in directing a verdict for the defendant, had excluded evidence that the pipe that was installed was the equivalent in every way to that specified and that failure to install Reading pipe was inadvertent. The Appellate Division reversed, holding that the evidence should have been admitted. The parties agreed that if the Court of Appeals affirmed the Appellate Division's judgment, a decree should be entered for the plaintiff for the balance due—apparently on the theory that any damages would be only nominal. The Court of Appeals did affirm, 4–3, in an opinion by Cardozo, with McLaughlin writing a dissent for himself, Andrews, and Pound.

The case could have been decided on the basis of a provision in the contract that stated that the specification of brands was to be considered as setting a standard and that other brands could be used with the architect's permission. Even though the architect's permission had not been obtained because the substitution was "inadvertent," the provision could have been used to demonstrate, as the plaintiff argued, that the breach was not material.[36] The suggested ground of decision was difficult, as the contractor had not complied with the provision upon which he relied. Instead, Cardozo turned to a much larger doctrinal and policy issue.

The law of conditions was the doctrinal battleground on which the case was fought. Without pursuing all the complexities of that law, the relevant doctrine is that promises to pay are either "independent" or "dependent," the answer turning on whether the particular promise is viewed as critical or not. When the promise is critical, performance of the dependent promise is said to be a condition of payment. When it is not critical, the failure to perform the independent promise will not justify a refusal by the promisee (the party to whom the promise was made) to pay the contract price, although the promisee may be able to recover damages for the failure to perform. This case was further complicated by another issue—whether and when "substantial" performance constitutes performance. In some jurisdictions, that issue was viewed along a continuum from most essential to most trivial promises, with perfect or near-perfect performance required for the most essential promises and more leeway granted as one descended toward the trivial. That characterization of the issues (which was more accurate for New York than for some other jurisdictions and was more accurate for construction contracts than for sale of goods contracts) still left open the additional questions of what was essential, what was trivial, and who decided.

Cardozo's opinion started from the premise that the contract was silent about whether use of Reading pipe was a dependent promise whose nonperformance justified nonpayment. He was not prepared to infer a purpose to make every requirement a dependent promise when "the significance of the default [the nonperformance] is grievously out of proportion to the oppression of the forfeiture."[37] Cardozo infused his statement of the doctrinal issue with a factual statement that was notably sympathetic to the contractor. Whether the promise to install Reading pipe was a dependent or an independent promise would be resolved by weighing "the purpose to be served, the desire to be gratified, the excuse for deviation from the letter, the cruelty of enforced adherence."[38]

Cardozo would not give the benefit of the substantial performance doctrine to a builder who had deliberately chosen not to comply with the brand name specification. But he concluded that the omission was neither "fraudulent nor willful." Rather, it was the result of "oversight and inattention."[39] The plaintiff's proposed evidence would have shown that the pipe he had installed was of the same quality, value, and appearance as Reading pipe, that failure to install Reading pipe was "inadvertent," and that replacing the pipe would have required tearing the building apart. In that factual setting, Cardozo viewed the promise to use Reading pipe as an independent promise, whose breach did not excuse the owner from payment of the contract price.

Turning to a consideration of the relative values of consistency and justice, with what looks like an uncharacteristic shot at his dissenting colleagues, he remarked, "Those who think more of symmetry and logic in the development of legal rules than of practical adaptation to the attainment of a just result will be troubled by a classification where the lines of division are so wavering and blurred. Something, doubtless, may be said on the score of consistency and certainty in favor of a stricter standard. The courts have balanced such considerations against those of equity and fairness, and found the latter to be the weightier."[40] Cardozo refused to adopt a rule that would hold a builder to performance of every single promise in a contract containing hundreds if not thousands of specifications before it would be entitled to payment. Considerations of fairness required a more flexible rule.

The dissenters took quite a different approach. Judge McLaughlin, seizing moral high ground of his own, began his opinion in a dramatically different way from Cardozo: "The plaintiff did not perform its contract. Its failure to do so was either intentional or due to gross neglect which, under the uncontradicted facts, amounted to the same thing, nor did it make any proof of the cost of compliance, where compliance was possible." The plaintiff, in his view, did not substantially perform the contract either. "The question of substantial performance of a contract of the character of the one under consideration depends in no small degree upon the good faith of the contractor."[41] The plaintiff installed 2,000 to 2,500 feet of pipe, of which only 1,000 feet at most complied with the terms of the contract. It gave no explanation of why it had failed to perform. Whether the home owner was motivated by whim or other reason in his demand was irrelevant. He had a right to get what he contracted for. The plaintiff whose omission was substantial could not invoke the rule regarding substantial performance. A rule that required payment for less than substantial performance would alter the parties' contract and encourage builders to break their contracts.

The opinions reflected different views of the law, different views of the facts, and different views of the application of the law to the facts. Cardozo had much the better of the argument over the law, for McLaughlin relied on an opinion that the Court of Appeals had long since repudiated.[42] Thus, with respect to the general legal principles that governed, Cardozo's opinion put them into a useful perspective but broke no new legal ground. Cardozo also had the better of the argument with respect to the culpability associated with the breach. Although the builder had "intended" to buy the other kind of pipe, it did not "intend" to break the contract.

Cardozo and McLaughlin also disagreed on what constituted substantial performance. Cardozo concluded that substantial performance was achieved when equivalent pipe was installed, at least with respect to pipe hidden in a building and absent any showing of special reasons for using Reading pipe. McLaughlin believed that substantial performance had not been achieved, as sixty percent of the pipe was nonconforming. Cardozo's view of substantial performance was more in tune with the prior relaxed New York view. He relied on the court's earlier decision in Woodward v. Fuller, in which it found substantial performance even though a house was built so "that the roof and chimneys were not well supported; that folding doors were not well hung, and the casings thereto well fastened; that the tar-paper and clapboards, in some few instances, were not well put on, and one door and casings not fitted so that the door would shut."[43] That conclusion easily supported the finding of substantial performance in Kent.[44]

Cardozo was usually concerned that people keep their promises, but Kent showed the practical limits of that consideration. When dealing with a commercial contract that involved a large objective, building a house, with a multitude of subordinate promises phrased in terms of the contract's specifications, Cardozo focused on the major purpose of the contract, building a satisfactory house. He was unwilling to penalize the builder for failure to comply with one specification when that failure did not affect the major purpose. The promise to use Reading pipe was of a much different order from the promise in Mirizio to have a religious marriage ceremony or the implied promise to offer a share in a proposed new deal to a coadventurer in Meinhard.[45] Those promises involved honorable conduct. The installation of a certain brand of pipe did not.

In these terms, Kent was not a novel case. The relaxation of the former strict rule enforcing construction contracts had already been accomplished, and the governing principles had been set forth forty years before. What, then, has made Kent special, the staple of most law school contracts casebooks, and the subject of intensive study long after the decision?[46] First, the facts presented a classic issue: the ability of a promisee to obtain a particular part of a promised performance when the part was easy to perform. Or at least the promise would have been easy to perform initially; afterwards, the promise was difficult and expensive to perform. Second, the conflicting views were presented in two lively opinions, and one of them, the majority, presented its conclusion in a historical-commercial-doctrinal combination that was, as Corbin said, "enlightening." Finally, the majority opinion was by Cardozo, whose reputation and arresting style gave, and still give, his opinions an audience and an authority.

Kent also had a special relation to the development of Cardozo's general views about law and judging. He had begun work on the lectures that were to become The Nature of the Judicial Process the summer before, and the opinion was handed down just three weeks before the first lecture.[47] As he wrote in the opinion, Cardozo thought of the case in terms of the conflict between logic and certainty on the one hand and the demands of justice on the other, a conflict that he discussed in his lectures. The decision in *Kent* became an example of the interplay among some of the decision-making forces that he would identify in the lectures: the clash between logic in the form of a definite and certain law of conditions, and justice or social welfare, which he identified both with "the good of the collective body" and with the more individualistic standards of "right conduct."[48] The right case had come along at the right time for Cardozo to demonstrate how the common law operated to accommodate both the need for rules and the needs of justice. Cardozo saw the substantial performance rule as a reaction against a too logical and mechanical application of the rules of contract. "I have no doubt," he said, discussing this case in his lectures, "that the inspiration of the rule is a mere sentiment of justice."[49] Rather than manipulating the rules of conduct to do justice in particularly appealing individual cases, courts had developed the substantial performance rule as a principle of justice that would cover many cases. The disagreement within the court, sharp but productive, honed Cardozo's reasoning and probably heightened his rhetoric. What might have been a routine opinion became a landmark of contract law in Cardozo's hands.

The same weapon that protected innocent contractors punished cheats. Much had turned in *Kent* on Cardozo's conclusion that there had been no deliberate breach of contract. When there was a deliberate breach, indeed, deceptive conduct, Cardozo's reaction to a "nice" technical argument on behalf of the deceiver was swift. In Suetterlein v. Northern Insurance Company of New York, a car insurance contract provided that no payment would be made if other insurance covered the loss.[50] The owner nevertheless took out a second policy in his wife's name, although the wife had no interest in the car. When the car was destroyed, both filed proofs of loss. Allowing both to recover would have meant double compensation. Cardozo wrote for the court denying recovery to the owner, who was claiming under the first policy. Noting that other insurance was prohibited "because the moral hazard is increased with the increase of temptation," Cardozo concluded that even if the wife's concealment of the fact that she was acting for her husband made the second policy void, that did not make the first policy valid. "We stick in the bark when we say that such conduct may be reconciled with the condition in the policy whereby other insurance is prohibited under penalty of forfeiture."[51] The dishonest claimant was entitled to nothing.

Cardozo was not always ready to subordinate the claims of certainty to those of justice. Even in *Kent* Cardozo was careful not to overstate what he thought the judge's role was. While Cardozo was often creative in reworking a doctrine or applying a doctrine to a new situation, he deliberately declined to innovate on many occasions—because of some sense that the time was not right for the law, or at least judge-made law, to take that step.

Murray v. Cunard Steamship Company, Ltd. was such a case.[52] The suit involved a contract defense to a tort cause of action. Luke Murray broke his knee on April 28, 1920, in a fall on the deck of the liner *Mauretania* while traveling from New York to Ireland. Alleging negligence, he brought suit on February 24, 1921, shortly after his return to New York. For most of the time between early May and mid-November 1920 Murray had been in the hospital because of his injury. The ticket that Cunard issued to all passengers conditioned suit for personal injury on delivery of written notice of the claim within forty days after debarkation. Murray had not complied with the requirement.

Cardozo wrote the opinion for a unanimous court, overturning a jury verdict for Murray that had been affirmed in the Appellate Division. Assuming sufficient evidence of negligence, he concluded that the failure to comply with the condition defeated the cause of action. The purpose of Cunard's regulation was reasonable. Because passengers scatter when the voyage is over, investigation of accidents becomes more and more difficult with the passage of time. Murray had no good excuse for noncompliance; there was no evidence that he had been physically or mentally unable to give notice. The fact that he had not read the terms of the ticket did not matter. A steamship ticket was a contract. "Here the condition is wrought into the tissue," and the passenger who neglects to read it takes his chances.[53] Moreover, the fact that the ticket was collected when he went on the ship was irrelevant. He should have read it beforehand or made a copy or note of the conditions or gotten a copy from the carrier. Although Cardozo did not say so, perhaps he was influenced by the fact that the "ticket" was no ordinary pasteboard stub. It was nearly one foot by one foot in size, with readable type, and a notice at the top calling passengers' attention to its terms.[54]

Cardozo was not always so unforgiving of failure to comply with contract terms requiring notice.[55] But in *Murray*, Cardozo was unwilling

to give the jury the opportunity to weaken the absolute notice requirement in a passenger ticket and so overturned its verdict. It made no
difference that a consumer might have less reason to understand language imposing a time limit for notice than a company in business.
Cardozo did not think in those terms. The plaintiff knew he had been
injured and hence was responsible for knowing the terms of his contract
relating to recovery for injuries. *Murray* long predates the age of consumer rights. It also predates early scholarship on contracts of adhesion,
contracts in which terms are imposed by one party on another on
virtually a take-it-or-leave-it basis.[56] The decision comported with the
standard view of contract doctrine as set forth in Williston's treatise and
even in the more practical work of Corbin.[57]

There was an opportunity here for a judge who was sensitive to the
practicalities of life to move the doctrine along. A big jump would have
been to recognize that passengers do not read all the terms in a passenger
ticket because they do not expect to find anything relevant to the main
purpose of buying the ticket. Making that jump would have threatened
a great deal of settled law. But it would have been typical of Cardozo
to find a special circumstance in the fact pattern that allowed him to
decide the case on a narrow ground and also to test the doctrinal waters.
For example, Cardozo could have found such a circumstance in the fact
that the company had collected the passenger's ticket when he boarded.
This fact had been strongly urged as a ground for decision not only by
the plaintiff but also by Joseph Paley, Cardozo's law secretary.[58]

One can almost hear Cardozo picking up the argument: true it is that
the general rule holds the passenger bound to read his contract. Here,
however, when the defendant has taken the passenger's contract from
him, how can it now contend that he must be held responsible for its
many paragraphs of terms and conditions? If it was so important for the
company to impose these conditions on its passengers, it should have
provided copies of the contract when it required passengers, as a condition of embarking, to surrender their tickets. The company's failure to
do so frees the plaintiff from any duty to give notice.

Cardozo, however, did not say anything like that. What he told Joseph
Paley and wrote in the opinion was that it was up to the passenger to
read the contract, remember it, or ask for a copy after it had been
collected. That conclusion was a stern approach to individual responsibility, but it was not grounded in a realistic view of human behavior.
Cardozo had previously used his practical knowledge of railroad travel

to conclude that passengers should not be bound by the terms of a posted sign.[59] He had also been on an ocean liner and could therefore have considered the passenger's situation more carefully than the lecture on responsibility indicated. For some unspecified reason, Cardozo simply was not moved by his knowledge of common behavior to apply the "method of sociology" in this case. The logic of the rules won out. Rightly or wrongly, and I think wrongly, Cardozo saw this case as he had seen the case of the woman who fell over the mechanic fixing the cash register. People had to take responsibility to look out for themselves sometimes, and Cardozo thought that this was one of these times.

Cardozo's contracts opinions contained a number of familiar features. He used the record in each case to produce a sharp vision of the relevant evidence. In the important cases at the crossroads of doctrine, he usually sought to write an opinion that dealt with the problem but that decided no more than necessary. Many Cardozo opinions therefore appear to have been decided on unique facts, for Cardozo usually did not emphasize which facts were decisive. "We know the value of the veiled phrase, the blurred edge, the uncertain line."[60] They preserved options for the future.

The Cardozo contracts opinions that had the most general application were those that dealt with the enforcement of commercial promises. Cardozo's experience and practical sense led him to make strong efforts to find enforceable agreements in the language and conduct of the parties. He also delivered striking opinions on the issue of consideration in cases involving government promises and some individual promises in unusual fact situations. As in other areas of the law, he was reluctant to impose new liability on government and indeterminate or unexpectedly large liability on private parties who had performed a service for a relatively small reward.

Cardozo made his reputation in part as the defender of judicial innovation. Innovation for him, however, did not proceed from a personal agenda of social change. Rather, it proceeded from the need to bring common law doctrine into line with evolving social or economic conditions—be it the commercial reality of business promises or the social reality behind promises relating to marriage or charitable subscriptions. As Corbin put it, Cardozo's contracts opinions did "not show the overthrow of old doctrine or the establishment of new." He carried on the evolutionary process "with wisdom and discretion . . . When Cardozo is through, the law is not exactly as it was before; but there has been no sudden shift or revolutionary change."[61] Cardozo made or supported innovations that matched innovations that had already made their way in the broader society; "modern" law, for him, kept pace with change and did not force it.

Although Grant Gilmore, Corbin's successor at Yale, and Karl Llewellyn saw Cardozo as a great, albeit masked, creator, Cardozo was cautious in innovating, more cautious even than Corbin thought.[62] Not only did Cardozo really mean all the qualifications that he put in his opinions, but he also meant to preserve future options. Those qualifications and reserved options made for difficult reading but were neither mask nor deception. So, too, does the vision of Cardozo as a thoroughgoing progressive, activist judge overshoot the mark. On the bench, as in his personal life, the values of tradition and order were important to Cardozo.

The contract cases help us to put Cardozo's views about appropriate sources of law, "the principle and practice of the men and women of the community whom the social mind would rank as intelligent and virtuous," into a practical application.[63] Although Cardozo's invocation of "right-minded men and women" could be both abstract and elitist, when it came to enforcing promises in the commercial context, he looked to contemporary commercial practice for enlightenment. When it came to enforcing promises relating to marriage or charitable subscriptions, he relied heavily on general social preferences and specific governmental policies. Sometimes, Cardozo solved the problem of discovering appropriate sources of common law by his own observation of events and ideas in the population at large, what he called making judgments based on life's experiences. The business and social practices that impressed Cardozo were consistent with his own personal world, in which duty and obligation played such a large role. Acting with honor, fulfilling a duty, accepting responsibility, and keeping promises were important themes in Cardozo's equity, torts, and contracts opinions.

Cardozo's approach to law gave judges some leeway to modernize doctrine to meet new problems and conditions, but only some. The lurking issues regarding enforcement of adhesion contracts and unconscionable contracts and consumer protection in general were for the next generation. Cardozo was not a believer in wholesale judicial change. Even though the time was approaching when courts would transform a contract law that was essentially laissez-faire into one that would involve substantial judicial oversight to prevent unfair contract terms as a result of inequality of bargaining power, Cardozo himself showed no interest in even beginning the process. He believed that the parties to a contract could and should look out for themselves.

Cardozo's general approach permitted eventual major change, in a bit-by-bit manner, but Cardozo himself never undertook any such agenda. He was careful not to intrude on the large-scale policy role of the legislature. Grant Gilmore characterized Cardozo as if he had been Samson in the Langdell-Williston temple of contract.[64] Cardozo would have appreciated the literary touch but not the conclusion. He did not believe in pulling down temples of the law. Instead, he believed in modernizing and refurbishing them, slowly, carefully, and on a modest budget.

19

Constitutional and International Law

The last six chapters have concerned issues of private law. The distinction between private law and public law was more clearly drawn in Cardozo's time than it is today. Private law involved cases that arose out of individuals' relations with one another. Public law involved cases that affected government or the public generally. Equity, contract, and tort cases were seen as private law because doctrine in those fields focused on the conduct of individuals more than on broader public issues, such as whether industry should bear the cost of injuries from its products or whether courts should take account of the inequality of bargaining power between workers and employers or between consumers and large corporate sellers. Constitutional law and labor law were paradigm public law subjects. The constitutionality of legislation and the lawfulness of strikes or picketing had obvious large-scale effects.

Constitutional law, especially federal constitutional law, and international law were an occasional feature rather than a major staple of the doctrinal diet of the Court of Appeals during Cardozo's tenure. He wrote enough opinions, however, to give an indication of his attitude toward the problems that would agitate court and country during his tenure on the Supreme Court of the United States. He had faced few of these issues in his private practice, but the clash between the regulatory power of government and the rights of private property, which had been in the forefront of political debate since shortly after the end of the Civil War, had reached a climax in the Progressive movement at the beginning of the twentieth century. As a student at Columbia, Cardozo had spoken the language of laissez-faire, Social Darwinism, and private property. Judge Cardozo would speak differently.

The court that Cardozo joined in 1914 was widely regarded as hostile to social and economic reform. Samuel Seabury's campaign for a Court of Appeals seat in 1913 had attacked the court as "reactionary."[1] That view of the court, spawned by its progressive critics and largely maintained by historians since, is not wholly accurate. The court upheld many regulatory statutes, and its total performance was considerably more balanced than indicated by the reactionary label pinned upon it.

No doctrine was more closely associated with reactionary jurisprudence during the first third of the twentieth century than that of substantive due process. Under this doctrine, the due process clauses of the Fifth and Fourteenth Amendments of the United States Constitution were interpreted as guaranteeing to individuals not only procedural rights but also "fundamental" substantive rights that are not explicitly spelled out in the Constitution. In the heyday of substantive due process from 1905 to 1937, these included such economic rights as the freedom of contract. In those years, the United States Supreme Court repeatedly struck down ameliorative social legislation, such as minimum wage and maximum hours laws for workers, for violating the freedom of contract of employees to enter contracts to work for long hours at low pay.

The New York Court of Appeals was one of the first courts in the country to interpret the Due Process Clause of its own constitution in a substantive as well as procedural fashion.[2] It did so even prior to the Civil War, and it elaborated its views in an influential series of opinions after the Civil War. The court stated quite early that the state's due process clause protected all rights that were "fundamental."[3] In 1885, in In re Jacobs, a unanimous Court of Appeals held unconstitutional a public health statute that in effect forbade the manufacture of cigars on any floor of a tenement house in New York City or Brooklyn if part of the floor was used for residential living.[4] Judge Robert Earl's opinion presaged the approach eventually adopted by the United States Supreme Court in Lochner v. New York[5] by rejecting the state's claim that the statute was a health measure. The Court of Appeals' worry was revealed in its prophecy of what might follow validation of the statute:

> if it can be sanctioned under the Constitution . . . we will not be far away . . . from those ages when governmental prefects supervised the

building of houses, the rearing of cattle, the sowing of seed and the reaping of grain, and governmental ordinances regulated the movements and labor of artisans, the rate of wages, the price of food, the diet and clothing of the people, and a large range of other affairs long since in all civilized lands regarded as outside of governmental functions. Such governmental interferences disturb the normal adjustments of the social fabric, and usually derange the delicate and complicated machinery of industry and cause a score of ills while attempting the removal of one.[6]

The court clearly saw itself as defending the social and economic progress achieved through free commerce from the restrictions, however benevolent, imposed by paternalistic government. The constitutional value protected by the court was the right of individuals to make economic decisions. But the major focus of the court's opinion was not an individual's right of choice, or "freedom of contract" as it later came to be called. Rather, it was the operation, for the sake of the "social fabric," of a free market. *Jacobs* and subsequent cases signaled that legislative regulation of economic activity would be subject to close and skeptical judicial scrutiny.[7]

The Court of Appeals, however, did not adopt a dogmatic philosophy opposed to all innovative social and economic legislation. It continued to recognize the power of the government to regulate private property to serve the public good, and it applied that principle to several important legislative initiatives. For instance, it upheld an important civil rights statute prohibiting racial discrimination in places of public accommodation.[8] The court in People v. Budd also upheld a statute that set maximum grain elevator charges.[9] Although Judge Charles Andrews (father of Cardozo's colleague Judge William Andrews) recognized the court's recent emphasis on personal economic liberty, he characterized the "virtual monopoly" of the Buffalo grain elevators as creating "exceptional" circumstances that justified the regulation.[10] Cardozo thought the senior Andrews was "take it all in all, the greatest judge that ever sat in the Court of Appeals."[11] Andrews saw the statute as a "check upon the greed of . . . consolidated interests" and not as an interference with a "rational liberty—liberty regulated by law."[12] Judge Rufus Peckham, Jr.'s, dissent attacked the statute as "vicious in its nature, communistic in its tendency, and . . . wholly inefficient to permanently obtain the result aimed at."[13] That was the same theme enunciated a few months earlier by the young

Benjamin Cardozo in his Columbia commencement address describing and attacking "The Altruist in Politics."

At the end of the nineteenth century, the Court of Appeals steered a wavering course between Andrews's approach in *Budd* and Earl's approach in *Jacobs,* examining the facts and context of each case carefully and upholding some regulations while striking down others.[14] When it came to the law setting maximum working hours for bakers in the famous *Lochner* case in 1904, a bare majority of the Court of Appeals upheld the statute by abjuring its economic regulatory aspects and focusing on the public health aspects.[15] In reversing the Court of Appeals, the United States Supreme Court held the statute to be an unreasonable interference with the bakers' freedom to make contracts. The name "Lochner" became a pejorative reference to the use by judges of personal political values to decide constitutional issues.

After *Lochner,* the Court of Appeals unanimously held unconstitutional a law prohibiting women from factory work before six in the morning or after nine in the evening.[16] In a brief opinion, Judge John Gray combined the language of liberty of contract with modern language forbidding discrimination against women. The court followed up this decision, striking down a statute requiring public dancing academies to be licensed and requiring the buildings in which they were located to comply with all building safety regulations and to have sufficient ventilation and toilet facilities.[17] The court held that the statute discriminated against public dancing academies by adding a license requirement on top of building safety obligations that were already mandatory and by not regulating dancing places where there was no instruction. Yet almost immediately thereafter the court upheld a statute prohibiting a railroad signal tower employee from being on duty more than eight hours in twenty-four.[18] This was a proper exercise of the police power to protect public safety. In general, the court examined health justifications carefully, and a selective regulation of dangerous conditions, as in the cigarmakers case, could be a fatal defect in a statute. The doctrine that legislatures were free to eliminate perceived evils one step at a time had not yet taken hold.

The decision that unleashed public wrath against the Court of Appeals was Ives v. South Buffalo Railway Company.[19] New York had passed the first general workers' compensation law in the country in 1909. A unanimous court in 1911 declared the act unconstitutional under both the federal and state due process clauses.[20] It regarded the principle of no liability without fault as a fundamental property right protected by the Constitution, whereas the statute provided employer-financed compensation regardless of fault. The court held that the legislature's "police power" did not save the statute, for its provisions did "nothing to conserve the health, safety or morals of the employees" and imposed "no new or affirmative duty or responsibilities" on the employer to make the business safer.[21] The court expressed its appreciation of the important social reasons for the statute. It simply found them constitutionally irrelevant.[22]

The important labor cases that came before the Court of Appeals in this period received the same mixed treatment. The court applied a fairly progressive doctrine of labor relations that recognized many, but not all, of the organizational rights sought by labor unions and some, but not all, of the defensive rights sought by employers and non-union employees.[23] Two opinions recognized the right of a union to take a variety of measures, including strikes, to force an employer to hire only its members.[24] These decisions permitted strikes for any competitive labor purpose that was sought by the union and also marked the rejection of the illegal-purpose doctrine that had permitted many state courts to enjoin strikes on very nebulous grounds. That new viewpoint in the common law of labor relations, which protected unionizing activities, eventually came to predominate.

The range of business and labor cases in the New York Court of Appeals prior to 1914 thus represented an assortment of doctrines, not a monolithic dogma. In modern terminology, the Court of Appeals generally used a fairly severe standard of scrutiny in judging the constitutionality of social and economic legislation. From an initial systemic opposition to statutory regulation on the basis of defending a free market, the court found itself torn between upholding individual freedom of contract and permitting legislative regulation in the name of safety, health, and protection of the public welfare. When persuasive arguments were made in favor of each rubric, the court was nearly always split, often in unpredictable ways, and the pattern of results was eclectic, almost erratic. All the judges thought that they had to assess the legislative means and goals against an elaborated constitutional standard, but the result was not predetermined for most of the judges most of the time.[25]

The year 1914 was a watershed for the court. Its personnel changed considerably in the next few years, and Cardozo was one of the members who led the court to be more open to legislative innovation. The court almost immediately pulled back from some of its more extreme pronouncements. It reconsidered its opinion in People v. Williams, which had struck down a statute prohibiting night work by women.[26] Cardozo was part of the unanimous court in People v. Charles Schweinler Press that upheld a new statute forbidding factory work by women between 10 P.M. and 6 A.M.[27] The opinion of Judge Hiscock, who had joined the earlier opinion, highlighted the difference in approach that lawyers as well as judges were beginning to take toward these issues. *Williams* was held not controlling because the statute in that case was not framed as a health measure and had not been defended as one. In setting *Williams* to the side, the court also avoided addressing the argument in that opinion that such statutes discriminated against women's access to employment. The new statute was based on a detailed factual investigation conducted by a legislative agency, and the court upheld it as a public health measure. In reaching that conclusion, it had the benefit of numerous similar health measures that had been passed by other states and countries.

Next, the *Ives* decision was overturned by a combination of constitutional amendment and court decision. At the same election that brought Cardozo to the bench, the voters approved a constitutional amendment that was designed to reverse *Ives* as a matter of state constitutional law. Cardozo thereafter joined the unanimous opinion of the court that upheld a new workers' compensation act in Matter of Jensen v. Southern Pacific Company.[28] Judge Nathan Miller first distinguished *Ives* on the ground of differences between the two statutes. He then upheld the new statute against attack under the Fourteenth Amendment. Since the United States Supreme Court had upheld a bank depositor insurance scheme that required compulsory contributions from the banks in order to compensate depositors, the requirement of compulsory contributions from employers to compensate injured employees was likewise constitutional.[29]

Cardozo would assert in *The Nature of the Judicial Process* that judges had more freedom to apply public policy considerations in the field of constitutional law than in ordinary common law cases. Precedent was less controlling. His sense, which he would make explicit when he joined the United States Supreme Court, was that the permanence of the United

States Constitution required that judges take a fresh look at the relation between precedent and current circumstances to make sure that constitutional interpretations served the underlying purposes of the constitutional provisions. He therefore felt no compunction about following his general democratic inclination to respect legislative power to deal with economic and social problems. But he also understood that constitutional provisions protected individuals against abuse of governmental power, and he examined each case carefully, especially with respect to the means chosen to achieve the apparent goals.

Early on, in a 1916 case, Klein v. Maravelas, Cardozo revealed his attitude toward legislative power in an opinion that overruled the 1905 decision of the Court of Appeals in Wright v. Hart.[30] *Wright* had held New York's bulk sales law unconstitutional. That law had sought to protect creditors by requiring a business proposing to sell a major part of its goods to give notice of the impending sale to all its creditors. In a relatively brief opinion for a unanimous court, Cardozo noted that the United States Supreme Court and numerous state courts had upheld such statutes since the decision in *Wright*. That made a difference: "In such circumstances we can no longer say . . . that the prohibitions of this statute are arbitrary and purposeless restrictions upon liberty of contract . . . Back of this legislation . . . there must have been a real need. We can see this now, even though it may have been obscure before."[31] Cardozo and his court drew heavily on the legislative statement of the needs of the age, whereas the previous court had adhered to an outmoded ideal of liberty of contract when it rejected the statute. Cardozo justified the overruling of *Wright* on the basis of changed circumstances and a clearer vision of the original circumstances. In his view, the underlying economic needs, supported by the legislature's judgment, were crucial.

Shortly after the unanimous *Klein* decision, however, the old divisions reasserted themselves within the court. The New York City Sanitary Code forbade the sale of proprietary medicines unless all active ingredients were registered, confidentially, with the department of health. A wholesaler and retailer of medicines sued to enjoin the enforcement of the ordinance by the board of health. Cardozo wrote for only four judges in Fougera & Company v. City of New York to affirm New York's general power to require such disclosure.[32] Cardozo concluded that the requirement of disclosure to officials charged with protection of public health satisfied the test that the ordinance have "a reasonable relation to the end to be attained." It would enable those officials to "prevent or punish sale of fraudulent or noxious compounds."[33] This reading, which seems so obvious today, was not obvious in 1918. Chase and Collin, the two remaining members of the *Ives* majority, and McLaughlin disagreed. They saw the relation of the ordinance to public health as too remote to justify it as a public health measure. The old doctrinal argument was still sharp. But by 1921, both Chase and Collin would be gone from the court, and "liberty of contract" ceased to be an effective counter to legislative regulatory power.

Cardozo's majority opinion found a fatal defect in the particular ordinance in *Fougera* on different grounds. Cardozo read the ordinance as applying to stocks of drugs in the hands of druggists and dealers who neither knew the ingredients nor had any way of learning them because the manufacturers would not disclose that information. The ordinance would therefore force a forfeiture of existing stocks. He concluded that the general grant of power in the New York City Charter to provide for security of life and health did not authorize a general prohibition of existing merchandise.

Cardozo refused to sever the retroactive portion of the ordinance, that is, to save the ordinance by simply holding unconstitutional the retroactive portion while letting the prospective, constitutional portion stand. In his view, the defect was "so deeply wrought into the substance of the law" that only a rewriting of the ordinance could save it.[34] Since public health was involved and since the drafters of the ordinance would likely have preferred half a loaf to none, Cardozo would have been justified in severing the retroactive portion of the ordinance. Perhaps he refused to do so because he thought that an ordinance was more easily amended, and therefore deserved less solicitude, than a statute.[35] Cardozo and the court had signaled to the city their approval of the ordinance's purposes and advised it about the necessary revisions.

Cardozo summed up his attitude toward legislative regulatory power in Roman v. Lobe in 1926. The occasion was his opinion upholding the power of the legislature to license real estate brokers.[36] His reasons were familiar. First was the strength of the policy behind the statute—to reduce the danger to the public of abuse of power by brokers, who enjoy "a relation of trust and confidence" with their customers. Second was the concurrent legislative judgment in other states, as expressed in the widespread adoption of similar statutes, which had generally been held constitutional. Finally, there was "the argument from history": for nearly a century the business of brokers had been marked off from other businesses, which were pursued without regulation as a matter of common right.[37] There was nothing startling about the result. Even the Supreme Court was prepared to uphold licensing regulation of this sort. But Cardozo's opinions were more vigorous in recognizing legislative power than most Supreme Court opinions in this era.

Cardozo wrote one final important opinion testing an innovative legislative requirement. People v. Teuscher considered a statute that provided that a farm might be quarantined when an owner of cattle refused to permit a tuberculin test of his herd after 90 percent of the herds in the town had been tested.[38] The statute was attacked as unconstitutional because of its uneven and therefore arbitrary operation. The owner argued that milk from towns where less than 90 percent of the herds had been tested could be sold and that there was no reason to believe that the defendant's milk was any less healthy. Rejecting the court's earlier opposition to one-step-at-a-time health legislation, Cardozo did not require statutory perfection as a condition of constitutionality. It was enough that the legislature was seeking to make progress in assuring healthy milk. "At least the local herds will be sound, and buyers from that source of supply will have a certificate of safety. A class may lawfully be restricted if the lines defining the restriction are not arbitrary altogether . . . Legislation is not void because it hits the evil that is uppermost. Equally it is not void because it hits the evil that is nearest."[39] Again, Cardozo supported his opinion by research into practices in other states where he found a great deal of similar legislation. This practical recognition that legislative solutions were often selective and incremental was critical in the Court of Appeals' movement toward an expanded view of legislative competence.

Cardozo looked carefully at the application of statutes in particular circumstances. In Municipal Gas Company v. Public Service Corporation, a statute had fixed the maximum charge for illuminating gas sold in Albany at $1 per 1,000 cubic feet.[40] After complying with the statute for many years, the company sued in 1918 to restrain its enforcement on the ground that it had become confiscatory. The question presented to the court was whether the plaintiff's complaint stated a valid cause of action. The lower courts concluded that it did not, but the Court of Appeals, with Cardozo writing its opinion, reversed. In recognizing that the passage of time and wartime conditions could make a statute that was constitutional when passed confiscatory and unconstitutional later,

Cardozo made a nice statement of the constitutional facts of statutory life. "The prediction" of the legislature, he wrote, "must square with the facts . . . at the beginning but equally at the end."[41]

The attitude in the Court of Appeals as a whole after 1914 was sympathetic to legislative regulation. It still undertook scrutiny of legislative ends and even more careful scrutiny of legislative means when reviewing economic legislation. But the terms of the constitutional debate were much different in the Court of Appeals from those in the United States Supreme Court. Not only was the discussion less strident in the Court of Appeals and less couched in ideological terms, but also the Court of Appeals, although subject to the overriding power of the United States Supreme Court when the United States Constitution was at issue, was much readier to recognize legislative power than was the Supreme Court. One testing case was the New York statute regulating the prices charged to ticket buyers by theater ticket brokers. Cardozo joined the Court of Appeals' opinion upholding the provision in 1924; however, the United States Supreme Court struck it down in 1927 on the ground that places of public entertainment were not so "affected with the public interest" as to justify interference with the liberty of brokers to sell tickets at whatever price they could command.[42]

Although Cardozo looked carefully at the particulars of regulation, his sympathy on the big issues was with the power of the legislature to regulate business. Indeed, he never wrote an opinion holding an economic regulation unconstitutional because the legislative goal was an impermissible subject of regulation. In private, he was critical of the Supreme Court's contrary approach. In 1923, when the United States Supreme Court struck down the District of Columbia's statute setting minimum wages for women and children in Adkins v. Children's Hospital, Cardozo wrote to Felix Frankfurter, who had argued on behalf of the statute in the Supreme Court, that "[t]he District of Columbia case left me speechless, or at least ought to have left me that way, for such speech as I uttered was not respectful."[43]

––––––––

Cardozo faced a number of cases that raised questions about the constitutional power of particular persons or groups to exercise governmental authority. The issues involved either the delegation of legislative power to private persons or the separation of powers among the various branches of government.

The *Teuscher* case, just discussed, was Cardozo's first meeting with the problem of delegation that would occupy him so conspicuously on the Supreme Court. The farmer-defendant argued that the requirement that his untested cattle be quarantined if the owners of 90 percent of the cattle in his town tested theirs, was an illegal delegation of legislative power to those owners. Relying on prior New York law, Cardozo concluded that this delegation of legislative power to a private group was not illegitimate. The decision to test cattle was beneficial to public health and was not solely for the personal good of those owners:

> Small use would there be in stimulating the many within a township to the care of the public health, if one or a few wiseacres or obstructionists could make the labor vain. More and more, in its social engineering, the law is looking to co-operative effort by those within an industry as a force for social good . . . Conspicuously is it doing this in its dealings with agricultural producers, spread often over wide areas, and thus deficient in cohesion, but yielding up new energies when functioning together.[44]

Cardozo usually asked only whether the legislative perception of the need for a particular means of regulation was valid. Here, unusually, he indicated that he supported both the goal and the cooperative process that was chosen. (What was not unusual was the series of inverted sentences.)

Cardozo also considered another kind of constitutional process question, the matter of separation of powers among the various branches of government. What kinds of powers may constitutionally be exercised by each branch? He wrote an opinion for a unanimous court in In re Richardson, which struck down a statute that permitted the governor to designate a judge to investigate charges against the borough president of Queens County.[45] He reviewed the duties laid on the judge and concluded that they were essentially investigative and prosecutorial, functions associated with the executive branch, as opposed to the case-deciding function of the judicial branch. A judge could therefore not be given such powers. Cardozo was not trying to protect the public against overbearing judges. To the contrary, he read the state constitution as protecting judges from being compromised. While noting that "exigencies of government have made it necessary to relax a merely doctrinaire adherence" to strict separation into a flexible and practical doctrine, "[e]lasticity has not meant that what is of the essence of the judicial function may be destroyed by turning the power to decide into a pallid opportunity to consult and recommend."[46] Judges were important figures in government. They decided cases. They were not investigators, and they did not simply recommend action to another government official.

Only when Cardozo reached the argument that a judge ought to be permitted to follow the federal example and perform the duty in an individual capacity did he turn to a specific provision of the state constitution, citing the provision that a state judge may not hold any other public office or trust. That provision distinguished the issue for state judges from that faced by their federal counterparts. Cardozo sought to bring some order out of a host of prior decisions that lacked an apparent common denominator. Distinguishing a prior case upholding a statute authorizing a state purchase of relics of George Washington on the certificate of a judge and two others that the relics were genuine, Cardozo viewed the cases as establishing a constitutional prohibition forbidding the execution of a continuing nonjudicial duty that was annexed permanently to the judicial office, as opposed to one, like the George Washington example, that conferred temporary power exhausted by a single act. He saw this construction as respecting the policy of the constitutional provision, which he described as conserving the time of judges for judicial work and protecting them from entanglements in partisan suspicions. But certification of the genuineness of George Washington relics was not much like deciding a case in a formal judicial proceeding.

Investigation of alleged wrongdoing provided the occasion for other separation of powers cases. In 1931, the Hofstadter Committee, a joint legislative committee, and its counsel, Cardozo's former colleague Samuel Seabury, began to investigate mounting evidence of corruption in Mayor James J. Walker's administration in New York City. The investigation was front-page news for several years. An important part of the investigation involved the Board of Standards and Appeals, the city's zoning board. A key witness was Dr. William ("Horse Doctor") Doyle, a veterinarian with impressive Tammany connections, who had a long record of success practicing before the board. (Lay people were permitted to do so.) At the committee hearings, Doyle pleaded the privilege against self-incrimination, refusing to answer questions relating to bribery of public officials and fee splitting. The joint committee took the position that since Doyle had been granted immunity from prosecution, he could not refuse to answer. It cited him for contempt, and the state Supreme Court sentenced him to jail for thirty days. The Appellate Division affirmed the sentence, and Doyle then appealed to the Court of Appeals. One of the critical issues involved the power of the legislature to grant a witness immunity by passing a joint resolution, without obtaining the governor's approval.

Doyle applied to Cardozo as chief judge for a stay of the jail sentence pending argument before the court. Cardozo heard the stay motion in his library at home. His questioning of counsel focused on the sufficiency of the immunity granted to Doyle, and he suggested, incautiously, that a pardon by Governor Franklin Roosevelt would cure any insufficiency. When the newspapers reported Cardozo's suggestion, Roosevelt sought advice from Cardozo on account of the "embarrassment" that the suggestion caused him. He thought that his ability to grant a pardon in those circumstances was quite doubtful and asked "[p]urely as a personal and non-official matter and for my own information," whether Cardozo thought that he had such power.[47] There is no record of any response by Cardozo, who doubtless did not want to write an advisory opinion, even privately. In the end, Cardozo denied Doyle's application. He was concerned that Doyle might flee New York. "If I had given him a stay he could have gone across the river into New Jersey and laughed at an adverse decision, which would have brought the administration of justice into contempt."[48] Cardozo did not want to have Seabury's investigation frustrated by the flight of a witness, and Doyle stayed in jail for the two weeks that it took the full court to hear and decide his expedited appeal.[49]

The appeal required the court to decide whether an individual subpoenaed to testify before a joint legislative committee had been given sufficient immunity so that he could be forced to testify despite his claim of self-incrimination.[50] Cardozo's majority opinion, reversing the contempt conviction with respect to some questions but affirming it as to others, began by setting out the important precedents—People ex rel. Lewisohn v. O'Brien from the Court of Appeals and Counselman v. Hitchcock from the United States Supreme Court. These opinions required the government to grant immunity from prosecution (rather than merely to refrain from using the compelled testimony itself) in order to force a witness to testify.[51] Cardozo then examined the immunity statutes carefully and concluded that they were sufficiently broad with respect to questions relating to bribes actually given to public officials, but not to those relating to conspiracies or attempts to bribe that had not been followed by payment. As to the latter, one of the legislative measures relied upon was broad enough, but it was a joint resolution of the legislature, which had not been presented to the governor for his approval.

Cardozo's majority opinion held that a grant of immunity from the penal laws was a legislative power that required passage of a statute and concurrence of the governor. Rejecting the argument in Judge Pound's dissent that the legislature ought to be able to grant immunity by itself in aid of its own investigations for legislative purposes, Cardozo held that such a power, while it might be useful, was not an inherent part of the legislature's investigative power or of its power to punish for contempt. Having reviewed English and American precedents, he found no instance where such immunity had ever been given without statute, although a few recent New York joint resolutions had claimed such power. Cardozo took seriously the tradition that law-making required the concurrence of the legislative and executive branches, and he was unwilling to allow experimentation even in the narrow way contemplated by the joint resolution.[52]

The Court of Appeals affirmed the contempt citations with respect to refusal to answer questions concerning bribes paid to public officials because the immunity statutes that had been signed by the governor were broad enough to cover them. Doyle then answered some questions, denying bribery and pleading a poor memory about other events. The committee attempted to hold Doyle in jail on the ground that his denial of bribery was false. He sought a discharge on habeas corpus. The trial court, the Appellate Division, and the Court of Appeals all directed his discharge. On Cardozo's last day on the Court of Appeals, that court handed down an unsigned per curiam opinion, probably written by Cardozo because he had written the original opinion. The court upheld the trial judge's finding that there was insufficient evidence of the falsity of Doyle's disclaimer of bribery.[53]

The *Doyle* opinion temporarily restricted a legislative investigation into an important public issue, but the legislature quickly passed, and Governor Roosevelt signed, the necessary immunity statute so that the committee could continue its work. Cardozo noted the "happy outcome": "The Governor has now sent in another message permitting the legislature to deal with the question of any upstate investigation. I think the Republicans will be in something of a hole if they oppose the Democrats' request."[54] Cardozo realized the political consequences of opposition to a widening of the corruption investigation.

Cardozo's concern for the proper procedures of lawmaking was, as he said, the key to the case, rather than any unstated purpose to give additional constitutional protection to persons under governmental investigation. Cardozo was not overly sympathetic to claims of the privilege against self-incrimination. After the case was over, he wrote that "[s]ome of the constitutional privileges seem pretty antiquated to-day, and very likely Counselman v. Hitchcock and People ex rel. Lewisohn v. O'Brien might better have been decided the other way. I did my best to apply the law as I understood it, convinced that more important than the result in the particular case was the proof to the public mind that the course of justice in the courts is impartial and serene."[55]

Cardozo's references to *Counselman* and *Lewisohn* suggest that as an original proposition, he thought it sufficient to require only that the witness's answers not be used against him. He did not explain his reasons, although his view fit his generally negative attitude toward expansion of defendants' procedural rights in criminal cases. But there was no hint of those views, however strongly felt, in his opinion in *Doyle.* Cardozo gave Doyle all the protection he thought the law required.

Cardozo wrote a revealing trilogy of constitutional cases involving the relation between cities and the state that is embodied in the principle of "Home Rule." The issue of state control versus local self-government had been seriously contested in American politics and in legal doctrine for a long time. The debate involved not only political and legal theory but also practical considerations relating to the trustworthiness of local versus state government. The argument over home rule was exacerbated by the argument over the disproportionately low representation afforded the cities, especially New York City, in both houses of the legislature. The cities argued for more power over their own affairs if they were not to be granted fair representation. Opponents compared rural virtue and urban vice as warranting both special protection of rural interests in the legislative apportionment and strict limits on home rule.[56] The Tweed Ring and Tammany Hall politics in which Albert Cardozo, Sr., had played such a notable role were examples used to argue for limitation of local autonomy.[57] Benjamin Cardozo construed the relevant constitutional and statutory provisions in a way that gave primacy to the sovereignty of the whole polity, the state, in contrast to localized polities, such as cities and towns.

The state of New York recognized the principle of local autonomy in a series of expansively worded constitutional amendments. The first effort imposed a limitation on legislative power as a way of protecting a city against "special" legislation. Laws had to be of "general application." The courts had held that the constitutional requirement was met so long as the legislation was general in form, even if applicable in effect only to one particular city. In 1923, however, a new Home Rule Amendment to the constitution required the courts to consider the effect as well as the form of legislation. In addition, it restricted the ability of the legislature to pass laws relating to the "property, affairs or government" of cities except upon a two-thirds concurrent vote of both houses of the legislature after an emergency message from the governor. It also conferred power on cities to adopt local laws relating to a wide variety of subjects.[58]

Cardozo wrote two of the leading opinions refusing to read the principle of home rule expansively. In Browne v. City of New York in 1925, he upheld a taxpayers' suit to enjoin the city from operating a municipal bus line. He rejected the city's argument that the constitutional amendment granting power to cities to adopt local laws relating to "the acquisition, care, management and use of its streets" and a statute using the same language authorized New York City's activity.[59] "In this State . . . municipal transportation upon a scale so extensive without supervision or restriction, is a notable innovation. The colorless words chosen were singularly inept if they were intended to express approval of a departure so momentous . . . A phrase so unobtrusive, so commonplace in the vocabulary of Legislatures, so freighted with other traditions . . . will not bear so great a burden."[60] Therefore, the city could not operate a bus line without a more specific grant of authority from the legislature.

An even more significant case, Adler v. Deegan, involved the power of the New York legislature to enact the Multiple Dwelling Law, which regulated the construction and occupancy of tenement houses. The act was enacted without complying with the provision of the Home Rule Amendment that required an emergency message from the governor and a two-thirds vote of the legislature to pass legislation relating to the "property, affairs or government" of cities.[61] A tenement house owner sued the Attorney General and the Tenement House Commissioner to enjoin enforcement of the law. The owner claimed that it was passed in violation of the Home Rule Amendment. The trial court agreed, and the defendants appealed. Many public and private organizations joined the appeal on each side. Various cities, including New York City, joined the plaintiff. The issue did not concern just state or local control of tenement houses. The court's interpretation of the Home Rule Amendment would affect a whole variety of state regulation of activities with local incidence.

The Court of Appeals split 5–2 in upholding the statute in a very unsatisfactory opinion by Judge Crane. Crane noted that the key words of the Home Rule Amendment restricting legislative power with respect to "property, government or affairs" of cities were the same words that had been given a narrow meaning by the court prior to 1923 as they related to general and special laws. He concluded that the narrow meaning was therefore incorporated into the 1923 Home Rule Amendment and that the legislature did not have to comply with the special constitutional procedures to enact the Multiple Dwelling Law.[62]

The rest of the court struggled with the powerful argument that the Home Rule Amendment had effected a constitutional revolution in New York by dividing sovereignty between the legislature and the cities. Cardozo presented his resolution of the debate in a separate concurring opinion.[63] He relied on "the basic principle that the power to adopt laws according to the usual forms of legislation resides with the Legislature except in so far as it has been limited or surrendered, and that neither limitation nor surrender will be inferred unless intention is revealed with reasonable clarity."[64] Cardozo found no such limitation or surrender because power was granted to cities in the Home Rule Amendment in words that had previously been given a narrow meaning. Cardozo observed that the legislative practice since the amendment, precedents in other states, and the views of commentators all pointed the same way. The only commentator he cited was Howard McBain, and he did not mention that others disagreed.[65] The presumption of state supremacy carried the day.

Cardozo attempted to be quite precise about the appropriate test to be applied in interpreting the Home Rule Amendment. He rejected, in polemical fashion, the argument of New York City that the test was whether the subject was "predominantly" of state or local concern:

[P]redominance is not the test. The introduction of such a test involves comparisons too vague and too variable, too much a matter of mere opinion, to serve as an objective standard. To adopt it is to infect our legislation with the virus of uncertainty . . . Considerations of "more or less" will lead us . . . into a morass of indecision. The test is rather this, that if the subject be in substantial degree a matter of State concern, the Legislature may act, though intermingled with it are concerns of the locality.[66]

Cardozo's scorn for the predominance test was overdone. He was himself a master of questions of "more or less." He had enunciated tests in other circumstances that were no more certain than a predominance test in the home rule context. Cardozo's test established a strong tilt toward legislative power that mirrored his narrow reading of the Home Rule Amendment. He sought to allay fears that his reading would gut the Home Rule Amendment by pointing out the "wide field" for local action that remained. But the field that he described was not so very wide. Laying out parks, building a recreation pier, and providing for public concerts were his examples. By comparison with the scope of state regulation in the Multiple Dwelling Law, these were puny powers.

Cardozo's test decided the case for him, for he had begun his opinion with an eloquent characterization of the state's purpose in passing the Multiple Dwelling Law. It was not merely a local measure aimed at regulating safety and health conditions in tenement houses.

The Multiple Dwelling Act is aimed at many evils, but most of all it is a measure to eradicate the slum. It seeks to bring about conditions whereby healthy children shall be born, and healthy men and women reared, in the dwellings of the great metropolis. To have such men and women is not a city concern merely. It is the concern of the whole State. Here is to be bred the citizenry with which the State must do its work in the years that are to come. The end to be achieved is more than the avoidance of pestilence or contagion. The end to be achieved is the quality of men and women.[67]

With that conception of the Multiple Dwelling Law, Cardozo had no problem in concluding that the subject was in substantial degree a matter of state concern and therefore that the legislature had acted properly.

In case of doubt, Cardozo preserved the power of the state, which represented all, over the power of the city, which represented only a portion of the state. Later Cardozo expressed himself in more caustic and exasperated terms about the amendment: "Home-rule is a slogan that has captivated the popular fancy, like arbitration and some others. For a thousand that cry hosanna when they hear the taking words, there is hardly one who has thought out the consequences of the policy so airily espoused."[68] He was sensitive to press and public criticism of the decision that he viewed as based on the substance of the statute, that is, its controversial governmental regulation of private property, and not based on the legal issue of legislative power to enact it.

The dissents by Lehman and O'Brien presented reasonable alternatives to Cardozo's view. Lehman found considerable meaning in the provision of the Home Rule Amendment that for the first time specifically vested legislative power in cities: "Every city shall have power to adopt and amend local laws not inconsistent with the constitution and laws of the State relating to . . . the government and regulation of the conduct of its inhabitants and the protection of their property, safety and health."[69] That section, in his view, divided sovereignty between the legislature and the cities. The appropriate test, which was set forth in the quoted section, was simply whether the law was "related to" the government of the city or its property or affairs. He saw the Multiple Dwelling Law as clearly falling within that definition because the act primarily affected New York City and those living in, or maintaining, multiple dwellings there.

O'Brien noted the overlapping nature of the relevant constitutional provisions. Both the legislative power and the cities' power were phrased in terms of a grant subject to noninterference in the power of the other. Judge O'Brien saw no way of resolving the clash except by looking at each individual statute and determining whether the interest of the city or the state prevailed. Here he thought the city's interest was predominant.

In the absence of any clear indication in the state constitution whether the scope of the power conferred by the Home Rule Amendment was to be as large as Lehman suggested or as limited as Cardozo perceived it, the judges chose three different ways to proceed. One was Cardozo's presumption of a basic constitutional preference for long-established state legislative power unless clearly circumscribed. Another was Lehman's perception that the Home Rule Amendment should be broadly construed to effect its purpose of increasing local autonomy. The third was O'Brien's ad hoc notion of determining predominant interest in each case.

Cardozo did not explain his preference for state authority. Possibly, he was influenced by Judge John Dillon's view that municipal governments were to be distrusted because they were likely to be corrupt. Corruption by Tammany Hall was the dark cloud that had hung over Cardozo's family, and Cardozo had begun his judicial career by running for office on an anti-Tammany ticket. He was critical of the government of New York in the 1920s under Mayor John Hylan.[70] Although he was fond of New York City as his home, he had little respect for its record in self-government.

But Cardozo gave no hint in his opinion or elsewhere that these experiences influenced his decision to prefer state to local control when the issue was doubtful. As we have seen, when Cardozo looked for decisional aids, he often looked to official expressions of public values—statutes and constitutional provisions and their purposes—and then to judicial precedents for assistance. Cardozo viewed the home rule movement in the context of a general preference in New York's constitution for a system that gave supreme legislative power to the legislature. He believed that that preference was a critical element of the state's constitutional system. If Cardozo's "method of sociology" encouraged pragmatic, flexible lawmaking in many areas, that was not the case when the basic constitutional structure was at stake. He saw no room for compromise between an interpretation that limited home rule to a rather small scope and one that expanded it to an enormous scope at the expense of the legislature. In the absence of a clear constitutional command, he preserved state legislative power.

When a less important principle was at stake, Cardozo was prepared to give more scope to the Home Rule Amendment. In one well-known opinion, he held unconstitutional a legislative attempt to circumvent the requirement that special or local laws could be passed only by two-thirds vote on an emergency message from the governor.[71] The Court of Appeals had earlier held that the American Express Company was barred from enforcing payment on a New York City voucher for payment of a condemnation award that the company had held without seeking payment for twenty-three years. The legislature then passed a statute, without an emergency message or the concurrent action of two-thirds of each house, that permitted enforcement of such claims.

In striking down the statute, Cardozo noted that it was worded as if it were of general application to all cities. That was not sufficient. "We close our eyes to realities if we do not see in this act the marks of legislation that is special and local in terms and effects. This group of conditions so unusual and particular is precisely fitted to the claimant's case, and only by a most singular coincidence could be fitted to any other."[72] Cardozo was ready to limit the legislature's power of action on the facts of this case, which affected only one particular local situation. On the larger substantive issue of the relations of city and legislative power, however, his tilt was heavily in the direction of the higher representative body, the state legislature, in its contest with city power.

Civil rights litigation was not a major staple of the Court of Appeals' calendar during Cardozo's years on the court, and he wrote but few opinions that touched on those issues. His New York opinions give only a hint of the cautious attitude toward constitutional protection of civil rights, except in free speech cases, that would characterize his position when he joined the United States Supreme Court.

People v. Crane was a major case early in Cardozo's career that tested the power of a state to prefer citizens to aliens when hiring workers on public construction projects. New York passed a statute that prohibited employers from employing aliens on public works projects.[73] A contractor who was convicted of hiring an alien argued that the statute unconstitutionally discriminated against aliens under the state and federal Due Process Clauses and the federal Equal Protection Clause. Cardozo was originally in a minority, but his views won over a majority to uphold the statute.[74] Even though he suggested disagreement with the policy of the statute, he upheld its prohibition. "To disqualify aliens is discrimination indeed, but not arbitrary discrimination, for the principle of exclusion is the restriction of the resources of the state to the advancement and profit of the members of the state. Ungenerous and unwise such discrimination may be. It is not for that reason unlawful."[75] Cardozo relied on a long series of cases in the United States Supreme Court, in New York, and in other jurisdictions that had upheld the power of a state to discriminate between citizens and aliens in the use of public resources.

Judge Collin, dissenting, saw the statute as an interference with the liberty of aliens to sell, and of contractors to buy, their labor and as such would have held it an unconstitutional interference with liberty of contract protected by both the Fourteenth Amendment and the state constitution's due process clause. Cardozo's opinion, recognizing legislative power to discriminate, was in line with the lack of constitutional protection given to aliens at that time. Use of the Equal Protection Clause to prevent discrimination against aliens was a half century away.[76] *Crane* was another instance when Cardozo apparently disagreed with legislative policy but upheld it as a matter of constitutional law.

Another case presented the Court of Appeals with an individual rights issue that would assume major proportions later in the century. *People v. Sanger* involved an appeal from the conviction of Margaret Sanger, the famous women's rights advocate, for violation of New York's Comstock Law, which made it a misdemeanor to sell, give away, or advertise any contraceptive device.[77] Sanger conceded the ability of the state to prevent the giving or advertising of contraceptive devices for use by unmarried persons. She contested the breadth of the statute, however, arguing that it prevented physicians from giving medical advice and that it applied to women whose life or health would be threatened by pregnancy. Cardozo joined Judge Crane's brief opinion for a unanimous court that affirmed the conviction. Crane rejected the argument regarding physicians, holding that their medical advice was protected by both this statute and other statutes. He did not address the remaining argument regarding the breadth of the statute's coverage, except to remark that Sanger's arguments "touching social conditions and sociological questions" were "matters for the legislature and not for the courts."[78] Sanger struggled to find an acceptable constitutional basis for her arguments, but the court was unwilling to find new constitutional rights in what would later be called the area of sexual privacy.

The final important individual rights opinions that Cardozo wrote while on the Court of Appeals were at the intersection of labor law and freedom of speech. *Nann v. Raimist* arose out of a dispute between two unions, one of which, International, began picketing an employer whose employees were represented by the other, Amalgamated.[79] The employer obtained relief against false and misleading statements but was denied relief against picketing. Thereafter, members of International engaged in violence against members of Amalgamated, which obtained a sweeping injunction, including an injunction against picketing any store where Amalgamated members were employed, against the use of a whole list of words (including calling Amalgamated a "scab" union), against seeking to persuade any Amalgamated employee to leave the union or the job, and against interfering with any business with which Amalgamated had a contract.

Cardozo, writing for a unanimous court, upheld the injunction against picketing because International had violated the first injunction and because it had engaged in violence. He indicated that the court might have preferred a less sweeping injunction but was unwilling to find the gross abuse of discretion by the lower court that was required for reversal. He did note, however, that the injunction had to be construed as being limited to acts done in connection with the current dispute or in pursuance of International's declared plan to destroy Amalgamated. Having upheld the injunction's provisions against misconduct, the court struck down its limitation of combative speech. The injunction against speech was too broad and also much less necessary since picketing had been banned. The law of equitable remedies would not enjoin false speech; a court would act only if personal safety or property interests were threatened by illegal acts of which words were the instruments. Therefore, only a false statement that a strike was in progress could be enjoined. Most of the speech in which International had engaged—praising itself, criticizing its rival in colorful fashion—was protected. "Courts have enough to do in restraining physical disorder without busying themselves with logomachies in which the embattled words are the expressions of the opinion of the writer or the speaker."[80]

Cardozo paid close attention to the context in which words were used—such as, Amalgamated is a scab—that came closer to the borderline of threatening illegal damage to property interests. "Standing by themselves, the statements may be unduly broad. Heard or read in the light of the context or in the setting of the occasion, they may wear another aspect . . . An injunction might draw a distinction between one context and another, yet the dividing line is one that it would be hard to make manifest by words."[81] With picketing prohibited, the danger of personal or property damage seemed insufficient to require the effort to draw a line between permitted and forbidden words. Finally, International could not be prohibited from peaceful efforts to persuade others to join it.[82] The union could be enjoined from provoking violence, but it had a right to state its case.

Thus the Court of Appeals stood out against the strong bias prevalent in much of the American judiciary against aggressive union-organizing methods. In particular, at a time when the right of free speech in labor controversies had not yet achieved much constitutional recognition, the court carefully protected the free speech rights of International despite its provocative behavior.[83]

Cardozo was also concerned with the free speech rights of individual union members in their dealings with a union. A member who had been fined and expelled by a union for suing and allegedly defaming union officers sought to restrain the union from enforcing those penalties. The member's original suit had claimed that union officials had misappropriated union funds. The lower court had ruled that the discipline against him was justified and that, in any event, the member had failed to exhaust internal remedies. The Appellate Division held that the union could impose discipline for slander but not for resort to the courts. On the member's motion for leave to appeal, Cardozo reported to the consultation that he needed more time to study the case before reaching a final conclusion, but he recommended allowance of the appeal because of the importance of the issues raised. He doubted that the union could punish a resort to the courts, and he advised that the member would probably have a defense in a libel action because his letters, albeit intemperate, dealt with matters relevant to the member's suit against the officials. Cardozo also raised a question of the fairness of the union's proceedings because the discipline was imposed by an executive committee composed exclusively of the union members who were the defendants in the court proceedings and who were the subject of the alleged libel.[84] The court followed Cardozo's recommendation and eventually ordered reinstatement of the expelled member, with Cardozo joining in Judge Kellogg's majority opinion.[85]

These cases indicate that of all the civil liberties issues that came before the New York Court of Appeals, Cardozo was most sympathetic to claims based on freedom of speech.[86] He made a start at explaining his views in a tribute that he wrote for Oliver Wendell Holmes's ninetieth birthday a year before he took Holmes's place on the Supreme Court. He began by characterizing Holmes's thought, but by the end of the passage he made it his own.

> Only in one field is compromise to be excluded, or kept within the narrowest limits. There shall be no compromise of the freedom to think one's thoughts and speak them, except at those extreme borders where thought merges into action. There is to be no compromise here, for thought freely communicated, if I may borrow my own words, is the indispensable condition of intelligent experimentation . . . There is no freedom without choice, and there is no choice without knowledge—or none that is not illusory. Here are goods to be conserved, however great

the seeming sacrifice. We may not squander the thought that will be the inheritance of the ages.[87]

Cardozo trumpeted the value of freedom of speech with a rhetorical flourish, without any deference to legislative and executive control and without any attempt to justify different standards for judicial scrutiny of governmental action in the economic and the civil liberties fields. It was easy to write so grandly in a tribute. Application of the principles in a judicial context when he was a Supreme Court Justice would be more difficult.

The other major public law field to which Cardozo made important contributions was international law. Although the field was more amorphous and less encumbered with precedent than most other areas of law, Cardozo still looked to history, precedent, and policy considerations in much the same fashion that he did in other cases. Techt v. Hughes required the court to decide a question of New York real property law with national and international aspects.[88] In 1911, Sara Hannigan, an American citizen, married Frederick Techt, a resident of New York but a citizen of the Austro-Hungarian Empire. By federal statute, she automatically took her husband's Austro-Hungarian nationality and lost her American nationality.[89] Her father, James Hannigan, an American citizen, died without a will while the United States was at war with the Austro-Hungarian Empire. Under a New York statute, Hannigan's New York real estate would "descend" to his two daughters, Sara and Elizabeth, that is, would pass to them by virtue of the statute in the absence of a will. Sara brought suit against Elizabeth to divide the property, and Elizabeth contended that Sara, as an enemy alien, was not entitled to anything under New York law. The lower court certified to the Court of Appeals the question whether Sara, as an enemy alien, could inherit real estate under the New York law.

Cardozo's opinion began with the rule that at common law, land could not descend to an alien although they could inherit by will. He accepted the rule as a given, even though he expressed doubt that the rule was sound historically and even though its policy might seem "[a]rtificial and far-fetched."[90] Since this rule of land law was "inveterate and undoubted," it governed, unless changed by statute or treaty.[91] "In the law of land . . . more than in any other field, the method of history supplies the organon of interpretation . . . Deep into the soil go the roots of the words in which the rights of the owners of the soil find expression in the law. We do not readily uproot the growths of centuries."[92] Thus, the public policy notions embodied in Cardozo's "method of sociology" yielded to the deeply rooted rules of real property, the method of history.

After reviewing a great deal of history, Cardozo first held that Sara could not qualify as an "alien friend," who was permitted by New York statute to take land by descent. Moreover, no one questioned the constitutionality of the federal statute that prescribed alien status for an American woman who married a foreign national. It would be another thirty-eight years before the United States Supreme Court limited Congress's power over citizenship under the Fourteenth Amendment.[93]

Cardozo then turned to an 1848 treaty between the United States and the Austro-Hungarian Empire and concluded that the treaty would protect Sara Techt's right to inherit the real estate if it was not abrogated by World War I. As he addressed that question, he warned that courts played "a humbler and more cautious" role in policy-making than the political departments of government did. After reviewing the scholarship and the cases concerning the effect of war on treaties, he concluded that the rule was that unless the political departments had taken clear action, "provisions [of treaties] compatible with a state of hostilities, unless expressly terminated, will be enforced, and those incompatible rejected." In determining compatibility, however, courts were free to choose "the conclusion which shall seem the most in keeping with the traditions of the law, the policy of the statutes, the dictates of fair dealing, and the honor of the nation."[94] The last two considerations indicate that he had a somewhat expansive notion of the role of courts, however humble and cautious he might name it, when it came to interpretation of principles of international law.

Cardozo was clear that his fourfold guide to interpretation—philosophy, history, custom, and public policy—were as valid in deciding international law questions as in common law and constitutional law questions. Indeed, public policy had perhaps a larger role to play here because judges were to look not only to principles of fair dealing but also to the honor of the nation. Moral sensibilities, in his opinion, were required of nations as well as of persons. Thus, he noted that the power of confiscation was now "seldom brought into play in the practice of enlightened nations." Aliens who were permitted to remain were generally allowed to retain employment and to buy and sell property. By analogy, a "public

policy not outraged by purchase will not be outraged by inheritance."[95]
Therefore, the treaty's protection of the right of inheritance was compatible with the state of war and was still in force. Cardozo's view of tradition, policy, fair dealing, and honor permitted Sara Techt to inherit from her father.

The Russian Revolution of 1917 created other legal problems with international aspects for the Court of Appeals to consider. The Soviet government's confiscation of private property, especially the property of private banks, led to considerable international litigation, much of which centered in New York. In 1924, Sokoloff v. National City Bank required Cardozo to consider the effect of the Soviet nationalization of banks.[96] In June 1917, Boris Sokoloff paid money to the National City Bank in New York so that it would open an account in his name in the bank's Petrograd branch. In November 1917 and February 1918, checks that Sokoloff drew on that account were dishonored. In the meantime, the Soviet government had nationalized the Petrograd branch and confiscated its assets. Sokoloff sued the bank for the amount of the dishonored checks. The bank argued that its agreement with Sokoloff was to be performed in Russia and was governed by the laws of Russia. The nationalization decree effected a seizure of the depositor's account and discharged the bank's liability to him.

Cardozo avoided all the difficult international law questions presented by the bank's defense. He viewed the business situation quite simply. He saw no reason to treat this bank account differently from other accounts. The depositor was a creditor of the American bank, and the assets that were seized in Russia were assets of the bank and not of the depositor. Sokoloff was entitled to restitution of the balance of his deposit.

The National City Bank did not fare any better when it attempted to retain funds deposited with it by a Russian bank that had been nationalized.[97] Surviving directors of the nationalized Russian bank fled and were attempting to gather up all its foreign assets in Paris. They requested payment of the bank's funds that were on deposit with National City Bank in New York. The National City Bank refused payment on the ground that the Russian bank had been dissolved and no longer had corporate existence; that even if it had, the surviving directors had no authority; and, finally, that the bank needed protection against the possibility of multiple liability. National City prevailed in the trial court and the Appellate Division, and the directors appealed to the Court of Appeals.

Cardozo wrote an opinion for a divided court, reversing the lower courts and directing that judgment be entered for the directors. He again adapted various principles of law to the novel situation of a nationalized Soviet bank when the refusal of the United States to recognize the Soviet government carried the consequence of not recognizing its nationalization decrees.[98] Cardozo reviewed the state of pre-Soviet Russian law, international law, general principles of corporate law, and the conflicting opinions of the plaintiff's and defendant's experts. He concluded that general principles of law provided that once a corporation came into existence, it was presumed to remain in existence until judicial decree or sovereign command ended its juridical life. Once the Soviet nationalization decrees were removed from the picture because of America's non-recognition policy, there was no clear law or exercise of power ending the bank's corporate life. Therefore its remaining directors had power to withdraw its funds from the defendant. The fact that the bank might be held liable to the Soviet government in a suit in another country was not relevant in the United States and was one of the risks of the bank's international business. Although Cardozo's opinion was filled with abstract principles of corporate law, the gist of the opinion was very practical. If the Soviet decrees were not recognized by this country, then the Russian corporation as it existed prior to the nationalization decree should still be recognized by our law and should therefore be able to collect its money from National City Bank.[99] Cardozo's international law opinions feature some of the same themes that characterize his opinions in other fields. They were practical and at the same time were influenced by the sense that governments, like individuals, ought to behave honorably.

The appropriate sources of "law" for judicial decision-making are a perennial issue of judging, and it is especially crucial with respect to constitutional and international law in which a decision carries so much weight and is difficult to overturn. In *The Nature of the Judicial Process*, Cardozo had viewed the process of decision-making as unitary. He had argued that his fourfold division of the forces shaping judicial decision-making—logic and analogy (the method of philosophy); history (the historical or evolutionary method); custom (the method of tradition); and justice, morals, and public policy (the method of sociology)—was as applicable to constitutional law as to common law adjudication. His argument was both descriptive and prescriptive: descriptive in the sense that Cardozo argued that the four methods he identified were those that judges had always used to decide cases, consciously or not; prescriptive in the sense that he was urging his colleagues to take conscious account of these methods each time they decided a case.

We have already seen that Cardozo was not specific in explaining when one of his methods should predominate over another. Nor did he expound a theory of jurisprudence. He was a judge trying to explain his view of what good judging was all about. Good judging, in his view, involved evaluating the claims of history, precedent, and certainty against the demands of justice, fairness, and the possible need for change, all in the particular context of each case. In the climate of the 1920s, Cardozo saw his major task as the justification of the method of sociology, the creative lawmaking function of the judge. At the same time, he was careful to balance this emphasis with cautionary reminders of the limits on the judge's lawmaking role and the importance of precedent and certainty in law.

Cardozo believed that the tools of the method of sociology, "justice, morals, and social welfare," were especially relevant to constitutional adjudication where major constitutional prescriptions—such as due process of law and equal protection of the laws—were so general. Moreover, in his view, the very nature of a constitution, designed as it was to last indefinitely, produced the result that "the content of constitutional immunities [that is, rights] is not constant, but varies from age to age."[100] That view left Cardozo with the problem of applying broad constitutional provisions and the rather abstract formulations he had employed in *The Nature of the Judicial Process* and other writings to the constitutional problems of his day.

Cardozo began with a general doctrinal principle, which he derived from his understanding of the purpose of the state and federal constitutions and from precedent. "Property, like liberty, though immune from destruction, is not immune from regulation for the common good. What that regulation shall be, every generation must work out for itself."[101] In the cases involving economic regulation, Cardozo's effort to look outside himself for governing values reinforced his strong respect for the democratic legislative process in choosing among competing economic principles. In answering the question whether the New York legislature had made a reasonable choice, he was influenced by legislative practice in other states and other industrialized countries, and by the factual situation underlying the particular regulation. But Cardozo did not give up scrutiny of legislative solutions completely, even in the realm of economic policy, and did not countenance legislation that in effect confiscated property.

The most intellectually challenging constitutional law cases that Cardozo considered in the Court of Appeals were the home rule cases. The constitutional language and history were susceptible to quite different readings. Cardozo broke the deadlock by reading the New York Constitution as generally favoring the state legislature, the sovereign body, over the local municipality. He was then able to resolve the ambiguity in specific constitutional provisions by resorting to a presumption favoring the power of the legislature over that of the city government.

Cardozo's constitutional record in New York foretold little about his attitude toward civil rights problems. People v. Crane, dealing with alien employment on public works projects, might have been seen as raising the issue, but aliens had yet to be recognized as having rights nearly akin to those of citizens. Cardozo and the court therefore did not treat the case as a typical individual rights case. The "liberty of contract" cases had been treated as individual rights cases, but Cardozo did not see them as such. He followed Holmes in seeing those cases as raising primarily questions of legislative regulatory power to preserve the health of workers, the public, or the economic system. The development of Cardozo's views on civil rights would have to await his elevation to the United States Supreme Court.

Cardozo's constitutional law opinions in the Court of Appeals foretold that when he joined the United States Supreme Court, he would regard sympathetically the far-ranging legislative efforts of the states and Congress to deal with the economic consequences of the Depression, and suggested also that he would be a champion of free speech.

20

Criminal Law

Cardozo came to criminal law cases with relatively little background. Although they were an important part of the Court of Appeals' docket—Cardozo estimated about 8 to 10 percent—they had not been a part of his practice, except for a few cases in which he had been engaged to argue an appeal.[1] Nor did he discuss criminal law in his extrajudicial talks until 1928 when an invitation to address the New York Academy of Medicine led him to consider, briefly, some issues: the system of punishment, especially the judge's sentencing function; the death penalty; the definition of premeditation and deliberation that marked the difference between first and second degree murder; and the law defining mental irresponsibility. His views on those subjects will become apparent as we consider his opinions.

Cardozo's criminal law opinions, especially the procedure opinions, were less literary and more sober than their civil law counterparts, but his concentration on the facts was equally strong. We have seen that in difficult civil cases, Cardozo's usual method was to state a legal issue in the context of the particular facts and then to examine how the pertinent rules and their underlying policies applied to those facts. Only rarely did he discuss legal rules at a more abstract level. We have also seen that he believed that there was some, but only some, flexibility in the rules that could be molded to fit his concept of justice. Sometimes he saw that concept as a matter of current practice—as when ordinary questions of business were concerned—but sometimes he saw it in distinctly moral terms of right and wrong. Many of these same practical and moral considerations were evident in Cardozo's criminal law opinions. For example, his sense of what constituted prejudicial trial error requiring the reversal of a conviction was grounded in practical judgments about the actual effect of the error on a jury's conclusion. His inclination to interpret a criminal statute to require a showing of willful conduct, that is, fault, came from his strong belief that as a general rule, fault was a requirement for punishment. One other quality that had characterized his practice at the bar appeared strongly in his criminal law decisions. Cardozo had been a tough lawyer who did not hesitate to make a personal attack on parties and lawyers who engaged in what he viewed as unseemly conduct. He was also a tough judge when he came to consider arguments for reversal of criminal convictions. He did not accept such arguments easily.

Cardozo addressed two kinds of criminal law issues. The first half of this chapter deals with matters of criminal procedure, matters relating to the way that cases are tried. The second half deals with matters of substantive law, the interpretation and constitutionality of criminal statutes—issues like the requirement of moral fault for criminal conviction, the existence of legitimate defenses, and the constitutionality of particular legislative prohibitions.

Cardozo had definite views about the type of trial error that would lead him to reverse a conviction. He was sensitive to errors that seemed likely to have caused significant prejudice to a fair trial for a defendant, but he did not strain to find prejudicial error, especially in cases in which evidence of guilt seemed overwhelming. In close cases, he was much more likely to vote to affirm than to reverse a conviction. Thus, in the thirteen criminal cases decided with an opinion in which Cardozo dissented, he dissented ten times from the reversal of a conviction and just three times from an affirmance, one of which related only to disagreement about the sentence.[2] Similarly, his opinions throughout demonstrate a substantial tendency to find that trial errors were harmless.

A typical case was People v. Kasprzyk in which Cardozo did not permit sympathy with a defendant's plight to affect his vote. Adam Kasprzyk had been convicted of second degree murder for shooting someone who had pursued him into his own house following a fracas. The jury rejected his plea of self-defense. The Appellate Division concluded that the trial judge had erred in accepting evidence of a prior occasion when the defendant had used a gun but concluded that the error was insubstantial. Two judges had dissented in a persuasive opinion that contended that the prejudice was real.[3] In recommending affirmance of the conviction to the consultation in 1924, Cardozo confessed "a certain degree of sympathy for the defendant." "He was evidently a member of a rough gang, and he met force with force, according to the standards which his own habits of thought and those of the men about him had led him to accept. The law, however, has standards of its own, which it enforces with rigor in aid of the sanctity of human life."[4] Cardozo kept his sympathy apart from his judgment when addressing the significance of the trial error and the need to enforce the law's command to punish the taking of life. The court accepted Cardozo's recommendation.

An even more telling example of Cardozo's reluctance to overturn a conviction was People v. Schmidt.[5] The defendant Hans Schmidt was accused of killing and dismembering a woman and throwing her remains into the Hudson River. Claiming that God had commanded the killing "as a sacrifice and atonement," he pleaded insanity.[6] The jury rejected the defense and found him guilty of murder in the first degree. Later, claiming new evidence, Schmidt filed a motion for a new trial in which he recanted his earlier confession. He asserted that the victim had died from an illegal abortion committed by another and that he and others had sought to conceal her death by throwing her body into the river. Schmidt had originally thought that a successful insanity defense would protect his confederates. He was wrong to have lied, but he argued that the new evidence justified a new trial because the crime he had committed was only manslaughter. Moreover, Schmidt claimed that error had been committed in the first trial in that the trial judge had erroneously charged the jury on the insanity defense. After his motion for a new trial was denied, his appeal in this capital case went directly to the Court of Appeals, as provided by statute.[7]

A first point of interest in Cardozo's opinion affirming the conviction was his statement of the facts. Many years later, in describing this case to his audience at the New York Academy of Medicine, Cardozo identified the defendant as a priest who had been sexually intimate with the victim.[8] He mentioned neither of those facts in his opinion, although they were relevant to judging the credibility of Schmidt's affidavit and to assessing Schmidt's initial claim that he had acted under God's command. They also helped explain the attempt at concealment of the crime. On the other hand, the record leaves considerable doubt whether Schmidt had actually been properly ordained, although he did perform many priestly functions. In his effort to present a succinct statement of the facts, Cardozo occasionally left out some that seem material to the issues, but he was not seeking to conceal anything from the general public in this case. The newspapers gave the trial extensive coverage. Perhaps Cardozo was a little squeamish about the story.

The major interest of *Schmidt* as a criminal process case—we shall consider its contribution to insanity defense law later—was Cardozo's refusal to reverse the conviction although he found that prejudicial error had been committed. Cardozo agreed with Schmidt's claim that the trial judge's charge on insanity was wrong. Schmidt, however, did not rely on just that claim. He wanted a new trial based on his new version of the facts. Cardozo relied on Schmidt's affidavit to conclude that the erroneous charge concerning insanity was a harmless error, for Schmidt now conceded his sanity. Cardozo was not willing to give any weight to the statements in the same affidavit about how the crime had really been committed. That was evidence that Schmidt had possessed at the original trial and had chosen to withhold. Because it was not newly discovered evidence, it could not be the basis for a new trial. In Cardozo's view, it was an ironic situation but not a matter for legal relief that Schmidt could have obtained a new trial on the basis of the erroneous charge about insanity if only he had kept silent about the abortion and therefore not conceded his sanity.

The logic of Cardozo's opinion was impeccable, and he had no patience with what he regarded as Schmidt's effort to gain an advantage on the basis of his own fraudulent defense. As in situations involving civil liability, Cardozo's view was that people had to take responsibility for the risks that they incurred. Schmidt could not get a second trial when his lie at the first trial failed. Yet Schmidt had been sentenced to death, and Cardozo indicated that the second story—describing a crime that was not punishable by death—had a ring of truth to it. "Strange to say, with all its incongruous features, the defendant's tale supplies a plausible explanation of some of the mysteries of this tragedy." Cardozo did not want to put the court in the position of sending a defendant to death when it believed that he had not committed a capital crime, and so he quickly added, "We do not mean to express a belief that the tale is true. All that we say is that in an appropriate proceeding it would merit earnest scrutiny." It was not for the courts to give that scrutiny at this point. Schmidt had had all the scrutiny to which he was entitled from the courts. "We do not doubt that such scrutiny will be given to it, and that right will be done, if hereafter an appeal for clemency is made to the Executive."[9] Although Cardozo's opinion comported with the general law about grounds for new trials, it affirmed the death penalty for someone who might have had a good defense to a death penalty charge if he had pleaded it in time, leaving Schmidt only the last chance of executive clemency. Schmidt made such an appeal, but Governor Whitman rejected it, and Schmidt was executed in February 1916.[10]

As an appellate judge, Cardozo was ready to leave a great deal of responsibility to the trial judge and jury. He understood from his years as a litigator that errors were inevitable in the course of trials, and he would not easily overturn a jury verdict. This was true even in capital cases, which presented the severest test to Cardozo's judicial philosophy because the death penalty went against his personal belief. Publicly he would say only that "[p]erhaps the whole business of the retention of the death penalty will seem to the next generation, as it seems to many even now, an anachronism too discordant to be suffered, mocking with grim reproach all our clamorous professions of the sanctity of life."[11] Privately he expressed clear opposition to the death penalty.

Cardozo did not often express views about controversial matters in his letters, but the famous case of the anarchists Nicola Sacco and Bartolomeo Vanzetti, who were executed after a trial whose fairness and verdict were widely challenged, led Cardozo to comment about capital punishment. Writing to Edgar Nathan, he commented, "We shall have such tragedies till we get rid of the death penalty."[12] Later, he set forth his reasons: "To me it is far from clear that weak-minded creatures would be more deterred by it than by some other form of punishment. Beyond and above all this, there is the ever-present chance of error. The risk is too great to be incurred by fallible mortals—a class large enough unfortunately to include judges, high and low."[13] As to the merits of the Sacco-Vanzetti case, he associated himself privately with a letter that Charles Burlingham wrote to the *New York Times*. Burlingham was very critical of a great number of the conclusions of the Lowell Committee, which was advising Massachusetts Governor Alvan Fuller whether to grant clemency, about the fairness of the trial. As far as the judicial issues then pending were concerned, Cardozo was cautious. Expressing no views on the merits, he simply stated that if his writs ran beyond the state, "I might have to make up my mind with a sense of responsibility. Making it up when one has no responsibility is a very different thing."[14] When Cardozo did have the responsibility, he did not flinch. He applied New York's death penalty statutes and voted to affirm numerous death sentences.

The personal opposition that he expressed to taking life did not carry over to the rules for taking life in self-defense. In People v. Tomlins, Cardozo had an opportunity in his first year on the bench to write an opinion modifying New York law in the direction of preserving life.[15] Newton Tomlins had been convicted of the first degree murder of his son. The killing took place in the family home, and Tomlins pleaded self-defense. The trial judge instructed the jury that even if the basic elements of self-defense were present, the homicide was justified only if the danger was so imminent that Tomlins could not safely retreat. The jury convicted Tomlins of murder in the first degree, and he appealed directly to the Court of Appeals. Cardozo, writing for the majority of a divided court, reversed the conviction and ordered a new trial.

There was no New York law that addressed the precise factual situation. Cardozo reviewed English and American cases and treatises for the previous two hundred years as well as New York statutes to conclude that it "is not now, and never has been the law that a man assailed in his own dwelling, is bound to retreat. If assailed there, he may stand his ground, and resist the attack. He is under no duty to take to the fields and the highways, a fugitive from his own home."[16] Even though the older law was as Cardozo stated it, the existing law in New York was uncertain at best, and Judges Collin and Cuddeback dissented, albeit without writing an opinion. Had Cardozo been moved to shift the law regarding the use of deadly force in self-defense in the home, even in the limited situation where a co-occupant of the home was the attacker, as some modern courts have done, the materials were at hand in the prior New York cases.[17] But Cardozo was not so moved. His opposition to the death penalty was based on his fear of making a mistake and on his uncertainty about the deterrent effect of the penalty, and apparently not on any deep-seated moral position about taking life. Tomlins's home was his castle, and he was not required to flee in order to escape attack.

Although Cardozo was tough where prejudicial error was alleged, he was not callous. People v. Zackowitz was one case in which Cardozo did find prejudicial trial error.[18] Joseph Zackowitz's wife was insulted by one of a group of young men on the street. Zackowitz did not hear the insult, but he saw his wife's reaction and shouted at the men that if they did not get off the street in five minutes, he would return and "bump them all off." When the couple got home, Zackowitz's wife told him that one of the men had offered her money "to lie with him."[19] Enraged, Zackowitz returned to the scene and found the group still there. There were words between Zackowitz and Frank Coppola, one of the group, followed by a fight. In the course of the struggle, Zackowitz pulled out a pistol and killed Coppola.

At the trial, the trial judge permitted the prosecution to introduce evidence that the defendant had three pistols and a tear-gas gun in his apartment. Zackowitz was convicted of first degree murder, and the Appellate Division affirmed the conviction. Zackowitz's major argument on appeal to the Court of Appeals was that the admission of the evidence about the four guns was prejudicial error: it might have helped the jury to conclude that the shooting was "deliberate" and "premeditated," the conditions for finding murder in the first degree.

Cardozo wrote for the majority that reversed the conviction and ordered a new trial. Cardozo, in his address to the New York Academy of Medicine, had recently discussed the presence of premeditation and deliberation as the distinguishing factor between first and second degree murder. In the address, he pointed out that case law had defined an act done with premeditation and deliberation as any act that was not "the result of immediate or spontaneous impulse." He viewed the test as a "mystifying cloud of words" that was designed in reality to give a "privilege" to the jury to find "the lesser degree [of guilt] when the suddenness of the intent, the vehemence of the passion, seems to call irresistibly for the exercise of mercy."[20]

Since Cardozo thought that the test of premeditation and deliberation was difficult for the jury to apply, it was not surprising that he viewed quite seriously any trial error affecting the issue that might have tipped the balance against the defendant. And that was exactly the way Cardozo set the scene for assessing the effect of the challenged evidence: "With only the rough and ready tests supplied by their experience of life, the jurors were to look into the workings of another's mind, and discover its capacities and disabilities, its urges and inhibitions, in moments of intense excitement. Delicate enough and subtle is the inquiry, even in the most favorable conditions, with every warping influence excluded. There must be no blurring of the issue by evidence illegally admitted and carrying with it in its admission an appeal to prejudice and passion."[21] Cardozo then noted that the only relevance of the evidence that Zackowitz owned several weapons was to demonstrate that he had criminal propensities. The introduction of such evidence would violate the rule that character was not an issue in a criminal trial unless the defendant introduced it. Cardozo rejected efforts to support the evidence as bearing on Zackowitz's homicidal state of mind when he selected the weapon, or as becoming admissible to impeach Zackowitz's credibility once he took the stand because his possession of the guns without a permit was felonious. The evidence was too prejudicial, and in any event it had not been presented simply for impeachment purposes. The conviction therefore had to be reversed.

In reaching his conclusion, Cardozo rejected Judge Pound's argument, which echoed the more usual Cardozo position that the trial error was harmless, that is, the evidence was not so prejudicial that justice required a new trial. Cardozo's contrary view may well have been affected by his doubts about the court's long-standing definition of the distinction between first and second degree murder. Rather than attacking the underlying substantive law, however, Cardozo factored those doubts into his view of the prejudicial effect of the error in admission of evidence. Since Zackowitz was already subject to the danger of a vague and mystifying standard to determine premeditation and deliberation, Cardozo apparently reasoned that he should be protected against improperly admitted evidence that would make the danger greater. This approach accounts for the fact that in this case, but in few others in which the court was divided over a prejudicial error issue, Cardozo voted for reversal of a conviction.

Other instances when Cardozo did not apply the harmless error rule were cases in which an examination of the record convinced him that the evidence of guilt was questionable. Cardozo wrote an eloquent opinion in People v. Dixon, in which he argued in dissent for reversal of a first degree murder conviction.[22] The case was sensitive because of suggestions of race and class prejudice. Hattie Dixon, an African-American subway porter, had been convicted as the instigator of the murder of a woman by Dixon's son and a friend. The son's friend, who confessed to the killing, gave the principal testimony against Dixon. New York law required corroboration. Although there was some other evidence, the major corroborative evidence relied on by the prosecution was that Dixon had told two other people that the victim had been killed by being struck on the head with a rock at a time when the only way she could have known that fact was if the killer had told her. In fact, Hattie Dixon had testified, without contradiction, that prior to the time she made that statement, a police officer at the station house had said that they had found the victim in the park with her hands tied and a stone lying on her head.

During deliberations, the jury returned to the courtroom and asked to have read the testimony relating to Dixon's conversation with two witnesses about the rock. After that was done, a juror asked whether there was any evidence that the defendant was told at the police station that the victim had been hit on the head with a stone. The judge replied that he did not remember that testimony and asked Dixon's counsel to point out the relevant testimony so that it could be read. Dixon's counsel stated that there was such testimony, but the judge adopted a suggestion of the prosecution that different testimony be read and sent the jury back to deliberate without hearing Dixon's testimony. In the Court of Appeals, the majority found no error because Dixon had never testified to being told that the victim was "hit" with a stone. Whatever slip the trial judge might have made did not constitute substantial error. The conviction was therefore affirmed.

There were two dissents. One by Judge Crane, joined by Judge Hogan, argued that the trial judge had committed error in the colloquy with the jury and also in the casual handling of the prosecution's reference to a confession by Dixon's son. Judge Crane also contrasted the Court of Appeals' reversal of a conviction of a "New York bank president because the jury panel had been drawn an hour early" with its affirmance in this case of a death sentence of "a colored woman porter on the subway." The suggestion of prejudice was pointed.[23]

Cardozo wrote his own dissent. He concentrated solely on the colloquy between the jury and the judge. He may well have been uncomfortable with Crane's public imputation of racial and class prejudice to colleagues, although he himself had voted to affirm the conviction of the bank president. Cardozo began his separate dissent with a statement of faith in jury deliberations that defined to a large extent his approach in criminal cases. "We are slow to reverse upon the facts a verdict of guilt rendered by intelligent jurors with understanding of the evidence." But he stated that an appellate court should not rely on a verdict when the jury had been misled about the state of the evidence. This was such a case.

Cardozo had a good trial lawyer's sense of the nature of the relation-ship between a judge and a jury, especially how a jury relied on a judge for guidance and the ease with which a jury might be misled. The jury, which had specifically asked whether there was evidence that Dixon had been told that the victim had been hit on the head with a stone, had been led to believe that there was none. But there was testimony that Dixon had been told that the victim was found with a stone lying on her head. "In this tangle of misconceptions, I am fearful that the truth may have been smothered . . . I think we should do wrong in upholding a verdict thus rooted in uncertainty."[24] Cardozo did not dissent in vain. As he explained later, "The Dixon woman was not executed. The Gov-ernor (largely because of the dissent) commuted the sentence to life imprisonment."[25]

In one case, Cardozo voted to reverse a conviction because of preju-dicial error in spite of overwhelming evidence against the defendant. People v. Moran involved a first degree murder conviction of Thomas Moran for killing two policemen.[26] There was clear evidence of guilt, evidence of premeditation and deliberation, a confession, and a demand from the defendant himself for the electric chair. Cardozo, for a unani-mous court, wrote to reverse the conviction because the trial judge had charged the jury only on the capital offense issue of felony murder and refused to charge the lesser degrees of homicide that the jury conceivably could have found. Cardozo's normal distaste for overturning a convic-tion when the evidence of guilt was clear, was overcome by his greater distaste for potential harm to the defendant from the egregious error committed by the trial judge.[27]

Another circumstance in which Cardozo's sympathy could be enlisted in the face of a jury decision to convict was the discovery of new evidence that cast doubt on a conviction. One such case was People v. Arata.[28] Cardozo had reported orally to the consultation in 1930 for affirmance of a first degree murder conviction on the ground that the verdict was supported by the evidence. He then filed a written report because of his doubts about the denial of a motion for a new trial based on new evidence. An accomplice, who had testified against Arata and who had refused to file an affidavit, stated out of court that Peter Arata was innocent. Cardozo suggested that the court consider whether testimony of the witness should be taken in the trial court before the Court of Appeals passed on Arata's appeal. He noted that the statute requiring production of witnesses referred to examination of "affiants," and there were none here. He questioned whether the statute could be interpreted liberally to include the accomplice as an "affiant." "Perhaps not as a matter of strict interpretation," he wrote, "yet it would be uncomfortable to limit too narrowly the power to do justice in a case where life is at stake."

Cardozo confessed that he found it hard to require the judge to do something not directly authorized by statute, but he crafted a neat solution. He prepared a draft per curiam opinion (an opinion, usually brief, issued by the court without identifying a principal author) for discussion. The draft stated that the cause of justice would be promoted by having the accomplice testify and withheld determination of the appeal "to the end that an opportunity may be given to the defendant to renew his motions for a new trial and an opportunity [given] to the trial judge to require the production of witnesses before him."[29] The proposal did not force the judge to hold a hearing, did not say that the evidence required a new trial, and did not interpret the word "affiants" in the statute. But it told the trial judge plainly what the court thought justice required.

The court adopted Cardozo's proposal, and the trial judge held a new hearing. The accomplice reaffirmed his original court testimony, and another accomplice who had been called to testify refused to answer any questions. The trial judge denied the motion for a new trial, concluding that there was no probability of a different verdict. The defendant filed a new appeal, and the Court of Appeals, in a per curiam opinion, affirmed the trial judge's decision. Per curiam opinions do not designate an author but are normally written by the chief judge. This opinion does indeed sound like Cardozo: "there can be no reversal of the judgment without breaking down the barriers that separate the functions of a jury from those of an appellate court." But the court made its uncertainty and unhappiness about the result clear, with the hope of obtaining relief of a different sort:

None the less, the weaknesses . . . revealed are circumstances which in the cautious administration of criminal justice the State should deeply ponder before putting into execution the irretrievable penalty of death. Contradictions and polluted sources [of testimony] might conceivably be insufficient to exact a mitigation of the penalty. When, however, we add the fact that two accomplices, whose guilt was no less than the defendant's, are serving terms for manslaughter . . . we think a case exists where the penalty to be suffered by the defendant should be reduced in some measure of equality . . . A recommendation to the Governor [Franklin Roosevelt] will be made to that effect.[30]

Two months later Cardozo wrote Felix Frankfurter, "I suppose that we may say of People v. Arata that it is magnificent, but that it isn't law . . . The Governor, so I am told, promptly commuted, as I felt sure he would."[31] Cardozo did not explain what he thought "wasn't law." If giving advice without ordering action is what Cardozo regarded as not being "law," he was of course correct. But the court's formal action was law. The first *Arata* opinion involved making law by suggestion; the second *Arata* opinion involved following law to an inexorable result because the facts had been weighed by a judge and jury with more power than the Court of Appeals to do so. At the same time, Cardozo and the court suggested that another lawmaker, the governor, exercise his separate powers. As in the first opinion, the court kept within its powers but helped other authorities reach the desired result by suggesting the appropriate course of action.

In the absence of blatant judicial misconduct or newly discovered evidence, Cardozo could deal quite summarily with technical issues, even in a capital case. In People v. Emieleta, John Emieleta and a confederate named Rys robbed and beat their victim with an iron pipe and a large iron bolt.[32] The trial judge charged the jury solely on the theory of premeditated murder, and the defendants were convicted. Emieleta argued on appeal that he could not be convicted of first degree murder because it had not been proved whether he or his confederate had struck the mortal blow. That made no difference to Cardozo. He concluded that if the defendant struck the crucial blow, there was enough evidence to support a finding of premeditated design to kill. If his confederate had done so, that willful act in the common plan of murder was the willful act of both. Cardozo conceded that it might have been made clearer to the jury that the common plan had to be for the murder and not just the robbery. However, the defendant's lawyer had made no objection to the instructions, and there was no reasonable basis for fear that justice had not been done on the whole case. The contrast between *Emieleta* and *Moran,* in which Cardozo voted to reverse a capital conviction because of egregious judicial error, underlines the exceptional circumstances of prejudice that were required before Cardozo would support reversal of a conviction in a capital case when guilt seemed clear.

———

Another set of questions related to the kind of evidence that courts should allow a jury to consider in a criminal case. Parties are not permitted to put whatever they wish before the jury. Even if evidence is relevant, other policy considerations may dictate that the evidence should be excluded. Because the rules are complicated, trial judges often make mistakes in permitting or denying the introduction of evidence. The question then arises whether the mistake should lead to reversal of a conviction. Cardozo's usual attitude was permissive with respect to admission of evidence in criminal cases and stringent with respect to reversal of convictions for erroneous rulings on evidentiary matters.[33]

Two evidence cases, one unknown and one famous, provide important insights into Cardozo's general approach to law. People v. Carey, a rape case decided in 1918 on an evidence issue, is unknown because Cardozo expressed his views privately.[34] It provides an instance in which a sense of Cardozo the human being helps to explain his particular stance. Cardozo's general desire to comprehend modern ideas struggled with his old-fashioned attitude toward women and sex. Raymond Carey's defense was that the victim, unnamed in the opinion, had consented to sexual intercourse on this occasion as she had done before. The law in New York was then that rape was "not committed unless the woman oppose the man to the utmost limit of her power."[35] Carey's conviction was affirmed by the Appellate Division. He appealed to the Court of Appeals, and that court unanimously reversed the conviction on the ground that the statutory requirement that the victim's testimony be corroborated by other evidence had not been met.[36] In addition, the court's opinion noted that some members of the court had also wanted to reverse because the trial judge had refused to admit Carey's evidence that the victim was unchaste, but that this view had not commanded a majority.

Since Cardozo was one of the members who wanted to use the additional ground, he had submitted a draft opinion urging his position in strong terms. He admitted that there was a split of authority in the country on the question whether testimony about victim misconduct was admissible to rebut the inference that she had resisted the man. More courts excluded the evidence than admitted it. The lower New York courts were divided, and Cardozo characterized the issue as "one of the vexed questions of the law." But he argued that while rules of evidence were "in the formative stage," the court's "duty was to shape them in such a way that right will be done and wrong exposed."[37] This was as explicit an argument for using public policy to achieve justice as Cardozo ever made.

He supported his argument for reversal with a stern reliance on traditional morals. "Unchastity is a fact that tends to disprove a constituent element of the crime . . . The truth remains that chastity has once been yielded, that honor has been lost, and that great motive which inspires resistance even unto death, has gone. To deny this is to ignore a truth which all history and all literature and all experience proclaim."[38] Cardozo's view may have been derived in part from some literature and some history. It was doubtful that it was derived from experience, certainly not his own.

Cardozo believed that his plea for change in the evidence rule was innovative and modern because he believed that his personal moral assumptions about chastity were generally accepted principles on which reasonable persons would rely in evaluating the issue of consent. His touchstone was community values, but he ignored the increasing public division about values concerning sex. At the time he wrote, public discussions about sexual morality were becoming more candid.[39] Cardozo's report reflected a thoroughly orthodox Victorian attitude about sex and the place of women in American society. He continued the discussion in *The Nature of the Judicial Process,* using *Carey* as an example for his argument that courts ought to be free to discard precedent when the rules came to be seen as "inconsistent with the sense of justice or with the social welfare."[40] But he changed the basis of his argument, retreating to the logical ground that it made no sense to permit evidence about the victim's reputation for chastity while rejecting evidence about specific acts of unchastity. "The one thing that any sensible trier of the facts would wish to know above all others in estimating the truth of his defense, is held . . . to be something that must be excluded from the consideration of the jury."[41] That formulation concealed his deep-seated belief that the "unchaste" woman had abandoned her honor, her motivation to refuse consent, and, in his eyes, her credibility.

———————

The famous evidence opinion, Cardozo's best known criminal law case, People v. Defore, involved a major principle of constitutional law and criminal procedure law—the admissibility of evidence obtained by an illegal police search and seizure of items from a suspect's room.[42] The son of the landlady of a boardinghouse found his missing overcoat in the closet of a roomer, John Defore. The landlady and her son called the police, who arrested Defore in the hallway. The police then searched Defore's room and found a blackjack in a bag. The police did not have a warrant for either the arrest or the search. Defore was prosecuted on two charges, theft of the overcoat and possession of an illegal blackjack. He argued that the evidence collected by the police from his room should be excluded because the failure to obtain a search warrant made the seizure illegal. The trial court denied the motion. The jury acquitted Defore on the theft charge but convicted him on the blackjack possession charge. The Appellate Division affirmed, and Defore then appealed to the Court of Appeals.

The Court of Appeals used *Defore* as an opportunity to reexamine the consequences of an illegal search and seizure. The issue was decided on state law grounds because the United States Supreme Court had not yet held that the federal constitution's Fourteenth Amendment incorporated the prohibitions against unreasonable searches and seizures and self-incrimination contained in the Fourth and Fifth Amendments as restrictions against the states. New York had its own prohibition against unreasonable searches and seizures. It followed that of the Fourth Amendment almost exactly, but it was embodied in a statute, not a constitutional provision. Interpreting that statute, the Court of Appeals had decided twenty-three years previously in People v. Adams that documents unlawfully seized from a defendant could be introduced in the defendant's criminal trial.[43] Although the police might be held liable in a separate civil or perhaps criminal action, their testimony as to what they saw and seized was not excluded in a prosecution of the defendant. Thus, the improper search and seizure was an offense to be punished separately rather than deterred by excluding the evidence from the defendant's trial. The Supreme Court of the United States affirmed that judgment.[44] Ten years later, however, it decided in Weeks v. United States that in federal prosecutions, exclusion was the appropriate remedy for evidence unlawfully seized by the police.[45] When *Defore* came to the Court of Appeals, the developments at the federal level, though not binding, led it to reexamine its earlier holding.

After reconsideration, the Court of Appeals unanimously reaffirmed the holding of *Adams* that illegally seized evidence could be admitted in a prosecution, and it upheld Defore's conviction. Cardozo's opinion did not break any new ground, except to add a much-quoted phrase to the literature. Cardozo characterized the contrasting federal rule in memorable fashion: "The criminal is to go free because the constable has blundered."[46] Cardozo's opinion was important for its explanation of the reasons for reaffirming *Adams*. Cardozo began his reconsideration of *Adams* by looking to the views of other jurisdictions and of the commentators. Only fourteen states had followed the *Weeks* federal exclusionary rule; thirty-one had rejected it. Moreover, most of the commentators favored the older *Adams* doctrine. "With authority thus divided, it is only some overmastering consideration of principle or of policy that should move us to a change. The balance is not swayed until something more persuasive than uncertainty is added to the scales."[47]

Cardozo urged the consistency of the New York rule as an argument in its favor. New York drew no distinction between official and private trespasses, forbidding and punishing both the same way. The federal rule prohibited a federal prosecutor from using evidence gathered by a federal marshal, but permitted the same prosecutor to use evidence illegally gathered either by a state official or by a private person. Cardozo saw the decisive factor as the "professed object of the trespass rather than the official character of the trespasser."[48] He observed that, as in the present case, there was often active cooperation between the police and a landlord, and that it was disingenuous to make the admissibility of the evidence turn on whether the intruder in the defendant's room was the police or the landlord. The consequences, whatever they were, should be the same for both.

Returning to the New York search and seizure statute, Cardozo relied on the fact that while it removed any privilege in the police to search without a warrant, it did not attach any consequences to violation of the statute. His canon of statutory construction was that interpretation could not attach consequences unless in furtherance of "some public policy, adequately revealed."[49] No such policy was revealed to him. Indeed, public policy looked in the opposite direction. The *Weeks* rule would immunize the most serious crime because of the overzealousness of the "pettiest peace officer." Nor was the statutory prohibition illusory without an exclusionary rule; historically, the prohibition of unreasonable searches and seizures had been enforced by a recovery of substantial damages against the intruding officers. Cardozo's clinching argument was that the legislature had acquiesced in the court's prior ruling in *Adams* by leaving the statute untouched. *Adams* had struck a balance between the social need that crime be suppressed and the social need that the statute not be flouted. "We must hold it to be the law until those organs of government by which a change of policy is normally effected, shall give notice to the courts that the change has come to pass."[50] The court had struck the original balance, and now it was up to the legislature and governor (or the United States Supreme Court) to change the balance, if it was to be changed.

The exclusionary rule has been the subject of constant debate over the decades that have followed *Defore*. In an opinion by Justice Felix Frankfurter that relied heavily on Cardozo's opinion as well as on the experience of many states, the Supreme Court held in Wolf v. Colorado in 1949 that the exclusionary rule of *Weeks* was not binding on the states.[51] Thereafter, in the wave of expansion of constitutional rights, especially in criminal procedure cases, during the Warren Court years, the Supreme Court overruled *Wolf* in Mapp v. Ohio in 1961.[52] The holding that the federal exclusionary rule was binding on the states did not end the debate. The Supreme Court now treats the exclusionary rule as a "judicially created remedy designed to safeguard Fourth Amendment rights generally through its deterrent effect, rather than a personal constitutional right of the person aggrieved," and has often applied a cost-benefit analysis in refusing to apply the exclusionary rule.[53] Even though the debate has gone far beyond the basic framework of Cardozo's opinion in *Defore,* his pithy warning about freeing the criminal solely "because the constable has blundered" captures the strong sentiment that still weighs against the exclusionary rule.

Cardozo's criminal procedure opinions show a judge whose general attitude was to enforce criminal statutes and to respect the roles of the jury and the lower courts. Although the rules of procedure existed to assure that the goals of justice were achieved by just means, they were not to be pursued so tenaciously as to defeat the larger goal of the legal system to punish the guilty. Thus, where there was clear evidence of guilt, Cardozo would not use technical errors to reverse a conviction unless reversal served a major public need, such as to correct an egregious error. Cardozo had seen in his years of litigating how easy it was for a judge to make an erroneous ruling, and he had to be convinced that a procedural error was in fact prejudicial. But Cardozo would vote to reverse a conviction if he found a procedural error that might have tipped the scale toward a jury verdict of guilty. In short, he was neither a "hanging judge" nor a "bleeding heart," but he was tough on the guilty.

Cardozo's major substantive criminal law opinions dealt with issues of moral fault. We have already seen that in tort law, Cardozo accepted negligence as the general standard of liability and that he focused rather narrowly on individual misconduct or failure of duty. But New York criminal law forced him to face the issues of strict and vicarious liability, that is, cases in which a statute made certain conduct criminal although the defendant had no intent to violate the proscribed standard (strict liability) and cases in which a statute imposed criminal liability on a defendant because of the criminal conduct of an employee (vicarious liability). Such cases defined the outer borders of criminal responsibility.

One case involved a conviction of a landlady because prostitution was occurring in her building. Tenement House Department v. McDevitt was an action brought to recover a statutory penalty of $50 under a statute providing that "[n]o tenement house . . . shall be used for the purpose of prostitution."[54] The trial judge, after finding that two women had engaged in prostitution in McDevitt's tenement on a single day, dismissed the action for lack of any willful or even negligent conduct by the landlord. The Appellate Division affirmed, and the Department appealed to the Court of Appeals, arguing that the facts found by the trial judge constituted a violation. Cardozo's lengthy opinion for a unanimous court affirmed the dismissal of the action. After considering the section in the context of other prohibited uses that suggested a requirement of continuous activity, as well as statutes from other jurisdictions reaching the same result, Cardozo rejected the contention that the statute was violated by a single use. He concluded that the word "used" in the statute required some element of permanence in the activity. As so construed, the statute was constitutional, but McDevitt had not violated it.

Cardozo's nervousness with the concept of strict liability was evident. He refused to state whether a statute that founded landlord liability on a single act of tenant prostitution would be constitutional, holding that if the legislature were to impose "a penalty so drastic," it "must say so in plain words."[55] He drew a distinction between "infamous" crimes, in which the element of conscious wrongdoing was generally required, and minor offenses, where there was a greater range of practice and power.

Where the latter were concerned, the legislature often acted by requiring an individual "at his peril to conform to the average standard of conduct and of knowledge" and did not allow individual lack of consciousness as a defense. Moreover, this particular statute, although criminal in form, did not charge the owner with a crime. The penalty was to be recovered through a civil action with a "trifling" penalty.[56]

Cardozo dealt with his concern about the ability of the legislature to make unintentional and nonnegligent conduct criminal in two ways. First, he characterized the statute as, in substance, the recovery of a civil penalty, and a minor one at that. Second, by interpreting the statute to require continuous misuse of the property, he was able to view a violation as the result of the landlord's failure to monitor the use of her property. The statute therefore required a finding of "guilt, whether due to design or to neglect, of the person by whom the penalty is payable," and hence it did not impose strict liability.[57] In other words, in Cardozo's view, liability under this statute was based upon fault.

Cardozo expounded this view more clearly in a second strict liability case, People ex rel. Price v. Sheffield Farms.[58] Section 162 of the New York Labor Law forbade specified businesses from employing anyone under the age of fourteen. Section 1275 of the Penal Law made violation of section 162 a misdemeanor, imposing fines between twenty and fifty dollars for a first offense, and heavier fines and even imprisonment for subsequent offenses. Sheffield employed drivers to deliver its dairy products. Those drivers, in violation of company rules, occasionally hired boys under fourteen to help them. Although the company had hired inspectors to prevent that practice, a state inspector caught a driver who had been employing a thirteen-year old boy for six months, and the state prosecuted Sheffield. The trial court convicted Sheffield of violation of the statute, and the Appellate Division affirmed. Although the Court of Appeals had previously, in dictum, indicated that section 162 provided for strict liability, Sheffield strongly attacked that construction in its appeal to the court.

Cardozo, writing for a court that was unanimous in deciding that the conviction should be affirmed, construed the statute as providing for strict liability, but he did so with several important qualifications. He first avoided the problem of vicarious liability by denying that the statute imposed it. Sheffield was not liable because of the liability of its driver; rather, it was liable because it broke the duty of supervision imposed directly upon it by statute. Cardozo equated the statutory term "permit" with the term "suffer," which appeared in others parts of the statute. He then discussed the prohibition in terms of sufferance, which he defined as he had defined "used" in *McDevitt*. "Sufferance . . . implies knowledge or the opportunity through reasonable diligence to acquire knowledge."[59] Even though the opportunity for supervision and hence for knowledge was lessened when the work was done off the company's premises, there was "some evidence of the defendant's negligence in failing for six months to discover and prevent the employment of this child," and that constituted a "sufferance" of the work.[60] Thus, although the typical requirement of subjective fault, the requirement of "willful" or "knowing" violation, was not present in this criminal statute, Cardozo's interpretation did infer a requirement of objective fault in its requirement of proof of negligent conduct, the failure to live up to the standard of care set out in the statute.

Cardozo did yield one step to legislative power. Unlike *McDevitt*, the statute in *Sheffield Farms* was explicitly a criminal statute. In upholding its prescription of criminal punishment without "willfulness," Cardozo emphasized that only a "moderate" fine was involved and concluded that the statute was "a reasonable regulation of the right to do business by proxy." Even though he left open the question whether the statute's imprisonment term would also be upheld, he gave some hint of his response by commenting that upholding "reasonable" regulations did not require upholding "extravagant" ones and that some of the statute's "penalties may be excessive."[61]

In dealing with the negligence issue in *McDevitt*, Cardozo had made it clear that although it would seldom occur, the legislature could constitutionally impose a civil fine even though the defendant was not at fault, either intentionally or negligently. In *Sheffield Farms*, however, in which a criminal violation was involved, Cardozo did not repeat the *McDevitt* language that the company could be punishable by a moderate fine even if not negligent. He left the question of imposition of a substantial fine or imprisonment without fault in a criminal case for another day. It is clear that he thought it presented a difficult issue.[62]

Cardozo's opinions in *McDevitt* and *Sheffield Farms* demonstrate his aversion to imposition of criminal responsibility without a requirement of some "moral" failing. Even when the penalty was recovered in a civil action, the statute had to be framed in terms of linking the prohibited conduct with a failing that would be negligent in the typical case. When the action was denominated criminal, negligence in the individual case had to be shown before the usual requirement of subjective fault, willful or knowing violation, could be dispensed with, and that omission was permissible only when the mandated penalty was modest. As in civil liability, Cardozo's usual measurement of criminal liability was grounded in a conception of fault, and departures from that standard were carefully scrutinized.

Believing that proof of individual moral fault was required in criminal statutes, Cardozo worked hard in People v. Mancuso to find that a statute that on its face seemed to presume the existence of fault in fact required the prosecution to prove it.[63] A New York statute provided that a corporate director who "[i]n case of the fraudulent insolvency of [a] corporation, shall have participated in such fraud . . . [i]s guilty of a misdemeanor." The statute further provided that the insolvency of a corporation was "deemed fraudulent unless its affairs appear upon investigation to have been administered fairly, legally and with the same care and diligence" that paid agents are bound to observe.[64]

Francis Mancuso was indicted under the New York statute. His motions to dismiss the indictment were granted, and the Appellate Division affirmed on the authority of Manley v. Georgia, in which the United States Supreme Court had held unconstitutional a similar Georgia statute that explicitly established a rebuttable presumption of fraud based on the insolvency. The Supreme Court had concluded that there was no rational connection between corporate insolvency and fraud by the directors.[65] The state appealed to the Court of Appeals, and Cardozo, writing for a divided court, upheld the statute and reversed the dismissal of the indictment.

The goal of the statute was to hold fiduciaries to high standards of conduct. *Mancuso* was the criminal law counterpart of Meinhard v. Salmon, the civil case in which Cardozo imposed on a joint venturer the obligation to include his coadventurer in a new deal.[66] First, he argued that the section deeming the insolvency fraudulent "unless" the corporation had been prudently managed set forth a definition of fraudulent conduct, not a presumption of fraud. But even if it were a presumption, Cardozo was prepared to sever the presumption, that is, to remove the unconstitutional language from the statute and uphold the remainder. Responding to an attack on the vagueness of the definition, he would have upheld all three tests. "Fairly" equaled good faith, and "legally" referred to existing state statutes. The third test simply established the long-known standard of the prudent and diligent fiduciary. This definition was sufficient because the standard was old and certain; it had been "sanctioned and defined by centuries of precept and example."[67] Having reshaped the statute so that it could be upheld, Cardozo summarized his conclusion for the benefit of the trial court that would then try Mancuso: "[T]he insolvency of a moneyed corporation resulting from the failure to administer its affairs with reasonable care and diligence is a fraudulent insolvency within the definition of the statute, and a director participates in the fraud when he participates in the negligence with ruin as the consequence."[68]

Cardozo's reading of the statute was not obvious. Judge Lehman, concurring, did not see the "unless" language as providing the crucially needed definition. All it provided, in his view, was a definition of fraudulent insolvency instead of a definition of the "participation" needed to impose criminal liability on directors. Lehman did not believe that the statute imposed criminal liability for mere negligence. Participation implied more, and Lehman was willing to save the statute by construing participation to mean conduct that aided and abetted fraud. Judge Kellogg's dissent attacked both opinions. The words "fraud" and "fraudulent conduct" had too many meanings in different contexts. Turning the "unless" language into a definition involved a complete rewriting of the statute to save it. Because the provisions were insufficient to state a crime, the statute violated due process.

Cardozo pushed hard to find a legislative desire to impose criminal liability on directors for failure to carry out their fiduciary responsibilities. His difference with Kellogg was technical—could the statute fairly be read to impose such liability? His difference with Lehman was more substantive. Lehman was willing to save the statute, but not by a construction that too easily imposed criminal liability on directors. Lehman's opinion shows more sympathy with the predicament in which the directors found themselves. "There but for the grace of God go I," he seemed to say. Cardozo was more interested in reading the statute to carry forward the underlying thrust of Meinhard v. Salmon to uphold high standards of fiduciary duty.

Another aspect of the issue of moral fault in criminal law was presented by the problem of insanity, which erases fault and hence creates a defense to criminal liability. In his second year on the Court of Appeals,

Cardozo wrote for the majority in interpreting the New York statute that provided an insanity defense for a person "laboring under such a defect of reason as: (1) not to know the nature and quality of the act he was doing; or (2) not to know that the act was wrong." The case was People v. Schmidt, which we have discussed earlier in connection with Cardozo's views about harmless error.[69] Hans Schmidt, the "priest" who threw his victim's body into the Hudson River, had pleaded insanity to a charge of murder in the first degree. The trial judge charged the jury that "wrong" meant "contrary to the law of the state." Thus, if the defendant knew that the homicide to which he had confessed was forbidden by state law, the jury should find him guilty even if he had been under the delusion that God had appeared to him and commanded him to sacrifice the victim.[70] The jury rejected his defense and found him guilty of murder in the first degree. He appealed to the Court of Appeals.

The Court of Appeals affirmed the conviction because of Schmidt's subsequent admission that he was not insane. Nevertheless, it considered the question of the proper interpretation of the statute "because the question is in the case, and the true rule on a subject so important ought not to be left in doubt."[71] Cardozo and the court were prepared to engage in dictum—a pronouncement not necessary to decide the case at hand—to settle an important unresolved question, whether the word "wrong" in the statute meant legal or moral wrong. Cardozo concluded that the insanity defense was available to one who knew that his action was prohibited by law but acted under a belief that it was not morally wrong. This dictum became a staple of criminal law casebooks for a number of years thereafter until developments in the medical view of insanity reshaped legal doctrine and made Cardozo's opinion obsolete.[72]

Cardozo used most of the interpretive techniques that he later laid out in *The Nature of the Judicial Process* to reach his conclusion. He first traced the growth of the insanity defense through hundreds of years of English and American law to "the famous decision of the House of Lords in *M'Naghten's Case*."[73] Much of that decision, including the Lords' confusing and somewhat contradictory pronouncements, was embodied in the New York statute. Cardozo began his consideration of the meaning of "wrong" by discussing numerous cases in which courts, including New York courts, explained the statutory requirement as requiring some knowledge that the act was morally wrong. His conclusion from the precedents was qualified:

In the light of all these precedents, it is impossible . . . to say that there is any decisive adjudication which limits the word "wrong" in the statutory definition to legal as opposed to moral wrong. The trend of the decisions is indeed the other way. The utmost that can be said is that the question is still an open one. We must, therefore, give that construction to the statute which seems to us most consonant with reason and justice.[74]

With this statement, he turned to public policy. He opened the discussion with the assertion that in the case in which a mother killed a child whom she loved under "an insane delusion that God has appeared to her and ordained the sacrifice," it would be "a mockery to say that, within the meaning of the statute, she knows that the act is wrong." His major policy argument was stated quite briefly: interpreting the statutory term "wrong" to include only legal wrong would "rob the rule of all relation to the mental health and true capacity of the criminal." He argued that an instruction to the jury that focused only on legal instead of moral wrong could lead to a conviction, an "abhorrent" conclusion in such a case.[75] The statutory word "wrong" required proof that the defendant knew that the act was morally wrong.

Cardozo's interpretation of the insanity doctrine reflected one of his major concerns in law. Although he was not at all squeamish about affirming even the harshest criminal punishments, he was, as we have seen in *McDevitt* and *Sheffield Farms,* reluctant to impose criminal liability without a finding of willful or knowing misconduct. Thus, his interpretation of the statute as requiring the state to prove knowledge of moral wrongdoing was quite consistent with his general approach to the role of fault in other criminal or civil law settings. Although fault was under some attack from policy-makers and theorists, it had been a central feature in civil and criminal law for centuries, and the concept was in accord with Cardozo's own sense of the importance of personal responsibility in life.

When we compare Cardozo's substantive criminal law decisions with his criminal procedure opinions, we see a significant difference in the way that Cardozo perceived his judicial role. In the substantive criminal law decisions, as in the civil law cases, Cardozo followed his prescription of using history, analogy, custom, and public policy to exercise the significant role accorded to the courts. Although respectful of precedent and generally deferential to the legislature, Cardozo occasionally gave priority to public policy arguments—especially those affirming the fault concept or high standards of fiduciary conduct. In the criminal procedure cases, Cardozo believed that the appellate court's responsibility for issues of law should not interfere with the primary responsibility of trial judges for conducting trials and of juries for determining guilt. He was loath to overturn a jury conviction, even in a capital case, when there was substantial evidence of guilt. A trial error had to be important and the prejudice had to be significant before Cardozo would do so.

Cardozo's substantive criminal law views proceeded from his general belief that it was his job as a judge to carry out the policies embodied in criminal law statutes, no matter what his personal view of that legislation was. He regarded penal legislation as rooted in a system based on punishment for fault, and he would not depart from that pattern without a clear mandate from the legislature. That focus on fault fit well with a judge who accepted the traditional doctrines of negligence law, with its emphasis on individual responsibility. It also fit well with a man who saw the essence of his personal creed and of his religious heritage as right conduct, responsibility, and duty.

21

Property, Corporations, the Legal Profession, and Legislative Policy

Cardozo was best known for his torts and contracts opinions, but, in addition, he wrote a number of important opinions dealing with the law governing property, corporations, and the conduct of lawyers. These opinions highlighted some of the characteristics we have already seen and added a few others. Most of Cardozo's property opinions were straightforward applications of well-settled real property law, as one might expect; however, the best example of Cardozo's combined use of history and custom and one of the best examples of public-policy reasoning occur in property cases. Fiduciary duty was a key element in Cardozo's decisions in both corporate law and the law governing lawyers. Finally, a number of cases illustrate that Cardozo's deference to other branches of government and his protective attitude toward the government treasury were broad-ranging concerns.

Cardozo recognized that history, and the expectations that are derived from history, played a major role in the law of real property.[1] One notable case, Beers v. Hotchkiss, called forth his legal talents in memorable fashion.[2] The case came to the court in 1931, near the end of Cardozo's career on the Court of Appeals, and he was then in peak form. He analyzed both history and custom, and their relation to legislation, to conclude that the eighteenth-century understanding of a specific form

416

of real-property transfer in a local community controlled the interpretation of statutes.

Two groups of claimants were fighting over land in Southampton, Long Island, that had been partly cleared for a landing strip and hangar for airplanes. The parties in possession (the appellants) had no claim of right other than possession. The out-of-possession claimants (the respondents) claimed ownership under an 1882 deed. In that deed the town conveyed unspecified, undivided land that, the respondents claimed, included the land in question. Under New York law, the respondents could not prevail by virtue of the weakness of the title of the possessors. The respondents had to demonstrate that their chain of title, which derived from the 1882 deed, gave them ownership of the land. The issue was whether this land had been owned by the town in 1882 or whether an allotment of these lands that had been noted in the town records in 1782 had previously transferred ownership from the town. If the town had already transferred title to the contested land, then the town could not have conveyed it in 1882, and the respondents would have no claim.

The lower courts had given judgment to the respondents on the ground that the English Statute of Frauds and a colonial New York statute of frauds invalidated the 1782 allotment to specified parties. The relevant statutes of frauds required written deeds to make transfers of land effective, and the Appellate Division held that the allotment did not constitute a written transfer of title. Therefore, the town retained title and conveyed it to the respondents in 1882. Since the Appellate Division had been unanimous, the occupants had to get permission from the Court of Appeals to file an appeal. Cardozo's report recommended granting the appeal because the question was interesting, "involving the antiquities of the colonial law of land," and because it was "important enough in view of its effect upon titles generally to call for a decision from our court that will set it at rest." He wanted "to study the case much more carefully before pronouncing about it one way or another . . . My impression is that the [occupants] will have trouble in sustaining their appeal, but that it is wise to hear them."[3]

Cardozo's colleagues accepted his recommendation, and after further study, he wrote for a unanimous Court of Appeals in reversing the Appellate Division and dismissing the respondents' claim against the occupants. He considered the original land grant to the Duke of York in 1664; the relationship of colonial statutes to similar English statutes; the upsetting effect on colonial laws of the English revolution of 1688;

various codifications of colonial law; and, finally, the effect of the American Revolution on the authoritative quality of English law in the new republic.

Cardozo's historical research was prodigious, and his handling of that history was the most interesting feature of the opinion. Cardozo had consulted Professor Julius Goebel of Columbia Law School, who was well versed in colonial legal history, about the issues. The memorandum that Professor Goebel sent Cardozo was skimpy compared with the wealth of material in Cardozo's opinion.[4] Cardozo either did the additional research himself or received other help.[5] He set out all the conflicting evidence with respect to the binding effect of English and colonial statutes of frauds and noted the uncertainty that had been explicitly recognized in New York all through the seventeenth and eighteenth centuries until 1787, when the legislature of the state of New York adopted its own law. After reciting the history, Cardozo concluded that the touchstone of decision was custom, usage, and the contemporary understanding at the time of the 1782 allotment. Referring to a 1774 New York statute that declared that the English Statute of Frauds had been received as law by usage in the colony, Cardozo stated, "If usage was potent to bring an act of Parliament into effect, usage must also have been potent to define the scope of its reception. This much at least is clear, the colonists were not conscious of any antagonism between the provisions of the statutes and the usage whereby town lands were parceled out to the proprietors by allotment noted on the records."[6] Thus, the specific practice of the colonists with respect to the land allotments coexisted with the more general recognition of the applicability of the statute of frauds.

The same argument applied to colonial statutes of frauds that supplanted earlier statutes of frauds that had excepted conveyances by towns from their operation: "A practical interpretation, too strong to be ignored, is evidence of the intention of the lawmakers that the exceptions should survive . . . We are not at liberty a century and half later to give to ancient statutes, whose very existence is and was in doubt, a meaning and operation at variance with the practice of the vicinage [the neighborhood]."[7] In the end, law in 1782 was what people thought to be law, as evidenced by their actions, so that statutes that might seem to dictate a contrary result gave way. Cardozo therefore upheld the validity of the 1782 allotment. Since the respondents received nothing from the 1882 deed, the occupiers of the land prevailed. This was the rare case in which Cardozo refused to give primacy to a statute that on its face seemed applicable.[8] *Beers* was the paradigm case for using custom—in the form of the popular understanding in 1782—to create law.

A different kind of case presented Cardozo with a conflict between the doctrines of property law and his personal sense of the obligations due to ancestors buried in a graveyard. In Lonby Realty Corp. v. Lane, a purchaser of property sought the return of its down payment on the ground that the title was rendered unmarketable by the existence of a burial easement that existed in a small part of the property, although the graveyard was no longer physically evident.[9] The trial judge had not accepted that argument, and his judgment for the seller was affirmed in the Appellate Division. After the case was argued in the Court of Appeals in 1928, Judge Hubbs reported orally to the consultation for affirmance on the ground that the reservation of a burial easement was too indefinite to be enforceable, but he later filed a written report recommending reversal. Hubbs relied on a finding in a 1917 action brought by the seller that the easement and the burial ground both existed, to conclude that the title was unmarketable.

Cardozo responded that he did not have a firm conviction that Judge Hubbs was wrong; however, since he tended the other way, he had written a memorandum. He concluded that the easement had expired because it had not been used. His memorandum mingled views on the law with an unusually personal rumination on the dead: "A burial ground will not cease to be such through mere neglect of the graves, the failure of the living to pay honor to the dead. A different result may follow where decay has gone so far that every trace of the identity of the cemetery has gone; the graves so obliterated that their existence and location can no longer be discovered . . . The living have postponed too long the offices of piety where the very place to be honored is unknown and unknowable." At such time, the failure to use became abandonment, and the easement was destroyed as irrevocably as "the obliteration of the resting places of the uncommemorated dead." Cardozo concluded that this had occurred and that therefore "[e]asement and dead alike are now buried in oblivion."[10]

At the time that Cardozo wrote, his sister Nellie was seriously ill. Having already lost the rest of his family, Cardozo was clearly concerned not only about the duties of care and honor that he bore as the survivor but also about the prospect that at his death, the whole family would be extinguished. His own will provided for the perpetual care of the family burial plot and that of his sister Emily. In his report to the consultation, he resurrected an opinion from 1844 by Judge Samuel Beardsley on the subject of abandonment of cemeteries and quoted its moving language: "When these graves shall have worn away; when they who now weep over them shall have found kindred resting places for themselves; when nothing shall remain to distinguish this spot from the common earth around . . . it will then have lost its identity as a burial ground."[11] The passage hints at Cardozo's sadness but also his acceptance of reality. In *Lonby,* the rules of property prevailed over the sentiment. If the facts showed an abandonment, then the burial easement had disappeared. The title was marketable, and the purchaser was bound to complete its contract. The court, including Judge Hubbs, agreed with Cardozo's conclusion and affirmed the judgment without an opinion.

Surprisingly, one of Cardozo's most explicit statements of the creative "method of sociology" came in connection with a property case. Stewart v. Turney involved the issue whether an 1812 deed from the state of New York that conveyed a lot bordering Lake Cayuga operated to extinguish the public right to walk along the shoreline.[12] The defendants were hunters who liked to shoot ducks from the cover of blinds along the shore. The plaintiffs, lessees of a portion of the lot, claimed that they could exclude the hunters because their ownership included the shore down to the low-water mark of the lake. The hunters argued that the lessees' ownership did not include the shore; the deed from the state should be interpreted as conveying ownership only to the ordinary line of upland vegetation, that is, the line higher up the shore marking the area kept free of vegetation by water action. The trial court agreed with the lessees and enjoined the hunters from walking along the shore. The Appellate Division reversed and dismissed the complaint.

In reporting to the consultation, Cardozo stated that the question was close and difficult and was an open one in New York. "We could decide either way with some support in precedent and reason. Viewing the question as still open, I am reporting in accordance with what seems to me to be the larger public policy."[13] Cardozo began his report by arguing that the court should not apply to large lakes the general presumption that the state's grant of land bordering rivers, ponds, and small lakes carried with it a grant to the center of the water bottom. The question then was to decide where to draw the boundary between the property of the state and that of the private landowner. Cardozo rejected the line of low water in favor of the line of upland vegetation, although conceding the landowner a right of access to the lake and the right to build piers and wharves. Cardozo defended his conclusion by noting that "considerations of public policy have had some place in shaping the conclusion." He spelled out what those considerations were: "If title to the shore is [in the plaintiffs], the public may be shut out by barriers at either end . . . The state pays its money to aid in propagating and protecting the fish and fowl within its borders. It has no thought in so doing of fostering exclusive privilege. The common lands and the common waters are held for the common good."[14] The public, and the hunters, should prevail.

The court agreed to hear the case. It was unanimous in agreeing with Cardozo's view that the state still owned the lake bottom. But Judge Andrews spoke for a four-judge majority in rejecting Cardozo's view of the boundary between state and private land. The majority followed precedent in other states and held that the boundary was at the low-water mark in order to give the purchaser of the land ownership rights that extended to the water, wherever it was at any time, low or high. It therefore enjoined the defendants from entering on the beach. Cardozo, Hogan, and Crane dissented without opinion. The dissenters, oddly, did not think that the important public policy question merited an explanation of their disagreement with the majority's opinion.

Cardozo's report made the basis for his own vote quite clear. In his view, the rights of the public should prevail over the claim of private property in order to protect public access to an important natural resource. This was not a case of taking property clearly owned by one person and devoting it to the use of many. He was dealing with uncertain ownership, unsettled expectations, and property on the geographical margin between public and private ownership. In that situation, Cardozo was inclined as a judge to prefer the rights of many over the rights of one.

Cardozo's opinions in these three property cases demonstrate that although he generally gave great weight to precedent in property disputes, he was ready to look to history and custom and to engage in policy analysis in situations in which there were no settled expectations and other interests were important. In the process, he gave us important insights into his prescription for lawmaking.

———

Cardozo's strong belief in enforcing obligations, which we have seen throughout, also informed his treatment of the responsibilities of corporate managers. Globe Woolen Company v. Utica Gas and Electric Company considered the validity of two contracts signed by an electric utility to supply electricity to Globe's worsted and woolen mills.[15] The contracts had been negotiated by John Maynard, the president and chief stockholder of Globe, with the general manager of the electric department of the utility. The problem arose from the fact that Maynard was also chairman of the executive committee of the utility, thus creating the possibility of undue pressure on the general manager and an unfair contract for the utility. When the contracts were presented to the directors of the utility, Maynard presided but took no part in the discussion or vote. Maynard also kept silent when questions were put about the profitability of the first proposed contract and later when the general manager stated that the terms in the second contract were practically the same as those in the first, although in fact they were not.

The contracts, which guaranteed savings to Globe, turned out to be losing propositions and, as time went on, financial disasters for the utility, with the result that the utility eventually rescinded them. Globe sued for "specific performance," that is, to require the utility to continue supplying electricity under the terms of the contract. The utility prevailed in the trial court on the ground that Maynard's dual role had led to an unfair contract for the utility. The Appellate Division affirmed the annulment of the contracts on condition that the utility reimburse Globe for certain installation costs. The Court of Appeals affirmed that judgment in an opinion by Cardozo.

The issue was whether Maynard had violated his fiduciary responsibility to the utility. Maynard argued that he had not participated in the approval of the contract and bore no responsibility for it. Cardozo rejected the argument that silence in the discussion and abstention from voting was sufficient. Noting that power could be exercised in other ways, he concluded that the evidence supported the trial judge's finding that Maynard had exercised a potent influence in negotiating with the utility's general manager, his own subordinate. Moreover, Maynard could not properly remain silent about dangers to the utility if the transaction was unfair. In these circumstances, there "must be candor and equity in the transaction, and some reasonable proportion between benefits and burdens." The unfairness of the transaction was "startling" and the consequences "disastrous." Maynard must have known that "he held a one-sided contract, which left the defendant at his mercy." He had ignored "the constant duty" that "rests on a trustee to seek no harsh advantage to the detriment of his trust, but rather to protest and renounce if through blindness of those who treat with him he gains what is unfair."[16]

The voltage of Cardozo's rhetoric signaled his personal emphasis on fiduciary responsibility. Even though the holding of *Globe Woolen* was not surprising, Cardozo used the opinion to send a message to the business world, a precursor of his later opinion in the joint venturers case, Meinhard v. Salmon.[17] Cardozo's opinion not only condemned the conduct of Mr. Maynard but also instructed other dual directors and, indeed, all directors about their responsibilities.

Cardozo's opinion in Berkey v. Third Avenue Railroad Company, which we noted earlier for its bearing on vicarious liability in tort law, also dealt with the important corporate law issue of the responsibility of a corporate parent for the actions of a corporate subsidiary.[18] Mr. and Mrs. Berkey had sued the parent company for negligence after Mrs. Berkey was injured while getting off the subsidiary company's streetcar. They argued that the parent company was not insulated from liability by the separate corporate organization of its subsidiary because all the railroad cars operating on the interconnected system of subsidiaries bore the parent's name and the parent company exercised significant operational control over the subsidiary. The trial judge dismissed the complaints on the ground that the parent was not liable for the subsidiary's negligence, but the Appellate Division reinstated them. The Court of Appeals reversed the Appellate Division and reinstated the trial court's judgment.

Cardozo's opinion for the majority relied on the fact that the parent company was not itself operating the subsidiary's line to conclude that the parent did not legally have operational control of the subsidiary. Cardozo argued that it would have been illegal for the company to have operated the subsidiary's line without approval of the Public Service Commission.[19] He therefore exempted the parent from liability for the subsidiary's negligence, although many other courts had extended the principle of vicarious liability to corporate parents in cases that were weaker than this. Cardozo refused to distinguish between control that would violate the statute and control that would make the parent liable in tort, and he concluded that ignoring the separation between the parent and its subsidiary would thwart the public policy of the state.[20]

Cardozo, himself a master of metaphor, warned against solving the issue by asking whether the subsidiary was a "dummy" of the parent:

> The whole problem of the relation between parent and subsidiary corporations is one that is still enveloped in the mists of metaphor. Metaphors in law are to be narrowly watched, for starting as devices to liberate thought, they end often by enslaving it. We say at times that the corporate unity will be ignored when the parent corporation operates a business through a subsidiary which is characterized as an "alias" or a "dummy." All this is well enough if the picturesqueness of the epithets does not lead us to forget that the essential term to be defined is the act of operation.[21]

In Cardozo's view, the parent-subsidiary form of business under which the two companies operated separately was sanctioned by statute. It should not be undermined, even in order to permit a party injured by the negligence of the subsidiary to recover from the parent, unless the corporate parties themselves had broken down the separate operation of the two entities. The Berkeys therefore could not recover from the parent company.

Judge Posner has cited *Berkey* as one of the cases in which Cardozo "substituted words for thought." Although Cardozo was guilty of that analytic flaw on occasion, *Berkey* does not seem to be a very good example of that trait. Posner says that Cardozo gave no reason for refusing to pierce the corporate veil in this case. Yet Posner himself noted that the general rule was that "a shareholder, even a corporate one, is not liable for the debts . . . of the corporation in which it owns shares," and Cardozo was clear about the kind of facts that would constitute an exception to the general rule. Cardozo recognized room for argument, but he was not convinced that the case for an exception had been made out here.

Posner argued that the railroad company's conduct during the lawsuit was a good reason for piercing the corporate veil. He relied on the opening argument of Berkey's lawyer at trial that negotiations between the parties had delayed the filing of the suit until just before the statute of limitations against the subsidiary would run; that the parent company got an extension to file an answer until after the statute ran; and that it then filed an answer denying liability on the ground that it did not operate the car in question.[22] The Berkeys, however, never pursued the issue and did not argue that the parent company's trial conduct was a ground for overturning the decision of the trial judge or the Appellate Division.

Even those moved by sympathy for Mrs. Palsgraf on the issue of liability for costs might pause here. The Berkeys were not poverty stricken or ignorant. Mr. Berkey was a professor of geology at Columbia University, and their lawyers were the well-connected firm of Satterlee, Canfield & Stone.[23] The firm neglected to investigate its case sufficiently to find out about the subsidiary, and it waited until just before the statute of limitations expired before bringing suit. Cardozo simply chose not to rescue the firm from its own mistakes. He decided the case on the substantive issue of corporate law as revealed by the record that the parties had made.[24]

Thus, Cardozo's two major corporate law opinions, *Globe Woolen* and *Berkey,* pursued familiar themes. The former imposed high fiduciary duty on a corporate manager, and the latter enforced a central precept of the governing law, the separateness of entities operating in the corporate form.

High fiduciary duty was also the centerpiece of Cardozo's opinions dealing with the responsibilities of lawyers. These cases, many of which involved attorney misconduct, came closer than any others to forcing Cardozo to think about his father's past conduct. Cardozo gave no hint of this factor in his handling of these cases, but he was uncompromising in his pursuit of responsible behavior and a clean image for the profession.

Cardozo's opinion for a unanimous court in In re Rouss subordinated the individual rights of an attorney to the standards of the profession.[25] Jacob Rouss, an attorney, had testified in a criminal case under a statutory grant of immunity that protected him from prosecution, penalty, or forfeiture on account of any transaction concerning which he testified. Rouss's testimony amounted to a confession that he had been involved in bribing a witness to stay out of the state so that he would not be available to testify against Rouss's client. Rouss was thereupon disbarred by the Appellate Division, but he appealed to the Court of Appeals on the ground that disbarment was a penalty or forfeiture under the immunity statute.

Cardozo accepted the then prevailing doctrine that disbarment did not violate the privilege against self-incrimination because disbarment was not punishment for crime. He saw only a question of interpretation of the breadth of the immunity granted by the statute. Cardozo concluded, after spending some time dealing with ancient English equity law, that the statute was designed to give immunity that was as broad as, but not broader than, the privilege against self-incrimination. There was, therefore, immunity from criminal punishment but not from disbarment.

Cardozo's opinion set forth his concept of the standards required for the practice of law. Using the then common language that "[m]embership in the bar is a privilege burdened with conditions," he stated that one of the conditions was that an attorney must have a "fair private and professional character." That standard had to be met not only at admission but also thereafter. Disbarment was therefore not an addition to the penalties for crime but rather a finding that the test of fitness was no longer satisfied. Cardozo reasoned that the claim being made by the disbarred lawyer would also apply to doctors. If the lawyer's view prevailed, two "great and honorable professions" would be "denied the right to purify their membership and vindicate their honor. The charlatan and rogue may assume to heal the sick. The knave and criminal may pose as a minister of justice. Such things cannot have been intended, and will not be allowed."[26] Not in Cardozo's court.

The clash of principle in *Rouss* was between a standard of professionalism that saw lawyers as bearers of important public responsibilities—ministers of justice—and the purpose of a statutory grant of immunity to compel the testimony of an important witness. We have already seen that Cardozo was not overly sympathetic toward the privilege against self-incrimination in the context of a grant of immunity, and he felt no imperative either to reexamine the rule or to interpret the statute broadly.[27] Using the grant of immunity to compel a confession and then disbarring the lawyer did not bother Cardozo. It was enough protection that the lawyer did not have to go to jail. A corrupt lawyer deserved the court's sanction, and the court had the right and obligation to vindicate its honor and to safeguard the health of the profession.

Cardozo had expressed a similar notion of attorney responsibility earlier in a case involving a contingent fee—an arrangement in which the lawyer gets paid a percentage of the award if successful and nothing if not. The clients had decided that their case was meritless and dropped it, but the lawyer sued them for the fee he would have collected if successful. He lost in the trial court and the Appellate Division, but persisted by appealing to the Court of Appeals. In a brief opinion in Andrewes v. Haas, Cardozo wrote that the law would not coerce an unwilling plaintiff to continue a suit for the lawyer's benefit. Cardozo was not content simply to reject the lawyer's claim. He went on to express his distaste emphatically: "The notion that such a thing [coercion of an unwilling plaintiff] is possible betrays a strange misconception of the function of the legal profession and of its duty to society."[28]

Cardozo attempted to translate his views about the professional obligations of attorneys to their clients into a broad right of lawyers and the public to protection from competition by persons and organizations who were not lawyers and hence were not similarly regulated. In People v. Title Guarantee and Trust Company, a four-judge majority reversed the conviction of a title corporation for practicing law without a license when its employees filled in the blanks on a chattel mortgage and deed in connection with the sale of a business.[29] The crucial vote was cast by Judge Pound, who wrote an interesting concurring opinion setting forth the complexities of deciding what constituted the practice of law in the twentieth century. Pound concluded that a corporation might prepare some basic legal documents when that work was ancillary to the main business of the company, as he believed it was in this case.

Cardozo, for the three dissenters, took a sterner view. In a one-sentence memorandum, he agreed with Pound's conception of legal services but thought there was sufficient evidence to sustain the conviction. Presumably, he believed that filling in the blanks on a chattel mortgage and deed was not ancillary to the business of furnishing title insurance but rather was the unlicensed practice of law. At the end of the twentieth century, the anticompetitive effects of regulating the "unauthorized practice" of law have put courts under great pressure in defining just what constitutes the practice of law. In Cardozo's time, when unmet legal needs because of high cost did not seem such an enormous problem, there was more support for the proposition that prevention of unauthorized practice protected the public as well as the profession. Cardozo certainly believed that it did.

Cardozo set forth his views about the profession most strongly in People ex rel. Karlin v. Culkin.[30] Responding to a petition from several bar associations, the Appellate Division for the First Judicial Department appointed Supreme Court Justice Isidor Wasservogel to conduct an investigation of "ambulance chasing" by members of the profession. Alexander Karlin, a lawyer who appeared in response to a subpoena, was held in contempt by Wasservogel after he refused to be sworn. The Appellate Division affirmed the conviction, and Karlin then appealed.

Cardozo, for a unanimous Court of Appeals, upheld the conviction and the Appellate Division's power to conduct an inquiry into the behavior of the profession. The commonplaces that lawyers were officers of the court and that membership in the bar was a privilege burdened with conditions had real meaning for him. Admission to the bar involved "something more than private gain."[31] Lawyers had a special duty to cooperate with the courts to serve justice. They could be assigned to serve without fee in both civil and criminal cases. They could be brought into court summarily in matters relating to clients. And they could be disciplined by the courts. Subject only to the privilege against self-incrimination, they could not refuse to be sworn and to testify at the command of the court.

Then Cardozo did what he liked to do in such cases. He turned to history, to 350 years of the power of courts over lawyers. He discussed New York's constitutional and legislative provisions beginning with the first New York constitution of 1777. Not satisfied with that, he then turned to the ancient roots of English practice, reviewing first the relations among barristers, the inns of courts, and the judges as "visitors" to the inns, and then the more direct relations between the courts and the attorneys in England. Cardozo demonstrated that the power to inquire into the bar's conduct had been exercised by courts in England and in this country for a long time.

Finally, he noted that the "argument from history is reinforced by others from analogy and policy."[32] His example was the operation of the legislature, which sometimes gathered information from the legislators' own knowledge, sometimes from voluntary affidavits or unsworn testimony, and sometimes by compulsory process from witnesses. Although the analogy was not decisive, it would be a "curious anomaly" if "the courts with all their writs and processes could do less in regulating and controlling the conduct of their officers than a legislative body can do in relation to a stranger."[33] Cardozo was responsive to the argument that an investigation could destroy the reputation of a lawyer summoned to testify. But that problem could be taken care of by holding the preliminary stages in secret. That opportunity had been offered to the lawyer in question.

Cardozo also referred to the more general problem of possible abuse of power, but that was a problem with any power. He assumed, and in so doing he cautioned the Appellate Division, that it should act "considerately and cautiously, mindful at all times of the dignity of the bar and of the resentment certain to be engendered by any tyrannous intervention." But in the long run, the power to investigate "will make for the health and honor of the profession and for the protection of the public. If the house is to be cleaned, it is for those who occupy and govern it, rather than for strangers, to do the noisome work."[34]

Cardozo addressed a number of important issues in the profession that were to become more troublesome over the years as the disciplinary process became more controversial. Cardozo cared greatly about the honor of the profession and the role of judges as traditional guardians of that honor. If the judiciary was to exert control over the profession, it needed to punish violations of its rules; otherwise, "strangers," that is, the legislature or an administrative board, would end up doing the task. We saw earlier his fear that administrative agencies would take over the work of courts if judges did not respect the role of juries.[35] His preference for judicial control was stronger where attorneys were concerned. Cardozo took this opportunity to make a public statement to the bar, to his judicial colleagues, and to the rest of the government that judges were responsible for the conduct of the profession.[36]

A highlight of the torts and contracts cases that we considered earlier was Cardozo's reluctance to impose financial costs on government or to innovate in areas where the legislature had already enacted legislation. These were characteristics of Cardozo's work across the board. As a judge in a democracy, Cardozo respected the legislature's power, exercised in conjunction with the executive and subject to constitutional limits, over the state's budget and over policy-making.

If a case presented a clash between current custom and a statute, custom gave way. In Manhattan Company v. Morgan, the issue arose whether Manhattan Company, a bank that had bought temporary certificates exchangeable for Belgian bonds, was entitled to obtain the bonds from the issuer of the certificates, J. P. Morgan & Company, when the certificates turned out to have been stolen.[37] Under the Negotiable Instruments Law, which was in force in New York, the Manhattan Company was entitled to the bonds if the certificates were negotiable, but not otherwise. Although the certificates did not meet the conditions of negotiability provided by the statute, the bank contended that the certificates were negotiable under the rules of the law merchant, which was the common law of commercial custom.

Cardozo concluded that although the statute provided that its provisions could be supplemented by the law merchant in cases not provided for by the statute, the statute did provide governing rules for this case by prescribing the conditions for negotiability. That was controlling.

> There is force in the argument that wider freedom of choice through the spontaneous flowerings of custom would work a social gain. One of the debit items to be charged against codifying statutes is the possibility of interference with evolutionary growth. It is the ancient conflict between flexibility and certainty. So far as the Negotiable Instruments Law is concerned, the remedy for the evil, if it be one, is an amendment of the statute that will add to the negotiable instruments there . . . described such other classes as the law merchant or the custom of the market may . . . establish. Until such an amendment shall be adopted, the courts . . . must take for granted that the Legislature is content with the law as it is written.[38]

Although custom was one of the sources for decision that Cardozo often considered, it did not prevail when the legislature had acted by adopting the Negotiable Instruments Law.

Likewise, Cardozo was reluctant to engage in creative use of public policy arguments in the face of opposing statutory policy. Hoadley v. Hoadley was an example.[39] In that case, Cardozo refused to annul a marriage at the request of a person married to a "lunatic." Although such a marriage had been void at common law, a New York statute made it voidable, and then only at the behest of the lunatic, or of the lunatic's relatives or friends. Cardozo concluded that the enumeration represented a complete list that excluded the sane spouse. He recognized that his interpretation left a legal problem of uncertain property rights and a human problem for the sane partner. The remedy, however, lay with the legislature, which could consider all the different situations and give a right of action to the sane partner with appropriate conditions.

Cardozo was most deferential to the legislature in matters involving government finances. O'Brien v. New York State Teachers' Retirement Board illustrates the consistency of Cardozo's position in the face of sympathetic facts for an opposite conclusion.[40] Helen O'Brien, a teacher with lengthy service in the New York public school system, filed a notice of her intention to retire as of February 20, choosing a retirement option that gave her sister a remainder interest in her pension. The teacher died twenty-eight days later, on March 20. The relevant statute provided that the retirement board fix a teacher's retirement date as of the date specified by the teacher or as of such time within thirty days thereafter as the retirement board might find advisable. Pursuant to that statute and to conserve the retirement fund, the board had adopted a general rule delaying the effective date of retirement thirty days in all cases. The board therefore refused to retire O'Brien, thus depriving her sister of any right to receive the actuarial equivalent of the sister's pension and limiting her entitlement to the amount that O'Brien had paid into the fund. The Appellate Division ordered the board to retire the teacher as of February 20, holding that although the board could delay retirement on an individual basis, it could not do so by general rule.[41] The retirement board appealed to the Court of Appeals. Judge Andrews reported to the consultation for affirmance. Cardozo circulated a dissenting memorandum to explain his vote, while noting that he would not file an opinion if the court accepted the Andrews report.

Cardozo thought that the sister should not prevail. The purpose of the statute in granting leeway was to permit the board to exercise its discretion with respect to the financial integrity of the fund. "The statute permits a leeway of thirty days, and leaves it to the Board to say whether the leeway is advisable . . . The courts are not to substitute their judgment for that of administrative officers to whom the power to judge has been confided by the law."[42] Cardozo saw nothing in the statute that required the board to exercise its judgment only on a case-by-case basis. Nor did he refer to the teacher who had earned her pension by working for thirty-five years and whose expectations had been dashed. Since the provisions with respect to the retirement fund were wholly a creature of statute, the paramount consideration was the legislature's purpose in enacting the thirty-day provision. Cardozo was quite clear that the purpose was to give the board discretion to protect the financial integrity of the fund rather than to facilitate the payment of pensions, and that ended the case, no matter how unfair its application seemed in the individual case. His view did not carry the court, and Chief Judge Hiscock and Judge Lehman joined him in dissenting without opinion.

Cardozo was consistent in his views about the teachers' retirement fund. Hannan v. Teachers' Retirement Board was an even more appealing case than *O'Brien* for recognizing the rights of a teacher's beneficiary.[43]

Nell Hannan died before she could sign the application necessary to process her disability retirement. Two members of the Retirement Board had gone to the hospital to help process the application, which made her sister a beneficiary. The teacher was too sick to sign the application, and when her sister offered to sign, she was told, apparently wrongly, that she needed a power of attorney. The teacher died before she was able to sign the application that would have triggered the medical examination and certificate needed to complete the retirement process. The Board refused to process the retirement. Then the sister sought an order from the Appellate Division to force the Board to do so, but that court denied her petition. The sister filed a motion in the Court of Appeals seeking leave to appeal.

Cardozo recommended to the consultation that her motion be denied. He was firm that failure to file the application ended the matter. It made no difference to him that the board was resisting payment on the basis of an error made by one of its members or that the sister, keeping a death watch in a hospital, had been in no position to discover and pursue a proper remedy. If the sister had received wrong advice, "she should have disregarded what he said, and submitted her application to the board in whatever form she pleased. She did not even protest, but acquiesced in his ruling, and left the document unsigned . . . I cannot say in such circumstances that petitioner has made out a clear legal right to receive the money that would be due her if the deceased teacher had been retired during life in accordance with the statute. The remedy is with the legislature if there are gaps in the statute that leave open the possibility of hardship or injustice."[44] Cardozo could have invoked the old equitable maxim that "Equity regards as done what should have been done" to treat the application as signed, thus warranting the issuance of the indispensable medical certificate. But the case involved statutorily mandated conditions for an entitlement to a pension from state funds, and Cardozo was not at all moved by the human consequences of the state's mistake to suggest any lessening of strict compliance with the terms of the statute. The whole court denied the sister's motion.[45] These cases show Cardozo at his most intransigent in refusing to find a little leeway in statutory conditions in order to do justice to long-term state employees. Protecting public funds was a bedrock rule for Cardozo.

He applied this policy in other kinds of cases involving state financial affairs as well. McCoun v. Pierpont and Cranz involved a contest between two claimants to a piece of land. McCoun claimed title through a tax sale of the property by Nassau County for inadvertent failure of the original owner to pay $11.04 in real estate taxes.[46] Cranz claimed title by purchase from the original owner. She had found some very small errors in the description of the property in the tax assessment and contended that the foreclosure was therefore illegal. Cardozo was not moved to use the errors to help her. "The case is, no doubt, a hard one. The tax is trivial in amount. The failure to pay it, we may assume, was inadvertent. The hardship does not justify us in magnifying microscopical defects and using them as an excuse for a refusal to enforce the statute. The statute authorizes sales for taxes. The period of redemption which it concedes is not indefinite, but limited. The power of dispensation is not confided to the courts."[47] The contrast with Cardozo's dissent in *Graf*, in which he found a way to excuse a delay in a mortgage payment, is striking.[48] That case involved an equitable remedy in a case involving solely the rights of private persons. However, in *McCoun*, there was a statute, and it enforced the government's power to collect taxes. That fact made all the difference for Cardozo.

Concern about the government's finances, whatever the setting, was a consistent theme in Cardozo's opinions. The City of Yonkers obtained a temporary injunction against a company on behalf of citizens whose comfort and property were affected because the company burned soft coal in its furnaces.[49] The injunction order was eventually reversed on the ground that the city had no authority to sue on behalf of its citizens. The company then sued the city for damages that it had sustained during the ten days that the injunction was in force. At common law, there was no such remedy for a party injured in such circumstances. A statute, however, provided for security to be given by a party seeking an injunction, either as provided by law or as set by the court. Municipal corporations had originally been given a statutory exemption from liability, but by amendment they were subjected to liability "to the same extent as sureties to an undertaking would have been if such an undertaking had been given." They were not required to give security before obtaining an injunction. A referee awarded damages to the company, and the Appellate Division affirmed in a reduced amount. Yonkers then appealed to the Court of Appeals.

Cardozo, writing for the majority, subjected the language of the statute apparently imposing liability on the municipality to a withering analysis. He noted that the statutory provisions enabled private parties seeking injunctions to know their maximum liability before proceeding.

Relying on the history of the imposition of municipal liability in these circumstances, he concluded that the statutory language imposing liability "to the same extent as sureties" required the injunction order to contain a provision setting a maximum damage limit in order to trigger municipal liability. Otherwise, the "special privilege" of the municipal corporation in not having to give security beforehand would be an "added burden," and an erroneous court order might impose a "crushing and indeterminate liability."[50] Cardozo was not willing to impose such liability without a clear indication that such was legislative policy. The court, with one judge dissenting, reversed the judgment for the company.[51]

Cardozo was not always inflexible in protecting the public treasury. In Jackson v. New York, the state condemned a warehouse and then resisted paying the owner for the machinery, elevators, and other items that were installed in it.[52] The state contended that it had the power to condemn only what it needed, and it did not need these things. The Board of Claims, which had jurisdiction in condemnation cases, and the Appellate Division agreed with the state's contention. Cardozo, for a unanimous court, reversed. The items constituted "fixtures," that is, personal property annexed to the real property that as a matter of law would ordinarily pass with the land in a real estate transaction. It would be "intolerable" and an "injustice," wrote Cardozo, if the state could take the warehouse and turn back a stock of second-hand machinery to the owner, paying only for the land and building.[53] Having said that, however, Cardozo took care to note that the court was not passing on the question whether the state could specifically and explicitly leave the fixtures out of the notice of appropriation. Leaving that question open, he hinted that it might make a difference if the fixtures retained substantial value when severed from the land. The question he left open suggests that his use of the words "intolerable" and "injustice" were rhetorical because the state might be able to save money in some cases by giving proper notice.

———

Cardozo's major opinions in the law of property, corporations, the legal profession, and public finance reaffirm earlier themes. Precedent, even ancient law, was important in land law, where people relied on the rules relating to title so heavily. But when the rules were in doubt, as they were with respect to the conflict between state and private title over shorelines, Cardozo preferred the rule that protected public over private use as a matter of policy. The corporate and legal profession cases demonstrate Cardozo's stress on high standards of fiduciary duty for corporate managers and lawyers alike. And a thread that ran through many areas of the law was Cardozo's reluctance to increase the cost of government without legislative approval. That was a major restraining factor on Cardozo's use of public policy considerations to make new legal doctrine. He saw the raising and spending of public money as the province of the legislature and governor, and he tried hard to respect their authority in those spheres. Cardozo modulated his approaches to decision-making—precedent, history and custom, policy, deference to the legislature and executive—according to his sense of his proper role as a judge in different areas of law. He was sometimes creative, sometimes quite limited, but he consistently matched his actions to the task at hand and to his place in a democratic government.

22

A Puzzle, Candor, and Style

This final chapter dealing with Cardozo's work on the Court of Appeals considers three different aspects of his work. The first part presents a Cardozo puzzle, a trio of similar cases exemplifying tensions among themes in Cardozo's work. The second part addresses an issue raised by many Cardozo critics, the candor—or lack of it—of his opinions. The third part looks at one of the most distinctive features of his opinions, their literary style.

The puzzle concerns a series of three family law torts cases. In each case Cardozo had to choose among the methods of philosophy, history, and sociology, for the methods pointed in different directions, and he took three distinct positions, using his methods of decision-making in different ways. In the first case, he initially suggested a creative public policy approach but ended up voting to apply prior precedent. In the second case, he applied a creative public policy approach, but then suppressed his opinion. In the third case, he rejected precedent in other jurisdictions in choosing between the conflicting policies embodied in two existing rules without ever giving reasons for his choice. The puzzle is to figure out what factors led him to different results in these similar cases.

All the cases were suits among close family members in situations in which the common law had previously prohibited such actions. The cases caused Cardozo enormous difficulty as he sought to assess the social and economic changes that undercut the reasons for the original rule, especially if the legislature had recognized some of the changes. A recent decision, which was relevant to the first case of the trio, was a leading case for equalizing the rights of wives with those of their husbands. Oppenheim v. Kridel, decided in 1923, was a suit by a wife for "criminal conversation" (in effect, alienation of affections) against a woman who had committed adultery with the plaintiff's husband.[1] The common law had permitted a husband but not a wife to bring such an action. Cardozo had joined Judge Crane's opinion, which held that so long as New York recognized an action for criminal conversation, it should be equally available to wives and husbands. Seven months later, Cardozo delivered his lectures that were later published as *The Growth of the Law.* He used *Oppenheim* as an illustration of the capacity and necessity of the law to change, explaining the decision in the following language: "Social, political, and legal reforms had changed the relations between the sexes, and put woman and man upon a plane of equality. Decisions founded upon the assumption of a bygone inequality were unrelated to present-day realities, and ought not to be permitted to prescribe a rule of life."[2] Cardozo was wrong about equality having been achieved in 1923, but *Oppenheim* pointed in that direction. Moreover, it presented a persuasive public policy argument for rejecting an old precedent founded upon an outmoded view of the status of women.

The first of the puzzle cases came to the court four years later. In Allen v. Allen, a wife brought suit against her husband for malicious prosecution after he had her jailed on a criminal charge without cause.[3] The trial judge granted the husband's motion to dismiss her suit on the ground that a wife could not sue her husband for malicious prosecution, and the Appellate Division affirmed. Its authority was the 1882 decision of the Court of Appeals in Schultz v. Schultz. The court there had reversed, without opinion, an order of arrest obtained by a wife against a husband in connection with an action for assault.[4] Two judges had dissented in *Schultz* on the ground that the Married Women's Property Acts had destroyed the notion of the unity of husband and wife that was the basis for the common law rule prohibiting the suit.[5] The wife in *Allen* filed a motion in the Court of Appeals for leave to appeal from the decision of the Appellate Division. The motion was assigned for report to Cardozo.

Cardozo recommended to the consultation that the wife's motion be allowed. He referred to the contrariety of views on the subject around the country and addressed the subject only in terms of a wife's ability to sue her husband for malicious prosecution, although a husband apparently was precluded from suing his wife in New York.[6] He then noted the changes in wording between the relevant statute governing the ability of wives to conduct litigation when the *Schultz* case had been decided and the current statute, although he added that he was hesitant to "stress the verbal differences." But he thought the issue of the ability of the wife to sue was "doubtful and important enough to call for a statement by this court as to the present state of the law." It was more than a matter of statutory interpretation:

> Even if the two statutes were verbally identical, I am not clear that Schultz v. Schultz should be followed today. A good deal of water has gone over the mill since that case was decided by this court forty-five years ago. A married woman may now contract with her husband . . . She may convey land to her husband . . . Apparently she may sue him and be sued by him for injuries to property . . . With so much of the old fiction abandoned, I doubt whether he is now immune from liability for tort (cf. Oppenheim v. Kridel, 236 N.Y. 156).[7]

Cardozo was seeking only to persuade his colleagues to hear the appeal, and he did not have to declare a position at this time. But the wording of Cardozo's report suggests that he was ready to follow the lead of *Oppenheim* and either overrule *Schultz* or perhaps distinguish it because of statutory changes. Cardozo was successful in getting the court to hear the case, but the majority refused to overrule or distinguish *Schultz*. Although the issue was important, the court chose not to write an opinion. It simply affirmed the dismissal of the wife's suit in one sentence, stating that "the later acts of the legislature have left unchanged the rule adopted by this court in Schultz v. Schultz."[8] Remarkably, Cardozo joined the majority, as did Judge Crane, the author of Oppenheim v. Kridel.

It was left to Judge Pound, joined by Judge Andrews, to dissent in a lengthy opinion. Pound argued that the changes in statutory wording freed the court to interpret broadly the statute that gave a married woman "a right of action for an injury to her person, property or character or for an injury arising out of the marital relation, as if unmarried." He followed the lines of Cardozo's report in elaborating the social and political changes that lay behind the legislation and urged the relevance of Oppenheim v. Kridel.[9]

Cardozo's apparent change of mind is hard to explain. Quite probably he concluded that the changes in the legislation were too insubstantial to justify distinguishing *Schultz*. But in his report he had seemed ready to overrule the case outright because the policy embodied in the common law unity of husband and wife had been overtaken by modern social and legislative changes. Cardozo's report had raised the question whether the reenactment of the statute, in similar language to that which had been in force when *Schultz* was decided, froze the court's earlier interpretation. The form in which he put the question, however, was rhetorical and implied a negative answer. "With the background of legislation what it was when the Domestic Relations Law was enacted, are we constrained to hold that the members of the Legislature, conferring upon a wife a right to sue in a different form of words from the form adopted in the act of 1862, must be presumed to have had in mind and to have intended to preserve the disabilities incidental to the common law concept of marital unity?"[10]

Perhaps Cardozo finally concluded that his question about the existence of legislation touching the issue was not so rhetorical after all and indeed indicated a conclusive reason for not following the path of *Oppenheim*.[11] Just the previous year, Cardozo had addressed a similar issue when a party suggested that the court overrule the interpretation it had given the Tenement House Law in Cardozo's opinion in Altz v. Lieberson: "The ruling in *Altz v. Lieberson* has been repeatedly acted upon by the trial courts, and if we construed the statute erroneously, the legislature should amend the provisions of §102 and thereby set us right."[12] That statement suggests that he may have concluded that deference to the legislature was the right path to follow in *Allen*.

Cardozo might also have concluded that the common law rule could be supported on the basis that actions between people still married to one another would disrupt any possible hope for future marital harmony and therefore should not be allowed. Cardozo had previously exhibited a shaky grasp of the realities of marital life, and perhaps he was sufficiently uncertain about the policy considerations that he concluded that the matter should be left to the legislature. His report, however, had not raised such considerations. In his report, Cardozo had laid the groundwork for abandoning the old common law rule and for adopting a new rule consistent with modern social policies. Two colleagues were prepared to do so, but Cardozo did not join them. He left no explanation, no hint, and no convincing grounds for inferring a reason why.

In 1928, one year after *Allen,* Cardozo was called on to report to the consultation in the case of Sorrentino v. Sorrentino, which concerned the right of a minor child to sue his father for injuries received in an automobile accident caused by his father's negligence.[13] The trial judge dismissed the child's lawsuit on the ground that a child could not sue a parent for negligence, and the Appellate Division affirmed. When the case was appealed to the Court of Appeals, Cardozo circulated a lengthy draft opinion for reversal with a cover sheet stating that he was not satisfied with it "either in form or in substance" and urging those with a different view to write dissents "so as to help us to a sound conclusion."[14]

Cardozo's draft opinion reviewed the precedents, noting that there were no relevant English cases, that there were a few recent American cases that had denied parental liability, albeit with some dissents, and that academic authorities were split. He concluded that the precedents "hostile to a remedy [for the child] have neither the continuity nor the volume requisite to a decision of the question on the basis of mere authority. We must seek an answer upon principle."[15] Cardozo started with the presumption that the law should provide a remedy for every wrong. Indeed, where the tort was willful, the liability of the parent had already been clearly established. He then turned to cases of negligence. He asserted that the nature of family relationships might exempt a parent from liability when the parent's negligence was passive, that is, a failure to act, or, if the negligence was active, when it was the negligence of another person for whom the parent might have responsibility, such as a servant. But the parent should be held responsible for personal, active negligence.

Turning to the present case, which involved the father's active, personal negligence, Cardozo sought a possible explanation for an exemption from the general rule of liability. "Filial piety" did not establish an exemption because a minor could already sue a parent for negligent damage to property. Nor was there any doubt that any disability to sue ended when minors reached adulthood or left home and lived on their own. The basis for an exemption "must be the interest of the State in the preservation of the family as a form of group life, a communal institution. The household is to be held intact during the years of nurture and training when its members should be kept together . . . Back of the disability is the fear that the structure will be undermined if the infant, while a member of the household, shall gain the right to sue."[16]

Cardozo rejected that argument. "The history of family law is strewn with the wrecks of predictions of disaster belied by the event . . . Here as often there must be a balancing of interests, with the burden on him who says that a wrong, though proved, must be borne without a remedy." He saw no reason to fear a "mad rush by children" to sue their parents.[17] Cardozo then broached a crucial subject, the relevance of insurance. For all the talk of children suing parents, he pointed out that in "the economic structure of modern life, a judgment recovered against the parent is likely in the vast majority of cases to be paid by an insurer."[18] He discussed the relevance of insurance to the rule to be adopted.

> The spread of insurance has changed the aspect of the picture . . . Insurance against accident, once solely a contract of indemnity, a means of reimbursement for the doer of the wrong, has lost much of its ancient quality, and, subject to conditions . . . has now become insurance for the protection of the sufferer . . . A method has thus been provided for minimizing loss by distributing the burden . . . A social growth is here, to be marked like any other, and weighed according to its value, before the word goes forth that an action against a parent is an affront to public policy.[19]

Putting the availability of insurance at the center of his reasoning was new for Cardozo and relatively unusual for judges in 1928. Courts had not figured out what impact, if any, the availability of insurance should have on traditional common law liability. Cardozo's only previous reference to insurance was the brief comment in Kerr Steamship v. RCA about the ability of a sender of a telegram to obtain insurance against the risk of nondelivery of its message.[20] In *Sorrentino,* Cardozo stopped his analysis with the simple point about the presence of insurance. He mentioned the possibility that the insurance company could adjust its rates or write in exemptions to counter a decision for the child, but he did not discuss the serious consequences of such a response to the social outcome that he favored. Although the presence of insurance was important, in Cardozo's view, to letting the child sue the parent, he used insurance only to explain why a parent should not receive any special exemption from ordinary liability for his negligence. Cardozo apparently did not believe that the presence of insurance should figure in the configuration of the basic negligence rules themselves. He took note of the possibility of collusion when the insurance company was the real defendant, but he minimized it. The insurance companies could protect themselves by the same means that they used elsewhere.

Thus, Cardozo rejected the various arguments against parental liability based on fears of family disruption, court congestion, and fraud. Just as competent families could be relied upon to avoid or solve most problems on their own, Cardozo relied on the trial courts to deal with any conflicts that might remain. "Juries will work out their rough justice hereafter as they have worked it out before."[21]

Finally, Cardozo had to confront the precedent of Allen v. Allen, in which he had joined the court in refusing to allow tort suits by wives against husbands. He distinguished that case quickly. "The disability is a relic of the old doctrine that in law the two [spouses] are one . . . No such identification exists between parents and their children." But Cardozo was candid with his colleagues about a possible argument that an identification did exist. "The only trace of it in that relation is to be gathered from the doctrine of imputed negligence when the child is too tender to be negligent itself. This is far short of its acceptance out and out as a concept to be carried to the limit of its logic . . . The doctrine of imputed negligence is today something of an anomaly, and one more or less discredited . . . The analogy is too weak to lead us to an isle of safety."[22] Cardozo therefore concluded that the child's suit should be allowed.

Cardozo's invitation to his colleagues to write dissenting memoranda was eagerly accepted. Pound, a dissenter in Allen, thought that that case was controlling. With an implicit dig at Cardozo, he wrote that the modern basis for the Allen decision was that the rights and duties existing between husband and wife prevent suit for personal injuries. The same sort of analysis, parental authority with relation to children, governed this case. Lehman also took a dig at Cardozo, noting that no cases in any common law country recognized the right of action. There was no wrong here for which a remedy had to be supplied. Palsgraf (Lehman did not need to specify Cardozo as the author) had defined negligence as absence of care according to the circumstances. The circumstances here involved the economic basis of family unity: a payment from parent to child would not be a net financial gain to the family but would be a destructive punishment to the parent. There was therefore no justification for bringing into the home the standard of care applicable in the world at large. Moreover, he offered a number of hypothetical cases to demonstrate that the distinction offered between active and passive negligence was neither logical nor practical. The final memorandum, by Judge O'Brien, relied on the absence of precedent and the danger of collusion to deny the remedy. Furthermore, O'Brien saw no basis for having the right turn on the existence of insurance.

This spate of draft opinions produced an anticlimactic result. The court voted to affirm the judgment of dismissal of the child's complaint, 4–3, with Judge Kellogg joining the three judges who had filed memoranda disagreeing with Cardozo's draft opinion. They filed no opinion. Cardozo, Crane, and Andrews dissented, but they too filed no opinion. The interesting and valuable exchange of views was suppressed. We do not know why.[23]

Cardozo's *Sorrentino* memorandum demonstrates his continuing commitment to bringing doctrine into line with developments in society, but it makes his previous behavior in *Allen* all the more puzzling. One difference is that it was easier to recognize a new cause of action in *Sorrentino* than in *Allen* because no prior New York case had to be overruled in *Sorrentino* and because no history of statutory interpretation was involved either. Nevertheless, *Allen* seems like an aberration, all the more so because of the tenor of Cardozo's report in that case. The explanation that he was deferring to a prior interpretation of legislative policy carries some weight, given Cardozo's institutional scruples, but his deference was misplaced. The rule against interspousal liability was not a legislative rule. It was a court rule. Cardozo's timidity carried a price. Having missed the opportunity for a socially well-grounded modern rule in *Allen,* the court was stuck with that decision in deciding not to take the even better opportunity in *Sorrentino.* The court took over forty years to reverse itself.[24]

The last part of this story occurred the year after *Sorrentino.* Schubert v. August Schubert Wagon Company raised the question of the liability of a company for its employee's negligence when the plaintiff could not sue the employee because the employee was her husband.[25] The jury found in the plaintiff's favor, but the trial judge took her verdict away on the basis of the interspousal immunity recognized in *Allen* and dismissed her complaint. The Appellate Division reinstated the verdict, and the Court of Appeals affirmed. Writing for a unanimous court, Cardozo refused to follow decisions in other states constricting the principles of vicarious responsibility because he saw no conflict between the principle of vicarious liability and the interspousal exemption in this situation. He argued that if the employee's act was unlawful, the company's liability to the plaintiff was established no matter what relation there was between the plaintiff and the employee. The company could in turn recover from the employee on the basis of his negligence, and that action would not contravene the exemption policy either. Liability of the employee to his employer would be based on the employee's duty to render faithful service. Although Cardozo argued that there was no conflict between the principles, they would collide if the wife recovered from the employer, who then recovered an equivalent amount from the employee. In effect, the wife would recover from her husband for the injuries that he negligently inflicted upon her.

Cardozo had a backup argument: if there was a conflict, the interspousal exemption, being "more or less anomalous," would have to give way to the company's responsibility, which was the general rule. In any case, the interspousal exemption to the statutory right of a married woman to bring suits should not be extended "by dubious construction."[26] Cardozo favored the policy of vicarious liability over the exception based on marital relationships. His comments about the anomaly of the interspousal immunity suggest that he was doubtful enough about the *Allen* result that he did not want to go beyond it.

The puzzle with which we began is Cardozo's conclusion that a family member injured by another family member should recover in *Sorrentino* and *Schubert,* but not in *Allen,* the case in which the wife sued her husband. The explanation for the different results appears to be that deference to the legislature, which lay at the heart of the older case relied on in *Allen,* apparently won out over his wish to modernize the law to protect the rights of family members. Cardozo's performance in *Allen* demonstrates the depth of his respect for the legislative role. *Sorrentino* and *Schubert* demonstrate Cardozo's willingness to justify recovery for a family member hurt by the negligence of another when he was not hemmed in by a combination of precedent and legislative action and when there was another pocket—an insurance company or employer—available to pay the damages. That factor complemented Cardozo's general belief that the law should provide remedies for wrongs and that this policy, with some exceptions, should apply inside families as well as outside.

The second task of this chapter is to examine Cardozo's candor, the extent to which he stated and explained his decisions accurately and openly. That subject has long been controversial. Opinions have ranged from Cardozo as paragon of candor to Cardozo as master of deception.[27] There are two kinds of candor at issue, candor in making decisions and candor in explaining them. The first relates to the application of doctrine in particular situations to resolve a case. Did Cardozo do so in straightforward fashion, in accordance with the doctrine's declared purpose, or did he purport to accept the doctrine but then manipulate it to reach a desired result? Examples of the latter would be judges who accept negligence principles but nearly always rule for the plaintiff or nearly always rule for the defendant in contested cases, or judges who accept the consideration requirement in contract law, but then manage always to find it.

The full range of Cardozo opinions demonstrates that he was candid in the matter of results. He acted on his belief that justice demanded evenhanded application of doctrine. Cardozo did not employ pretense in order to avoid a harsh result; he accepted harsh results. Since the system demanded fault in negligence cases, he saw it as his job, as Helen Palsgraf learned, to take a verdict away from an injured plaintiff if he could not find anything that fit the definition of fault. So long as the law mandated the death penalty, which he personally opposed, he saw it as his duty to affirm the sentence if the case fell within the rules that called for it. Likewise, when he changed a particular doctrine but set forth qualifications, he would come out the other way when a case involved the qualifications. Cardozo was fundamentally honest in his opinions. He said what he meant, and he meant what he said.

The second type of candor relates to Cardozo's ability to explain his results. Did he relate fully the governing legal reasons for his conclusions? This question is harder to answer. Candor did not require Cardozo to identify the psychological and cultural influences that predisposed him to prefer one value over another. Such public self-analysis has never been viewed as part of opinion writing. The question is whether Cardozo sorted out and identified the relevant facts and legal considerations that he relied on in reaching his decision.

Cardozo's desire to write with "style" affected his presentation of the facts in many cases. He disdained lengthy factual statements, perhaps for literary reasons, perhaps because he found them distracting. He had a fondness for pithy presentations of the details of a case. The best of them, like Wood v. Lucy, Lady Duff Gordon and Jacob & Youngs v. Kent, are masterpieces. But sometimes, as in *Palsgraf* and *Allegheny College,* he left out some facts that now seem important to a full understanding of the problem, especially from the perspective of the losing party. This situation did not happen often, and I see no evidence that Cardozo was being manipulative. Either his literary bent may have led him astray, or he may simply have made a mistake in assuming that he had stated everything needed for the reader to understand the case. But most of the time Cardozo's factual statements let the reader know what he considered important in reaching a decision.

Cardozo's reasoning was sometimes hard to understand. Often the decision turned on a combination of factors, and Cardozo left it at that, without identifying which ones were crucial. That trait seems to have been a habit of thought. If the result was stronger when supported by four factors than by three, he didn't decide which three would be enough. Likewise, occasionally he read precedents for more than they were worth and did not present contrary authority as strongly as he might have.[28] Sometimes a flaw in analysis led him not to support a conclusion as forcefully as he might have.[29]

Cardozo's opinions have spawned a cottage industry of critical analysis, especially in recent years. There are good reasons why his style of reasoning, which generally focused on the particular case and discussed many variables, has left so many academics dissatisfied in the controversial cases. The business of academics and of judges is quite different. Academics are always trying to fit a case into a larger picture, imagining where particular holdings and forms of reasoning lead; also, academics come to their views after they have studied and taught cases for years. No wonder they have a different perspective. As a working judge, Cardozo avoided large questions of doctrine most of the time. It was hard enough to get agreement in the court on a difficult case within the short time in which he and his colleagues had to decide it before moving on to the next one. Occasionally, he considered hypothetical cases to which a present solution might apply, but not often. Only rarely, most notably in *Palsgraf,* did Cardozo bring a fully developed doctrinal analysis to a case and fit the case into the theoretical framework. Sometimes it was apparent that he was unsure how he would decide the next relevant case, didn't want to commit himself in advance, and therefore was careful to explain the current case in a way that left himself and the court flexibility for the next one. Cardozo's candor consisted in trying to explain the present result without encumbering the future. It was a difficult job, and, on the whole, he did it well.

The last subject of this final chapter on Cardozo's Court of Appeals work is the style of his judicial writing. Cardozo saw part of his job as persuading his readers that his conclusions were correct, and he thought that the style of the opinion was an important part of persuasion. Cardozo worked at that style. The briefs that he wrote while at the bar were well written, but their sole function was to persuade judges. The distinctive literary features, the metaphors, and the striking phrases that mark his judicial writing came later. He read widely, had a prodigious memory, and kept commonplace books in which he stored items for future use. Once he became a judge, he had greater opportunity to let his literary bent develop, and it did.

Cardozo addressed the literary style of judicial opinions in a talk that he gave in 1925. The "sovereign quality" was clarity, but other qualities were needed for an opinion to be remembered, to "win its way." It "will need persuasive force, or the impressive virtue of sincerity and fire, or the mnemonic power of alliteration and antithesis, or the terseness and tang of the proverb and the maxim."[30] He classified opinions into six categories: "the type magisterial or imperative; the type laconic or sententious; the type conversational or homely; the type refined or artificial, smelling of the lamp, verging at times on preciosity or euphuism; the type demonstrative or persuasive; and finally the type tonsorial or agglutinative, so called from the shears and the pastepot which are its implements and emblem."[31] He admired the magisterial type, which eschewed analogy or illustration and spoke from on high. John Marshall and Lord Mansfield were judges who often wrote in that vein. Cardozo did not fit himself into that category, which seemed no longer possible because a "changing philosophy of law has tended . . . to the use of other methods more conciliatory and modest."[32] The modern counterpart of the magisterial opinion, and the one to which Cardozo himself aspired, was the "demonstrative or persuasive" opinion: "It is not unlike the magisterial or imperative, yet it differs in a certain amplitude of development, a freer use of the resources of illustration and analogy and history and precedent, in brief, a tone more suggestive of the scientific seeker for the truth and less reminiscent of the priestess on the tripod."[33] Cardozo saw himself in that vein, although in his view the "scientific seeker of the truth" was seeking a pragmatic, not an absolute, truth.

Cardozo admired the laconic and conversational styles of Holmes and of some English judges, which featured epigrams and maxims to make their points. He found them becoming rare as cases reflected the greater complexity of modern life. Also, he found that the refined, very precise style was useful in cases that required exposition of shades and nuances of difference, as in the interpretation of a will. But he scorned the scissors and paste opinion, put together with lengthy quotations and little explanation, and welcomed its predicted disappearance.

Cardozo's talk was a plea for judges to pay attention to the communication of a result to a reader. An opinion was an exercise in education, and style helped reach the reader and impress the message in the reader's mind. The judge was "expounding a science, or a body of truth which he seeks to assimilate to a science, but in the process of exposition he is practicing an art." Literary style was part of judicial achievement. The Muses "know that by the lever of art the subject the most lowly can be lifted to the heights. Small, indeed, is the company dwelling in those upper spaces, but the few are also the elect."[34] Cardozo's elitism was evident, but he had earned the vanity. *Palsgraf, Wood, De Cicco, Defore,* and other Cardozo opinions would not have remained in public discourse as long as they have if Cardozo had not practiced the art of writing well.

Cardozo's style has aroused the whole spectrum of opinion. Everyone has agreed that it is arresting. Jerome Frank, a former admirer with a grudge, was at one end of the spectrum. After Cardozo's death, Frank wrote an anonymous article that criticized Cardozo's style. After paying formal obeisance to Cardozo's "greatness as a judge, a philosopher . . . a scholar," Frank turned to a psychiatric explanation of the writing: Cardozo was deeply hurt in his youth by his father's disgrace. He therefore retreated from the twentieth century and "re-entered it disguised as an 18th Century scholar and gentleman . . . The result was by no means ugly. His writings have grace. But it is an alien grace." His witticisms were "pedantic"; his language was "semi-archaic"; his style was "awkward" and "sometimes ornate, baroque, rococo"; his ornaments were sometimes "annoyingly functionless"; and his metaphors were "elaborate." Frank preferred the writing of Justices Black, Douglas, and Jackson because they wrote as they spoke, and in the current American idiom.[35] It was not only Jerome Frank who did not like the style. Mark De Wolfe Howe found it marked by a "humorless streak of pretentiousness." Even Felix Frankfurter, who much admired Cardozo, found his style "fluffy," or as he put it in public, "elegantly diffuse," and "Corinthian, not Doric."[36]

At the other end of the spectrum, Professor Zechariah Chafee, something of a stylist himself, echoed the views of many Cardozo contemporaries when he wrote that "Cardozo possesses one of the best prose styles of our times."[37] More recently, Richard Weisberg, describing Cardozo as his "favorite judicial author," has written several appreciations of the "architectonics" (Cardozo's word) of Cardozo's opinions. He saw Cardozo's style as part of an aesthetic structure that synthesized law and fact, vitalized his opinions, and contributed to their persuasive effect.[38] Weisberg's word for the distinctive combination of form and substance in Cardozo's opinions was "poetics." Beryl Levy, an earlier admiring critic, used the term "artist" broadly to capture the same thought.[39]

A middle view is that of Judge Richard Posner, who admired Cardozo's writing at its best but found that it was not always at its best. "Sometimes Cardozo writes tersely and lucidly, sometimes fancily and preciously. The former style dominates in his judicial opinions; the latter is far more marked (though not dominant) in his nonjudicial writings . . . True, with his inversions of word order and his archaisms Cardozo violates the standard precepts of good writing. But a great writer does not write to rule . . . and Cardozo's prose occasionally . . . rises to greatness."[40]

Judge Posner has said it well. Cardozo wrote many opinions in which the words not only fix the opinion in our memory but also help persuade us that his chosen result is preferable. Some sentences and paragraphs belong in legal writing's Hall of Fame. The statements of facts in Wood v. Lucy, Lady Duff Gordon and Jacob & Youngs v. Kent fall in that category. The blundering constable of *Defore* is another. There are other memorable expressions:

"Not lightly vacated is the verdict of quiescent years."[41]

"Metaphors in law are to be narrowly watched, for starting as devices to liberate thought, they end often by enslaving it."[42]

"The tendency of a principle to expand itself to the limit of its logic may be counteracted by the tendency to confine itself within the limits of its history."[43]

"Danger invites rescue."[44]

"The timorous may stay at home."[45]

"The assault upon the citadel of privity is proceeding in these days apace."[46]

"A trustee is held to something stricter than the morals of the market place. Not honesty alone, but the punctilio of an honor the most sensitive, is then the standard of behavior."[47]

"One who is a martyr to a principle . . . does not prove by his martyrdom that he has kept within the law."[48]

"[Of freedom of thought and speech] one may say that it is the matrix, the indispensable condition, of nearly every other form of freedom."[49]

"We are not to close our eyes as judges to what we must perceive as men."[50]

"Justice is not to be taken by storm. She is to be wooed by slow advances."[51]

"[A] great principle of constitutional law is not susceptible of comprehensive statement in an adjective."[52]

When Cardozo wrote his tribute to Holmes in 1931, he quoted a number of memorable lines that Holmes had written. He then referred to Matthew Arnold's prescription for separating "the gold from the alloy in the coinage of poets by the test of a few lines which we are to carry in our thoughts."[53] As Holmes had written many such lines, so did Cardozo.

There were stylistic problems in Cardozo's later published lecture series. Replaying the major themes of *The Nature of the Judicial Process* in these later talks, he appears to have felt the need to dress them up with analogies drawn from his wide nonlegal reading and with fancier phraseology. The one serious talk following *The Nature of the Judicial Process* that did not replay the old themes, his lecture on "Jurisprudence" at the New York State Bar Association meeting in 1932, was written in the plainer, clearer style of the first lecture series.

Cardozo cared about language and its relation to thought. His style was a striking feature of everything he wrote. Sometimes that style concealed problems. Sometimes it even created them. Most often it helped the reader along to a resolution of them. Certainly, it helped to keep the substance of his thought alive for future generations of lawyers, judges, and scholars.

This chapter concludes our consideration of Cardozo's Court of Appeals work. Although a final discussion of his legal work is reserved for the last chapter in order to include his career on the United States Supreme Court, all the major themes and characteristics were developed during his long tenure in New York. The doctrinal themes of duty, responsibility, and honor; the political theme of deference to the legislature and executive; and the theoretical accommodation of logic, precedent, and history with the pragmatic considerations of public policy were all products of his eighteen years on the New York Court of Appeals. Cardozo's memorable opinions were complemented by lectures and writings in which he set forth his judicial philosophy.

In 1932, Cardozo stood for something in the judicial world. His defense of judicial lawmaking that brought legal doctrine into line with modern social, economic, and political events paralleled the work of progressive politicians and the legal realists. They gave one another mutual support in the struggle for the popular mind. But Cardozo also stood for caution in judicial lawmaking. For all his elitist outlook with respect to his social and intellectual position, he was a democrat when it came to assigning the judiciary a place in government. He accorded great respect to the other branches of government. Yet he knew how to make law when appropriate, and he did it. Cardozo took this creed to Washington.

The Supreme Court: 1932–1938

23
Appointment

At the opening of 1932, Cardozo was the preeminent judge in the country who was not sitting on the Supreme Court. Only Learned Hand, who was not so well known, was his equal in ability and accomplishment. The first-rate lawyer had become a first-rate judge. In his eighteen-year career on the New York Court of Appeals, Cardozo had shown himself to be a thoughtful, creative, judicious man who wrote with style. He had a wide-ranging intellect that he used to deliver an innovative series of lectures that explained a judge's decision-making process to a wide audience. He was also a good colleague, respected, admired, and beloved by his fellow judges and the academic world. Moreover, Cardozo was chief judge of an able court in New York, which was then the most populous, wealthy, and prominent state in the country.

After six years as Chief Judge, Cardozo's career was at its zenith. During the previous ten years, he had already been mentioned several times, but not seriously considered, as a possible nominee for the Supreme Court of the United States.[1] Although he was now sixty-one, many justices had been appointed in their sixties and had lived long enough to give valuable service. The leading example was Oliver Wendell Holmes, who in 1902 had been appointed at the age of sixty-one and was still on the bench at the age of ninety. Holmes's colleagues, however, had come to believe that his mental and physical frailty was seriously impeding his ability to perform his work. Chief Justice Charles Evans

Hughes, at the request of a majority of the Court, undertook the unpleasant task of visiting Holmes at his home in Washington on Sunday, January 11, 1932, to suggest that he ought to resign. Holmes immediately wrote a letter of resignation to President Hoover.[2]

At once, newspapers began reporting that Cardozo's name was under consideration to take Holmes's place. The *New York Sun* expressed the hope that he would remain in New York where he had made his reputation.[3] For the next several days, the newspapers were filled with reports about various suggestions. Cardozo was featured so prominently that by January 22 Mark Sullivan wrote in his syndicated column that the "universality of the applause for Judge Cardozo constitutes a unique condition, almost a phenomenon."[4]

On the very day that Sullivan was proclaiming unanimous praise, Cardozo involved himself in a controversy that might have hurt his chances for selection. He delivered a lecture entitled "Jurisprudence" to an audience of over two thousand lawyers at a meeting of the New York State Bar Association.[5] In what was to be his last such lecture, he uncharacteristically involved himself in a war of words that had recently broken out between Roscoe Pound, one of the earliest advocates of sociological jurisprudence, which was a precursor of legal realism, and a group of younger, more thoroughgoing realists, especially Karl Llewellyn and Jerome Frank.[6] Cardozo knew that he was under consideration as Holmes's successor. Former Chief Judge Frank Hiscock, in introducing Cardozo, referred to the possibility that the Court of Appeals might lose him. Cardozo gave his talk, heedless of the possibility that involvement in controversy might impede his candidacy.

Although he usually shunned public debate, Cardozo had two reasons for intervening in this one. The first was his view that the combatants all were on the same side, his side, in the struggle to break out of a too-strict adherence to the dogma of precedent. He thought that he might mediate the dispute. The second was the hope that he could moderate what he saw as the nihilist tendencies of some realists, especially their exaggeration of the indeterminacy of legal principles. As Cardozo wrote to Felix Frankfurter, "Recent talks with Llewellyn make me feel that the bark of the realists is worse than their bite, and that the differences are largely verbal. I am trying in my bar association address to reconcile the factions and bring the contending groups together."[7]

The way that Cardozo went about the task of reconciliation, however, ensured its failure. It was one thing to write privately to Frankfurter that "Most of what is good in the writings of the realists is not new,"[8] and quite another to say that publicly. Cardozo simply got carried away. He denominated the new group "neo-realists," because there "were brave men before Agamemnon; and before the dawn of the last decade there were those in jurisprudence [he named, among others, Holmes and Pound] who strove to see the truth in the workings of the judicial process . . . and to report what they had seen with sincerity and candor."[9] Indeed, he saw his own opinions and writings as embodying the realists' call for the abandonment of rules when those rules stood "condemned as mischievous in the social consciousness of the hour."[10] Cardozo intended to embrace the "neo-realists" as part of a larger and older realist tradition; however, he did not realize that this gesture might be seen as a veiled insult to people who considered themselves pioneers and who were flush with the enthusiasm of their "discovery."[11]

Having put the neorealists in their place, Cardozo proceeded to point out particular shortcomings. He commented on "the style that the faithful have appropriated to themselves" as perhaps "a bit over-pretentious"—not simply pretentious, but "over-pretentious." Calling them "the faithful" was a description of dogmatic zealots. Then he characteristically reversed direction by suggesting that perhaps the war was chiefly one of words and that the core of neorealist philosophy was accurate. He did not want to "exaggerate unduly the differences that divide the forces of enlightenment and truth when there is need to present a united front to . . . prejudice and error." Cardozo dismissed some neorealist writings that seemed to reject completely the value of order, certainty, and rational coherence in favor of ad hoc judicial subjectivism, "the visceral reactions of one judge or another." He simply asserted that the neorealists did not really mean to go that far. Those writings merely expressed "the derision and impatience that betray themselves here and there among the priests of the new gospel of juridical salvation," and they did not represent the more moderate and fundamental assertions of mainstream neorealist thought.[12]

Cardozo rejected the position of a growing number of neorealists that law includes only what judges do, not what they say. He saw considerable force for the development of law in the explanations that judges gave for the results that they reached. He found the neorealists' prescription of the need for far-reaching change in legal doctrine misleading, and

he saw the major innovations in current juristic thought as being "chiefly
the candor of its processes." Cardozo ended by defending the eclectic
approach to decision-making that he had set out in his earlier lectures.
His closing sentence underlined his commitment, in a self-congratulatory
fashion, to all the elements in the process that he had described, with an
emphasis on the cautions and limits. "If I have not lost the road altogether, if my feet have not sunk in a quagmire of uncoordinated precedents, I owe it not a little to the signposts and the warnings, the barriers
and the bridges, which my study of the judicial process has built along
the way."[13]

It was a provocative performance by a judge whose name was already
being mentioned for the Supreme Court, for he took on the vanguard
of the academic community that had supported him. If Cardozo was
"perhaps the premier Realist judge," his talk demonstrated that there
was a difference between a realist judge and realist academics.[14] The
emphasis on the policy-making and intuitive factors in judicial lawmaking made Cardozo a realist. But Cardozo, who came to his realism from
practice and from judging, knew, in a way that most of the academics
did not, that precedent, logic, analogy, dispassionate application of rules,
and other institutional considerations also played an important role in
decision-making. Cardozo rejected the notion that judicial decision-
making should embody a specific ideological bent and thus opposed
those realists who tended in that direction.

Although Cardozo's talk was reported fully in the daily press, he did
not receive any public criticism.[15] The criticism came in a private letter
nearly eight months later. After Cardozo had been sitting on the Supreme
Court for six months, he received a thirty-one-page letter from Jerome
Frank, with a thirty-one-page postscript.[16] Frank was a practicing lawyer
whose law review articles and recent, psychologically oriented book,
Law and the Modern Mind, made him a major figure on the legal scene.
Frank had admired Cardozo and had previously corresponded with him.
Indeed, in *Law and the Modern Mind,* Frank had praised Cardozo for
his "adult emotional stature," his efforts "to do away with legal mys-
teries," and his education of the public about the realities of judicial
lawmaking.[17]

Frank had learned in advance about Cardozo's talk to the bar association from Oscar Cox. Cox was a young New York City lawyer who
had begun a book on Cardozo's jurisprudence.[18] Cox engaged in flatter-
ing correspondence with Cardozo in which he passed along admiring

comments from others about Cardozo and at the same time occasionally repeated Cardozo's comments to others. Having learned about Cardozo's planned talk, Frank chose Cox as a go-between to reach Cardozo. Frank sent Cox copies of a two-part article that he had published and asked Cox to send them to Cardozo with the suggestion that Cardozo read them "before he makes his proposed public comment on my book as I think they will help to remove some possible misunderstandings of my position." Cox forwarded the copies and then tried some mediation of his own. He reported that "Jerome Frank is suffering some qualms" that Cardozo might comment publicly on the book without having read the recent article. Cox advised Cardozo to "suspend public comment until you have had a more comprehensive view of his work." Cardozo responded politely that he had already read the first installment and that he did not "expect to refer by name to the book by Jerome Frank, though I will deal to some extent with its theme."[19]

When Frank finally saw Cardozo's talk in print, he felt both misunderstood and mistreated. The year before, he had taken on Roscoe Pound in angry correspondence, and he now attacked Cardozo.[20] Although the opening paragraphs of his long letter to Cardozo expressed reverence for Cardozo's integrity and path-making in legal thought, the rest of the letter was a strong defense against what he regarded as Cardozo's attack on the "sceptics" (Frank's term for the realists) and especially on himself. Frank's defense boiled down to two propositions. First, Cardozo's criticism of the "sceptics" for exaggerating the amount of uncertainty that existed in law was based on an incomplete conception of what constituted "law." Cardozo's view and indeed the view of most legal thinkers proceeded from a study of opinions written by appellate courts; from that perspective, Frank conceded, legal rules might appear fairly certain. But that perspective neglected the uncertainties arising out of the "facts" to which legal rules had to be applied in trial courts. He criticized Cardozo for not acknowledging that the power of judges and juries to "find" facts gave them an enormous area of discretion in deciding particular cases and that the result was a great deal of uncertainty. Frank's second proposition was that the sceptics were merely describing the large amount of uncertainty and irrationality that they saw in the system, not applauding it. He then set forth his own views at great length, emphasizing the virtues of the rational social planning of the new twentieth-century "Enlightenment."[21]

Having argued his case for thirty-one pages, Frank could not rest it.

Not only was Cardozo wrong, he should have known he was wrong, as Frank tried to prove with another thirty-one pages of appendix extracted from his own works. Clearly Frank felt that Cardozo had not only slighted him but, worse, had also ignored him. Frank was angry. A hero had betrayed him. If the length of Frank's letter was obsessive, the tone was accusatory. One passage was especially pointed: "[T]hose judges who are most lawless, or most swayed by the 'perverting influences of their emotional natures,' or most dishonest, are often the very judges who use most meticulously the language of compelling mechanical logic, who elaborately wrap about themselves the pretense of merely discovering and carrying out existing rules, who sedulously avoid any indications that they individualize cases."[22] That passage could have been meant to apply to Cardozo's techniques of using precedent as well as to the so-called "judicial conservatives" who used precedent to stifle reform. A denunciation of weak and dishonest judges, which doubtless was intended by Frank to refer to contemporaneous conditions, was a tactless reminder to Cardozo of his own father's disgrace.

Cardozo let it all pass. He took advantage of the workload involved in his new Supreme Court appointment to avoid personal confrontation. With the excuse of having to get settled in a new apartment and the imminent beginning of a new term of court, Cardozo wrote back that he had time only to "skim over" Frank's letter. Although he found it "full of interest and suggestion," he had no time to reply in detail. Then, in typical disarming fashion, he proceeded to deprecate his own work, perhaps seeking to dissuade Frank from attacking him publicly: "I am sorry that you have found so much to criticize in my address; but I do not think very highly of it myself and so I have no reason to complain that it is unsatisfactory to others. I refused to send it to the law reviews, preferring to bury it in the yearbook of the bar association . . . If you write about it, you will be investing it with an importance which I am quite ready to believe that it does not deserve."[23] Although Cardozo clearly hoped to soothe Frank's feelings by forgoing a rebuttal, his reply probably added further insult to Frank's injuries. Frank had sent Cardozo sixty-two pages of heartfelt argument; Cardozo merely skimmed over it and offered excuses for his inattention. Frank took his revenge years later, after Cardozo's death, by publishing his criticisms.[24] Frank's letter and later article were the extreme reaction of a volatile man who felt that he had been criticized publicly when he should have been praised.

In his address, Cardozo had seized what turned out to be his final opportunity to restate his judicial creed and to distance himself from some "followers" who ignored its qualifications. He also saw an opportunity to use his conciliatory talents to effect an accommodation between judicial realism and some elements of academic realism. Cardozo succeeded in his first goal but failed badly in his second. In part, he failed because for all his contacts with the academy, and for all his efforts to keep up with new ideas, his deepest engagement was in a different part of the legal enterprise. His job was the practical job of deciding cases, and the learning to which he was most attuned was that which was most relevant to his daily task. Jerome Frank was simply too ethereal for Benjamin Cardozo.

In those days, newspapers were not quick to see the connection between jurisprudential disputes and the current political scene, so that Cardozo's talk on January 22, 1932, did not provoke any public controversy. In the following days, the attention paid to Cardozo as a possible replacement for Holmes grew. A Supreme Court vacancy is always an event in the life of the nation, and this vacancy was extraordinary because of the stature of the retiring justice. In public reputation, Holmes was first among American judges. His judicial philosophy was adopted as a model by much of the profession, especially in academic circles and the younger generation of lawyers. His service beyond the age of ninety and the magnificent way in which he had aged into the visual ideal of a judge caused Holmes's public position to transcend his philosophy. Chief Justice Hughes, a model of correct, reserved behavior, expressed a general view in a radio address on Holmes's ninetieth birthday: "We honor him, but, what is more, we love him."[25]

Many people expressed the view that a giant should be replaced by a giant. In a political world, that consideration rarely prevails, and, in any event, an heir is usually not apparent. Yet this time the heir was apparent to many professional and public leaders, and it was Benjamin Cardozo. There were, however, serious obstacles to his appointment. Cardozo was a Democrat. Moreover, the distributive arithmetic was awkward. There were already two justices from New York City, and there was another Jew, Louis Brandeis, on the Supreme Court. However, in terms of the politics of the pressing constitutional issues before the Court, Holmes counted as a progressive, and they were a minority in the membership of the Supreme Court. Hoover was looking to keep some balance on the Court, and powerful political reasons counseled the replacement of Holmes with another progressive. The composition and mood of the Senate in 1932 would have made it difficult to force the nomination of a judge who was hostile to legislative regulation of the economy—a replica of either Justice Sutherland, Butler, McReynolds, or Van Devanter. After all, largely on ideological grounds, twenty-six votes had been mustered against Chief Justice Hughes's confirmation in 1930, and the forty-one votes against Judge John Parker the same year had been enough to reject him.

Moreover, the President and his advisers could take two kinds of ideology into account in their evaluation of Cardozo. One was his political orientation; the other was his institutional orientation. In a judge, the latter may curb the former. Cardozo's view that in most cases, the state or federal constitution had given the choice of governmental regulatory action to another branch of government led him on occasion to a result that was contrary to his own personal view of wise action. Cardozo had written enough, both judicially and extrajudicially, so that Attorney General William Mitchell and Hoover's other advisers should have known that, in constitutional matters, Cardozo was a cautious and moderate progressive, not a radical activist. A political conservative with a long-range view might well have seen Cardozo's institutional sense as a positive factor. Finally, unless the pattern of Hoover's appointments to the Court was highly coincidental, he and his advisers were not interested in appointing justices like Sutherland, Butler, McReynolds, or Van Devanter. The justices whom Hoover nominated—Charles Evans Hughes, John Parker, Owen Roberts, and Benjamin Cardozo—were, albeit in different measure, much more accommodating to legislative regulation of the economy. Erwin Griswold, then a young lawyer in the Justice Department, later Dean of Harvard Law School and Solicitor General of the United States, believed that Hoover and Mitchell "got what they wanted, that is, a judge of liberal outlook, restrained by a careful and philosophical conception of the judicial process."[26]

One version of the story has credited Senator William Borah of Idaho, who had broken with other Progressive leaders in 1928 to campaign for Herbert Hoover, with decisive influence in persuading Hoover to name Cardozo.[27] Hoover denied this story: "Judge Cardoza's [sic] selection was determined upon by myself and the Attorney General. Judge Cardoza was asked to come to the White House and discuss the appointment. Upon his acceptance, I notified various Senators that the appointment would be sent up to the Senate, and suggested that they support it. Therefore, [neither] Senator Borah nor any other Senator had a part in that selection."[28] In a subsequent letter, Hoover asserted that he had made his decision "within a few hours after the vacancy occurred," but changed his original story by reporting, accurately, that his only contact with Cardozo was a telephoned offer of appointment.[29]

The story of the Cardozo appointment was a good deal more complicated than Hoover's brief account. Hoover was faced with a number of problems. There was the pressure to replace Holmes with someone who approached his stature, the belief that some balance of views should be maintained on the Supreme Court, and the obvious availability of Mitchell, who had done a first-rate job as Attorney General.[30] Finally, many other names were being pressed upon Hoover, including some with definite political or geographic advantages. Members of the Supreme Court were also vitally interested in Holmes's replacement. Lobbying on behalf of Mitchell had begun even before Holmes's resignation was made public. Justice Van Devanter discussed the situation in a letter to his sister:

> Most of us are wishing that Mr. Mitchell be made the successor. This probably would be rather certainly done, save that the President might have much embarrassment in selecting a new Attorney General . . . Mitchell realizes the President's situation and has urged that we do not present his name and thus bring embarrassment to the President. [His?] name has been presented, and if the President [resolves the?] matter in Mitchell's favor and distinctly asks him to take the place we feel sure Mitchell will accept; but if the President hesitates or manifests any embarrassment we fear that Mitchell will ask that his name be not considered.[31]

Hoover needed Mitchell near the White House. As Van Devanter later wrote, Hoover had "come to believe strongly in Mitchell and recognizes that Mitchell has kept him out of trouble." Van Devanter thought that Mitchell would have had the nomination if he had not taken himself out of the running to save Hoover the difficulty of losing him as Attorney General.[32]

The "most of us" mentioned by Van Devanter as wanting Mitchell must have included Pierce Butler, George Sutherland, and James Mc-

Reynolds along with Van Devanter. Louis Brandeis and Harlan Stone surely preferred a more progressive nominee than Mitchell. We do not know the stance of Chief Justice Hughes or Owen Roberts. Another Van Devanter letter three days after Holmes's resignation states that when Hughes presented Holmes's resignation, he told the President that "most" of the justices wanted Mitchell.[33] What Hughes actually said is not known, but after Cardozo's appointment, Hughes told his son that he was delighted with the appointment and that he "had hoped that this would be possible."[34]

Another person who influenced the result was Mark Sullivan, a syndicated newspaper columnist with the New York *Herald-Tribune* and a close friend of Hoover. He sent a memorandum of a conversation he had had with Borah to the President's special secretary, Larry Richey, and asked him to pass it on to the President: "Borah called me on the phone and asked if I knew anything about that Judgeship. He is extremely strong for Cardozo. I asked him how Mitchell would fare. He spoke slowly and thoughtfully to the effect that he did not know . . . His attitude toward Mitchell was purely one of speculating objectively on how the Senate would take it. . . . Borah is, however, extremely strong for Cardozo." On the bottom of the page Sullivan added his own handwritten recommendation: "I am very much impressed by the support of Cardoza [sic] in all areas. I do not believe that in this one case geography would raise any objection. Cardoza is in unique class by himself. Borah would be put in a mood to support the administration by putting it up to him to get Cardoza through the Senate. Borah at just this time would probably be glad of justification to get behind the administration."[35] Sullivan's memorandum indicates that Hoover had probably already used him as a sounding device. Political insight was Sullivan's forte. This support from someone who was not a friend of Cardozo and whose judgment Hoover trusted was probably very helpful to Cardozo's cause.

The vacancy also provoked a flurry of activity on the part of those seeking to influence the selection. As with the three earlier steps in Cardozo's judicial career—his nomination to run for the Supreme Court of New York, his appointment to the Court of Appeals, and his selection as Chief Judge of that court—his friends and admirers in and out of the legal community lobbied on his behalf.

Cardozo's old friend, Rabbi Stephen Wise, used his many personal and political connections, kept in close touch with Borah, who had mobilized him, and recruited other friends to promote Cardozo's candidacy.[36] Felix Frankfurter had been personal assistant to Henry Stimson between 1906 and 1913 when Stimson was the United States Attorney in New York and then Secretary of War.[37] Four days after Holmes's resignation, Frankfurter visited Stimson, who was then Secretary of State, and the two men talked about the Supreme Court vacancy. During the following week, Stimson discussed the vacancy with Hoover, and not for the first time. Stimson told Hoover that he had canvassed many people for suggestions of candidates from the West and the South but had come up with no one who would be a good successor for Holmes. "Under these circumstances," Stimson noted, "I told him pretty strongly that I thought his safest bet was Cardozo, although [Learned] Hand would also be a good candidate."[38] Hand might have been as apt a successor to Holmes as Cardozo; but Hand, a maverick Republican, had many political liabilities and was not a serious candidate.[39] He was also not nearly so well known nationally as Cardozo, who gained nearly unanimous faculty support from many major law schools, which sent petitions to the President.[40] The signatures included leading realist scholars, who either did not know of Cardozo's recent talk or were not sufficiently bothered by it to withhold their support.

Justice Stone, an adviser to Hoover on all sorts of matters and a member of his "medicine ball" cabinet, also pressed Cardozo's cause.[41] Stone later stated that in order "to emphasize both the importance of the appointment and Judge Cardozo's fitness," he even "intimated" to Hoover that he would be willing to retire in order to reduce the objection that the appointment of Cardozo would put three justices from New York City on the bench.[42] But as close as Stone was to Hoover, by his own account he did not know what was in Hoover's mind. Throughout the month between Holmes's retirement and Cardozo's nomination, Stone first thought that Mitchell would be appointed, then suspected that a search was being made "for someone who will satisfy the supposed sectional requirements," then stated that Judge Orie Phillips of the Tenth Circuit had the inside track, and finally proclaimed his lack of knowledge on the very date of the appointment.[43] Even though Stone was not in on the decision, his opinion doubtless carried weight with Hoover.

If all the President was waiting for, as subsequently claimed by Walter H. Newton, his secretary, was an "expression of opinion . . . throughout the country as to Judge Cardozo's fitness and general acceptability," it was not long in coming.[44] Cardozo's friends and supporters flooded the White House with messages of support. Because Senator Robert Wagner, a Democrat, was from Cardozo's home state, his support was therefore important to Cardozo and Hoover both. Almost immediately, "on his own initiative," Wagner recommended Cardozo to Hoover.[45] Even more important may have been the views of another Progressive, Senator George Norris of Nebraska, who was chairman of the Committee on the Judiciary, which would vote on the nomination. Norris was reported as stating that "a man holding the economic and social views of Justice Holmes" should replace him.[46] In addition, many other prominent individuals forwarded expressions of support for Cardozo to Hoover and Mitchell.[47]

Senator Borah's role remains to be clarified. One story concluded that Borah's last-minute intervention with Hoover was crucial, and the President's own records confirm a meeting with Borah on Sunday night before he offered the position to Cardozo on Monday.[48] But Borah's visit probably confirmed rather than caused Hoover's decision. Hoover saw Chief Justice Hughes on the preceding Friday evening, Attorney General Mitchell on Saturday morning, Borah on Sunday, and then called Cardozo on Monday. That chronology strongly suggests that Hoover had determined to appoint Cardozo before Borah's Sunday evening visit. Hoover may well have let Borah believe that he influenced the choice in order to gain political advantage with a powerful senator. It is extremely unlikely that Hoover would have made his decision after meeting with Borah and not have discussed it with Mitchell before sending in the nomination. Mitchell was Hoover's trusted and principal adviser on judicial appointments. Later, Hoover stated that he overrode Mitchell's recommendation only once—and it was not this appointment.[49] Had Borah changed Hoover's mind, the President would have needed to talk with Mitchell, and perhaps Hughes, again, and he did not do so before offering Cardozo the appointment. The record indicates that Hoover made the decision with Mitchell and then gained Borah's support.

Several factors were influential in Hoover's decision to appoint Cardozo. First was the fact that Justice Holmes occupied a unique position in American law. Only Cardozo had a reputation approaching that of Holmes. In addition, Hoover was inclined to appoint a Democrat. Mitchell was as obvious a Democrat to appoint as Cardozo, and a Mitchell appointment would have been personally satisfying to Hoover, for Mitchell had given him good service—too good service, because Hoover needed Mitchell to stay where he was.

Hoover was aware that a "nonpolitical" selection of a progressive Democrat had political problems, which he acknowledged in a letter to former Attorney General George Wickersham immediately after announcement of the appointment. He wrote that it "was a difficult matter from many points of view. It contains more political liabilities than assets but I felt that I must disregard such questions." Hoover was responding to a letter from Wickersham congratulating Hoover on the appointment. Wickersham wrote that Cardozo "was the outstanding figure on the bench of the State Courts and I think he has no equal on the federal district or Circuit Courts."[50] The obvious political liabilities included disappointment felt by some Republicans at the appointment of a Democrat, especially one believed to be a "liberal," disappointment in the selection of a third justice from New York City felt by those who believed their own areas of the country were due for an appointment, and disappointment engendered by the appointment of a second Jew to the Court. This last was a touchy issue. One did not have to be an anti-Semite to have views about the desirability of some sort of balance on the Supreme Court. Rabbi Wise heard that Hoover alluded to the problem in his Sunday evening conversation with Borah.[51] These issues must have been on Hoover's mind.[52] But, as Zechariah Chafee put it, "President Hoover ignored geography and made history."[53]

Shortly before noon on Monday, February 15, Herbert Cone, confidential clerk to the New York Court of Appeals, went to the Albany train station to pick up Cardozo and to give him a message. He told Cardozo that Lawrence Richey, special secretary to President Hoover, had tried to reach him at his New York office earlier that morning and had asked that he call the President as soon as he reached Albany. When Cardozo returned Hoover's call from his office at the Court of Appeals, he received an offer of appointment as a Justice of the Supreme Court of the United States. He accepted immediately.[54]

What was Cardozo himself doing all through this time of scurrying about by his friends? He had written a short note to Holmes on January 13. He had seen Holmes's response to his colleagues' warm letter of tribute. Holmes had written to his fellow justices, "For such little time as may be left for me I shall treasure [your letter] as adding gold to the sunset."[55] Cardozo's note picked up the reference. "The sunset moves me deeply. I send you the assurance of my loving homage."[56]

Cardozo was well aware that he was being considered to replace Holmes. His personal mail increased so much that he began a letter to his cousin, Annie Nathan Meyer, by apologizing that he had had "so many letters to answer" that he was "resorting to the hateful type-writer."[57] Substantive comment was reserved for Frankfurter and Stone. In the course of expressing joy that Frankfurter was being considered for the Massachusetts Supreme Judicial Court, Cardozo commented, "I wish they wouldn't talk about taking me to Washington. I don't want to go and have little thought that I could go if I wished. I have suffered a great upheaval in my home life [the death of his sister Nellie], as you know, and I cannot tolerate with equanimity the thought of another."[58] To Stone he added, "I have brought myself over to the belief that I can accomplish more for the development of the law in the office that I hold than I could in the Supreme Court."[59] Each Saturday, when he entered his New York office after a week's session in Albany, he heaved a sigh of relief and said, "No news from Washington."[60]

When Rabbi Wise wrote to Frankfurter about the activity that he was promoting on Cardozo's behalf, he warned that Cardozo "knew nothing of all this, and what is more that no one could discuss the thing, in the terms in which we were speaking 'with this august being.'"[61] Wise thought that political maneuvering to obtain a judgeship was not Car-dozo's conception of the way a judge should be appointed and that he would disapprove. He was probably right that Cardozo would have disapproved had he been asked to sanction such tactics. A tactful silence spared Cardozo's feelings and preserved Wise's freedom to lobby without restraint. Cardozo understood this as well as Wise did. The events surrounding his election to the Supreme Court of New York in 1913 and his elevation to the chief judgeship of the Court of Appeals in 1926 indicate that Cardozo understood quite well how the political machinery operated, that usually judges did not just happen to be appointed by acclaim, and that work had to be done by supporters. He did not do what Judge Hough had done and tell his supporters to stop working on his behalf.[62] He let his friends help him.

Cardozo did not relish the personal wrench that leaving New York would entail and the change in the nature of the work that would be involved. He would have to give up the familiar common law problems and the collegiality of his state court to immerse himself in the interpretation of federal statutes and to join the bitter constitutional disputes that had wracked the Supreme Court for years. He would also lose his position as leader of the Court of Appeals to become one of a minority, and the junior member as well, on the Supreme Court. He expressed a desire not to be asked and stated that he did not believe he "ought to take it."[63] Afterwards, he stated that he had balanced the pros and cons before being asked and concluded that if the position was offered, he would accept it "as one must accept sickness or death."[64]

That explanation was typical Cardozo—treating a serious, emotional matter with a light touch. But the offer was a great honor, the highest honor that can come to a judge. Being a judge was Cardozo's whole life. No one turns down such an office lightly, and as pride and vanity were part of his makeup, they added their weight, too. There was also the silent influence of Cardozo's desire to enhance the family name. Personal and professional reasons to stay in New York gave him misgivings, but still he wanted the job. When the summons came, he immediately accepted.

Cardozo's appointment was greeted with an outpouring of approval, and Hoover received volumes of letters applauding his selection.[65] Learned Hand put it eloquently: "His wisdom, his learning, his penetration, his outlook, and, above all, the purity and elevation of his character, set him in a class apart."[66] Augustus Hand, Learned's first cousin and colleague on the Court of Appeals for the Second Circuit, was known for his spare language, but he could not resist a burst of enthusiasm in reacting to Cardozo's appointment. Writing to his friend and Cardozo's colleague Henry Kellogg, Gus Hand wrote, "What an incomparable man you have lost! I have never known a more wonderful and deeply spiritual character. His character, I think, has been the real source of his eminence and success."[67]

The Senate hearing on Cardozo's appointment was quite brief.[68] One disgruntled person, whose forgery conviction had been affirmed by the Court of Appeals, testified that his conviction was the product of a Tammany plot and that Cardozo had paid too little attention to his arguments. Samuel Seabury, president of the New York State Bar Association and Cardozo's former colleague on the Court of Appeals, wrote a warm letter of support. The subcommittee and the full Judiciary

Committee approved the nomination unanimously.[69] The Senate confirmed Cardozo without discussion, without a roll call, and without objection on February 24, 1932.

Cardozo sat for a few more days on the Court of Appeals to wind up some business before retiring on March 3. At a session in his honor, Cuthbert Pound, his successor as Chief Judge, presented him with a silver loving cup from his colleagues in a short address that referred, simply and without exaggeration, to his power, grace, calm, industry, and kindness.[70] Cardozo used the next few days in New York to prepare for his move to Washington and to begin to answer some of the hundreds of letters of congratulations that he had received. Even Jerome Frank rejoiced that "the angel of wisdom led President Hoover to perform the finest action thus far in his administration," although Frank might not have regarded that as his highest praise.[71] In responding, Cardozo expanded beyond his typical short letter of thanks, perhaps in an attempt to mollify Frank after his Bar Association talk: "You are pointing a way of life for the judges of the coming years; and even though I am too fixed in modes of thought to follow you completely, I admire to the full your brilliant and arresting thought . . . Perhaps there isn't much difference between us except a slightly variant shade of emphasis."[72] Frank's subsequent diatribe indicates that Cardozo's conciliatory gesture was unsuccessful.

Cardozo understood that the demands of his new position would not permit him to continue his extrajudicial activities. He therefore resigned his positions as a trustee of Columbia and as a member of various Jewish organizations and of the Law School Visiting Committee at Harvard. He also decided that he ought not publish an essay commenting on the current relevance of Alexis de Tocqueville's observations about the relation between judicial power and democracy in the United States.[73] Then, on March 8, a number of writers and painters at the Century Club gave a dinner for him as a fellow artist.[74] At the end of the week, the Wises gave him a surprise party, and he went off to Washington the weekend before he took his seat.[75]

Stephen Wise had perceived the personal meaning of the appointment even while it hung in the balance: "[T]he glory of it will be . . . that [although his father] came under the malign influence of Tweed [and] made the name Cardozo synonymous with shame, [in] twenty years, Cardozo has effaced the memory of his father and his name can never more be used save in terms of reverence and honor. What an achievement for a man!"[76]

Cardozo was sworn in as a Justice of the Supreme Court of the United States in a ceremony at the Supreme Court attended by many relatives and friends on March 14, 1932.[77] It was a triumphant moment for Benjamin Cardozo. The one thing missing was that Nellie was not there to savor it with him.

24

Life in Washington

Appointment to the Supreme Court was a recognition of Cardozo's stature in American law, but it carried a heavy cost. Cardozo had dreaded the personal upheaval that a move to Washington would bring, and he was right in his apprehension. He had managed to put his life back together after Nellie's death with the assistance of his household staff and his New York family and friends. Even though he eventually re-created his household in Washington, he left his family and friends behind. Also, he missed the regular meetings of the Philosophers at Fred Coudert's house and of the Round Table. He lost the professional and social collegiality of the Court of Appeals and entered the stressful and uncollegial existence of the Supreme Court. There was some recompense in that his friends and extended family did not forget him and that he gained the companionship of a series of intelligent, young law clerks and secretaries, but he never felt at home in Washington.

Cardozo came to Washington with just a few months left in the Court's 1931–1932 term. He rented a three-room suite at the Mayflower Hotel until he could find more permanent quarters. Joseph Paley came with him as law clerk for the remainder of the term, but the rest of his household remained in New York.[1] He was "wretchedly homesick" and despondent. "I don't think there is much to live for when the people who have really mattered in one's life are all dead. I'm too old to make new friends who can replace those with whom I have lived for a lifetime."[2] The demands of his new job were the best antidote to despondency. With no advance preparation time for the new subjects of federal law, he threw himself into his work and kept himself busy.

Cardozo's New York friends delighted him with visits. "The Kelloggs were here last night, and I was hysterical with joy at the sight of them." Or, as he wrote to Aline and Lafayette Goldstone after they had paid him a visit, "The sight and sound of you lifted me out of my slough of despond." He used the dining room of the Mayflower as a social center, although he warned visitors that he would have to "resume [his] labors" after dinner was over.[3] In early May, when the American Law Institute held its annual meeting at the Mayflower, Cardozo was able to renew acquaintances with many friends, including some of his former colleagues on the Court of Appeals. He had an emotional tie to New York, and he looked forward to the end of the term. As soon as it ended, he was on the first train to New York City. He spent a month at his house on West 75th Street before moving to a cottage in Rye, New York, that Sissie Lehman, Irving Lehman's wife, had selected for him.[4]

Cardozo used part of his summer vacation to travel around more than he had in years. He went from upstate New York to western Massachusetts, New Jersey, and Pennsylvania as he collected honorary degrees from St. Lawrence, Williams, Princeton, and Pennsylvania.[5] Finally, he settled down in Rye, where he was constantly entertained at lunch and dinner by friends and family, and he did some entertaining himself. Cousin Addie Cardozo and Learned Hand came for a few days in July. He went to Albany for a day with his old court and had dinner with his former colleagues.

When not socializing, Cardozo spent some time working on the petitions for certiorari that had been filed by litigants requesting the Supreme Court to hear their cases, and he read books that he had not had time for while the Court was in session. He had decided to rent an apartment at 2101 Connecticut Avenue in Washington, overlooking Rock Creek Park, in the same building where Justice Van Devanter lived. Throughout the summer, he fussed over the moving arrangements, constantly reminding Joseph Paley about details, especially the transportation of his library.[6] Despite the social activity and work, Cardozo reported that he spent a great deal of time idling and that friends found him looking better than he had in years. He clearly enjoyed his vacation.

Over the summer, Joseph Paley decided not to remain as law clerk—

"wisely," Cardozo concluded, for Paley did not have the academic ability of the other Supreme Court law clerks. Cardozo turned to Felix Frankfurter at Harvard Law School to find a new one. Many of the justices sought help from law schools in recruiting able graduates as law clerks, and Felix Frankfurter had already performed that task for Holmes and Brandeis. Frankfurter suggested Melvin Siegel, who had recently obtained an LL.B. and an S.J.D. at Harvard, although Frankfurter had originally told Siegel that he was to be clerk to Brandeis. After meeting Siegel, Cardozo accepted the recommendation. At the suggestion of Charles Cropley, clerk of the Supreme Court, Cardozo also hired Percy Russell, another Harvard Law School graduate, as a combination secretary and law clerk.[7] Thereafter, he yielded to the importunities of friends at Yale and Columbia and adopted a rotation system for selecting clerks. Ambrose Doskow from Columbia followed Siegel, and Alan Stroock of Yale came next. Cardozo asked Stroock to stay a second year. Then it was Harvard's turn again, and Joe Rauh was selected by Frankfurter. He also stayed for two years, although most of the second year was consumed with Cardozo's final illness. Cardozo was so taken with Rauh that he abandoned his selection routine and asked Frankfurter to find someone comparable for the following year, but his illness and death cut short that assignment.[8]

Only two people occupied the second position of the secretary-clerk. Percy Russell stayed until 1936 when he was replaced by Chris Sargent. Sargent was a Harvard Law School graduate who had done well and had been elected an editor of the Harvard Law Review. Frankfurter had recommended Joseph Fanelli for the position. Frankfurter did not think that Sargent was good enough, and he had an animus against Sargent's father, who was rector of St. Bartholomew's Episcopal Church on Park Avenue in New York City. At the last minute, however, Cardozo switched and hired Sargent. He was a little defensive about his motives, commenting that it wasn't a bad idea for church-society people to know that Jews didn't have horns. Sargent was hard-working and a good lawyer, and he stayed until it became apparent during Cardozo's final illness that he would not return to the bench.[9]

Cardozo's first order of business when he returned from his summer vacation in 1932 was getting settled in his new eight-room apartment. In trying to re-create as much of his New York life as he could, he furnished the apartment with his old furniture from the 75th Street house. Kate Tracy and Catherine Walsh returned with him from New York and moved into the apartment. They were permanent fixtures for the rest of his life, except for one year that Catherine spent in her former home in Ireland. Catherine's sister Mary, who had been the cook, did not move with them, and Anna Barthek replaced her. Harry Hayes was hired to serve as chauffeur and general valet both in Washington and in Westchester every summer. Aside from his driving duties, he did a variety of household tasks. He shaved Cardozo every day, pressed his suits, and ran household errands for Miss Tracy.[10] The Court supplied each justice with a messenger to deliver draft opinions to the other justices and to the Court's printer and to run other professional errands. Elmer Jones became Cardozo's messenger; he was the only black aide Cardozo ever had.

Kate Tracy ran the household as before. Except for financial matters that Cardozo saw to himself, the staff did everything for Cardozo and tried to do it perfectly, shielding him from all the cares of daily life. Cardozo ate his dinner with Kate Tracy, but it was a rapid affair, not a sociable event. However, he did occasionally unburden himself to her, even to the point of saying once during his first year in Washington that he wished he were dead.[11] Loneliness and dislocation produced that moment of despair, but he persevered and gradually worked out a life for himself in Washington.

The apartment at 2101 Connecticut Avenue was office as well as home. The Supreme Court did not yet have a separate building of its own. The justices conferred and heard argument of cases in the Capitol, and they used their homes as their chambers. Cardozo was quite formal when working at home, wearing a coat and tie even in hot weather. He got up early, often as early as 5:00 A.M., and had breakfast around 7:30.[12] Then he did his correspondence. Although he had his business and judicial correspondence typed, he wrote out almost all his personal correspondence in longhand. His law clerk and secretary would arrive around nine o'clock. Cardozo would have a brief chat with them, bringing them up to date on the work he had done since he saw them last. Except for meals and time spent with occasional visitors, he worked all day up until dinnertime, which was around seven o'clock. When there was more work to do, Cardozo continued after dinner, often working as late as eleven o'clock. If he had finished working, he spent his free time reading. Cardozo often reported that he had trouble sleeping when he was working on an opinion. He kept a pad by his bedside and jotted down thoughts that occurred to him during the night. Sometimes he would get a book and read in the middle of the night. He was not strong physically even when he first came to Washington, and his work habits wore him out. It was no wonder that his doctors often found him run down at the end of the term.

Cardozo's law clerk and his secretary used a room in his apartment as their working space, and they answered the telephone for him. When the Court was in session, Harry Hayes would chauffeur Cardozo back and forth on a regular routine, leaving the apartment at 11:20 A.M. and returning immediately after the conclusion of argument. Sometimes Cardozo would take the law clerk with him to hear a particular argument, but Cardozo would not deviate from his weekday routine even to see the cherry trees in bloom on a beautiful day. Once in a while, though, he would go for a drive in the country with Hayes or sometimes with a law clerk on Sunday if there were no opinions to work on. Cardozo followed the Washington protocol of leaving his calling cards at the homes of people who had left their cards for him. Although Hayes could have done that, Cardozo often went with Hayes in the car on Sunday afternoon to do that task. Sometimes he spent part of a Sunday afternoon paying what was known as "a dinner call," that is, stopping by a friend's home two weeks after he had been there for dinner.[13]

One other visit that Cardozo made a few times each year was to Justice Holmes, until Holmes's death in 1935. He was, in fact, the last regular visitor at Holmes's Washington home before Holmes contracted a fatal bout of pneumonia. They were not "intimate friends," but Cardozo had an affection for Holmes and recognized that Holmes had been an important influence in his thinking.[14] "Many a time," Cardozo wrote, "in turning the pages of an opinion devoted to a humdrum theme, some problem perhaps of contract or of negligence, I have come across a winged sentence that seemed with its wings to chase obscurity away. Curious, I have gone back to the beginning, to find the name of Holmes."[15] Cardozo put up on the wall of his apartment a framed letter from Holmes to him that expressed his own creed as well as that of Holmes. It also contained a compliment that Cardozo must have treasured above all others: "I always have thought that not place or power or popularity makes the success that one desires, but a trembling hope that one has come near to an ideal. The only ground that warrants a man for thinking that he is not living in a fool's paradise if he ventures such a hope is the voice of a few masters, among whom you hold a conspicuous place . . . I feel it so much that I don't want to talk about it."[16]

The biggest professional change for Cardozo was in his personal relations with the other members of his court. By contrast with the New York Court of Appeals, the Supreme Court was not a collegial body. The justices mostly worked alone. Although the new Supreme Court building was completed in 1935, Cardozo did not use his office there often, preferring to keep his chambers in his apartment as before. Most of Cardozo's colleagues also retained their offices at home, and even Chief Justice Hughes used his office in the new building only for appointments and administrative work.[17] The justices generally got together only during the weeks of oral argument during the Court's term from October to June. The Court heard argument Monday through Friday from twelve noon to four-thirty with a half-hour break for lunch at two. Cardozo's participation in the argument of cases was also different from his practice in the Court of Appeals. In that court, he had become an active questioner who helped to channel the argument. As junior justice on the Supreme Court for almost the entire period of his service, he did not ask many questions.

With the justices working in different places, Cardozo did not mingle much with his colleagues. The justices did eat lunch together on argument days. The other justices noticed that Cardozo had a bit of a sweet tooth, as Miss Tracy regularly included a piece of cake with his sandwich. When they teased him about this indulgence, Cardozo told Miss Tracy to stop the cake. She ignored his request, but he repeated it with some asperity. Evidently he did not appreciate being teased, at least not by his Supreme Court colleagues.[18] The justices also got together at noon on Saturday after an argument week to discuss and vote on the cases that had been argued during the week.

With one exception, Cardozo rarely went to a colleague's home office, and his colleagues rarely came to his. Comments on one another's draft opinions were usually made by letter. Brandeis used to send Cardozo volumes of materials, usually economic materials, as background reading for various cases, but Cardozo generally ignored them. Starting in the 1936 term, however, he met with Brandeis and Stone for a half hour or so at Brandeis's apartment on Friday evenings before a Saturday conference as a response to the regular habit of the conservative bloc of four—Butler, McReynolds, Sutherland, and Van Devanter—to have a meeting while driving to Court together before arguments and the Saturday conference.

Cardozo's closest relationship on the Court was with Harlan Stone. He had known Stone from New York days. Stone had been dean of Columbia Law School between 1910 and 1923, and in the later years of his deanship, he used to come to see Cardozo almost weekly to talk about law school matters.[19] After Stone went to Washington in 1923, they occasionally saw one another socially and at meetings of the American Law Institute, and they corresponded about professional matters once in a while. Cardozo knew that Stone had supported his appointment to the Supreme Court. Furthermore, Stone had helped him with his move to Washington. Although Cardozo did not often go out socially, he traded dinners with the Stones several times a year, and they occasionally called on one another. He had a more extensive correspondence with Stone than with any of his other colleagues, and his constitutional philosophy was closest to Stone's.

Cardozo saw something of Brandeis, too. The Brandeises regularly invited lonely bachelors to dinner on Thanksgiving and before Christmas. Cardozo was on that list.[20] On rare occasions he attended one of Brandeis's regular Sunday afternoon teas for young government employees. He did not like to go to the Brandeis apartment, though, because he found it so overheated as to be uncomfortable. Although Cardozo respected and admired Brandeis, he realized that Brandeis's passionate attachment to causes set them apart. From time to time, he poked a little fun at Brandeis about a variety of things: the heat in the Brandeis apartment; the way he had his law clerks work on one opinion for several months, compiling a compendium of the law of all the states; the teas; and even Zionism. Once Cardozo applied an old joke to Brandeis in claiming that Brandeis ought to pay for a statue of Hitler because Hitler had done so much for Zionism. Cardozo had a tendency to treat weighty matters lightly; however, it was never clear whether that was a way of keeping his feelings private or a way of distancing himself from troubling subjects. He certainly had a deep antagonism toward Hitler, but his feelings about Zionism were mixed.

The other justice that Cardozo saw socially was Owen Roberts. He liked Roberts, and he and the Robertses traded dinners and afternoon calls once in a while. When Cardozo received an honorary degree from the University of Pennsylvania, he spent the night at the Roberts's farm nearby. He also knew Chief Justice Hughes from New York days; also, Hughes's son had been Cardozo's law clerk for a month when he first went on the bench in New York. Cardozo admired Hughes's forcefulness and the way that Hughes ran the Court, although he was not happy about the small number of interesting and important opinion assignments that he received from Hughes. But he saw very little of Hughes outside the official sessions of the Court. Hughes visited Cardozo in his apartment on a handful of occasions when he wanted to persuade Cardozo not to file a proposed opinion, but rarely otherwise.

Cardozo had very little contact with the other justices of the Court. He respected Willis Van Devanter's ability and special expertise in matters of western law, especially water and mining law. Even though they lived in the same apartment building, they almost never spent time together outside the Court. Cardozo thought George Sutherland was a nice man, but he also never saw anything of him outside official Court business. Neither did he have any social contact with Pierce Butler, whom he thought lacked the requisite judicial disinterestedness in some cases. Butler, in his view, pressed the Court to grant railroad petitions for certiorari in order to reverse verdicts for injured workers. Cardozo thought this a misuse of the certiorari jurisdiction. He was so upset at the practice that he proposed to issue an extraordinary written dissent from the granting of a petition for certiorari in such a case. Hughes talked him out of publishing on the promise that no more such petitions would be granted. That incident may well have soured relations between Cardozo and Butler, although Butler later traveled to New York to attend Cardozo's funeral.[21]

Cardozo had virtually no relationship with James McReynolds. McReynolds did not like Jews, and he particularly did not like his two Jewish colleagues on the Court, who entertained constitutional views so different from his own. Fred Coudert was a friend of both Cardozo and McReynolds, and when Cardozo was appointed to the Supreme Court, Coudert extolled him to McReynolds. McReynolds replied that he would remember Coudert's opinion but that Cardozo represented the "most subversive elements" in the country.[22] A story gained wide circulation that McReynolds directed a gratuitously nasty remark at Cardozo during his first year on the Court. When Aaron Steuer, son of the celebrated and controversial criminal defense lawyer Max Steuer, became a New York Supreme Court justice in 1932, the event was mentioned at some gathering when all the United States Supreme Court Justices were present. McReynolds commented that all one needed in order to get on the bench was to be the son of a crook. Another version reports McReynolds as having said "a Jew" and the son of a crook.[23] Cardozo surely understood that the comment included himself as well as Judge Steuer.

McReynolds emphasized his hostility. He often held a brief or record in front of his face when Cardozo delivered an opinion from the bench on opinion day,[24] and he sometimes did not even return a notation of agreement on Cardozo draft opinions. Cardozo for his part would write "I concur" on McReynolds drafts, but usually no more.[25] When Cardozo died, McReynolds did not attend any of the three sessions at the Supreme Court honoring him. The enmity of McReynolds added to the contrast between working conditions in Albany and in Washington. Cardozo had seen rational debate as the real strength of the Court of Appeals. Writing just after he left it in 1932, he said, "I don't find the 'conferences' [of the Supreme Court] as satisfactory as the 'consultations' at Albany—observe the difference in terminology. There is nothing like the genuine debate—the painstaking and willing interchange of views—that gave my old court whatever strength it had . . . I don't believe that I'll ever have the influence here that I had at Albany."[26]

Cardozo's closest collaborator in the work of the Court was his law clerk. Since he had had no previous experience with a first-class clerk, he experimented with how to make best use of the able law school graduates who served him. He had the law clerk read and prepare brief memoranda on the facts and issues in all the petitions for certiorari, the petitions by losing parties requesting the Court to review lower courts' decisions. The secretary–law clerk would also work on a few of the petitions. Cardozo sometimes had the law clerk prepare memoranda for him in advance of argument on those difficult cases in which he thought that the law clerk could give him some help. Before a case was argued, he read all the briefs himself and then discussed the cases with the clerks the morning before they were to be heard. When he returned from argument, he reported on anything interesting that had occurred. On Saturdays when there was a conference, the clerks would wait at his apartment for his return shortly after 4:30 P.M. to hear the results of the day's work and to learn about the assignment of opinions. The Chief Justice, if he was in the majority, would assign the majority opinion, and those assignments would be delivered to the individual judges by messenger Saturday night. If the Chief Justice was in the minority, the assignment would be made by the senior Associate Justice in the majority. After Cardozo suffered a heart attack in the summer of 1935, Hughes delayed sending him assignments until Sunday morning to give him more time to rest.[27]

Once Cardozo had received his assignment of an opinion, he began to work on it immediately, writing out a draft in longhand on pads of white lined paper. He had the unusual ability of being able to write while walking up and down, which he often did. Cardozo worked so fast that he usually had enough of a draft ready that it could be typed by the secretary on Monday morning. Indeed, he generally had a draft roughed out if the law clerk came in on Sunday afternoon. Once in a while, Cardozo had a law clerk do some research on a particular point. The law clerk could also write a memorandum or discuss a particular point if he disagreed with the draft, but in the main the law clerk's principal contribution was made before argument. Rarely did words of a law clerk find their way into a Cardozo opinion. Law clerks were free, though, to discuss any line of argument and to give him their views. He was also willing to rewrite his opinions on the basis of these discussions. The only impatience Cardozo showed was with repeated objections on the same point. The law clerks learned quickly, so that those were rare occasions.

Cardozo appreciated the quality of his new law clerks and he lavished praise on them. All of them, on reflection, regarded themselves as vastly overpraised because they thought that they made relatively little contribution to his thinking or to his opinions. Overpraise was a part of Cardozo's behavior. In this case, it may also have reflected his perception of the difference in ability between his Supreme Court clerks and his two Court of Appeals law clerks.[28]

Although Cardozo treated his clerks well, he was not on intimate terms with any of them. He was a private man, and the age difference was too great. The talk was mostly of law and current events. No one asked him about personal matters, and he offered them little insight into that side of his life. Only his last clerk, Joe Rauh, got up enough nerve, when asked to stay a second year, to ask Cardozo to call him by his first name instead of Rauh or Mr. Rauh. Cardozo complied, yet it was hard for him to break the habit. After Rauh had agreed to stay a second year, Robert Jackson asked Rauh to work for him in the Solicitor General's office. That was one of the best jobs that a young lawyer could hope for. Jackson thought Cardozo would not want Rauh to turn it down. Rauh felt caught between the Solicitor General, who was "close to God," and the Supreme Court Justice, "who was God."[29] He mentioned the job offer "gingerly" to Cardozo, who made it clear instantly that he didn't want to change clerks. That response ended the discussion. Cardozo understood the importance of the opportunity offered by Jackson, but he had a prior commitment from Rauh and felt entitled to hold him to it.

Cardozo socialized a bit with his present and former clerks and secretaries. He had them to dinner once or twice a year, and they in turn usually invited him to dinner at their homes. The clerks also took him to theater on occasion. The first such episode was a disaster. Mel Siegel and Herbert Wechsler, a Stone clerk, took Cardozo to Noel Coward's *Design for Living* to see what his reaction would be. The play featured adulterous living arrangements. Cardozo was uncomfortable throughout, although he made light comments about the play during the intermission. He thought it probably would not have been banned in New York, even though many would have liked to ban it. When Wechsler arrived at Cardozo's apartment the next day for Sunday tea, Miss Tracy was furious with him for having taken the Justice to such a play. Cardozo reciprocated the invitation by taking them to Marc Connelly's *Green Pastures,* a Pulitzer Prize–winning version of biblical stories done in the fashion of a Negro spiritual. He enjoyed that play a great deal.[30] The Noel Coward story must have been passed along to subsequent law clerks because they restricted themselves to inviting Cardozo to performances of Gilbert and Sullivan.

Working so closely with Cardozo, his law clerks felt the force of his personality and character. Mel Siegel saw him as "not only a great jurist," but as "physically beautiful. Looked like a saint, acted like a saint, and really was a saint. And who was so utterly removed and gentle that everybody . . . would have felt . . . you should protect this fragile little angel . . . [who had] great strength of character of course."[31] Ambrose Doskow, his second clerk, was more balanced: "Cardozo had a saintly quality to him in that he didn't like to hurt people and was very gentle and very considerate. But he had his opinions of people too and sometimes spoke out; for example, he was often quite critical and openly so of some of the lawyers who argued before the Court."[32] Learned Hand put more strongly the sense that Cardozo's gentle appearance masked strong views. Hand commented that "very few have ever known what went on behind those blue eyes."[33] Joe Rauh, Cardozo's last law clerk, shared Siegel's view: "[A]t that time I thought he was a saint, and came as close to being a saint as I would ever in my lifetime meet."[34]

Alan Stroock had a different perspective from the other law clerks. Although not a Sephardic Jew, he came from the same social background in New York as Cardozo and had a long family connection with him. Stroock's father and uncle were professional and personal friends of Cardozo; Stroock's wife, Katherine, was related to many members of the Nathan family. Familiarity allowed room for some criticism. Stroock perceived Cardozo's "extraordinary self-esteem" and "sensitiveness to adverse comments or to any lack of respect from others" as significant characteristics. When asked about "saintliness," Stroock replied, "Not at all. He was a very vain and in some ways intolerant man." Stroock remembered that Cardozo did not like jokes about himself; that he spent a good deal of time combing his hair to achieve an effect; and that even though he liked to seem simple and frugal, he always made sure to have "the right wine" on the table for guests.[35] Although Stroock overemphasized Cardozo's foibles, he recognized the elitist strain and sense of entitlement. But like the other clerks, Stroock's overall assessment was strongly positive. He considered his clerkship years as an "extraordinary experience" with a "brilliant, wise, cultured, and gracious . . . human being. In both law and manners, he was the greatest teacher I have ever known."[36] Cardozo derived a good deal of pleasure from his daily contact with his law clerks and secretaries. It was not the same as the close life he had shared with his colleagues in Albany; still, it was an unexpected pleasure, and it provided some warmth in the cold atmosphere of the Supreme Court.

———

Cardozo's social life also changed when he moved to Washington. In New York, his cousins and their adult children had made it a point to keep in regular touch after Nellie died. There had also been lunches with friends at the Century Club, regular meetings of the Philosophers and the Round Table, lecturing and informal talks at professional meetings, and other professional and extrajudicial activities that took up a good deal of time. Although Cardozo may have welcomed the opportunity to eliminate some of his extrajudicial activities when he went to Washington, he missed the frequent contact with family and friends, especially the exciting talk and ideas of people like Charles C. Burlingham, Felix Frankfurter, and Learned Hand. Even though they got to Washington once in a while and occasionally corresponded, he lost the pleasure of more frequent meetings. "I long for the sight of you" is a familiar refrain in Cardozo's letters to good friends during his Washington years.

Cardozo continued to refer to Washington as his place of "exile," but his life there, even though lonely, was not empty of social contact. People sought him out, and there were many visitors to 2101 Connecticut Avenue. Irving and Sissie Lehman, Charles Burlingham, and Learned Hand, as well as family members Henry and Rosalie Hendricks, Michael Cardozo (IV), and Sidney and Eva Cardozo, came from New York. There were some new friends, too. He got to know the diplomat Robert Woods Bliss and Mildred Bliss, who were collectors of pre-Columbian art and were prominent in the Washington scene. They traded dinners with Cardozo and occasionally took him to an evening concert. He would go to their house "when he would go to no other."[37]

Cardozo was willing to spend time with many other people whom his friends regarded as dull. He once confided to Joe Rauh that he found certain guests, whom he saw almost more than anyone else in Washington, "boring."[38] It may be that he enjoyed having company and so was willing to put up with some friends who were not scintillating. He noted in his commonplace books a passage from Galsworthy's *Forsyte Saga* concerning Mrs. Septimus Small, who loved to drone on for hours about the blows that she had endured from fortune. She did not ever perceive "that her hearers sympathized with Fortune, for her heart was kind."[39] Cardozo knew boring people like Mrs. Small; he spent time with those whom he liked and treated them with respect. He was lonely, and his heart was kind.

Cardozo also became friendly with Jane Perry Clark, professor of political science at Barnard. She was the daughter of a New York colleague, John C. Clark, who had been a New York Supreme Court Justice. Professor Clark, who was interested in the Supreme Court professionally, saw Cardozo several times a year. They corresponded often—but not about the work of the Supreme Court—and Cardozo progressed from "Miss Clark" to "Jane" in his salutations. Other new friends were Ben Cohen and Tom Corcoran, two young lawyers who were deeply involved in bill-drafting, speech-writing, and political work for Franklin

Roosevelt.[40] A favorite visitor was Robert Marshall, son of Louis Marshall and an important figure in the American conservation movement before his early death. Marshall, who was then in the Bureau of Indian Affairs, spent much of his time tramping all over Alaska. Cardozo greatly enjoyed the tales with which Marshall regaled him. On one visit, responding to a joking challenge from Miss Tracy, Marshall did a somersault in the doorway. Cardozo, who came out of his office at just that moment, loved it.[41]

Cardozo's letters made it perfectly clear that the life he looked forward to was his life in the country during the summer vacations of the Court. Sissie Lehman found places for him to rent every summer in Rye or White Plains, New York. Often he would go out to lunch or dinner, and he would have friends over for meals on a regular basis. He saw a great deal of the Lehmans, Edgar Nathan's widow Sallie, and their children, Emily Nathan and Rosalie Nathan Hendricks and her husband Henry. In addition, he spent a fair amount of his summertime with the Goldstones, the Hirschs, C. C. Burlingham, Learned Hand, Eugene Meyer, publisher of the *Washington Post,* Irwin Edman, the philosopher, his former law clerks, many relatives, and a wide variety of other people. During one summer, Albert Einstein was staying at the Lehmans, and Cardozo had many lunches and dinners with him.

Cardozo would see almost anyone. One summer day he returned from the barber shop to find that a man who appeared to be insane had visited and promised to return. Cardozo rejected the notion that the police should be called, telling Harry Hayes, "I'll talk to any man, even a crazy man." When the man returned, Cardozo saw him alone in his library. Hayes stood by the door, but after a half-hour's conversation, the man left peacefully.[42]

The long summer months from late May or early June until the end of September were a real vacation. Cardozo socialized, read, and rested under the watchful eye of Kate Tracy. He even went to the movies occasionally, usually to see light fare like the Marx Brothers films. Every once in a while he went to New York City to meet friends at the Century Club, to do some shopping, and to see the tailor who made his suits.[43] On June 27, he would visit the Shearith Israel cemetery in Cypress Hills, Long Island, on the anniversary of Nellie's "blessed birthday."[44] His correspondence was filled with joy at his escape from Washington. Only a constant stream of certiorari petitions and an occasional need to deal with an emergency request impinged upon his free time.

During the 1934 term, he had been ill occasionally and was exhausted at the end of the term. A visitor to the Court reported that Cardozo barely got through delivering several opinions in late April 1935. "His eyes began to twitch so violently that his glasses fell off and it was only by putting his finger over one eye that he was able to continue."[45] When he arrived in Rye for his summer vacation in June 1935, his doctors put him to bed for two weeks. After he had a number of heart spasms and a severe attack on June 27, a day and a night nurse were brought in to care for him. He was allowed to move around a bit by the middle of July, but he overdid it and was sent back to bed again at the beginning of August for ten days. By the end of September, however, new medicine had quieted his spasms, so that he was ready to return to work. He was not, however, prepared to follow doctors' orders. "I have been cautioned to moderate my pace, but you know that is an impossibility for me." He treated his problem by taking his glycerine pills not only whenever he had a pain but also preventively, with the result that his doctors thought he was overdosing himself.[46]

But he managed the work of the next two terms well and thus could spend the summer vacations of 1936 and 1937 as he had prior to his heart attack of 1935. In 1937, after a turbulent session that saw the excitement of the Court-packing plan and the Court's veering in a new constitutional direction, he even ventured to Cape Cod to spend ten days with the Irving Lehmans in a cottage that they had rented there.[47] During that summer, he cut a cherished tie to New York by selling his Manhattan house at 16 West 75th Street. The house and land were assessed for $41,000, but real estate values were still depressed. Cardozo sold the house for only $17,000, taking back a $12,500 mortgage. He regarded the price as "little more than a gift."[48] He returned on September 28 to what he now called the "concentration camp" for his final few months of active participation in the work of the Court.[49]

During his six years in Washington, Cardozo had a strong interest in events outside the courtroom. He read the *New York Times* and the *Washington Post* the first thing every day. When he joined the Court in 1932, the country was in economic turmoil, and political change was in the air. An exciting political campaign swept Hoover out of office and brought Franklin Roosevelt and the New Deal to Washington. Cardozo had had official dealings with Franklin Roosevelt in New York when he was chief judge and Roosevelt was governor; however, he was not excited when the Democrats made Roosevelt their presidential candidate in 1932. He confided to Learned Hand that the "nomination of F.D.R. leaves me cold, though I like him personally."[50] Having moved to Washington, Cardozo could not vote in that election. As he wrote to C. C. Burlingham, "It is a glorious thing to be disfranchised as I have been by moving to Washington. I can look Hoover and Franklin D. squarely in the eye and not flinch with the thought that I have betrayed either one of them."[51] Although it is difficult to imagine that he would have abandoned the Democratic Party during the depression election of 1932, he certainly was not beating the same drum against Hoover that he had done in 1928. Perhaps gratitude for his appointment dampened some of those feelings; perhaps also his own selection made him feel guilty about his statements that Republicans did not nominate Jews to positions of importance.

Cardozo quickly changed his mind about Roosevelt as president. At Roosevelt's request, he swore in the cabinet. Just two days after the inauguration, he wrote to C. C. Burlingham that "Franklin D. made a stirring speech, and I think is taking hold in fine shape. He seems ready to do things, and announces his purpose with a set jaw and a mighty voice which Hoover never could attain."[52] Even though he later wondered whether Roosevelt was moving things too fast and commented that he wanted to keep the wealth that he had, he also expressed the opinion, quite in contrast to his anti-Socialist talk at his own college graduation, that if he were a young man in 1932, he'd be a Socialist.[53] Cardozo did not see much of Roosevelt in Washington except on formal occasions. However, when Cuthbert Pound, Cardozo's friend and successor as chief judge of the Court of Appeals, died suddenly, Roosevelt telephoned to give Cardozo the bad news and to console him. In 1938, when Cardozo had suffered the first round of illness that would later prove fatal, Roosevelt wrote to invite him to tea or dinner at the White House, commenting that he had thought it unwise to do so while the court-packing fight had been going on.[54]

When he was appointed to the Court, Cardozo had resigned his connections with Jewish organizations, but both the times and specific incidents forced him to deal with anti-Semitism and his role as a Jewish judge. In 1935, a group of demonstrators boarded the German liner *Bremen* and tore down a Nazi flag. A fight ensued, and one of the demonstrators struck a policeman with brass knuckles. Magistrate Louis

Brodsky created an international uproar when he dismissed the charge of unlawful assembly against five defendants, binding over for grand jury action only the defendant who had hit the policeman. Concluding that there had been no proof of unlawful assembly, he wrote an inflammatory opinion in which he set forth what might have been in the minds of the defendants in seeking to tear down the Nazi flag. Brodsky wrote that they might have viewed the flag as emblematic of all the acts, which he listed, of the Nazi regime's destroying human freedom.[55] Aline Goldstone sent Cardozo a newspaper clipping about the incident and apparently commented favorably on Brodsky's action. Cardozo responded sharply, "I am disappointed that you and Maud [doubtless his cousin Maud Nathan] approve of Brodsky and his shameful utterance. What is the use of striving for standards of judicial propriety if you and she condone such lapses! It would have been bad enough if he had been a Gentile; but for a Jew it was unforgivable. Now our traducers will say—and with some right if such as you and Maud approve—that these are the standards of the race. Never mind; you're a great poet anyhow."[56] That put-down to a good friend, especially the double-edged final sentence, was unusually sharp for Cardozo. He clearly believed that Brodsky had failed to give the German ship the protection that it was owed under our law and that he had done so because of his own political views. Cardozo viewed the matter all the more seriously because Brodsky was a Jew whose performance cast Jews, particularly Jewish judges, in a bad light.

Cardozo's jurisprudential point was that Brodsky had no business letting his own personal views as a Jew affect his judicial judgment. This was not one of those situations in which the judge was called upon or entitled to be creative, a situation when judicial lawmaking was appropriate. The law, in Cardozo's view, was clear, and the German shipowners were entitled to its protection irrespective of the judge's personal reaction to Nazism.

Cardozo expressed his own antagonism to Nazism in a letter to Felix Frankfurter shortly after the Brodsky incident: "[T]here are few, even among the intellectuals that are burning with indignation about [Hitler's] treatment of the Jews. They deprecate such narrowness; they would put an end to the persecution if they could do so with a word; but they do not lie awake at night about it. I found a man the other day who said it made him sleepless. But there are not many of his type. We need another Garrison who will cry out unceasingly until all the world shall hear."[57]

Although Cardozo's notions of judicial propriety or perhaps his own lack of a crusading spirit kept him from public action in attacking Adolph Hitler's policies, he did join a number of Jewish judges in 1933 in asking President Roosevelt to change government policy so that refugees from Nazi Germany could more easily be admitted to the United States.[58]

When anti-Semitism struck closer to home, Cardozo was ready to take a stand. His law clerk, Alan Stroock, signed an agreement to purchase a home in Spring Valley, in the northwest section of the District of Columbia. When the real estate agent later told Stroock that the agreement violated a restrictive covenant against Jews, Stroock cancelled it. Cardozo was outraged. He asked whether the agent knew that Stroock was his law clerk. When Stroock replied affirmatively, Cardozo became even more angry, taking the incident as a personal attack. He encouraged Stroock to bring a lawsuit, saying that he would issue a public statement of support. Cardozo's resolve was not tested because Stroock did nothing. The passionate response that Stroock described was uncharacteristic because Cardozo the judge sought to avoid both controversy and the public eye, but it was reminiscent of his combativeness as a practicing lawyer.[59]

Yet Cardozo did not react strongly to a letter from Learned Hand praising conditions in Fascist Italy. While traveling in Benito Mussolini's Italy, Hand had written a racy letter about wonderful restaurants and exciting people. He also praised what Mussolini had done for Italy, including the cliché about making the trains run on time, while muting his disapproval of some of Mussolini's methods. Cardozo showed this letter to Joe Rauh, who expressed surprise about the references to Mussolini. Cardozo simply passed the issue off in a "light vein."[60] The restrictive covenant had involved Cardozo's identity as a Jew, whereas Mussolini's activity did not. Moreover, Cardozo generally avoided criticizing his friends, especially to others, and his lack of reaction to Hand's letter may only reflect that pattern of behavior.

One issue that Cardozo did not pass off was the love affair between King Edward VIII and Wallis Simpson in 1936. He was absolutely consumed by it. He read every newspaper article and even listened to the news on the radio to keep up with the most recent events, which was not something he did regularly. Initially, he sided with Edward VIII. This was not the Cardozo who stuck with ancient traditions and voted to keep separate seating for men and women in his synagogue. Whatever romantic vein was within him prevailed over his respect for ancient rules about monarchy and divorce. The Court heard argument the day that the King abdicated. At the end of argument, Cardozo rushed home to turn on the radio. He, Kate Tracy, Joe Rauh, and Chris Sargent pulled chairs out into the hallway, where the radio was, and Cardozo listened spellbound to the King's address. A month later, however, when the subject came up at lunch, Cardozo reportedly said that Edward's highest duty was to his country and that that duty should not have been relinquished. When Miss Tracy suggested that Edward could have followed a royal tradition by making Mrs. Simpson his mistress, Cardozo disagreed. His respect for duty and family proprieties prevailed over his first impulsive reaction.[61]

Cardozo shared his absorption in that event with his household. In former days, he would have shared it with Nellie and his New York friends. His move to Washington cost him most of the New York relationships that had given him a life outside his work. When he moved, he managed to cobble together a form of social life, especially in the summer, that gave him a human existence. But Cardozo was a lonely man, and the center of his life in Washington was his judicial work.

25

State Regulatory Power and the Constitution

Cardozo had a short career of just five and a half years on the Supreme Court, but it came during a tumultuous struggle between the majority of the Supreme Court on the one hand and the state governments, Congress, and President Roosevelt on the other. The big issue was the constitutionality of legislation enacted to meet the economic and social problems of the Depression of the 1930s. The Supreme Court invalidated many important federal and state laws regulating the economy, such as legislation governing the wages and hours of workers, usually with Justices Harlan Stone, Louis Brandeis, Benjamin Cardozo, and sometimes Chief Justice Charles Evans Hughes, dissenting. Finally in 1937, the Court reversed direction, with a new majority accepting the constitutional standard of greater deference to the economic and social power of government that had been outlined by the former dissenters.

Cardozo was an important participant in the constitutional drama that accompanied the political drama. The struggle to create the welfare state, initiated during the Progressive Era and expanded greatly by the New Deal, changed the constitutional law map enormously. A vast increase in the power of the national government, both absolutely and relative to the states, was legitimated. Administrative power, especially federal administrative power, achieved constitutionally protected status, with extraordinary consequences for our system of checks and balances.[1]

Cardozo's contribution to the change is the subject of the following chapters.

————

Cardozo joined a court that saw itself, and was perceived by the public generally, as divided into conservatives or reactionaries and liberals, progressives, or radicals, depending on who was doing the classifying. The major issue dividing the justices was the extent of the government's power to regulate the economy—and the justices were sharply split. Justices Willis Van Devanter, George Sutherland, Pierce Butler, and James McReynolds sought to restrain new forms of governmental intervention in the economy. They adhered to the strict scrutiny of governmental regulation that was exemplified in the majority position in Lochner v. New York, which in 1905 struck down New York's maximum working hours legislation in the baking industry.[2] The justices examined with suspicion both the goals and the particular means of governmental action, using all available constitutional provisions—the Contract Clause, the Due Process and Equal Protection Clauses of the Fourteenth Amendment, the Commerce Clause, separation of powers notions, and the Tenth Amendment—to preserve the constitutional universe of limited government that they had inherited.

Justices Brandeis and Stone were much readier to accept government regulation, both as to ultimate ends and as to means selected. Chief Justice Hughes and Justice Owen Roberts were poised between the two groups. Hughes often voted with Brandeis and Stone, but Roberts was completely unpredictable. The Cardozo appointment was therefore critical. A fifth vote for the conservative bloc would have given it a consistent majority. That knowledge colored Van Devanter's reaction. "His decisions do not commend him to me," he wrote to his sister shortly after Cardozo's appointment. He was also familiar with Cardozo's recent talk on "Jurisprudence" to the New York State Bar Association. It confirmed Van Devanter's fears: "I think the address stamps him as unstable and as wishing to depart from old landmarks and take up with new and uncertain experiments."[3] Ironically, Van Devanter had decided in 1932 that he was going to retire following the November election, whatever the outcome, but then Congress passed a statute limiting the retirement pay of judges to $10,000 per year. Since that amount would have cut Van Devanter's retirement pay in half, he decided to stay on.[4] Had he carried through with his original intention, a Roosevelt appointment in

1933 would probably have changed the result in a great many important cases and would have avoided the struggle over the role of the Supreme Court that marked the whole of Cardozo's service on the Court.

Cardozo believed, accurately, that he made his major contribution to American law during his years on the New York Court of Appeals. Early in his Supreme Court career, discouraged by the "minor importance" of most of his opinions, he wrote that in Albany he "did really accomplish something there that gave a new direction to the law," but a judge of this court "must be satisfied" if "he accomplishes something by his vote."[5] As the junior justice on the Supreme Court during almost the whole period of his service, he was not often assigned a major opinion, even when he was in the majority. Thus, the subject matter of many of his majority opinions involved specialized questions of taxation or bankruptcy law or even common law issues much like those that he had faced on the Court of Appeals.[6]

Nevertheless, Cardozo's Supreme Court opinions are important for two reasons. First, he wrote several important constitutional law opinions, both for a majority and in dissent, and two of his most important opinions, though unpublished, substantially influenced the majority opinion. Although he followed a pattern of constitutional results laid out previously by Holmes, Brandeis, and Stone, he made some particular additions of his own to the development of twentieth-century constitutional thought. Second, his Supreme Court opinions add a dimension to his earlier work. Cardozo had a unified theory of judging that subsumed constitutional law questions within the general framework of decision-making that he had outlined in *The Nature of the Judicial Process.* Cardozo had named the field of constitutional interpretation as one in which the "primacy" of the method of sociology—public policy—was "undoubted."[7] Yet his Supreme Court opinions demonstrated that for him, constitutional law decisions were not determined only by public policy considerations. The other factors in decision-making exerted substantial power here as they had in his major Court of Appeals opinions. Finally, as Cardozo realized himself, his service was important simply because at this critical time, his vote was important.

In cases dealing with governmental regulatory power, Cardozo's Supreme Court opinions followed the general pattern of his Court of Appeals opinions. He began from the proposition that constitutional provisions granting power to government should be interpreted sympathetically to permit it to respond to the enormous economic problems that were threatening the social fabric. He therefore voted, often in dissent, to uphold most, but not all, state economic legislation and most major pieces of the New Deal program. He rejected a rigid adherence to precedents that crippled the power of the government to govern; moreover, it made no difference whether they were precedents applying the precisely worded Contract Clause or the broadly worded Fourteenth Amendment.

Cardozo's use of the common law method, including the analysis of each case in the context of its precise facts, the problems faced by the legislature, and the means chosen to resolve them, produced a familiar pattern of results. Just as the cases that arrived in the Court of Appeals so often produced pairs in which Cardozo first announced an expanded principle and then showed its limitations, so too in the Supreme Court a great many cases announcing generous principles of legislative power were balanced by opinions showing its limits.

After Cardozo's first conference, his new colleague Willis Van Devanter noted that Cardozo was "well educated, very pleasant and modest in his demeanor," but he was quick to perceive gloomily that "[h]is general attitude is in full keeping with what I had anticipated."[8] On the Court of Appeals, Cardozo had contributed to a reversal of position that expanded substantially the court's acceptance of the regulatory efforts of the legislature and executive. From the outset, Van Devanter believed that Cardozo shared the sympathetic attitude of Brandeis and Stone toward government. Van Devanter's assumption was largely confirmed by Cardozo's position in Coombes v. Getz, which was argued on March 21, 1932, one week after Cardozo joined the Court.

Coombes was the subject of Cardozo's first Supreme Court opinion, a dissent.[9] A provision of the California Constitution imposed liability on directors of corporations to creditors for monies embezzled by an officer of the corporation. A creditor sued a director for its debt, alleging that the conditions of liability had been met. He lost at trial, and while the case was on appeal to the California Supreme Court, California repealed the constitutional provision by a referendum, which was the equivalent of the exercise of legislative power. The California Supreme Court then dismissed the creditor's appeal because the provision on which the suit was based had been repealed. The issue was whether this exercise of legislative and judicial power could constitutionally extinguish the creditor's property right. Justice Sutherland for a six-judge majority held that the repeal violated the Contract Clause and the Due

Process Clause, although the latter had not been invoked. The constitutional provision imposing liability was part of the creditor's contract with the corporation. Although the California Constitution had reserved the power to amend corporate charters, California could not apply that provision to rights, such as these, that had vested as a matter of federal constitutional law.

Cardozo, joined by Brandeis and Stone, drew on his common law experience to argue that calling the director's liability contractual was fictitious. The liability of the corporation to the creditor was contractual, but the liability of the directors arose from the provision of California's Constitution. Cardozo concluded that the creditor's cause of action against the directors evaporated because the California courts had already held that that sort of liability could be extinguished at any time before it ripened into a judgment. "Either the petitioner took his cause of action subject to such infirmities . . . as were attached to it by the law of the State . . . or he did not take anything."[10] Felix Frankfurter wrote to Cardozo after *Coombes* to congratulate him on the "hard sense" of his opinion and to comment about the grip that "formula and formalism" had on even able judges.[11] But of course Cardozo's description of the creditor's cause of action was "formalistic" too. The real issue was how to accommodate, as a policy matter, the constitutional right conferred by California on the creditor with California's power to take it away. The issue would come to a head two years later in the much more important *Minnesota Mortgage Moratorium* case. It is apparent that Van Devanter was distressed both by Cardozo's less-than-reverential attitude toward the absoluteness of private property rights and by his sympathy for the law-making power that had been exercised by the voters in the referendum.

Cardozo addressed the constitutional standards to be applied to economic legislation in several cases early in his Supreme Court career. He differed sharply with the close analysis of state and federal tax statutes given by the majority of his colleagues under the provision of the Fourteenth Amendment forbidding states to deny to any person the "equal protection of the laws." The majority had held in many instances that various tax statutes were unconstitutional because they classified businesses in a discriminatory fashion. Cardozo thought that the legislatures had the power and the responsibility to weigh the competing economic and political considerations that led them to create different levels of taxation, with the judiciary playing the limited role of ascertaining that a plausible balance had been struck.

His major opinion on this issue was written in Louis K. Liggett Company v. Lee in 1933.[12] The case involved the constitutionality of Florida's chain store tax, which imposed a licensing tax on the operation of most retail stores. The tax on each store increased with the number of stores operated and even more if the operations were conducted in more than one county. Justice Roberts wrote for a six-judge majority in holding that the statute was an infringement of the equal protection of the laws. In the majority's view, the statute discriminated against chain stores because there was no reasonable ground for increasing the per-store tax on the basis of the number of counties in which the business operated.

Justice Brandeis used his dissent to make a major statement of his economic as well as his constitutional philosophy.[13] Since the plaintiffs were all corporations, he focused on the legislation's effect on them. Referring to the giant corporation as a "Frankenstein monster," he saw no constitutional requirement that governmental charges for doing business in the corporate form must be reasonable.[14] Moreover, receiving permission to do business in more than one county was a privilege that justified a higher charge. Finally, Brandeis delivered an economics treatise on the chain store, especially the giant chain store, and justified the tax as socially and economically desirable to preserve the competition of independent stores with chain stores or even to eliminate chain stores. In short, Brandeis publicly approved the wisdom of the tax.

Cardozo did not join Brandeis's opinion. He prepared a dissent along more conventional lines. His initial draft relied heavily on the fact that the county was the historical unit of government in the South. Further research by Melvin Siegel, his law clerk, disclosed that chain stores were often classified as local, sectional, or national, and that the transition from local to either sectional or national tended to come when the chain store crossed the county line:[15] "The question is how it [a business] *does* develop in normal or average conditions, and the answer to that question is to be found in life and history. When the problem is thus approached, the movement from one county to another becomes in a very definite sense the crossing of a frontier, a change as marked as the difference between wholesale trade and retail . . . So at least the Legislature might not unreasonably believe, and act on that belief in the formulation of the law."[16] Whether the differential tax was a good thing or not, Cardozo emphasized that the tax was within the legislature's discretion because there was a reasonable basis for it. That basis was grounded in "life and history," which were motifs in many Cardozo opinions.

Having formulated a rational basis for the Florida statute, Cardozo believed that his function as judge was ended. He would not follow the Brandeis course. Not that he disregarded the purpose of the statute. But instead of applauding it with moral fervor, as Brandeis had done, Cardozo viewed the statutory purpose neutrally. A statute that differentiated levels of taxation on the basis of a legislative weighing of the social utility of one business organization against another corresponded to an intelligible, widely prevalent belief "among honest men and women," those ideal persons whose judgment was a source for decision in the common law setting.[17] That was enough.

Cardozo's approach was quite different from the Brandeis dissent, which set forth Brandeis's personal, social, and economic views in a powerful opinion that Professor Paul Freund described as a "labor of love."[18] Cardozo's view of Brandeis's opinion was ambivalent. On the one hand, he stated that the opinion would be "referred to again and again in the years to come by forward-looking students of the law," and would be "a source of inspiration and enlightenment." On the other, he thought that it was "not an opinion that one should 'swallow whole,' so to speak, without making it one's very own by deep inspection. It should represent one's innermost and profound convictions." Clearly, Brandeis's opinion did not represent Cardozo's profound convictions, and he therefore would not join it. "To have concurred in it airily would have been a profanation as well as a blunder."[19] Cardozo concluded his dissent with a veiled criticism of Brandeis for indulging in personal advocacy: "Holding these views, I find it unnecessary to consider whether the statute may be upheld for the additional reasons that have been stated by Mr. Justice Brandeis with such a wealth of learning. They present considerations that were not laid before us by counsel either in the briefs or in the oral argument, and a determination of their validity and weight may be reserved with propriety until the necessity emerges."[20] Cardozo's vote showed his support for legislative regulatory power; the nature of his argument showed his restrained sense of the judge's role.

Cardozo later wrote an opinion for a bare majority of the Court in Fox v. Standard Oil Company of New Jersey that upheld a West Virginia chain store licensing tax that was progressive on the basis of the number of outlets.[21] A three-judge district court first decided that gas stations were not "stores" under the statute but that even if they were, it found a violation of equal protection in the tax's harsher application to gas station chains that operated a large number of small volume outlets as compared with the smaller number of high volume stores operated, say, by food store chains.

Cardozo viewed prior law, including Liggett v. Lee, as justifying the conclusion that the commercial advantages of chain store operation made it permissible to tax them differently from stores separately owned. The rates were neither arbitrary nor oppressive. Cardozo refused to require a greater precision in the operation of a legislative rule than in the operation of a judge-made common law rule. "The operation of a general rule will seldom be the same for every one. If the accidents of trade lead to inequality or hardship, the consequences must be accepted as inherent in government by law instead of government by edict."[22] That insight was critical in Cardozo's idea of lawmaking.

Cardozo's approach to statutory interpretation in Fox is also interesting. He reviewed a number of interpretive aids to help decide whether a gas station was a "store" under the statute. He rejected the argument that popular understanding was relevant in this case. The legislature, which had decided to define the term itself, included all establishments in which "goods, wares, or merchandise of any kind, are sold." Gas stations fit within that definition. Another circumstance, "not conclusive" in itself but a "circumstance to be weighed," was that an amendment to except gas stations from the definition of stores had been rejected. Finally, the contemporaneous interpretation of the Tax Commissioner, the agent charged with enforcement, to which "respectful consideration" was owed, included gas stations. The deference given to the vote of the legislature on the amendment and the interpretation of the administrator are probably more controversial today than they were in 1935, but Cardozo was eager to look for help in interpreting a statute from whatever sources gave light.[23]

Cardozo was quite consistent in this area, and he wrote and joined opinions that upheld many different kinds of tax statutes against a variety of claims. Thus, he wrote a dissent from the holding in Steward Dry Goods v. Lewis that a progressive gross sales tax violated the Equal Protection Clause.[24] In Cardozo's view, it was rational for the legislature to believe, as so many businesses believed, that the capacity to pay generally increased with the volume of receipts. Cardozo also dissented from the Court's decision in United States v. Constantine to strike down a federal statute that made it unlawful to conduct a liquor business in violation of state law without paying a federal excise tax aimed exclusively at illegal liquor businesses.[25] The majority held that the Tenth Amendment, which reserved to the states and people all powers not delegated to the federal government, forbade the federal government from enacting a statute whose purpose was to punish violation of state law. Cardozo saw the majority's attribution of a hidden motive to Congress as inappropriate. "Thus the process of psychoanalysis has spread to unaccustomed fields." He relied on the "wise and ancient doctrine" of statutory construction that courts do not inquire into the motives of legislatures and do not find unconstitutionality unless manifestly necessary.[26] The tax should be upheld as based on a rational belief that an illegal business was likely to have larger profits than a legal business would have. So long as the statute could be justified as based on the exercise of a legitimate constitutional power, the Court should not entertain a claim that Congress had an illegitimate reason for enacting the legislation.

––––––––

When the issue moved from taxation to a state's power to regulate, Cardozo was part of a 5–4 majority in the first part of his Supreme Court career that often found that constitutional restrictions did not prevent states from dealing with the enormous economic problems created by the Depression. The two major cases, both decided in 1934, were Home Building & Loan Association v. Blaisdell (the Minnesota Mortgage Moratorium case) and Nebbia v. New York.[27] In *Blaisdell,* Minnesota had passed emergency legislation that was designed to stem a flood of real estate foreclosures and dispossessions. It permitted a court to extend the time in which a property owner could redeem property from a foreclosure. A delinquent owner was required to pay a reasonable rental value to the holder of the mortgage during the delay, and the mortgagee's debt and right to an eventual deficiency judgment remained unimpaired. When the statute was upheld by the Minnesota Supreme Court, the losing mortgagee appealed to the Supreme Court.

The major constitutional argument was that the statute violated the

Contract Clause, the provision in Article 1, Section 10, of the Constitution prohibiting a state from "impairing the Obligation of Contracts." The case was hotly debated by the justices in their conference. Van Devanter took the lead for the opponents of the statute and spoke for an hour.[28] At the end of the debate, the justices voted 5–4 to uphold the statute. Although half of Cardozo's personal investments were in real estate mortgages, and statutes like the Minnesota law made life harder for mortgagees like himself, Cardozo voted with Chief Justice Hughes, Brandeis, Stone, and Roberts to uphold the statute.

Chief Justice Hughes assigned the majority opinion to himself. The crucial part of his draft opinion distinguished between statutes that impaired a mortgagee's substantive rights under its contract and those that, as here, merely impaired the remedy. Both Cardozo and Stone were distressed at what they regarded as Hughes's weak defense of the statute. Cardozo prepared a draft concurring opinion, and Stone wrote a long memorandum concerning his views.[29] Cardozo's draft opinion addressed the immediate issues of constitutional doctrine that divided the court, and it also discussed some major issues of constitutional theory. He wrote a little essay on the transformation of the meaning of constitutional provisions over time, using the Fourteenth Amendment to interpret the Contract Clause. Cardozo began by noting the vast change in the law relating to governmental power that had been accomplished by the Fourteenth Amendment:

> Upon the basis of that amendment a vast body of law unknown to the fathers has been developed and expounded by the judges of the nation. The economic and social changes wrought by the industrial revolution and by the growth of population have made it necessary for government at this day to do a thousand things that were beyond the experience or the thought of a century ago. With the growing recognition of this need, courts have awakened to the truth that the contract clause is perverted from its proper meaning when it throttles the capacity of the states to exert their governmental power to deal with matters which are basically the concern of government . . . A gospel of *laissez-faire*—of individual initiative—of thrift and industry and sacrifice—may be inadequate in the great society that we live in to point the way to salvation, at least for economic life. The state when it acts today by statutes like the one before us is not furthering the selfish good of individuals or classes as ends of ultimate validity. It is furthering its own good by maintaining

the economic structure on which the good of all depends. Such at least is its endeavor, however much it miss the mark.[30]

This was as close as Cardozo ever came in an opinion to setting forth his personal support for the welfare state. His language went far beyond support for the Minnesota statute that delayed creditors' foreclosure rights. Perhaps moved by the consequences of the Depression, Cardozo now leaned in the direction of expressing the kind of sweeping opinion that he had forsworn earlier in his dissent in Liggett v. Lee. He addressed directly whether the words of the Contract Clause must be taken literally and noted that the Supreme Court had refused to do so from the beginning, drawing a distinction between permissible impairment of remedies and impermissible impairment of rights. But the real accommodation was between "private rights and public welfare," and the route to interpretation of the Contract Clause was found in the respect for legislative judgments about economic and social policy that Cardozo saw as the touchstone for interpreting the general language of the Fourteenth Amendment: "Contracts were still to be preserved. There was to be no arbitrary destruction of their binding force, nor any arbitrary impairment. There was to be no impairment, even though not arbitrary, except within the limits of fairness, of moderation, and of pressing or emergent need. But a promise exchanged between individuals was not to paralyze the state in its endeavor at times of direful crisis to keep its life-blood flowing."[31]

Cardozo's language foreshadowed future Contract Clause analysis. The focus was no longer to be solely on the effect of a statute on a particular contract between two parties. The effect was to be examined in the context of the statute's social need and fairness. Cardozo addressed explicitly the question whether the court was justified in interpreting a provision of the Constitution in a way different from what was understood in 1787. He acknowledged that his interpretation

> may be inconsistent with things that men said in 1787 when expounding to compatriots the newly written constitution. They did not see the changes in the relation between states and nation or in the play of social forces that lay hidden in the womb of time. It may be inconsistent with things that they believed or took for granted. Their beliefs to be significant must be adjusted to the world they knew. It is not in my

judgment inconsistent with what they would say today, nor with what today they would believe, if they were called upon to interpret "in the light of our whole experience" the constitution that they framed for the needs of an expanding future.[32]

This was a forceful and candid justification for reinterpreting constitutional provisions in light of their purposes and in light of changing conditions in society. No justice of the Supreme Court had ever written anything like it in an opinion. It presaged the modern debate about the reinterpretation of constitutional provisions in light of changing conditions in society. That debate has focused on the open-ended Due Process and Equal Protection Clauses of the Fourteenth Amendment. Cardozo believed that continuing reinterpretation was necessary not only with respect to the Fourteenth Amendment but even with respect to the Contract Clause, despite its more specific language and its narrower historical focus. The terms of the Contract Clause did not invite creativity. That fact did not give Cardozo any pause at all. The world was a far different place in 1934 from what it had been in 1787. Constitutional interpretation simply had to take account of the difference. That was the reason Cardozo began his opinion by referring to John Marshall's classic statement that "We must never forget, that it is a *constitution* we are expounding . . . a constitution intended to endure for ages to come, and, consequently, to be adapted to the various *crises* of human affairs."[33]

Cardozo clearly continued to believe strongly in the creative judicial function. His unpublished *Blaisdell* opinion argued that the meaning of constitutional provisions could change as society changed, and he applied his view in the context of expanding governmental power at the expense of the property rights of creditors. If Cardozo had published his concurring opinion in *Blaisdell*, it would surely have been controversial. It would also have been much quoted by subsequent justices because it expressed so well a dominant theory of constitutional interpretation in the twentieth century. But the opinion, although influential within the Court, was not published. After Cardozo showed his draft to Chief Justice Hughes, Hughes incorporated much of Cardozo's theoretical argument into his own opinion, and Cardozo decided not to publish his concurring opinion.[34] The draft was nevertheless important in two respects. It induced Hughes to insert the substance of Cardozo's thought, albeit in summary fashion, into his majority opinion, and once it came to light, it gave posterity a clear statement of Cardozo's support for change in constitutional interpretation.

Cardozo's reading of the Contract Clause was not meant to read that clause out of the Constitution as a limit on state power. He spoke in his unpublished *Blaisdell* opinion about the requirement that the state observe "the limits of fairness, of moderation, and of pressing or emergent need." Cardozo believed that Arkansas had failed to do so when it exempted life insurance proceeds from seizure by creditors and applied its legislation retroactively to a lien that had been obtained prior to its passage. He therefore joined Chief Justice Hughes's opinion in W. B. Worthen Company v. Thomas, striking down the Arkansas statute.[35] The difference between the statutes, for those who had constituted the *Blaisdell* majority, was the absolute destruction of the creditor's property interest in *Thomas*.

Cardozo also wrote for a unanimous Court in W. B. Worthen Company v. Kavanaugh, a case that was similar to *Thomas*.[36] *Kavanaugh* involved the rights of holders of bonds issued by Arkansas Municipal Improvement Districts on the security of assessments levied against real property in the improvement districts. Earlier statutes, which had given the secured creditors substantial protection, required lot owners to pay assessments within thirty days. In the event of a default, there was a 20 percent penalty, local assessment commissioners were to institute foreclosure proceedings against defaulting lot owners at once, and costs and attorneys' fees were to be paid by the defaulter. There was to be prompt sale of foreclosed property, and the purchaser could obtain immediate possession. The lot owner could redeem the property within two or five years; the statute was unclear on the point. A new statutory scheme enlarged the payment period from thirty to ninety days, reduced the penalty to 3 percent, eliminated payment of costs and attorneys' fees, fixed the time for redemption at four years, and prevented a purchaser at a foreclosure sale from taking possession during the redemption period. The result of all the changes was to delay a foreclosure sale for at least two-and-a-half years and the right to possession an additional four years, during which time the creditor received nothing. The purpose was to give the lot owners considerably more time to pay their debts and keep their property in hard times.

There were defaults, and the bondholders sued to foreclose their security, the assessments on the lots of delinquent owners. The bondholders claimed that they were entitled to a decree based on the terms of the earlier statutes because the subsequent statute impaired the obligation of their contracts in violation of the Contract Clause. Cardozo looked at the facts of this case, and without stating any rule or stating whether any particular modification was crucial, he concluded that the totality of the changes took from "the mortgage the quality of an acceptable investment for a rational investor."[37] Just as Cardozo's view in *Blaisdell* was that the Contract Clause should not be read literally to deprive the state of power to deal with the problem of massive foreclosures during the Depression, his opinion in *Kavanaugh* made it clear that the earlier case was not a license for the state to destroy existing creditors' property rights.

Cardozo had tried many cases involving mortgage law during his years as a practicing lawyer. His professional experience and his personal investments in real estate mortgages gave him a sense, perhaps tinged by self-interest, of what amounted to a forbidden destruction of mortgagees' rights and what was a permissible regulation in the public interest. Although today his investments would raise an ethical issue regarding the propriety of his sitting in *Blaisdell* and the *Worthen* cases, they were not seen as raising such an issue then.

Cardozo's opinions in *Blaisdell* and *Kavanaugh* marked out instances where governmental interference with private mortgage contracts was permissible and where it was not, leaving to subsequent cases the task of delineating the area in between. That was a typical common law approach, and it was typical Cardozo. He made no effort to fashion general rules or guidelines at the beginning of what he assumed would be a period of accommodation. No accommodation has yet taken place; the Court extended the *Blaisdell* approach and let the *Kavanaugh* limitations lapse. Once analysis under the Contract Clause was assimilated to the Fourteenth Amendment approach, it followed the interpretation of the Fourteenth Amendment that became extremely deferential to legislative judgments about economic and social regulation.[38] But Cardozo sought a flexible approach that recognized both the need for government power and the need for constitutional limitation.

––––––––––

The major issue in the Supreme Court for the half century before Cardozo joined the Court was the restraining effect of the Fourteenth Amendment on state regulatory power. The battle to recognize substantial legislative power to regulate the economy and the conditions of labor, which had been won in the New York Court of Appeals during Cardozo's tenure, was still ongoing in the United States Supreme Court when Cardozo arrived. Cardozo's opinions in regulatory cases under the Fourteenth Amendment followed the pattern of generous, but not absolute, deference to legislative judgment that marked his Court of Appeals opinions and his Supreme Court opinions on state tax and Contract Clause issues. Shortly after *Blaisdell,* Cardozo joined Justice Roberts's important opinion for a five-judge majority in Nebbia v. New York. *Nebbia* upheld New York's milk control act, which established a board empowered to fix minimum retail selling prices.[39] Earlier Supreme Court cases had indicated that legislative price-fixing was permissible only in a restricted category of businesses "affected with the public interest." One such case in 1927 had nullified a New York Court of Appeals decision, in which Cardozo had joined, that upheld price-fixing of the sale of theater tickets by brokers.[40] The crucial part of Roberts's opinion in *Nebbia* adopted a realistic and broad definition of businesses affected with the public interest as including any business that was subject to control for the public good.

Cardozo wrote two opinions after *Nebbia* in which he expressed the view that the legislature and the milk control board were entitled to substantial discretion in the exercise of their power. In Hegeman Farms Corp. v. Baldwin, he rejected the claim of a dealer that the milk board's orders violated due process because the spread between the price paid to the farmer and the price collected from the customer was so small that the dealer was losing money. Cardozo, for a nearly unanimous court, found the complaint insufficient. It contained no charges demonstrating arbitrariness, no showing that the industry was about to perish. Perhaps the weaker dealers would be forced out of business; Cardozo's attitude toward them resembled the tough-minded attitude that he had exhibited in tort cases: "it is their comparative inefficiency, not tyrannical compulsion, that makes them laggards in the race."[41] In Cardozo's view, it was up to legislators and administrators, not judges, to decide the economic issues of the milk industry.

But another case under the New York Milk Control Act demonstrated that for the majority of the Court, close judicial scrutiny of the details of regulation was still the order of the day. Mayflower Farms, Inc. v. Ten Eyck considered a section of the New York Milk Control Act that, in effect, permitted milk dealers without well-advertised trade names to sell milk to stores in New York City at one cent per quart below the price fixed for dealers with well-advertised trade names if the former were already in business when the statute was passed.[42] Roberts and Hughes joined the *Nebbia* dissenters and struck down the statute under the Equal Protection Clause of the Fourteenth Amendment because it denied the lower price advantage to new dealers and effectively closed the milk business to them without any relation to public welfare.

Cardozo dissented on the ground that it was not arbitrary for the legislature to have struck a balance between maintaining the price differential that had grown up before passage of the Act and extending it to newcomers who had not invested anything in the milk business prior to the Act. He saw the majority's conclusion that the price advantage must be extended to all businesses that were not well advertised as essentially a judgment about the equities and policies of business regulation that was for the legislature and not for the judiciary to make.[43]

Perhaps the biggest struggle over state legislative power concerned state minimum wage legislation. The obstacle to such legislation was the case that had left Cardozo "speechless," the Supreme Court's 1923 decision in the *Adkins* case holding that a District of Columbia minimum wage law for women was unconstitutional.[44] The issue came before the Supreme Court again in 1936 in Morehead v. New York ex rel. Tipaldo, which involved a statute setting minimum wages for women employees.[45] The Court struck the statute down in a 5–4 decision. Justice Butler's majority opinion argued that New York had not asked that *Adkins* be overruled, and since it could not be distinguished, the New York statute fell. His opinion also contained language indicating support for the principles of *Adkins*. Hughes dissented, distinguishing *Adkins;* and Stone, writing for Cardozo and Brandeis as well, argued that *Adkins* should be overruled. The public reaction to the Court's decision was hostile, and even the Republican party adopted a plank at its national convention stating that such legislation was constitutional.[46] At the end of the term, Cardozo commented on the reaction in a letter to Stone: "I think we should be more than human if we failed to sit back in our chairs with a broad grin upon our faces as we watch the reaction to the minimum wage decision. Is it possible that both political parties hold the view that legislation condemned by the majority of our brethren as an arbitrary and capricious assault upon liberty is so necessary and beneficent that we cannot get along without it? Perish the thought!"[47]

During the following term the constitutionality of state minimum wage legislation for women and minors came up once again in West

Coast Hotel Company v. Parrish.[48] This time Roberts joined the four dissenters from *Morehead* to uphold the statute and overrule *Adkins* in an opinion by Hughes. Justice Roberts later claimed that he did not "switch" his vote in the Minimum Wage Cases and that he would have voted to overrule *Adkins* in *Morehead* if only the parties had asked the Court for an overruling. The accuracy of his claim has been quite controversial.[49] Whether Roberts was accurate or not, Cardozo and Stone did not understand that Roberts had been ready to overrule *Adkins*. After the decision, Cardozo told his friend Charles Burlingham that "nothing could separate O.J.R. et ces autres [and those others]" in *Morehead*.[50]

Parrish was one of a trilogy of 1937 cases—National Labor Relations Board v. Jones & Laughlin and the *Social Security Cases* were the other two—that put the Supreme Court firmly on the path of deference to state and federal legislative judgments (with the concurrence of the executive) about the need for, and the direction of, economic and social regulation. Cardozo's treatment of state legislative power in his Supreme Court career mirrored his Court of Appeals opinions—deference to the legislature's choice of goals and substantial deference to its choice of means, although he considered carefully whether the means went too far in destroying private property rights. What was new was Cardozo's explicit justification of continuous reinterpretation of the constitutional text, which he supplied in his *Blaisdell* concurrence. Cardozo's argument was more complete and impassioned than was Hughes's summary of it. If it had been published, it would have been a major contribution to constitutional debate both then and in the ensuing years.

26

National Regulatory Power and the Constitution

Although state efforts to regulate the economy raised constitutional issues for the Supreme Court, the major response to the Depression came from the national government. The biggest issues in the Supreme Court throughout Cardozo's tenure involved the constitutionality of the New Deal legislation proposed by President Roosevelt and passed by Congress to deal with the economic crisis. The major constitutional stumbling blocks for New Deal legislation were separation of powers doctrine, the Commerce Clause, the Tenth Amendment, and the Due Process Clause of the Fifth Amendment. Cardozo again was generous in validating governmental power, but he was also ready to apply the constitutional restrictions in a few limited circumstances.

One obstacle related to the procedures chosen by Congress to carry out its substantive regulation: did it delegate so much authority to an agency or private group that it violated basic separation of powers principles? This was a critical issue in the New Deal's establishment of an administrative state. Cardozo had already faced the problem in the Court of Appeals and had expressed sympathy for cooperative lawmaking between government and private groups in the public interest.[1] The other obstacles to New Deal legislation related to the legitimacy of the regulation: was it authorized under the powers conferred on Congress by the Constitution—the Commerce Clause issue? Was it prohibited by explicit provisions of the Constitution—the Tenth Amendment and Due Process Clauses? The due process issue was the same that the Court faced when considering the constitutionality of state economic legislation.

Cardozo's first consideration of the delegation of powers issue came in 1933 in *Norwegian Nitrogen Products Company v. United States.*[2] The context was Congress's effort to divest itself of constant involvement in the contentious issue of the tariff. Section 315 of the Tariff Act had given the President the flexible power to raise or lower the tariff duties specified in the Act to equalize differences between costs of production in the United States and elsewhere. The United States Tariff Commission was to assist the President in making such determinations under procedures of its own making, but the Commission was required to give notice of its hearings and to afford reasonable opportunity for interested parties to be present, produce evidence, and be heard. The President increased the duty on sodium nitrate. Subsequently, an importer of that commodity challenged that action on the ground that the procedures of the Tariff Commission did not comply with the statute. Specifically, the importer had not been permitted to examine data used by the Commission or to question the investigators and competitors regarding the cost figures that they produced at the hearing.

Cardozo's opinion for the eight-judge majority that upheld the President's decision took quite an innovative tack.[3] The flexible nature of the tariff provision suggested that Congress had empowered the President to make essentially an unreviewable political decision within certain set boundaries. The establishment of a Tariff Commission, on the other hand, suggested a model of a nonpolitical decision constrained by rules that would be uniformly applied to all cases. Cardozo synthesized the two notions to produce a lasting rule. The meaning of "hearing" varied with the context. His consideration of history, analogy, administrative practice, and the wording of the statute suggested that what Congress delegated to the Tariff Commission was the process that had been followed by Congress, except that it made the hearing a legal right. He was fortified in his judgment by the advisory nature of the Tariff Commission's role. Cardozo rejected the notion that a formal hearing, like that conducted by the Interstate Commerce Commission, was required.

Cardozo, as Professor Louis Jaffe commented, "was one of the first to recognize that rule making powers were essentially legislative in character," and it therefore followed that judicial procedures were not required.[4] His recognition placed a good deal of faith in the Commission:

"[T]here is a command by implication to do whatever may be necessary to make the hearing fair . . . The appeal is to the sense of justice of administrative officers, clothed by statute with discretionary powers. Their resolve is not subject to impeachment for unwisdom without more. It must be shown to be arbitrary."[5] Cardozo reviewed the process and the conduct of the parties and concluded that the refusal of the importer's procedural requests was not arbitrary.

Cardozo's solution interpreted an ambiguous statute as giving substantial discretion to the Tariff Commission and the President, subject only to minimum procedural guarantees. Much of the model approved by Cardozo in *Norwegian Nitrogen* was enacted into law in the provisions of the Reciprocal Trade Agreements Act of 1934.[6] It has been criticized for overreliance on the wisdom of the President and his advisers and its removal of the political issue of tariff-setting from the democratic political process. Cardozo might have made the process more judicial; however, given the delegation contained in the statute, he did not have the choice of remitting the tariff issue to the legislature—unless he was willing to declare unconstitutional the whole idea of giving the President the power to vary the tariff. Cardozo, who was more sympathetic to delegation than his colleagues, did not even contemplate the possibility. He was willing to read the statute as giving the President and the Commission the power to do the job.

Cardozo was alone in employing *Norwegian Nitrogen's* sympathetic approach to delegation issues in the first Supreme Court case to consider the constitutionality of a major New Deal statute. He dissented in 1935 in Panama Refining Company v. Ryan, the so-called "Hot Oil" case, when the Court, by a vote of 8–1, held Section 9(c) of the National Industrial Recovery Act unconstitutional.[7] The majority concluded that the section unlawfully delegated legislative power to the President by permitting him to prohibit the shipment of oil in interstate commerce when it had been produced in excess of state-imposed quotas. The crucial element for the majority was that the legislation imposed no standard whatsoever to guide the President's decision whether to issue an order prohibiting the transportation of oil.

Cardozo did not quarrel with the majority's assertion that the Congress had to set forth a standard to guide the president's discretion, but he did quarrel with its conclusion that the Congress had not done so. Examining the entire statute, he found the required standard in the express purpose of the provision, not in any specific procedure. The prohibition was required to be in furtherance of the explicitly declared purposes of the Act to prevent unfair competition, conserve natural resources, stabilize prices, decrease unemployment, or increase workers' purchasing power. Therefore, Cardozo concluded, with a typical metaphor, "Discretion is not unconfined and vagrant. It is canalized within banks that keep it from overflowing."[8] Paralleling his interpretation of the Contract Clause, he asserted that "separation of powers between the Executive and Congress is not a doctrinaire concept to be made use of with pedantic rigor. There must be sensible approximation, there must be elasticity of adjustment, in response to the practical necessities of government."[9] Finally, he buttressed his conclusion with several examples of congressional delegations going all the way back to 1794 that were similar to Section 9(c). Cardozo understood that the Congress had given the President power to choose between enforcing the state quotas or not. He was "one of the first judges explicitly to recognize and sanction this factor of choice."[10] In Cardozo's view, the President, acting under a delegated power, was to be guided by the standard of delegation. Cardozo assumed, optimistically, that a President would behave as a judge was supposed to behave. But the constitutionality of the delegation did not turn on whether the President so acted. Instead, it turned on the adequacy of the standard.

Cardozo was careful in *Panama Refining* to require Congress to supply a standard for presidential action. He proved that he meant it shortly thereafter in A. L. A. Schechter Poultry Corporation v. United States, the "Sick Chicken" case.[11] That case considered the constitutionality of the Live Poultry Code that had been promulgated by the National Recovery Administration for the metropolitan New York area. The code set minimum wages and maximum hours of work and also governed working conditions and trade practices in the slaughterhouses. On May 27, 1935, called "Black Monday" because three unanimous decisions struck down three important New Deal actions on one day, the Court held major portions of the National Industrial Recovery Act unconstitutional.[12] Chief Justice Hughes's opinion held that the act's authorization to the President to promulgate "codes of fair competition" for industry was an excessive delegation of legislative power because it contained no definition of the content of those codes. Moreover, Congress had no power under the Commerce Clause to regulate these businesses. The codes under attack covered poultry that had already finished its interstate journey, and the practices regulated had only an "indirect" effect on interstate commerce. The decision generated enormous public interest, and it was a severe blow to the New Deal.

Cardozo, the lone dissenter in the *Hot Oil* case, wrote a separate concurring opinion, which was joined by Stone.[13] Although he agreed that the statute could not stand, the case still troubled him—even at the opinion-writing stage, which was unusual. He produced draft after draft of his concurring opinion. He tried out first the delegation issue and held the code, not the statute, unconstitutional. Then he wrote an opinion based solely on invalidity under the Commerce Clause. Finally, he held both the code and the statute unconstitutional on both grounds.[14] Even though he later said that as between his dissent in *Panama Refining* and his concurrence in *Schechter*, he would take his dissent any time and that he was really proud of it,[15] nevertheless he wrote a very strong opinion in *Schechter*. Cardozo relied not only on the lack of standards of guidance but also on the connected issue of the vast amount of power delegated at one time. In contrast to the situation in *Panama Refining*, he found "an attempted delegation not confined to any single act nor to any class or group of acts identified or described by reference to a standard. Here in effect is a roving commission to inquire into evils and upon discovery correct them." The problem was that the codes of fair competition were not codes aimed at fraudulent, tricky, or unfair business practices but rather sought to promote the health and well-being of industries. The codes covered in essence the whole field of industrial regulation: "This is delegation running riot. No such plenitude of power is susceptible of transfer."[16]

Panama Refining and *Schechter* were decided at the dawn of a new administrative age that marked a fundamental shift in power among the various branches of government. They represented an effort by the Court to require the legislature to maintain some semblance of control, at least in a supervisory capacity, over the substance of the rules whose promulgation was delegated to the executive branch. These were not like other cases in which the Court forbade certain legislative goals and means as unconstitutional. The Court was not cutting the government off from achieving its goals. It was simply saying that the Constitution gave Congress and not the executive branch the legislative power. Congress therefore had to give more directions to those expected to carry out its policies. In historical context, the effort now appears to have been futile, although the Court's fear that the executive and administrative branches of government would gain great power at the expense of the legislature has been realized.

Cardozo was less moved than his colleagues were by a desire to impose some procedural discipline on the legislature. He was more sympathetic to the New Deal than all his colleagues. Of the so-called liberal grouping on the Court, Stone was a Republican and wary of the sweep of the New Deal reforms,[17] and Brandeis was distrustful of large economic units. But Cardozo too had his limits, in this as in most other doctrinal matters, and he reached them in *Schechter.*

————

One critical early piece of New Deal legislation, embodying a key feature of New Deal monetary policy, was the Joint Resolution of 1933, which invalidated contract provisions calling for payment of debts in gold or measured by gold and which required payment dollar for dollar in any currency that was legal tender at the time of payment. Shortly thereafter, the Gold Reserve Act of 1934 reduced the gold content of the dollar from the value set by the gold act of 1900. Many creditors under contracts calling for payment of dollars measured by the 1900 statute sought to enforce payment of their debts in the larger dollar amounts as called for by the contracts. Enforcement of such contracts would have required payment of $1.69 for every $1.00 of debt. The debtors answered that the Joint Resolution forbade the enforcement of the gold payment clauses. The creditors argued that the Joint Resolution was unconstitutional under the Due Process Clause of the Fifth Amendment because it destroyed their property rights without compensation and that they were therefore entitled to have their debts paid in the larger dollar amounts provided by their contracts. A group of cases that raised the constitutionality of the Joint Resolution, the *Gold Clause Cases,* came to the Supreme Court together in 1935.

Cardozo joined Chief Justice Hughes's 5–4 majority opinion in Norman v. Baltimore & Ohio Railroad Company, the major case, which upheld the Joint Resolution. In reasoning much like that urged by Cardozo in his unpublished opinion in *Blaisdell,* Hughes concluded that enforcement of the gold clause provision in private contracts would interfere with the purpose of devaluation and the dominant constitutional power of Congress to establish a monetary system.[18] All private payment contracts were entered into subject to the power of Congress to alter monetary policy.

Cardozo had no difficulty separating his personal views about the propriety of the legislation from its constitutionality. Writing privately to his friend Aline Goldstone about the cases after the decision, he remarked, "I don't wonder you are troubled by them." Cardozo understood that it might seem unfair to deprive a party of the bargain it had made based on its foresight of the possibility of devaluation. "The difficulty is that most people fancy it to be the business of a court to condemn as 'unconstitutional' everything that is unfair. Nothing of the kind! There is room for a lot of immorality within the confines of the constitution and of constitutional law."[19] That response comported with Cardozo's general view that such unfairness was one of the risks of doing business under a system where government needed to be free to make effective financial policy.

He made the point explicit two years later in another gold clause case when he was assigned to write the opinion for a 5–4 majority in Holyoke Water Power Company v. American Writing Paper Company.[20] A lease provided for payment of the rent in a quantity of gold equal to $1,500 in gold coin of the United States of the standard of weight and fineness of 1894 or the equivalent in United States currency. When the lessee went into bankruptcy, the lessor, seeking to fix the rent due it, sought to distinguish its case from *Norman* on the ground that what it was owed was the commodity value of the gold. Cardozo disagreed. The transaction was a contract to lease property, not a contract to sell gold. The result in *Norman* controlled. The lessor argued that outlawing such a covenant was arbitrary and a violation of the Fifth Amendment. This form of covenant was so exceptional, it contended, that it could be enforced without undermining the government's control of the monetary system. Cardozo's response was prescient. "A particular covenant, if viewed in isolation, may have a slight, perhaps a trivial, influence upon the effectiveness and symmetry of a new monetary policy. The aggregate of many covenants, each contributing its mite, may bring the system to destruction." Then he added, with a characteristic metaphor, "Rivulets in combination make up a stream of tendency that may attain engulfing power."[21] The argument was an important insight, later much used by the Supreme Court, for supporting legislative power.[22] The trick was in knowing when to use it. As we shall see shortly, he did not apply it to a similar situation under the Commerce Clause.

Cardozo saw the issue of gold clauses differently when public contracts were involved. He joined Chief Justice Hughes's opinion in Perry v. United States, which explicitly stated that Congress did not have power to repudiate the substance of the government's own obligations.[23] It was implicit in the power to borrow money on the credit of the United States, that having exercised that power in issuing specific obligations, Congress could not then destroy those obligations. But Hughes concluded that the bondholder was not entitled to any recovery because he had not shown any damage, any loss of purchasing power as measured by the dollars that he actually received. Allowing recovery, in his view, would have given the bondholders a windfall. Cardozo, who generally added a sentence of praise when he joined a Hughes opinion, referred to this one as "finely worked out."[24] He did not comment on Hughes's failure to refer to the inconvenient fact that the government's contractual promise was to repay in dollars based on a certain gold content and not on purchasing power and that the promise was a hedge against the devaluation that occurred.[25] Justice Stone cast the fifth vote for the government's position. He argued that since a majority had decided that Perry had no cause of action, it was unnecessary to conclude that the obligation of a gold clause was binding in a government bond although not in a private bond. The Court should say nothing on that score at that time. Cardozo's decision to join Hughes's opinion and not Stone's indicated that he wished to declare that the government's breach of faith was unconstitutional.[26] Cardozo balanced his reluctance to impose large liabilities on the government with his desire to promote a high standard of good faith and honor in the government.

Panama Refining and *Schechter* involved issues of the separation of powers among different branches of the federal government. The Court also resurrected the constitutional division of powers between the state and national governments to strike down New Deal legislation. The Tenth Amendment, which reserves the powers not delegated to the national government to the states and the people, had previously been used occasionally to protect state sovereignty against national legislation.[27] Cardozo invoked it again in 1936 in Hopkins Federal Savings & Loan Association v. Cleary.[28] Writing for a unanimous Court, he held unconstitutional a statute of Congress that permitted a state-chartered building and loan association to convert itself into a federally chartered savings and loan association without state consent. Cardozo acknowledged that the field of the Tenth Amendment was "a new one."[29] Nevertheless, without any discussion of the history or purposes of the Tenth Amendment, he treated the transformation of these associations from creatures of the state to creatures of the federal government as an obvious violation of state sovereignty and hence of the Tenth Amendment. The only caution he expressed was that the case had not raised any question of the effect of the war, commerce, or eminent domain powers on the Tenth Amendment.

Cardozo was generally sympathetic to governmental efforts to deal with economic crises, and the statute had been passed in the aftermath of the numerous failures of state building and loan associations. But *Hopkins* raised an additional issue. Congress was not just seeking to regulate private activity. It was doing so by authorizing private stockholders to remove these institutions from state control. The states and Congress had concurrent jurisdiction to establish banking institutions, and the Tenth Amendment foreclosed transformation of a state bank into a federal bank without state acquiescence. As the former chief judicial officer of a state, Cardozo respected the sovereignty of states as separate agencies of government, and he was not about to sanction the destruction of state-established institutions just because Congress found it convenient. Deferential as he was to congressional power, he was not prepared to accord it complete constitutional leeway.

Shortly afterwards, Cardozo demonstrated that he was also not prepared to read the concept of state sovereignty as a broad limit on federal power. On the same day in 1936 that the decision in *Hopkins Savings* was announced, the Court heard argument in United States v. Butler, which dealt with the constitutionality of the Agricultural Adjustment Act, another major New Deal statute.[30] Later that year, Cardozo dissented when the Court used the Tenth Amendment to hold that statute unconstitutional. *Butler* invalidated a tax that was laid upon processors of agricultural goods in order to pay subsidies to farmers to reduce crop acreage and thus to raise farm prices. Justice Roberts's opinion for the majority recognized a broad power under Article 1, section 8, of the Constitution to impose taxes to "provide for the . . . general Welfare." He resolved an ancient debate between Alexander Hamilton and Joseph Story on the one hand and James Madison on the other by deciding with Hamilton and Story that the power to tax for the general welfare was plenary and not limited to the purposes specified in Article 1, section 8.[31]

Roberts concluded, however, that the power was limited by the Tenth Amendment and that Congress could not tax in order to regulate an area in which Congress had no regulatory authority. The tax was part of a plan to regulate agricultural production, which was not within congressional power. Furthermore, the federal government could not save the act's constitutionality by coercing farmer compliance or by purchasing state submission on a subject reserved to the states.

Cardozo did not find the Tenth Amendment controlling. He joined Stone's dissent, which saw no limitation in the Tenth Amendment on the explicit grant of the power to tax for the general welfare. Moreover, the dissenters found no economic coercion of farmers in the offer of payment to reduce acreage. The power to tax and spend included "the power to relieve a nationwide economic maladjustment by conditional gifts of money."[32] Cardozo was ready to invoke the Tenth Amendment when Congress used a concurrent power to deprive states of their jurisdiction over state-created entities. However, he was not ready to use it to deprive Congress of the power given in the Constitution to tax for the general welfare when tax proceeds were used for the regulation of agricultural production, even assuming that Congress could not regulate it directly under its Article 1 powers.

Cardozo continued to resist an expansive notion of the Tenth Amendment. A five-judge majority in Ashton v. Cameron County Water Improvement District struck down a provision of the federal Bankruptcy Act permitting a local subdivision of a state to file a petition in bankruptcy, but also allowing states to require their approval of such action.[33] Justice McReynolds's majority opinion held that the statute violated the Contract Clause because it permitted states to impair the obligation of their own contracts. The statute also violated the Tenth Amendment because it interfered with the freedom of states to manage their own affairs, and state consent could not enlarge the powers of Congress. Cardozo wrote a dissenting opinion that was joined by Hughes, Brandeis, and Stone.[34] He was willing to assume that *Hopkins Savings* stood for the proposition that a federal statute that allowed private parties to bring bankruptcy proceedings against a state subdivision without its consent would dislocate the essential balance between the state and the central government. But Cardozo saw no such threat in this statute because the state's action was voluntary.

The Contract Clause argument in *Ashton* presented a different problem. The state's decision to use the bankruptcy court was an effort to scale down its obligations. The Court's majority, with a constitutional philosophy that sought to hold the state strictly to its promises, found that to be a violation of the Contract Clause. Cardozo subscribed to a different view of the Contract Clause, one that did not disable government to that degree. He had learned in his law practice how to use technical arguments to serve his purpose, and he used one here. Cardozo drew on common law notions of causation in arguing that any impairment of contract came not from the state in filing for bankruptcy relief but rather from the federal court in approving a plan of "composition"—an agreement between the municipality and its creditors to pay scaled-down debts. "There [in the federal courts], and not beyond in an ascending chain of antecedents, is the cause of the impairment to which the law will have regard . . . The [federal] court, not the petitioner, is the efficient cause of the release."[35] While the Contract Clause forbade states from impairing the obligation of contracts, it did not forbid the federal government from doing so. That was what the bankruptcy power was all about. Cardozo's refusal to see the state's invocation of bankruptcy as a forbidden "impairment" was spurred by his perception that if voluntary bankruptcy was not available, then "municipalities and creditors have been caught in a vise from which it is impossible to let them out."[36] Here as elsewhere, Cardozo's sense of the practicalities of the economic situation informed his legal conclusion that the Constitution ought not to be interpreted as forbidding a solution to the problem of municipal insolvency.

Cardozo's tendency to accommodate conflicting doctrines, that is, to leave some scope for one doctrine even though in a particular case he favored the other, was exemplified in his treatment of the final stumbling block for New Deal legislation, the Commerce Clause, which gave Congress power to "regulate Commerce . . . among the several States."[37] For over a century, the Supreme Court had wavered back and forth in its definition of congressional power under that provision. Many decisions had proceeded on the theory that some activities were so inherently local, such as mining or the production of goods or crops, that they represented exclusively intrastate commerce and hence were beyond the scope of congressional power. As Chief Justice Melville Fuller put it in the 1895 *E. C. Knight* case in holding that the Sherman Antitrust Act did not reach an attempt to monopolize the sugar manufacturing industry,

"Contracts, combinations, or conspiracies to control domestic [i.e., intrastate] enterprise in manufacture, agriculture, mining, production in all its forms, or to raise or lower prices or wages, might unquestionably tend to restrain external as well as domestic trade, but the result would be an indirect result, however inevitable."[38] Fuller relied heavily on geography instead of economic impact in determining the extent of congressional power. He believed that the result of the alternative approach "would be that Congress would be invested, to the exclusion of the States, with the power to regulate . . . every branch of human industry."[39]

The competing conception of the Commerce Clause was advanced by Charles Evans Hughes in the 1914 *Shreveport Rate Case*.[40] Upholding an Interstate Commerce Commission order that regulated the intrastate charges of an interstate railroad, Hughes concluded, after examining the economic effect of the intrastate rates on interstate commerce, that Congress could regulate intrastate commerce "in all matters having such a close and substantial relation to interstate traffic that the control is essential or appropriate to security of that traffic."[41]

The competing conceptions came before the Supreme Court again in 1935 in Railroad Retirement Board v. Alton Railroad Company, which considered the constitutionality of a federal statute mandating the establishment of retirement and pension plans by all railroads subject to the Interstate Commerce Act.[42] The restrictive conception of interstate commerce prevailed in Justice Roberts's opinion for a 5–4 majority. Roberts held that the statute was social legislation, having nothing to do with commerce, and hence could not be justified under Congress's commerce power.[43]

Cardozo had no difficulty in concluding that the legislation could be supported under the commerce power. After Roberts's opinion had circulated within the Court and while Hughes was preparing a dissent, Cardozo had a discussion with Stone and then sent Hughes a long letter suggesting that the best way to tie the pension proposal to the business of running railroads in interstate commerce was

> to view the statute as analogous to a workmen's compensation act. I suppose no one would deny that such an act could be adopted by Congress for the protection of workers on interstate railroads . . . It is an attempt to make the industry bear the attendant risks of the employment.

If that is the rationale of such an act, wherein does it differ from the act in controversy? What is the distinction between compensating men who have been incapacitated by accident (though without fault of the employer), and compensating men who have been injured by the wear and tear of time, the slow attrition of the years? What is the difference between replacing worn out machinery and replacing worn out men? Is not each a legitimate incident of the business?

Cardozo concluded by putting the issue in human terms, arguing in inflammatory and not wholly accurate language that if his analogy was correct, "what is left of the argument of Roberts, J., that the Government should instruct the railroads to dismiss their superannuated workers without payment or pension, throwing them out helpless into the world?"[44] Hughes incorporated Cardozo's legal argument and some of the supporting language into his own dissent.[45] Cardozo had clearly adopted Hughes's *Shreveport* approach to the Commerce Clause, which defined the commerce power broadly to ensure effective national regulation of the economy.

But Cardozo also believed that Congress's commerce power had its limits and that there was validity to the notion that some intrastate commerce was exempt from national regulation. Three weeks after the *Alton* decision, the commerce power reappeared as an issue in the *Schechter* case, which has already been considered for its treatment of the doctrine of delegation of powers.[46] The Schechter Poultry Corp., which operated a slaughterhouse in Brooklyn, New York, bought chickens that had traveled in interstate commerce, but it sold only to local retailers. A Live Poultry Code governing industry conditions had been adopted by the industry and approved by the President under the National Industrial Recovery Act. Schechter was convicted of violating the provisions governing minimum wages, maximum hours of work, and various trade practices. The Supreme Court, after unanimously holding the statute unconstitutional because of an impermissible delegation of legislative power, also unanimously held that these provisions could not constitutionally be applied to Schechter's slaughterhouse under the Commerce Clause. Chief Justice Hughes, author of previous opinions interpreting the commerce power broadly, concluded that interstate commerce in the poultry came to an end when the chickens reached the slaughterhouse, a local business. Moreover, wages and hours in local industry did not have a "direct" effect on interstate commerce. If they did, everything that affected prices of interstate goods would then fall within congressional power.

Cardozo's concurring opinion agreed with Hughes's effort to set a limit on the reach of the commerce power. His opinion was based on the view that the national government could not regulate all aspects of business, that there were both a category consisting of interstate commerce and intrastate commerce that substantially affected interstate commerce and a category consisting of intrastate commerce that did not substantially affect interstate commerce. Otherwise, the Constitution would have simply granted Congress the power to regulate commerce instead of limiting the power to commerce "among the several States." It was the duty of the Court to examine the context and to define the reach of federal commerce power. Again he turned to his common-law learning on the issue of causation:

> There is a view of causation that would obliterate the distinction between what is national and what is local in the activities of commerce . . . The law is not indifferent to considerations of degree. Activities local in their immediacy do not become interstate and national because of distant repercussions . . . To find immediacy or directness here is to find it almost everywhere. If centripetal [i.e., national] forces are to be isolated to the exclusion of the [local] forces that oppose and counteract them, there will be an end to our federal system.[47]

In short, Cardozo's resolution of the question whether the intrastate commerce at issue sufficiently affected interstate commerce to permit congressional regulation was to ask whether the impact of the activity was predominantly local or not. If it was, as he deemed it in the operation of the slaughterhouses in *Schechter,* then the federal regulation was unconstitutional. He did not offer the insight that he would later proclaim in *Holyoke Power,* the gold clause case, that the impact of Schechter's violations on interstate commerce might be trivial but that the impact of the violations of all the Schechters of intrastate commerce taken together might well be substantial. This was, in fact, the tack that the Supreme Court itself took a few years later in United States v. Darby, which, with Wickard v. Filburn, virtually eliminated the category of an exclusively intrastate commerce immune from federal regulation.[48] *Schechter* preceded *Holyoke Power,* but the fact that state power and not private rights lay in the balance in *Schechter* was probably critical for Cardozo. It was important to preserve at least some state power over commerce.

But there was a large difference for Cardozo between the regulation of a local slaughterhouse and the regulation of the coal mining industry, which was at issue in Carter v. Carter Coal Company the following term.[49] The Guffey Coal Act fixed wages and hours of workers in the bituminous coal industry and also contained provisions for fixing the sales price of coal. Justice Sutherland, for six judges, including Chief Justice Hughes, held the labor provisions unconstitutional because of their "indirect" connection to interstate commerce and the price-fixing provisions unconstitutional because they were inseparable from the labor provisions. Sutherland, following the theory of Chief Justice Fuller in the E. C. Knight case, sought a bright-line distinction between interstate and intrastate commerce. Using the language of "proximate cause" from tort doctrine, he argued that the requirement that there be a "direct" effect on interstate commerce to invoke congressional power "implies that the activity or condition invoked or blamed shall operate proximately—not mediately, remotely, or collaterally—to produce the effect." Questions of degree of impact were irrelevant. "The distinction between a direct and an indirect effect turns, not upon the magnitude of either the cause or the effect, but entirely upon the manner in which the effect has been brought about."[50] Production was local. Interstate commerce had not yet begun, and the incidents of production could therefore not be regulated by Congress.

Cardozo, writing for Stone, Brandeis, and himself, regarded the attack on the labor provisions as premature and would have upheld the price-fixing provisions on their own merits. Without referring explicitly to Sutherland's statement of the appropriate test, Cardozo discussed the general principles that should govern the decision whether price regulation might constitutionally extend to the intrastate sales of coal at the mines. For him the test was the magnitude of the effect upon interstate commerce. As he had often done in the New York Court of Appeals, Cardozo approached the issue pragmatically, relating the purposes of the provision in question, here a constitutional provision, to the particular facts before him. His long-standing distrust of labels was also apparent. He began by addressing the conclusory term often used to permit regulation: "Sometimes it is said that the relation must be 'direct' to bring that power [the power to regulate intrastate commerce] into play. In many circumstances such a description will be sufficiently precise to meet

workload. After consulting with Brandeis and Van Devanter, Hughes wrote a letter on March 21, 1937, to Senator Burton Wheeler, leader of the opposition to the President's plan. Hughes stated that the Court was up to date in its work and that the proposal would impair its efficiency.[56] Cardozo was upset with Hughes's letter. He thought that the Court ought to remain aloof from the political struggle over the plan.[57]

Cardozo kept his disagreement with the plan and with Hughes's action private. He refused to discuss the issue with most people, but he did make his views clear to his friend Charles Burlingham. Burlingham delivered a talk on the radio in which he recounted the history of British attempts to control the colonial judges as forming the background for American efforts to assure judicial independence. He saw the lessons of that history as the key issue in Roosevelt's proposal and opposed the plan as a threat to the Supreme Court's independence. Burlingham sent Cardozo a copy, and Cardozo responded that Burlingham had "hit the nail on the head unerringly."[58] Cardozo's disagreement with the Court-packing plan did not affect his admiration for the President. Once Roosevelt began emphasizing his view that the Court's majority was substituting its view of the wisdom of legislation for the legislature's judgment, that view sounded very much like Cardozo's own opinion.[59]

While the debate over Roosevelt's proposal was raging throughout the country in the winter and spring of 1937, the wavering course of Supreme Court decisions finally turned decisively in favor of government power to regulate the economy in three major cases. The state minimum wage case, West Coast Hotel Co. v. Parrish, had been argued between the reelection of President Roosevelt and his proposal of the Court-packing plan. In March, eight days after Hughes's letter to Senator Wheeler, the Supreme Court overruled the *Adkins* case and upheld the power of the states to set minimum wages for women and minors.[60] Then in April, the Court decided a group of cases in which it turned away from its restrictive commerce power decisions in *Alton* and *Carter* and returned to the broader Hughes formulation of the *Shreveport* line of cases. National Labor Relations Board v. Jones & Laughlin Corp. had been argued just five days after President Roosevelt proposed the Court-packing plan.[61] In that case and two companion cases, the Supreme Court upheld the constitutionality of the National Labor Relations Act not only as applied to a large manufacturer of iron and steel products but also to a large Michigan trailer manufacturer and a moderate-sized Virginia manufacturer of men's clothing.[62]

The National Labor Relations Act cases faced the obstacles of the holding in *Carter* that Congress's commerce power did not reach the labor policies of producers and manufacturers of goods no matter how great their effect on commerce. Before the Court met in conference, Cardozo tried to write a memorandum demonstrating that this group of cases was sufficiently different from *Carter* that the Court could reach a different result. Unable to find a satisfactory distinction, he gave up the effort. He was therefore amazed when both Hughes and Roberts voted at conference to uphold the statute in its application to these three industries.[63] Hughes's 5–4 majority opinion in *Jones & Laughlin,* which Cardozo joined, simply noted *Carter* as one of a group of cases that "are not controlling here."[64] Hughes dealt with the Commerce Clause attack on the statute in a powerful argument that stressed "the close and intimate relation which a manufacturing industry may have to interstate commerce."[65] Cardozo, delighted at Hughes's return to the broad Commerce Clause fold, congratulated him on his "magnificent opinion."[66] Many people deserved credit in the struggle to establish the constitutional power of government to deal with the economic crisis of the 1930s; but as Professor Richard Friedman, the scholar who is writing the volume on this period in *The History of the Supreme Court of the United States* series, has reminded us, "in the darkest time, Cardozo was the prime bearer of the torch."[67]

The day after the National Labor Relations Act opinions were handed down, Cardozo, writing to Felix Frankfurter, felt good enough about the Court to include a pun in his assessment of recent events: "What a change in the centre of gravity—and perhaps of humor too—since the previous term ended a year ago."[68] And the third major change in direction, the *Social Security Cases,* was still more than a month away when he wrote that letter.

Even before the opinions in those cases were announced, there was another dramatic event. On May 18, Willis Van Devanter informed President Roosevelt of his intent to retire at the end of the term. The upcoming vacancy would give Roosevelt the opportunity to nominate his first Supreme Court justice and to solidify the new balance on the Court. Six days later, the Supreme Court, in Steward Machine Company v. Davis and Helvering v. Davis, upheld a cornerstone of the New Deal, the Social Security Act.

Cardozo was assigned to write the opinions in both cases.[69] The Social Security Act imposed a tax on employers of more than eight workers but gave a credit of up to 90 percent for taxes paid into a state unemployment fund that met stated criteria. One of the criteria was that states pay over the taxes collected by the state fund to the Secretary of the Treasury's Unemployment Trust Fund. The Act authorized federal grants to the states to assist them in administering their unemployment compensation funds. Steward Machine Company paid the federal tax and then sued to recover its payment on the ground that the Social Security Act was unconstitutional. It claimed that an excise tax could not be laid upon employment, which was a right and not a privilege; that the tax did not meet the constitutional requirement of uniformity; that it was arbitrary and hence violated the Fifth Amendment's Due Process Clause; that it violated the powers reserved to the states under the Tenth Amendment; and that the states had been unlawfully coerced into surrendering their sovereignty. After the federal district court and circuit court of appeals had rejected Steward's arguments, the Supreme Court granted review.

Cardozo, as the junior justice and so often in the minority, had rarely been assigned to write the majority opinion in an important case. He was therefore very pleased when Hughes gave him the assignment in the *Social Security Cases,* even though he was in dissent on a procedural point in one of them, Helvering v. Davis.[70] The major issues were the Tenth Amendment and coercion of the states, and Cardozo had to deal with United States v. Butler. *Butler* had contained two themes. The first theme was the acceptance of a broad notion of the power of Congress to tax for the general welfare; however, the second theme was an expansive reading of the Tenth Amendment so as to restrict Congress's ability to impose a tax in order to regulate an area not within federal regulatory authority, or to purchase state acquiescence or to coerce private party compliance. What the first theme granted, the second tended to restrict. Cardozo narrowed the second theme to permit a greater exercise of federal taxing and spending power.

Cardozo brought the Act within the scope of providing for the general welfare by invoking the national character of the unemployment crisis and the fear of individual states that acting on their own would place their industries at a disadvantage. The credit granted by the statute was related to the fiscal need served by the tax and therefore operated as inducement or persuasion to action by the states and not as coercion. The states were free to choose whether or not to have an unemployment compensation system of their own, and, indeed, the state in this case had not argued that it was coerced. Alabama chose to obtain a tax credit for its citizens by consenting to conditions that did not impair its sovereignty: "[T]o hold that motive or temptation is equivalent to coercion is to plunge the law in endless difficulties. The outcome of such a doctrine is the acceptance of a philosophical determinism by which choice becomes impossible. Till now the law has been guided by a robust common sense which assumes the freedom of the will as a working hypothesis in the solution of its problems."[71] In true common law fashion, Cardozo recognized that it would be difficult to attempt a formula to differentiate between inducement and coercion. "Enough for present purposes that wherever the line may be, this statute is within it. Definition more precise must abide the wisdom of the future."[72]

Having made an affirmative case for upholding the statute, Cardozo then disposed summarily of the second theme of *Butler.* Relief of unemployment was the concern of the nation as well as the states. The state statute that was a condition of the credit had to be passed by the state, which also had the option of repealing it. The proceeds of the tax were not earmarked for any special group.[73] Thus, the state sovereignty theme of *Butler* did not condemn the statute because the subject matter of regulation was national and the states could choose whether or not to join the federal program, as they pleased.

The coordination of the federal program with state legislation made the *Social Security Cases* sufficiently different from *Butler* that Cardozo's opinion generated support even within the conservative bloc of four. Justice Sutherland, writing for himself and for Justice Van Devanter, wrote that he concurred "with most of what [was] said" in Cardozo's opinion. But he concluded that the administrative provisions of the Act constituted an unconstitutional surrender by the state of its power to administer its own unemployment compensation law and its own funds.[74] Justice Butler disagreed completely with Cardozo's view of the statutory scheme. First, he saw no delegated power in the Constitution that would permit Congress to pay unemployment compensation. Second, where Cardozo saw inducement and free choice, Butler saw coercion. Practically, the states with compensation laws were under a compulsion to save their taxpayers from double payments, and such coercion violated the Tenth Amendment.[75] Justice McReynolds, in a dissent that mostly reprinted an 1854 veto message of President Franklin Pierce, added angrily that "no cloud of words or ostentatious parade of irrelevant statistics should be permitted to obscure [the] fact" that Title IX interfered with state sovereignty.[76]

Cardozo also wrote for the Court in the companion case, *Helvering v. Davis*, decided with *Steward Machine*. His opinion upheld Titles II and VIII of the Social Security Act, imposing a tax on employers and employees to provide for payment of old-age benefits. Sutherland and Van Devanter joined the five-judge majority of *Steward Machine* to make a 7–2 majority. Cardozo's opinions in the *Social Security Cases* opened the way for a new mechanism of federal power—the provision of federal funds to the states tied to the condition that they comply with detailed federal regulation of the funded program. Wisely—perhaps more wisely than he realized, for the issue has been very troublesome—Cardozo did not attempt to mark out the line between coercion and inducement; he did, though, establish a presumption that favored governmental power. The *Social Security Cases* were the last major cases of a tumultuous term.

The final chapters of the Court-packing controversy were written that summer. While the Senate was debating the fate of Roosevelt's plan, Senator Robinson, leader of the administration's forces, had a heart attack and died on July 13. The bill was then recommitted to the Judiciary Committee where it too died.[77] One month later, Roosevelt nominated Senator Hugo Black, an ardent New Deal supporter, to replace Van Devanter. Although the opponents of the Court-packing plan were furious, the Senate confirmed Black, one of their own.[78]

During his service on the Court, Cardozo made a substantial contribution to another part of Commerce Clause jurisprudence that, in this instance, did not make national headlines. For over one hundred years following Chief Justice Marshall's suggestion in Gibbons v. Ogden, the Supreme Court had held not only that the Commerce Clause authorized the affirmative use of congressional power but also that it had a negative effect on state power. Under this so-called "dormant commerce power," the states were prohibited in particular instances from regulating interstate commerce even when Congress had not acted.[79] Most of the justices agreed that Congress's commerce power prohibited the states from outright discrimination against interstate commerce in favor of local business. Nevertheless, there had been sharp differences of opinion about whether the commerce power also prohibited states from unduly burdening interstate commerce even when there was no discrimination. There was also disagreement over what constituted an undue burden. Cardozo added two important opinions to the debate. The first opinion was Baldwin v. G. A. F. Seelig, Inc., dealing with the power of New York to apply its milk control law to interstate transactions.[80] New York denied a milk license to Seelig, a New York milk dealer buying Vermont milk from a Vermont dealer, unless Seelig agreed not to sell it in New York if the Vermont farmers had been paid less than the minimum price set by New York law.

Cardozo employed his formidable analytical and rhetorical skills for a unanimous court in striking down this application of the New York program. He viewed the New York statute as wiping out any competitive advantage that Vermont milk might have had in the New York market. "If New York, in order to promote the economic welfare of her farmers, may guard them against competition with the cheaper prices of Vermont, the door has been opened to rivalries and reprisals that were meant to be averted by subjecting commerce between the states to the power of the nation." New York sought to justify the application of its legislation to Vermont milk by arguing that the purpose was to assure a supply of pure and healthy milk that was threatened when cutthroat competition resulted in prices that were so low that farmers could not survive. Cardozo responded that the exception would "eat up the rule" and "invite a speedy end of our national solidarity. The Constitution was framed under the dominion of a political philosophy less parochial in range. It was framed upon the theory that the peoples of the several states must sink or swim together, and that in the long run prosperity and salvation are in union and not division."[81] If there were problems with the purity of the milk or the conditions under which it was produced, those problems should be dealt with more directly than by regulating Vermont prices.

Cardozo dealt with the doctrinal issue by concluding that application of the New York statute to Vermont prices violated both branches of "dormant commerce power" analysis. The restrictions were both discriminatory and unduly burdensome to interstate commerce. They were "hostile in conception as well as burdensome in result," and an injunction should be granted forbidding enforcement of the statute against Seelig.[82] Just as Cardozo leaned toward recognition of state sovereignty over local sovereignty in case of doubt, so too he leaned toward recognition of national sovereignty over state sovereignty.

As in so many other areas of the law, Cardozo did not press his views about economic isolationism to a logical extreme. He was more sympathetic, in his second important dormant commerce opinion, when a state that imposed a sales tax sought to avoid a loss of business from its own residents. The state of Washington imposed a 2 percent sales tax on retail sales and a compensating use tax of 2 percent on goods purchased elsewhere and brought into Washington, subject to a credit for sales tax paid in the state of purchase. In Henneford v. Silas Mason Company, Inc., Silas Mason claimed that Washington's compensating use tax was an effort to prevent its sales tax from putting Washington sellers at a disadvantage in the same way that New York's denial of a license to Seelig unless he paid the New York milk price to Vermont farmers was an effort to prevent New York's price-fixing law from disadvantaging New York dairy farmers.

Cardozo, writing for a majority in the first case to consider the effect of dormant commerce doctrine on this type of tax, upheld the constitutionality of the compensating use tax.[83] Thomas Reed Powell, trenchant analyst of the Court's commerce cases, remarked that Cardozo's "skill was adequate for the task [of distinguishing this case from his own opinion in *Baldwin*], or nearly so."[84] Ernest Brown, Powell's successor in Commerce Clause analysis, complimented Powell on his "nice turn of ironical phrase," but thought the measurement inaccurate: "The opinion . . . is not one of the ornaments of the Justice's judicial career."[85] The problem was an apparent inconsistency between Cardozo's permitting Washington to protect its own industry from harm by equalizing the economic effects of its sales tax legislation with a compensatory use tax while forbidding New York from protecting its own industry from harm by equalizing the economic effects of its minimum price legislation by imposing the same requirement on out-of-state purchases.

Cardozo's effort in *Henneford* was indeed weak. He differentiated *Baldwin* solely on the ground that that case involved an attempt by New York to project its legislation beyond its borders.[86] That was a jurisdictional objection, a due process problem, and there was more to *Baldwin* than a jurisdictional problem. If New York had not allowed Vermont milk into New York without inspection by either Vermont or New York inspectors and if Vermont did not inspect health conditions at Vermont farms, the same jurisdictional objection could have been made. Cardozo would doubtless not have rejected an effort by New York to inspect Vermont farms in such circumstances with the simple assertion that New

York was projecting its legislation beyond its borders. He would have made a dormant commerce power analysis like the one he made in *Baldwin. Henneford* needed such an analysis too, and Cardozo did not make it.

But there was a basis for harmonizing *Baldwin* and *Henneford*. The use tax in *Henneford* preserved the prior competitive status quo by taxing a local incident—use in the taxing state—whereas the price regulation in *Baldwin,* operating on an out-of-state incident—the price paid in the producing state—eliminated the preexisting possibility that industry in the producing state could retain or gain any advantage from lower costs. Cardozo had pointed the way to this explanation in his *Baldwin* opinion. Referring to New York's efforts to guard its farmers "against competition with the cheaper prices of Vermont" and to New York's attempt "to neutralize advantages belonging to the place of origin," he emphasized that the New York statute had eliminated the Vermont milk's price advantage.[87] Inexplicably, he failed to make use of this insight in *Henneford*. These dormant commerce power cases presented as great a challenge to the intellect as any that Cardozo had faced in Albany. That Cardozo failed to articulate clearly the difference he instinctively seems to have felt between *Baldwin* and *Henneford* indicates that even a powerful mind needs more than sporadic exposure to the intricate problems of economic analysis and federalism. Cardozo had reached a good result, but he bungled the analysis in *Henneford*.

———

Cardozo was a Supreme Court justice during a momentous period of its history, and he lived to see his major constitutional beliefs become incorporated into its decisions. His survey of judicial decision-making in *The Nature of the Judicial Process* had recognized the great discretion that judges had in constitutional cases to look to public-policy considerations. In choosing among the competing theories of governmental power and constitutional restriction, Cardozo chose the theory that gave great deference to legislative choice. That choice was in line with his belief that law should, with some qualifications, represent community values. Thus, he voted to uphold the constitutionality of most of the major pieces of New Deal legislation: the Railroad Retirement Act, the Guffey Coal Act, the Agricultural Adjustment Act, the Wagner Act, and the Social Security Act; and similar state legislation: minimum wage laws, New York's Milk Control Act, and Minnesota's Mortgage Moratorium Act.

Cardozo also believed that there were limits to the legislative powers, so that occasionally, as in *Schecter, Hopkins,* and *Kavanaugh,* he read the Commerce Clause, the Contract Clause, and the Tenth Amendment as forbidding particular government regulation. His opinions made clear that although he gave great scope to legislative choice, he was balancing and combining constitutional principles that looked in different directions, not choosing one to the exclusion of the others.[88] The Constitution should be interpreted so as to protect a measure of state autonomy and of personal liberty and property rights while at the same time—and this was the critical issue for Cardozo and the Court in the 1930s—interpreting the Constitution so as to enable government to govern.

27

Civil Liberties, Race, and Other Supreme Court Issues

Cardozo was a "liberal" justice. In the parlance of the day, that designation meant that he generally voted to uphold state and federal economic and social legislation against constitutional attack. In other words, it was called "liberal" judging to uphold liberal legislation. The constitutional struggle that ended in 1937 with victory for his views had been fought out primarily over the meaning of the Due Process Clauses of the Fifth and Fourteenth Amendments, which prohibited government from depriving any person of "life, liberty, or property" without due process of law. But another issue was beginning to surface that would involve a different definition of liberal judging. It was not called liberal for a judge to uphold the exercise of governmental power when it impinged upon civil liberties. The contradiction was not just a question of semantics. The issue was a difficult one for all those who had taken sides in the long battle over how much deference to give governmental decisions in the shaping of a democratic society. Life, liberty, and property were linked together in the Due Process Clauses. Should judges give the same deference to governmental decisions that affected life and liberty as they gave decisions that affected property? And if not, why not? These issues had not been in the forefront of constitutional debate during Cardozo's years on the Court of Appeals; they slowly emerged while he was on the Supreme Court. The pattern of results in his civil liberties opinions was mixed.

An irony of modern civil liberties law is that it owes a great deal to

534

two opinions of Justice James McReynolds in the mid-1920s. McReynolds was widely excoriated as a reactionary for his hostility to state and federal economic regulation. But he was sometimes hostile to governmental regulation of personal liberty, and he wrote two opinions that are civil liberties landmarks. In Meyer v. Nebraska and Pierce v. Society of Sisters, the Supreme Court held state efforts to restrict the teaching of German in public schools and to require children to attend public schools unconstitutional under the Fourteenth Amendment. The Court concluded that those statutes unreasonably interfered with the liberty of parents to direct the upbringing of their children.[1] In the former case, McReynolds outlined the "liberty" protected by the Fourteenth Amendment. "Without doubt, it includes not merely freedom from bodily restraint but also the right of the individual to contract, to engage in any of the common occupations of life, to acquire useful knowledge, to marry, establish a home and bring up children, to worship God according to the dictates of his own conscience, and generally to enjoy those privileges long recognized at common law as essential to the orderly pursuit of happiness by free men."[2] The issue for the justices in the 1930s was the application of these generalities in particular cases.

A second civil liberties issue was the extent to which the Fourteenth Amendment incorporated the individual protections of the Bill of Rights. There was considerable evidence that the Privileges or Immunities Clause of the Fourteenth Amendment was expected by the drafters to be the major provision giving substantive protection to individuals against the state, even applying to the states the protections that the Bill of Rights afforded against the federal government.[3] But in 1873, the Supreme Court had reduced that clause to a dead letter, leaving the Due Process and Equal Protection Clauses to protect civil liberties against state infringement.[4] By the time that Cardozo came to the Supreme Court, the Court had refused to incorporate some of the provisions of the Bill of Rights, including the requirement of indictment by grand jury and the privilege against self-incrimination, into the Fourteenth Amendment; however, it had incorporated other provisions, including the freedom of speech.

In New York, Cardozo's record on civil liberties had been meager and mixed. He was fairly tough in criminal law cases. Even though he personally opposed the death penalty, he regularly affirmed convictions in death penalty cases. He did not stretch to find reasons to reverse convictions, and he reversed them only when there had been substantial error in the trial. In the few cases when there were federal constitutional questions, he was not sympathetic to expansion of the protections afforded by the search and seizure clause or the privilege against self-incrimination. Cardozo had encountered the constitutional problem of explicit racial discrimination just once on the bench and once in his practice. Only where free speech was involved did he exhibit special interest in protecting a civil liberty, and he did so both in his opinions and in his extrajudicial writing. Free speech was a matter close to Cardozo's heart. But civil liberties cases were few and far between in New York, and Cardozo had not definitively committed himself to a theory or to a course of decision before he went to Washington.

Cardozo's record in civil liberties cases on the Supreme Court was also mixed. Sometimes his general inclination to defer to a governmental decision or to a Supreme Court precedent prevailed. At other times, he was ready to enforce the civil liberties policy embodied in a constitutional provision to invalidate a governmental judgment.

The Court experimented in the 1930s with an expansion of the Fourteenth Amendment's protections of individual liberty against government. Just before Cardozo came to the Court, it had decided several cases unambiguously applying the First Amendment's freedom of speech and press protections to the states for the first time.[5] Whereas Cardozo had extolled the virtues of freedom of speech in his tribute to Justice Holmes in 1931, he was cautious in applying the First Amendment. His approach was familiar. On a case-by-case basis, he looked at the aim to be served by the constitutional provision through the prism of history and precedent. Even though he saw great scope for public policy considerations in constitutional cases and even though precedent so often looked two ways, he habitually looked for some constraint on the exercise of the Court's discretion.

Cardozo's mixed approach to First Amendment issues may be seen by comparing two opinions. In the first case, Hamilton v. Regents in 1934, Cardozo concluded that it was constitutional for the University of California to require that all students take military science courses in peacetime without any exemption for conscientious objectors.[6] In the second case, Grosjean v. American Press Co. in 1936, Cardozo concluded that it was unconstitutional for Louisiana to impose a gross advertising receipts tax on certain newspapers and periodicals.[7]

In *Hamilton,* conscientious objector students refused to take the required courses, which included military training in uniform and instruction in the use of weapons, and they were suspended. The Supreme Court denied their petition to compel the University to permit them to complete their studies without taking the courses. A major claim was that the regulation violated their right to freely exercise their religion. Cardozo joined Pierce Butler's opinion for a unanimous court that upheld the regulation. But Cardozo also wrote a separate opinion for himself and Justices Brandeis and Stone. Cardozo's concurrence took a somewhat different tack from Butler's opinion, which relied principally on the voluntary nature of attendance at the university and the duty of citizens to serve in the military forces.

Cardozo did not proclaim the same status for the free exercise of religion clause of the First Amendment that he had enunciated for freedom of speech in his tribute to Justice Holmes. Although the majority regarded it as settled that the religious liberty protected by the First Amendment against national government encroachment was also protected against state encroachment by incorporation of the First Amendment into the Fourteenth Amendment, Cardozo was ready only to "assume" that proposition. His purpose was to mark out a narrower ground for decision than the majority. The University of California required less than military service. "Instruction in military science, unaccompanied here by any pledge of military service, is not an interference by the state with the free exercise of religion when the liberties of the constitution are read in the light of a century and a half of history during days of peace and war."[8] Although Cardozo also concurred in Justice Butler's opinion, he distanced himself from its comments about the duty of compulsory military service, at least in peacetime.

In determining the meaning of free exercise of religion, Cardozo relied heavily on a historical approach. He detailed the treatment of conscientious objectors from colonial times to the present, noting that the constitutions and the laws of many states had contained exemptions for conscientious objectors from military service but only on the condition that a substitute or the money to hire one be supplied instead. His judgment was that the study of military science without a pledge of service was a lesser affront to the conscientious objector than the furnishing of either money or a substitute to wage war. The state requirement could be avoided by going to a different school, but that fact may not have been critical to Cardozo, for he did not view the requirement of training as an infringement on free exercise of religion in any event.[9]

Cardozo separated his personal from his legal views. When he first prepared a concurring memorandum, he seemed moved by sympathy for the objectors. Asking Justice Stone whether he thought it wise to circulate his draft, Cardozo commented, "All through the land conscientious and hard principled young men—for ethical if not religious reasons—are opposed to military training. I think it is oppressive to make them submit to it in these times of peace, though I am satisfied the state has the power to be oppressive if it chooses. The opinion of the Court seems to be quite without sympathy for their attitude."[10] In his published opinion, Cardozo was much more guarded, saying only that the state's policy "may be condemned by some as unwise or illiberal or unfair when there is violence to conscientious scruples, either religious or merely ethical."[11] But his study of the history of governmental treatment of conscientious objection and his analysis of the impact of the university's requirement of military training convinced him that this particular "violence to conscientious scruples" was not sufficient to violate the free exercise of religion.

Cardozo usually did not foresee a parade of horrible consequences of a particular course of action because he knew how to draw distinctions. Here he predicted that creation of an exemption would lead to refusal to pay taxes to support a war or any other policy objected to as irreligious or immoral. Analogizing the present case to those fears, he concluded, rather unsympathetically given his correspondence with Stone, that "[t]he right of private judgment has never yet been so exalted above the powers and the compulsion of the agencies of government. One who is a martyr to a principle—which may turn out in the end to be a delusion or an error—does not prove by his martyrdom that he has kept within the law."[12]

He sounded the same theme in a letter to Rabbi Wise when responding to a request for a copy of his opinion:

> I understand the feeling of the anti-militarists. Unfortunately it is not the function of the court to pass upon the fairness or wisdom of the rule adopted by the Regents. We have only to say whether there is anything in their action which is in conflict with a provision of the Constitution of the United States.

I rather think you will agree with the court that such a conflict was not made out.[13]

Hamilton was another in a long line of cases in which Cardozo refused to transform his personal sympathy for an individual's situation into legal support.

Cardozo's other major First Amendment opinion, *Grosjean,* also involved a long look at history and an analysis of the impact of state regulation in the form of a tax on a First Amendment freedom. The result was the most innovative civil liberties opinion that Cardozo ever wrote. Unfortunately, like his *Blaisdell* opinion, it never saw the light of day. Governor Huey Long, the charismatic political leader of Louisiana, had proposed, and the legislature had adopted, a tax on the advertising receipts of newspapers and other periodicals with a circulation of over twenty thousand copies per week. Nine newspapers had won an injunction against enforcement of the tax on the ground that it was unconstitutional both under the Louisiana Constitution and under the Equal Protection Clause of the Fourteenth Amendment, although the discussion was almost entirely about the violation of the Fourteenth Amendment. The lower court did not pass on the contention that the statute also violated the First Amendment.[14]

The state appealed to the Supreme Court, which unanimously concluded that the statute was unconstitutional. Justice Sutherland wrote a draft opinion holding the statute an unconstitutional violation of the Equal Protection Clause of the Fourteenth Amendment because it made taxation turn on the size of a newspaper's circulation. Because Cardozo had strong views supporting the power of the legislature to adopt reasonable classifications in exercise of its taxing power, he could not agree with the basis for Sutherland's conclusion. He drafted a concurring opinion that rejected the conclusion that the statute violated the Equal Protection Clause but asserted that a "tax discriminating against newspapers in favor of other forms of business, and discriminating against some newspapers in favor of others, is an unconstitutional abridgment of the freedom of the press." The tentativeness that marked Cardozo's *Hamilton* concurrence had disappeared. He recognized that it was settled that the Fourteenth Amendment incorporated the First. He rejected the argument that corporations did not enjoy Fourteenth Amendment "liberty," relying on *Pierce* for the proposition that once a corporation had been formed, liberty was closely associated with "the integrity of an established business, which is in the nature of a right of property . . . Freedom of expression in the conduct of a newspaper is the very life-blood of the business."[15]

The newspapers' attorneys had provided an extensive discussion of the history of taxes on newspapers in England and in the colonies before passage of the First Amendment, and Cardozo recounted that history in his draft. He saw the First Amendment as a response to official efforts to control the press. "Here was indeed a case where a power to tax would be a power to destroy."[16] The Louisiana tax, then, was a modern counterpart of the ancient repressive system of taxation.

Cardozo referred to the allegations that the circulation standard where taxation began had been chosen in order to punish those newspapers and periodicals that were critical of Huey Long, but he concluded that courts could not conduct a trial of the motivations of the legislature in passing a law. He also used the "incapacity of courts in that regard" as "a warning of possibilities of favoritism and tyranny" in order to set the stage for a far-ranging defense of freedom of the press: "Experimentation there may be in many things of deep concern, but not in setting boundaries to thought, for thought freely communicated is the indispensable condition of intelligent experimentation, the one test of its validity. The duty of the courts to ward off encroachments upon the freedom of the press is thus proportionate to the danger and its insidious approaches."[17] This is as passionate a statement about civil liberty as Cardozo ever wrote. There was no talk of the needs of the state or deference to the legislature. He concluded unambiguously—and innovatively—that newspapers could be required to pay their fair share of expenses of the state, but that it had to be on the basis of equality with other businesses and other newspapers. The statute did not do that; on the contrary, it singled out some newspapers and periodicals for special taxation. The opinion was a splendid combination of history and reason with a sympathetic appreciation of the setting in which the press functions and of modern requirements of its freedom.

Cardozo's stirring interpretation of the First Amendment produced an unusual result. Sutherland rewrote his opinion, placing the unconstitutionality of the statute on the grounds of the freedom of the press without passing on the equal protection argument. He adopted Cardozo's historical argument about the purpose of the First Amendment but muddied the waters in applying the First Amendment to the facts of the case. In his view, the tax was "bad because, in the light of its history and of its present setting, it is seen to be a deliberate and calculated device in the guise of a tax to limit the circulation of information to which the public is entitled in virtue of the constitutional guaranties." Part of that setting was the suspicious form of the tax in its aim at selected newspapers. It is unclear whether Sutherland meant to suggest that the statute was bad because of its bad motive, a ground that Cardozo had rejected, or that it was bad because of the ground that Cardozo asserted, the levying of a tax only on newspapers.[18] John Ely, writing in 1980 on the use of motive in testing legislative classifications, believed that the real ground of Sutherland's opinion was its condemnation of the classification of newspapers to be taxed so as to punish certain ideas. He thought it anachronistic to attribute to a 1936 opinion the more general and lofty notion that protection of First Amendment freedom required that taxes on newspapers be universal and uniform.[19] But Cardozo's 1936 opinion made just that argument. Unfortunately, when Sutherland recast his opinion, Cardozo withdrew his draft, and Sutherland thus spoke for a unanimous Court.

Cardozo's opinions in *Hamilton* and *Grosjean* are instructive. He was influenced by history and by the practical impact of the challenged governmental action in both cases. In *Hamilton,* his reading of the history told against recognition of the claimed right; in *Grosjean,* it told in favor of its recognition. In *Hamilton,* the impact of the military training on the objectors' religious beliefs was viewed as not substantial. Moreover, recognition of the individual right would have too great an impact on the ability of the state to carry out the essential function of military preparedness. In *Grosjean,* the potential for destruction of freedom of the press through a selective tax on newspapers was great, and the state's need for such a tax had not been shown. The different history and different impacts led to different results. *Grosjean* was a landmark result in the history of the First Amendment, and Cardozo deserves a large share of the credit.

A different type of First Amendment issue involved efforts of state and federal governments to punish seditious speech. Political assassinations throughout the world followed by the Communist Revolution in Russia produced a variety of legislation in the first two decades of the twentieth century aimed at the preaching of anarchy and revolution. These new statutes in turn produced a major constitutional debate about the limits placed by the First Amendment on the ability of government to punish advocacy of illegal action, such as politically motivated violence. The Supreme Court in the 1920s and 1930s steered a middle course between, on the one hand, immunizing speech entirely and punishing only the criminal activity and, on the other, permitting punishment of all speech with a "bad tendency," that is, any speech that might possibly produce criminal activity. Civil liberties forces eventually coalesced around various formulations of Justice Holmes's 1919 test that words could not be punished unless they created a "clear and present danger that they will bring about the substantive evils that Congress has a right to prevent."[20] However, until 1951, the Supreme Court used that test only in cases in which the legislature itself had not defined the conduct that presented such a danger.[21]

The Supreme Court's seditious speech cases in the 1920s mostly resulted in affirming convictions. The divisions reflected differences of opinion on the formulation of the proper test and its application to the evidence in particular cases. Only in Fiske v. Kansas in 1927 was there a reversal of a conviction. There a unanimous court concluded that the Kansas Syndicalism Act was unconstitutional when applied to a union organizer without proof of any advocacy of illegal activity. As written, the Court's opinion sounds more like a procedural due process opinion—a conviction based on no relevant evidence may not stand—than a First Amendment opinion.[22]

While on the New York Court of Appeals, Cardozo had been involved in this early free speech debate because one of the major cases came from his court. New York prosecuted and convicted Benjamin Gitlow under its Criminal Anarchy Act for his publication of the "Left Wing Manifesto," a pamphlet of a splinter group of the Socialist Party. The Act made criminal the advocacy of the overthrow of organized government by force, violence, assassination, or other unlawful means. In 1922, Judge Frederick Crane, for a five-judge majority, upheld the constitutionality of the statute on the basis that it was a basic right of government to protect itself against overthrow by force, and freedom of speech did not include freedom to advocate such overthrow. Crane also held that the evidence supported the application of the statute to the defendant.[23]

Cuthbert Pound dissented. Pound agreed with the majority that the Left Wing Manifesto advocated the overthrow of government by force and that such advocacy could constitutionally be punished. His opinion, like Crane's, adopted something like the bad tendency test as the measure of the constitutionality of this statute. But Pound read the Criminal Anarchy Act, passed in 1902 in the aftermath of the assassination of President William McKinley by an anarchist, as directed only at advocacy of the overthrow of all organized government. Although that was Gitlow's eventual hope, Pound read the Manifesto as urging the supplanting of the current government with a dictatorship of the proletariat, which was another form of organized government. Gitlow therefore could not be convicted under the New York statute. Cardozo, who was an admirer of Holmes and of Holmes's views on the First Amendment, simply joined Pound's dissent. He did not perceive, or at least did not raise, the serious constitutional problem that Gitlow was convicted on the basis of his publication of the Left Wing Manifesto without any showing of its danger. The failure of the prosecution to show "clear and present danger" that the words would bring an attempt at violent overthrow of the government, was the basis of the Holmes and Brandeis dissent when the Supreme Court affirmed Gitlow's conviction.

Cardozo had a chance to revisit the seditious speech issue when he joined the Supreme Court. The first case involved Georgia's conviction of Angelo Herndon, a young Communist leader in Atlanta, for violating a Georgia criminal statute by attempting to induce others to join in resistance to the lawful authority of the state. Not only was Herndon a committed Communist, but also he was black, although none of the opinions in the two United States Supreme Court cases dealing with his conviction mentioned that fact. Given the state of the constitutional law of sedition, the trial judge had given a charge that was very favorable to Herndon. The judge told the jury that it could not convict Herndon unless it concluded that he intended his advocacy to be acted upon immediately and that the evidence must show that immediate serious violence against the state was to be expected or was advocated. The jury found Herndon guilty. In affirming the conviction, the Georgia Supreme Court construed its statute as requiring only that Herndon be found to have intended that acts of violence occur at any time as a result of his influence. Herndon appealed to the Supreme Court, arguing that the Georgia statute as so construed was an unconstitutional impairment of his freedom of speech.

Justice Sutherland, in a 6–3 decision, held in 1936 that the Court had no jurisdiction because Herndon had not raised any federal constitutional question until the petition for rehearing in the Georgia Supreme

Court. That timing was too late under that court's settled rules. Herndon claimed that there had been no federal constitutional issue to raise until the Georgia Supreme Court had rejected the trial court's interpretation of the statute. Sutherland responded that a Georgia Supreme Court opinion delivered in another case after Herndon's conviction but while his motion for a new trial was pending in the trial court should have made it apparent how the Georgia Supreme Court would rule in his initial appeal. Herndon should therefore have raised the constitutional question then.[24]

Cardozo wrote a powerful dissent, joined by Brandeis and Stone, in which he contended that the Court should have considered the merits of Herndon's appeal. Cardozo first rejected the state's argument that the free speech issue should have been raised at trial. It would be novel to require a defendant who has received a favorable charge from the trial judge to preserve an objection on the chance that an appellate court would later decide that the charge was too favorable. The more serious issue was whether Herndon should have anticipated the Georgia Supreme Court's ruling because of that court's recent decision in another case under a different statute. Cardozo's comprehensive analysis of Georgia case law demonstrated that the intervening Georgia decision did not determine whether the Georgia Supreme Court would approve or disapprove the trial judge's charge in Herndon's case. Herndon had raised a serious First Amendment issue at the first moment when it was appropriate. The "great securities of the Constitution" should not "be lost in a web of procedural entanglements." The Court should decide Herndon's constitutional challenge to the Georgia criminal statute as it applied to his case.[25]

Herndon v. Georgia had a surprising aftermath. Herndon again challenged his conviction in the Georgia courts by seeking a writ of habeas corpus. The Georgia courts demonstrated that their procedural objections had not been a pretext to foreclose Herndon from raising his constitutional issues by agreeing to consider them in a habeas corpus suit.[26] The trial court rejected Herndon's claim that his conviction violated his liberty of speech and assembly, but it decided that the statute as applied was too vague to afford a clear enough standard of guilt. It ordered Herndon discharged from custody. The Georgia Supreme Court disagreed and remanded Herndon to custody. He appealed to the Supreme Court. In January 1937, a month before Herndon's appeal was argued, the Supreme Court in De Jonge v. Oregon reversed a conviction under a criminal syndicalism act in which the only evidence was that the defendant assisted in a public meeting of the Communist Party held for a lawful purpose. Chief Justice Hughes's opinion in *De Jonge,* for a unanimous court, held that the conviction violated the defendant's right of free speech and peaceable assembly.[27]

Three months later, in April 1937, two weeks after the momentous opinion in *Jones & Laughlin,* the Supreme Court decided Herndon's appeal. In Herndon v. Lowry, it reversed the Georgia Supreme Court, 5–4.[28] Roberts and Hughes joined Cardozo and the other two dissenters from Herndon v. Georgia, and Cardozo joined and contributed to Roberts's majority opinion. That opinion, which is wordy and imprecise in its holding, was apparently even more so in its original draft. Roberts followed the pattern of Hughes's opinion in De Jonge v. Oregon, reviewing the evidence to determine whether the statute as interpreted and applied violated Herndon's constitutional rights. Roberts concluded that it did. The evidence showed that Herndon belonged to the Communist Party and solicited members for it. It also demonstrated that he possessed Party literature advocating, among other things, proletarian revolutionary action and the establishment of Negro rule in the Black Belt of the South, where blacks were a numerical majority. Roberts concluded that this evidence failed to establish any attempt by Herndon to incite others to insurrection and therefore that his conviction under the statute violated his right of freedom of speech.

A final part of Roberts's opinion, probably added by Cardozo, was that the statute as applied also failed to furnish an ascertainable standard of guilt.[29] This part of the opinion was praised by Zechariah Chafee, a leading free speech proponent, as setting forth "better than anybody hitherto the importance of the procedure in a sedition proceeding."[30] As interpreted by the Georgia Supreme Court, the statute permitted a jury to speculate that Herndon's activity on behalf of the Communist Party might at some unknown time in the future lead others to commit violence against the state. Permitting a conviction on that basis violated both the freedom of speech and of assembly comprehended in the Fourteenth Amendment's protection of liberty. In prior years, convictions based on similar evidence had been affirmed. The reversal of the convictions of De Jonge and Herndon indicated that in applying statutes directed at advocacy of illegal activity against the state, the Supreme Court was ready to take a close look at what the defendant had said and done in order to determine whether the defendant's expression fell within the clear and present danger test. Cardozo's position in *De Jonge* and in Herndon v. Lowry indicates that he was now ready to support more constitutional protection of antigovernment speech than he contemplated when he had joined Pound's dissent in *Gitlow* in 1922.

One final First Amendment case in 1937 tested the interaction of the Court's growing deference to the legislature in economic matters with its growing scrutiny of legislation impinging on First Amendment freedoms. Associated Press v. National Labor Relations Board involved the application of the National Labor Relations Act to the Associated Press.[31] More particularly, the Board found that the AP had discharged one Morris Watson for union activities, and the Board ordered his reinstatement. When the case came to the Supreme Court, the AP's First Amendment contention was the major issue. AP contended that its effort to distribute the news in an impartial fashion to its members required that it have freedom to discharge any editors, like Watson, who manifested bias. It claimed that the Act's protection of the union activity of editors violated its freedom of the press.

The three "liberal" justices, Cardozo, Brandeis, and Stone, combined with Hughes and Roberts to uphold the challenged statute as economic regulation. The four conservatives would have struck it down as violating the First Amendment. Cardozo joined the opinion of Justice Roberts rejecting the AP's contention. Roberts, in an opinion that was as pithy as his opinion in Herndon v. Lowry was verbose, concluded that the freedom of the press did not exempt the AP from the application of general laws. There was no impact on AP's freedom because it could discharge Watson if he failed to follow the AP policy regarding nonpartisan editing of the news. The only thing it could not do was fire him for union activities.

Justice Sutherland's dissent spoke in eloquent terms about the absoluteness of the phrasing of the First Amendment and of the need to interpret its proscriptions broadly. He saw the compulsion on the AP to retain a union organizer as a news editor as an interference with the editorial discretion that was at the heart of freedom of the press, and the compulsion was only confirmed by the necessity of proving a concrete instance of bias before removal was possible.

The majority and the dissent clearly viewed the impact of the statute very differently. For the majority, there was no reason to exempt a news organization from the NLRA any more than from libel laws or the antitrust laws. Its legitimate interests were protected by enabling it to discharge Watson for failure to follow company rules. The statute was a general labor law and was not directed at the press in the way that the tax statute in *Grosjean* had been. For the dissenters, the First Amendment, which was directed toward a high public policy, protected the AP and took primacy over labor policy. Subtle biased editing would be difficult to prove, and imposing that test on editorial discretion was an encroachment on freedom of the press that would encourage other encroachments.

Although it is possible that the dissenters were using the First Amendment to mask antilabor feelings, they did have the advantage of logical consistency. They had applied the Bill of Rights broadly, if sporadically, in a variety of other situations. And there was more to their argument than Roberts acknowledged because, as the dormant Commerce Clause cases indicated, even a law of general applicability might have a substantial burden on an important constitutional value. The majority, however, was in the grip of deference to legislative power in April 1937, and the cause of civil liberties, which was of growing importance, had not yet engaged the Court strongly. The *AP* case is a good example of a clash between two "liberal" causes, and the reasoning of the resolution was unsatisfactory. In denying that any problem existed, the majority failed to explore the impact of the labor policy on the freedom of the press. Even though it is not fair to tax Cardozo with the failings of Roberts's opinion, it is apparent that he was sufficiently satisfied with its conclusion to join in that opinion.

Likewise, Cardozo saw no substantial First Amendment problem when Oregon regulated advertising by dentists to forbid advertising of prices, free services, superiority of performance, and the like. He joined Chief Justice Hughes's unanimous opinion that upheld the legislature's judgment that "bait advertising" posed enough of a threat of fraud that it was not unreasonable to outlaw it for all dentists.[32] The Court quite clearly saw the issue as one of economic regulation and not of free speech. Indeed, the words "free speech" do not appear in the opinion. Protection of commercial speech was still a long way off.[33]

The 1930s were a time of cautious exploration by the Supreme Court of the meaning of the First Amendment, and there were some notable advances in using that amendment to protect individual rights. Cardozo, who joined the growing number of opinions giving life to the First

Amendment, made one stirring contribution, his draft opinion in *Grosjean,* although its impact remained unknown because it was not published.

———————

Cardozo also addressed a number of criminal procedure constitutional issues. Unlike other issues that Cardozo had to decide as a member of the Supreme Court, he had long experience with criminal law questions in the New York Court of Appeals. He had given great weight to the interests of society in effective law enforcement. Also, he was not sympathetic to expansion of Fourth Amendment search and seizure doctrine or of the Fifth Amendment privilege against self-incrimination.

Cardozo heard his first major criminal case in 1932, his first year on the Court. It was Powell v. Alabama, one of the famous Scottsboro cases, involving the capital conviction of seven black men for the rape of two white women in an open gondola car on a train.[34] Walter Pollak, who had assisted Cardozo twenty years before in defending a theater's segregated seating policy, argued the case for the defendants. Cardozo joined Justice Sutherland's majority opinion reversing the convictions. The Court held for the first time that in certain circumstances, due process required the appointment of counsel for defendants in state criminal proceedings. Those circumstances were a capital case in which the defendants were unable to employ counsel and were incapable of defending themselves adequately. In addition, the Court examined the proceedings at the trial and determined that the requirement of counsel had not been met by a last-minute assignment without the opportunity to investigate the facts.[35] Cardozo also joined the unanimous opinion in 1935 in Norris v. Alabama that reversed a later conviction of these same defendants on the ground that evidence demonstrated the systematic exclusion of Negroes from jury service in the relevant Alabama counties. The Court, and Cardozo, recognized that issues of race and the ability of defendants' counsel to prepare for trial had to be considered in deciding whether a defendant had been afforded due process. A fair trial was a factual and not just a theoretical concept.[36]

Cardozo's first major criminal law opinion in the Supreme Court was in a case that split both the liberal and conservative blocs on the Court. In Snyder v. Massachusetts, Cardozo wrote for a majority of five that included Hughes, Stone, Van Devanter, and McReynolds in upholding a state court conviction of murder in the first degree resulting from the commission of a homicide during the course of a robbery.[37] The constitutional issue arose from the trial judge's ruling that Snyder's counsel, but not Snyder, could be present when the jury was taken to view the scene of the crime. Although Cardozo had originally voted in the Court's conference to reverse the conviction and had been assigned to write an opinion to that effect for a five-judge majority, he changed his mind while writing the opinion. He concluded that the state's procedure did not affect the fairness of the trial and hence did not involve a deprivation of due process. Perhaps reflecting the need to convince himself as well as his colleagues, Cardozo produced an intricate opinion that took the reader step-by-step through his reasoning process.[38]

Cardozo's doctrinal starting point was the Court's previous holdings that the Fourteenth Amendment limited only those state procedures that offended "some principle of justice so rooted in the traditions and conscience of our people as to be ranked as fundamental." His review of the cases led him to conclude that a defendant in a felony case had a constitutional right to be present personally only at those moments when his presence had "a relation, reasonably substantial, to the fulness of his opportunity to defend against the charge."[39]

Cardozo then considered a hypothetical situation. He argued that if the jury had conducted just a bare inspection, there would have been no Fourteenth Amendment violation because there would have been nothing that Snyder could have done at the viewing. Only if the jury had been shown the wrong place would there have been a problem, but constitutional rights should not depend on "so shadowy a risk."[40] In any event, Snyder did not claim that any particular injustice occurred. Snyder admitted at trial that he was part of the group that committed the theft and claimed that only larceny, not robbery, was the purpose of the crime. If that had been the case, the charge would have been reduced. On those facts, Cardozo concluded, Snyder's absence from the viewing caused no injustice and no due process violation.

Having set up and demolished that straw man, Cardozo moved on to the real case. Massachusetts allowed the lawyers to point out features of the crime scene to the jury without comment. What the jury saw was part of the evidence in the case. Cardozo downplayed the difference between a bare inspection and an inspection with participation by counsel as "one of degree and nothing more." Turning to history, he referred to the old practice of judges' appointing "showers" who were not counsel. His argument was that such a viewing was no different from a bare inspection insofar as Snyder's ability to participate was concerned. If there was no constitutional violation with a bare inspection or with "showers" who were not counsel, then the Fourteenth Amendment was not violated by a practice of using counsel, which was an additional assurance that nothing would be overlooked by either side. At that point, Cardozo finally got to a situation where Snyder's presence might have made a difference: Snyder, had he been there, might have been able to give advice to his counsel about what to show the jury. Cardozo's response focused on the facts of this case: "Constitutional immunities and privileges do not depend upon these accidents . . . The least a defendant must do . . . is to show that in the particular case in which the practice is exposed to challenge, there is a reasonable possibility that injustice has been done . . . No one can read what was said at this view in the light of the uncontroverted facts . . . and have even a passing thought that the presence of Snyder would have been an aid to his defense."[41]

Cardozo turned from the facts of the case to history to buttress his argument and to attack the approach of those contending for the existence of a constitutional right. Transferring to a "view" the privileges associated with a trial was "to be forgetful of our history" and was an example of that "fertile source of perversion in constitutional theory . . . the tyranny of labels."[42] In Cardozo's opinion, it was a mistake to conclude that just because a "view" occurred during a trial, it was part of the trial for purposes of requiring the presence of the defendant. He pointed out that in England, where the practice of allowing a "view" grew up, the judge was not required to attend and that, indeed, a committee of the jury could represent the whole body at the viewing. That history demonstrated that a "view" was something different from the trial itself, where a defendant's presence was required.

Cardozo finally addressed the difficult question of why Snyder had to show prejudice in order to demonstrate violation of a constitutional right and to obtain a reversal of his conviction. His answer was that prejudice did not have to be shown when the constitutional privilege or immunity was explicitly granted by the Constitution or was "obviously fundamental." But here the

> Fourteenth Amendment had not said in so many words that [Snyder] must be present every second . . . of the trial. If words so inflexible are

to be taken as implied, it is only because they are put there by a court, and not because they are there already, in advance of the decision. Due process of law requires that the proceedings shall be fair, but fairness is a relative, not an absolute concept. It is fairness with respect to particular conditions or particular results . . . The law . . . is sedulous in maintaining for a defendant charged with crime whatever forms of procedure are of the essence of an opportunity to defend. Privileges so fundamental as to be inherent in every concept of a fair trial that could be acceptable to the thought of reasonable men will be kept inviolate and inviolable, however crushing may be the pressure of incriminating proof. But justice, though due to the accused, is due to the accuser also. The concept of fairness must not be strained till it is narrowed to a filament. We are to keep the balance true.[43]

Without much support in precedent, Cardozo created two categories of due process protections, one in which violation required reversal of a conviction without any showing of prejudice and one in which prejudice was required. Cardozo did not draw the line between explicit and implied rights. He was willing to put some implied due process rights, like the opportunity to answer and to be heard, in the same category with explicitly mentioned rights because they were "fundamental" to the system. Other implied rights, such as the right claimed by Snyder, were of lesser importance and would only receive due process protection if their denial in particular circumstances thwarted a fair hearing.[44]

Roberts, joined by Brandeis, Sutherland, and Butler, wrote a strong dissenting opinion that took a different view of every aspect of the case. In Roberts's view, tradition, the Bills of Rights in state and federal constitutions, and state and federal law in all states but Massachusetts supported a defendant's right to be present at the inquiry from beginning to end. Under Massachusetts law, the jury's view of the scene was an important piece of evidence and was a part of the trial. That circumstance should have ended the matter. Roberts was not clear whether there was prejudice or not, but he concluded that prejudice did not have to be shown. The right to be present was the substance of the constitutional protection, and the court should not conduct any further inquiry. The whole point of procedural due process was that the manner of the trial be fair; the guarantee was not concerned with the justness of the result.[45]

Cardozo's treatment of Roberts's arguments carried into the constitutional sphere his prior attitude on the Court of Appeals that convictions should not be reversed unless substantial error or prejudice had occurred. He made a judgment that the right claimed by Snyder was not important enough to be recognized without a showing of prejudice, and he was confident that there was nothing Snyder could have done to help his cause by being present. His focus was the circumstances of this case, not the constitutional rights of defendants generally.

What became Cardozo's most famous Supreme Court criminal law opinion was Palko v. Connecticut, although in 1937, when it was decided, it did not attract much attention either inside or outside the Court.[46] Palko was another case in which the Court had to decide whether a particular provision of the Bill of Rights would be applied to the states by reason of incorporation within the due process protection of the Fourteenth Amendment.[47] In Palko, the state had charged Frank Palka (misnamed Palko throughout the proceedings) with first degree murder for killing two policemen who had sought to question him about a robbery. The trial judge excluded a confession and other important evidence offered by the prosecution, and the jury convicted Palko only of murder in the second degree.[48] Under Connecticut law, the state, with the permission of the trial judge, was permitted to appeal the verdict, and the Connecticut Supreme Court of Errors reversed the conviction for errors in instructions to the jury and in excluding evidence. There was a complete new trial. Palko was convicted of murder in the first degree and sentenced to death. The conviction was affirmed by the Connecticut Supreme Court. Palko appealed to the United States Supreme Court, raising the issue that the statute permitting a retrial after an appeal by the state violated due process.

Cardozo wrote the opinion for the Supreme Court rejecting Palko's contention. He held that the double jeopardy provisions of the Fifth Amendment were not binding on the states in toto, if at all, and that, therefore, Connecticut could constitutionally give the state, with permission of the presiding judge, a right of appeal on a question of law in a criminal case. Only Justice Butler would have held the statute unconstitutional, and he dissented without writing an opinion. Justice Hugo Black, who had recently been appointed to replace the retired Justice Van Devanter, joined the majority opinion, although he later repudiated his vote and the theory of Palko.

Cardozo followed earlier cases in concluding that the only provisions of the Bill of Rights that were applicable to the states were those that were "of the very essence of a scheme of ordered liberty."[49] The protections of the Bill of Rights not made applicable to the states were those that "might be lost, and justice still be done." Jury trials, the right to an indictment, and the privilege against self-incrimination had all been held not to be applicable to the states, and rightly so, said Cardozo. He drew on his own judgment of how "right-minded people" would regard these rights. "Few would be so narrow or provincial as to maintain that a fair and enlightened system of justice would be impossible without them."[50] That was a considerable overstatement. Although these provisions of the Bill of Rights might not survive a popular referendum, many of the "elect" whom Cardozo habitually talked about would have disagreed with his estimate of those rights on the basis of their familiarity with unfair prosecutions. But his view was consistent with his general belief that people should be punished when the evidence of guilt was strong.

Cardozo then described the characteristics of those Bill of Rights provisions that had been incorporated into the Fourteenth Amendment. Our political and legal history taught that they stood on "a different plane of social and moral values." Liberty and justice would not exist if they were sacrificed. Freedom of thought and speech, for example, were "the matrix, the indispensable condition, of nearly every other form of freedom." Likewise, it was "fundamental" to due process and liberty that there be no condemnation without a trial and that the hearing be real, and not a sham.[51]

This notion that incorporation of the Bill of Rights should be handled on a case-by-case, issue-by-issue basis was very congenial to Cardozo's incremental common law approach to decision-making. He carried the approach one step further, for he avoided deciding whether or not the Fifth Amendment's immunity from double jeopardy was "fundamental" and hence applicable against the states. Cardozo deliberately chose not to address the situation of a new prosecution for the same crime after an error-free first trial. He dealt only with the facts of this case, relying on a Supreme Court case that looked in the direction of incorporation to demonstrate that there was no Fourteenth Amendment violation in this case. In 1904, the Supreme Court had held that a retrial in federal court after an appeal by the government violated the Fifth Amendment's prohibition against double jeopardy.[52] Justice Holmes, joined by Justices White and McKenna, had dissented on the ground that there was no additional jeopardy in a retrial after a government appeal because it was all one case. Cardozo used Holmes's dissent to argue that "right-minded men could reasonably believe that in espousing that conclusion they were not favoring a practice repugnant to the conscience of mankind."[53] That is a plausible enough argument until one realizes that Cardozo did not apply it in situations when he concluded that due process had been denied and other members of his own Court dissented. In *Palko,* Cardozo simply declared, without arguing the point, that giving the state the same right to an error-free trial that the defendant had was not a "seismic" innovation and did not deny due process. "The edifice of justice stands, its symmetry, to many, greater than before."[54] In *Palko,* as in *Snyder,* Cardozo's conscience was not easily shocked.

Cardozo's formulation of the guiding principle of selective incorporation of the provisions of the Bill of Rights is still accepted by a majority of the Court today, although its application has been greatly expanded to include many provisions that Cardozo would have excluded. Today, a particular Bill of Rights provision either is or is not "fundamental." If fundamental, it applies to the states in the same measure as it applies to the federal government. Thus, when the Court decided in 1969 that protection against double jeopardy was "fundamental," the holding of *Palko* was overruled.[55] What remains of Cardozo's opinion is the concept that the Due Process Clauses of the Fifth and Fourteenth Amendments protect "fundamental" rights. In that regard, *Palko* is part of a long line of individual rights cases that culminated in the abortion case, Roe v. Wade.[56]

––––––––

Issues concerning race began to appear on the Supreme Court's calendar more frequently during Cardozo's tenure, although they were still not a major focus of litigation. Cardozo had had some exposure to racial problems before joining the Court. As the Shubert theater's lawyer, he had made a powerful argument to preserve their segregated seating policy, but on the bench he had voted to uphold the applicability of a public accommodations law to the same conduct. In private, Cardozo sympathized with the plight of black Americans in a general fashion, but he had expressed strong negative views about interracial relationships. There was no indication in his past that he brought any special experience or concern to constitutional claims of race discrimination.

That issue formed the background in the due process/right to counsel issue in the first Scottsboro case and in the due process/First Amendment challenge of Angelo Herndon. The issue was central in the equal protection argument raised in the second Scottsboro case, but the holding regarding the method of proof of discrimination broke no new ground. However, there were some cases in which new legal issues regarding racial discrimination were raised. They involved the efforts of the Democratic Party in the South to structure the election process to prevent African Americans from voting in the Democratic primaries that were effectively the final elections in many places.

Nixon v. Condon dealt with one in a series of efforts by Texas to enable the Democratic Party to achieve that result. It was reargued in 1932 at the first session of the Supreme Court at which Cardozo sat, presumably because the Court had divided 4–4 after the earlier argument.[57] Texas had once enacted a statute that explicitly made African Americans ineligible to vote in Democratic primaries. In 1927, the Court held that statute unconstitutional in Nixon v. Herndon as a clear violation of the Equal Protection Clause of the Fourteenth Amendment.[58] Texas then repealed the offending statute and enacted a new statute giving to the State Executive Committee of every political party the power to prescribe the qualifications of its own members who would be permitted to vote in the primary. The purpose of the statute was to remove the state from participation in any discrimination by a political party, since the Fourteenth Amendment prohibited denials of equal protection and due process by "any State" and not by any "private person." Nixon, again prohibited from voting, brought a new suit.

In the Supreme Court, the party functionaries who had forbidden African Americans to vote argued that the discrimination occurred not by any action of the state but by the action of a private voluntary association not covered by the prohibitions of the Fourteenth Amendment. Meeting that argument required a doctrinal reach, and Nixon provided one. He argued that the political parties, especially the Democratic Party, had become the custodians of political power, real instruments of government, and hence agencies of the state. After the case was reargued, Cardozo provided the decisive vote for invalidating this second, and more subtle, Texas effort to permit the Democratic Party to discriminate, and he was assigned to write the majority opinion.[59]

The Court was not prepared to break the boundaries between state and private action in the fashion suggested by the plaintiff and so Cardozo declined to pass on that contention. He found a narrower way in the technicalities of the law of voluntary associations to view the discrimination as that of the state. In his view, the state had not given back to the party the untrammeled authority to prescribe the qualifications of its members. Having originally taken the power to impose qualifications away from the party in the statute that had previously been declared unconstitutional, the state returned it by lodging the power in the party's State Executive Committee. That committee therefore acted not by virtue of authority delegated by the party but by virtue of authority delegated by the state. That circumstance was enough to bring the case within the authority of Nixon v. Herndon.

McReynolds, joined by Sutherland, Butler, and Van Devanter, dissented on the ground that nothing in the challenged statute discriminated against African Americans. Texas had left political parties free to determine their own members, and under state law, the executive committee spoke for the party and not for the state. Abstracting the case from the political reality, the dissenters' position was perfectly rational. Cardozo's opinion sounds like a strained effort to read the legal situation in light of his knowledge of the political reality of voting in Texas without, however, facing the ultimate question that the plaintiff had raised: would the state violate the Fourteenth Amendment if it created primary election machinery and left the issue of voter qualification to the parties that used it?

The Texas Democratic Party proceeded to reshape its membership rules to eliminate the basis for Cardozo's opinion. Immediately after the decision in Nixon v. Condon, it adopted a resolution limiting membership in the party to whites. When Albert Townsend, a county clerk, refused to give R. R. Grovey, a black would-be voter, an absentee ballot to vote in a Democratic primary election, Grovey sued Townsend for ten dollars in damages. The local Justice Court dismissed the suit, which went straight to the United States Supreme Court because no review was available in any Texas court for a ten-dollar claim. The Supreme Court in 1935 unanimously affirmed the dismissal in Grovey v. Townsend.[60] Justice Roberts's opinion found no basis for attributing the discrimination of the Democratic Party to the state. The fact that the state permitted the party to prescribe the qualifications for membership did not make the state responsible for the private discrimination. Nor was the party an agency of the state. Nor was the fact that a primary victory was tantamount to election relevant. What was relevant was the difference between the primary run by a private party and the official election run by the state.

Nixon v. Condon was yet another example in which the qualifications that Cardozo put into an opinion were real. When the issue of state responsibility arose in *Grovey,* the qualifications of *Condon*—that the state was responsible only if it participated in the discrimination—limited its antidiscrimination principle. Cardozo and the Court were not ready to move Fourteenth Amendment doctrine further into the realm of private discrimination to reach this instance of racial discrimination. In Nixon v. Condon, the Court had reached the limit of its willingness to find state responsibility in private discrimination. No justice was then ready to break the boundaries between state and private action by accepting the innovative arguments that the whole voting process involved the exercise of state sovereignty or that the reality of the situation in Texas was that the only election that counted was the primary and that it was part of the state's responsibility. That expansion of doctrine came in the 1940s and 1950s when the Court was willing to expand the bounds of state responsibility in voting cases and in a very few other areas, but not beyond.[61]

Different racial issues were involved in adjudicating the constitutionality of California's Alien Land Law, which restricted land ownership by persons who were ineligible to become citizens. Two cases arose out of the lease of California land by George Morrison, a Caucasian, to H. Doi, a person of Japanese ancestry. In Morrison v. California, *(Morrison I),* the Supreme Court in 1933 had unanimously upheld §9b of the Alien Land Law. That section made criminal the use of land by a member of a race ineligible for citizenship and put the burden on a defendant to prove his own citizenship once the state had proved use of land by a member of a race ineligible for citizenship. Morrison and Doi were convicted under §9b, and the Supreme Court dismissed their appeals as not raising a substantial constitutional question.[62] In the second Morrison v. California case, *(Morrison II),* Morrison and Doi appealed their conviction under §9a of the statute, which made criminal a conspiracy to violate the Alien Land Law.[63] A stipulation of facts stated only that Doi had gone on the land with Morrison's permission. It did not refer to Doi's race or to his ineligibility for citizenship. The California courts had affirmed the convictions on the ground that the burden was on the defendants to prove Doi's citizenship or eligibility for citizenship. The only issue raised in the Supreme Court related to the constitutionality of requiring Doi and Morrison to prove Doi's citizenship, not to the underlying law regarding his ineligibility to own land in California.

Cardozo wrote the opinion for a unanimous Supreme Court, reversing the conviction. He distinguished *Morrison I* on the ground that once the state had proved in the earlier case that the defendant belonged to a race ineligible for citizenship, it was not unfair to make the defendant prove his citizenship. The information was peculiarly within his possession. In *Morrison II,* by contrast, the state had only shown possession by Doi and had not proved anything with respect to his race. Since the charge was conspiracy, it was arbitrary and a violation of due process to impute guilty knowledge to Morrison that putting Doi in possession of the land was a crime without proving anything beyond Doi's possession. As far as Doi's conviction was concerned, the state should be made to prove his race. In Cardozo's view, stated in stereotypical fashion but carefully thought out, there was a significant factual issue. Although in "the vast majority of cases the race of a Japanese or a Chinaman will be known to any one who looks at him,"[64] in cases of mixed race, many defendants might not know enough of their own heritage to raise a defense. If ignorant, they might be convicted for failure to carry the burden of proving eligibility: "family traditions are not always well preserved, especially when the descendants are men and women of humble origin, remote from kith and kin."[65] It was therefore required that the normal rule placing the burden of proof on the prosecution be maintained.

Morrison was announced the same day as *Snyder,* but Cardozo mentioned neither case in the other. His *Snyder* opinion was filled with stirring references to the idea that due process protected only the essentials of the opportunity to defend. He refused to constitutionalize every aspect of a common law trial. His *Morrison* opinion, although it held that putting the burden of proof on the defendants to prove Doi's race was a violation of the Fourteenth Amendment, was more modest in tone. Not only was the state's change in the normal burden of proof rules troublesome with respect to Morrison, who might have difficulty proving Doi's race and citizenship, but also it was troublesome with respect to Doi himself, and this in the face of *Morrison I.* Cardozo was unwilling to state simply that placing the burden of proof on a defendant with respect to an essential element of a crime was unconstitutional. He limited his holding to the existing case, which led him to the justification that changing the burden of proof was unfair because poor immigrants might sometimes not know enough about their own heritage. That was a big stretch for the author of *Snyder.* Perhaps what really bothered Cardozo was that the burden was changed when there was no initial proof of criminality. He had stated in *Snyder* that the fundamentals of a fair trial would "be kept inviolate and inviolable, however crushing may be the pressure of incriminating proof."[66] Here there was no incriminating proof at all.

Although *Morrison II* was not controversial within the Court, it was so outside. Professor Edmund M. Morgan, one of the country's leading evidence experts, was very critical. He saw no constitutional basis on which to deny states the ability to modify the rules regarding burden of proof and thought that Doi had not been deprived of his opportunity to defend himself. Morgan, who was struck by the relation between *Snyder* and *Morrison II,* published an imaginary opinion reaching the opposite result in the latter, using Cardozo's own words from the former.[67] Writing privately, he stated that he actually felt more strongly than his article disclosed. He thought that Cardozo's result was wrong, his approach "worse than wrong," and his standard for constitutionality false and capable of "producing much harm."[68]

Cardozo's opinion announced a favorable result for Doi and Morrison, but there was a trace of condescension from the man, not of humble origin and with plenty of kith and kin, whose family traditions were very well preserved. Cardozo's language was reminiscent of the views he had expressed earlier about the sexual mores of the lower classes in *Mirizio.*[69] He gave Mr. Doi justice, but he also put him in his place. Cardozo had not lost his aristocratic instincts.

Like the other "liberal" justices on the Court, Cardozo was feeling his way on the appropriate deference owed to the government in civil liberties cases. Cardozo had strong feelings about the importance of freedom of speech and the press, and he joined in the Court's cautious expansion of the constitutional guarantees of free speech and free press. He never made a theoretical justification for the Court's First Amendment decisions that was comparable to his *Blaisdell* concurrence; nor did he address the reasons for a difference in approach between economic and civil liberties cases. But his *Grosjean* opinion was a major doctrinal statement. Underlying it was his conclusion that state tax classifications based on newspaper circulation were not entitled to the same degree of deference as those based on the number of counties in which a chain store operated (Liggett v. Lee). In *Grosjean,* it was the First Amendment that was entitled to deference. Cardozo's overall approach saw the Constitution as an instrument that was designed both to allow the government to govern the practical affairs of society and to preserve freedom of speech and other "fundamental rights" at the same time.

Cardozo came to the field of constitutional criminal procedure with his own well-developed sense of the balance between what was allowable to the state and what was essential to assure a fair trial for a defendant. He was not inclined to innovate in the direction of mandating expanded procedural rights for defendants. His major constitutional opinions in that field—*Defore, Snyder,* and *Palko*—all rejected that argument, although he accepted it in the *Scottsboro Cases* and in *Morrison II.*

In constitutional law cases, as in other cases, Cardozo gave substantial weight to history and precedent when he could find them. *Hamilton, Palko,* and *Snyder* are cases in which those limiting conditions on creativity were important factors in denying constitutional claims. In general, Cardozo was at the center of gravity of the Supreme Court civil liberties decisions during his tenure, whether they involved seditious speech, free exercise of religion, criminal procedure, or race issues. He did not dissent in any of them, whether they recognized the claimed constitutional right, as in *Grosjean, Herndon, De Jonge, Morrison II, Condon,* and *The Scottsboro Cases,* or denied it, as in *Hamilton, Grovey, Snyder, Palko, Semler,* or *Associated Press.*

Cardozo's remaining Supreme Court opinions dealt with a wide variety of topics. Some opinions were in common law cases resembling the staples of the docket of the Court of Appeals. Some involved interpretation of peculiarly national statutes and policies—taxation, bankruptcy, and federal jurisdiction; and some reflected the problems of the new field of administrative law that derived from the activity of a growing regulatory bureaucracy. These opinions should be considered, briefly, to give some hint of Cardozo's contributions to these fields.

One of the features of Cardozo's opinions, both in New York and in Washington, was their common law approach. He dealt with cases one by one and not in groups. That practice meant that he eschewed broad rules and focused on factual settings in the context of the issue at hand, whether it was an issue of judge-made, legislative, or constitutional law. His opinions were like chairs with six legs. It was often difficult to know which of the factual and legal props were essential to support his decision. A problem with this style of judging is that his opinions sometimes failed to provide much specific guidance to courts and lawyers. Sometimes an opinion caused confusion when a different style of opinion might have promoted clarity.

Professors of taxation have such a candidate in Welch v. Helvering, a Supreme Court case that we have already considered in connection with Cardozo's feelings about his father.[70] The issue was the deductibility, as an "ordinary and necessary" business expense, of moneys paid by commission agents of a bankrupt corporation to its creditors in order to safeguard the agents' own credit standing. In discussing whether the payments met the statutory definition, Cardozo wrote that there was no "verbal formula that will supply a ready touchstone . . . Life in all its fullness must supply the answer to the riddle."[71] Tax professors regard that much-quoted language as quite mischievous. Cardozo was dealing with a statute that had to be administered every day. Guidance and touchstones for business people and government agents were needed in the form of factors that would make the payment a personal expense, a business expense, or a capital expense. But there was something in Cardozo's opinion for everyone, and the opinion has only caused confusion.[72]

One of the better-known Cardozo opinions was his upholding of the concept of prospective overruling of precedent in Great Northern Railway Co. v. Sunburst Oil & Refining Co.[73] The Montana Railroad Commission had approved a tariff schedule of the Great Northern Railroad, and a shipper made payments to the railroad according to its terms. Since the Montana statute permitted an attack on the schedule, the shipper filed a complaint with the Commission. After the Commission found the schedule unreasonable, the shipper sued in a Montana state court and recovered a portion of its payments. In a previous case, the Montana Supreme Court had held that shippers could recover payments lawful when made if the tariff schedule was later held unreasonable. The railroad appealed the judgment for the shipper in *Sunburst,* and the Montana Supreme Court held that its earlier decision was wrong. Henceforth, a finding by the Commission that a rate previously established was unreasonable was not to be applied retroactively, so that shippers would not be able to recover excess payments. But the Montana Supreme Court decided that its former view was law until reversed and hence governed the relations between the shipper and the railroad that had acted on the basis of that view in this case. The court announced that it would apply its new rule of nonliability only prospectively. The shipper was therefore entitled to recover the overcharges. The railroad filed a petition for certiorari requesting the Supreme Court to exercise its discretion and review the Montana decision. It argued that the court's refusal to apply its new rule in this case violated the Fourteenth Amendment.

The petition was filed with the Court during the summer of 1932, a few months after Cardozo had joined the Court. He studied it over the summer and noted on the petition that "there is grave doubt whether this [position of the Montana Supreme Court that it would not apply its new rule retroactively to cover the present case] is due process."[74]

The Supreme Court granted the petition for review and heard argument in the 1932 term. Cardozo, having resolved his doubts, voted with a unanimous court to uphold the decision of the Montana Supreme Court. His opinion for the Court concluded that there was no violation of due process when the Montana court followed a precedent that it thought was wrong. Although the "ancient dogma" was that the court's latest decision always had been "law," the state was free to choose for itself whether it would accept that view or decide that its new view would be law only in the future. There was no one meaning, as far as constitutional due process was concerned, of stare decisis (following past precedent). "The choice for any state may be determined by the juristic philosophy of the judges of her courts, their conceptions of law, its origins and nature."[75] That view of the freedom accorded to Montana was in line with Cardozo's pragmatic approach to law. The law was a social construct, certainly not something that was immanent and just waiting to be perceived. Cardozo's stamp of approval on prospective overruling gave an impetus to the technique.[76]

Federal administrative law was one of the new topics to which Cardozo was exposed when he came to Washington. Jones v. Securities & Exchange Commission dealt with the ability of a party under investigation by the SEC to thwart the proceeding.[77] Jones had filed a registration statement with the SEC covering a proposed issue of securities. The SEC, which had started an investigation concerning the accuracy of the statement, subpoenaed Jones to produce numerous documents. Jones withdrew the statement and contended that his action ended the jurisdiction of the SEC to continue its proceeding. The SEC obtained an order from the federal district court requiring Jones to testify and to produce the subpoenaed documents.

When the case finally reached the Supreme Court in 1936, Justice

Sutherland, for a six-judge majority, concluded that the withdrawal deprived the SEC of jurisdiction to continue its investigation. Absent some specific prejudice to the public, the registrant had an absolute common law right to withdraw his statement. Sutherland was wary about the exercise of administrative power and saw the effort of the SEC to enforce its subpoena as embodying the entering wedge of arbitrary power infringing on ultimate principles of personal liberty.

Cardozo, who had revealed some concerns of his own about administrative power earlier, dissented for himself, Brandeis, and Stone. His focus was on the conduct of the registrant and the protection of the public. He saw the statutory investigative power of the SEC as directed to safeguarding the public interest by punishing past misconduct and preventing future harm. When wrongs like these have been committed, they "must be dragged to light and pilloried." If the wrongdoer can stop an investigation by withdrawing the application, then the "statute and its sanctions become the sport of clever knaves."[78] Cardozo took issue with the constitutional references in the majority opinion, finding no specific provision that was relevant and nothing in "the spirit of the Constitution" that protected an applicant to a regulatory body from inquiry into deceptive conduct. He mocked the constitutional allusions of the majority opinion in striking, if florid, language. A commission, with power only to report but not to coerce, "is likened with denunciatory fervor to the Star Chamber of the Stuarts. Historians may find hyperbole in the sanguinary simile."[79] Cardozo did not let his reservations about administrative agencies cloud his understanding that the purpose of the statute was the protection of the investing public and the unmasking of those who might seek to deceive it. *Jones* was a federal counterpart to his famous Court of Appeals opinion in Meinhard v. Salmon. In *Meinhard,* he had imposed a high standard of duty on a fiduciary. In *Jones,* he would have given strong enforcement power to the agency charged with monitoring the performance of issuers of securities—a form of statutory fiduciary obligation.

After the opinions in *Jones* were delivered, the *Chicago Tribune* ran a biting editorial attacking the Supreme Court dissenters who refused to condemn tyrannical New Deal regulatory legislation. Under the headline "Justice Brandeis and Justice Cardozo," it noted the "strange" element that these Jewish justices were so insensitive to the importance of the Bill of Rights, not just in property cases but in a personal liberty case like *Jones.* The point of the editorial was that the dissent was clearing the way for prejudiced majorities to attack minorities and that those "considerations should have great weight [for Jewish judges] where they seem to have the least."[80] Cardozo was a reader of newspaper commentary about his decisions, and this one upset him. Showing the editorial to Frankfurter, he asked him, literally in tears, whether the writer expected him to vote against his conscience when he concluded that a statute was constitutional.[81] Perhaps at one level he understood that a newspaper that was violently opposed to the New Deal would be hostile to his constitutional views. At another, he was a little naive and was occasionally surprised and upset by unpleasant criticism, especially when directed at him personally. He exhibited a different emotion to Alan Stroock, angrily telling him that the editorial writer, "who has not got his roots as deeply in America as I have dares to speak of me as if I were not an American."[82] Cardozo was entitled to be angry, but his reaction also underlined two other aspects of his personality: thin-skinned sensitivity and an aristocratic sense of his place in the country.

Jones, together with the delegation of powers cases and the state administrative law decisions discussed earlier, demonstrates that Cardozo caught on quickly to a variety of legal problems presented by that relatively new area of the law. Even though he brought some reservations with him from his New York experience, he was ready to let Congress and the President experiment with vesting considerable power in administrative agencies. He helped begin the task of marking out their relation to the judiciary, other branches of government, private parties, and the public.

––––––––

Cardozo's Supreme Court career produced few surprises. He had already declared himself in New York as being deferential to legislative judgment with respect to regulation of the economy. He occasionally found both in New York and in Washington that the legislature had overstepped constitutional bounds, usually in the means chosen to effect a legitimate goal. Because the Depression produced a great social and economic dislocation, the New Deal statutes that he addressed on the Supreme Court were more far-reaching and comprehensive than those he had considered on the Court of Appeals. Cardozo responded by producing a ringing statement of support for a powerful, activist government and of the need for a changing Constitution in his unpublished *Blaisdell* concurrence. His argument that changes in society justified reinterpretation of particular constitutional provisions in order to preserve their underlying purposes—which found its way into Chief Justice Hughes's majority opinion—was a benchmark for constitutional law throughout the rest of the century.

The major impact of Cardozo's insight about continuous constitutional reinterpretation was in the area of the regulatory power of democratically elected state and federal government. Whereas his voting record virtually mirrored that of Stone and Brandeis, he did not share Brandeis's distaste for bigness in business and government, and he was more sympathetic toward governmental experiments than Stone. At a time of great constitutional ferment, his voice and his vote mattered.[83] Cardozo was much less certain about reinterpretation in the emerging field of civil liberties. He justified his doctrinally innovative *Grosjean* opinion by an appeal to history that showed the need to protect freedom of the press, not by an appeal to the need for change in a modern society. It would be left to the next generation of judges and scholars to develop Cardozo's insights about "fundamental" rights and an evolving Constitution into modern civil liberties law.

28

Legacy

At the end of September 1937, Cardozo returned to Washington from his summer vacation in White Plains, New York. He had a new Supreme Court colleague, Hugo Black, who was being criticized because of the disclosure that early in his political career he had joined the Ku Klux Klan. Although Cardozo was upset that Black's problem involved the Court in controversy, he told his law clerk Joe Rauh that "any young man can make a mistake and must be given another chance."[1] Cardozo immediately paid a call on Black and paid him another one the day before Black was to take his seat. He was the only Justice to do that, Black reported.[2]

Cardozo was sixty-seven years old that fall, and two years had passed since his last heart attack. The work of a Supreme Court justice in the late 1930s was stressful, but Cardozo was determined to keep working at his usual pace. On Monday, December 6, he handed down his opinion in Palko v. Connecticut, in which he elaborated his view of the relation between the Bill of Rights and the Fourteenth Amendment. He felt ill all that week. On Friday, he stayed in bed until eleven o'clock, when he got up to go to court. When he returned after argument, Kate Tracy insisted that he rest. Cardozo did so, but he could not be deterred from going to Brandeis's apartment at six o'clock for the regular Friday evening meeting with Brandeis and Stone. He returned at quarter-past seven and shortly thereafter had a heart attack, which was followed by a case of shingles. After a few days in critical condition, in which he was treated at home, he showed marked improvement and was allowed to sit up. His doctors predicted that he would be able to return to work by the February session.

Meanwhile, Cardozo had completed his assignment to write the Court's opinion in Smyth v. United States, and it was ready to come down. Stone was writing a concurring opinion. Consequently, when Cardozo fell ill, Joe Rauh asked Stone whether he would simply note a concurrence. Stone, however, circulated his concurring opinion, which made an argument that needed a response. The doctors said that Cardozo was not to be bothered with the opinion and that it should be gotten out of the way. Rauh inserted a two-sentence response with Chief Justice Hughes's approval, and the opinion came down on Monday, December 13, although Cardozo was not present. It was his last opinion.[3]

In the first week of 1938, Cardozo's situation took a disastrous turn. He had a stroke that paralyzed his left side and affected his speech. Cardozo remained in his apartment, with responsibility for making decisions about his care being shared among the Lehmans, William Freese, Kate Tracy, and Rosalie Hendricks and Edgar Nathan, children of Edgar Nathan, Sr. Dr. Worth Daniels, who was credited with saving Justice Stone's life two years before, was brought in to take charge of Cardozo's treatment. Joe Rauh stayed on to cheer up Cardozo, to read to him when that was possible, and to respond to letters and telephone calls. Eventually, Cardozo recovered enough so that he was able to see a few friends once in a while, but he remained weak and depressed.

In May, Sissie Lehman suggested that Cardozo be brought to the Lehman home in Port Chester, New York. She hoped that living in the country would help his recovery. He was taken on a stretcher through the window of a train and made the trip in a private compartment with Dr. Daniels, a nurse, Kate Tracy, Catherine Walsh, and Joe Rauh. When the train stopped in New York City, Cardozo asked where he was. On being told, he replied, "This is the place I love. I feel better." He did improve somewhat after he got to the Lehmans' home, and he could even be taken by wheelchair to a car for a drive in the countryside. But in July, Cardozo failed quickly, and he died on July 9, 1938.[4]

Cardozo's great interests in life had been his immediate family, his professional work, and ideas. He liked to socialize with people singly or in small groups, and he met with a substantial number of men and a few women in that way. But he was exceedingly private. Learned Hand's comment that "very few have ever known what went on behind those blue eyes" was accurate.[5] Nellie, with whom he shared his life, knew most. Cardozo led a sheltered life, but neither a cold nor an empty one. Never a husband or a father, nevertheless he experienced a large part of the closeness of those relationships in his life with Nellie. He had the experience of devoting himself fully to another.

When Cardozo went on the bench, he made an enormous personal impression on those with whom he worked. Although he had faults— vanity, excessive love of praise, sensitivity to criticism, and an aristocratic sense of entitlement to the service and deference of others—he impressed people with his kindness, his personal and intellectual integrity, and a serenity that projected extraordinary character. Felix Frankfurter captured the elements of a striking presence: "Great courtesy, accentuated by the slight stoop of the cloistered scholar, a face, according to Holmes, 'beautiful with intellect and character' . . . a fine head with silken white hair."[6]

Cardozo became a commanding figure in the law. He had intelligence, judgment, and style, all in large measure. His family situation left him with time to lecture and write, and his messages commanded attention. His accomplishments and his personality brought him many influential friends, and those friends were crucial in advancing his career at every step. His clear and persuasive defense of the lawmaking aspect of his job endeared him to liberal lawyers and judges, as well as to the academics who taught successive generations of law students and who made him known to a wider public. Several lengthy articles and books studied his approach to law both during his lifetime and immediately after his death.[7] In an unprecedented action in 1939, the law reviews at Columbia, Harvard, and Yale published a joint issue devoted to an examination of his work.[8]

Cardozo emphasized that part of the judicial task involved a choice among conflicting precedents or a choice to overrule existing precedents when they no longer served society well. This was a theme that was becoming central to modern legal education. He also found important issues hidden in humdrum factual situations and brought them into the open with thoughtful discussion. Cardozo wrote with flair. His opinions "taught well" in class. He openly appreciated the work being done by academics and was one of the first judges to cite their work regularly in his opinions.[9] In return, they applauded him loudly and muted their criticism.

The new generations that have appeared since Cardozo's death have not experienced the spell of his personality; their criticism has been louder. Yet Cardozo's reputation has endured. Although the passage of time has made many of his opinions obsolete, his major opinions, his theoretical writings, and his approach to judging have remained a subject for study. In 1961, on the fortieth anniversary of *The Nature of the Judicial Process,* the *Yale Law Journal* reconsidered that lecture series in half of an issue.[10] In the 1970s, John Noonan devoted a portion of a book to Cardozo's *Palsgraf* case, and the *Cardozo Law Review* devoted its first issue to Cardozo's life and contributions to law.[11] In the 1980s and 1990s, many articles studied specific aspects of Cardozo's work.[12] In 1990, Richard Posner's *Cardozo: A Study in Reputation* made a quantitative analysis of citations to his opinions that confirmed that Cardozo still remained influential, and he advanced a number of reasons for that status. Posner's effort provoked further writing about Cardozo's work.

Cardozo deserves the high place that he has held in the judicial hall of fame. He delivered important opinions with a memorable style. Given his reputation as a progressive, the surprising element about the totality of his opinions is the balance between innovative opinions, in which he modernized law by bringing a legal doctrine into line with current social or economic conditions, and noninnovative opinions. Cardozo did not use public policy considerations to modernize law in all those instances where he might have done so. He lived by the limits that he thought hedged in a judge. Sometimes he believed that modernization was the responsibility of other institutions of government. Sometimes he simply rejected the proposed change as not warranted. And sometimes he took a tough view of the facts to deny recovery to what seems the more deserving party as a matter of then-existing legal doctrine. Although Cardozo justified a pragmatic progressivism, he justified it in moderation and applied it with a measured, skillful touch. Cardozo's record and reputation have made him a point of comparison for other judges, usually in terms of a judge or judicial nominee falling short of the mark, as being "no Cardozo."[13] Cardozo remains in the public memory as a standard of judicial excellence.

Cardozo's enduring importance has derived from both his opinions in particular cases and his approach to judging. He left succeeding generations several messages about the purposes and limits of judging that are as important in our day as they were in his.

The initial message was simply descriptive. Cardozo reflected on the elements of judicial decision-making—logical reasoning from precedent; history; custom; and policy considerations—and explained them clearly to the profession and to the public. Some judges have commented that his writings do not help them to decide particular cases.[14] That was not his purpose. As the constitutional scholar Thomas Reed Powell said, Cardozo "tells us how much easier it is to find the ingredients than to fix the proportions of the blend . . . Judge Cardozo, like wise men generally, has no general rule."[15] He did not tell judges precisely what to do; rather, he described different elements that they should keep in mind. Cardozo understood that individual judges would weigh the elements differently in hard cases and reach varying results. The important thing was to reflect on the elements conscientiously to see how they played out. Cardozo's explanation in his lectures about how he decided a case when logical analysis, history, and public policy pointed to a variety of possible results was quite general. He spoke of intuition and life experience as helping him reach a conclusion.

But his judicial opinions contained further messages. They indicate that there were additional, more specific considerations that helped Cardozo to decide particular cases. In almost every substantive field, Cardozo approached doctrinal problems with a general acceptance of the fundamental legal principles that had previously been developed, whether it was negligence doctrine in torts, the general principles of contract in business dealings, or the selective incorporation of provisions of the Bill of Rights into the Fourteenth Amendment. He looked to see where the law was, that is, how far the precedents went toward resolving the particular dispute. That approach narrowed the issues in most cases, sometimes to the point at which a particular precedent, if followed, was decisive.

A second consideration was often crucial. Cardozo examined the record in each case, including the findings of the trial judge or jury, to create a picture of the factual situation. His conclusions in many of his best-known cases were heavily influenced by his particular vision of the facts. For example, MacPherson v. Buick is famous because Cardozo cast aside the privity concept; however, his conclusion was driven by his perception that the car manufacturer ought to have foreseen that the person who bought a new Buick from a Buick dealer was the person most likely to be injured by a defective part. Likewise, Cardozo's judgment in *Palsgraf* depended on his assessment that Mrs. Palsgraf was standing too far away to be within any foreseeable range of harm from the railroad guard's negligent conduct. The result in *Dougherty,* the case of the window washer without a safety belt, was determined by Cardozo's factual decision that the employee had "voluntarily" assumed the risk of the dangerous working conditions. The perception in *MacPherson* was gifted; the opinion has won general acclaim. The perception in *Palsgraf* was problematic; the opinion has been controversial. The perception in *Dougherty* seems wrong; the opinion has not been much noted, but it is not an ornament to Cardozo's reputation.

Cardozo's sense of the factual situation also influenced his opinions in other fields. For all the doctrinal discussion about consideration in *Allegheny College,* involving Mary Johnston's promised gift to the college, his vision of the nature of the pledge, the obligation undertaken by the college, and the relation between the partial payment and the attempted cancellation of the gift by the donor played a large role in the eventual outcome. Likewise, in all the contract formation cases, Cardozo sought to determine what the parties had really undertaken to do, which was a substantial component of determining their reasonable expectations. Cardozo made similar judgments in most of the equity cases and in many others as well. Although principles of law were often mixed in with fact questions and were sometimes the dominant, or even the sole, issue in a case, his vision of the facts was an important element in his actual decisions.

Once Cardozo had melded the legal issues and the factual setting, most cases were over. Either the facts or the governing case law indicated clearly what the outcome should be for an appellate judge who was respectful of the prior law and the fact-finding power of the trial judge or jury. Understood in that fashion, Cardozo was right in asserting that most of his cases could have been decided only one way. But he recognized that even with the facts settled and general doctrinal principles accepted, there were a small percentage of cases, amounting to a large number over the years, in which the proper result was not so clear.

In such cases, one element that did not receive significant attention in his lectures, although it has been much discussed in this book, was the deference that Cardozo paid to the legislature. His respect for the democratically elected legislature as a major source of social values helped shape Cardozo's decisions both in some obvious and in some less obvious ways. That respect was evident in cases in which he refused to consider reforming a legal doctrine because that decision was the prerogative of the legislature, with the concurrence of the governor or president. That was the case when the proposed reform involved too great a break with established rules that formed the basis of many parties' expectations or when the court could not obtain the factual information needed to decide whether or to what extent change was needed. Only the legislature should change the rules in those situations. Another area where Cardozo followed legislative policy was the criminal law. Those statutes expressed a strong social decision that certain behavior should be punished. Cardozo would not reverse a conviction when there was substantial evidence of guilt unless there was an important trial error that constituted significant prejudice. Although he opposed capital punishment, he enforced the death penalty because it was the law.

Cardozo also understood that there were limited resources available to government, and he respected the legislature's power over the purse. He was reluctant to have the courts impose substantial new costs on the state. Also, he shared the Progressives' faith in the betterment of society through government regulation and was wary of judicial interference through imposition of substantial financial liabilities. Politically, he was a progressive in the sense that he believed in the need for government regulation to redress economic and social ills, and his judicial philosophy generally found no constitutional bar to such regulation. Rejecting the tendency of the preceding generation of judges to engage in close oversight of the goals and the means of regulation, Cardozo gave substantial, but not unlimited, deference to the combined vision of the legislature and executive regarding economic and social needs. But he gave considerably less deference to governmental action that impinged on free speech because he saw the First Amendment as fundamental to his notion of human freedom in a democratic society.

Another feature of Cardozo's decision-making was his sense that, except for cases involving specific equitable principles that called for doing justice on an individualized basis, justice was best served by either upholding or modifying the general rules across the board. He did not attempt to remedy the harsh application of fair rules in hard cases, as judges sometimes do, by manipulating the facts or ignoring relevant doctrine in order to evade the rule. One possible exception was *Hynes,* in which Cardozo upheld the cause of action of a boy swimmer injured while technically a trespasser, but even there Cardozo did modify the governing legal principle a little bit to cover the case. Usually, when Cardozo did not think that the rule should be altered, he followed it and accepted the consequences, as in the teachers' pension cases in which the strict enforcement of procedural rules deprived the beneficiaries of benefits. Sometimes, especially in his private memoranda to his colleagues on the Court of Appeals, Cardozo was explicit that the result called for by applicable legal principles was harsh, but that the court had no power to alter it. His eventual refusal to recognize a remedy for the wife in Allen v. Allen, whose husband had her jailed without cause, was just such a case.[16]

Cardozo's sense that equitable principles focused on justice at retail and that the common law focused on justice at wholesale captured the different histories and traditions of those two branches of law.[17] Justice at wholesale addressed the question whether a particular rule was a just rule. When Cardozo did vote to alter an established doctrine, it was because in his view, the doctrine demonstrably failed to comport with current public values, not because it produced an unwelcome result in one case.

Cardozo often faced the question of the relation between his personal value system and his judicial solution. When it came to the large political, economic, and social components of a decision, he tried hard to let what he conceived to be dominant societal values govern. As a human being, he might sympathize with the plight of an injured worker or he might vote against a bonus for war veterans or he might oppose the death penalty or he might favor a religious exemption from military instruction at a state university. His job as a judge required him to apply a different set of norms—principles of law that were derived from a judge's professional view of societal norms or that were declared by another governmental body. In cases involving those issues, he often voted against his personal predilections, although once in a while his personal beliefs blinded him to a serious conflict over governing values.

People v. Carey, the rape case in which he discussed the evidential value of the victim's loss of chastity, was one such case. His sense was that there was a relation between the victim's prior loss of chastity and proof of her consent to intercourse. Since she had consented once before, he felt that she had lost her honor and that there was less reason for her to refuse consent later and less reason to believe her testimony that she had refused. Cardozo did not know or acknowledge that, with a growing change in sexual mores, his view was controversial. If he had realized it, he would have had to put aside his own Victorian views about sex and gender and consider, as a judge, how to choose among competing societal values in deciding the evidence issue.

When Cardozo saw the issue in a case in terms of individual responsibility, he was most likely to fuse his personal values with his conception of dominant societal values. Acting honorably, doing one's duty to others, behaving responsibly, carrying out obligations of loyalty, and keeping promises were parts of Cardozo's value system that he also found in, or imputed to, the larger society because of their general moral worth. Cardozo's opinions reflect these substantive values. He required people—like the man who got on the Flopper—to avoid foreseeable risks or to bear the consequences if they did not. He assumed that people who engaged in business with one another generally meant to assume enforceable contractual obligations, and he worked hard to spell them out when the terms were not clear. When obligations and duties were undertaken, he expected people to fulfill them. In such cases, when Cardozo's values were in harmony with well-established social values, the force of the language in his opinions—for example, "the punctilio of an honor the most sensitive"—indicated that the subject was close to his heart.

Cardozo's philosophizing about law made him a self-conscious judge. His philosophy did not result in decisions driven by abstractions, however, but rather in decisions crafted with a disciplined carefulness. His philosophy was one of method, not ideology. He examined each case on the basis of his vision of the governing facts, and he gave a fair hearing to each argument made by each of the parties. He thought carefully about every case, and although he sometimes went wrong on the law or the facts, it was not because he was careless. Cardozo tried hard to decide cases impartially, without predispositions based on the nature of the parties. His opinions did not favor, as his father's had, those who advanced his judicial career. It was these qualities of impartiality and disinterestedness that he saw as the core of the judicial temperament.

A corollary of these messages about the judge's job was equally important. Cardozo reminded the public and the profession that although judges make law, they are different from legislators. The political element in judicial lawmaking is different from the politics of lawmaking by legislators, for judges work within stricter limits. The slogan "all law is politics" is often heard in academia, and it has found its way into journalism and political rhetoric as a statement that judges manipulate legal doctrine to achieve whatever result they wish. It is certainly possible for judges to do so. Cardozo agreed with the realist insight that law had links to politics; however, he rejected the more extreme form of that argument, put forth by some realists and by some recent critical theorists, that denies or greatly diminishes the difference between judges and legislators and denies also the difference between law and politics.

As Cardozo put it, building on Holmes, a judge "legislates only between gaps. He fills the open spaces in the law. How far he may go without traveling beyond the walls of the interstices cannot be staked out for him upon a chart . . . [R]estrictions . . . are established by the traditions of the centuries, by the example of other judges, his predecessors and his colleagues, by the collective judgment of the profession, and by the duty of adherence to the pervading spirit of the law."[18] Since Cardozo's time, the self-consciousness of judges has grown considerably, so that judges must make a deliberate choice about their own place on the creative lawmaking spectrum. The struggle over the appropriate judicial role is renewed in every generation. There is nothing sacrosanct about the Cardozo messages, even though they are the messages that by and large most judges have attempted to live by for centuries.

Another related message was that judges should understand their place in a democratic society. Their lawmaking function was modest. Judges were free to take public policy considerations into account, but they should do so only at the edges of doctrine and to further a developing public policy. A court might modify privity so as to allow the purchaser of a defective product to sue the manufacturer in certain circumstances; it could not abolish the fault requirement to allow all injured persons to recover damages irrespective of the manufacturer's negligence. A court might strain to find consideration and hence to enforce a promise in a charitable subscription case; it could not abolish the consideration standard totally. Cardozo saw much more scope for judicial lawmaking in the field of constitutional interpretation because the generality of many of the Constitution's most important provisions indicated that the Constitution was designed to be updated constantly. He would therefore uphold a state-imposed mortgage foreclosure moratorium during the Depression in spite of the language of the Contract Clause. But even in matters of constitutional interpretation, Cardozo sought guideposts and limitations and found them in the power of the other branches of government, in the history and purposes of particular constitutional provisions, and in the concept of fundamental principles of justice. In his hands, those guideposts restrained judges and limited the creation of new constitutional doctrine.

Just as Cardozo resisted the argument that law was all politics, so he resisted the argument that judicial choice was all subjective. The opposite of "subjective" in this context was not really "objective," although Cardozo sometimes used that word. He used the term to mean that judges should be looking for some collective judgment, whether it was expressed in the guideposts of history, custom, the action of the legislature, or what he called the views of "right-minded men and women." At other times, Cardozo sought help from commonsense notions of what was reasonable to ordinary people or what would be understood in a particular trade or business.

Cardozo resisted subjectivity because he thought that it would lead to the nihilism that he glimpsed in the more extreme writings of some realists. His vision required that judges respect the powers of other institutions even as they modernized those legal rules that were their primary responsibility. His references to "right-minded" people as models of judgment had an aristocratic cast, but his reaching out to community values and to other institutions of government, especially the legislature, blended a strong respect for democracy into his judicial vision. Thus, in Jewel Carmen v. Fox Film Corp. he put aside his subjective opinion that the young actress who broke her contract had behaved dishonorably and decided in her favor because the legislature had given her the absolute statutory right to repudiate a contract signed as a minor.[19]

The balance in Cardozo's messages—the justification of judicial lawmaking and the insistence on important restrictions—has made it possible for judicial theorists with divergent views to find supporting language in Cardozo's writings. This quality is the ambiguity that many have perceived in Cardozo's work. It is possible to find ambiguity because Cardozo did not supply a single formula for making decisions. But Cardozo was not ambiguous about his own position. He believed that judges should be disciplined and moderate in their ongoing creative work of modernizing law. His counsel that a judge should be respectful of precedents, other institutions, and the work of the trial court and jury; should be well informed about social conditions and trends; and should be resolutely impartial, was neither liberal nor conservative. That counsel was equally useful for both causes in appropriate circumstances. He furnished argument both for those who wanted maximum, and for those who wanted minimum, judicial creativity. Thus, he was the exemplar of the "serene optimism of Progressive jurisprudence,"[20] the "premier Realist judge,"[21] a pragmatist with a "moralistic streak," who occasionally engaged in "proto-economic" analysis.[22] Nonetheless, he also provided a text on judicial caution for Supreme Court Justice Ruth Bader Ginsburg to use at her confirmation hearing: "Justice is not to be taken by storm. She is to be wooed by slow advances."[23]

Cardozo's final message was that all the other messages were not just theoretical but were capable of achievement. The judicial task as he described it was doable; it was the way he believed that good judges had always done their job, restated for his time. It required conscientious hard work in every case in order to take all the contending elements into account and then to determine which should dominate. It required first learning from the lesson of Albert Cardozo that personal and partisan favor be checked at the courtroom door, and then consulting a series of sources in the decision-making process to keep personal values in check—not eliminated, but in check. Cardozo brought his intelligence, self-confidence, aristocratic notions of duty and honor, and practical experience to the judgment about justice that he exercised in every case. He also brought a theory of government and a philosophy of law that was heavily infused with a democratic respect for the roles of other agencies of government and the values of society. His performance of this difficult and complex task made him a great judge.

In his will, Cardozo left his own final word about his affections—his family, Jewish causes, loyal employees, a few friends, Columbia University, and the law. The first gift was for perpetual care of the graves of his parents, siblings, and himself in the Shearith Israel cemetery in Cypress Hills, Long Island, and the separate plot in Woodlawn Cemetery, in the Bronx, of his twin sister Emily. He gave Mt. Sinai Hospital, with which his father had been associated, $7,500 to endow a bed "to the sacred memory of my sister Ellen Ida Cardozo." He left $25,000 to the Federation for the Support of Jewish Philanthropic Societies, the umbrella Jewish charitable organization in New York City.

Cardozo also remembered those who had been loyal to him. He left generous gifts of $2,250 to the cook and the chauffeur who had joined the household in Washington, $7,500 to Catherine Walsh, and the magnificent gift of $75,000 to Kate Tracy "in grateful recognition of her devoted service during many years to my deceased sisters Elizabeth and Ellen, and since their death to me." He also left money gifts to several friends: George Engelhard, his former partner ($7,500 and his china and silverware); William Freese, the manager of his former office and his own financial manager and executor ($5,000 and his jewelry); Irving Lehman ($2,000 and his library); and Sissie Lehman (the loving cup presented to him by the Court of Appeals).

Cardozo's final gift was to leave the remainder of his estate, approximately $188,000—over $2,000,000 in mid-1990s dollars—in a form that combined his long association with Columbia, his devotion to law, and his name. The bequest was made to Columbia with the hope that it would be "applied to the foundation or maintenance of a chair of jurisprudence in the Law School of the University, to be associated with my name, and to perpetuate the scientific study of a subject which has been one of my chief interests in life." Columbia honored the wish, and the Cardozo Professorship of Jurisprudence is the result.[24]

On July 11, 1938, two days after Cardozo died, there was a funeral service at the Lehmans' home in Port Chester. The service was brief, spoken in Hebrew, and consisted of prayers, the 23rd Psalm, and readings from Proverbs. More than two hundred family members, friends, lawyers, judges, and political leaders attended. Cardozo's Supreme Court colleagues Pierce Butler, Owen Roberts, and the newly appointed Stanley Reed were there, but Harlan Stone and Charles Evans Hughes were out of the country on vacation.[25] Cardozo had requested that there be no eulogy, and there was none. After the service, the funeral procession made its way down the Hutchinson River Parkway, detoured to Manhattan and paused in front of Shearith Israel, which opened its doors and gates wide in respect, and then continued on to the Shearith Israel cemetery in Long Island.[26]

There was a short service at Cypress Hills, and then Benjamin Cardozo was buried with his ancestors in the family plot next to his beloved Nellie.

Notes

Index of Cases

General Index

Notes

I acknowledge with thanks the permission granted by the following individuals and institutions to cite and quote the named sources:

The American Jewish Archives, Cincinnati, Ohio with respect to the Annie Nathan Meyer Papers.

The American Jewish Historical Society, Waltham, Massachusetts, with respect to the papers of Stephen S. Wise.

The American Law Institute with respect to minutes of a meeting of the Torts Advisers to the Restatement of Torts.

The Barnard College Archives with respect to the Annie Nathan Meyer Papers.

The Court of Appeals of the State of New York and the New York State Archives with respect to internal memoranda of the Court of Appeals between 1914 and 1932.

Jonathan Hand Churchill with respect to the Learned Hand Papers and excerpts from Judge Hand's remarks at a meeting of the American Law Institute's advisers to the Restatement of Torts.

Trustees of Columbia University in the City of New York, as the residuary legatee of the estate of Benjamin N. Cardozo, with respect to all writings of Benjamin N. Cardozo.

Rare Book and Manuscript Library, Columbia University, with respect to the Benjamin Cardozo Papers.

Oral History Research Office, Columbia University, with respect to their interviews with Charles C. Burlingham, Frederic Coudert, Jr., Charles H. Tuttle, Stanley Isaacs, James M. Landis, and John Lord O'Brian.

Harvard Law School Library, Special Collections, with respect to the Charles C. Burlingham Papers, the Learned Hand Papers, the Oliver

Wendell Holmes Papers, the Edmund M. Morgan Papers, the Joseph Paley Papers, the Roscoe Pound Papers, and the Thomas Reed Powell Papers.

Jonathan Marshall with respect to the Louis Marshall Papers.

The New York Public Library with respect to the Charles P. Daly Papers.

Congregation Shearith Israel with respect to Benjamin Cardozo material in the archives of the Congregation.

Yale Collection of American Literature, Beinecke Rare Book and Manuscript Library, Yale University, with respect to a letter from Horatio Alger to E. C. Stedman and quotations from the James Weldon Johnson and Alfred Stieglitz Papers.

Yale University Library, Manuscript and Archives, with respect to the Jerome N. Frank Papers, the Henry L. Stimson Papers, and the Thomas Walter Swan Papers.

I have used the following abbreviations for frequently cited materials in these notes. I have cited box or folder locations only for difficult-to-find items.

ABCNY   Association of the Bar of the City of New York.

CCB   Charles C. Burlingham Papers, Harvard Law School Library, Cambridge, Massachusetts.

CCC   Columbia Cardozo Collection. The collection includes the papers that Columbia received as residuary legatee of Benjamin Cardozo's estate; papers collected by George Hellman in connection with his biography of Cardozo; and miscellaneous contributions from family members and others. They are stored in the Rare Book and Manuscript Library, Butler Library, Columbia University, New York, New York.

CM   Cardozo Memoranda. These are internal memoranda written by Benjamin Cardozo to his colleagues on the New York Court of Appeals in cases assigned to him for reporting purposes. They are confidential memoranda that were made available to the author under special arrangement with the Court of Appeals. They have been placed by the Court in the New York State Archives, Albany, New York, and have been designated New York State Court of Appeals, Internal Case Reports Files, New York State Archives series J2003. Albany, New York. The Court of Appeals is in the process of depositing memoranda written by other judges in the State Archives.

COHP   Columbia Oral History Project, Butler Library, Columbia University, New York, New York.

FF   Felix Frankfurter Papers, Harvard Law School Library, Cambridge, Massachusetts.

HHP   Herbert Hoover Papers, The Herbert Hoover Library, West Branch, Iowa.

HLS   Harvard Law School Library, Cambridge, Massachusetts.

JP   Joseph Paley Papers, Harvard Law School Library, Cambridge, Massachusetts.

KCC   Kaufman Cardozo Collection. This is a collection of Benjamin Cardozo correspondence, interviews of Cardozo friends and acquaintances, and miscellaneous other materials relating to the preparation of this biography. These materials have been deposited in the Andrew L. Kaufman Papers, Harvard Law School, Cambridge, Massachusetts.

LC   Library of Congress, Manuscript Division, Washington, D.C.

LH   Learned Hand Papers, Harvard Law School Library, Cambridge, Massachusetts.

LM   Louis Marshall Papers, American Jewish Archives, Hebrew Union College, Cincinnati, Ohio.

SSW   Stephen S. Wise Papers, Farber Library, Brandeis University, Waltham, Massachusetts.

There are frequent references to briefs that Cardozo wrote as a lawyer in cases in the Court of Appeals and the Appellate Division of the Supreme Court and to the record of proceedings in those cases. There are also references to similar materials regarding cases on which Benjamin Cardozo sat as a judge. These materials may be found in the Association of the Bar of the City of New York, New York, New York, and the New York State Archives, Education and Cultural Hall, Empire Plaza, Albany, New York. Harvard Law School has the set of briefs used by Cardozo in Court of Appeals cases from 1921 to 1932.

A few conventions should be noted with respect to quotations and citations in these materials. Ellipses denote the omission of internal material in a quotation, but ellipses are not used at the beginning or the end of quoted materials. The first citation of a work in a chapter gives the full bibliographic information in the form generally used in legal scholarship. Subsequent citations in that chapter are made in shortened form. The volume number of periodicals is indicated in arabic numerals before the title. The volume number of books is given in roman numerals after the title. Legal cases are cited according to legal convention. A citation to Meinhard v. Salmon, 249 N.Y. 458 (1928) gives the name of the parties, the volume number (249) and page number (458) of the New York Reports in which the opinion appears and the year in which the case was decided (1928). A citation to Steward Machine Company v. Davis, 301 U.S. 548 (1937), gives the same information for decisions of the United States Supreme Court reported in the United States Reports.

1. Cardozo's Heritage

1. Memorandum of N. Taylor Phillips, a second cousin of Benjamin Cardozo, October 2, 1929, containing a genealogy of, among others, the Cardozos and Nathans, CCC, Box 6. Writing in 1932, Jacob de Haas noted that at that time, there were still members of the Cardozo family living in Amsterdam. *Jewish Ledger* (Feb. 29, 1932). The genealogist Walter Max Kraus traced the probable origin of Cardozo's Seixas ancestors to "Vasco Gomez de Seixas who was knighted by King John of Portugal in 1385." *New York Sun* (Feb. 22, 1932).

2. Letter of Samson Mears to Aaron Lopez, 1779, printed in Jacob R. Marcus, *Early American Jewry: The Jews of New York, New England, and Canada, 1649–1794,* I, 173 (1951). Jacob Ezekiel, "The Jews of Richmond," 4 *Publications of the American Jewish Historical Society,* 21 (1896).

3. Malcolm H. Stern, *First American Jewish Families: 600 Genealogies, 1654–1988,* 29 (3d ed. 1991).

4. Jacob R. Marcus, *Early American Jewry: The Jews of Pennsylvania and the South, 1655–1790,* II, 226–274 (1953).

5. For information on the genealogy of the Cardozo family, see Stern, *First American Jewish Families,* 29. On David N. Cardozo, see Barnett A. Elzas, *The Jews of South Carolina,* 84, 87, 95, 142–143, 154 (1905); Leon Huehner, *The Jews of South Carolina,* 50 (1904). On Isaac Nunez Cardozo (1751–1832), see 24 *American Genealogical-Biographical Index to American Genealogical, Biographical, and Local History Materials (Fremont Rider, ed. 1958); The Universal Jewish Encyclopedia,* III, 43 (1941); Elzas, *Jews of South Carolina,* 95; Huehner, *The Jews of South Carolina,* 56; David and Tamar de Sola Pool, *An Old Faith in the New World: Portrait of Shearith Israel, 1654–1954,* 505 (1955). On Jacob Newton Cardozo, see Alexander Brody, "Jacob Newton Cardozo, American Economist," 15 *Historia Judaica,* 135–166 (1953); Charles Reznikoff and Uriah Engelman, *The Jews of Charleston,* 84–86 (1950); Harry Simonhoff, *Jewish Notables in America: 1776–1865,* 265–267 (1956); Elzas,

The Jews of South Carolina, 141, 176–179. On the African American branch of the Cardozo family, see Bertram Korn, "Jews and Negro Slavery in the Old South, 1789–1865," 50 *Publication[s] of the American Jewish Historical Society* 151, 171–180 (Mar. 1961), sources cited therein, and materials contained in the Francis Lewis Cardozo Papers, LC. See also genealogical chart of the white and black branches of the Cardozo families prepared by Michael H. Cardozo IV, copy in KCC.

6. Uzal W. Condit, *The History of Easton, Penn'a from the Earliest Times to the Present,* 15–16 (ca. 1895); Herbert Ezekiel and Gaston Lichtenstein, *The History of the Jews of Richmond,* 132–133 (1917); Stern, *First American Jewish Families,* 103.

7. Eli Faber, *A Time for Planting: The First Migration, 1654–1820,* 60–66 (1992); Hyman B. Grinstein, *The Rise of the Jewish Community of New York, 1654–1860,* 165–173 (1945); Malcolm H. Stern, *New York's Early Jews: Some Myths and Misconceptions,* 6–17 (Jewish Historical Society of New York 1976). Dr. Marc Angel, rabbi at Congregation Shearith Israel, contends there was never the hostile relationship between Sephardim and Ashkenazim in New York that existed in other communities abroad and even in other places in this country. He points to the large intermarriage rate between the two communities and the majority status of the Ashkenazim in Shearith Israel itself as evidence. Yet his explanation of why the Ashkenazim did not impose their ritual in Shearith Israel is revealing: "The Ashkenazim looked up to the Sephardim for whatever reasons—they acculturated with the Sephardim . . . and they wanted to be Sephardim." Angel, Response to Malcolm Stern, in id. at 25–26. For a discussion of the history, language, and culture of Sephardic Jews, see Paloma Diaz-Mas, *Sephardim: the Jews from Spain* (1992).

8. Pool, *An Old Faith,* 1–44, 81–83, 458–464.

9. Oscar Handlin, *Adventure in Freedom: Three Hundred Years of Jewish Life in America,* 8–11 (1954); Jacob R. Marcus, *The Colonial American Jew, 1492–1776,* II, 583–652 (1970); and Joseph A. Scoville [pseud. Walter Barrett], *The Old Merchants of New York City,* 122 (2d ser. 1863).

10. The best estimate is that, as late as 1812, there were only about 400 to 500 Jews in a city of 96,000. Pool, *An Old Faith,* 472, citing Rabbi Gershom Seixas. One scholar has estimated that in 1840 there were 10,000 Jews in the country. Stern, *First American Jewish Families,* vii.

11. Maud Nathan, *Once Upon a Time and Today,* 91 (1933). See also Frances Nathan Wolff, *Four Generations: My Life and Memories of New York,* 21 (1939) for a similar story.

12. Annie Nathan Meyer, *It's Been Fun: An Autobiography,* 11 (1951).

13. *New York Times,* 5 (Nov. 9, 1885).

14. Two of Albert's brothers also married into prominent Sephardic families, one into the Seixas family and one into the Peixotto family. The information

on Albert Cardozo in this paragraph is derived from *New York Times,* 5 (Nov. 9, 1885); *New York Herald,* 10 (Nov. 9, 1885); *The Universal Jewish Encyclopedia,* III, 38 (1941); Michael H. Cardozo, "Communication," 67 *American Jewish Historical Quarterly* 284–285 (1978); Edgar J. Nathan, Jr., "Benjamin N. Cardozo," 41 *American Jewish Year Book* 25 (1939); Pool, *An Old Faith,* 317, 319, and 391; *Trow's New York City Directory* for the years 1856–1885; *Doggett's New York City Directory* for the years 1848–1851; *Rode's New York City Directory* for the years 1850 and 1851; and *Doggett & Rode's New York City Directory* for the years 1851–1856.

15. *Pennsylvania Packet* (June 3, 1783), as quoted in Wolf and Whiteman, *Philadelphia Jews,* 109. See also id. at 100, 115, 116, 129, 155–156, 173, 422.

16. *The New York Directory for 1786,* 44; Pool, *An Old Faith,* 503.

17. See N. Taylor Phillips, "The Levy and Seixas Families of Newport and New York," 4 *Publications of the American Jewish Historical Society,* 189, 212 (1896) for a memoir of this remarkable woman. See also Wolff, *Four Generations,* 4–5.

18. David de Sola Pool, *Portraits Etched in Stone: Early Jewish Settlers, 1682–1831,* 344–375 (1952).

19. Pool, *An Old Faith,* 318, 503; Francis L. Eames, *The New York Stock Exchange,* 25 (1894).

20. Pool, *An Old Faith,* 178–182.

21. See *The Diary of George Templeton Strong,* III, 363 (Allan Nevins and Milton Halsey Thomas, eds., 1952) (entry of Oct. 13, 1863); Pool, *An Old Faith,* 318.

22. See id. at 393; Grinstein, *Rise of the Jewish Community,* 138, 149, 153, 158, 169, and 188; and Wolff, *Four Generations,* 39–40.

23. *Trow's New York City Directory for 1847–48.* See also Walter Max Kraus, "A Jurist's Ancestry," *The New York Sun* (Feb. 22, 1932), for a discussion of other Benjamin Cardozo ancestors, the Myers, Seixas, Hart, and Levy families, all of whom arrived in America before the Revolution.

24. Wolff, *Four Generations,* 10–12, 16, 21, 22, 28, 31, and 36.

25. See R. W. B. Lewis, *Edith Wharton: A Biography,* especially 3–61 (1975).

26. Pool, *An Old Faith,* 390–391; *New York Herald,* 1 (May 18, 1855).

27. In the family plot in the Shearith Israel cemetery at Cypress Hills, Long Island, there are two tiny graves that give no names but list dates of death as June 25, 1855, and August 29, 1856. Stern, *First American Jewish Families,* 29, does not list the first two children who died immediately, but he does list a twin of Albert, Jr., named Isaac. There is no grave for Isaac in the family plot and no mention of him in family records.

28. See *Trow's New York City Directory 1860–61,* 140; Wolff, *Four Generations,* 7; and Grace M. Mayer, *Once Upon a City,* 24 (1958).

29. Meyer, *It's Been Fun,* 85.

30. See Andrew L. Kaufman, "The First Judge Cardozo: Albert, Father of Benjamin," 11 *Journal of Law and Religion* 271 (1995) for the complete story of Albert Cardozo's professional and political career.

31. Pool, *An Old Faith*, 314–328.

32. James W. Brooks, *History of the Court of Common Pleas of the City and County of New York*, 32 (1896); Charles P. Daly, *History of the Court of Common Pleas* (1855).

33. *New York Leader*, 4 (Oct. 17, 1863).

34. The opinion was reported in full in *New York Times*, 8 (June 22, 1866). See also Matthew P. Breen, *Thirty Years of New York Politics*, 107–112 (1899), and Jerome Mushkat, *The Reconstruction of the New York Democracy, 1861–1874*, 93 (1981) on some of the political aspects of the 1866 law.

35. The Governor had power to appoint judges from among the justices of the Supreme Court to the General Term, which was an intermediate appellate court that heard appeals from Trial Term and Special Term of the Supreme Court.

36. Letter from Albert Cardozo to John R. Brady, July 26, 1866, 1866 Box, Charles P. Daly Papers, Rare Books and Manuscripts Division, The New York Public Library, Astor, Lenox, and Tilden Foundations, New York, N.Y.

37. A Court of Appeals decision in another case upheld the constitutionality of the statute before Cardozo's opinion could be reviewed. Board of Excise v. Barrie, 34 N.Y. 657 (1866).

38. But see [T. G. Shearman], "The Judiciary of New York City," 105 *North American Review* 148, 156 (1867). On the authorship of this unsigned article, see Kaufman, "The First Judge Cardozo," 280, note 50.

39. John I. Davenport, *New York Election Frauds and Their Prevention*, 91, 94 (1881).

40. Breen, *Thirty Years*, 121.

41. Fernando Wood's speech nominating Cardozo, as reported by Charles Francis Adams, Jr., "A Chapter of Erie," reprinted in Charles Francis Adams, Jr., and Henry Adams, *Chapters of Erie*, 1, 82–83 (1956 ed.). The essay originally appeared in 109 *North American Review* 30 (July 1869). Adams gave no source for the quotation.

42. *The World*, 4 (Oct. 19, 1867). See Kaufman, "The First Judge Cardozo," 288, note 83 for the full text.

43. *The World*, 5 (Nov. 5, 1867).

44. Testimony of Richard Beamish, William C. Barrett, Gratz Nathan, and Peter Wimmer, in *Charges against Justice Albert Cardozo, and Testimony Thereunder*, 196, 297, 659–660, 715–716, and 859–860 (1872).

45. See "The Ermine in the Ring," *Putnam's Supplement* (Dec. 1868) for a lengthy article, apparently based on information from counsel for the city, making specific charges of improper conduct against Cardozo; see also Samuel

A. Pleasants, *Fernando Wood of New York,* 172–175 (1948), and Mayor of New York v. Wood, 3 Abbott Practice Reports (N.S.) 467 (Sup. Ct. 1868).

46. Adams, "A Chapter of Erie," 82–83.

47. See Shearman, "Judiciary of New York," and *Diary of George Templeton Strong,* IV, 236 (Dec. 19, 1868); id. at 273–274 (Feb. 2, 1870).

48. A referee was appointed by a judge to perform certain judicial functions, from conducting a foreclosure sale of property to acting as a "judge" in a complicated case and rendering a report on the facts and the law to the appointing judge.

49. *Charges against Albert Cardozo,* 386–387, 689–692, 830, and 834.

50. See Kaufman, "The First Judge Cardozo," 296.

51. Meyer, *It's Been Fun,* 85.

52. Charles F. Wingate, "An Episode in Municipal Government," 119 *North American Review* 359, 395–396 (Oct. 1874).

53. *Cap and Gown* (Jan. 26, 1870).

54. Shearith Israel Register, III, 216 (1858–1907), Congregation Shearith Israel Archives.

55. Pool, *An Old Faith,* 391; Edgar Nathan, Jr., "Benjamin Nathan Cardozo," in 41 *American Jewish Yearbook 5700,* 25.

56. Pool, *An Old Faith,* 390–391; Wolff, *Four Generations,* 6.

57. The incident is described in George Martin, *Causes and Conflicts: The Centennial History of the Association of the Bar of the City of New York,* 46 (1970).

58. See Martin, *Causes and Conflicts,* 68–86; *Charges against Albert Cardozo,* 15; *Charges against Judge J. H. McCunn, and Testimony Thereunder,* 198 (1872).

59. See *Charges against Albert Cardozo,* 1–14.

60. *Charges against Albert Cardozo,* 3–8.

61. I have told the story of the Gold Conspiracy and set forth the evidence and my conclusions in Kaufman, "The First Judge Cardozo," 304–308.

62. See *Charges against Albert Cardozo,* 8–14 (second, third and fourth charges).

63. See Kaufman, "The First Judge Cardozo," 309.

64. See the full report in *New York Times,* 4 (Apr. 10, 1872).

65. Report of the Judiciary Committee, New York Assembly Doc. No. 173, 6 (1872).

66. *New York Times,* 8 (May 2, 1872).

67. Meyer, *It's Been Fun,* 86.

68. *New York Times,* 8 (Sept. 6, 1872).

69. Note written by Judge Daly on a letter from Albert Cardozo to Judge Brady, July 28, 1866, in 1866 Box, Charles P. Daly Papers, The New York Public Library, Astor, Lenox and Tilden Foundations, New York, N.Y.

70. See *New York City Directory for 1872–1873,* listing his office at 84 Nassau Street, and *Wilson's New York Business Directory for 1873,* listing 258 Broadway; *New York Times,* 8 (Oct. 9, 1872).

71. *New York Times,* 1 (Nov. 27, 1883), 4 (May 26, 1884), and 5 (July 27, 1891). The description of his handling of a divorce case in von Wallhoffen v. Newcombe and Leventritt, 10 Henn 277 (Gen. Term 1st Dept. 1877), a malpractice suit against him and another lawyer, demonstrates that he was not a careful lawyer. In another divorce matter, the judge commented that it was "a mild form of description to say that the act of the attorney [Newcombe] was a gross irregularity." *New York Times,* 4 (May 26, 1884).

72. *Trow's New York City Directory for 1878,* 221, 1080.

2. Young Cardozo

1. See letter of Albert Cardozo to Judge John R. Brady, July 28, 1866, referring to Rebecca's continuing high state of nervous anxiety. 1866 Box, Charles P. Daly Papers, The New York Public Library, Astor, Lenox and Tilden Foundations, New York, N.Y.

2. See Maud Nathan, *Once Upon a Time and Today,* 37, 101 (1933); Frances Nathan Wolff, *Four Generations,* 1–41 (1939).

3. See *Charges against Justice Albert Cardozo and Testimony Thereunder,* 294 (testimony of William C. Barrett) and 678–679 (testimony of Gratz Nathan) (1872). See also Charles F. Wingate, "An Episode in Municipal Government," 119 *North American Review* 359, 396 (Oct. 1874).

4. Author interview with Aline Goldstone (June 11, 1962), KCC. Aline Goldstone was the great-niece of Benjamin Nathan, and her parents had known Cardozo's parents.

5. Annie Nathan Meyer, *It's Been Fun: An Autobiography,* 92 (1951); Municipal Archives of the City of New York, New York Department of Records and Information Services, Death Certificate No. 332098.

6. Author interview with Aline Goldstone, KCC; George Hellman, *Benjamin N. Cardozo: American Judge,* 11 (1940). This is the only previous biography of Cardozo, and it is substantially personal, not professional, in its treatment. Mr. Hellman deposited the notes of his interviews and research with Columbia, and they are in CCC.

7. George Hellman interview with Annie Nathan Meyer (Feb. 13, 1939), CCC, Box 9.

8. Author interview with Aline Goldstone, KCC; George Hellman interview with William Cardozo, a first cousin (1938 or 1939), CCC, Box 9. The quotation is from the latter. For an appreciation of Emily by Ben, see chap. 4, text at note 51.

9. Author interview with Alan Stroock (Apr. 19, 1961), KCC. There seem

to have been at least 76 first cousins who lived beyond infancy, and many were either much older or much younger than Ben. See list in BNC Genealogy file, KCC. The figure is derived from Malcolm Stern, *First American Jewish Families: 600 Genealogies, 1654–1988* (3d ed. 1991), and Michael H. Cardozo IV, *Leaves From a Family Tree* (2d ed. 1976) (privately printed), KCC.

10. Author interview with Joseph L. Rauh, Jr., 34–35 (July 2, 1958), KCC.

11. Hellman, *Cardozo,* 40.

12. Wolff, *Four Generations,* 7.

13. Letter from Michael H. Cardozo, IV, Ernest's son, to author, Apr. 8, 1981, KCC.

14. Henry C. Brown, *Brownstone Fronts and Saratoga Trunks,* 324 (1935); Lady Duffus Hardy, *Through Cities and Prairie Lands,* 307–308 (1881).

15. See text at note 29. Hellman's notes indicate that a Michael Optar told him that he went to a public school on East 57th Street with Ben Cardozo. Hellman did not credit the story since he states that all the Cardozo children except Emily were educated at home. Hellman, *Cardozo,* 14.

16. Meyer, *It's Been Fun,* 35.

17. George Hellman interview with Kate Tracy (Nov. 18, 1938), CCC, Box 9.

18. Quoted in Hellman, *Cardozo,* 16. A reproduction of the original handwritten version appears in id. after 86, and the original album is in the Benjamin Cardozo Papers, Box P-138, at the American Jewish Historical Society, Waltham, Mass.

19. Congregation Shearith Israel announcement of the death of Benjamin N. Cardozo, July 9, 1938, Clerk's Office Correspondence, Congregation Shearith Israel Archives.

20. Hellman, *Cardozo,* 12–13. See also the obituary of Albert Cardozo, Sr., *New York Times,* 5 (Nov. 9, 1885).

21. Hellman, *Cardozo,* 12–13. Hellman recounts this story in connection with Albert Cardozo's first election to the bench and then states that Albert did not know that the Supreme Court met Saturday mornings when he accepted the nomination. Hellman also states that Cardozo intended to resign from the bench rather than do work on Saturday. It is very difficult to credit this version of the story, as any experienced lawyer in New York City surely would have known that the Court of Common Pleas followed the common practice in New York courts of meeting on Saturdays.

22. Letter from Cardozo to Sallie Nathan, widow of Edgar Nathan, Sr., Apr. 8, 1934, original in possession of the family of Rosalie Nathan Hendricks, copy in KCC.

23. The description in this and the following paragraph is based on Nathan, *Once Upon a Time,* 27–30.

24. See David and Tamar de Sola Pool, *An Old Faith in the New World: Portrait of Shearith Israel, 1654–1954,* 192–201 (1955).

25. Nathan, *Once Upon a Time,* 30.

26. Shearith Israel Register, III, 391 (1858–1907). Cardozo's Hebrew name was Binyamin bar Yaakob Nunes Cardozo, Benjamin Son of Jacob Nunes Cardozo, which was his father's Hebrew name. Letter from Victor Tarry, Assistant to the Clerk, Congregation Shearith Israel to Abraham Greenwald, Dec. 8, 1938, in Clerk's Office Correspondence, Congregation Shearith Israel Archives.

27. Hellman, *Cardozo,* 13; Hellman interview with David de Sola Pool (Nov. 9, 1938), CCC, Box 9.

28. Letter to Charles C. Burlingham, May 25, 1931, CCB. Or as Cardozo put it to relatives on the death of their brother: "You are better than I am and have religion too." Letter to Sally Nathan and Elvira Nathan Solis, Aug. 12, 1935, original in possession of the family of Rosalie Nathan Hendricks, copy in KCC.

29. Letter from Cardozo to Milton Halsey Thomas, partly quoted in Hellman, *Cardozo,* 15.

30. Gary Scharnhorst, with Jack Bales, *The Lost Life of Horatio Alger, Jr.,* 100, 125–126 (1985). The material on Alger is all derived from this book.

31. Scharnhorst and Bales, *Horatio Alger,* 64–67, tell the story in full, as detailed in the records of the American Unitarian Association.

32. Letter from Gary Scharnhorst to author, Feb. 15, 1992, KCC.

33. See letter from Horatio Alger to E. R. A. Seligman, July 1, 1885, referring to a letter from "Bennie" Cardozo. E. R. A. Seligman Papers, Rare Book and Manuscript Library, Columbia University, New York, N.Y.

34. *Columbia College Handbook, 1885,* 16.

35. Scharnhorst and Bales, *Horatio Alger,* 99.

36. See ibid., translating from Seligman's autobiography in German.

37. Charles Evans Hughes, *The Autobiographical Notes of Charles Evans Hughes,* 62 (David Danelski and Joseph Tolchin, eds., 1973); see also Hellman, *Cardozo,* 221.

38. Municipal Archives of the City of New York, New York Department of Records and Information Services, Death Certificate No. 517613. Grace died Feb. 3, 1885, ten months before the death of Albert, Sr.

39. *Columbia College Handbook, 1885,* 16.

40. See Nicholas Murray Butler, *Across the Busy Years,* I, 63 (1939).

41. *President's Annual Report for 1890,* 20, 25; *Columbia Register for 1885/86,* 12–13; *Columbia Register for 1889/90,* 22. Including the Schools of Mines, Law, Political Science and Medicine, the student body of the whole College exceeded 1,400 students, and the faculty numbered 160 professors, instructors, and assistants. *Columbia College Handbook, 1885,* 14.

42. Municipal Archives of the City of New York, New York Department of Records and Information Services, Death Certificate No. 545480.

43. Author interview with Charles C. Burlingham (Nov. 13, 1957), KCC.

44. *New York Times,* 8 (Nov. 17, 1885).

45. *Columbia College Handbook, 1885,* 32–35; Butler, *Across the Busy Years,* I, 63–68.

46. See Frederick Keppel, *Columbia,* 1–27 (1914).

47. Munroe Smith, "The University and Non-Professional Graduate Schools," in *A History of Columbia University 1754–1904,* 222–240; Keppel, *Columbia,* 18–23, 28–32; Butler, *Busy Years,* I, 134–148.

48. John W. Burgess, *Reminiscences of An American Scholar,* 180 (1934).

49. See Albert Payson Terhune, of the class of 1893, in *Columbia Stories,* 10 (1897).

50. See Burgess, *Reminiscences,* 183–187.

51. Butler, *Across the Busy Years,* I, 62–91.

52. Id. at 65, 68, 90–91.

53. The notes are collected in CCC, Boxes 3, 3A, 4, and 13.

54. An example of the speed-written version remains in his Constitutional History of England notebook for April 1889, just before he graduated. CCC, Box 13.

55. Cardozo, "Tribute to Nicholas Murray Butler," 8 (Feb. 11, 1932), manuscript in KCC.

56. Cardozo, Lecture Notes for Alexander, History of Philosophy, 2–139 (undated), in CCC, Box 4.

57. Cardozo, Lecture Notes for Butler, History of Philosophy, 99–110, in CCC, Box 4.

58. Cardozo, Lecture Notes for Butler, Ethics, 200–201, in CCC, Box 4.

59. Cardozo, Lecture Notes for Burgess, Lectures on Political Science and Comparative Constitutional Law, July 1890, 36–252, in CCC, Box 3A.

60. Cardozo, Lecture Notes for Burgess, Lectures on Political Science and Comparative Constitutional Law, July 1890, 31, in CCC, Box 3A.

61. See Cardozo, Lecture Notes for an unnamed professor's Administrative Law course; Lecture Notes for Bernheim, Comparative Constitutional Law of Commonwealths, Aug. 1890; and Lecture Notes for Munroe Smith, History of European Jurisprudence, Aug. 1890, CCC, Box 3.

62. Cardozo, "The Moral Element in Matthew Arnold," in Benjamin N. Cardozo, *Selected Writings of Benjamin Nathan Cardozo,* 61, 64–65 (Margaret Hall, ed., 1947).

63. Id. at 70.

64. Cardozo, "Some Notes on George Eliot," 20, CCC, Box 3.

65. Id. at 3–4.

66. Id. at 6.

67. Id. at 16, 19.

68. Id. at 25.

69. Id. at 30–32.

70. Id. at 35.

71. Id. at 53.

72. Id. at 43–44.

73. Author interview with Judge William Speer (Oct. 27, 1958), KCC.

74. Letter from George Warren to George Hellman, Nov. 3, 1938, in CCC, Box 6.

75. Nicholas Murray Butler, quoted in Hellman, *Cardozo,* 21.

76. Thomas B. Fiske, Professor Van Amringe's assistant, quoted in Hellman, *Cardozo,* 24.

77. George Odell, who later became Professor of English at Columbia, quoted in id. at 26.

78. Letter of Cardozo's classmate Remsen Johnson to George Hellman, undated but written in 1938 or 1939, CCC, Box 6.

79. Columbia College, "Roll of Merit," for the four years of the Class of 1889.

80. *Columbia Annual Register for 1888–89,* 14.

81. *Columbia Annual Register for 1889–90,* 17.

82. *Columbia Annual Register for 1887–88,* 13; *Columbia Annual Register for 1888–89,* 13. See also Remsen Johnson letter to George Hellman, undated but written in 1938 or 1939, CCC, Box 6.

83. Remsen Johnson, quoted in Hellman, *Cardozo,* 24.

84. Hellman, *Cardozo,* 27–28, relying on undated handwritten notes from E. H. Hornbostel of the class of 1890 written in response to a letter from Hellman, Oct. 22, 1938, CCC, Box 6. An account of the 1885 cane rush is also contained in the autobiography of one of Cardozo's classmates. James W. Gerard, *My First Eighty-Three Years in America,* 25–26 (1951).

85. A description of the kind of pressure exerted is contained in Terhune, *Columbia Stories,* 116–132.

86. *1890 Columbiad,* 57 (1889); Hellman, *Cardozo,* 22.

87. Id. at 26.

88. Interview with Frederic Coudert, Jr., 119 (1949–1950), COHP part I. Coudert was a son of a trustee of Columbia and a member of the class of 1890. Later a lawyer and member of the House of Representatives, he was friendly with Cardozo from college days, and belonged to an informal conversation group called "The Philosophers" with Cardozo for 30 years. See chap. 9, text at note 10.

89. The use of Cardozo's middle name was probably intended to tie in with

the required reading of Gotthold E. Lessing's *Nathan the Wise* in the junior year German class. See Hellman, *Cardozo,* 27.

90. Id. at 25. See E. H. Hornbostel notes on reverse side of letter from Hellman to Hornbostel, Oct. 22, 1938, CCC, Box 6.

91. Frederic Coudert remembered seeing Cardozo's posted perfect marks. Interview with Coudert, 119 (1949–1950), COHP part I.

92. Hellman, *Cardozo,* 25.

93. The valedictorian was selected by the students from a list submitted by the faculty, *Columbia College Handbook, 1888,* 31; *1891 Columbiad,* 103; 24 *Columbia Spectator 95* (June 25, 1889).

94. Cardozo, "Commencement Speech—1915," manuscript in KCC.

95. Cardozo, "The Altruist in Politics," in Cardozo, *Selected Writings,* 47–51.

96. Letters from Cardozo to Oscar Cox, Apr. 15, 1932, and Oct. 19, 1932. Box 135, Correspondence (II), Oscar Cox Papers, Franklin D. Roosevelt Library, Hyde Park, N.Y.

3. Columbia Law School

1. Author interview with Justine Wise Polier (July 11, 1958), KCC. She remembered hearing Professor Seligman tell this story to her father, Rabbi Stephen Wise. Others who knew Cardozo have assumed that redemption of the family name helps explain his choice of career. See, for example, Joseph L. Rauh, Jr., "A Personal View of Justice Benjamin N. Cardozo," 1 *Cardozo Law Review* 5, 9 (1979), referring to the views of others but disclaiming any personal knowledge.

2. George Hellman, *Benjamin N. Cardozo,* 211 (1940).

3. Welch v. Helvering, 290 U.S. 111, 115 (1933).

4. Theodore Dwight, "Address to the Graduating Class," 1 *Columbia Law Times* 1 (Oct. 1887).

5. These notes were taken by students but always "officially revised" by the respective professor. Some of the professors' notes were merely scanty statements of propositions set out in outline form followed by case citations. The Dwight notes, however, were obviously substantially his work, written as a supplemental text. See, for example, 3 *Columbia Law Times* 74 (1889) for an exegesis by Dwight on a passage in *Parsons on Contracts,* dealing with an agent's powers.

6. Dwight's exposition of his method appears in *Columbia College Handbook of Information on Several Schools and Courses of Instruction, 1889–1890,* 171–172 (1889). See also Dwight, "Columbia College Law School," 1

Green Bag 141 (1889), and Thomas F. Taylor, "The Dwight Method," 7 *Harvard Law Review* 203, 206–207 (1894). For the students' perspective, see Theron Strong, *Landmarks of a Lawyer's Lifetime,* 252–263 (1914); and 4 *Columbia Law Times* 1, 3 (No. 9, The Dwight Tribute, June 1891), containing 25 commentaries on Dwight as a teacher.

7. See *President's Annual Report for 1890,* 17.

8. *Columbia College Handbook, 1889–1890,* 185.

9. *Ibid.*

10. 3 *Columbia Law Times* 64 (1889). William Blackstone was the Vinerian Professor of Jurisprudence at Oxford. His lectures, compiled in the 1760s into a treatise entitled *Commentaries on the Laws of England,* were the major comprehensive treatment of English law in his day and became the primary text for generations of English and American students in the eighteenth and nineteenth centuries.

11. See William Blackstone, *The American Students' Blackstone: Commentaries on the Laws of England,* abridged and annotated by George Chase, (2d ed. 1888).

12. Id. at iii–vi.

13. Cardozo, "Modern Trends in the Study and Treatment of the Law," address at the installation of Dean Huger Jervey, Nov. 17, 1924, manuscript in KCC. The printed version in 16 *Columbia Alumni News* 151 (Dec. 19, 1924) was abridged.

14. Theophilus Parsons, *The Law of Contracts,* 3 (7th ed. 1883).

15. See Dwight's lecture notes published in 3 *Columbia Law Times* (1889–1890).

16. 3 *Columbia Law Times* 88 (1889).

17. Cardozo, "Modern Trends in Law," KCC.

18. *Columbia College Handbook, 1889–90,* 185; on Benjamin Lee, see *A History of the School of Law, Columbia University,* 94–95, 119 (1955), this portion largely adapted from J. Frederick Kernochan, "Memorial of Benjamin F. Lee," *1908 Year Book of the Association of the Bar of the City of New York,* 162–164.

19. Munroe Smith, "The School of Law and The School of Political Science," 1 *Columbia Law Times* 15 (Oct. 1887). The question whether there is one right decision has remained to bedevil philosophers of law. See, for example, Ronald Dworkin, "Is There Really No Right Answer in Hard Cases?" in Dworkin, *A Matter of Principle,* 119 (1985).

20. See 1 *Columbia Law Times* 23 (1887).

21. Columbia College, "Matriculation Book, Faculty of Philosophy," 30 (1890–1891), archives of Columbia University.

22. 3 *Columbia Law Times* 60 (1889); *History of the School of Law,* 108–

119; "Report of the Warden for the academic year ending June 30, 1891," in *Annual Report of President Low, Oct. 5, 1891, 54–55.*

23. *Columbia College Handbook, 1890–1891,* 189 (1890), as supplemented by *History of the School of Law,* 120.

24. *History of the School of Law,* 138; *The Centennial History of the Harvard Law School, 1817–1917,* 40–41 (1918).

25. 4 *Columbia Law Times* 41 (1890).

26. For Keener's view of the aims of teaching, see William Keener, "The Inductive Method in Legal Education," 17 *Report of the Seventeenth Annual Meeting of the American Bar Association* 473 (1894).

27. Author interview with Judge William Speer (Oct. 27, 1958), KCC.

28. Cardozo, "The Comradeship of the Bar," an address to the New York University Law School Alumni Association in 1927, reprinted in Cardozo, *Selected Writings of Benjamin Nathan Cardozo,* 422, 423 (Margaret Hall, ed., 1947).

29. Thomas M. Cooley, *A Treatise on the Law of Torts,* 635–642 (2d ed. 1888).

30. Id., chap. 2.

31. Id. at 15.

32. James Stephen, *A Digest of the Law of Evidence* (Am. ed. with annotations by George Chase, 1887).

33. *History of the School of Law,* 150–151.

34. Letter from Cardozo to his cousin, Ernest A. Cardozo, Nov. 21, 1932, CCC, Box 1. He remembered that the trustees had added on the third year during the middle of his second year, but he was mistaken. *History of the School of Law,* 113, 119; "Report of Dean Keener, June 30, 1892," in *Third Annual Report of President Low to the Trustees,* 55. The *History* gives the figure of returning students as 68. *History of the School of Law,* 446. The story of the controversy is contained in id. at 120–131 and 4 *Columbia Law Times* 153, 177–180, 184–189, 244–251 (1891).

35. 4 id. 248 (1891); George Chase, "Columbia Law School—A Sketch of Its History," 4 id. 1 (No. 9, The Dwight Tribute, June 1891); *History of School of Law,* 99–101. The records preserved in the archives of Columbia University for those years contained two penciled numbers after each student's name. One appears to be tuition. Whatever the other may be, it does not appear to represent grades. See Columbia College Law School, Registers for the Years 1889 to 1890 and 1890 to 1891, Columbia University Archives, New York, N.Y.

36. Cardozo, "The Bench and the Bar," Address before the Broome County Bar Association, 1929, reprinted in 34 *New York State Bar Journal* 444, 448 (Dec. 1962).

37. Cardozo, "Modern Trends in Law," KCC.

38. Ibid.

4. Apprenticeship

1. George Hellman interview with Annie Nathan Meyer (Feb. 13, 1939), CCC, Box 9; author interview with Adele Dobson, former secretary in Simpson, Werner & Cardozo, later secretary to Judge Froessel of the Court of Appeals (June 23, 1958), KCC.

2. The certificate is in CCC, Box 10, along with his certificate of admission to the United States District Court for the Southern District of New York five years later.

3. The lawyer Theron Strong, who wrote the best first-hand account of life at the New York bar between the Civil War and World War I, gave a vivid picture of Donohue the judge: "He regarded no precedents; followed no established rules . . . in his charges to juries, almost always fair and impartial, he would present the issue of fact . . . without any rules to guide them." He would also sign virtually any order presented him on the theory that if it was not accurate, it could always be vacated on application of the other side. This careless attitude finally led the Bar Association to petition the legislature to do something. As there was no suggestion of any dishonest conduct, nothing came of that effort. Theron Strong, *Landmarks of a Lawyer's Lifetime,* 126–128 (1914).

4. Interview with Charles H. Tuttle, a leading New York lawyer, 89 (1964), COHP part I; *Trow's New York City Directory* for 1882 to 1894.

5. *Trow's New York City Directory* for 1892–1898.

6. Strong, *Landmarks of a Lawyer's Lifetime,* 346–354. See also Robert Swaine, *The Cravath Firm,* I, chaps. 4 and 5, especially 369–371 (1946). "Rainmakers" are the big producers of business in a law firm.

7. George Martin, *Causes and Conflicts: The Centennial History of the Association of the Bar of the City of New York, 1870–1970,* 187–195 (1970); James Willard Hurst, *The Growth of American Law: The Law Makers,* 300–305, 333–352, and 366–375 (1950); *Davis Polk Wardwell Gardner & Reed: Some of the Antecedents,* 1–27 (1935); Walter K. Earle, *Mr. Shearman and Mr. Sterling and How They Grew,* 20–23, 122–145 (1963); and Henry W. Taft, *A Century and a Half at the New York Bar,* 174–179, 191–201 (1938). The quotation is from Martin, at 195.

8. See Martin, *Causes and Conflicts,* 191–193; Swaine, *Cravath Firm,* I, 448–452; Earle, *Mr. Shearman and Mr. Sterling,* 125–126; Bayrd Still, *Mirror for Gotham: New York,* 206, 209, 231–232 (1956).

9. Letter from Henry M. Powell to George Hellman, Oct. 25, 1938, CCC, Box 6. The source of the story was Richard S. Newcombe, son of the Newcombe who was a partner in Donohue, Newcombe & Cardozo. Hellman repeated the story in his biography, George Hellman, *Benjamin N. Cardozo,* 42 (1940), but changed the subject matter of Cardozo's study to torts.

10. See Alfred Z. Reed, *Training for the Public Profession of the Law,* 273–287 (1986).

11. A list of these cases is contained in the BNC Practice File, KCC. Cardozo compiled a collection of his briefs and memoranda and donated it to St. John's University in 1932 when he was appointed to the Supreme Court. *New York Times* 18 (Oct. 23, 1932). As long ago as 1938, however, the collection could not be located. Efforts by his biographer George Hellman to find them at that time, and subsequent efforts by members of his family and by me, have proven unsuccessful.

I have reconstituted Cardozo's private practice by utilizing the official and unofficial New York Court reports, the docket books and clerk's minutes of the Appellate Division, First Department, the miscellaneous indices and papers of various New York courts maintained in the Old Records Division of the New York County Clerk's Office, and the *New York Law Journal,* which published daily calendars in the period of Cardozo's law practice. When Cardozo was called in to argue a case in the Court of Appeals, it was fairly easy to decide, by examining the brief in the lower court, what he contributed and what he borrowed from the previous argument. In addition, his brief-writing style was fairly distinctive. For an earlier look at Cardozo's law practice, see Jerome Hyman, "Benjamin N. Cardozo: A Preface to His Career at the Bar," 10 *Brooklyn Law Review* 1 (1940).

12. 61 Hun 496 (Gen. Term 1st Dept. 1891), rev'd, 135 N.Y. 275 (1892).

13. 127 N.Y. 673 (1891).

14. 135 N.Y. at 278 (1892).

15. 139 N.Y. 432 (1893).

16. 65 Hun 619 (1st Dept. 1892), opinion printed in Record on Appeal in Court of Appeals, ABCNY.

17. 9 Ex. 341 (1854).

18. One of those counsel was his first cousin, Gratz Nathan, who had split receiver's fees with Albert Cardozo, Sr. The case was Hardt v. Levy, 79 Hun 351 (Gen. Term, 1st Dept. 1894).

19. Letter from Remsen Johnson, Cardozo's classmate, to George Hellman, undated but written in 1938 or 1939, CCC, Box 6. On Patterson, see Strong, *Landmarks,* 107–112.

20. Michael H. Cardozo was the second to bear that name. The first was Albert Cardozo's father.

21. Letter from Cardozo to Sallie Nathan, wife of Edgar Nathan, Sr., June 27, 1929, original in possession of Rosalie Nathan Hendricks family, copy in KCC; Edward S. Greenbaum, *A Lawyer's Job,* 28–31 (1967); letter from Learned Hand to Cardozo, June 26, 1929, LH. Michael Cardozo was nominated by a good government Lawyers Committee to run for a Supreme Court

of New York vacancy in 1906, but he died before the election. *New York Times*, 7 (July 20, 1906).

22. Matter of Baer, 147 N.Y. 348 (1895).

23. Author interview with Rosalie Nathan Hendricks, daughter of Edgar Nathan, Sr. (June 5, 1958), KCC; *Trow's New York City Directory* for 1901 and 1902.

24. Author interview with Mrs. William H. Freese and William G. Freese (June 20, 1962), KCC. William H. Freese rose from office boy to become the managing clerk of the law firm of Simpson, Werner & Cardozo and, after he became a lawyer in 1921, he acted as Benjamin Cardozo's lawyer, investment manager, and executor. Mrs. Freese worked as a secretary in Simpson, Werner & Cardozo. William G. Freese is their son.

25. Galle v. Tode, 148 N.Y. 270 (1896).

26. A "confession of judgment" gives a creditor consent to enter judgment against a debtor if the debtor defaults in its payments.

27. Supplemental Memorandum for Respondents, 3, ABCNY.

28. Julius Goldman was an older lawyer whose family included the members of the banking firm of Goldman, Sachs & Co.; Paul Sachs, the well-known art historian; and Felix Adler, founder of the Society of Ethical Culture. The friendship that began at this time lasted until Cardozo's death and included Mrs. Goldman and their daughter Agnes Goldman Sanborn. Cardozo spoke at the service on the occasion of Mrs. Goldman's death. See Cardozo-Goldman correspondence, 1913–1937, Goldman Papers, HLS.

29. Ladenburg v. Commercial Bank of Newfoundland, 5 App. Div. 219 (1st Dept. 1896).

30. Brief for Respondents, Appellate Division, 7–8, ABCNY.

31. In this tabulation, I have counted only matters in which there was a reported result. My figures are considerably higher than those reported in Hyman, "Benjamin N. Cardozo," 13.

32. Willard Hurst attributed the nineteenth century's "excessive insistence on local peculiarities of doctrine and procedure" to, "in large part . . . the loss of professional standards at the bar, and the victory of a rule-of-thumb attitude toward the administration of justice." Hurst, *Growth of American Law*, 352. The press of the Court of Appeals' business caused the court to lose some of its interest in procedural matters at the end of the nineteenth century, although it took a little while, as it usually does, for the procedural reforms to catch up to the need for efficiency. See Henry Cohen, *The Powers of the New York Court of Appeals*, 1–6, 118–131 (1934).

33. 14 *New York Law Journal* 788 (Dec. 26, 1895).

34. 13 id. 29 (Apr. 2, 1895). Charles Evans Hughes, who practiced law in New York before becoming Governor, Secretary of State, and Chief Justice of

the United States, gave a good description of this aspect of the law business. Charles Evans Hughes, *The Autobiographical Notes of Charles Evans Hughes,* 77–78 (David J. Danelski and Joseph S. Tulchin, eds., 1973).

35. Cardozo, "Identity and Survivorship," in Allan Hamilton and Lawrence Godkin, eds., *A System of Legal Medicine,* 213 (1st ed. 1894).

36. Id. at 231–232.

37. Id. at 242.

38. George Hellman interview with Kenneth Hayes Miller (Jan. 1939), CCC, Box 9. See also author interview with Justine Wise Polier (July 11, 1958), KCC.

39. Lizzie referred to the "wastes of Pain" that she suffered in a poem entitled "To My Sister Ellen." Elizabeth Cardozo, *Salvage,* 48 (1912).

40. Hellman, *Cardozo,* 39.

41. Hellman interview with Kenneth Hayes Miller (Jan. 1939), CCC, Box 9; see also Hellman interview with Kate Tracy (Nov. 1939), ibid.

42. Letter from Horatio Alger to E. R. A. Seligman, July 1, 1885. E. R. A. Seligman Papers, Rare Book and Manuscript Library, Butler Library, Columbia University. Letter from Alger to E. C. Stedman, Jan. 9, 1888, Stedman Papers, Yale Collection of American Literature, Beinecke Rare Book and Manuscript Library, Yale University, New Haven, Conn.

43. George Hellman interview with Kate Tracy (Nov. 1939) and with Kenneth Hayes Miller (Jan. 1939), both in CCC, Box 9. "To My Sister Ellen," in Elizabeth Cardozo, *Salvage,* 48.

44. George Hellman interview with Kate Tracy (Nov. 18, 1938), CCC, Box 9. (I have followed Hellman's interview notes instead of the version in Hellman, *Cardozo,* 40–41, which changes a few details.) See also author interview with Justine Wise Polier (July 11, 1958), and notes of Michael H. Cardozo IV on a draft of this chapter, KCC.

45. Author interview with Alan Stone, M.D., and Professor of Law, Harvard Law School, July 1990.

46. Rabbi Stephen Wise regarded her as "almost audacious." George Hellman interview with Rabbi Stephen Wise, noted in his interview with Mr. and Mrs. William Cardozo (1938 or 1939), CCC, Box 9.

47. Annie Nathan Meyer, *It's Been Fun,* 86 (1951).

48. See *Trow's New York City Directory* for the year 1898. His residence is listed as Flushing, New York.

49. The one letter in existence from Ben to Nellie—in 1916—refers to Emily's illness in a way that makes it seem more than just temporary. Letter from Benjamin Cardozo to Ellen Cardozo, 1916, in private hands, extract in KCC.

50. Letters from Cardozo to Charles C. Burlingham, Apr. 15, 1922, CCB, and from Cardozo to Felix Frankfurter, May 3, 1922, FF. The material on Emily Cardozo Bent is based on the author's interviews with Aline Goldstone (June 11, 1962) and Justine Wise Polier (July 11, 1958), KCC; and George Hellman

interviews with Mr. and Mrs. William Cardozo (1938 or 1939) and Adeline Cardozo (Nov. 6, 1938), CCC, Box 9. (See also letter from Frederick W. Rothschild to Hellman, Nov. 2, 1938, in which he mentions that he used to visit Emily at her home, CCC, Box 6.) Stephen Birmingham, *The Grandees: America's Sephardic Elite,* 299 (1971) contains a chapter on the Cardozos that discusses the effect of Emily's marriage on her immediate family. He states that they cut criah for her, that is, held a service as if she had died, and literally turned her picture to the wall. He cites no authority for this or any other statement in the chapter, which on the whole is so full of misinformation as to be utterly unreliable. Such a story had some currency among more distant relatives in Cardozo's family, see letter from Michael H. Cardozo to author, Apr. 8, 1988, KCC, but it seems quite false.

Ben also had enough of a relation with Frank that he invited him to his vacation home in Allenhurst after Emily's death. See letters from Cardozo to Joseph M. Paley instructing Paley to purchase and send railway tickets to Frank Bent, July 16, 1922, and July 26, 1926, JP.

51. Stephen Wise was the rabbi at the Free Synagogue in New York, a leading figure in American Jewry and the Zionist movement, and very active in progressive causes for a half century.

52. Handwritten notes prepared by Benjamin Cardozo for the use of Rabbi Stephen Wise at the funeral of Emily Cardozo Bent, attached to letter from Cardozo to Stephen S. Wise, Apr. 8, 1922, SSW.

53. Hellman interview with Kate Tracy (Nov. 11, 1938), CCC, Box 9; letter from Joseph Rauh to author, Nov. 25, 1990, KCC.

54. See chap. 24, text at note 32.

55. Author interview with Aline Goldstone (June 11, 1962), KCC.

56. Ibid.

57. Hellman interview with Kate Tracy (Nov. 1939), CCC, Box 9.

58. He copied it into one of his commonplace books, in which he noted his readings. Commonplace Book, I, [78], CCC, Box 5. See chap. 9, note 56, for a description of those books. The quotation is from John Galsworthy, *The Forsyte Saga,* 13 (1922).

59. Author interview with Justine Wise Polier (June 11, 1962), KCC. Louise and Ben met in 1893 when he was twenty-three. Letter from Stephen Wise to Kate Tracy, July 18, 1939, SSW.

60. Letter from Ethel Siesfeld to author, Nov. 24, 1967, KCC.

61. Hellman interview with Adeline Cardozo (Nov. 6, 1938), CCC, Box 9.

62. Future genetic research may provide clues as to whether the fragile health of Albert and Rebecca Cardozo's family was due in part to substantial intermarriage in the small Sephardic community and especially in the Cardozo-Nathan clan, as has been suggested, see Richard A. Posner, *Cardozo: A Study in Reputation,* 4 (1990), or to some other genetic weakness, or to chance.

63. The letter from Ben to Nellie cited in note 49 refers to playing chess together. Kate Tracy remembered listening to them playing classical music together. Hellman interview with Tracy (Nov. 19, 1938), CCC, Box 9.

64. Author interviews with Aline Goldstone (June 11, 1962) and Justine Wise Polier (July 11, 1938), KCC; George Hellman interview with Adeline Cardozo (Nov. 6, 1938), CCC, Box 9. The quotation is from the Justine Polier interview.

65. Hellman interview with Kate Tracy (Nov. 18, 1938), CCC, Box 9.

66. George Hellman interview with William McKenna (1938 or 1939), CCC, Box 9.

67. Author interview with Learned Hand, 20 (Nov. 12, 1957), KCC.

68. Author interview with Alan Stroock (Apr. 19, 1961), KCC.

69. His first cousin, twice removed, Michael H. Cardozo, IV, remembers using Cardozo's seat at Shearith Israel during High Holidays in the 1930s. Letter from Michael H. Cardozo, IV, to author, June 14, 1988, KCC.

70. Anyone in good standing over the age of twenty-one, whose parents had been members and who retained his own membership, could become an elector of the Congregation simply by signing the electors' book. Cardozo did so. Author interview with Victor Tarry, former clerk of Shearith Israel (Dec. 3, 1990), KCC.

71. Letter from N. Taylor Phillips to George Hellman, Nov. 23, 1938, CCC, Box 6.

72. On Solomons, see David and Tamar de Sola Pool, *An Old Faith in the New World: Portrait of Shearith Israel, 1654–1954*, 394 (1955).

73. George Hellman interview with David de Sola Pool (Nov. 9, 1938), CCC, Box 9. Dr. Pool did not become the rabbi of the congregation until later and must have reported what he had been told.

74. Congregation Shearith Israel, Electors Minutes, June 5, 1895, 94 (June 1878–May 1932), Congregation Shearith Israel Archives. The clerk of the meeting who recorded these events was another Cardozo relative, N. Taylor Phillips. He later made some rather severe comments on Ben's devotion to Judaism. See chap. 7, text at note 35. See also Pool, *An Old Faith*, 99–101.

5. Developing a Practice

1. A list of these cases is contained in the BNC Practice File, KCC.

2. The Importers and Traders National Bank v. Werner, 54 App. Div. 435 (1st Dept. 1900). Cardozo Brothers handled that case from the outset.

3. Croll v. Empire State Knitting Co., 17 App. Div. 282 (3d Dept. 1897); Papers on Appeal in In re Simpson, Account of Angel J. Simpson, 158 N.Y. 720 (1899), ABCNY. For a definition of the duties of an assignee for the benefit of creditors, see chap. 4, text at note 34.

4. In re Simpson, 36 App. Div. 562, aff'd, 158 N.Y. 720 (1899). For a discussion of "receivers," see chap. 1, text after note 45.

5. 54 App. Div. 637 (1st Dept. 1900).

6. Brief for Respondent, 9, ABCNY.

7. Id. at 12.

8. Id. at 17.

9. Id. at 18.

10. Id. at 21.

11. 51 App. Div. 639 (1st Dept. 1900).

12. Brief for Respondent, 7–8, ABCNY.

13. See 63 App. Div. 134, 63 App. Div. 140, and 63 App. Div. 615 (1st Dept. 1901) (two cases).

14. 73 App. Div. 627 (1st Dept. 1902).

15. See Griswold v. Caldwell, 13 *New York Law Journal* 364 (C. P. Gen. Term 1895), 5 App. Div. 622 (App. Div. 1896).

16. Brief of Respondents, 5, in Lamprecht v. Mohr, 73 App. Div. 627 (1st Dept. 1902), ABCNY.

17. See McCarty v. The Altonwood Stock Farm, 68 Hun 551 (1st Dept. 1893) and the Case on Appeal, ABCNY.

18. Brief for Respondent, 70, in Parham v. Burns, 201 N.Y. 559 (1911), ABCNY.

19. Edgar J. Nathan, Sr., "Michael H. Cardozo," in Association of the Bar of the City of New York, *1907 Yearbook,* 134.

20. Letter from Cardozo to Edgar Nathan, Sr., Mar. 22, 1907, original in possession of the Rosalie Nathan Hendricks family, copy in KCC.

21. Letter from Cardozo to Edgar Nathan, Sr., Aug. 29, 1907, original in possession of the Rosalie Nathan Hendricks family, copy in KCC.

22. Parham v. Burns, 135 App. Div. 884 (2d Dept. 1909), order resettled, 136 App. Div. 946 (2d Dept. 1900).

23. Brief for Respondent, 70–72, ABCNY.

24. See Parham v. Burns, 135 App. Div. 884 (2d Dept. 1909), aff'd, 201 N.Y. 559 (1911), for a description of the proceedings. See also K. Webber Parker v. Altonwood Park Co., 121 App. Div. 908 (2d Dept. 1907).

25. 13 App. Div. 624 (1st Dept. 1897). The later case in which he established the principle was Meinhard v. Salmon, 249 N.Y. 458 (1928), chap. 13, text at note 50.

26. Brief for Appellants, 18–19, ABCNY.

27. See Charles Reznikoff ed., *Louis Marshall: Champion of Liberty* (1957).

28. 45 App. Div. 499 (1st Dept. 1899), aff'd, 169 N.Y. 589 (1901).

29. Brief for Appellants in the Court of Appeals, ABCNY.

30. In re Snyder, 29 Misc. 1 (Sup. Ct. Sp. Term 1899) was the case in which Cardozo and Marshall opposed one another.

31. Lewisohn Bros. v. Anaconda Copper Mining Corp., 26 Misc. 613 (Sup. Ct. Sp. Term 1899).

32. Robert Raymer, *A History of Copper Mining in Montana*, 27–52 (1930).

33. There are no papers to indicate the extent of Cardozo's contribution to the suit, just the official notation that he was "of counsel."

34. Finkel v. Kohn, 38 App. Div. 199 (1st Dept. 1899).

35. Record in Finkel v. Kohn, 56, 58, 60–69, ABCNY.

36. Id. at 84–96, 101–112, and 124.

37. 38 App. Div. at 205.

38. See State Bank v. Silberman, 87 App. Div. 631 (1st Dept. 1903) for another case in which Cardozo prevailed both at trial and on appeal by demonstrating the falsity of the plaintiff's testimony. That was another case referred to Cardozo by the Lyons firm.

39. 17 App. Div. 329 (1st Dept. 1897).

40. See Edward H. Warren, *The Rights of Margin Customers*, 220–225 (1941), discussing *Douglas* at length.

41. Id. at 224–225.

42. Record on Appeal, In re Simpson, 158 N.Y. 720 (1899), ABCNY.

43. See Matter of Cornell, 17 Misc. 468, 471 (Surr. Ct. 1893); Matter of Young, 17 Misc. 680, 684 (Surr. Ct. 1896); and Matter of Young, 23 Misc. 223 (Surr. Ct. 1898).

44. See Matter of Young, 15 App. Div. 285 (3d Dept. 1897) and 160 N.Y. 705 (1899) and the record on appeal in the latter, ABCNY; and Carpenter v. Romer & Tremper Steamboat Co., 48 App. Div. 363 (3d Dept. 1900).

45. See, for example, Jenkins v. John Good Cordage Co., 56 App. Div. 573 (2d Dept. 1900), aff'd, 168 N.Y. 679 (1901).

46. 172 N.Y. 90 (1902).

47. See Robert Wiebe, *Businessmen and Reform: A Study of the Progressive Movement*, 6–10, 43–56 (1962).

48. The partnership announcement was dated April 1, 1903, CCC, Box 10.

49. Cuddy v. Clement, 187 U.S. 647 (1902).

50. Hatch v. Ketcham, 198 U.S. 580 (1905). Cardozo had handled this case below as well. 135 Fed. 504 (2d Cir. 1905).

51. Kendall v. Automatic Loom Co., 198 U.S. 477 (1905).

52. Memorandum from William H. Freese to George Hellman, Jan. 5, 1939, CCC, Box 6. Allie Cardozo lived there too, but I could find no evidence of the role he played in Cardozo family life.

53. Annie Nathan Meyer, *It's Been Fun: An Autobiography*, 87 (1951).

54. Author interviews with William Rosenblatt (Feb. 13, 1958), Carl Stern (June 14, 1962), and Julian Hess (Mar. 17, 1990), KCC.

55. George Hellman, *Benjamin N. Cardozo*, 49 (1940).

56. Author interview with Justine Wise Polier (July 11, 1958), KCC; author

interview with Aline Goldstone (June 11, 1962); George Hellman interview with Adeline Cardozo (Nov. 6, 1938), CCC, Box 9.

57. Handwritten note addressed "To whom it may Concern," Aug. 20, 1898, in possession of Joseph Rauh family, copy in KCC.

58. See chap. 4, text at note 60.

59. Author interview with Julian Hess (Mar. 17, 1990), KCC. Ms. Content, who never married, was a friend of Mr. Hess's mother, and Mr. Hess remembered hearing Ms. Content make the claim.

60. George Hellman's notes on his interview with Alan Stroock (Nov. 6, 1938) also contain a number of notes from his conversation with Adeline Cardozo, CCC, Box 9.

61. See chap. 2, note 9, for the calculation that there were at least seventy-six.

62. George Hellman interview with David de Sola Pool (Nov. 9, 1938), CCC, Box 9.

63. 61 *American Hebrew* 184–187 (June 11, 1897). Members were required to be engaged in "one of the recognized professions or in literature, art or science," or be "actively identified with Jewish interests." The Judaeans: Constitution and List of Members, Art. V, §2 (1931), microfilm A304.807, Widener Library, Harvard University.

64. See text at chap. 10, note 25, for the events surrounding Cardozo's election to membership in the Century.

65. 94 *The American Hebrew* 126 (Nov. 28, 1913), noting a meeting of the Judaeans to honor Cardozo and another of its members who had been victorious members of the Fusion ticket. See also The Judaeans, Constitution and List of Members, 7.

66. Cardozo, "The Earl of Beaconsfield: A Jew As Prime Minister," in Michael Selzer, ed., *Disraeli The Jew* (1993). The manuscript of the talk is in CCC, Box 3A.

67. Cardozo, "Earl of Beaconsfield," 41.

68. Id. at 47–49.

69. Id. at 61.

70. Id. at 65.

71. Selzer's example is that Cardozo "always invested his funds in bonds, for example, because he thought there was something sleazy about trying to make money in the stock market." Id. at 22. The only evidence I have found disagrees with that comment. Cardozo told Robert Marshall that he did not own stocks because their value was "too intimately affected by court decisions." Notes of Robert Marshall, Mar. 21, 1937, original in the possession of the George Marshall family, copy in KCC. When Cardozo told his friend Doris Webster that he had never lost money in the market because he never bought stock, she asked whether he disapproved of making money in the stock market.

He responded, "Oh, no indeed, I don't mind making money." Hellman interview with Doris Webster (Nov. 23, 1938), CCC, Box 9.

72. Cardozo, *The Jurisdiction of the Court of Appeals of the State of New York,* v (1903).

73. Letter from Louis Marshall to A. Bleecker Banks, Dec. 4, 1902, and letter from Louis Marshall to Benjamin Cardozo, Dec. 4, 1902, LM.

74. Henry Cohen's later book, *The Powers of the New York Court of Appeals* (1934), is an example of how a scholar, with time, can treat the same subject with a broader perspective and deeper analysis.

75. Id. at 295.

76. 163 N.Y. 505, aff'd, 186 U.S. 70 (1902).

77. Cardozo, *Jurisdiction of the Court of Appeals,* 92.

78. Letter from Louis Marshall to A. Bleecker Banks, Mar. 28, 1903, LM.

79. "The power to tax involves the power to destroy." McCulloch v. Maryland, 4 Wheat. 316, 431 (1816).

80. Quoted in letter from Louis Marshall to A. Bleecker Banks, Mar. 28, 1903, LM.

81. The Alton Parker Papers, LC, contain no correspondence with Louis Marshall. That collection may not be complete since it seems more likely that Banks would have sent a manuscript on the powers of the Court of Appeals to the Chief Judge of that court than to a Presiding Judge in the Appellate Division.

82. Letter from Louis Marshall to A. Bleecker Banks, Mar. 28, 1903, LM. We do not know exactly what Parker's criticism was because Marshall returned the Parker letter to Banks. Marshall's advice to Cardozo to remove the offending sentences is a little surprising. Marshall was a feisty lawyer who spoke out in blunt language on all kinds of subjects. Perhaps he was attempting either to protect the young Cardozo or to protect his own standing with the Court.

83. See Cardozo, *Jurisdiction of the Court of Appeals,* 277 in a Note at the end of the book; see also Cardozo, *The Jurisdiction of the Court of Appeals of the State of New York,* 279–283 (2d ed. 1909).

84. Learned Hand, who later had a distinguished career on the federal Court of Appeals for the Second Circuit, had begun writing such a book in his early years as a practicing lawyer, but he never completed it. Letter from Frederick Townsend to Learned Hand, Nov. 5, 1904, in LH, Box 108, Folder 3.

6. Lawyer's Lawyer

1. Whereas he had been retained in twenty-four cases in the Court of Appeals in his first fifteen years of practice, he was retained in fifty cases during his last eight years. By comparison, Charles Evans Hughes argued twenty-five cases in the Court of Appeals from 1894 to 1904, his last ten years of private

practice before he became Governor of New York and Supreme Court Justice. Edwin McElwain, "The Business of the Supreme Court as Conducted by Chief Justice Hughes," 63 *Harvard Law Review* 5, 8 (1949); Charles Evans Hughes, in *Autobiographical Notes of Charles Evans Hughes,* 108, note 17 (David Danelski and Joseph Tulchin, eds., 1973).

2. 184 N.Y. 504 (1906).

3. 97 App. Div. 416 (2d Dept. 1904).

4. 115 App. Div. 552 (1st Dept. 1906).

5. 198 N.Y. 592 (1910).

6. The issue is discussed fully in chaps. 14–16.

7. 198 N.Y. at 594.

8. George Hellman interview with William H. Freese (Dec. 1938), CCC, Box 9. Freese dated the trip as 1905. He was probably mistaken, however, as Cardozo's letters do not suggest that he had ever been to Europe before.

9. Letter from Cardozo to Edgar Nathan, Sr., Aug. 3, 1907, original in possession of the Hendricks family, copy in KCC.

10. Robert Herrick, *The Common Lot* (1904).

11. Letter from Cardozo to Edgar Nathan, Sr., Aug. 29, 1907, copy in KCC. These letters are the earliest existing nonprofessional Cardozo correspondence. His closing, "Always affectionately yours," is one that he used only with some members of the Cardozo-Nathan family and a few others with whom he had close personal relations. One was Charles Burlingham, whom he knew for twenty-nine years before he used that warm closing. Another was Joseph Rauh, his last law clerk, who achieved that status in less than a year of devoted service.

12. His letters do not mention time spent in England, except for a brief stopover at Plymouth, but George Hellman wrote that Cardozo spent the "happiest [days] of his life" on the Thames during this trip. See Hellman, *Benjamin N. Cardozo,* 48 (1940). Perhaps, as William Freese thought, he took another European trip later. George Hellman interview with William Freese (Dec. 1938), CCC, Box 9.

13. Author interview with Learned Hand, 5–6 (Nov. 12, 1957), KCC; George Hellman interview with Learned Hand (Nov. 15, 1938), CCC, Box 9; interview with Charles C. Burlingham, 9 (1949), COHP part I.

14. The records in cases in which there are published opinions demonstrate that in 1909, for example, Cardozo was in court on at least 48 days, sometimes arguing several matters on a single day. Since the results of so many trials and motions were not reported, Cardozo must have been in court considerably more than one day a week.

15. See Merlo J. Pusey, *Charles Evans Hughes,* I, 132–168 (1951); Alfred Lief, *Brandeis: The Personal History of an American Ideal,* 58–344 (1936); Allon Gal, *Brandeis of Boston,* 46–65, 96–136 (1980).

16. See Julius Henry Cohen, *They Builded Better Than They Knew* (1946).

17. Cohen, who was thirteen years older than Cardozo, was an outstanding trial specialist who was often called in by other lawyers. He had been a New York Supreme Court Justice for a few years and was close to Theodore Roosevelt. Cohen was active in public life and performed a number of governmental tasks at the state and federal level. Judge Cohen died Feb. 27, 1938. Paragraph 11th of his will provided: "Since his early boyhood I have known Benjamin N. Cardozo, and before he entered public life I realized the effort he was making for the highest standards both in character and learning in his profession. Since then he has fully established a name second to none in both. He has not been lured by material advancement as he might have been, but has adhered to the work that he loved with a singleness of purpose and loftiness of aim that are rare indeed. As a mark of my deep affection and high regard, I give Benjamin N. Cardozo $5,000." *New York Times,* 2 (Mar. 4, 1938). The correspondence between the two men did not begin until Cardozo went to Washington, but Cardozo always addressed his older friend with the salutation "Dear Judge Billy." See Cardozo-Cohen correspondence, CCC, Box 6.

18. Colby v. The Equitable Trust Co., 192 N.Y. 535 (1908).

19. 120 App. Div. 218 (1st Dept. 1907), rev'd, 193 N.Y. 486 (1908), motion for reargument denied, 194 N.Y. 564 (1909).

20. Brief for Appellants in the Court of Appeals, 50, ABCNY.

21. 193 N.Y. at 495.

22. Burlingham was a leading figure in New York reform movements for over half a century. He knew everyone and almost everything, good and bad, that was occurring in New York politics. Many prominent persons, including Cardozo, owed their positions, at least in part, to his support.

23. Author interview with Charles C. Burlingham (Nov. 13, 1957), KCC; interview with Charles C. Burlingham, 9 (1949), COHP part I. Learned Hand also recalled having asked Cardozo whether he would take a federal district judgeship and having been turned down in the same way. He could remember only that the date was prior to 1913, and hence this may well have been the same offer referred to by Burlingham. Author interview with Learned Hand, 1 (Nov. 12, 1957), KCC. For the salary figure, see 32 *Report of the New York State Bar Association* 353 (1909).

24. Throughout this book, I occasionally make rough dollar comparisons between early and late twentieth century dollar amounts. There are many complex methods and comparisons that could be made. For crude approximations, I have deemed it sufficient to use the changes in the Bureau of Labor Statistics consumer price index, as variously figured, since 1913 and the Federal Reserve Bank's cost of living index before that date. See 118 *Monthly Labor Review* 106 (Mar. 1995); United States Bureau of the Census, *The Statistical*

History of the United States from Colonial Times to the Present, 210–212 (1976).

25. 199 N.Y. 544 (1910), aff'g, 128 App. Div. 925 (1st Dept. 1908). See also 121 App. Div. 786 (1st Dept. 1907) and 126 App. Div. 953 (1st Dept. 1908).

26. Record and Brief on appeal in the Court of Appeals, 8, ABCNY.

27. Ziegfeld v. Norworth, 148 App. Div. 185 (1st Dept. 1911); Cardozo had also appeared in the last stage of the injunction proceeding. See 202 N.Y. 580 (1911).

28. Municipal Archives of the City of New York, Death Certificate No. 2561, New York City Department of Records and Information Services.

29. Author interview with Mae (Mrs. William H.) Freese (June 20, 1962), KCC. Other interviews confirmed that Mr. Werner had had some trouble but added no details. Author interview with Carl Stern, member of a successor firm (June 14, 1962), KCC. He reported a conversation in which George Engelhard, friend and, subsequently, partner of Cardozo, had stated that Werner had been a "bad actor." Judge Proskauer also remembered "some scandal," but no details. Author interview with Joseph M. Proskauer (Feb. 19, 1962), KCC.

30. Memorandum from William G. Freese to George Hellman, Jan. 5, 1939, CCC, Box 6; author interview with Adele Dobson, former secretary in Simpson, Werner & Cardozo, later secretary to Judge Froessel of the Court of Appeals (June 23, 1958), KCC; and partnership cards of the various firms in CCC, Box 10.

31. George Hellman interview with Walter Pollak (Jan. 1939), CCC, Box 9.

32. Author interview with Adele Dobson (June 23, 1958), KCC.

33. 154 App. Div. 932 (1st Dept. 1913).

34. New York Civil Rights Law, §514.

35. Thompson v. New Academy, 149 App. Div. 932 (4th Dept. 1912). See Appendix to appellant's brief in *Levy,* ABCNY.

36. Brief for Appellant, 6–7, ABCNY.

37. 109 U.S. 3 (1883).

38. Brief for Appellant, 8, ABCNY.

39. 163 U.S. 537 (1896).

40. But see Hall v. De Cuir, 95 U.S. 485 (1878), which interpreted the Commerce Clause to deny state power to apply its antisegregation law to Mississippi River steamboats operating in interstate commerce.

41. Brief for appellant, 8, ABCNY.

42. Brief for appellant, 18, ABCNY.

43. 152 App. Div. 266 (4th Dept. 1912).

44. The reply brief in *Levy* also marks the appearance of Walter Pollak as an associate in Simpson, Werner & Cardozo. Ironically, one of the first appellate appearances of this talented lawyer, who later appeared in a number of impor-

tant civil liberties cases, arguing appeals for the Scottsboro defendants and the Communist leader Earl Browder, was on behalf of a segregationist position in *Levy.*

45. 211 N.Y. 522 (1914). Cardozo apparently saw little problem in sitting on the *Joyner* appeal. He had taken no role at all in the *Joyner* litigation, but the fact that he had to deal with the *Joyner* case so fully in arguing *Levy* because of their near identity ought to have given him some pause.

46. Author interview with Mae (Mrs. William H.) Freese (June 20, 1962), KCC. There was probably more to the inquiry and the advice than Mrs. Freese remembers, but the incident made a big impression on her, and there is no reason to doubt that she got the substance of the inquiry and the advice correct.

47. People v. Katz, 209 N.Y. 311 (1913).

48. Id. at 316–317.

49. Brief for Appellants in the Court of Appeals, 1–3, ABCNY.

50. 205 N.Y. 409 (1912).

51. A random examination of the *New York Law Journal* calendars for the federal courts and a Lexis search of the federal reports indicates that Cardozo's federal practice was probably quite small. The records of the federal courts are kept in such fashion that only a file examination of every item of litigation would turn up the matters in which he was involved. I have not undertaken that task.

52. Meyerson v. Hart, 214 U.S. 516 (1909); Blake v. William Openhym & Sons, 216 U.S. 322 (1910); In re Leaf Tobacco Board of Trade, 222 U.S. 578 (1911). *Blake* did produce an opinion from the Court accepting Cardozo's argument that the appeal should be dismissed for lack of jurisdiction.

53. 206 N.Y. 688 (1912).

54. Brief for Respondents, 1–2, ABCNY.

55. Hellman, *Cardozo,* 46; author interview with attorney Emil Weitzner (May 6, 1958), KCC.

56. Letters from Louis Marshall to Cardozo, Nov. 22, 1911 and January 20, 1913, LM; American Jewish Committee, *Seventh Annual Report,* 32–33 (1913); and In re Schiff, 48 *New York Law Journal* 1462 (Dec. 21, 1912).

57. In re Schiff, id. at 2061 (July 31, 1913).

58. Minutes of Group for Consideration of Problems of Professional Responsibility, December 4, 1908, in LH, Box 3, Folder 2. I have found no other information about the group and do not know the extent of its meetings or of Cardozo's participation.

59. He did not join the Association even when he became a judge. It was not until 1928, after he had become chief judge of the Court of Appeals, that he became a member by reason of being elected to honorary status. *The Association of the Bar of the City of New York Year Book 1928,* 23.

60. New York County Lawyers' Association, *Year Book 1911*, 9; id., 1912, at 7, 17; and id., 1913, at 7, 15.

61. See George Martin, *Causes and Conflicts: The Centennial History of the Association of the Bar of the City of New York*, 19–20 (1970).

62. New York Law Institute, *Officers, Charter, By-Laws, Rules and Members*, 22 (1908).

63. Jerome Hyman, "Benjamin N. Cardozo: A Preface to His Career at the Bar," 10 *Brooklyn Law Review* 1, 28 (1940).

7. New York Supreme Court

1. For a discussion of reform movements in New York City, especially the relationship of politics, decision-making, and the power of various groups, see David Hammack, *Power and Society: Greater New York at the Turn of the Century* (1982).

2. The story of the 1913 Fusion campaign and Charles C. Burlingham's part in it are based in large part on Charles C. Burlingham, *Nomination of John Purroy Mitchel for Mayor of the City of New York in 1913* (privately printed 1943), copy in CCB; interview with Charles C. Burlingham, 7 (1949), COHP part I; and author interview with Charles C. Burlingham (Nov. 13, 1957), KCC, as supplemented by other cited sources. See also Charles Bernheimer, *Treasurer's Report of the Citizens' Municipal Committee for the Campaign of 1913*, in Joseph M. Price Papers, Rare Book and Manuscript Library, Columbia University. The report contains a short history of the Fusion Movement, the votes for the mayoral nominees in the Executive Committee, and a list of committee members, contributors, and amounts contributed. It also details the $143,000 spent by the committee on the campaign.

3. Letter from Charles C. Burlingham to Learned Hand, Aug. 8, 1913, in LH [parenthesis in original letter].

4. See Joseph Price Papers; letter from Joseph M. Price to Charles C. Burlingham, May 26, 1930, CCB.

5. *New York Times*, 1, 3 (July 12, 1913).

6. See *New York Times*, 2 (July 22, 1913); 2 (Aug. 5, 1913); and 1 (Aug. 10, 1913).

7. Interview with Burlingham, 9, COHP part I.

8. Letter from Abraham Tulin to George Hellman, Nov. 4, 1938, CCC, Box 9.

9. Interview with Charles C. Burlingham 9, COHP part I. On Moskowitz, see *New York Times*, 25 (Dec. 18, 1936).

10. Stanley Isaacs, a well-known liberal and later Manhattan Borough President, proposed Holden Weeks, a Progressive lawyer, for the nomination.

Burlingham asked him what he thought of Cardozo. "Naturally I had to say 'I think he'd be magnificent if you could get him to run.'" Isaacs later learned that Burlingham used this technique with others. Interview with Stanley M. Isaacs, 26 (1949–1950), COHP, part I.

11. Letter from Charles C. Burlingham to Learned Hand, Aug. 8, 1913, LH.

12. Ibid. See also author interview with Burlingham (Nov. 13, 1957), KCC.

13. Interview with Charles C. Burlingham, 9 (1949), COHP part I; Author interview with Burlingham (Nov. 13, 1957), KCC.

14. The career of Michael H. Cardozo, Benjamin's first cousin and Albert's nephew, was also part of the process of redemption of the family name. See chap. 4, text at note 4. Michael Cardozo was overjoyed when nominated by a committee of lawyers for the Supreme Court in New York County in 1906 because of his own desire to restore the family's reputation. Interview with Charles C. Burlingham, 9 (1949), COHP part I.

15. *New York Times*, 3 (Aug. 21, 1913).

16. Burlingham and Bannard had served together on the Board of Education in the anti-Tammany administration of Mayor William Strong, 1895–1897. Interview with Charles C. Burlingham, 3 (1949), COHP part I.

17. Author interview with Charles C. Burlingham (Nov. 13, 1957), KCC.

18. *New York Times*, 3 (Aug. 13, 1913); 1 (Aug. 16, 1913); 1, 2 (Aug. 17, 1913); 1 (Aug. 25, 1913); 1 (Aug. 26, 1913); 1 (Aug. 27, 1913); and 1 (Aug. 28, 1913).

19. *New York Times*, 1, 4 (Sept. 12, 1913); 1, 2 (Sept. 14, 1913); and 2 (Sept. 24, 1913).

20. *New York Times*, 1 (Oct. 22, 1913); 1 (Oct. 23, 1913); 2 (Oct. 24, 1913); and 2 (Oct. 28, 1913).

21. Some judicial candidates in 1913 did allow advertisements supporting their candidacy to be published in the newspapers.

22. George Hellman interview with Walter Pollak (Jan. 1939), CCC, Box 9.

23. George Hellman, *Benjamin N. Cardozo*, 54–55 (1940) and Hellman interview with Walter Pollak (Jan. 1939), CCC, Box 9. See letter from William N. Cohen to Louis Marshall, Oct. 17, 1913, soliciting Marshall's endorsement, LM, and *New York Times*, 5 (Oct. 31, 1913).

24. *New York Tribune*, 1 (Nov. 3, 1913).

25. Letter from Walter E. Meyer to Louis Marshall, Oct. 8, 1913, LM. Indeed, after Cardozo's nomination, Marshall had written him immediately. "Do not hesitate to call upon me for such assistance as it is within my power to render, to advance your candidacy." Letter from Louis Marshall to Benjamin N. Cardozo, Aug. 15, 1913, LM.

26. Letter from Louis Marshall to Editor of the *Jewish Morning Journal*, Oct. 27, 1913, LM. The same letter was sent on the same date to the editors of the *Jewish Daily News* and the *Warheit*. Ibid.

27. See, for example, *New York Evening Journal,* 28 (Oct. 24, 1913).

28. See *New York Herald,* 14 (Nov. 3, 1913).

29. See Hellman interview with Pollak (Jan. 1939), CCC, Box 9; Hellman, *Cardozo,* 56; *New York Sun,* 8 (Oct. 31, 1913); *New York Tribune,* 1 (Nov. 3, 1913); *New York Herald,* 4 (Nov. 3, 1913) (referring to Mitchel's endorsement of Cardozo as "the finest made by any party"); and *New York Times,* §3, 6 (Nov. 2, 1913) (urging voters to support the entire Fusion ticket on the Republican Party line but not mentioning Cardozo specifically).

30. He would later be selected parnas, the chief lay administrative officer, of Shearith Israel several times. See David and Tamar de Sola Pool, *An Old Faith in the New World,* 318, 503 (1955).

31. Letter from Joseph H. Cohen to Louis Marshall, Oct. 28, 1913, LM.

32. Letters from Louis Marshall to Harry Fischel, N. Taylor Phillips, and Joseph H. Cohen, Oct. 27, 1913, LM.

33. Letters from Joseph H. Cohen to Louis Marshall, Oct. 28, 1913, and from Louis Marshall to Cardozo, Oct. 29, 1913, LM.

34. Letter from Cardozo to Louis Marshall, Oct. 30, 1913, LM. Marshall then communicated that request to Fischel. Letter from Louis Marshall to Harry Fischel, Oct. 30, 1913, LM.

35. Letter from N. Taylor Phillips to Louis Marshall, Oct. 28, 1913, LM.

36. See chap. 4, note 74.

37. The story of the formation of the Jeffersonian Union party and its effect on Cardozo's election was later recalled by James Donnelly in "How Cardozo Came to the Bench," 11 *The Advocate* 141 (June 1964). (*The Advocate* is a publication of the Bronx County Bar Association.) This account is based partly on that brief piece, partly on stories in the *New York Times,* 9 (June 16, 1913); 2 (Aug. 3, 1913); 2 (Aug. 23, 1913); 3 (Aug. 25, 1913); and partly on the accounts in the *Bronx Home News,* 1, 6 (Oct. 2, 1913); 1 and 3 (Oct. 5, 1913); 1 and 7 (Oct. 9, 1913); 1 (Oct. 12, 1913); 10 (Oct. 16, 1913); 6 (Oct. 19, 1913); 1 (Oct. 30, 1913); 9 (Nov. 2, 1913); and 11 (Nov. 6, 1913).

38. *Official Canvas of Votes Cast in the City of New York, Nov. 4, 1913,* 28–33.

39. Hellman, *Cardozo,* 56–57, quoting a comment made to George Farnum. The legend had apparently made the rounds. Charles Burlingham referred to it many years later: "Considering that you owe your own judicial life to some 1200 Italians in the Bronx." Letter from Charles Burlingham to Cardozo, Nov. 13, 1933, CCB.

40. The election statistics taken from *Official Canvas of Votes Cast in the City of New York, November 4, 1913,* 28–33, and the figures relating to Italian-Americans taken from *Thirteenth Census of the United States—1910— Population,* III, 253–255 (1913) demonstrate this point. These statistics and figures may be found in the BNC Election file in KCC.

41. The official canvas and the newspaper reports list only the total votes for each candidate. The vote by political party must have been available unofficially at the time, for "Onlooker," the political columnist of the *Bronx Home News,* analyzed the returns and determined the approximate vote for each party in the Bronx. On the basis of an approximate total vote of 78,000, "Onlooker" estimated the following breakdown:

Tammany—26,000
Republican—18,000
Progressive—12,500
Jeffersonian Union—6,000
Independence League—6,500
Socialist—6,000
Anti-Tammany Jeffersonian Alliance—2,500
Bronx County Independent Union—500

Bronx Home News, 9 (Dec. 11, 1913). Using this estimated vote tabulation would have given Cardozo 39,000 Bronx votes and Weeks 33,000. Cardozo actually polled 900 less than the estimate and Weeks 500 more, but the fact that the totals are so close indicates the likelihood that Onlooker's estimates are quite accurate.

42. Letter from Cardozo to Agnes Goldman (later Mrs. Agnes Sanborn), Dec. 13, 1913, Agnes Goldman Sanborn Papers, HLS.

43. Letters from Cardozo to Louis Marshall, Nov. 10 and 20, 1913; letter from Marshall to Cardozo, Nov. 15, 1913, LM. With all that Marshall had done for Cardozo, their correspondence never advanced beyond "Dear Mr. Marshall" and "Dear Judge." See, for example, letter from Cardozo to Marshall, Apr. 19, 1926, and letter from Marshall to Cardozo, Apr. 20, 1926, LM.

44. 50 *New York Law Journal* 1707–1708 (Jan. 6, 1914).

45. Holmes v. St. Joseph Lead Co., id. at 1799 (Jan. 10, 1914) (stockholder's suit to set aside a contract to purchase company gold notes at 90% of face value); Allen v. Watt, id. at 1821 (Jan. 12, 1914) (procedural issues in suit against directors for neglect of duty); Kamm v. Kamm, id. at 1894 (Jan. 16, 1914) (complaint and counterclaim for separation); Golland v. Harris, id. at 2259 (Feb. 5, 1914) (enforcement of secret trust of property by beneficiaries after devisee's bankruptcy); and Drucklieb v. Harris, id. at 2259 (Feb. 5, 1914).

46. Felberbaum v. Union Ry., id. at 2230 (Feb. 4, 1914), papers on file in Municipal Reference Library, Municipal Bldg., New York, N.Y.

47. The Governor was empowered to appoint up to four Supreme Court judges to sit in the Court of Appeals for such purpose. New York Constitution of 1894, Article VI, §7, as amended 1899. Three judges had regularly been designated.

48. Frank H. Hiscock, "The Court of Appeals of New York: Some Features of Its Organization and Work," 14 *Cornell Law Quarterly* 131, 133, 137 (1929).

49. George Hellman interview with Walter Pollak (Jan. 1939), CCC, Box 9. Irving Lehman, Cardozo's politically well-connected friend and colleague on both the New York Supreme Court and Court of Appeals, reported that some of Governor Glynn's "close friends" also urged Cardozo's appointment. Lehman, "Judge Cardozo in the Court of Appeals," 52 *Harvard Law Review* 364, 365 (1939).

50. Edward Greenbaum, *A Lawyer's Job*, 39 (1967). The author was Samuel Greenbaum's son.

51. See Herbert Mitgang, *The Man Who Rode the Tiger: The Life and Times of Samuel Seabury*, 107–108 (1996 ed.); Walter Chambers, *Samuel Seabury: A Challenge*, 170 (1932).

52. 201 N.Y. 271 (1911). See discussion in chap. 19, text at note 19.

53. Greenbaum "was an excellent judge, and his standards have always been the highest in all the affairs of life." Letter from Cardozo to Annie Nathan Meyer, Aug. 19, 1925, Annie Nathan Meyer Papers, Barnard College, New York, N.Y.

54. Greenbaum, *A Lawyer's Job*, 39. Although I believe the story of Cardozo's designation to be more complicated than Greenbaum's report, I do believe that the quoted conversation did take place at some point. The words attributed to Cardozo certainly sound like something he would have said.

55. Glynn's official designation, dated February 2, 1914, is in CCC, Box 10. The designation was to last until the backlog of cases in the Court of Appeals was reduced to 200.

56. Irving Lehman, *Benjamin Nathan Cardozo: A Memorial*, 7 (1938).

57. 50 *New York Law Journal* 2232 (Feb. 4, 1914). Charles Burlingham told quite a different story, but for once he seems to have been mistaken. Burlingham stated that Governor Glynn wanted to appoint a Catholic and first offered the post to William D. Guthrie of the Cravath firm. After Guthrie turned him down, Glynn then offered it to Cardozo's Columbia classmate and friend, Frederic Coudert. After Coudert turned him down, Glynn offered it to Justice William Kelley of the Appellate Division of the Supreme Court. Kelley declined when he learned that he was being offered the position because he was a Catholic. Only then, Burlingham said, did Glynn turn to Cardozo. Interview with Charles C. Burlingham, 9 (1949), COHP part I. I believe that Burlingham confused two appointments that Glynn had to make in 1914. Neither Guthrie nor Coudert were sitting Supreme Court justices and therefore could not have been designated to the Court of Appeals. Glynn also had a regular appointment to make to the Court of Appeals because Willard Bartlett, a sitting judge of that court, had been elected chief judge of the court at the November 1913 elections. Glynn

probably offered that position to Guthrie, Coudert, and Kelley before he finally appointed William Hornblower.

58. Minutes of the Board of Trustees, VIII, 457 (meeting of Feb. 3, 1914), Congregation Shearith Israel Archives.

59. Letter from Cardozo to the Trustees of the Congregation, Mar. 6, 1914, in Clerk's Office Correspondence, 1912–1914, Congregation Shearith Israel Archives.

60. This ex parte consultation with judges of a higher court would raise an interesting ethical question today under the current *Model Code of Judicial Conduct* (1990). Canon 3B(7)(c), which contains an exception to the general prohibition against ex parte communications by permitting a judge to "consult . . . with other judges," but the Commentary suggests that consultation with a judge of a reviewing court is ordinarily problematic. Ethical sensibilities were less strict in Cardozo's time, and apparently no one questioned his right to consult the Court of Appeals.

61. Record in Drucklieb v. Harris, No. 8041–13, Municipal Reference Library, Municipal Bldg., New York. The reference to Cardozo's report of his conversations with judges of the Court of Appeals appears in an affidavit of George Ferris, attorney for the defendant. No record of the eventual outcome of the case remains.

8. The Job of a Judge

1. Judge Seabury thought that Pound's views were equally important with Cardozo's in swinging the Court of Appeals "from its former reactionary nature." George Hellman interview with Samuel Seabury (Apr. 10, 1939), CCC, Box 6. John Lord O'Brian, who had a long career at the bar in both public and private practice and was highly regarded as one of the country's wise lawyers, regarded Pound as "one of the original liberals of this country." Interview with John Lord O'Brian, 62, 381, COHP part I. And Dean James Landis of Harvard Law School thought him one of the great state judges. Interview with Landis, 85 (1963–1964), COHP part II. See also Henry Edgerton, "A Liberal Judge: Cuthbert W. Pound," 21 *Cornell Law Quarterly* 7 (1935).

2. Palsgraf v. The Long Island R. Co., 248 N.Y. 339, 347 (1928).

3. This brief estimation of some of Cardozo's colleagues is based on my own reading of their opinions supplemented by the views of Justice Frankfurter (author interviews of Aug. 20 and 21, 1960, KCC), Judge Learned Hand (author interview, Nov. 12, 1957, KCC), Judge Edward Finch (author interview, June 19, 1962, KCC), Jay Leo Rothschild, a perceptive New York lawyer (author interview, May 12, 1958, KCC); and John Lord O'Brian, (interview, COHP part I).

4. Alden Chester, *Courts and Lawyers of New York: A History, 1609–1925*,

II, 824–825 (1925). There is a picture of the old courtroom in 2 *Green Bag* 341 (1890).

5. This description is taken from Henry Cohen, *The Powers of the New York Court of Appeals,* 291–351 (1934).

6. Chester, *Courts and Lawyers,* II, 822.

7. Frank H. Hiscock, "The Court of Appeals of New York: Some Features of Its Organization and Work," 14 *Cornell Law Quarterly* 131 (1929).

8. The discussion of the Court's "reporting" practice is based on my examination of the 646 folders of Cardozo's reports from 1914–1932 that still exist. CM. The description of court procedure seems accurate with respect to cases reported by other judges because there are a few reports from other judges in the Cardozo files. No official court files containing judges' drafts and memoranda exist for cases in which the original decision was to write an opinion.

9. See chap. 10, text at note 14, for a quantitative survey of Cardozo's opinions and votes during his service on the Court of Appeals.

10. 211 N.Y. 241 (1914), rev'g 151 App. Div. 198 (4th Dept. 1912).

11. Id. at 263–264.

12. Id. at 257.

13. In that regard, however, he did not mention the plaintiffs' claims for damages. Technically, he did not have to, since the damage claim had been lost because of failure of proof and because of inability to separate the acts of the defendants from the acts of others. Still, insofar as Cardozo was announcing general rules, he could have adverted to the question of the availability of damages even though equity might not order the tearing down of urban development.

14. See Critten v. Vredenburgh, 151 N.Y. 536 (1897) where Cardozo replaced Simon W. Rosendale, who had argued the cause in the Appellate Division but had then been named Attorney General of New York. Cardozo filed basically the same brief, word for word, that Rosendale had used in the Appellate Division, adding only a few sentences to discuss a new case and to meet some argument made below. But he deliberately changed one sentence to suit his own literary taste. Rosendale had written, "There is no inconsistency between these two positions; and the plaintiffs are entitled to the benefit and the protection of them both." Brief for Respondents in the Appellate Division, 25, ABCNY. Cardozo changed the sentence to read, "There is no inconsistency between these two positions; and to the benefit and protection of both, the plaintiffs are entitled." Brief for Respondents, Court of Appeals, 29, ABCNY.

15. Letter from Thomas Reed Powell to Cardozo, Oct. 16, 1935, Thomas Reed Powell Papers, HLS.

16. Letter from Cardozo to Thomas Reed Powell, Oct. 18, 1935, ibid.

17. Letter from Cardozo to Charles C. Burlingham, Jan. 7, 1933, CCB.

18. 211 N.Y. 465 (1914), rev'g 149 App. Div. 934 (4th Dept. 1912).

19. 211 N.Y. at 468.

20. See letter from Cardozo to Felix Frankfurter, May 8, 1924, FF; author interview with Andrew J. Lynch (July 1, 1958), KCC.

21. Author interview with Louis Feldman, bellman at the Hotel Ten Eyck (June 23, 1958), and author inspection of the premises, June 23, 1958, KCC.

22. During most of Cardozo's service on the Court of Appeals, the card clerk, William B. Estabrook, attended all the consultations. Part of his job was to digest, for the court's use only, all cases decided by the Court without opinion. In connection with that job, Mr. Estabrook, who was also a stenographer, recorded the discussions. His job was described by Cardozo at the ceremony honoring Estabrook's forty years of service with the Court when he retired. See the clipping from the newspaper *The Knickerbocker Press,* Jan. 15, 1931, in CM, Box 5, Folder 5373.

23. See letter from Cardozo to Charles C. Burlingham, Mar. 15, 1921, referring to Friday afternoon consultations, CCB. See also Cardozo, "The Bench and the Bar," Address before the Broome County Bar Association, 1929, reprinted in 34 *New York State Bar Journal* 444, 446 (Dec. 1962).

24. Author interviews with Raymond Cannon, Clerk, New York Court of Appeals, and Richard Lewis, stenographer in Clerk's office (June 23, 1958), KCC.

25. See letters from Cardozo to Joseph Paley, July 13 and 15, 1922, JP.

26. Author interview with Chris Bogiages (June 23, 1958), KCC. This picture of Cardozo's life in Albany is a composite drawn from author's interviews (June 23, 1958) with members of the staff of the Hotel Ten Eyck: Chris Bogiages, Ray Billsborrow, room clerk, and Louis Feldman, bellman; members and former members of the staff of the Clerk's office at the Court of Appeals: Raymond Cannon, Clerk, Richard Lewis, stenographer, Floyd Melius, staff member; and especially author interview with Andrew Lynch, confidential assistant to the court (July 1, 1958), KCC.

27. See chap. 9, note 56, for a discussion of the commonplace books.

28. Commonplace Book, II, 1–2, CCC, Box 5.

29. Commonplace Book, I, [17], CCC, Box 5, quoting Bertrand Russell, *The Problems of Philosophy,* 163 (1912).

30. Commonplace Book, II, 137, CCC, Box 5, quoting Lawrence P. Jacks, *Constructive Citizenship,* 76 (1928).

31. Commonplace Book, II, 165, CCC, Box 5, quoting Irwin Edman, *Adam, the Baby, and the Man From Mars,* 177 (1929).

32. Commonplace Book, II, 174–175, CCC, Box 5, quoting Edward F. Benson, *As We Were: A Victorian Peep Show,* 175 (1930).

33. Commonplace Book, II, 177, CCC, Box 5, quoting the *New York Times,* §5, 1 (July 26, 1931).

34. Commonplace Book, II, 225, CCC, Box 5, quoting Henry W. Nevinson, *Goethe: Man and Poet,* 152 (1932).

35. Commonplace Book, I, [76], CCC, Box 5, quoting Herbert Asquith, *Memories and Reflections,* I, 55–56 (1928).

36. Cardozo, "The Bench and the Bar," 446; author interview with Mary Hun Sears (Dec. 22, 1958), KCC.

37. See Cardozo memorandum in Day v. Ceder, 228 N.Y. 588 (1920), CM, Box 1, Folder 1039.

38. This comment is based on the several transcripts of discussions in the consultation found in the Cardozo files at the Court of Appeals. The transcripts are from the consultations in Byrnes v. Owen, CM, Box 3, Folder 2820 (1926); Resigno v. F. Jarka Co., Inc., 248 N.Y. 225 (1928), CM, Box 4, Folder 3829; In re Zirpola v. Casselman, Inc., 237 N.Y. 367 (1924), CM, Box 2, Folder 2159.

39. Cardozo report in People v. Bressen, 212 N.Y. 578 (1914), CM, Box 1, Folder 261.

40. Cardozo report in Goldberger v. Fidelio Brewing Co., CM, Box 2, Folder 1528 (motion no. 5, May 30, 1923).

41. Cardozo memorandum accompanying his report in Lee v. Erie R. Co., 225 N.Y. 727 (1919) (judgment affirmed without opinion), CM, Box 1, Folder 689.

42. Cardozo report in Fulton Co. Gas & Elec. Co. v. Rockwood Mfg. Co., Inc. (motion for leave to appeal denied), CM, Box 2, Folder 1738 (motion no. 20, Jan. 15, 1924).

43. Cardozo report in Warner v. Lucey, 238 N.Y. 638 (1924) (judgment affirmed without opinion), CM, Box 2, Folder 1943.

44. Cardozo report in Brannen v. Union Stock Yards Bank, 215 N.Y. 652 (1915) (judgment affirmed without opinion), CM, Box 1, Folder 325.

45. Wikoff v. New Amsterdam Cas. Co., 226 N.Y. 596 (1919) (judgment affirmed without opinion), CM, Box 1, Folder 705.

46. Cardozo report in In re Tessier and Sullivan, 230 N.Y. 660 (1921) (judgment affirmed without opinion), CM, Box 1, Folder 846.

47. Cardozo report in Mandell v. Moses, 239 N.Y. 555 (1924) (judgment affirmed without opinion, Cardozo and Lehman dissenting), CM, Box 2, Folder 2032.

48. Cardozo memorandum in Neumond v. Farmers Feed Co., 244 N.Y. 202 (1926), CM, Box 3, Folders 3004 and 3188.

49. Memorandum in In re People ex rel. Woodin v. Ottaway, 247 N.Y. 493, motion for reargument denied, 4–3, 248 N.Y. 527 (1928), CM, Box 3, Folder 3614.

50. See, for example, Cardozo memorandum in In re Transfer Tax upon the Estate of Hawes, 221 N.Y. 613 (1917) (order affirmed without opinion when

original vote was for reversal), CM, Box 1, Folder 517; Cardozo memorandum in D'Aprile v. The Turner-Looker Co., 239 N.Y. 427 (1925) (opinion by Cardozo, with Lehman and Crane dissenting), CM, Box 2, Folder 2262 (Cardozo's memorandum was in response to Lehman's original draft opinion for the Court); Cardozo memorandum in Richard v. Credit Suisse, 242 N.Y. 346 (1926) (order affirmed in opinion by Cardozo when original vote was for reversal), CM, Box 3, Folder 2924.

51. See, for example, Cardozo memorandum in Kettell v. Erie R. Co., 225 N.Y. 727 (1919), CM, Box 1, Folder 1029; letter from Cardozo to William Andrews in Phelps-Stokes Estate, Inc. v. Nixon, 222 N.Y. 93 (1917), CM, Box 1, Folder 1067; Cardozo memorandum in Schwartz & Co. v. Aimwell Co., Inc., 227 N.Y. 184 (1919), CM, Box 1, Folder 1090; Cardozo memorandum in American Lithographic Co. v. Sullivan, (1925), CM, Box 2, Folder 2504; Cardozo memorandum in Kittredge v. Grannis, 244 N.Y. 182 (1926), Box 3, Folder 3003.

52. Foster v. City of New York, 222 N.Y. 581 (1917) (affirming without opinion the judgment of the Appellate Division that had reversed a judgment for a plaintiff in a personal injury case because the required notice of intention to sue was defective), CM, Box 1, Folder 554.

53. Cardozo report in People ex rel. City of New York v. Voris, 238 N.Y. 548 (1924) (motion for reargument denied), CM, Box 2, Folder 1829.

54. Cardozo report on motion for leave to appeal in Boer v. Garcia, 240 N.Y. 9 (1925) (judgment affirmed, Cardozo joining in unanimous opinion by Chief Judge Hiscock), CM, Box 2, Folder 1960.

55. Report on motion for leave to appeal in Lichtenthal v. Jacob Cohen, CM, Box 4, Folder 4711 (motion 49 of Feb. 10, 1930) (recommending denial of motion).

56. People ex rel. Boyle v. Cruise, 231 N.Y. 650 (1921) (motion denied in a per curiam adopting Cardozo's suggested wording), CM, Box 1, Folder 907.

57. Letters from Cardozo to Learned Hand, Sept. 21, 1922, LH, and to Felix Frankfurter, Dec. 4, 1922, FF.

58. Author interview with Joseph Andrews, secretary to the Librarian of the Association of the Bar of the City of New York (June 8, 1958), KCC.

59. Letter from Cardozo to Felix Frankfurter, Oct. 17, 1931, FF.

60. Although not explicitly forbidden in the Code of Judicial Conduct even in 1995, such conduct would doubtless raise a serious issue now.

61. Author interview with Joseph Paley (Jan. 23, 1958), KCC.

62. George Hellman, *Benjamin N. Cardozo,* 57–58 (1940), reporting similar testimony by Walter Pollak and Charles E. Hughes, Jr. See also transcript of the consultation in Byrnes v. Owen, 243 N.Y. 211 (1926), CM, Box 1, Folder 2820, in which Cardozo referred to three older cases, two by volume number and one

by volume and page, during discussion of a case not assigned to him. See also author interview with Joseph Paley (Jan. 23, 1958), KCC.

63. Letters from Cardozo to Joseph Paley, Oct. 29, 1918, Nov. 11, 1918, JP.

64. Author interview with Joseph Paley (Jan. 23, 1958), KCC.

65. Letter from Cardozo to Abraham Paley, July 13, 1918, JP; letter from Cardozo to Joseph Paley, July 19, 1922, JP.

66. See, for example, letters from Cardozo to Joseph Paley, June 24, 1919, Sept. 11 and 12, 1920, and Aug. 16, 1927, JP. Joseph Paley kept Cardozo's handwritten drafts of many of his lectures and speeches. After Paley died, the material surfaced and was acquired jointly by Harvard Law School, Columbia University, and Cardozo Law School. The originals are at Cardozo Law School, with photocopies in CCC and JP.

67. See, for example, letters from Cardozo to Joseph Paley of July 20, 22 (two letters), and 23, 1921, JP.

68. See, for example, letter from Cardozo to Joseph Paley, Sept. 14, 1927, JP.

69. There were dozens of letters containing such requests. See, for example, letters from Cardozo to Joseph Paley, Feb. 3, 1919, Jan. 7, 1923, Aug. 21, 1925, and July 26, 1926, JP.

9. Private Life and Private Views

1. The description of the house and the living arrangements is from author interview with Catherine Walsh (June 17, 1958), KCC.

2. Author interviews with Justine Wise Polier (July 11, 1958) and Aline Goldstone (June 11, 1962), KCC; George Hellman interview with Kate Tracy (Nov. 18, 1938), CCC, Box 9. See letter from Cardozo to Mrs. E. R. A. Seligman, May 12, 1919, referring to some bad heart attacks that Nellie had had recently, E.R.A. Seligman Papers, Butler Library, Columbia University, New York, N.Y. Hellman's notes have Miss Tracy's remembering Nellie as being an "invalid" from 1911, but because there are some chronological errors in those notes, that date may not be exact.

3. George Hellman interview with Adeline Cardozo (Nov. 6, 1938), CCC, Box 9.

4. Author interviews with Floyd Melius (June 23, 1958) and Andrew Lynch (July 1, 1958), KCC. George Hellman interview with Kate Tracy (Nov. 18, 1938), and letter from Kate Tracy to Robert Marshall, Apr. 28, 1939, original in possession of George Marshall family, copy in KCC.

5. In 1932, during the summer after his first few months on the Supreme Court, Cardozo went through his correspondence files in preparation for moving into his new Washington apartment. In so doing, he engaged "in the

gruesome task of sorting out old papers and consigning many to the flames with the pangs inseparable from a parting with old and trusted friends." Cardozo letter to Felix Frankfurter, Sept. 10, 1932, FF. It seems likely that he burned his letters to Nellie at that time. After Cardozo died, William H. Freese, his lawyer and one of his executors, and Kate Tracy, supposedly on Cardozo's instructions and after discussion with Irving Lehman, destroyed not only Cardozo's Supreme Court papers but also his remaining personal correspondence and other personal papers. Author interview with Mae (Mrs. William H.) Freese and Mr. William G. Freese, the widow and son of William H. Freese (June 20, 1962), KCC; note of William H. Freese, Oct. 11, 1938, in private possession. Of course, insofar as correspondence was concerned, the destruction encompassed primarily letters written by others to Cardozo since most of his own correspondence was handwritten and remained in the files of the recipients.

6. Letter from Benjamin Cardozo to Ellen Cardozo, 1916, in private possession, read to author.

7. See James Waterman Wise, *Legend of Louise: The Life Story of Mrs. Stephen S. Wise,* 41–42 (1949) for commentary on the close relationship that existed between Louise Wise and Nellie.

8. Judge Elkus was one. Children of some friends were others. Burlingham, Hand, and Frankfurter became CCB, LH, and FF eventually; and finally FF became Felix, but it took 18 years. Even joint letters to Louise and Stephen Wise were most often addressed as "Dear Louise and Dr. Wise" and never as "Dear Louise and Stephen."

9. Author interview with Justine Wise Polier (July 11, 1958), KCC.

10. Interview with Frederic Coudert, 113 (1949–1950), COHP part I. Virginia Veenswijk, *Coudert Brothers: A Legacy in Law,* 218–219 (1994).

11. See, for example, Cardozo letter to Learned Hand, Dec. 4, 1920, LH, and letter from Michael H. Cardozo, IV, to author, June 14, 1988, KCC, referring to lunches with Cardozo and his own father, Cardozo's first cousin Ernest.

12. Several of his books of marriage certificates, with the stubs showing the names of the married couples, survive. See CCC, Box 11.

13. See Cardozo letter to Maud Nathan, Dec. 14, 1923, CCC, Box 9, and letter from Charles C. Burlingham to Learned Hand, June 11, 1925, LH.

14. The Bea Lillie performance was "Charlot's Revue," and the Galsworthy play was *Escape.* George Hellman interview with Hortense Hirsch (1938 or 1939), CCC, Box 9, and Cardozo letter to Aline Goldstone, Nov. 6, 1927, explained in author interview with Aline Goldstone (fall 1962), copy in KCC.

15. Interview with Frederic R. Coudert, Jr., 121 (1949–1950), COHP part I.

16. Author interview with Rosalie Hendricks (June 5, 1958), KCC; author interview with Emily Nathan (June 11, 1958), KCC.

17. Letter from Cardozo to Mrs. E. R. A. Seligman, May 12, 1919, Seligman Papers, Butler Library, Columbia University, New York, N.Y.; letter from Cardozo to Stephen Wise, Dec. 19, 1923, SSW.

18. Letter from Cardozo to Felix Frankfurter, Sept. 4, 1927, FF.

19. Author interview with Catherine Walsh (June 17, 1958), KCC; letter from Cardozo to Agnes Goldman, July 3, 1918, Agnes Goldman Sanborn Papers, HLS; and letter from Cardozo to Felix Frankfurter, July 1, 1927, FF.

20. Report in Wikoff v. New Amsterdam Cas. Co., 226 N.Y. 596 (1919), CM, Box 1, Folder 705.

21. Hellman interview with Tracy (Nov. 18, 1938), CCC, Box 9.

22. Estate Tax Return of Benjamin N. Cardozo, Surrogate's Office, Westchester County, File No. 1372–1938.

23. The information in this paragraph and the next one is based on Cardozo's correspondence with his secretary Joseph Paley; Estate Tax Return of Benjamin N. Cardozo, Surrogate's Office, Westchester County, File No. 1372–1938; and privately held documents.

24. See letter from Cardozo to Joseph Paley, June 4, 1927, JP.

25. See letters from Cardozo to Joseph Paley, Sept. 12, and Sept. 28, 1919, JP.

26. See, for example, letters from Cardozo to Joseph Paley, Sept. 28, 1919, Oct. 11, 1919, Nov. 30, 1925, and Feb. 8, 1931, JP.

27. See, for example, letter from Cardozo to Joseph Paley, July 19, 1922, asking him to check whether Freese had Cardozo's mortgage investment reports, JP.

28. See, for example, letter from Cardozo to Joseph Paley, July 18, 1920, JP.

29. George S. Hellman, *Benjamin N. Cardozo,* 67–68 (1940).

30. Letter from Cardozo to Joseph Paley, Oct. 9, 1927, JP.

31. See the references in letter to Joseph Paley, July 31, 1919, JP, and letter to Annie Nathan Meyer, Jan. 17, 1933, American Jewish Archives, Cincinnati, Ohio.

32. Author interview with Aline Goldstone (June 11, 1962), KCC.

33. Letter from Cardozo to Dean Roscoe Pound, Harvard Law School, Apr. 2, 1921, Roscoe Pound Papers, HLS. But Cardozo's effusiveness was not hypocritical. He remarked to Frankfurter that he had written Pound "in a white heat of enthusiasm on reading some of his articles. I owe more to him than to anyone else except Holmes." Letter from Cardozo to Felix Frankfurter, Sept. 16, 1921, FF.

34. Letter from Cardozo to Frederic Coudert, Dec. 22, 1921, Coudert Papers, Butler Library, Columbia University.

35. Letter from Cardozo to Felix Frankfurter, June 11, 1921, FF.

36. Letter from Cardozo to Felix Frankfurter, Feb. 4, 1922, FF.

37. Letter from Cardozo to Learned Hand, Feb. 11, 1922, LH.

38. Letter from Cardozo to Learned Hand, June 26, 1927, LH.

39. Letter from Cardozo to Learned Hand, Aug. 20, 1927, LH.

40. Letter from Learned Hand to Harlan Fiske Stone, July 18, 1938, just after Cardozo's death, LH.

41. Maud was a strong suffragette and active in the Consumers League. See Anne L. Kaufman, "Maud Nathan," in Deborah Moore and Paula Hyman, eds., *Jewish Women: An Historical Encyclopedia* (New York: Routledge, 1997). Annie was a founder of Barnard College, a playwright, and antisuffragette.

42. Author interview with Aline Goldstone (June 11, 1962), KCC. The bulk of the respective correspondence is some indication of closeness, and the bulk of the correspondence with Annie is substantially greater than that with Maud. Likewise, he appears to have seen her more often, at least in later years.

43. Letter from Robert Nathan to Michael Cardozo, July 1, 1967, copy in KCC.

44. Letter to Annie Nathan Meyer, Dec. 29, 1924, Annie Nathan Meyer Papers, American Jewish Archives, Hebrew Union College, Cincinnati, Oh., and Annie Nathan Meyer Collection, Barnard College, New York, N.Y. The portion of the letter quoted here is in the former collection, the rest of the letter is in the latter collection.

45. Letter to Annie Nathan Meyer, Aug. 26, 1932, Annie Nathan Meyer Papers, American Jewish Archives, Hebrew Union College, Cincinnati, Oh.

46. See letter from Cardozo to James Weldon Johnson, Sept. 28, 1929, James Weldon Johnson Papers, series I, folder 81, Yale Collection of American Literature, Beinecke Rare Book and Manuscript Library, Yale University, New Haven, Conn. On the remarkable career of Johnson, see Eugene Levy, *James Weldon Johnson* (1973).

47. Letter from Cardozo to Oliver Wendell Holmes, Aug. 6, 1930, Oliver Wendell Holmes Papers, HLS. The sermon-poem "Go Down Death" was published with other poems in Johnson's *God's Trombones* (1927). It may also be found in Nathan Huggins, ed., *Voices From The Harlem Renaissance*, 342 (1976). Cardozo's letter did not mention the name of the author of the book of sermons, and I am grateful to my colleague Randall Kennedy for supplying the name of the writer of "Go Down Death."

48. A typed version of Holmes's letter to Cardozo of Aug. 8, 1930, labeled "copy," appears in the James Weldon Johnson Papers, Yale Collection of American Literature, Beinecke Rare Book and Manuscript Library, Yale University, New Haven, Conn., without any cover letter. The source was probably Cardozo, for it seems unlikely that the 89-year-old Justice, vacationing without any staff at Beverly Farms, Mass., made the effort to send the copy.

49. Letter from Cardozo to Felix Frankfurter, Mar. 30, 1933, FF.

50. Author interview with Henry Cohen (June 9, 1958), KCC. Cohen served as Irving Lehman's law clerk between 1930 and 1934.

51. Letter from Dale Bosley, marshal of the Supreme Court of the United States, to author, June 1, 1995, KCC; letter from Joseph L. Rauh, Jr., to author, Jan. 29, 1991, KCC. See letter from Cardozo to Judge and Mrs. Kellogg and Mary Hun, Dec. 24, 1932, KCC, referring to his "colored messenger."

52. Letter from Cardozo to Learned Hand, Sept. 19, 1929, LH.

53. Letter to Professor Cassius J. Keyser of Columbia, Feb. 6, 1932, Cassius J. Keyser Papers, Butler Library, Columbia University, New York, N.Y.

54. Letter from Cardozo to Edgar Nathan, Sr., Sept. 17, 1925, original in possession of the Hendricks family, copy in KCC. See *New York Times*, 1 (Sept. 16, 1925), for a report of the election results.

55. Letter from Cardozo to Charles C. Burlingham, Jan. 1, 1934, CCB. See chap. 19, text preceding note 47, for the ironical outcome of Cardozo's vote and his subsequent judicial involvement in Walker's tribulations.

56. His correspondence and his writings from the previous years indicate that this sample is representative of his lifelong reading habit. The list comes from the period from 1924 to 1937 when he kept commonplace books in which he recorded excerpts from his current reading, and also occasionally stories told by friends and comments of his own. The three handwritten commonplace books are in CCC, Box 5. I do not know whether these are survivors of a more complete set or whether these are the only ones he ever kept. The first items in volume one and a separate scrapbook preserve extensive clippings of newspaper articles from a wide variety of sources reviewing his books, reporting on his talks, and recording a variety of events in which Cardozo's name was mentioned. CCC, Box 11.

57. Michael H. Cardozo IV's notes on a draft of this book, KCC.

58. Commonplace Book, II, 142, CCC, Box 5. Cardozo thereafter used the term to describe Nicholas Murray Butler at a dinner given in Butler's honor. Cardozo, "Address at a Dinner to Nicholas Murray Butler," Feb. 11, 1932, CCC, Box 5, and KCC.

59. Commonplace Book, II, 15, CCC, Box 5, quoting from Alfred North Whitehead, *The Aims of Education & Other Essays*, 1 (1929).

60. See chap. 27, note 54, for a negative comment about Spinoza's *Ethics*.

61. Letter from Cardozo to Annie Nathan Meyer, Aug. 8, 1927, Annie Nathan Meyer Papers, Barnard College, New York, N.Y.; letter from Cardozo to Learned Hand, Aug. 20, 1927, LH.

62. Letter from Cardozo to Learned Hand, Aug. 20, 1927, LH.

63. See Edward A. Purcell, *The Crisis of Democratic Theory*, 47–73 (1973).

64. Letter from Cardozo to Annie Nathan Meyer, July 21, 1924, Annie Nathan Meyer Papers, Barnard College.

65. Letter from Cardozo to Mary Hun, Aug. 3, 1929, KCC.

66. Commonplace Book, II, 90, 91, quoting from Holmes's comments to him during his visit at Beverly Farms, Mass., Aug. 5, 1930, and from Russell's article, "Heads or Tails," in *Atlantic Monthly*, 163, 169 (Aug. 1930).

67. Letters from Cardozo to Alfred Stieglitz and Georgia O'Keefe, Sept. 22, 1931, Sept. 24, 1931, Oct. 3, 1931, Feb. 21, 1932, and Mar. 24 (or 27) 1933, Alfred Stieglitz Papers, Yale Collection of American Literature, Beinecke Rare Book and Manuscript Library, Yale University, New Haven, Conn.

68. Letter from Cardozo to Annie Nathan Meyer, July 3, 1925, Annie Nathan Meyer Papers, Barnard College, New York, N.Y.; letter from Cardozo to Edgar Nathan, Sr., July 8, 1925, original in possession of Hendricks family, copy in KCC.

69. Letter from Cardozo to Sallie (Mrs. Edgar) Nathan, Feb. 3, 1926, original in possession of Hendricks family, copy in KCC; letter from Cardozo to Professor John Erskine, Feb. 3, 1926, CCC, Box 9; letters from Cardozo to Learned Hand, Feb. 7 and March 26, 1926, LH; letter from Cardozo to Justice Harlan Stone, Mar. 6, 1926 (misdated 1925), LC; and author interview with Catherine Walsh (June 17, 1958), KCC.

70. Letter from Cardozo to Harlan Stone, Apr. 17, 1926, LC.

71. Letter from Cardozo to Felix Frankfurter, Apr. 29, 1926, FF.

72. Letter from Cardozo to Maud Nathan, July 24, 1926, Maud Nathan Papers, Barnard College, New York, N.Y.

73. Letter from Cardozo to Annie Nathan Meyer, June 6, 1926, Annie Nathan Meyer Papers, Barnard College, New York, N.Y.

74. Letter from Cardozo to Joseph Paley, July 16, 1926, JP.

10. A Judge's Service

1. 217 N.Y. 382 (1916).

2. Letter from Cardozo to Louise Wise, Nov. 11, 1916, SSW.

3. 215 N.Y. 126, reargument denied, 215 N.Y. 721 (1915). A previous conviction had been overturned by the Court of Appeals, with Cardozo not sitting. 210 N.Y. 274 (1914). See Andy Logan, *Against the Evidence: The Becker-Rosenthal Affair*, 291 (1970), and also 17, 283, and 290.

4. The story of Ingraham's involvement in the maneuvering that led Cardozo to accept the appointment was related in a letter by Sidney Bobbé to the editor, *New York Times*, A22 (Jan. 12, 1979), as amplified by subsequent letters to the author, Jan. 18, 1979, and Feb. 23, 1979, KCC. Bobbé had been Judge Ingraham's law clerk in 1915 during the judge's last year as Presiding Justice of the Appellate Division, First Department, and became his associate when Ingraham returned to private practice. Bobbé took the call from Governor Whitman in Ingraham's absence and was given the message that Cardozo had rejected the

temporary appointment. Bobbé also remembers having seen a subsequent letter from Cardozo to Ingraham thanking Ingraham for his efforts in making the necessary arrangements that led to Cardozo's election.

5. Although I have found nothing to substantiate any connection between Cardozo's vote in the *Becker* case and his appointment by Whitman, Sidney Bobbé disclosed a connection between Ingraham and Whitman in that regard. Mr. Bobbé reported: "I was reliably informed that Whitman was greatly indebted to Ingraham for advice that Ingraham had given to him in connection with the prosecution of the Becker case, which brought Whitman into such prominence that he became Governor as a result. Since Whitman was prosecuting Becker . . . for first degree murder, and in case of a conviction and an appeal therefrom, that appeal would go directly to the Court of Appeals, there was no ethical impediment for the Presiding Justice of the Appellate Division that would prevent him from helping in a murder prosecution." Letter from Sidney Bobbé to author, Feb. 23, 1979, KCC. If Bobbé's information is correct, the story would help explain Ingraham's ability to help Cardozo and McLaughlin. Whether his statement that there was no "ethical impediment" is correct is another matter.

6. Letter from Cardozo to Learned Hand, Jan. 24, 1917, LH.

7. Letter from Cardozo to the Association of the Bar of the City of New York and the New York County Lawyers Association, Jan. 18, 1917, reprinted *New York County Lawyers' Association Year Book 1917*, 166 (1917).

8. Samuel Seabury, quoted in Herbert Mitgang, *The Man Who Rode the Tiger: The Life and Times of Judge Samuel Seabury*, 109 (1996 ed.).

9. Learned Hand, "Tribute to the Memory of the Late Justice Benjamin N. Cardozo of the Supreme Court of the United States," 2–3 (July 19, 1938) (delivered over Radio Station WHN), in FF.

10. Author interview with Ambrose Doskow (Jan. 18, 1961), KCC.

11. Irving Lehman, *The Influence of Cardozo on the Common Law*, 14–20 (1942) (this was the first annual Benjamin N. Cardozo lecture, delivered in 1941 to the Association of the Bar of the City of New York). The Lehman opinion based on Cardozo's work is People v. Mummiani, 258 N.Y. 394 (1931). Joseph Paley, Cardozo's law secretary, told the story of that case quite differently, but both versions indicate that Cardozo was open to persuasion even after the initial vote on the case. Author interview with Joseph Paley (Jan. 23, 1958), KCC.

12. See former Chief Judge Hiscock's reference to the collegiality of the court when introducing Cardozo's address to the New York State Bar Association, Jan. 22, 1932, *55 Report of the New York State Bar Association* 262 (1932).

13. Cuthbert W. Pound, "Address to Chief Judge Benjamin N. Cardozo," 258 N.Y. v (1932). See also Irving Lehman, "Judge Cardozo in the Court of Appeals," *52 Harvard Law Review* 364 (1939).

14. The figures in this paragraph and the next one were compiled by Lexis

searches of the New York Reports. The figures do not include the motions, which were handled summarily, and the New York Reports do not list the judges who considered them. For the purpose of comparing the judges' dissents in cases decided with majority opinions, I used the Lexis definition of a dissenting opinion. In fact, only half of Cardozo's sixteen so-called dissenting opinions are full-fledged opinions. The rest are short statements of the grounds for dissenting. Visual examination of the Reports turned up a number of Cardozo dissents that were not denominated as such, and these are included in the figures in the text. The figure in the text for majority opinions written by Cardozo includes one, People v. Shilitano, 215 N.Y. 715 (1915), that appears in the section of the New York Reports that contains the memorandum decisions.

15. Interview with Charles C. Burlingham, 9 (1949), COHP part I.

16. Author interview with Jay Leo Rothschild (May 12, 1958), KCC.

17. Author interview with Charles C. Burlingham (Nov. 13, 1957), KCC.

18. Interview with Frederic R. Coudert, Jr., 118 (1949–1950), COHP part I.

19. Author interview with Felix Frankfurter, 36 (Aug. 21, 1960), KCC.

20. City of New York v. South Brooklyn Ferry & Steam Transportation Co., 231 N.Y. 18 (1921), and In re Niagara Falls v. Public Service Comm'n, 229 N.Y. 333 (1920).

21. 241 N.Y. 7 (1925).

22. Hiscock memorandum to the Court in Ader v. Emil and Blau, CM, Box 2, Folder 2366 (1925).

23. Cardozo memorandum in Bailey v. Betti, 241 N.Y. 22 (1925), CM, Box 2, Folder 2365.

24. Hiscock memorandum in Bailey v. Betti, attached to his memorandum in Ader v. Emil and Blau, CM, Box 2, Folder 2366.

25. Letter from Charles C. Burlingham to Elihu Root, June 24, 1925, CCB.

26. Letter from Charles C. Burlingham to John Milburn, June 5, 1925, CCB.

27. Ibid.

28. Letter from Charles C. Burlingham to Elihu Root, June 24, 1925, CCB.

29. J. B. (John Brooks), in the *Century Bulletin* (February, 1979).

30. Letter from Cardozo to Charles C. Burlingham, June 26, 1925, CCB.

31. Author interview with Felix Frankfurter, 16 (Aug. 20, 21, 1960), KCC.

32. Letter to Edgar Nathan, Sr., July 17, 1923, original in possession of the Hendricks family, copy in KCC.

33. Letter from Cardozo to Louis Marshall, Sept. 19, 1923, responding to letter to him from Louis Marshall, Sept. 14, 1923, LM. The reference to Judge Alonzo Clearwater is to that judge's address, "The Under-Valuation of American Citizenship," which disparaged the immigrants who had been coming to the country since 1880. See 55 *Report New York State Bar Association* 315 (Clearwater's address) and 355 (Marshall's impromptu response) (1923).

34. The Overseers together with the President and Fellows (who are known as the Corporation) make up the legal governing structure of the university. The Corporation has charge of the management of the university and, except in times of trouble, the Overseers are less active. One of the responsibilities of the Overseers is to establish visiting committees to inspect the operations of the various schools and certain departments of the university. The tasks of these committees vary greatly, depending on the health and needs of the school or department being visited, but the committees are an available "outside" resource to assist in the event of trouble. Cardozo served on the visiting committee to the Law School from 1920 to 1932. Letter from Michael Roberts, secretary to the Corporation, to author, Apr. 17, 1995, KCC.

35. Zechariah Chafee, Jr., "A Contemporary State Trial—The United States versus Jacob Abrams et al.," 33 *Harvard Law Review* 747 (1920).

36. Id. at 754–764. The case in the United States Supreme Court was reported as Abrams v. United States, 250 U.S. 616 (1919).

37. See Peter Irons, "'Fighting Fair': Zechariah Chafee, Jr., the Department of Justice, and the 'Trial at the Harvard Club,'" 94 *Harvard Law Review* 1205, 1233 (1981).

38. Report of the Committee to Visit the Law School, reprinted in Chafee, "A Contemporary State Trial," 9.

39. Abbott L. Lowell, quoted in Henry Yeomans, *Abbott Lawrence Lowell*, 323 (1948). This account of the trial at the Harvard Club is based on id. at 317–323; Donald Smith, *Zechariah Chafee, Jr., Defender of Liberty and Law*, 36–57 (1986); Irons, "Fighting Fair," 1230–1234; and correspondence and reports in the Abbott Lawrence Lowell Papers, Harvard University Archives, Cambridge, Mass.

40. Andrew L. Kaufman, "Cardozo's Appointment to the Supreme Court," 1 *Cardozo Law Review* 23, 28 (1979).

41. See N. E. H. Hull, "Restatement and Reform: A New Perspective on the Origins of the American Law Institute," 8 *Law and History Review* 55 (1990). The account in this and the following paragraph relies heavily on Professor Hull's work.

42. See 20 *Handbook of the Association of American Law Schools* 54 (1922).

43. 19 *Handbook of the Association of American Law Schools* 117–121, 123 (1921).

44. Hull, "Restatement and Reform," 74.

45. Id. at 83.

46. The information about Cardozo's relationship to the Institute is drawn from a letter from William Draper Lewis to George Hellman, Dec. 14, 1938, CCC.

47. Cardozo, "Address at Second Annual Dinner," in American Law Institute, *Minutes of the Second Annual Meeting and Address at the Second Annual Dinner,* 104, 110 (1924).

48. See chap. 16, text at notes 7–14, for an example of his extensive participation in conferences relating to the Restatement of Torts.

49. Herbert Goodrich, "Judge Learned Hand and the Work of the American Law Institute," 60 *Harvard Law Review* 345–346 (1947). The minutes of the various meetings that he attended disclose that Cardozo was often an extremely active participant. See American Law Institute, Torts Conference Minutes, I, Oct. 23, 1927, Nov. 10, 1928, May 2 and 3, 1930, and Nov. 12 and 13, 1930, HLS.

50. Before his involvement in the ALI projects, Cardozo had also urged New York to establish a ministry of justice to survey the work of the courts and draft legislative proposals for reform where the work of the courts suggested that such reform was advisable. Cardozo, "A Ministry of Justice," 35 *Harvard Law Review* 113 (1921). Prompted by Cardozo, the New York Legislature established the Law Revision Commission in 1934 to deal with substantive law reform proposals. Bernard Shientag, "A Ministry of Justice in Action: The Work of the New York State Law Revision Commission," 22 *Cornell Law Quarterly* 183 (1937).

51. Letter from Abraham Tulin to George Hellman, Nov. 4, 1938, CCC, Box 9.

52. Letter from Cardozo to Louise Wise, Nov. 21, 1916, SSW.

53. Letter from Louis Brandeis to Jacob de Haas, Dec. 25, 1917, *Letters of Louis D. Brandeis,* IV, 331 (Melvin Urofsky and David Levy eds., 1975).

54. Judge Mack, who was a member of the Court of Appeals for the Second Circuit, was prominent in Jewish affairs.

55. Letter from Cardozo to Stephen S. Wise, Sept. 10, 1918, SSW.

56. Letter from Cardozo to Stephen S. Wise, Sept. 19, 1918, SSW.

57. Letter from Cardozo to Elvira N. Solis, Sept. 5, 1929, original in possession of Rosalie Nathan Hendricks family, copy in KCC.

58. Letter to Felix Frankfurter, Nov. 15, 1930, FF.

59. Letter from Louis Brandeis to Felix Frankfurter, Jan. 1, 1927, *Letters of Louis D. Brandeis,* V, 258.

60. Letter to Aline Goldstone, Nov. 13, 1927, original in possession of Goldstone family, excerpt in KCC.

61. *New York Times,* 33 (Oct. 9, 1929).

62. Letter to Stephen Wise, Oct. 19, 1929, SSW. The letter from Rabbi Wise questioned whether Cardozo had understood the implications of becoming a member of the executive committee. Letter from Stephen S. Wise to Cardozo, Oct. 12, 1929, SSW. When Cardozo was appointed to the Supreme Court, he resigned from the Committee because its "activities . . . touch too closely the

field of Federal jurisdiction to make my continued membership appropriate." Letter to Dr. Cyrus Adler, Feb. 26, 1932, published in American Jewish Committee, *26th Annual Report,* 35 (1933).

63. Edgar J. Nathan, Jr., "Benjamin N. Cardozo," 41 *American Jewish Year Book* 28 (1939).

11. Chief Judge

1. Francis Bergan, *The History of the New York Court of Appeals 1847–1932,* 246–247 (1985). Bergan, who was a judge of the Court of Appeals himself from 1964–1973, cited no authority for this statement.

2. Letters from Samuel Seabury to Abram Elkus, Nov. 17, 1925; from Adelbert Moot to Elkus, Nov. 30, 1925; from Adolph Ochs to Elkus, Dec. 11, 1925; from Charles Evans Hughes to Elkus, Dec. 4, 1925; and from William D. Guthrie to Elkus, Nov. 17, 1925, all in CCC, Box 9.

3. Letter from Alfred E. Smith to Abram Elkus, Dec. 8, 1925, CCC, Box 9.

4. Letter from Cardozo to Abram Elkus, Dec. 12, 1925, copy in CCC, Box 9.

5. See chap. 9, text at note 69.

6. Letter from Cardozo to Felix Frankfurter, June 21, 1926, FF.

7. Letter from Charles Burlingham to Felix Frankfurter, June 12, 1926, CCB.

8. Ibid.

9. See chap. 9, text at note 74.

10. Letter from Cardozo to Learned Hand, Aug. 17, 1926, LH. He wrote a somewhat similar letter to Paley about the same time: "Somehow or other I fancy that things are tending [Pound's] way. I'm trying to forget the whole matter. Maybe I'll be happier as associate judge." Letter from Cardozo to Joseph Paley, Aug. 5, 1926, JP.

11. Letter from Cardozo to Joseph Paley, Sept. 17, 1926, JP.

12. See Carl H. Voss, ed., *Stephen S. Wise, Selected Letters,* 145–150 (1969); letter from Louis Marshall to Charles Hilles, Sept. 21, 1926, LM.

13. Author interview with Joseph Paley (Jan. 23, 1958), KCC.

14. Letter from Stephen S. Wise to Alfred E. Smith, Sept 15, 1926, SSW; letters from Louis Marshall to Adolph Ochs, Sept. 12, 1926, and to Julius Ochs Adler, Sept. 15, 1926, LM.

15. Letter from Louis Marshall to Charles Hilles, Sept. 21, 1926, LM. Further Marshall efforts are detailed in his letters to Governor Smith, Sept. 16, 1926; to Senator James Wadsworth, Sept. 20, 1926; to William D. Guthrie, Sept. 20 and 21, 1926; to Senator John G. Saxe, Sept. 20, 1926; to Meier Steinbrink, Sept. 21, 1926; and to Judge Henry Kellogg, Sept. 21, 1926, LM. Apparently also, the deal involved a joint nomination of a Democratic associate

judge to the vacancy that would occur the following year. Alfred E. Smith, *Up to Now: An Autobiography,* 363–364 (1929).

16. Letter from Charles Burlingham to Felix Frankfurter, Sept. 27, 1926, CCB. Burlingham added that "Pound acted very handsomely . . . as might have been expected" in response to the selection of Cardozo.

17. Author interview with New York attorney, Emil Weitzner (May 6, 1958), KCC.

18. Library of Congress, Brander Matthews Dramatic Museum Collection, Sound Recording of Speeches given at Columbia University Alumni Dinner, Feb. 12, 1932, copy in KCC.

19. Author interview with Carl Stern, partner in the successor law firm to Cardozo & Engelhard (June 14, 1962), KCC, quoting someone whom he could not remember. Stephen Baldwin, who had been Cardozo's colleague in practice, also used a similar expression. Author interview with Alfred Schaffer (June 16, 1958), KCC. Schaffer, a New York lawyer with offices on the same floor as Cardozo's chambers, concurred.

20. Gerald Gunther, *Learned Hand: The Man and the Judge,* 414 (1994); Grant Gilmore, *The Ages of American Law,* 75 (1977); Richard H. Weisberg, "Law, Literature, and Cardozo's Judicial Poetics," 1 *Cardozo Law Review* 283, 284–287 (1979); and interview with John Lord O'Brian, New York and Washington lawyer, 62, 381, COHP part I.

21. George Hellman interview with John O'Brien (Feb. 4. 1939), CCC, Box 8. O'Brien added that Governor Smith told him that he appointed O'Brien because Cardozo told him to.

22. Author interview with Harry Hayes (Jan. 25, 1958), KCC.

23. Author interviews with Catherine Walsh (June 17, 1958) and Harry Hayes (Jan. 25, 1958), KCC, and letter from Kate Tracy to Robert Marshall, April 28, 1939, original in possession of George Marshall family, copy in KCC.

24. Richard A. Posner, *Cardozo: A Study in Reputation,* 8 (1990).

25. Letter from Cardozo to Thomas Reed Powell, Apr. 29, 1931, Thomas Reed Powell Papers, HLS.

26. George Hellman interview with Adeline Cardozo (Nov. 6, 1938), CCC, Box 8; Alan Stroock, "A Personal View of Justice Benjamin N. Cardozo: Recollections of Four Cardozo Law Clerks," 1 *Cardozo Law Review* 20, 21 (1979); author interview with Alan (Bill) Stroock (April 19, 1961), KCC.

27. Author interview with Carl Stern (June 14, 1962), KCC.

28. Letter from Cardozo to Felix Frankfurter, Mar. 22, 1933, FF.

29. Posner, *Cardozo,* 9.

30. Author interviews with New York attorney Jay Leo Rothschild (May 12, 1958), and with Weitzner, KCC.

31. See *Boston Evening Transcript,* pt. 2, 3 (Feb. 17, 1932), describing the

last day of arguments at which Cardozo presided as chief judge before leaving for Washington.

32. Author interviews with Rothschild and Weitzner, KCC; letter from Judge Simon Rifkind to Richard Posner, Oct. 14, 1993, copy in KCC, recounting the story of his first argument in the Court of Appeals when Cardozo came to his rescue in similar fashion.

33. George Hellman interview with Judge John F. O'Brien, CCC, Box 8.

34. Author interview with Weitzner, KCC.

35. Author interview with Henry Cohen (June 9, 1958), KCC.

36. Author interview with Felix Frankfurter, 32, 36 (Aug. 20 and 21, 1960), KCC.

37. Author interview with Charles C. Burlingham (Nov. 13, 1957), KCC, reporting a story told to him by Irving Lehman.

38. Irving Lehman, "Judge Cardozo in the Court of Appeals," 52 *Harvard Law Review* 364, 369–370 (1939).

39. Letter from Cardozo to Charles Evans Hughes, Sept. 8, 1927, CCC.

40. Letters from Louis Marshall to Cardozo, Aug. 26, Sept. 27, and Oct. 14, 1926, and letters from Cardozo to Marshall, Aug. 30 and Oct. 2, 1926, LM.

41. Letter from Cardozo to Herbert Cone, confidential clerk of the Court of Appeals, Aug. 11, 1918, copy in KCC.

42. George Hellman interview with Augustus Tack (Feb. 10, 1939), CCC, Box 9.

43. Letter from Cardozo to Moses Grossman, Dec. 27, 1936, and George Hellman interview with Grossman (Oct. 20, 1938), both in CCC, Box 9.

44. Letter from Frank D. Fackenthal, Provost, to George Hellman, Oct. 20, 1938, and letter from Cardozo to Nicholas Murray Butler, Feb. 26, 1932, both in CCC, Box 9.

45. Letter from Nicholas Murray Butler to George Wickersham, another member of the Round Table nominating committee, Oct. 30, 1927; letter from Cardozo to Butler, Dec. 20, 1927, indicating his acceptance of an invitation to join. Both letters are in CCC. See Gunther, *Learned Hand*, 408.

46. Letters from Charles C. Burlingham to Cardozo, Feb. 3 and Nov. 13, 1933, and March 4, 1938, CCB; Gunther, *Learned Hand*, 408.

47. 19 *Columbia Alumni News* No. 21 (Mar. 9, 1928); *Who's Who in New York (City and State) 1929*, 282 (1929); and letter from Cardozo to Learned Hand, Dec. 4, 1920, LH.

48. *The Association of the Bar of the City of New York Yearbook 1994–1995*, 103 for a list of its honorary members.

49. Letter from Cardozo to Aline Goldstone, Aug. 20, 1928, original in the possession of the Goldstone family, extract in KCC.

50. Letter from Cardozo to Archie M. Palmer, Sept. 23, 1925, CCC, Box 1.

51. Letters from Cardozo to Aline Goldstone, Aug. 20 and Aug. 25, 1928, originals in the possession of the Goldstone family, extracts in KCC.

52. Letter from Cardozo to Felix Frankfurter, Sept. 10, 1928, FF.

53. See chap. 10, text at note 2.

54. William Allen White, *The Autobiography of William Allen White*, 367 (1946).

55. See letter from Cardozo to Joseph Paley, June 20, 1927, JP.

56. Cardozo, "Address at the Reception for Dr. Mendes," 3 (June 5, 1927), manuscript copy in KCC.

57. Id. at 6.

58. *Free Synagogue Announcements*, "Address of Judge Cardozo at the Dinner" (Apr. 10, 1927).

59. His reaction to Dante's *Inferno* reflected the same thought. Referring to Dante's idea that spirits who had lived blameless lives before Jesus and hence were not able to have become Christian were nevertheless consigned to Hell, Cardozo recorded his own reaction: "The curious morality of Dante's Inferno reflects the curious morality of the Church." Commonplace Book, II, 25, CCC, Box 5.

60. Letter from Cardozo to Louise Wise, Sept. 21, 1929, SSW.

61. "Values" is reprinted in Cardozo, *Selected Writings of Benjamin Nathan Cardozo*, 1 (Margaret Hall, ed., 1947). See also Commonplace Book, II, 138–139, CCC, Box 5, where six months before he had reproduced a portion of Noyes's poem.

62. Commonplace Book, II, 138–139, CCC, Box 5.

63. Cardozo, "Values," 4.

64. See chap. 9, text at note 39.

65. Letters from Cardozo to Annie Nathan Meyer, June 28 and July 11, 1934, American Jewish Archives, Cincinnati, Ohio. Sarah Lyons was the daughter of Reverend Jacques Judah Lyons and of Cardozo's aunt Grace Nathan Lyons. She had served as principal and superintendent of the Shearith Israel Sunday School for many years. David and Tamar de Sola Pool, *An Old Faith in the New World: Portrait of Shearith Israel, 1654–1954*, 225 (1955).

66. Remarks of Cardozo at the funeral of Morris J. Hirsch, Nov. 12, 1925, copy in KCC.

67. Cardozo, "A Word of Good-Bye and Blessing," Dec. 9, 1934, copy in KCC.

68. Author interviews with Catherine Walsh (June 17, 1958) and with Justine Wise Polier (July 11, 1958), KCC.

69. Letter from Cardozo to Nicholas Murray Butler, Feb. 4, 1928, CCC. Cardozo referred to Nellie's speech as "variable." Letter from Cardozo to Aline

Goldstone, July 28, 1928, original in the possession of the Goldstone family, excerpt in KCC.

70. Letter from Cardozo to Felix Frankfurter, June 30, 1929, FF; letter from Cardozo to Mary Hun, July 10, 1929, KCC.

71. Letter from Cardozo to Felix Frankfurter, Aug. 5, 1928, FF; letters from Cardozo to Aline Goldstone, Aug. 12, 20, and 25, 1928, originals in the possession of the Goldstone family, excerpts in KCC.

72. The information about the family plot is based on personal observation.

73. Letter from Cardozo to Learned Hand, Nov. 30, 1929, LH.

74. Author interview with Learned Hand, 12 (Nov. 12, 1957), KCC.

75. Letter from Cardozo to Learned Hand, Nov. 30, 1929, LH.

76. Author interview with Catherine Walsh (June 17, 1958), KCC.

77. Letter from Cardozo to Felix Frankfurter, Feb. 6, 1930, FF.

78. Letter from Cardozo to Learned Hand, Mar. 16, 1930, LH.

79. George Hellman interview with Kate Tracy (Nov. 18, 1938), CCC, Box 9.

80. Letter from Cardozo to Joseph Paley, Mar. 30, 1930, JP; *New York Times,* 23 (Mar. 10, 1938). Cardozo's checks for the last nine months of his life are privately held.

81. Author interview with Catherine Walsh (June 17, 1959), KCC.

82. Letter from Cardozo to Rabbi Stephen Wise, May 9, 1930, SSW.

83. Hellman interview with Tracy, CCC, Box 9; letter from Cardozo to Elvira Solis, June 7, 1930, original in possession of the Hendricks family, copy in KCC. Within a week, Cardozo made lunch plans with Felix Frankfurter. Letter from Cardozo to Felix Frankfurter, June 14, 1930, FF.

84. Letter from Felix Frankfurter to Harlan Stone, Aug. 6, 1938, Harlan Fiske Stone Papers, LC, recounting a conversation with Dr. Alfred Cohn.

85. Letter from Cardozo to Aline Goldstone, July 27, 1930, original in the possession of the Goldstone family, excerpt in KCC.

86. Letter from Cardozo to his cousin Elvira N. Solis, Aug. 14, 1930, original in Hendricks family possession, copy in KCC; author interview with Rosalie Hendricks (June 5, 1958), KCC.

87. Letter from Cardozo to Aline Goldstone, Aug. 27, 1930, original in possession of Goldstone family, excerpt in KCC.

88. Letter from Cardozo to Stephen and Louise Wise, Nov. 26, 1930, SSW.

89. The talk was entitled "Faith and a Doubting World" and is reprinted in Cardozo, *Selected Writings,* 99.

90. The Holmes article is discussed in chap. 19, text following note 86.

91. Commonplace Book, II, 183–184, CCC, Box 5. The ceremony was noted in the *New York Times,* 25 (Sept. 3, 1931).

12. The Nature of the Judicial Process

1. See Richard A. Posner, *Cardozo: A Study in Reputation* (1990), and *The Problems of Jurisprudence*, 26, 28–29 (1990).

2. See Stanley Brubaker, "The Moral Element in Cardozo's Jurisprudence," 1 *Cardozo Law Review* 229 (1979); Thomas G. Barnes, introduction to Benjamin N. Cardozo, *Cardozo on the Law*, 7–17 (1982).

3. Cardozo, *The Nature of the Judicial Process* (1921).

4. For commentary by judges, see David A. Nelson, "The Nature of the Judicial Process Revisited," 22 *Northern Kentucky Law Review* 563 (1995); Shirley S. Abrahamson, "Judging in the Quiet of the Storm," 24 *St. Mary's Law Journal* 965 (1993); Judith S. Kaye, "The Human Dimension in Appellate Judging," 73 *Cornell Law Review* 1004 (1988); Patricia Wald, "Some Thoughts on Judging as Gleaned from One Hundred Years of the *Harvard Law Review* and Other Great Books," 100 *Harvard Law Review* 887 (1987). A bibliography of relevant writings is Shirley S. Abrahamson, Susan M. Fieber, and Gabrielle Lessard, "Judges on Judging: A Bibliography," 24 *St. Mary's Law Journal* 995 (1993). See also Harry Wellington, "Common Law Rules and Constitutional Double Standards: Some Notes on Adjudication," 83 *Yale Law Journal* 221 (1973).

5. It is easier to state that some critical legal theorists make that contention than to find the claim put that way in print. Reports are that the claim has commonly been made orally and in classrooms. Printed assertions are usually more elliptical.

6. See Robert Bork, *The Tempting of America* (1990); Robert Bork, "Neutral Principles and Some First Amendment Problems, 47 *Indiana Law Journal* 1 (1971); and Henry Monaghan, "Our Perfect Constitution," 56 *New York University Law Review* 353 (May–June 1981).

7. Oliver Wendell Holmes, *The Common Law*, 5 (1881); Benjamin Cardozo, "Mr. Justice Holmes," 44 *Harvard Law Review* 682, 683 (1931). See Mark DeWolfe Howe, ed., introduction, Holmes, *Common Law*, xxii–xxvii (1963), and Morton J. Horwitz, *The Transformation of American Law, 1870–1960*, 109–143 (1992).

8. Oliver Wendell Holmes, "The Path of the Law," in *Collected Legal Papers*, 181, 184 (1920).

9. John Chipman Gray, *Restraints on the Alienation of Property* (2d ed. 1895) and *The Rule Against Perpetuities* (3d ed. 1915).

10. John Chipman Gray, *The Nature and Sources of the Law*, 118 (1909).

11. This paragraph is based on David Wigdor, *Roscoe Pound: Philosopher of Law*, 3–131 (1974).

12. Roscoe Pound, "Mechanical Jurisprudence," 8 *Columbia Law Review* 605, 614–615 (1908). See also Pound, "Liberty of Contract," 18 *Yale Law*

Journal 454 (1909) and "The Scope and Purpose of Sociological Jurisprudence," 24 *Harvard Law Review* 591 (1911) and 25 id. 489 (1912).

13. See Wigdor, *Roscoe Pound*, 103–205, and Morton Horwitz, "The Conservative Tradition in the Writing of American Legal History," 17 *American Journal of Legal History* 275 (1973).

14. Letter from Cardozo to Roscoe Pound, July 31, 1920, Roscoe Pound Papers, HLS.

15. See William W. Fisher, III, Morton J. Horwitz, and Thomas A. Reed, *American Legal Realism* (1993); Edward Λ. Purcell, *The Crisis of Democratic Theory*, 74–94 (1973).

16. Arthur L. Corbin, "The Judicial Process Revisited: Introduction," 71 *Yale Law Journal* 195, 197–198 (1961).

17. Yale Weekly Bulletin & Calendar, Feb. 14, 1921.

18. Corbin, "Judicial Process," 197–198.

19. Id. at 198.

20. Letters from Annette Beetz and Linda Norton, of the Yale University Press, publisher of the book, to author, Nov. 9, 1994, and July 30, 1984, KCC.

21. Cardozo, *Nature of the Judicial Process*, 10.

22. Id. at 28.

23. Id. at 164.

24. Id. at 165.

25. Id. at 30–31. Cardozo's four methods followed the categories of analysis used by John Chipman Gray in *The Nature and Sources of the Law*.

26. Cardozo, *Nature of the Judicial Process*, at 31.

27. For a catalog of the many different things called formalism, see Robert W. Gordon, "The Elusive Transformation," 6 *Yale Journal of Law & the Humanities* 137 (1994) (reviewing Morton J. Horwitz, *The Transformation of American Law, 1870–1960* (1992)).

28. Cardozo, *Nature of the Judicial Process*, at 31.

29. Id. at 33. We may wonder, however, whether Holmes would have agreed with the premise that experience is ever truly silent.

30. Id. at 35–36.

31. Id. at 43.

32. Id. at 65.

33. Id. at 60.

34. Ibid.

35. Id. at 65–66.

36. Id. at 63.

37. Id. at 102.

38. Id. at 66.

39. Id. at 67.

40. Id. at 71–72.

41. Id. at 112.
42. Id. at 149.
43. Id. at 66.
44. Id. at 113.
45. Id. at 77–78, quoting from Roscoe Pound "Juristic Science and Law," 31 *Harvard Law Review* 1047, 1048 (1918).
46. Cardozo, *Nature of the Judicial Process,* at 87.
47. Id. at 91–93. One of the critics to whom this passage was addressed was his good friend Learned Hand whose article, "Due Process of Law and the Eight-Hour Day," 21 *Harvard Law Review* 495 (1908), he cited as an attack on the institution of judicial review. Fifty years later Hand's lectures, published as *The Bill of Rights* (1958) sparked another controversy among the friends and foes of judicial review.
48. Cardozo, *Nature of the Judicial Process,* 135.
49. Id. at 10.
50. Cardozo, *The Growth of the Law,* 133–134 (1924).
51. Id. at 135.
52. Cardozo, *Nature of the Judicial Process,* 63.
53. Id. at 104, 107–110.
54. Letter from Thomas Reed Powell to Cardozo, quoted in Cardozo, *Growth of the Law,* 64–65.
55. Cardozo, *Nature of the Judicial Process,* 112–113.
56. Ambrose Doskow, in "A Personal View of Justice Benjamin N. Cardozo," 1 *Cardozo Law Review* 5, 18–19 (1979).
57. Cardozo, *The Nature of the Judicial Process,* 116.
58. Id. at 136–137 and 113–114. See Holmes J., in Southern Pacific Co. v. Jensen, 244 U.S. 205, 218, 221 (1919) (dissenting): "I recognize without hesitation that judges do and must legislate, but they can do so only interstitially; they are confined from molar to molecular motions."
59. Cardozo, *Nature of the Judicial Process,* at 129.
60. Id. at 133–134.
61. Id. at 136.
62. Id. at 108–109.
63. Id. at 106.
64. Cardozo, *The Paradoxes of Legal Science,* 37 (1928).
65. Id. at 18–19.
66. Ernest Nagel, "Reflections on 'The Nature of the Judicial Process,'" 1 *Cardozo Law Review* 55, 59–60 (1979).
67. Cardozo, *Nature of the Judicial Process,* 108.
68. Id. at 105–106.
69. Letter from Cardozo to Learned Hand, June 25, 1929, LH. Hand's response took up the challenge: "No, I did not mean that you or other sages

did not interpret a common will. I think you do. 'Interpret' is a baffling word. I am by no means sure that I know just what it means, but I should say that what you succeeded in doing was expressing ideas to which people would assent when they became aware of them. If you are disposed to be a mystic you may say that the idea was there already; I should prefer to say that it was not, but that you made your beliefs theirs. That people in general have any thought or will about most things I do not believe, and the law is only one instance." Letter from Cardozo to Learned Hand, June 25, 1929, and letter from Hand to Cardozo, June 28, 1929, LH.

70. Cardozo, *Nature of the Judicial Process*, at 12.

71. Id. at 171–173.

72. Id. at 174–176.

73. Id. at 177–178.

74. See Daniel Boorstin, *The Americans: The National Experience* (1965) and Richard Hofstadter, *The Progressive Historians*, 438 (1968). For a modern update, see G. Edward White, "Reflections on the 'Republican Revival': Interdisciplinary Scholarship in the Legal Academy," 6 *Yale Journal of Law & the Humanities* 1 (1994).

75. In his own day, Cardozo's views were publicly criticized by Henry Edgerton, who preferred John Chipman Gray's position that in doubtful cases, judges should follow their own opinions. See Edgerton, "A Liberal Judge: Cuthbert W. Pound," 21 *Cornell Law Quarterly* 7, 12–14 (1935).

76. Learned Hand, Book Review, 35 *Harvard Law Review* 479, 480 (1922).

77. Harlan Stone, Book Review, 22 *Columbia Law Review* 382, 385 (1922).

78. Charles Hough, Book Review, 7 *Cornell Law Quarterly* 287, 289 (1922).

79. Felix Frankfurter, "Benjamin Nathan Cardozo," in *Dictionary of American Biography*, 93 (Supp. 2, 1958).

80. Edwin Patterson, "Cardozo's Philosophy of Law," 88 *University of Pennsylvania Law Review* 71, 156 (1939).

81. Grant Gilmore, *The Ages of American Law*, 76 (1977).

82. Posner, *Cardozo*, 28; Posner, "What Has Pragmatism to Offer Law?," 63 *Southern California Law Review* 1653, 1658–1661 (1990); and Posner, *Problems of Jurisprudence* (1990).

83. Learned Hand, Book Review, 35 *Harvard Law Review* 479, 480 (1922).

84. The lectures were an expansion of two talks that he had given in 1922 as the Irvine Lecture at Cornell. Cardozo commuted back and forth between New Haven and New York because he needed to work on opinions during the mornings of the three days when he gave the lectures. His honorarium for the three lectures was $400, not a small sum in 1923. Letters from Cardozo to Dean Thomas Swan, July 30 and Dec. 1, 1923 and letter from Swan to Cardozo, Dec. 22, 1923, Thomas W. Swan Papers, Manuscripts and Archives, Yale University Library.

85. Letters from Cardozo to Dean Thomas Swan, Dec. 1, 1923, and Jan. 12, 1924, and from Swan to Cardozo, Jan. 10, 1924, Apr. 21, 1924, and May 9, 1924; letter from H. G. Deane, secretary to editor of Yale Press to Swan, June 5, 1924, all in Thomas W. Swan Papers, Manuscripts and Archives, Yale University Library.

86. Letter from Cardozo to Felix Frankfurter, Apr. 26, 1924, FF.

87. Cardozo, *Growth of the Law,* 1.

88. Cardozo, *The Paradoxes of Legal Science* (1928).

89. Id. at 4–5.

90. Id. at 5, quoting René Demogue, *Analysis of Fundamental Notions,* 570 (1911).

91. Cardozo, *Paradoxes of Legal Science,* at 99.

92. United States v. Carolene Products Co., 304 U.S. 144, 152, note 4 (1938), in which Justice Stone suggested a double standard of review in which the Court would scrutinize much more strictly legislation restricting the political processes, including those where prejudice against "discrete and insular minorities" may be involved, than it would ordinary economic legislation. The suggestion has been the source of vast academic writing. The most imaginative is John H. Ely, *Democracy and Distrust: A Theory of Judicial Review* (1980).

93. Cardozo, *Paradoxes of Legal Science,* at 99, citing Meyer v. Nebraska, 262 U.S. 390 (1923); Bartels v. Iowa, 262 U.S. 404 (1923); and Pierce v. Society of Sisters, 268 U.S. 510 (1925).

94. Cardozo, *Paradoxes of Legal Science,* 99.

95. Roe v. Wade, 410 U.S. 113 (1973).

96. Cardozo, *Paradoxes of Legal Science,* 104.

97. Id. at 117.

13. Equity, Individual Justice, and the Punctilio of Honor

1. See Morton J. Horwitz, *The Transformation of American Law, 1780–1860,* 265–266 (1977) (formalization of rules marked the end of equity as an independent source of legal standards).

2. 249 N.Y. 122, cert. denied, 278 U.S. 647 (1928).

3. Id. at 139.

4. Since there was no opinion, Cardozo did not address the form of relief that he would have ordered. In particular, he did not address the fact of urban development in the interim that made such a difference to him in *Howard,* chap. 8, text at note 10.

5. 254 N.Y. 1, 7 (1930).

6. Id. at 6.

7. Id. at 8.

8. Id. at 12.

9. Ibid.

10. Id. at 14–15.

11. Cardozo reached a somewhat similar result in a contract case in which a buyer of land sought to get its deposit back when the seller had not made promised street repairs by August 1 in a contract where time was of the essence. The buyer, however, had not made the required monthly payment for July. The trial court concluded that buyer could not recover its deposit because he was in default, and the Appellate Division affirmed. Friedman v. TenBroeck Realty Co., 225 App. Div. 858 (1st Dept. 1929). Cardozo concluded that the buyer was playing "a pretty sharp game." Most of the improvements had been made in time, and if he had wanted to take advantage of the time requirement, he should "have seen that his own conduct was impeccable." The case "seems to be one of diamond cut diamond," and the parties should be left where they stood. Report in Friedman v. TenBroeck Realty Co., CM, Box 4, Folder 4321.

12. Theodore F. T. Plucknett, *A Concise History of the Common Law,* 697–699, 704–707 (1956).

13. Brooklyn City R. Co. v. Whalen, 229 N.Y. 570 (1920).

14. Report in Schafer v. New York City, CM, Box 2, Folder 1551 (1923).

15. Report in East New York Elec. Co. v. Petmaland Realty Co., 243 N.Y. 477 (1926), CM, Box 2, Folder 2694.

16. Report in Jewel Carmen v. Fox Film Corp., CM, Box 4, Folder 4000 (motion 12, Feb. 21, 1927). The main Appellate Division opinion is at 204 App. Div. 776 (1st Dept. 1923). The judgment appealed from was an affirmance without opinion at 218 App. Div. 764 (1st Dept. 1926).

17. See 204 App. Div. 776 (1st Dept 1923).

18. 248 N.Y. 175 (1928) (hereafter Mirizio (II)).

19. Mirizio v. Mirizio, 242 N.Y. 74 (1926) (hereafter Mirizio (I)). Cardozo is listed as "absent," although he sat in several other cases that were heard on the same day.

20. Record in *Mirizio (II),* 28, 29, 33–36, HLS.

21. In the first case, the issue came up in quite a different way. Members of the husband's family filed an affidavit asserting that the husband had offered to take up married life in a room in his parents' home. Responding by affidavit, the wife stated that "they all knew full well that it would be an impossibility for deponent [the wife] to remain in her own estimation a chaste woman if she lived with the defendant prior to the religious ceremony." Record in *Mirizio (I),* 21, HLS.

22. 248 N.Y. at 178.

23. Record in *Mirizio (I),* 45, HLS. Record in *Mirizio (II),* 28, HLS.

24. 248 N.Y. at 180.

25. Id. at 180, 181.

26. In an analogous case, Cardozo recommended denial of a husband's

motion for leave to appeal from a judgment that granted separation to a wife. The husband's actions in inducing the wife to come from Germany, ostensibly to resume their married life after a period of sea duty, and then bringing a baseless suit for annulment as soon as she arrived, supplied a sufficient basis for a finding of cruelty. Report in Comfort v. Comfort, CM, Box 4, Folder 4645 (motion 49, Jan. 6, 1930).

27. Maud Nathan, *Once Upon a Time and Today,* 178–179 (1933). She was doubtless referring to voting on state suffrage amendment proposals in New York in 1915, when the proposal lost, and 1917, when it carried. Eleanor Flexner, *Century of Struggle,* 281, 300–301 (1975). There was no popular vote on the federal Nineteenth Amendment in 1919 and 1920.

28. Report to the consultation, CM, Box 3, Folder 3880 (motion 28, Oct. 1, 1928).

29. 211 App. Div. 646 (1st Dept. 1925).

30. Report in In Re McKenna, CM, Box 2, Folder 2285 (motion 6, May 4, 1925).

31. 254 N.Y. 161 (1930).

32. Id. at 167.

33. Id. at 168.

34. 253 N.Y. 1 (1930).

35. Id. at 7–8. For a recent case dealing with constitutional issues surrounding this ancient presumption, see Michael H. v. Gerald D., 491 U.S. 110 (1989).

36. Coler v. Corn Exchange Bank, 250 N.Y. 136 (1928), aff'd sub nom. Corn Exch. Bank v. Coler, 280 U.S. 218 (1930).

37. Letter from Cardozo to Felix Frankfurter, Mar. 16, 1929, FF.

38. 250 N.Y. at 141.

39. Id. at 143.

40. 235 N.Y. 245 (1923).

41. Another Cardozo opinion reaching a similar result was Foreman v. Foreman, 251 N.Y. 237 (1929).

42. 235 N.Y. at 253.

43. Cardozo report in Falk v. Hoffman, CM, Box 2, Folder 2344 (motion 13, June 1, 1925).

44. 241 N.Y. 569 (1925).

45. 123 Misc. Rep. 332 (Sup. Ct. Sp. T. 1924), aff'd, 215 App. Div. 702 (1st Dept. 1925).

46. Cardozo report in Klaw v. Erlanger, CM, Box 2, Folder 2586 (motion 13, Jan. 11, 1926).

47. 243 N.Y. 525 (1926).

48. 243 N.Y. 439 (1926).

49. Id. at 444. See also Cardozo's later opinion in a United States Supreme Court case, Rogers v. Guaranty Trust Co., 288 U.S. 123, 150, 151 (1933), a

stockholders' suit against directors of a company for breach of fiduciary duty in appropriating company stock to themselves under a stock option plan. The majority dismissed the suits because they should have been brought in the state of incorporation. Cardozo dissented, believing that the case should have been heard on the merits. "The overmastering necessity of rebuking fraud or breach of trust will outweigh competing policies and shift the balance of convenience. Equity, it is said, will not be over-nice in balancing the efficacy of one remedy against another when action will baffle, and inaction may confirm, the purpose of the wrongdoer."

50. 249 N.Y. 458 (1928).

51. Id. at 463–464.

52. Id. at 464. In 1974, Dean Russell Niles regretted Cardozo's use of the expression "undivided loyalty." "The more traditional terminology of 'conflict of interest' is less charged with emotion and is more accurate. Every trustee is subject to some actual or potential conflict between his duty and his selfish interest." Russell Niles, "A Contemporary View of Liability for Breach of Trust," 29 *The Record of the Association of the Bar of the City of New York* 573, 587 (Oct. 1974).

53. 249 N.Y. at 466.

54. Id. at 467.

55. Id. at 468.

56. Duncan Kennedy, "Form and Substance in Private Law Adjudication," 89 *Harvard Law Review* 1685, 1689, note 9 (1976).

57. 249 N.Y. at 473.

58. Niles, "Contemporary View of Liability," 574, 575–576.

59. Richard A. Posner, *Cardozo: A Study in Reputation,* 104–105 (1990).

60. Letter from Cardozo to Felix Frankfurter, Feb. 23, 1929, FF. Much of the commentary about Cardozo's poetry related to his use of the word "punctilio." Cardozo must have liked the sound of the word, for he also used it in the *Coler* case, which came down the same day.

61. McCandless v. Furlaud, 296 U.S. 140, 163, petition for rehearing denied, 296 U.S. 664 (1935).

14. The Law of Negligence: Duty to Strangers

1. 51 N.Y. 476 (Commission on Appeals 1873).

2. There is a debate in the tort literature about the causal relationship between industrialization and the rise of tort litigation. See Randolph Bergstrom, *Courting Danger: Injury and Law in New York City, 1870–1910* (1992) for an empirical discussion.

3. The systemization of tort law in the last half of the nineteenth century is vividly demonstrated by a comparison of the rudimentary organization and

analysis contained in the first edition of the Shearman and Redfield torts treatise with the sophisticated discussion in later editions. For general discussions of the phenomenon, see Lawrence M. Friedman, *A History of American Law*, 467–487 (2d ed. 1985); G. Edward White, *Tort Law in America*, 37–62 (1980); and Gary T. Schwartz, "The Character of Early American Tort Law," 36 *UCLA Law Review* 641 (1989). Compare Morton J. Horwitz, *The Transformation of American Law, 1870–1960*, 51–60 (1992).

4. See chap. 19, text at note 19.

5. See Jeremiah Smith, "Tort and Absolute Liability—Suggested Changes in Classification," 30 *Harvard Law Review* 241, 409 (1917). For later discussion of the problem, see Richard Epstein, "A Theory of Strict Liability," 2 *Journal of Legal Studies* 151 (1973); George P. Fletcher, "Fairness and Utility in Tort Theory," 85 *Harvard Law Review* 537 (1972); and Gary T. Schwartz, "The Vitality of Negligence and the Ethics of Strict Liability," 15 *Georgia Law Review* 963 (1981).

6. See, for example, Walton Hamilton, "Justice Cardozo: The Great Tradition," *The New Republic*, 328 (July 27, 1938).

7. See William Powers, Jr., "Reputology," 12 *Cardozo Law Review* 1941, 1944, 1946–1949 (1991); see also Richard A. Posner, *Cardozo: A Study in Reputation*, 11–19 (1990), where he summarized but ultimately did not agree with the criticism.

8. 233 N.Y. 16 (1922). Judge Andrews dissented, without opinion. The quotation is from Judge David Bazelon, a noted innovator who could be counted on to recognize a landmark case, in Whetzel v. Jess Fisher Management Co., 282 F.2d 943, 945 (D.C. Cir. 1960).

9. 191 App. Div. 888 (1st Dept. 1921).

10. 233 N.Y. at 18–19.

11. 256 N.Y. 287 (1931).

12. Id. at 291.

13. 217 N.Y. 382 (1916).

14. 247 N.Y. 340 (1928).

15. Report in McFarlane v. City of Niagara Falls, CM, Box 4, Folder 4130 (motion 7, Jan. 7, 1929).

16. Fiocco v. Carver, 234 N.Y. 219 (1922).

17. Id. at 223.

18. But see Fallon v. Swackhamer, 226 N.Y. 444 (1919).

19. 211 N.Y. 125 (1914).

20. 240 N.Y. 328 (1925).

21. Report in Nichitta v. City of New York, 250 N.Y. 530 (1928). The Appellate Division had reversed a judgment for an injured plaintiff, and the Court of Appeals affirmed without opinion. CM, Box 4, Folder 4115.

22. Berkey v. Third Avenue R. Co., 244 N.Y. 84 (1926) (5–2), reargument

denied, 244 N.Y. 602 (1927). See chap. 21, text at note 18, for further discussion of this case.

23. Palsgraf v. Long Island R. Co., 248 N.Y. 339, 341 (1928).

24. See chap. 8, text at note 5.

25. See BNC Torts file, KCC, for a list of eight examples.

26. See BNC Torts file, KCC, for a list of those cases.

27. Report in Leahy v. Jordan, 254 N.Y. 566 (1930), reversing, 228 A.D. 43 (3rd Dept. 1930), CM, Box 5, Folder 5137.

28. Cardozo, *The Paradoxes of Legal Science*, 74–75 (1928).

29. 225 N.Y. 727 (1919).

30. Memorandum in Kettell v. Erie R. Co., 225 N.Y. 727 (1919), CM, Box 1, Folder 1029.

31. 224 App. Div. 759 (2d Dept. 1928), motion for reargument denied, id. at 849.

32. Cardozo report, CM, Box 4, Folder 3953 (motion 14, Nov. 19, 1928). The court accepted Cardozo's recommendation.

33. 257 N.Y. 190 (1931).

34. Report in Greene v. Sibley, Lindsay and Curr Co., 257 N.Y. 190 (1931) (Pound and Crane dissenting), in CM, Box 5, Folder 5694 (1931).

35. 257 N.Y. at 191–192.

36. Report in Rath v. Texas Co., 240 N.Y. 598 (1925) (judgment for plaintiff in property damage negligence case affirmed without opinion, Andrews dissenting), CM, Box 2, Folder 2208.

37. The doctrine had been discussed quite critically by Professor Bohlen shortly before Cardozo came to the Court of Appeals. Francis H. Bohlen, "Voluntary Assumption of Risk," 20 *Harvard Law Review* 14, 91 (1906).

38. Id. at 115.

39. Knisley v. Pratt, 148 N.Y. 372, 380, reargument denied, 149 N.Y. 582 (1896).

40. Fitzwater v. Warren, 206 N.Y. 355 (1912).

41. See Dollard v. Roberts, 130 N.Y. 269 (1891) (no assumption of risk as a matter of law when tenant's daughter injured by plaster falling from ceiling in hallway despite fact that tenant had complained of dangerous condition); Wasmer v. D., L., & W. R. Co., 80 N.Y. 212 (1880) (impulsive attempt of plaintiff killed trying to save his horse, which had been frightened by defendant's negligence, does not bar recovery).

42. 244 N.Y. 111 (1926).

43. 250 N.Y. 179 (1929).

44. See Charles Labatt, *Commentaries on the Law of Master and Servant*, III, §§960–964 (2d ed. 1913).

45. 244 N.Y. at 113.

46. See Zurich Gen. Acc. & Liab. Ins. Co. v. Childs Co., 253 N.Y. 324

(1930), and Caspersen v. La Sala Bros., Inc., 253 N.Y. 491 (1930). The employee plaintiffs in the latter case were injured in a manner strikingly similar to the way the plaintiff was injured in a case that Cardozo had lost as a practicing lawyer many years before. See Devine v. Alphons Custodis discussed in chap. 6, text at note 5.

47. 250 N.Y. at 483.

48. 250 N.Y. at 482.

49. Id. at 482.

50. Cardozo, *The Nature of the Judicial Process*, 33 (1921).

51. 250 N.Y. at 483.

52. See Farwell v. Boston & W. R. Corp., 4 Metc. 49 (Mass. 1842) (Shaw, C.J.). The leading early case was Priestly v. Fowler, 3 M. & W. 1, 150 Eng. Rep. 1030 (1837), which was also the leading early case on assumption of risk generally.

53. See Thomas M. Cooley, *A Treatise on the Law of Torts*, 637–642 (2d ed. 1888).

54. Coon v. Syracuse and U. R. Co., 5 N.Y. 492 (1851).

55. See Flike v. Boston and A. R. Co., 53 N.Y. 549 (1873), and Crispin v. Babbitt, 81 N.Y. 516 (1880). A restrictive decision of the United States Supreme Court that was frankly hostile to the vice-principal rule, was followed in a number of states. Baltimore & Ohio R. Co. v. Baugh, 149 U.S. 368 (1893). For further discussion, compare White, *Tort Law in America*, 52–55, with Thomas G. Shearman and Amasa A. Redfield, *A Treatise on the Law of Negligence*, I, 661–685 (6th ed. 1913).

56. Shearman and Redfield, *Treatise on the Law of Negligence*, I, 415–416, note 1 (5th ed. 1898).

57. See Shearman and Redfield, *Treatise on the Law of Negligence*, III, 2170–2174 (6th ed. 1913), where some of the early statutory modifications of the common law of employer liability to employees are set forth.

58. See Record on Appeal, in Fitzgerald v. O'Rourke Engineering Construction Co., 211 N.Y. 65 (1914), ABCNY.

59. See Sun Printing & Publishing Association v. Remington, chap. 17, text at note 24.

60. Butterfield v. Forrester, 11 East 60, 103 Eng. Rep. 926 (K. B. 1809); Smith v. Smith, 2 Pick. 621 (Mass. 1824). See W. Page Keeton et al., *Prosser and Keeton on the Law of Torts*, 451–462 (5th ed., student ed., 1984), for a survey of the doctrine and the critical literature.

61. See Grippen v. New York Central R. Co., 40 N.Y. 34 (1869).

62. Shearman and Redfield, *Treatise on the Law of Negligence*, I, 266–273 (6th ed. 1913) (citing numerous cases).

63. 250 N.Y. 610 (1929), reversing 224 App. Div. 845 (2d Dept. 1928). Cardozo's report is in CM, Box 4, Folder 4297.

64. Updating eventually came from the legislature. It abolished the defense of contributory negligence, which wiped out a plaintiff's recovery, and substituted a rule of comparative negligence. New York Civil Practice Law and Rules §§1411, 1412. (McKinney).

65. 292 U.S. 98 (1934).

66. 275 U.S. 66 (1927).

67. 292 U.S. at 104–106.

15. Liability and Duty: MacPherson v. Buick

1. W. Page Keeton et al., *Prosser and Keeton on the Law of Torts*, 264 (5th ed., student ed., 1984).

2. William L. Prosser, *Handbook of the Law of Torts*, 244 (4th ed. 1971).

3. 6 N.Y. 397 (1852).

4. 10 M. & W. 109 (Ex. 1842).

5. 6 N.Y. at 410.

6. Loop v. Litchfield, 42 N.Y. 351 (1870) (defective balance wheel in circular saw arrangement not a dangerous instrument); Losee v. Clute, 51 N.Y. 494 (1873) (defective boiler not a dangerous instrument).

7. Coughtry v. The Globe Woolen Co., 56 N.Y. 124 (1874) and Devlin v. Smith, 89 N.Y. 470 (1882) (scaffold); Torgeson v. Schultz, 192 N.Y. 156 (1908) (aerated water) and Statler v. Ray Mfg. Co., 195 N.Y. 478 (1909) (coffee urn). Still later, when the "general rule" came under attack, Professor Bohlen viewed it as extraordinary that the *Thomas* doctrine should have "been thought a novel principle. It was because of the nature of his business, because unless properly carried on danger to such persons as the one injured was reasonably probable, that the defendant was liable. This liability was as old as the common law." Bohlen, "The Basis of Affirmative Obligations in the Law of Tort," 53 *University of Pennsylvania Law Review* 209, 273, 361 (1905).

8. Robert E. Keeton, *Legal Cause in the Law of Torts*, 3–36 (1963).

9. 35 N.Y. 210 (1866).

10. Id. at 212, 213, and 217. New York's fire rule represented a minority position among the states. Keeton, *Prosser and Keeton on Torts*, 282–283. A series of New York cases in the late nineteenth century restricted *Ryan* by formatting recovery by the adjacent property owner, but no other. See Webb v. Rome, W. & O. R.R., 49 N.Y. 420 (1872); O'Neill v. New York, O. & W. R. Co., 115 N.Y. 579 (1889); and Hoffman v. King, 160 N.Y. 618 (1899). These holdings were later changed by statute, but the Court of Appeals limited the statute to forest land. Rose v. Pennsylvania R. Co., 236 N.Y. 568 (1923).

11. 217 N.Y. 382 (1916) and 248 N.Y. 339 (1928).

12. See Morton J. Horwitz, *The Transformation of American Law, 1870–1960*, 51–61 (1992).

13. See Swords v. Edgar, 59 N.Y. 28 (1874).

14. 213 N.Y. 404 (1913).

15. Id. at 405, 408, and 409.

16. Cardozo was unwilling to extend landlord liability for nonpublic use in the absence of a statute. See Altz v. Leiberson and Cullings v. Goetz, discussed in chap. 14, text at notes 8–13.

17. 215 N.Y. 488 (1915).

18. Id. at 492.

19. Id. at 491.

20. 217 N.Y. 382 (1916).

21. Id. at 384–385.

22. See David W. Peck, *Decision at Law,* (1961), at 59, quoting from Buick's brief, and 38–69, for the history of the case.

23. 160 App. Div. 55 (3d Dept. 1914).

24. Huset v. J. L. Case Threshing Machine Co., 120 Fed. 865 (8th Cir. 1903); see Thomas M. Cooley, *A Treatise on the Law of Torts,* II, 1486–1492 (3d ed. 1906); Francis Wharton, *A Treatise on the Law of Negligence,* 364–373 (2d ed. 1878). The rule was usually traced to Winterbottom v. Wright, 10 M. & W. 109 (Ex. 1842). Thomas G. Shearman and Amasa A. Redfield, *A Treatise on the Law of Negligence,* 298–300 (6th ed. 1913), took a different view. They argued that the view of Lord Esher in Heaven v. Pender, L. R. 11 Q. B. Div. 503 (1883), imposing a broad duty of care, was correct and would eventually be accepted everywhere. The same argument had previously been made in Melville Bigelow, *Leading Cases on the Law of Torts,* 613–619 (1875).

25. 217 N.Y. at 395, 400. Bartlett had written the opinion that had found liability in Torgeson v. Schultz, the exploding water bottle case. See text at note 7. A case similar to *MacPherson* had just been decided in favor of nonliability by the United States Circuit Court of Appeals for the Second Circuit. See Cadillac Motor Car Co. v. Johnson, 221 Fed. 801 (1915).

26. Even such cases as Loop v. Litchfield and Losee v. Clute, see note 6, accepted the principle, although they took a narrow view of it and therefore found the risk remote.

27. 217 N.Y. at 387; see text at note 7.

28. L.R. 11 Q.B.D. 503 (1883).

29. One critic was Francis Bohlen, who nevertheless was also a leading critic of *Winterbottom*. See Bohlen, "The Basis of Affirmative Obligations," 279–285, 289–310.

30. Edward Levi described the movement of the legal concepts that resulted in the *MacPherson* decision in a way that interweaves New York case law with more general law. He ascribes somewhat more creativity to Cardozo's opinion than I do, while also noting how the results in earlier cases had gotten the New

York courts close to the *MacPherson* result before Cardozo's opinion. Edward H. Levi, *An Introduction to Legal Reasoning*, 8–25 (1949).

31. 217 N.Y. at 391. The rhetorical flourish was appropriate to the state of New York law where Cardozo could focus on the need to show "imminent danger." Elsewhere in the country, he would have had to contend with "inherent" danger, a much more difficult task.

MacPherson would have not been so important if Donald MacPherson could have recovered damages for his injury from the dealer on a breach of contract theory. Recovery for personal injuries in a breach of warranty action was not, however, well-recognized in 1916, although there was some authority for the possibility of recovery in New York. Compare Swain v. Schieffelin, 134 N.Y. 471 (1892) with Birdsinger v. McCormick Harvesting Machine Co., 183 N.Y. 487, 492 (1906). Many years after *MacPherson*, in 1931, Cardozo allowed a recovery for personal injuries against a seller of a defective food product in a contract action by generalizing the foreseeability point in a way similar to *MacPherson*. Ryan v. Progressive Grocery Stores, Inc., 255 N.Y. 388 (1931).

32. 217 N.Y. at 392.

33. Id. at 390.

34. Prosser, *Handbook of the Law of Torts*, 642–643; Warren A. Seavey, "Mr. Justice Cardozo and the Law of Torts," 52 *Harvard Law Review* 372, 379 (1939).

35. 235 N.Y. 468 (1923). The Appellate Division had unanimously affirmed a verdict for the plaintiff without opinion. 200 App. Div. 864 (1st Dept. 1922).

36. It took a while for the *MacPherson* principle to make its way into contract law. See the three alternatives to §2–318 of the Uniform Commercial Code that were offered in the 1966 amendment and that have not been changed since.

37. Prosser, *Handbook of the Law of Torts*, 500 (2d ed. 1955).

38. Lawrence M. Friedman, *A History of American Law*, 685 (2d ed. 1985); but see Robert M. Davis, "A Re-examination of the Doctrine of MacPherson v. Buick and its Application and Extension in the State of New York," 24 *Fordham Law Review* 204 (1955), for the view that the scope of Cardozo's opinion was broader than most courts had recognized.

39. See, for example, Johnson v. Cadillac Motor Car Co., 261 Fed. 878 (2d Cir. 1919), discussed in note 25. The Court of Appeals for the Second Circuit, on the strength of the reasoning of Cardozo's opinion in *MacPherson*, reversed its earlier holding in the same case, which had denied liability on facts virtually identical to those in *MacPherson*. 221 Fed. 801 (2d Cir. 1915).

40. 219 N.Y. 60, 62 (1916). The decision was unanimous, although Judge Hogan, as in *MacPherson*, merely concurred in the result.

41. Id. at 63, 64.

42. For a case in which violation of a statute designed for the protection of the one who complained was held to constitute not just evidence of negligence but negligence itself, see Cardozo's opinion in Martin v. Herzog, 228 N.Y. 164 (1920). There the violation was by the plaintiff, driver of a buggy without required lights, who was hit by a car being driven on the wrong side of the road. Still to be shown was causation between the (contributory) negligence and the accident, but Cardozo put the burden on the plaintiff to show no causation given the fact of the accident and the time, one hour after sundown.

43. 219 N.Y. 439 (1916).

44. Id. at 442.

45. After a retrial, the court reversed another verdict for the plaintiff, 4–3, with Cardozo in the majority. Prior to *Perry*, the court had also denied liability as a matter of law in Gaines v. City of New York, 215 N.Y. 533 (1915), in which a car hit the center truss of an unlighted bridge in a dense fog. Cardozo's opinion held that defendant would have carried out its duty by lighting both sides of the bridge, but there was no evidence that such light would have penetrated the fog and so have lighted the center truss. The defendant had no duty to light the center truss because light on either side would have been entirely adequate but for the peculiar atmospheric conditions that existed on that occasion. Thus, the defendant's negligence did not "cause" the accident.

46. 224 N.Y. 47 (1918).

47. Id. at 49.

48. See 180 App. Div. 470, 474.

49. 224 N.Y. at 51, 52.

50. Id. at 53. He cited an article by Jeremiah Smith and two English cases for that proposition. The purpose of discussing the torts cases was to rely on the New York fire cases, which used a geographic standard to limit potentially enormous liability in property destruction actions. Cardozo did not refer to two contracts theories that might have been used to reach an opposite conclusion. The first was the well-known proposition that insurance contracts are construed against the party, here the insurance company, that prepared it. The second was to rely on the contract language that provided coverage against "perils" of the river as well as against fire damage and to conclude that damage from an explosion was a covered "peril."

51. See also his report in Aktiebolaget Malareprovinsernas Bank v. Globe and Rutgers Fire Ins. Co., 241 N.Y. 551 (1925). These were consolidated cases involving a vessel that had been insured by many insurance companies against losses except those resulting from seizure by the British government. The vessel had in fact been seized by the British but later released on condition that it make a certain voyage. It was sunk on that voyage. Cardozo, recommending grant of the insurance companies' motion for leave to appeal a judgment for the insured,

stated that there was "much force in the argument that this loss was a proximate result of the capture and restraint." That statement reflects a broader notion of what constituted proximate cause than he had recognized in *Bird*. CM, Box 2, Folder 2258. The court took the appeal and reversed the insured's judgment on the basis of Judge Crane's opinion in a related case. The grounds for the reversal were different, but in dicta the court expressed sympathy with the position espoused by Cardozo in his report. Aktiebolaget Malareprovinsernas Bank v. American Merchant Marine Ins. Co., 241 N.Y. 197 (1925), reargument denied, 242 N.Y. 538 (1926).

52. 224 N.Y. 18 (1918).

53. Id. at 20–21.

54. 231 N.Y. 229 (1921) and 232 N.Y. 176 (1921).

55. See Nicholson v. The Erie R. Co., 41 N.Y. 525 (1870).

56. 231 N.Y. at 235.

57. Id. at 233.

58. Id. at 236.

59. Ibid.

60. He might have added to his *Hynes* list of factors, that of custom (the method of tradition) from his *Nature of the Judicial Process* list, for the discussion of protection of bathers in public waters was grounded in their traditional rights.

61. See the good discussion of *Hynes* in G. Edward White, *Tort Law in America*, 121–124 (1980). See also Richard H. Weisberg, "Law, Literature and Cardozo's Judicial Poetics," 1 *Cardozo Law Review* 283, 304, 324–326 (1979) and "Judicial Discretion, or the Self on the Shelf," 10 *Cardozo Law Review* 105, 108–110 (1988) and Richard A. Posner, *Cardozo: A Study in Reputation*, 48–55 (1990).

62. Cardozo's suggestion that there ought not to be a difference in result between the actual case, where the boy was on the plank, and the hypothetical case of the boy leaning against the springboard with his feet on the ground on public land suggests a different result in the "cutting across defendant's land" case.

63. 227 N.Y. 208 (1919).

64. Weisberg, "Judicial Discretion," 108.

65. 231 N.Y. at 235.

66. 232 N.Y. 176, 180 (1921).

67. 232 N.Y. at 180.

68. Id. at 180–181, citing Ehrgott v. Mayor, 96 N.Y. 264 (1884) for the latter proposition. See chap. 16, text at note 39, for discussion of *Ehrgott*.

69. Seavey, "Mr. Justice Cardozo and the Law of Torts," 381.

70. 232 N.Y. 220 (1921).

71. Letter from Cardozo to Felix Frankfurter, Mar. 18, 1922, FF.

72. Moore v. Van Beuren and New York Bill Posting Co., 208 App. Div. 352 (1st Dept. 1924).

73. 240 N.Y. 673, reargument denied, 241 N.Y. 504 (1925).

74. CM, Box 2, Folder 2328 (1924).

16. Fireworks and Foreseeability: *Palsgraf*

1. *New York Times,* 1 (Aug. 25, 1924).

2. Ibid.

3. Dean William Prosser relied on testimony that the explosion occurred below the platform level and on the lack of testimony about injuries to others to argue that the scale "was in fact knocked over by the stampede of frightened passengers." William Prosser, "Palsgraf Revisited," 52 *Michigan Law Review* 1, 3, note 9 (1953). But the *New York Times* story indicated that there was plenty of damage done to persons and property above platform level, and it seems more likely that the explosion blew over the scale.

4. 248 N.Y. 339, reargument denied, 249 N.Y. 511 (1928). The quotation is from Prosser, "Palsgraf Revisited," 1. The discussions of *Palsgraf* are collected in W. Page Keeton, et al., *Prosser and Keeton on the Law of Torts,* 284, note 31 (5th ed., student ed., 1984) and in John T. Noonan, Jr., *Persons and Masks of the Law,* 114–122, 191–192 (1976). The latter contains an extensive critique, attacking Cardozo and the commentators on their failure to relate the individual human beings who were involved in the case, especially the poor plaintiff and the rich defendant, to the formulation of the abstract rule.

5. Anyone interested in a more detailed exploration of the facts as they appear both in the record and outside the record should consult Richard A. Posner, *Cardozo: A Study in Reputation,* 33–37 (1990); Noonan, *Persons and Masks,* 111–151; and Jorie Roberts, "Palsgraf Kin Tell Human Side of Famed Case," *Harvard Law Record,* 1 (April 14, 1978).

6. The trial judge's charge was reproduced in the papers filed on the ultimate appeal to the Court of Appeals. Case on Appeal, 55–58, HLS. The other technical information about the course of the proceeding comes from the same source.

7. American Law Institute, Restatement of Torts Minutes of Conferences, 1925–30, I, Proceedings of Oct. 20–23, 1927, copy in HLS. During the course of writing this biography, I discovered a mass of materials, largely uncatalogued, in the Harvard Law School Library pertaining to the Restatement of Torts. It includes not only minutes of the advisers' meetings but also copies of the drafts of various segments of the project that were used as working documents by Professor Warren Seavey and Professor Edward Thurston. The collection was donated by the former. Conversation of author with Assistant Librarian Mar-

garet Moody, 1976. See also Harvard Law School Library Accession Book for 1957. Because the American Law Institute has apparently destroyed its own collection of minutes from that period, see letter of Professor Eldredge to Professor Noonan, Mar. 16, 1976, KCC, this may be the only collection of minutes relating to the drafting of the Restatement of Torts.

I have assumed the general accuracy of the minutes because the ALI hired trained reporters to take notes. As far as this particular reporter, R. M. M. (probably the Ralph M. Mullin whose name appears on a copy of Draft No. 18-R) was concerned, I was able to make some assessment of the accuracy of his work, and I found that he was quite accurate.

8. American Law Institute, "Torts Restatement Draft No. 18-R," §2(2) and accompanying Note to Advisers (Oct. 4, 1927), contained in a bound volume at HLS entitled American Law Institute, "Torts Preliminary Drafts 17–26" (1941); see Henry Terry, *Some Leading Principles of Anglo-American Law,* 542–549 (1884).

9. Leading efforts were those of Henry Terry: *Some Leading Principles,* 165–200, 391–434, and 538–606; "Proximate Consequences in the Law of Torts," 28 *Harvard Law Review* 10 (1914); and "Negligence," 29 *Harvard Law Review* 40 (1915); Francis H. Bohlen, "The Probable or the Natural Consequence as the Test of Liability in Negligence," 40 *American Law Register* (N.S.) 79, 148 (Feb., Mar., 1901), reprinted with a supplementary Note in Bohlen, *Studies in the Law of Torts,* 1 (1926); Joseph W. Bingham, "Some Suggestions Concerning 'Legal Cause' at Common Law," 9 *Columbia Law Review* 16, 136 (1909); Jeremiah Smith, "Legal Cause in Actions of Tort," 25 *Harvard Law Review* 103, 223, 303 (1911, 1912); Joseph H. Beale, "The Proximate Consequences of an Act," 33 *Harvard Law Review* 633 (1920); Henry Edgerton, "Legal Cause," 72 *University of Pennsylvania Law Review* 211, 343 (1924); and Leon Green, *Rationale of Proximate Cause* (1927).

10. American Law Institute, Torts Conference Minutes, 36 (Oct. 23, 1927), HLS. The hypothetical bore a striking resemblance to the facts of the *Perry* case (the box with blasting caps left on the Erie Canal), text at chap. 15, note 40, in which Cardozo found no liability. Presumably, he would have distinguished the cases by the fact that in *Perry,* the blasting caps were not left in the open and the children stole the caps.

11. 248 N.Y. at 346–347.

12. American Law Institute, *Restatement of Torts,* §281, comment e (1934).

13. American Law Institute, Torts Conference Minutes, I, 39–43 (Oct. 23, 1927), HLS.

14. The memorandum was given by Professor Seavey to Professor Robert Keeton, who quoted it in Keeton, "A *Palsgraf* Anecdote," 56 *Texas Law Review* 513 (1978). Seavey identified the meeting as "NY meeting Torts Advisors around 1926–27?" Examination of the minutes of the meetings of the Torts

Advisers suggests that the memorandum may well have referred to the same Oct. 23, 1927, meeting just discussed. Keeton notes that the reference by Andrews in his *Palsgraf* dissent to a hypothetical example in "an unpublished manuscript by a distinguished and helpful writer on the law of torts" sounds very much like the two Seavey hypotheticals, and he suggests that Andrews had access to one of Bohlen's memoranda prepared for the advisers that contained these hypotheticals or ones close to it. That observation seems quite plausible, and if accurate, the conference must have preceded *Palsgraf*. That fact narrows down the field to the conference of Oct. 20–23, 1927, which is the only one at which all the participants named by Seavey were present. The only problem with that hypothesis, and it is a big problem, is that Cardozo attended that conference only on October 23 and that Professor Green is reported to have left the conference on October 22 "not to return the following day." American Law Institute, Torts Conference Minutes, I, 27 (meeting of Oct. 22, 1927), HLS. It is still possible that the conversation could have occurred at that conference in some informal setting, perhaps at dinner, or that it could have occurred over two days, with Seavey reporting Green's views from one day and Cardozo's from another. If Seavey's memory about the date is faulty, another possible meeting date was the meeting of Feb. 20 and 21, 1931. See American Law Institute, Torts Conference Minutes, II, HLS. But it seems more likely to me that the report concerns pre-*Palsgraf* events.

15. 222 App. Div. 166 (2d Dept. 1927).

16. Prosser, "Palsgraf Revisited," 4–5.

17. Id. at 5, note 21.

18. See letter of Laurence Eldredge to John T. Noonan, Jr., Mar. 16, 1976, KCC; Eldredge, "*Palsgraf*, Chief Judge Cardozo and Restatement of the Law of Torts §281," *Torts and Retorts*, 7 (No. 5 Oct. 1976) (publication of the Association of American Law Schools Torts-Compensations Systems Section). Professor Eldredge's inquiry was stimulated by the reporting of the Prosser story in Noonan, *Persons and Masks of the Law*, 147–149. I should take the occasion to make a public apology to my friend Judge Noonan. I read a draft of the relevant chapter of his book, but it was at a time when I had no reason to doubt the accuracy of the Prosser story. Shortly thereafter, I discovered the minutes of the torts advisers' meetings and came to believe that the Prosser story was not true.

19. See, for example, People v. Ecker, 247 N.Y. 538 (argued Dec. 12, 1927) and People v. Lewis, 247 N.Y. 541 (argued Dec. 13, 1927).

20. American Law Institute, "Restatement of Torts, preliminary draft no. 23, for the meeting of Sept. 28, 1928," §165, illustration 3, HLS.

21. That copy is in the Harvard Law School's collection of Restatement of Torts materials, but the collection contains no minutes of the June 19–22, 1928, conference. Cardozo might have attended the last day of that conference. He

was in Albany hearing arguments on Monday, June 18, through Thursday, June 21. See 248 N.Y. 645–657 (1928). Since that was the last argument week of the term, the court might have held its consultation on Thursday instead of the usual Friday, because Cardozo wrote Felix Frankfurter the next week that he had closed his Albany work on Thursday. Letter from Cardozo to Felix Frankfurter, June 25, 1928, FF. If so, he could have made the Friday Advisers meeting in New York City. Although nothing was pending in *Palsgraf* at that time, a petition for reargument was filed later and was denied on Oct. 9, 1928. See note 32.

22. 248 N.Y. 339 (1928).

23. Id. at 341, 343.

24. 248 N.Y. at 344, citing Warren A. Seavey, "Negligence—Subjective or Objective?," 41 *Harvard Law Review* 1, 6 (1927). Cardozo dealt with language of expansive liability that appeared in some cases by restricting such liability to situations in which acts are so imminently dangerous "as to impose a prevision not far from that of an insurer." 248 N.Y. at 344.

25. Id. at 342.

26. Id. at 352.

27. Id. at 354.

28. Id. at 341.

29. Cardozo, "Law and Literature," in *Law and Literature and Other Essays*, 1, 7–8 (1931).

30. Case on Appeal, 46, HLS. Her older sister Elizabeth also testified that the newsstand was "at the other end of the station." Id. at 42.

31. 248 N.Y. at 356. Lillian also testified that the newsstand was approximately 29 feet away from her mother. Case on Appeal, 47, HLS. There was also testimony that the platform was 12 to 15 feet wide. Id. at 17, 37. On that basis, if the newsstand was nearly perpendicular to the location where the guard pushed the passenger, that would place Mrs. Palsgraf approximately 25 to 40 feet from that location.

32. 249 N.Y. 511 (1928). The one-sentence opinion was "per curiam." Since Cardozo had written the earlier majority opinion, he was probably the author of the response.

33. See text at chap. 15, note 40.

34. See text at chap. 15, note 46.

35. See text at chap. 14, note 33.

36. Cardozo had long been aware of the possibility of this sort of analysis, for he had used a somewhat similar analysis in deciding whether damage to property was "caused" by fire for purposes of insurance coverage. See the *Bird* case, text at chap. 15, note 46, in which he concluded that 1,000 feet was too far away for a ship to recover under a marine fire policy when damaged by an explosion caused by fire.

37. 248 N.Y. at 345.

38. Id. at 346.

39. 96 N.Y. 264 (1884). The opinion was written by Judge Robert Earl, who had previously written the famous liability-restricting opinion in Losee v. Buchanan, chap. 14, text at note 1.

40. 248 N.Y. at 346–347.

41. William Powers, "Reputology," 12 *Cardozo Law Review* 1941, 1947, and 1949 (1991). In subsequent correspondence, Powers regretted the use of the word "tricky," finding it too pejorative and not based on study of a significant body of Cardozo's work. Letter from William Powers to author, Jan. 14, 1992, KCC.

42. Cardozo, *The Paradoxes of Legal Science,* 85 (1928).

43. This order later subjected Cardozo and the court to severe criticism for imposing an obligation on Mrs. Palsgraf to pay the Long Island Railroad what amounted to nearly a year's income. Noonan, *Persons and Masks,* 144. But in fact her lawyer never asked the court to alter the normal award of these costs to the winning party. Posner, *Cardozo,* 16–17 and 36–37. Judge Posner also suggests the possibility that the railroad never attempted to collect the award. Cardozo's reports to the consultation indicate that on occasion, the Court of Appeals did discuss the award of costs. Sometimes Cardozo recommended that the court exercise its discretion not to award costs against a losing party. Reports in Dickey v. Gortner, 236 N.Y. 641 (1923), CM, Box 2, Folder 1619 (motion 54, Oct. 2, 1923); Voss v. W. J. Martin Coal Co., 243 N.Y. 592 (1926), CM, Box 3, Folder 2865; and Tecla Corp. v. Salon Tecla, Ltd., 249 N.Y. 513 (1928), CM, Box 4, Folder 3903. It does not appear whether any of these changes of the normal award of costs occurred without a request to do so by the losing party.

44. American Law Institute, *Restatement of Torts,* §281, comment g (1934), using the *Palsgraf* facts as an illustration; Keeton, *Prosser and Keeton on the Law of Torts,* 288.

45. This was the burden of Professor Albert Ehrenzweig's critique of the *Palsgraf* rule—"Loss-Shifting and Quasi-Negligence: A New Interpretation of the *Palsgraf* Case," 8 *University of Chicago Law Review* 729 (1941)—where he urged a theory of "enterprise liability" for "typical" damage caused by the enterprise wholly apart from fault. (Ehrenzweig was later identified by Dean Prosser as the originally anonymous author of that piece. Prosser, "Palsgraf Revisited," 31.) See also Noonan, *Persons and Masks,* 111–151, and Morton J. Horwitz, *The Transformation of American Law, 1870–1960,* 61–63 (1992).

46. G. Edward White, *Tort Law in America,* 101–102 (1980); see also Horwitz, *Transformation of American Law,* 62–63, for an elaboration of this view.

47. G. Edward White, *The American Judicial Tradition,* 279–280 (Expanded ed. 1988).

48. 247 N.Y. 160 (1928).

49. Cardozo distinguished prior cases in which municipal contracts had been used as the basis for recovery by private citizens on the ground that a benefit to individual citizens had been contemplated when the contract was made. One such case was New York Pneumatic Service Co. v. P. T. Cox Contracting Co., 235 N.Y. 567 (1923) (Cardozo and Hiscock dissenting without opinion). In a memorandum to the consultation in that case, Cardozo indicated his general unwillingness to give third parties rights under contracts between the city and a supplier of services. CM, Box 1, Folder 1458.

50. 247 N.Y. at 164.

51. Id. at 165. See chap. 15, text at note 9, for discussion of New York's fire rule.

52. 247 N.Y. at 168.

53. Cardozo had one year earlier expressed his reluctance to impose extensive liability in such a situation, and the only surprise in his opinion in *Moch* is that he failed to refer to that earlier statement as authority. See Kerr Steamship Co. v. Radio Corporation of America, discussed in chap. 18, text at note 23.

54. See chap. 14, text at note 8.

55. Warren A. Seavey, "Mr. Justice Cardozo and the Law of Torts," 52 *Harvard Law Review* 372, 391–393 (1939).

56. The issue continues to trouble the courts. See Edwards v. Honeywell, 50 F.3d 484 (7th Cir. 1995), where Judge Richard Posner held that a fire alarm service company had no duty of care to a firefighter killed in the home of the company's customer while fighting a fire. The service company had delayed sending the alarm. Judge Posner discussed Cardozo's opinions in *Moch, Palsgraf,* and *Kerr,* see note 53, extensively.

57. Seavey, "Mr. Justice Cardozo," 394–395.

58. 233 N.Y. 236 (1922).

59. Id. at 239.

60. Ibid.

61. Seavey, "Mr. Justice Cardozo," 396.

62. 233 N.Y. at 240.

63. Compare Jaillet v. Cashman, 235 N.Y. 511 (1923) and Courteen Seed Co. v. Hong Kong and S.B. Corp., 245 N.Y. 377, reargument denied, 246 N.Y. 534 (1927) (both denying recovery for negligent statements) with International Products Co. v. Erie R. R., 244 N.Y. 331, cert. denied, 275 U.S. 527 (1927) and Doyle v. Chatham & Phoenix Nat. Bank, 253 N.Y. 369, reargument denied, 254 N.Y. 548 (1930) (both allowing recovery in carefully limited opinions). This series of cases is discussed in Seavey, "Mr. Justice Cardozo," 397–398.

64. 255 N.Y. 170 (1931).

65. 233 N.Y. at 240.

66. See Seavey, "Mr. Justice Cardozo," 400.

67. 255 N.Y. at 179.

68. 255 N.Y. at 187.

69. Seavey, "Mr. Justice Cardozo," 398–404, discusses many analytical problems with the opinion and gives a sense of the state of the law at the time the opinion was written. See also Keeton, *Prosser and Keeton on the Law of Torts,* 745–749. The New York Court of Appeals continues to apply the principles, and the distinctions, set forth in *Glanzer* and *Ultramares.* See the majority and dissenting opinions in Security Pacific Business Credit, Inc. v. Peat Marwick Main & Co., 79 N.Y.2d 695, motions denied, 80 N.Y.2d 918 (1992), for a discussion of the history of the privity doctrine since Cardozo's earlier opinions.

70. See chap. 15, note 31.

71. 258 N.Y. 462 (1932).

72. See his report in Moore v. Van Beuren, discussed in chap. 15, text at note 72.

17. Contracts and Promises

1. See Samuel Williston, *The Law of Contracts* (1st ed. 1920).

2. Corbin eventually embodied his ideas in his own treatise, Arthur L. Corbin, *Corbin on Contracts* (1st ed. 1950).

3. Professor Charles Fried reviewed the debate and the literature in *Contract as Promise,* 4–5 (1981). Compare Patrick Atiyah, *The Rise and Fall of Freedom of Contract,* 771–778 (1979) and Lon L. Fuller and William Perdue, "The Reliance Interest in Contract Damages," 46 *Yale Law Journal* 52, 373 (1936, 1937). For a different view, see Lawrence A. Cunningham, "Cardozo and Posner: A Study in Contracts," 36 *William and Mary Law Review* 1379, 1391–1392 (1995).

4. See Grant Gilmore, *The Death of Contract,* 57 (1974) for a published characterization.

5. Scott used the expression in McCall Co. v. Wright, 133 App. Div. 62, 68 (1st Dept. 1909). Cardozo used it in Moran v. Standard Oil Co. and Wood v. Lucy, Lady Duff Gordon, which follow, and in Sinclair v. Purdy, chap. 13, text at note 40.

6. 211 N.Y. 187, 198 (1914).

7. 217 N.Y. 223, 233 (1916) (dissenting in part).

8. 222 N.Y. 88 (1917), reargument denied, 222 N.Y. 643 (1918), reversing 177 App. Div. 624 (1st Dept. 1917).

9. Id. at 90. *Wood* is included in twelve of the thirteen leading contracts casebooks. Cunningham, "Cardozo and Posner," 1459.

10. A selection of the writings on the problem of consideration that was available in Cardozo's time is contained in Association of American Law Schools, *Selected Readings on the Law of Contracts*, 320–608 (1931) (with an introduction by Cardozo).

11. 217 N.Y. at 91, citing *McCall* and *Moran*.

12. Id. at 92.

13. Professors Farnsworth and Fried disagree on whether inference of a "best efforts" clause in an exclusive dealing contract was the more usual rule. Compare E. Allan Farnsworth, *Contracts*, II, 314 (2d ed. 1990) (one vol. ed.) with Fried, *Contract as Promise*, 31. An article that places *Wood* in the broader setting of changes in the American economy is Walter F. Pratt, Jr., "American Contract Law at the Turn of the Century," 39 *South Carolina Law Review* 415 (1988).

14. See, for example, Arthur Rosett, *Contract Law and Its Application*, 37, question 3 (5th ed. 1994).

15. 231 N.Y. 459 (1921).

16. 189 App. Div. 843, 849, 856–857 (1st Dept 1919) (Judge Page dissenting from the majority opinion, which upheld the validity of the contract).

17. 232 N.Y. 112 (1921).

18. Cohen v. Lurie Woolen Co., 232 N.Y. at 113, 114.

19. Karl Llewellyn, *The Common Law Tradition*, 116 (1960).

20. Ibid.

21. From a commercial standpoint, the distinction that McLaughlin drew between *Schlegel* and *Wood* appears sound, as the practical situations in *Wood* and *Schlegel* were quite different. Wood was not making money by buying Duff Gordon's goods at a fixed price and reselling them at a profit, as the jobber in *Schlegel* was. The *Schlegel* court also relied on the fact that the absence of a standard by which the jobber's obligation could be measured meant there was no legal limit on the sales he could make. In *Schlegel*, the court confronted a buyer who had made too many contracts, nearly bankrupting the seller in the process. It was one thing to find that the grant in *Wood* of an exclusive dealing privilege to the agent justified an inference that he was required to use reasonable efforts. There was no similar lever, no custom or usage, in *Schlegel* either to impose a duty to buy or, more importantly, to impose a limit on the amount purchased. The buyer's demand therefore was not enforceable. Viewed from that perspective, *Schlegel* was not out of the mainstream.

22. 232 N.Y. at 114.

23. Llewellyn, *Common Law Tradition*, 116, 358.

24. 235 N.Y. 338 (1923).

25. Id. at 342.

26. 235 N.Y. at 344–345.

27. Llewellyn eventually approved, and Farnsworth did too, at least as the

case was presented. Corbin and Gilmore did not. Compare Llewellyn, *Common Law Tradition*, 242 and 242, note 243, and Farnsworth, *Contracts*, 221–222 (1990 ed.) (one vol. ed.) with Arthur L. Corbin, *Corbin on Contracts*, I, 92, note 35 (1963 ed.) (Cardozo's conclusion was "in all probability not liberal enough") and Gilmore, *Death of Contract*, 62, 128, note 137.

28. Arthur L. Corbin, "Mr. Justice Cardozo and the Law of Contracts," 52 *Harvard Law Review* 408, 409–410, note 1 (1939).

29. Cardozo, *The Growth of the Law*, 110–111 (1924) (footnotes omitted).

30. 210 App. Div. 875 (1st Dept. 1924).

31. Report in *Sun Printing*, CM, Box 2, Folder 2114 (motion 6, Jan. 19, 1925).

32. Stewart Macaulay, "Non-Contractual Relations in Business: A Preliminary Study," 28 *American Sociological Review* 55, 60 (1963), as quoted in Farnsworth, *Contracts*, 222, note 15 (2d ed. 1990) (one vol. ed.).

33. Gilmore, *Death of Contract*, 62.

34. 227 N.Y. 200 (1919).

35. Id. at 202.

36. 221 N.Y. 431 (1917). The court was unanimous in its conclusion, but Judge Crane filed a concurring opinion.

37. That policy is recognized in American Law Institute, *Restatement (Second) of Contracts* §90(2) (1981), which regards promises in connection with marriage settlements and charitable subscriptions as binding even without consideration if justice so requires even "without proof that the promise induced action or forbearance."

38. 221 N.Y. at 433–434.

39. Id. at 435.

40. It would require a footnote of several pages to state the facts of each of these cases and to argue why they were not controlling. Since Cardozo did not pursue the point, neither shall I. The original suggestion that these cases did not support the proposition for which they were cited was made to me by Professor Harry Wellington of the Yale Law School many years ago, and I am grateful for that insight. See letter from Harry H. Wellington to author, Jan. 15, 1959, KCC. See Joshua Davis, "Cardozo's Judicial Craft and What Cases Come to Mean," 68 *New York University Law Review* 777, 789 (1993) for the argument that Cardozo's four cases all involve situations in which one person entered into a contract with a second person to fulfill that person's contract with a third person. But that is somewhat different from Cardozo's proposition.

41. Hamer v. Sidway, 124 N.Y. 538 (1891) and Shadwell v. Shadwell (1806) 9 C.B. [N.S.] 159.

42. 221 N.Y. at 435 (emphasis in original).

43. That conclusion, with its emphasis on reliance, contains intimations of the modern idea of promissory estoppel. See text at note 62.

44. 221 N.Y. at 437. One scholar viewed this argument as "empirically" being "among Cardozo's silliest." He contends that there was nothing in the Record "to indicate Blanche and the Count ever contemplated rescission or delay," and therefore the case confirms the charge that Cardozo made up facts. Robert Birmingham, "A Study After Cardozo: *De Cicco v. Schweizer,* Noncooperative Games, and Neural Computing," 47 *University of Miami Law Review* 121, 130 (1992). Although Cardozo's opinion is problematic, I do not think he made up facts. He never said that the couple contemplated rescission or delay, and such an assertion was not necessary to his argument. All he said was that delay or retraction was an option and that the natural tendency of the promise was to induce them to go ahead. Given the public policy consideration for upholding marriage settlements, that was enough to constitute consideration.

45. 221 N.Y. at 438.

46. In addition, Cardozo also stated that the consideration must be regarded as such by the parties, citing both Holmes's *Common Law* and a pre–Civil War Supreme Court case for this "bargain theory" notion.

47. 221 N.Y. at 439.

48. Arthur L. Corbin, "Does a Pre-existing Duty Defeat Consideration?," 27 *Yale Law Journal* 362 (1918), revised and reprinted in Association of American Law Schools, *Selected Readings on the Law of Contracts,* 504 (1931).

49. Letter from Cardozo to Arthur Corbin, Jan. 17, 1918, reprinted in George Hellman, *Benjamin N. Cardozo,* 87–88 (1940). The date of the letter appears in a letter from Corbin to Professor Michael Cardozo, Nov. 30, 1938, copy in KCC. Corbin's correspondence, except for scattered items, has not been found, despite a diligent search. Letter from Professor Morris Cohen, Librarian, Yale Law School, to author, June 28, 1984, KCC.

50. Lon L. Fuller, "Consideration and Form," 41 *Columbia Law Review* 799 (1941).

51. Justice Oliver Wendell Holmes, dissenting in Southern Pacific Co. v. Jensen, 244 U.S. 205, 218, 221 (1917).

52. We have no copy of Corbin's response, if any.

53. In re Slocum, 204 App. Div. 877 (1st Dept. 1922).

54. Report in In re Slocum, CM, Box 1, Folder 1483 (motion 1, Mar. 23, 1923).

55. Cardozo also pointed out in his report that the claim that there was a contract could not be sustained for another reason. The Society had not met the time limit set by Mrs. Sage for matching her gift, and so her promise was no longer binding when she decided to make the payment.

56. 246 N.Y. 369 (1927).

57. Id. at 371, 372. This endorsement was in Mary Johnston's handwriting. Opinion of Judge Crosby, the trial judge. Record on Appeal, 18, HLS.

58. 124 N.Y. 538 (1891).

59. 246 N.Y. at 373.

60. Corbin, "Mr. Justice Cardozo and the Law of Contracts," 417–418.

61. Gilmore, *Death of Contract,* 60–64.

62. American Law Institute, *Restatement of Contracts,* I, §90 (1932); see Stanley Henderson, "Promissory Estoppel and Traditional Contract Doctrine," 78 *Yale Law Journal* 343 (1968).

63. 246 N.Y. at 374. Michael Townsend suggests that Cardozo's support for the doctrine of promissory estoppel was designed to assist the proponents of §90, which was under heavy attack in the discussions of the Restatement of Contracts in the American Law Institute. Townsend, "Cardozo's *Allegheny College* Opinion: A Case Study in Law as an Art," 33 *Houston Law Review* 1103 (1996).

64. Barnes v. Perine, 12 N.Y. 18 (1854). In later cases that followed *Barnes,* the connection between the promise and action by the promisee in reliance on it were more attenuated. See, for example, Keuka College v. Ray, 167 N.Y. 96 (1901).

65. 246 N.Y. at 374.

66. Id. at 375.

67. Ibid.

68. Ibid.

69. Id. at 379.

70. Richard Danzig's research turned up a witness who suggested a link between the partial payment and the letter of repudiation, but Cardozo and Kellogg cannot be faulted for their conclusions on that ground because they were limited to the record on appeal. Richard Danzig, unpublished Contracts teaching materials, IV-32—IV-33, KCC.

71. 246 N.Y. at 376–377.

72. The will that was probated was executed in 1935, subsequent to *Allegheny,* but there were doubtless earlier versions. A copy of Cardozo's will is in KCC.

73. Leon Lipson, "The Allegheny College Case," 23 *Yale Law Report* 8 (1977); Corbin, "Mr. Justice Cardozo and the Law of Contracts," 418; and Richard A. Posner, *Cardozo: A Study in Reputation,* 14, 93, note 2, 99, note 8 (1990).

74. Professor Alfred Konefsky, who has done a sentence-by-sentence analysis of Cardozo's opinion, agrees that the basis of the opinion was Cardozo's finding of consideration and that the major problem for Cardozo was the factual setting. But he also thinks that Cardozo expanded consideration while purporting to respect conventional doctrine. Alfred Konefsky, "How to Read, or at Least Not Misread, Cardozo in the *Allegheny College* Case," 36 *Buffalo Law Review* 645 (1987). Professor Konefsky's novel and interesting analysis exposes

every detail in the opinion. Although Konefsky discloses many flaws, he had considerably more time to analyze the opinion than Cardozo had to write it.

75. 233 App. Div. 753 (2d Dept. 1931).

76. Report in *Howard,* CM, Box 5, Folder 5852 (motion 42, Nov. 16, 1931).

77. See American Law Institute, *Restatement (Second) of Contracts* §90(2) (1981), text at note 38, where the relevant language is set forth.

18. Moral Obligation and Damages

1. 231 N.Y. 465 (1921).

2. Id. at 484, 486.

3. Id. at 491.

4. Letter from Cardozo to Felix Frankfurter, Sept. 16, 1921, FF. On the issues raised by a judge's confessing that she is voting to uphold what she believes to be bad policy, see Shirley Abrahamson, Susan Craighead, and Daniel Abrahamson, "Words and Sentences: Penalty Enhancement for Hate Crimes," 16 *University of Arkansas at Little Rock Law Journal* 515 (1994).

5. 231 N.Y. at 491.

6. 233 N.Y. 1 (1922).

7. N.Y. Const. 1894, Art. III, §28.

8. 234 N.Y. 377 (1923).

9. Id. at 385.

10. Id. at 390.

11. Blakeslee v. The Board of Water Commissioners, 106 Conn. 642, 655–656 (1927).

12. Walton Water Co. v. Village of Walton, 238 N.Y. 46, reargument denied, 238 N.Y. 555 (1924).

13. Id. at 50.

14. Id. at 51.

15. 231 N.Y. at 492.

16. 228 N.Y. 447 (1920).

17. See generally E. Allan Farnsworth, *Contracts,* 396–426 (2d ed. 1990) (one vol. ed.).

18. 228 N.Y. at 455.

19. Ibid.

20. Beatty v. Guggenheim Exploration Co., 225 N.Y. 380, 387 (1919). In Cammack v. Slattery & Bro., Inc., 241 N.Y. 39, 49 (1925), Cardozo, dissenting, would have allowed oral modification of a contract under seal.

21. 233 N.Y. 230 (1922).

22. Id. at 233–235.

23. 245 N.Y. 284, cert. denied, 275 U.S. 557 (1927).

24. 9 Exch. 341 (1854).

25. Case on Appeal in *Kerr,* 23, 55, and 56, HLS.

26. Case on Appeal, Exhibits A and B, 10, HLS.

27. 245 N.Y. at 287.

28. Id. at 291.

29. Id. at 290.

30. See chap. 16, text at notes 48 and 64.

31. See American Law Institute, *Restatement (Second) of Contracts,* III, §351(3), comment f, illustration 17 (1981), which adopts this notion of disproportionate results. The Reporters' Note states that the illustration was based on *Kerr.*

32. 245 N.Y. at 292.

33. 230 N.Y. 239 (1921). See Arthur L. Corbin, *Corbin on Contracts,* IIIA, 326–327 (1960).

34. 230 N.Y. at 240–241.

35. Further factual background of the case has been gathered in Richard Danzig, *The Capability Problem in Contract Law,* 108–128 (1978). His investigations suggest that other difficulties between the owner and the builder and not the use of non-Reading pipe were the main reasons for the refusal to pay the balance due. See also Todd D. Rakoff, "The Implied Terms of Contracts: Of 'Default Rules' and 'Situation Sense,'" in Jack Beatson and Daniel Friedmann, eds., *Good Faith and Fault in Contract Law,* 191 (1995) for a discussion of Cardozo's opinion in *Kent* as a good example of the useful method of analysis that Rakoff follows Karl Llewellyn in calling "situation sense."

36. These facts are discussed in Danzig, *Capability Problem,* 108–128, and Richard A. Posner, *Cardozo: A Study in Reputation,* 106–107 (1990).

37. 230 N.Y. at 243–244.

38. Id. at 243.

39. Id. at 241.

40. Id. at 242–243.

41. Id. at 245, 246.

42. McLaughlin quoted at length from Judge Comstock's opinion in Smith v. Brady, 17 N.Y. 173, 179, 186–187 (1858), to the effect that an owner has a right to have his building constructed as he wished, that the builder has no right to change the specifications, and that the owner is under no obligation to pay until the contract has been performed. Referring specifically to Comstock's opinion, the Court in Woodward v. Fuller stated, "But there has been a relaxation of that rule, and now on such a contract there may be a recovery without a literal or exact performance of it. It is now the rule, that where a builder has in good faith intended to comply with the contract, and has substantially complied with it, although there may be slight defects caused by inadvertence or unintentional omissions, he may recover the contract price, less the damage

on account of such defects . . . The defects must not run through the whole, or be so essential as that the object of the parties, to have a specified amount of work done in a particular way, is not accomplished." 80 N.Y. 312, 315–316 (1880). See also Nolan v. Whitney, 88 N.Y. 648 (1882), and Spence v. Ham, 163 N.Y. 220 (1900), reiterating the same legal principles.

43. 80 N.Y. at 316.

44. A motion for reargument urged the relevance of the explicit requirement that defective work be replaced. A per curiam three-sentence response stated that the court had not overlooked that specification. Like the original promise, it was an independent promise whose breach, when the defect was "trivial and innocent," gave rise only to a damage remedy. 230 N.Y. 656, 657 (1921).

45. See chap. 13, text at notes 18 and 50.

46. Danzig, *Capability Problem,* 108. *Kent* is included in eleven of the thirteen leading contracts casebooks. Lawrence A. Cunningham, "Cardozo and Posner: A Study in Contracts," 36 *William and Mary Law Review* 1379, 1459 (1995).

47. Letter from Cardozo to Dean Roscoe Pound, July 31, 1920, Roscoe Pound Papers, HLS.

48. Cardozo, *The Nature of the Judicial Process,* 71–72 (1921).

49. Id. at 44.

50. 251 N.Y. 72 (1929).

51. Id. at 77, 78. See also Brody v. Pecoraro, 250 N.Y. 56 (1928), for an opinion in which Cardozo unwrapped the facts to demonstrate a transfer of property in fraud of creditors. This was not a difficult task for one who had dealt with S. Webber Parker.

52. 235 N.Y. 162 (1923).

53. Id. at 166.

54. Exhibit attached to Record on Appeal in *Murray,* HLS.

55. In Haas Tobacco Co. v. American Fidelity Co., Cardozo in dissent would have excused an insured from giving a required notice of an accident to its insurer when a boy, knocked down by the insured's driver, had not seemed to be injured and had walked away. 226 N.Y. 343 (1919).

56. See Karl Llewellyn, "The Effect of Legal Institutions upon Economics," 15 *American Economic Review* 665 (1925) and Todd D. Rakoff, "Contracts of Adhesion: An Essay in Reconstruction," 96 *Harvard Law Review* 1173 (1983).

57. Samuel Williston, *The Law of Contracts,* §90B, note 14 (1st ed. 1920); Corbin, *Contracts,* III, §607, note 17 (1960 ed.).

58. Author interview with Joseph Paley (Jan. 23, 1958), KCC.

59. See discussion of Kettel v. Erie R. Co., chap. 14, text at note 29.

60. Cardozo, "Address at the Third Annual Meeting, American Law Institute," reprinted in 11 *American Bar Association Journal* 294, 296 (May 1925).

61. Arthur L. Corbin, "Mr. Justice Cardozo and the Law of Contracts," 52 *Harvard Law Review* 408–409 (1939).

62. See also Paul Gewirtz, "Remedies and Resistance," 92 *Yale Law Journal* 585, 666 (1983): "judges such as Cardozo are often praised for their ability to secure change in legal doctrine through a 'creative'—but not fully candid reading of precedent."

63. Cardozo, *The Paradoxes of Legal Science,* 37 (1928).

64. "I have credited Holmes and Williston with the design and execution of the great theory [the classical theory of contract]. It is tempting to set Cardozo and Corbin over against them as the engineers of its destruction. Tempting and by no means untrue." Grant Gilmore, *The Death of Contract,* 57 (1974).

19. Constitutional and International Law

1. See chap. 7, text at note 52.

2. In the celebrated case of Wynehamer v. People, 13 N.Y. 378 (1856), the court had held a general liquor prohibition statute unconstitutional under the New York Due Process Clause on the ground that its provisions forbidding sale except for sacramental or medicinal purposes made liquor that had already been lawfully purchased for general sale virtually worthless.

3. Bertholf v. O'Reilly, 74 N.Y. 509, 515 (1878).

4. 98 N.Y. 98 (1885). See Arnold Paul, *Conservative Crisis and the Rule of Law,* 1–18 (1969 ed.); Clyde Jacobs, *Law Writers and the Courts* (1954); and Edward Corwin, "The Doctrine of Due Process of Law Before the Civil War," 24 *Harvard Law Review* 366, 460 (1911) for a discussion of the debate over "freedom of contract" before 1914.

5. 198 U.S. 45 (1905).

6. 98 N.Y. at 114–115.

7. See also People v. Marx, 99 N.Y. 377 (1885) (holding unconstitutional a statute forbidding the manufacture or sale of any butter substitute) and People v. Gillson, 109 N.Y. 389 (1888) (holding unconstitutional a statute that prohibited any seller of an item of food from giving away any other item with it). But see People v. Arensberg, 105 N.Y. 123 (1887) (upholding, on the basis of preventing deception, a statute prohibiting butter substitutes that were colored to make them look like butter).

8. People v. King, 110 N.Y. 418 (1888).

9. People v. Budd, 117 N.Y. 1 (1889), aff'd, 143 U.S. 517 (1892). The statute was similar to the one that the United States Supreme Court had upheld in Munn v. Illinois, 4 Otto 113 (1876).

10. 117 N.Y. at 27.

11. Letter from Cardozo to Charles C. Burlingham, Aug. 14, 1936, CCB.

12. 117 N.Y. at 22.

13. Id. at 71.

14. Compare People ex rel. Nechamcus v. Warden, 144 N.Y. 529 (1895); Health Department v. Rector, 145 N.Y. 32 (1895); and People v. Havnor, 149 N.Y. 195 (1895), writ of error dismissed, 170 U.S. 408 (1898), all upholding regulatory efforts, with Forster v. Scott, 136 N.Y. 577 (1893); Colon v. Lisk, 153 N.Y. 188 (1897); People ex rel. Tyroler v. Warden, 157 N.Y. 116 (1898); and People v. Coler, 166 N.Y. 1 (1901), all striking down legislation.

15. 177 N.Y. 145 (1904), rev'd, 198 U.S. 45 (1905).

16. People v. Williams, 189 N.Y. 131 (1907).

17. People ex rel. Duryea v. Wilber, 198 N.Y. 1 (1910).

18. People v. Erie R. Co., 198 N.Y. 369 (1910), rev'd, 233 U.S. 671 (1914).

19. 201 N.Y. 271 (1911).

20. Workers' compensation or accident insurance laws were passed in twelve states by 1911. For a discussion of such legislation, see James Weinstein, *The Corporate Ideal in the Liberal State, 1900–1918,* 40–61 (1968).

21. 201 N.Y. at 302.

22. See Francis Bergan, *The History of the New York Court of Appeals, 1847–1932,* 245–246, 284–287 (1985) for further discussion of the events surrounding the *Ives* case and the effect of the case on the defeat of Judge Werner in the 1913 election contest for chief judge.

23. Charles O. Gregory, *Labor and the Law,* 76–82 (2d ed. 1961).

24. See National Protection Assn. v. Cumming, 170 N.Y. 315 (1902) (4–3) and Jacobs v. Cohen, 183 N.Y. 207 (1905), reargument denied, 184 N.Y. 524 (1906). But see People v. Marcus, 185 N.Y. 257 (1906), holding unconstitutional New York's anti–yellow dog criminal statute that prohibited employers from refusing to employ union members.

25. See Janet Lindgren, "Beyond Cases: Reconsidering Judicial Review," *1983 Wisconsin Law Review* 583, for a review of the constitutional due process cases in the New York Court of Appeals between 1870 and 1920 that explains the court's wavering path in terms of a dialogue between the court and the legislature.

26. 189 N.Y. 131 (1907).

27. 214 N.Y. 395 (1915), appeal dismissed, 242 U.S. 618 (1916).

28. 215 N.Y. 514 (1915). Only Chief Judge Bartlett and Judge Collin of the *Ives* court sat in Jensen, and both joined Miller's opinion.

29. Noble State Bank v. Haskell, 219 U.S. 104 (1911). The Court of Appeals decision in *Jensen* was reversed by the Supreme Court insofar as it applied the New York workers' compensation law to a stevedore engaged in maritime work because of conflict with federal admiralty jurisdiction. 244 U.S. 205 (1917). By then, the Supreme Court had already upheld the constitutionality of New York's workers' compensation law in New York Central R. Co. v. White, 243 U.S. 188 (1917), aff'g 216 N.Y. 653 (1915).

30. 219 N.Y. 383 (1916), overruling 182 N.Y. 330 (1905).

31. 219 N.Y. at 386.

32. 224 N.Y. 269 (1918).

33. Id. at 278.

34. Id. at 283.

35. See People ex rel. Alpha Portland Cement Co. v. Knapp, 230 N.Y. 48 (1920), reargument denied, 231 N.Y. 516, cert. denied, 256 U.S. 702 (1921) for an example of Cardozo's ingenuity in severing an unconstitutional portion of a tax statute to save the rest.

36. 243 N.Y. 51 (1926).

37. Id. at 54–56.

38. 248 N.Y. 454 (1928).

39. Id. at 459–460.

40. 225 N.Y. 89 (1919).

41. Id. at 96.

42. Compare People v. Weller, 237 N.Y. 316 (1924) (opinion by Lehman, joined by Cardozo, upholding licensing and price fixing provisions), aff'd, 268 U.S. 319 (1925) (upholding licensing provisions but not passing on price-fixing provisions) with Tyson v. Banton, 273 U.S. 418 (1927) (opinion by Sutherland, with Holmes, Brandeis, Stone, and Sanford dissenting, striking down the price-fixing provisions). But compare People ex rel. Durham Realty Co. v. La Fetra, 230 N.Y. 429 (1921) (opinion by Pound, joined by Cardozo, upholding, 6–1, the New York Rent Laws which forbade the ejectment of a defaulting tenant who was prepared to pay a reasonable rent fixed in a judicial proceeding) with Block v. Hirsh, 256 U.S. 135 (1921) (upholding a similar law).

43. 261 U.S. 525 (1923); letter from Cardozo to Felix Frankfurter, July 4, 1923, FF.

44. 248 N.Y. at 463.

45. 247 N.Y. 401 (1928).

46. Id. at 410.

47. Letter from Franklin Roosevelt to Cardozo, July 30, 1931, CCC, Box 1.

48. Letter from Cardozo to Harlan Fiske Stone, Aug. 13, 1931, LC.

49. *New York Times*, 1, 2, and 3 (July 28, 1931); 1, 2, and 4 (July 29, 1931); 1, 5 (Aug. 1, 1931); and 1, 16, and 17 (Aug. 11, 1931).

50. Matter of Doyle, 257 N.Y. 244 (1931). The story of the *Doyle* case and of the entire Seabury investigation is told in Herbert Mitgang, *The Man Who Rode the Tiger,* 159–310 (1966 ed.).

51. 176 N.Y. 253 (1903) and 142 U.S. 547 (1892). Actually, the holding in *Counselman* was that the immunity statute was insufficient since it did not even grant what has come to be known as "use" immunity, that is, it did not prohibit use of any information derived directly or indirectly from the compelled testi-

mony. But the Court went on to suggest that "transactional" immunity, that is, immunity covering any transaction relating to the testimony, was required. Cardozo's opinion followed the same course, pointing out first that immunity was not sufficient if clues from the testimony could form the links in establishing a chain of guilt, and then stating that in order to force disclosure, "the immunity must be so broad that the risk of prosecution is ended altogether." 257 N.Y. at 251. The constitutionality of "use" immunity has since been upheld in Kastigar v. United States, 406 U.S. 441 (1972).

52. INS v. Chadah, 462 U.S. 919 (1983) and Bowsher v. Synar, 478 U.S. 714 (1986) are modern cases involving a similar issue. In another case involving legislative power, Cardozo held for a unanimous court in his final opinion on the Court of Appeals that the statutory immunity from arrest in a civil action or proceeding did not shield a legislator from answering a subpoena to testify before a joint legislative investigation committee, although Cardozo also held that imprisonment as punishment for contempt of court for failure to answer the subpoena was not authorized by statute and hence was illegal. People ex rel. Hastings v. Hofstadter, 258 N.Y. 425 (1932).

53. People ex rel. Falk v. Sheriff, 258 N.Y. 437 (1932).

54. Letter from Cardozo to Joseph Paley, Aug. 28, 1931, JP.

55. Letter from Cardozo to Felix Frankfurter, Aug. 12, 1931, FF.

56. See W. Bernard Richland, "Constitutional City Home Rule in New York City," 54 *Columbia Law Review* 311, (1954), 55 id. 598 (1955).

57. See Gerald Frug, "The City As a Legal Concept," 93 *Harvard Law Review* 1059, 1109–1120 (1980) and Terrance Sandalow, "The Limits of Municipal Power Under Home Rule: A Role for the Courts," 48 *Minnesota Law Review* 643 (1964), for a summary of the development of legal doctrine and its relation to political theory and public events. The leading work on municipal corporations was Judge John F. Dillon, *Treatise on the Law of Municipal Corporations* (5th ed. 1911). His experience led him to contend that municipal governments were often run extravagantly and unwisely by those unfit to govern, and his remedy was strict legislative and judicial control over municipal governments.

58. See Joseph McGoldrick, *Law and Practice of Municipal Home Rule, 1916–1930,* 265–281 (1933) and Richland, "Constitutional City Home Rule," 327–328.

59. 241 N.Y. 96 (1925). The amendment was contained in New York Constitution, Art. XII, §§2 and 3 (1923).

60. 241 N.Y. at 124. When the issue had been less momentous, however, Cardozo was more friendly toward the exercise of local power. In People ex rel. New York City v. N.Y. R. Co., 217 N.Y. 310 (1916), Cardozo, joined by Seabury, would have allowed a city, which had been granted power to regulate

the streets, to compel a railroad to relocate its tracks on a street by virtue of that delegated power.

61. 251 N.Y. 467, reargument denied, 252 N.Y. 574 (1929).

62. Richland, "Constitutional City Home Rule," 330–331, notes that the cases relied on by Judge Crane were decided after the 1907 Constitution changed the key words "property, affairs or government" to "property, affairs of government" and that it was not accurate to state, as both Crane and Cardozo did, that those cases precisely governed the 1923 Amendment, which used the original form of the words. The courts simply ignored the change, which appears to have been made deliberately in 1907: the relevant enacting document bracketed the "or" and inserted the "of."

63. 251 N.Y. at 484.

64. Id. at 490.

65. Howard McBain, "The New York Proposal for Municipal Home Rule," 37 *Political Science Quarterly* 655 (1922). See Frug, "The City," 1113–1115, citing the work of Judge Thomas Cooley, Amasa Eaton, and Eugene McQuillen as contrary to McBain. Frug noted that the academic challenge to the McBain thesis, which built on the work of Judge Dillon, was rejected by the courts.

66. 251 N.Y. at 490–491.

67. Id. at 484.

68. Cardozo, "Jurisprudence," address before the New York State Bar Association, reprinted in Cardozo, *Selected Writings of Benjamin Nathan Cardozo*, 42–43 (Margaret Hall, ed., 1947).

69. New York Constitution, Art. XII, §3 (1923).

70. See chap. 9, text at note 54.

71. In Re Mayor of New York (Elm Street), 246 N.Y. 72 (1927). See also text at note 58.

72. Id. at 77–78.

73. 214 N.Y. 154 (1915).

74. George Hellman interview with Samuel Seabury (Apr. 10, 1939), CCC.

75. 214 N.Y. at 161.

76. The Supreme Court affirmed the decision of the Court of Appeals unanimously, on the ground that the state had power to prescribe the conditions under which public work might be accomplished. 239 U.S. 195 (1915), decided with Heim v. McCall, 239 U.S. 175 (1915). Strict scrutiny of classifications based on alienage began with Graham v. Richardson, 403 U.S. 365 (1971).

77. 222 N.Y. 192 (1918), writ of error dismissed, 251 U.S. 537 (1919).

78. Id. at 195.

79. 255 N.Y. 307 (1931).

80. Id. at 318.

81. Ibid.

82. On another occasion, Cardozo would have given some protection to

picketing itself. Steinkritz Amusement Co. v. Kaplan, 257 N.Y. 294 (1931) and Brooklyn United Theater v. International Alliance, 257 N.Y. 555 (1931).

83. The court itself recognized, in an opinion by Judge Pound shortly after Cardozo was appointed to the Supreme Court of the United States, that its labor law was "perhaps more favorable to the defendant [union] than that of the United States Supreme Court or other jurisdictions." Stillwell Theatre, Inc. v. Kaplan, 259 N.Y. 405, 410 (1932).

84. Report in Polin v. Kaplan, CM, Box 5, Folder 5484.

85. Polin v. Kaplan, 257 N.Y. 277, motion for reargument denied, 257 N.Y. 579 (1931).

86. See also Cardozo's concurrence in Pound's dissent in People v. Gitlow, 234 N.Y. 132, 154 (1922), chap. 27, text at note 23.

87. Cardozo, "Mr. Justice Holmes," 44 *Harvard Law Review* 682, 688 (1931).

88. 229 N.Y. 222, cert. denied, 254 U.S. 643 (1920).

89. This statute was repealed in 1922, two years after *Techt*. See Savorgnan v. United States, 338 U.S. 491, 501 (1950).

90. 229 N.Y. at 227.

91. Ibid.

92. Id. at 240.

93. Trop v. Dulles, 356 U.S. 86 (1958) (statute depriving a native-born soldier of citizenship upon military conviction of wartime desertion is unconstitutional). See also Afroyim v. Rusk, 387 U.S. 253 (1967) (statute removing citizenship from citizens who vote in foreign elections is unconstitutional).

94. 229 N.Y. at 243, 241, and 247.

95. Id. at 244–245.

96. 239 N.Y. 158, motion for reargument denied, 239 N.Y. 171 (1924). See 250 N.Y. 69 (1928) for further proceedings.

97. Petrogradsky M. K. Bank v. National City Bank, 253 N.Y. 23, motion for reargument denied, 254 N.Y. 563, cert. denied, 282 U.S. 878 (1930).

98. After the United States recognized the Soviet government, it recognized its decrees as well. For some of the consequences, see United States v. Belmont, 301 U.S. 324 (1937).

99. Similar principles led Cardozo to hold liable a Russian insurance company that had reinsured a British company's marine risks. The defense of nationalization was rejected on the ground that the unrecognized nationalization did not terminate the ability of the British company to reach the defendant's American assets. Nor did Great Britain's recognition of the Soviet government and the terms of its trade agreement with that government operate by eminent domain to wipe out the hitherto enforceable claims of its nationals. Fred S. James R. Co. v. Second Russian Ins. Co., 239 N.Y. 248, motion for reargument denied, 240 N.Y. 581 (1925). See American Law Institute, *Restatement (Second)*

of the Foreign Relations Law of the United States, §113, Reporters' Note (1965), stating that the rule of the section was "suggested by the reasoning of Judge Cardozo . . . in Sokoloff" and citing *Petrogradsky* and *James.*

100. Cardozo, *The Nature of the Judicial Process,* 76–94 (1921).

101. Id. at 87.

20. Criminal Law

1. Cardozo, "What Medicine Can Do for Law" (1928) in Cardozo, *Law and Literature and Other Essays and Addresses,* 70, 78 (1931).

2. See BNC Criminal Cases file, KCC, for a list of these cases.

3. 209 App. Div. 449 (4th Dept. 1924).

4. Report to the consultation in People v. Kasprzyk, 238 N.Y. 633 (1924) (affirming the judgment of the Appellate Division without opinion), CM, Box 2, Folder 1935.

5. 216 N.Y. 324 (1915), reargument denied, 216 N.Y. 762 (1916).

6. Id. at 327.

7. See Cardozo, *The Jurisdiction of the Court of Appeals,* 174 (2d ed. 1909).

8. Cardozo, "What Medicine Can Do for Law," 105.

9. 216 N.Y. at 329.

10. Whitman, who had been district attorney, had actually entered a personal appearance when Schmidt was tried, although one of his assistants tried the case. See Record on Appeal, ABCNY, and *New York Times,* 12 (Feb. 19, 1916). When the Court had stronger feelings that executive action was warranted, it said so explicitly. See text at note 31.

11. See Cardozo, "What Medicine Can Do for Law," 70, 93–94.

12. Letter from Cardozo to Edgar Nathan, Sr., Aug. 9, 1927, original in the possession of the Hendricks family, copy in KCC.

13. Letter from Cardozo to Victor Morawetz, Sept. 29, 1928, copy in FF.

14. Letter from Cardozo to Learned Hand, Aug. 20, 1927, LH, referring to Burlingham's letter published in the *New York Times,* 14 (Aug. 20, 1927).

15. 213 N.Y. 240 (1914).

16. Id. at 243, distinguishing People v. Sullivan, 7 N.Y. 396 (1852) and other cases.

17. See Cooper v. United States, 512 A.2d 1002 (D.C. App. 1986) and cases cited therein.

18. 254 N.Y. 192 (1930).

19. Id. at 194.

20. Cardozo, "What Medicine Can Do for Law," 98–100.

21. 254 N.Y. at 195.

22. 231 N.Y. 111, 128 (1921).

23. Id. at 127. The case referred to by Judge Crane was People v. Damron, 212 N.Y. 256 (1914).

24. 254 N.Y. at 129.

25. Letter from Cardozo to Felix Frankfurter, Sept. 14, 1921, FF.

26. 246 N.Y. 100 (1927). After a retrial, Cardozo joined a per curiam affirmance of a conviction of murder in the first degree.

27. Id. at 105. In two other cases in which Cardozo wrote opinions reversing convictions because of prejudicial trial error, the possibility of conviction of a capital crime was a factor. See People v. Van Aken, 217 N.Y. 532 (1916) and People v. Galbo, 218 N.Y. 283 (1916).

28. 254 N.Y. 565 (1930).

29. Report and draft in *Arata*, CM, Box 5, Folder No. 5140 (1930).

30. 255 N.Y. 374 (1931).

31. Letter from Cardozo to Felix Frankfurter, Apr. 4, 1931, FF.

32. 238 N.Y. 158 (1924).

33. See, for example, People v. Grutz, 212 N.Y. 72 (1914) and People v. Buffom, 214 N.Y. 53 (1915), in which Cardozo dissented from reversal of convictions for erroneous admission of evidence.

34. 223 N.Y. 519 (1918).

35. Id. at 520.

36. The court's per curiam opinion was substantially in the language of a portion of Cardozo's report to the consultation.

37. Report in People v. Carey, CM, Box 1, Folder 1060.

38. Ibid. Cardozo was willing to imagine situations in which the evidence would have "slight weight." He was prepared to deal with those when they arose. "An innocent defendant is not to suffer in one case lest perchance the complainant's sensibilities may be wounded in another." Ibid.

39. Radical feminists like Margaret Sanger, whose conviction he had just voted to uphold, proclaimed the social need for sexual equality. Perhaps more importantly, the availability of automobiles and the increasing independence of teenagers heralded a change in attitudes toward sexual activity. See John D'Emilio and Estelle Freedman, *Intimate Matters: A History of Sexuality in America,* 150–154, 233–235, and 239–242 (1988).

40. Cardozo, *The Nature of the Judicial Process,* 150 (1921).

41. Id. at 156.

42. 242 N.Y. 13 (1926), cert. denied, 270 U.S. 657 (1926).

43. 176 N.Y. 351 (1903).

44. 192 U.S. 585 (1904).

45. 232 U.S. 383 (1914).

46. 242 N.Y. at 21.

47. Ibid.

48. Id. at 22.

49. Id. at 23.

50. Id. at 23, 25.

51. 338 U.S. 25 (1949).

52. 367 U.S. 643 (1961).

53. United States v. Calandra, 414 U.S. 338, 348 (1974). See United States v. Leon, 468 U.S. 897 (1984).

54. 215 N.Y. 160, 163 (1915).

55. Id. at 166.

56. Id. at 169.

57. Ibid.

58. 225 N.Y. 25 (1918).

59. Id. at 30.

60. Id. at 33. Cardozo's interpretation of statutes phrased in terms of sufferance and permission continues to be cited and followed in modern New York case law. See, for example, Martin v. Sarafan, 35 N.Y.2d 83 (1974).

61. 225 N.Y. at 32, 33. Judge Crane, concurring, would have explicitly struck down the provision for imprisonment as unconstitutional. Judge Pound, while avoiding the issue in his concurrence, gave an opposing hint by noting that there was an argument that personal fault could be found whenever an underage child was found working in a company's business from the fact that the company had chosen to engage in a business in which child labor was not permitted. Id. at 34. Cardozo, somewhat surprisingly, did not let Pound's hint go unanswered. Perhaps there were some companies to which Pound's principles might apply, he wrote, but this was not one of them. Id. at 33.

62. The issue of the criminal responsibility of company officers for statutory violations when they lack the usual conscious awareness of fault that is implied by a requirement of "willful" or "knowing" violation continued to provoke controversy. See United States v. Dotterweich, 320 U.S. 277 (1943) and United States v. Park, 421 U.S. 658 (1975) for Supreme Court cases dealing with that issue in the context of federal statutes. See also Francis Sayre, "Criminal Responsibility for the Acts of Another," 43 *Harvard Law Review* 689 (1930) and Richard Wasserstrom, "Strict Liability in the Criminal Law," 12 *Stanford Law Review* 731 (1960).

63. 255 N.Y. 463 (1931).

64. Id. at 467.

65. 279 U.S. 1 (1929).

66. See chap. 13, text at note 50.

67. 255 N.Y. at 471.

68. Id. at 475.

69. 216 N.Y. 324, 329 (1915), reargument denied, 216 N.Y. 762 (1916), discussed in text at note 5.

70. Id. at 329–330.

71. Id. at 340.

72. For example, Francis Sayre, *A Selection of Cases on Criminal Law,* 502 (1927); Augustin Derby, *Cases on Criminal Law,* 318 (3d ed. 1930); and Jerome Michael and Herbert Wechsler, *Criminal Law and its Administration,* 814 (3d ed. 1940).

73. 216 N.Y. at 332.

74. Id. at 338.

75. Id. at 339. See Sheldon Glueck, *Mental Disorder and the Criminal Law,* 221–225 (1925) for some criticism of the assumptions in Cardozo's opinion regarding the ability of a mentally deluded person to reason normally on subjects unconnected with the delusion.

21. Property, Corporations, the Legal Profession, and Legislative Policy

1. Cardozo, *The Nature of the Judicial Process,* 54–56 (1921).

2. 256 N.Y. 41 (1931).

3. Report in Beers v. Hotchkiss, CM, Box 5, Folder 5331 (motion 14, Jan. 5, 1931).

4. "Memorandum on the status of New York Colonial Laws published or enacted prior to 1691; recording acts and the Statute of Frauds in New York Province, 1665–1775; town land and recording laws," from the Foundation for Research in American Legal History, signed by Julius Goebel, Jr., to Cardozo, undated, in Manuscripts, Addresses, and Essays, III, JP.

5. Professor Richard B. Morris of Columbia, another expert in colonial legal history, thought he had written a memorandum to Judge Cardozo about early American legal history, but he did not remember what the case or subject matter was. Letter from Richard B. Morris to author, Feb. 2, 1971, KCC. Today, communication of this sort by a judge with a legal historian would violate the Canons of Judicial Ethics unless the historian were appointed an expert by the court and the results of the research were disclosed to the parties. See Canon 3(B)(7)(a) and (b) of the Model Code of Judicial Conduct (1990) and Canon 3(A)(4) of the former Model Code of Judicial Conduct (1972). In Cardozo's time, however, there was no explicit prohibition and, on the basis of what judges and professional colleagues have told me, I believe that consultation between judges and academics was common. For a modern instance, see In re Fuchsberg, 43 N.Y.2d j, u–y (New York Court on the Judiciary 1978).

6. 256 N.Y. at 56.

7. Id. at 62–63.

8. Doctor v. Hughes, 225 N.Y. 305 (1919), was another well-known case in which Cardozo sought to put something of a modern face on ancient land law.

9. 250 N.Y. 554 (1929).

10. Report to the consultation in _Lonby,_ CM, Box 4, Folder 4173 (1928).

11. Hunter v. Trustees of Sandy Hill, 6 Hill 407, 414 (1844), as quoted in Cardozo's report to the consultation in _Lonby,_ CM.

12. 237 N.Y. 117 (1923).

13. Memorandum from Cardozo to the consultation, Sept. 5, 1923, accompanying his report in Stewart v. Turney, CM, Box 2, Folder 1652 (1923).

14. Ibid.

15. 224 N.Y. 483 (1918).

16. Id. at 490, 491, and 492.

17. See chap. 13, text at note 50.

18. 244 N.Y. 84 (1926) (5–2), discussed in chap. 14, note 22.

19. This was a point that he had made previously in Doran v. New York City Interborough R. Co., 239 N.Y. 448 (1925), in upholding a negligence suit by an employee of one railroad comprising the Third Avenue Railway System against another of the system's railroads. He rejected the argument that since the plaintiff was the employee of all the railroads comprising the system, his only remedy was workers' compensation. Cardozo's view of the separateness of the parent and subsidiary corporations was therefore not always antiplaintiff.

20. 244 N.Y. at 95. On reargument, the plaintiffs attempted to avoid the problem of the statute by arguing that the control contemplated by the statute required an agreement between the parent and subsidiary, whereas they were arguing that liability arose simply because the subsidiary acquiesced in direction by the parent of its activity. Cardozo rejected that proposed limitation of the statute as subversive of its purpose. 244 N.Y. 602 (1927). He followed what one contemporary commentator called the orthodox "corporate entity" view. Burt Franklin, "Corporations: Parent and Subsidiary," 12 _Cornell Law Quarterly_ 504 (1927). This approach viewed the purpose of the Public Service Commission Act as the protection of stockholders and creditors of the parent against diminution of assets and also the furtherance of the public's interest in "cheap, continuous and efficient operation" by prohibiting railroad companies from engaging in "improvident extensions" of their business without regulatory approval. 244 N.Y. at 92.

21. Id. at 94–95. See Robert C. Clark, _Corporate Law,_ 83–85 (1986) on the continued viability of the agency theory of parent liability in _Berkey_ situations.

22. Richard A. Posner, _Cardozo: A Study in Reputation,_ 119 (1990). The railroad's lawyer, in his opening statement, asserted that he had requested an extension of time to answer the complaint in order to decide whether to move to compel plaintiffs to file a bond. A motion had to be made before an answer was filed. Record on Appeal, 69, HLS.

23. Satterlee was J.P. Morgan's son-in-law and Stone was Harlan Fiske Stone, who was Dean of Columbia Law School when the suit was filed but also

managed to conduct a "moderately active practice" at the same time. Alpheus T. Mason, *Harlan Fiske Stone,* 89 (1956). Stone resigned as Dean and accepted a partnership at the Wall Street firm of Sullivan & Cromwell before the Berkeys' suit went to trial.

24. Cardozo was a strong believer in applying *Berkey* strictly. In Vampa v. Erie R. Co., 257 N.Y. 519 (1931), the court affirmed, without opinion, a judgment of the Appellate Division that permitted a passenger injured on a subsidiary of the Erie to go to the jury in a suit against the Erie. Cardozo was one of three who dissented without opinion. His memorandum to the consultation argued first that there was no evidence of negligence by the Erie dispatcher in connection with the accident, but he spent more time arguing the applicability of *Berkey* on the ground that it was plain that the Erie had not used the subsidiary as its agent. CM, Box 5, Folder 5686.

25. 221 N.Y. 81, reargument denied, 221 N.Y. 667 (1917), cert. denied, 246 U.S. 661 (1918).

26. Id. at 84, 91.

27. See chap. 19, text at note 55.

28. 214 N.Y. 255, 258–259 (1915).

29. 227 N.Y. 366 (1919), reargument denied, 228 N.Y. 585 (1920).

30. 248 N.Y. 465 (1928).

31. Id. at 470.

32. Id. at 477.

33. Id. at 478.

34. Id. at 480.

35. See chap. 14, text at note 36.

36. See also In re Kaufmann, 245 N.Y. 423 (1927), for which Cardozo wrote an opinion reversing the Appellate Division's conclusion that it had no power to undo the disbarment of two lawyers convicted of crime, even after they had been pardoned by President Coolidge on the basis of Attorney General Stone's report that they were innocent. Cardozo concluded that the pardon removed the bar to reconsideration. The "honor of the profession does not demand the sacrifice of the innocent." Id. at 429. See also In re Schwarz, 231 N.Y. 642 (1921), where he joined Pound's dissent from the disbarment of a lawyer for solicitation by letter of former clients. Pound thought disbarment appropriate only for serious offenses relating to character defects and questioned whether mass solicitation by letters addressed to 4,500 former clients of a collection business could be regarded as any violation of professional ethics at all.

37. 242 N.Y. 38 (1926).

38. Id. at 52.

39. 244 N.Y. 424 (1927).

40. 244 N.Y. 530 (1926), motion for reargument denied, 244 N.Y. 603 (1927).

41. 215 App. Div. 220 (3d Dept. 1926).

42. Report in *O'Brien,* CM, Box 3, Folder 3009 (1926).

43. 226 App. Div. 656 (1st Dept. 1929).

44. CM, Box 4, Folder 4370 (motion 14, May 27, 1929).

45. Wilcox v. The Teachers' Retirement Board is a nearly identical case in which Cardozo reached the same conclusion and recommended denial of a motion for leave to appeal. CM, Box 4, Folder 4623 (motion 21, Jan. 6, 1930). When the court considered a similar issue in a written opinion, it was equally rigid. See Matter of Creveling v. Teachers' Retirement Board, 255 N.Y. 364 (1931).

46. 232 N.Y. 66 (1921). Pierpont claimed through McCoun and did not contest McCoun's title.

47. Id. at 71.

48. See chap. 13, text at note 5.

49. Yonkers v. Federal S.R. Co., 221 N.Y. 206, reargument denied, 222 N.Y. 586 (1917).

50. Id. at 210–211.

51. In another case Cardozo protected government finances against unlawful charges by government employees by labeling innocent, but mistaken, conduct as "fraud." Smith v. Hedges, 223 N.Y. 176 (1918).

52. 213 N.Y. 34 (1914).

53. Id. at 35, 36.

22. A Puzzle, Candor, and Style

1. 236 N.Y. 156, reargument denied, 236 N.Y. 643 (1923).

2. Cardozo, *The Growth of the Law,* 105–106 (1924).

3. 246 N.Y. 571 (1927).

4. 89 N.Y. 644 (1882).

5. The dissenting opinion was not published but was later discussed in Abbe v. Abbe, 22 App. Div. 483 (2d Dept. 1897).

6. Or at least so Cardozo later said in Schubert v. August Schubert Wagon Co., 249 N.Y. 253, 255 (1928).

7. Report in Allen v. Allen, CM, Box 3, Folder 3294.

8. 246 N.Y. 571 (1927).

9. Ibid.

10. Report in Allen v. Allen, CM, Box 3, Folder 3294.

11. *Allen* was eventually overturned not by the Court but by the legislature. See New York Laws 1937, chap. 669.

12. Report on motion for leave to appeal in Forman v. J. Weil Holding Co., CM, Box 3, Folder 2622 (motion 13, February 23, 1926).

13. 248 N.Y. 626 (1928), CM, Box 3, Folder 3833 (1928).

14. Memorandum, July 9, 1928, attached to draft opinion in *Sorrentino*, CM.

15. Draft opinion in *Sorrentino*, CM.

16. Ibid.

17. Ibid.

18. Ibid.

19. Ibid.

20. See chap. 18, text after note 28.

21. Draft opinion in *Sorrentino*, CM.

22. Ibid.

23. The issue recurred. In Cannon v. Cannon, 287 N.Y. 425 (1942) and Badigian v. Badigian, 9 N.Y.2d 472 (1961), the Court of Appeals reaffirmed *Sorrentino*. In the latter case, Judge Fuld dissented and resurrected portions of Cardozo's memorandum in *Sorrentino* as part of his opinion. Finally, in Gelbman v. Gelbman, 23 N.Y.2d 434 (1969), the Court of Appeals overruled *Sorrentino*.

24. After *Sorrentino*, Cardozo had an opportunity to reconsider his position in *Allen*. He declined to do so, recommending that the court deny a motion for leave to appeal in Clayburgh v. Clayburgh, which involved a tort suit by a wife, who was separated from her husband, against her husband for malicious prosecution of a divorce. CM, Box 4, Folder 4655 (motion 7 of Jan. 13, 1930).

25. 249 N.Y. 253 (1928).

26. Id. at 258.

27. See Karl Llewellyn, *The Common Law Tradition*, 358 (1960) and Richard A. Posner, *Cardozo: A Study in Reputation*, 11–19 (1990), summarizing the critique.

28. *Allegheny College* seems to fit that category and some would add MacPherson v. Buick, although I would not.

29. Jacob & Youngs v. Kent and De Cicco v. Schweizer seem to me to be examples of that sort.

30. Cardozo, "Law and Literature," published in 14 *Yale Review,* 699 (July 1925), and reprinted in Cardozo, *Law and Literature and Other Essays and Addresses,* 3 (1931). Id. at 9.

31. Id. at 10.

32. Id. at 14–15.

33. Id. at 25–26.

34. Id. at 40.

35. Anon Y. Mous [Jerome Frank], "The Speech of Judges: A Dissenting Opinion," 29 *Virginia Law Review* 625, 629–634, 639–641 (1943). See G. Edward White, *The American Judicial Tradition*, 272, 499, note 102 (Expanded ed. 1988).

36. Mark De Wolfe Howe, Book Review, *New York Herald Tribune*, 14

(Mar. 31, 1940); author interview with Felix Frankfurter, 41 (Aug. 20 and 21, 1960), KCC; and Frankfurter, "Benjamin Nathan Cardozo," in *Dictionary of American Biography,* 95 (Supp. 2 1958).

37. Zechariah Chafee, Jr., "Mr. Justice Cardozo," *Harpers Magazine* 40 (June 1932). See Richard H. Weisberg, *When Lawyers Write,* 249 (1987), citing Chafee as an example of a writer on legal language who wrote well.

38. Id. at 253–255; Richard H. Weisberg, "Law, Literature and Cardozo's Judicial Poetics," 1 *Cardozo Law Review* 283, 308–320 (1979).

39. Beryl Levy, *Cardozo and Frontiers of Legal Thinking,* 83–111 (rev. ed. 1969).

40. Posner, *Cardozo,* 22, 57.

41. Coler v. Corn Exchange Bank, 250 N.Y. 136, 141 (1928).

42. Berkey v. Third Avenue Railway, 244 N.Y. 84, 94 (1926).

43. Cardozo, *The Nature of the Judicial Process,* 51 (1921).

44. Wagner v. International R. Co., 232 N.Y. 176, 180 (1921).

45. Murphy v. Steeplechase Amusement Co., 250 N.Y. 479, 483 (1929).

46. Ultramares Corp. v. Touche, 255 N.Y. 170, 180 (1931).

47. Meinhard v. Salmon, 249 N.Y. 458, 464 (1928).

48. Hamilton v. Regents of the University of California, 293 U.S. 245, 265, 268 (1934).

49. Palko v. Connecticut, 302 U.S. 319, 327 (1937).

50. People ex rel. Alpha Portland Cement Co. v. Knapp, 230 N.Y. 48, 63 (1920).

51. Cardozo, *Growth of the Law,* 133.

52. Carter v. Carter Coal Co., 298 U.S. 238, 327 (1936).

53. Cardozo, "Mr. Justice Holmes," 44 *Harvard Law Review* 682, 686 (1931).

23. Appointment

1. For a more detailed account of Cardozo's appointment, including his earlier consideration, see Andrew L. Kaufman, "Cardozo's Appointment to the Supreme Court," 1 *Cardozo Law Review* 23 (1979).

2. Merlo J. Pusey, *Charles Evans Hughes,* II, 680–682 (1951); Sheldon M. Novick, *Honorable Justice,* 375 (1989).

3. *New York Sun,* 24 (Jan. 14, 1932).

4. *New York Herald-Tribune,* 10 (Jan. 22, 1932).

5. Cardozo, "Jurisprudence," reprinted in Cardozo, *Selected Writings of Benjamin Nathan Cardozo,* 7–46 (Margaret Hall, ed., 1947).

6. The most important pieces were Roscoe Pound, "The Call for a Realist Jurisprudence," 44 *Harvard Law Review* 697 (1931) and Karl Llewellyn, "Some Realism About Realism: Responding to Dean Pound," id. at 1222. See

also William W. Fisher, Morton J. Horwitz, and Thomas A. Reed, eds., *American Legal Realism*, 49–52 (1993) for a concise summary of the debate. Although Jerome Frank helped in the conception and research on Llewellyn's article, he did not think he should receive credit as an author because he did no actual writing. Edward A. Purcell, *The Crisis of Democratic Theory: Scientific Naturalism & the Problem of Value*, 285, note 37 (1973).

7. Letter from Cardozo to Felix Frankfurter, Aug. 21, 1931, FF.

8. Letter from Cardozo to Felix Frankfurter, Aug. 29, 1931, FF.

9. Cardozo, "Jurisprudence," 10–11.

10. Id. at 13.

11. Letter from Cardozo to Felix Frankfurter, Aug. 29, 1931, FF.

12. Cardozo, "Jurisprudence," 11, 15.

13. Id. at 37, 46.

14. Fisher, Horwitz, and Reed, eds., *American Legal Realism*, 3.

15. *New York Herald Tribune*, 4 (Jan. 23, 1932); *New York Times*, 5 (Jan. 23, 1932).

16. Letter from Jerome N. Frank to Cardozo, Sept. 9, 1932, Jerome N. Frank Papers, Group No. 222, Series No. 1, Box 2, Manuscripts and Archives, Yale University Library, New Haven, Conn.

17. Jerome N. Frank, *Law and the Modern Mind*, 134, 236, and 237 (1930).

18. Cox never completed the book. His papers contain the beginnings of drafts of various chapters, but it is apparent that he never progressed very far. He did send some early draft chapters to Cardozo, who replied, "I was tempted to read your manuscript, though really it was wrong to do so. No man should read such things about himself, or seem to give them his approval. That is the view Holmes took about some of the books that were written about him. He refused to cooperate in advance of the event. Well, I fell anyhow, if reading is a fall . . . What you have said about the law in general, I like. But I fear my philosophy comes out as a pretty thin product, or no philosophy at all. Thanks, my dear man, but don't send me the later instalments. Let me have a surprise—a pleasurable shock—when I read the published book." Letter from Cardozo to Cox, April 18, 1933, Oscar Cox Papers, Box 134, Cox Drafts (II), Franklin D. Roosevelt Library, Hyde Park, N.Y.

19. Letter from Jerome Frank to Oscar Cox, Dec. 6, 1931; letter from Cox to Cardozo, Dec. 7, 1931; and letter from Cardozo to Cox, Dec. 8, 1931, all in ibid., Box 135, Correspondence (I).

20. See N. E. H. Hull, "Some Realism about the Llewellyn-Pound Exchange Over Realism: The Newly Uncovered Private Correspondence, 1927–1931," *1987 Wisconsin Law Review* 921, 940–953.

21. Letter from Jerome Frank to Cardozo, Sept. 9, 1932, 28–30, Frank Papers, Group No. 222, Series No. 1, Box 2, Manuscripts and Archives, Yale University Library, New Haven, Conn.

22. Ibid., Appendix, 23, quoting from Frank, *Law and the Modern Mind,* 137.

23. Letter from Cardozo to Jerome Frank, Sept. 16, 1932, Frank Papers, Manuscripts and Archives, Group No. 222, Series No. 1, Box 2, Yale University Library, New Haven, Conn.

24. He even attacked the title of *The Nature of the Judicial Process* as misleading because the text was limited to the appellate judicial process. Frank argued that Cardozo's views were severely defective for ignoring the very different judicial processes of the trial courts. Jerome Frank, "Cardozo and the Upper-Court Myth," 13 *Law and Contemporary Problems* 369 (1948). But Cardozo had made it abundantly clear in his lectures that he was addressing the role of an appellate judge. He was, after all, explaining his own job.

25. Silas Bent, *Justice Oliver Wendell Holmes,* 322 (1932); Francis Biddle, *Mr. Justice Holmes,* 192 (1942).

26. Erwin N. Griswold, "The Judicial Process," 28 *The Record of the Association of the Bar of the City of New York* 14, 15 (1973).

27. See Leroy Ashby, *The Spearless Leader: Senator Borah and the Progressive Movement in the 1920's,* 260–283 (1972).

28. Letter from Herbert Hoover to Irving Dilliard, July 22, 1938, in "Appointment of Cardozo—Judiciary—Supreme Court" folder in Presidential Papers, HHP.

29. Letters from Herbert Hoover to author, May 25 and May 28, 1958, KCC. Hoover's secretary did some research after he had written Dilliard and discovered that there was no White House visit. Letter from Bernice Miller to Lawrence Richey, Oct. 12, 1939, in "Cardozo Appointment" file, HHP.

30. Mitchell had earned a reputation as a first-rate Attorney General after also having served as Solicitor General. He had spoken sympathetically of the recent emphasis on the quality, as opposed to the politics, of potential appointees. See William D. Mitchell, "Appointment of Federal Judges," 17 *American Bar Association Journal* 569 (1931). Mitchell was also aware that, to some degree, "the predilections of the Justices, born of their experiences with human affairs, have tended to affect their conclusions." Address by William D. Mitchell, "Proceedings in Memory of Mr. Justice Van Devanter," reprinted in 316 U.S. at xvi, xxi (1942). Although Mitchell was a Democrat, he favored retaining the states as a primary locus of power in dealing with social and economic problems. See Mitchell, "The Abdication by the States of Powers Under the Constitution," 17 *American Bar Association Journal* 811 (1931).

31. Letter from Willis Van Devanter to Mrs. J. W. Lacey, Jan. 11, 1932, in Van Devanter Papers, LC.

32. Letter from Willis Van Devanter to Frank Kellogg (former Senator from Minnesota and Secretary of State under President Coolidge), Mar. 10, 1932, in Van Devanter Papers, LC.

33. Letter from Willis Van Devanter to Frank Kellogg, Jan. 14, 1932, in Van Devanter Papers, LC.

34. Letter from Charles E. Hughes to Charles E. Hughes, Jr., quoted without date in Pusey, *Hughes,* II, 682.

35. Memorandum attached to letter from Mark Sullivan to Lawrence Richey, Jan. 18, 1932 (unsigned and typed), requesting Richey to pass it on to the President, in "Cardozo Appointment" file, HHP; see letter from Mark Sullivan, Jr., Mark Sullivan's son, to author, Feb. 26, 1973, KCC, identifying the handwriting as that of his father. In the period between Jan. 11 and Feb. 15, 1932, Sullivan is recorded as the most frequent guest at the White House, having had breakfast with the President six times and dinner once. See "Calendar," in Presidential Papers, HHP.

36. Telegram from William E. Borah to Stephen S. Wise, Jan. 15, 1932, SSW; letter from Stephen Wise to Felix Frankfurter, Jan. 19, 1932, FF. This letter and a subsequent memorandum from Wise to Frankfurter and Judge Julian Mack of the Court of Appeals for the Second Circuit, dated Mar. 8, 1932, are the sources of many of the accounts of Cardozo's nomination. Kaufman, "Cardozo's Appointment," 44–45. Wise, who realized the importance of drumming up support for Cardozo from the West and the South, spurred such activity. See telegrams from Stephen Wise to Richard W. Montagu, Portland, Oregon, and Sidney Herold, Shreveport, Louisiana, Jan. 16, 1932, SSW.

37. Liva Baker, *Felix Frankfurter,* 13–34 (1969).

38. Diary of Henry Stimson, entry for Jan. 22, 1932, in Henry L. Stimson Papers, Manuscripts and Archives, Yale University Library, New Haven, Conn.; letter from Felix Frankfurter to Henry Stimson, Feb. 9, 1932, ibid.

39. Gerald Gunther, *Learned Hand,* 428 (1994).

40. There were petitions signed by nearly all members of the faculties of the Columbia, Yale, Pennsylvania, Chicago, Indiana, and Illinois Law Schools. Petitions from all but Indiana Law School are in the "Benjamin Cardozo" file in Department of Justice Records, National Personnel Center, General Services Administration, St. Louis, Mo. The Indiana Law School petition accompanied a letter from Professor Hugh Willis to Walter Newton, Jan. 26, 1932, in "Cardozo Appointment" file, HHP. The impetus for this outpouring came from Dean Albert Harno of Illinois and Dean Young B. Smith of Columbia law schools. See the exchange of telegrams between Dean Harno and Dean Smith, Jan. 14, 1932, and Jan. 15, 1932, copies in SSW.

41. Alpheus T. Mason, *Harlan Fiske Stone,* 266–289 (1956). The "medicine ball" cabinet was a group of Hoover's friends who threw a medicine ball around with him in the early morning.

42. Letter from Harlan F. Stone to George Hellman, Nov. 30, 1939, quoted in Mason, *Stone,* 336.

43. Letter from Harlan F. Stone to Felix Frankfurter, Jan. 28, 1932, in the

Harlan Fiske Stone Papers, LC; Alpheus Mason interview with Professor Walter Gellhorn of Columbia Law School, then Stone's law clerk, quoted in Mason, *Stone,* 336. See letter from Stone to Felix Frankfurter, Feb. 9, 1932, Stone Papers, LC, thanking him for producing a memorandum on Phillips's opinions.

44. Letter from Walter Newton to the Editor, *New York Times,* 22 (Nov. 22, 1938).

45. *New York Times,* 2 (Jan. 15, 1932). See also Ira Carmen, "The President, Politics and the Power of Appointment: Hoover's Nomination of Mr. Justice Cardozo," *55 Virginia Law Review* 616 (1969).

46. *New York Times,* 15 (Jan. 14, 1932). The day after Cardozo's nomination, the *Times* reported that Norris had favored Cardozo's selection from the moment of Holmes's retirement. Id. at 1 (Feb. 16, 1932).

47. Letters and telegrams came from Newton Baker, Cleveland lawyer and former Secretary of War in the Wilson administration; an individual letter and a telegram came from Samuel Seabury, Cardozo's former colleague on the Court of Appeals and, at the time, president of the New York State Bar Association, reporting the formal endorsement of Cardozo by the State Bar at its annual meeting; and a letter from William Green, president of the AFL, supporting Cardozo as well as some others. In addition, there were letters from New Orleans (Monte Lemann, well-known lawyer, Harvard Law School classmate and friend of Felix Frankfurter); Michigan (Judge Henry Butzel of the Michigan Supreme Court); Oregon (the president and six former presidents of the Oregon Bar Association, two judges, and an ex-United States Senator); San Francisco (former Judge M. C. Sloss of the California Supreme Court); Chicago (Lessing Rosenthal); and from other cities throughout the country. See the "Benjamin Cardozo" file in Department of Justice Records, National Personnel Center, General Services Administration, St. Louis, Mo.

48. See Kaufman, "Cardozo's Appointment," 46.

49. Herbert Hoover, *Memoirs,* II, 268 (1952).

50. Letter from Herbert Hoover to George W. Wickersham, Feb. 17, 1932, and letter from Wickersham to Hoover, Feb. 15, 1932. "Cardozo Appointment," file, HHP.

51. Kaufman, "Cardozo's Appointment," 44–45.

52. Stone reported that Hoover had mentioned receiving an objection that Cardozo as a Jew was not "socially" acceptable but that Stone had replied to Hoover that Cardozo was a member of the exclusive Century Club to which the objector, who was not named, could never gain admission. Mason, *Stone,* 337.

53. Zechariah Chafee, "Mr. Justice Cardozo," *Harpers,* 34 (June 1932).

54. Author interview with Joseph Paley, (Jan. 23, 1958), KCC; Telephone Memorandum of President Hoover's calls for Feb. 15, 1932, in "Telephone Calls," HHP.

55. Letter from Oliver W. Holmes to "My Dear Brethren," Jan. 12, 1932, 284 U.S. at vi (1932).

56. Letter from Cardozo to Oliver W. Holmes, Jan. 13, 1932, in Oliver W. Holmes Papers, HLS.

57. Letter from Cardozo to Annie Nathan Meyer, Jan. 23, 1932, in Annie Nathan Meyer Papers, American Jewish Archives, Cincinnati, Ohio.

58. Letter from Cardozo to Felix Frankfurter, Jan. 19, 1932, FF.

59. Letter from Cardozo to Harlan F. Stone, Jan. 30, 1932, in Stone Papers, LC.

60. Author's interview with Joseph M. Palcy (Jan. 23, 1958), KCC.

61. Letter from Stephen Wise to Felix Frankfurter, Jan. 19, 1932, FF.

62. See chap. 10, text at note 40.

63. Letter from Cardozo to Harlan F. Stone, Jan. 20, 1932, in Stone Papers, LC.

64. Notes of Robert Marshall after dinner with Cardozo, Apr. 16, 1932, original in possession of George Marshall family, copy in KCC.

65. See the selection of commentary from all over the country in *New York Times,* 3 (Feb. 16, 1932); "Benjamin Cardozo" file, Department of Justice Records, National Personnel Center, General Services Administration, St. Louis, Mo.

66. Letter from Learned Hand to Herbert Hoover, Feb. 24, 1932, ibid.

67. Letter from A. N. Hand to Henry T. Kellogg, Feb. 18, 1932, copy of extract in Cardozo file, FF.

68. Although there was no official report of the hearing before the subcommittee of the Judiciary Committee, it was summarized in the *New York Times,* 2 (Feb. 20, 1932).

69. *New York Times,* 3 (Feb. 24, 1932).

70. 258 N.Y. v (1932).

71. Letter from Jerome Frank to Cardozo, Feb. 18, 1932, Frank Papers, Group No. 222, Series No. 1, Box 2, Manuscripts and Archives, Yale University Library, New Haven, Conn.

72. Letter from Cardozo to Jerome Frank, Feb. 19, 1932, ibid.

73. Letter from Cardozo to Nicholas Murray Butler, Feb. 26, 1932, copy in CCC, Box 9; letter from Cardozo to Cyrus Adler, American Jewish Committee, *26th Annual Report,* 35 (1933). The de Tocqueville essay, which was entitled "The Judicial Power," discussed many Supreme Court decisions. A copy is in CCC, Box 13. See also letter from Butler to George Hellman, Oct. 13, 1938, mentioning Cardozo's decision not to publish it. The essay put much of Cardozo's earlier extrajudicial writing into a constitutional law setting.

74. Letter from Rodman Gilder to George Hellman, Mar. 21, 1939, CCC, Box 1.

75. Letter from Cardozo to Louise Wise, Mar. 11, 1932, SSW.

76. Letter from Stephen S. Wise to Richard W. Montague, Jan. 20, 1932, SSW.

77. 75 Cong. Rec. 4632 (Feb. 24, 1932); 258 N.Y. v (1932); *New York Times,* 15 (Mar. 4, 1932), and 23 (Mar. 15, 1932).

24. Life in Washington

1. Notes of Robert Marshall, made after dinner with Cardozo, Apr. 16, 1932, original in possession of George Marshall family, copy in KCC. Except where otherwise specifically noted, the remaining information in this chapter about Cardozo's life in Washington is a composite of the author's interviews with Cardozo's law clerks Melvin Siegel (June 26, 1958), Ambrose Doskow (Jan. 18, 1961), Alan Stroock (April 19, 1961), and Joseph Rauh (July 2, 1958), and with his secretary Percy Russell (June 16, 1961), all in KCC. The law clerks recounted some of the same information in Joseph Rauh, Melvin Siegel, Ambrose Doskow, and Alan Stroock, "A Personal View of Justice Benjamin N. Cardozo: Recollections of Four Cardozo Law Clerks," 1 *Cardozo Law Review* 5 (1979).

2. Notes of Robert Marshall, Apr. 16, 1932, original in possession of George Marshall family, copy in KCC.

3. Letter from Cardozo to Mary Hun, Apr. 16, 1932, copy in KCC; letter from Cardozo to Aline Goldstone, May 17, 1932, original in possession of Goldstone family, excerpt in KCC; letter from Cardozo to Annie Nathan Meyer, Apr. 23, 1932, Annie Nathan Meyer Papers, American Jewish Archives, Cincinnati, Oh.

4. Letter from Cardozo to Felix Frankfurter, May 27, 1932, FF.

5. Columbia had given him an honorary degree in 1915, and Harvard, Yale, Michigan, Chicago, New York University, Brown, Yeshiva, Brooklyn, and the University of London also conferred honorary degrees upon him. CCC, Box 10.

6. Letters from Cardozo to Joseph Paley, June 11, July 25, and Aug. 1, 1932, JP.

7. Letters from Cardozo to Felix Frankfurter, July 23, Aug. 3, and Aug. 29, 1932, FF; author interviews with Siegel, 4, and Percy Russell, KCC.

8. Letters from Cardozo to Felix Frankfurter, Oct. 4 and Nov. 2, 1937, FF. Rauh became a leading civil rights lawyer and chairman of the Americans for Democratic Action.

9. Author interview with Joseph L. Rauh, Jr., 2, KCC; letters from Cardozo to Felix Frankfurter, Dec. 2 and 6, 1935, Feb. 26, 1936, Mar. 4, 1936, Apr. 9 and 18, 1936; letters from Frankfurter to Cardozo, Dec. 13, 1935, Mar. 3, 1936, and Apr. 13 and 30, 1936, FF.

10. Author interview with Harry Hayes (Jan. 25, 1958), KCC.

11. Author interview with Siegel, 34, KCC. Siegel heard the comment inadvertently.

12. George Hellman interview with Kate Tracy (Nov. 18, 1938), CCC, Box 9.

13. Author interview with Rauh, 39–40, KCC.

14. Letter from Cardozo to Elvira Solis, Mar. 7, 1935, original in possession of Rosalie Nathan Hendricks family, copy in KCC.

15. Cardozo, "Mr. Justice Holmes," 44 *Harvard Law Review* 682, 690 (1931).

16. Letter from Oliver Wendell Holmes to Cardozo, Dec. 15, 1928, original in possession of the family of Joseph L. Rauh, Jr., copy in KCC.

17. Merlo Pusey, *Charles Evans Hughes,* II, 690 (1951).

18. George Hellman, *Benjamin N. Cardozo,* 273 (1940).

19. Author interview with Joseph Paley (Jan. 23, 1958), KCC.

20. Author interview with Paul Freund (July 1961), KCC; see Cardozo, appointment book for 1937 (Nov. 25 and Dec. 24, 1937), original in possession of Joseph Rauh family, copy in KCC.

21. Author interview with Siegel, 43–46, KCC; *New York Times,* 19 (July 12, 1938).

22. Interview with Frederic Coudert, 122 (1949–1950), COHP part I.

23. The first version derives from author interview with Siegel, 29–31, KCC. Siegel reported hearing the story from Herbert Wechsler, Stone's law clerk. Wechsler remembered being told the story but did not remember the details. Letter from Wechsler to author, undated, in response to letter from author to Wechsler, Aug. 29, 1984, KCC. See also James E. Bond, *I Dissent: The Legacy of Chief Justice James Clark McReynolds,* 54 (1992) ["Chief Justice" is an error], which quotes McReynolds as saying that "one need only be a Jew and the son of a criminal to be appointed to this Court." The original source of the story was Justice Stone, but he never wanted to be quoted directly. Letter from George Hellman to Harlan F. Stone, May 23, 1939, and letter from Stone to Hellman, May 29, 1939, Harlan F. Stone Papers, LC, Container 16.

24. Paul A. Freund, at a talk delivered before the Harvard Law School Forum, Mar. 7, 1977, KCC (author's notes).

25. Author interview with Russell (June 16, 1961), KCC.

26. Letter from Cardozo to Felix Frankfurter, Apr. 7, 1932, FF.

27. Letter from Harlan Stone to Felix Frankfurter, Oct. 18, 1935, Stone Papers, Container 13; author interviews with Stroock and Joseph Rauh, KCC.

28. Joseph Paley, his longtime Court of Appeals law clerk, did not report excessive praise of his work, and there was no hint of it in Cardozo's lengthy correspondence with Paley.

29. Author interview with Rauh, 64, KCC.

30. Author interview with Herbert Wechsler (Mar. 26, 1962), KCC; author interview with Siegel, 39–40, KCC.

31. Author interview with Siegel, 31, KCC.

32. Author interview with Doskow, KCC.

33. Author interview with Learned Hand, 19 (Nov. 12, 1957), KCC. The actual color of his eyes was an issue: "It has always been a subject of contention in my family as to just what sort of eyes I have. The prevailing opinion has been that they are colored like unto a cat's." Letter from Cardozo to Rosalie Nathan Hendricks, Mar. 4, 1935, original in possession of the Rosalie Nathan Hendricks family, copy in KCC. Later, he told Judge Pound that they were "hazel." *Boston Evening Transcript* (Feb. 17, 1932).

34. Author interview with Rauh, 4, 60–61, KCC. During his interview, Rauh wondered whether, considering what he had since learned about life and about people's motivations, he would have the same reactions to Cardozo if he could go through his experience again.

35. Stroock's observations about meals for guests being elegantly served were echoed by Dean James M. Landis of Harvard Law School. Interview with Landis, 84 (1963–1964), COHP part II. Cardozo did not drink or serve alcohol at his home during Prohibition. Hellman, *Cardozo*, 65–66, 225.

36. Stroock, "Recollections," 1 *Cardozo Law Review* 20, 22 (1979); author interview with Stroock, KCC. See Hellman notes of a meeting with Alan Stroock (Nov. 6, 1938), CCC, Box 8, also reporting some comments that were critical of Cardozo. Stroock knew Cardozo before becoming his law clerk. See Cardozo, Commonplace Book, II, 2, CCC, Box 5, recording that in 1929 Cardozo had read an essay on Plato that Stroock had written while in college.

37. Letter from Margaret Chanler to George Hellman, Mar. 3, 1939, CCC, Box 1.

38. Author interview with Rauh, 52, KCC.

39. 1 Commonplace Book [36], CCC, Box 5. The quotation is from John Galsworthy, *The Forsyte Saga*, 36 (1922).

40. See Cardozo, appointment book for 1937, original in possession of Joseph Rauh family, copy in KCC.

41. Robert Marshall notes of a lunch with Cardozo (Mar. 21, 1937), original in possession of George Marshall family, copy in KCC; author interview with Rauh, 51, 52, KCC.

42. Author interview with Hayes, KCC.

43. See appointments with Gifford Mabie listed in Cardozo, appointment book for 1937, original in possession of Joseph Rauh family, copy in KCC.

44. Id., June 27, 1937.

45. Letter from Harry Shulman to Felix Frankfurter, May 4, 1935, FF. It was traditional for the Justices to announce their decisions on Monday "opinion

days" at that time. The opinion writers read or summarized their opinions in open court.

46. Letter from Cardozo to Joseph Paley, Sept. 11, 1935, JP. See also letter from Cardozo to Learned Hand, June 25, 1935, LH, and letter from Cardozo to Hortense and Walter Hirsch, Aug. 13, 1935, copy in KCC. As to the glycerine pills, see author interview with Rauh, 51, KCC.

47. Letter from Cardozo to Joseph Rauh, Sept. 1, 1937, original in possession of Joseph Rauh family, copy in KCC.

48. Letter from Cardozo to Rupert Joseph, July 27, 1937, CCC, Box 1; *New York Times,* 38 (June 29, 1937).

49. Letter from Cardozo to Felix Frankfurter, Sept. 21, 1937. The reference was to the German camps of the 1930s, largely for political opponents and not yet the instruments of horror that they became in the 1940s.

50. Letter from Cardozo to Learned Hand, July 6, 1932, LH.

51. Letter from Cardozo to Charles C. Burlingham, Nov. 17, 1932, CCB.

52. Letter from Cardozo to Charles C. Burlingham, Mar. 6, 1933, CCB.

53. Author interview with Siegel, 36, KCC.

54. Author interview with Rauh, 15, KCC; letter from Franklin Roosevelt to Cardozo, Jan. 4, 1938, CCC, Box 1.

55. *New York Times,* 1 (Sept. 7, 1935). See *New York Law Journal,* 1 (Sept. 11, 1935) for Brodsky's full opinion. For more on Brodsky, see Herbert Mitgang, *The Man Who Rode the Tiger,* 190–191 (1966 ed.).

56. Letter to Aline Goldstone, Sept. 14, 1935, original in possession of Goldstone family, excerpt in KCC.

57. Letter from Cardozo to Felix Frankfurter, Jan. 31, 1936, FF.

58. Interview with Charles Wyzanski, 242 (1954), COHP Part V.

59. Author interview with Stroock, KCC. Further discussion of Cardozo's relation to Judaism is contained in Andrew L. Kaufman, "Benjamin N. Cardozo, Sephardic Jew," in *The Jewish Justices of the Supreme Court Revisited,* 35 (Jennifer Lowe, ed. 1994).

60. Author interview with Rauh, 42–43, KCC. See letter from Cardozo to Learned Hand, Sept. 26, 1937, LH, referring to Hand's "interesting and charming letter" from Italy. Hand's more considered views were strongly anti-Fascist. See Gerald Gunther, *Learned Hand,* 479–481 (1994).

61. Author interview with Rauh, 43–44, KCC; George Hellman interview with Doris Webster (Nov. 23, 1938), CCC, Box 9.

25. State Regulatory Power and the Constitution

1. See Cass Sunstein, "Constitutionalism After the New Deal," 101 *Harvard Law Review* 421 (1987); Bruce Ackerman, "The Storrs Lectures: Discovering the Constitution," 93 *Yale Law Journal* 1013 (1984).

2. See chap. 19, text at note 15.

3. Letter from Willis Van Devanter to his sister, Elisabeth V. Lacey, Feb. 29, 1932, Willis Van Devanter Papers, LC, Container 13.

4. Letter from Willis Van Devanter to Elisabeth V. Lacey, Sept. 29, 1932, Van Devanter Papers, LC. Two years later when he was again thinking of retiring, Brandeis paid a special visit to persuade him not to do so. Letter from Van Devanter to Elisabeth V. Lacey, June 23, 1934. Ibid.

5. Letter from Cardozo to Felix Frankfurter, Mar. 22, 1933, FF.

6. For a good analysis of Cardozo's opinions in common law issues in Supreme Court cases, see David N. Atkinson, "Mr. Justice Cardozo: A Common Law Judge on a Public Law Court," 17 *California Western Law Review* 257 (1981).

7. Cardozo, *The Nature of the Judicial Process,* 76. (1921).

8. Letter from Willis Van Devanter to Elisabeth V. Lacey, March 28, 1932, Van Devanter Papers, LC, Container 13.

9. 285 U.S. 434, 448 (1932).

10. Id. at 451. See Arnett v. Kennedy, 416 U.S. 134, rehearing denied, 417 U.S. 977 (1974), for more sophisticated analysis of that kind of positivist thinking.

11. Letter from Felix Frankfurter to Cardozo, Apr. 15, 1932, FF.

12. 288 U.S. 517 (1933).

13. 288 U.S. at 541.

14. Id. at 567.

15. Author interview with Melvin Siegel, 23–25 (June 26, 1958), KCC; Siegel, "A Personal View of Justice Benjamin N. Cardozo: Recollections of Four Cardozo Law Clerks," 1 *Cardozo Law Review* 5, 11, 14 (1979).

16. 288 U.S. at 580, 583.

17. Id. at 585–586.

18. Paul A. Freund, *The Supreme Court of the United States,* 124 (1961). See Lewis J. Paper, *Brandeis,* 331–335 (1983), for a discussion of this case from the perspective of Brandeis's law clerks.

19. Letter from Cardozo to Felix Frankfurter, Mar. 22, 1933, FF. Justice Stone joined Cardozo, but not Brandeis, because he thought it inappropriate to discuss the merits of the statute as opposed to the state's power to enact it. Alpheus T. Mason, *Harlan Fiske Stone,* 349–350 (1956).

20. 288 U.S. at 586.

21. 294 U.S. 87, rehearing denied, 294 U.S. 732 (1935).

22. Id. at 102.

23. Id. at 95–97. For an insightful modern discussion of aids to statutory interpretation, see David Shapiro, "Continuity and Change in Statutory Interpretation," 67 *New York University Law Review* 921 (1992) (also citing much of the recent academic discussion).

24. 294 U.S. 550, 566, rehearing denied, 295 U.S. 768 (1935). Brandeis and Stone joined Cardozo's dissent.

25. 296 U.S. 287, 297 (1935). Brandeis and Stone joined Cardozo's dissent.

26. Id. at 299.

27. 290 U.S. 398 (1934) and 291 U.S. 502 (1934).

28. Letter from Willis Van Devanter to Elisabeth V. Lacey, Jan. 23, 1934, Van Devanter Papers, LC, Container 13.

29. Mason, *Harlan Fiske Stone,* 360–365.

30. Unpublished concurring opinion of Cardozo in Home Building & Loan Association v. Blaisdell, 290 U.S. 398 (1934), 3–4, in Harlan Fiske Stone Papers, LC, Container 60. There are a few handwritten changes in the typewritten text that I have assumed were inserted by Cardozo or his clerk and not by Stone, but they do not change the substance of the typewritten views in any event. An excerpt from Cardozo's draft opinion has been published in Paul Brest and Sanford Levinson, *Processes of Constitutional Decisionmaking,* 349 (3d ed. 1992).

31. Cardozo unpublished concurring opinion in *Blaisdell,* 5–6, Stone Papers, LC.

32. Id. at 6.

33. Id. at 1, quoting from Marshall's opinion in McCulloch v. Maryland, 4 Wheat. 316, 407 (1819).

34. Letter from Charles Evans Hughes to Harlan F. Stone, Jan. 4, 1934, including three new paragraphs that appear in Hughes's final version of the opinion at 290 U.S. 442–444. Stone Papers, LC, Container 60. See also Mason, *Harlan Fiske Stone,* 360–365.

35. 292 U.S. 426 (1934).

36. 295 U.S. 56 (1935).

37. Id. at 60.

38. There was an abortive revival of Contract Clause jurisprudence in the late 1970s. See United States Trust Co. of New York v. New Jersey, 431 U.S. 1 (1977); Allied Structural Steel v. Spannaus, 438 U.S. 234, rehearing denied, 439 U.S. 886 (1978); and Laurence Tribe, *American Constitutional Law,* 619–628 (2d ed. 1988).

39. 291 U.S. 502 (1934).

40. Tyson v. Banton, 273 U.S. 418 (1927). See discussion in chap. 19, text at note 42.

41. 293 U.S. 163, 171 (1934).

42. 297 U.S. 266 (1936).

43. Id. at 274. Brandeis and Stone joined Cardozo's dissent.

44. See chap. 19, text at note 43.

45. 298 U.S. 587 (1936).

46. Richard Friedman, "Switching Time and Other Thought Experiments:

The Hughes Court and Constitutional Transformation," 142 *University of Pennsylvania Law Review* 1891, 1947 (1994).

47. Letter from Cardozo to Harlan F. Stone, June 9, 1936, Stone Papers, LC. Stone responded, noting that a motion to reargue *Morehead* had been filed on the ground that the petition for certiorari had requested a reconsideration of *Adkins*. "Curious that our brethren, with their firm conviction as to the merits, should have resorted to such a flimsy evasion." Letter from Stone to Cardozo, June 30, 1936, Stone Papers, LC. The petition for rehearing was denied. 299 U.S. 619 (1936).

48. 300 U.S. 379 (1937).

49. Roberts's claim was embodied in a memorandum that he gave to Justice Frankfurter, who subsequently published it. Roberts's version of the facts was subjected to a withering attack in Michael Ariens, "A Thrice-Told Tale, or Felix the Cat," 107 *Harvard Law Review* 620 (1994), which also suggested that Frankfurter might have fabricated the Roberts memorandum for his own purposes. The fabrication possibility was convincingly refuted in Richard Friedman, "A Reaffirmation: The Authenticity of the Roberts Memorandum, or Felix the Non-Forger," 142 *University of Pennsylvania Law Review* 1985 (1994). A companion piece considers the accuracy of Roberts's claim quite sympathetically. Friedman, "Switching Time," 1939–1953. I was one of Frankfurter's law clerks when he published the Roberts memorandum. Professor Friedman's description of the memorandum jogged my memory, and I now think that in 1956 I saw the memorandum, conceivably for the purpose of proofreading Frankfurter's manuscript. The memorandum and other material have disappeared from the Frankfurter Papers in the Library of Congress.

50. Letter from Charles C. Burlingham to Harlan F. Stone, June 11, 1936, Stone Papers, LC.

26. National Regulatory Power and the Constitution

1. See chap. 19, text at note 44.

2. 288 U.S. 294 (1933).

3. This analysis of *Norwegian Nitrate* is based on the insights of Daniel Tarullo in "Law and Politics in Twentieth Century Tariff History," 34 *UCLA Law Review* 285, 333–345 (1986).

4. Louis Jaffe, *Judicial Control of Administrative Action*, 63, note 104 (1965).

5. 288 U.S. at 321.

6. See 19 U.S.C. §1351 (1982) for the current version.

7. 293 U.S. 388 (1935).

8. Id. at 433, 440.

9. Id. at 440.

10. Jaffe, *Judicial Control of Administrative Action*, 63.

11. 295 U.S. 495, 551 (1935).

12. The second unanimous decision invalidated the Frazier-Lemke Act, the federal farm bankruptcy act, in Louisville Joint Stock Land Bank v. Radford, 295 U.S. 555 (1935) because the statute in *Radford* substantially modified the ability of a mortgagee to realize upon its security. Although the federal government was not limited by the Contract Clause, federal power under the Bankruptcy Clause was limited by the due process clause of the Fifth Amendment. The third unanimous decision denied the president power to remove a Federal Trade Commissioner. Humphrey's Executor v. United States, 295 U.S. 602 (1935).

13. 295 U.S. at 551.

14. Copies of the many drafts are in KCC. Percy Russell, Cardozo's secretary-clerk, kept Cardozo's handwritten draft opinions during his period of service and made copies available to the author.

15. Author interview with Joseph L. Rauh, Jr., 20 (July 2, 1958), KCC.

16. 295 U.S. at 551, 553. For further discussion of the delegation issue, see Todd Rakoff, "The Shape of Law in the American Administrative State," in 11 *Tel Aviv University Studies in Law* 9, 21–25 (1992).

17. See Alpheus T. Mason, *Harlan Fiske Stone*, 369–374 (1956).

18. 294 U.S. 240 (1935).

19. Letter from Cardozo to Aline Goldstone, Mar. 15, 1935, original in possession of Goldstone family, excerpt in KCC.

20. 300 U.S. 324 (1937).

21. Id. at 340.

22. See, for example, Wickard v. Filburn, 317 U.S. 111 (1942).

23. 294 U.S. 330 (1935). Hughes's opinion was a majority opinion because eight Justices thought the repudiation unconstitutional, and Justice Stone joined the four who concurred in Hughes's opinion on the damage issue.

24. Note from Cardozo to Charles Evans Hughes, undated, on the *Perry* opinion, Charles Evans Hughes Papers, LC.

25. For further discussion, see Richard Friedman, "Switching Time and Other Thought Experiments: The Hughes Court and Constitutional Transformation," 142 *University of Pennsylvania Law Review* 1891, 1923–1927 (1994), and authorities collected therein.

26. Stone later concluded in another case that the constitutional power to regulate the value of money gave the government the same power to abrogate gold clauses in government bonds as it had in private contracts. Smyth v. United States, 302 U.S. 329, 360 (1937). In *Smyth*, Cardozo wrote for the Court in

permitting the federal government to redeem its own bonds early pursuant to the contract although it was repudiating its obligation to pay a fixed gold value. Cardozo, who thought the repudiation unconstitutional, had a much harder time reaching that conclusion than Stone, who did not think so. In conference, Cardozo reported, Stone "sure rubbed it in." Author interview with Rauh, 28, KCC.

27. See Laurence Tribe, *American Constitutional Law,* 381 (2d ed. 1988).

28. 296 U.S. 315 (1935).

29. Letter to Felix Frankfurter, Dec. 14, 1935, FF. It is possible that he meant that the field was a new one to him, but I do not think so, for he contrasted the opinion to that in United States v. Constantine, which he did not regard as "a new one," although it was certainly new to him.

30. 297 U.S. 1 (1936).

31. Justice Frankfurter wrote in the margin of his copy of 297 U.S. 1, 66 (1936), the following report of a subsequent colloquy between himself and Justice Roberts: "F.F.: I hope you now realize what a door you opened in your shall I say much-discussed Butler decision as to scope of 'general welfare.' O.J.R.: I do realize it, and often wonder why the hell I did it just to please the Chief." Justice Frankfurter's set of United States Reports, which he kept in his study at home, is in the author's possession.

32. 297 U.S. at 78, 88.

33. 298 U.S. 513, rehearing denied, 299 U.S. 619 (1936).

34. Id. at 532.

35. Id. at 542.

36. Id. at 541. Two years later, the Court restricted the scope of *Ashton* by upholding the constitutionality of a portion of the Bankruptcy Act passed after *Ashton* that also permitted various state instrumentalities, with state consent, to compose their debts in bankruptcy court proceedings. United States v. Bekins, 304 U.S. 27, rehearing denied, 304 U.S. 589 (1938). Cardozo, who was then quite ill, did not participate in the case.

37. United States Constitution, art. 1, §8, cl. 3.

38. United States v. E. C. Knight Co., 156 U.S. 1, 16 (1895).

39. Id. at 14. See also Hammer v. Dagenhart, 247 U.S. 251 (1918), holding unconstitutional a congressional statute prohibiting the transportation in interstate commerce of goods manufactured by a factory employing children under a certain age. The holding was based on a conclusion that the aim of the statute was to regulate manufacturing, to which the commerce power did not reach.

40. Houston, East and West Texas R. Co. v. United States, 234 U.S. 342 (1914).

41. Id. at 351.

42. 295 U.S. 330 (1935).

43. He also concluded that certain provisions violated the Due Process Clause of the Fifth Amendment.

44. Letter from Cardozo to Charles Evans Hughes, Apr. 19, 1935, copy to Justice Stone, Stone Papers, Container 61, LC. I believe that this letter, the copy of which is unsigned, is from Cardozo and not from Brandeis, the other dissenter. Alpheus Mason so identified it, Mason, *Harlan Fiske Stone*, 393, and Cardozo worked often with Stone in this fashion.

45. See 295 U.S. at 381–384.

46. 295 U.S. 495 (1935).

47. 295 U.S. at 554. Cardozo also used the common law treatment of problems of causation as an analogy to help decide when a case "arose under" federal law so as to confer jurisdiction on federal courts. Gully v. First National Bank, 299 U.S. 109 (1936). Countless claims could "arise under" the Constitution or some federal statute if one searched hard enough. Causation problems had been resolved by "a selective process which picks the substantial causes out of the web and lays the other ones aside." The federal jurisdiction problem was resolved by formulating "the distinction between controversies that are basic and those that are collateral, between disputes that are necessary and those that are merely possible." Id. at 118.

48. 312 U.S. 100 (1941) *(Darby)* and 317 U.S. 111 (1942) *(Filburn)*. But see United States v. Lopez, 115 S. Ct. 1624 (1995), in which the Supreme Court took a small step toward resurrecting an area of private conduct immune from congressional regulation under the Commerce Clause.

49. 298 U.S. 238 (1936).

50. Id. at 307–308.

51. Id. at 324, 327–328.

52. See, for example, United States v. Darby, 312 U.S. 100, 117–124 (1941) and Wickard v. Filburn, 317 U.S. 111, 125–129 (1942).

53. 298 U.S. at 329.

54. Letter from Cardozo to Learned Hand, July 31, 1936, LH.

55. Letter from Harlan F. Stone to Helen Stone Willard, June 2, 1936, Stone Papers, LC, Container 4, quoted in Mason, *Harlan Fiske Stone*, 425.

56. See Merlo J. Pusey, *Charles Evans Hughes*, II, 754–757 (1951).

57. Author interview with Rauh, 16–17, KCC.

58. Letter from Cardozo to Charles Burlingham, Apr. 2, 1937, CCB.

59. Author interview with Rauh, 16–17, KCC.

60. See chap. 25, text at note 44.

61. 301 U.S. 1 (1937).

62. The companion cases were National Labor Relations Board v. Fruehauf Trailer Co., 301 U.S. 49 (1937) and National Labor Relations Board v. Friedman-Harry Marks Clothing Co., 301 U.S. 58 (1937).

63. Author interview with Rauh, 18–19, KCC.

64. Id. at 41.

65. Id. at 43. The argument echoed his earlier landmark opinion in the *Shreveport* case.

66. Note from Cardozo to Charles Evans Hughes on *Jones & Laughlin* opinion, Box 157, Hughes Papers, LC. Roberts's vote, however, was not a return to the fold. It represented a new direction for him. Whether his vote was a reaction to the Court-packing plan, the 1936 elections, or other causes is discussed with insight in Friedman, "Switching Time," 1967–1974.

67. Richard Friedman, "On Cardozo and Reputation: Legendary Judge, Underrated Justice?" 12 *Cardozo Law Review* 1923, 1936 (1991).

68. Letter from Cardozo to Felix Frankfurter, Apr. 13, 1937, FF.

69. 301 U.S. 548 (1937) and 301 U.S. 619, opinion amended 301 U.S. 672 (1937).

70. 301 U.S. at 639; author interview with Rauh, 7–8, 11, KCC.

71. 301 U.S. at 589–590.

72. Id. at 591.

73. Cardozo also rejected other arguments made by Steward. He used history to demonstrate numerous instances going back to colonial times when taxes had been laid on employment. Id. at 579–580.

74. Id. at 609.

75. Id. at 616.

76. Id. at 599.

77. See Pusey, *Charles Evans Hughes*, II, 749–765.

78. Roger K. Newman, *Hugo Black*, 237–239 (1994).

79. 9 Wheat. 1 (1824).

80. 294 U.S. 511 (1935).

81. Id. at 523.

82. Id. at 527.

83. 300 U.S. 577 (1937).

84. Thomas Reed Powell, *Vagaries and Varieties in Constitutional Interpretation*, 190 (1956).

85. Ernest J. Brown, "The Open Economy: Justice Frankfurter and the Position of the Judiciary," 67 *Yale Law Journal* 219, 233–235 (1957).

86. 300 U.S. at 585–586.

87. 294 U.S. at 522, 527. Professor Brown's comment that "normally no price competition arises between farmers in the sale of milk" was not supported by any reference to testimony in either case or in any other source of information. Brown, "Open Economy," 235.

88. See Felix Frankfurter, "Mr. Justice Cardozo and Public Law," 52 *Harvard Law Review* 440 (1939) for a review of Cardozo's public law decisions from the perspective of 1939.

27. Civil Liberties, Race, and Other Supreme Court Issues

1. 262 U.S. 390 (1923) and 268 U.S. 510 (1925).

2. 262 U.S. at 399. Holmes and Sutherland dissented in *Meyer,* but the Court was unanimous in *Pierce.*

3. "No State shall make or enforce any law which shall abridge the privileges or immunities of citizens of the United States." Amend. XIV, §1.

4. See the Slaughter-House Cases, 16 Wall. 36 (1873). Cardozo dissented from the Court's resuscitation of the Privileges or Immunities Clause to strike down a discriminatory state tax in Colgate v. Harvey, 296 U.S. 404 (1935), but *Colgate* was quickly overruled in Madden v. Kentucky, 309 U.S. 83 (1940).

5. Stromberg v. California, 283 U.S. 359 (1931) and Near v. Minnesota, 283 U.S. 697 (1931).

6. 293 U.S. 245, 265 (1934), rehearing denied, 293 U.S. 633 (1935).

7. 297 U.S. 233 (1936).

8. Id. at 266.

9. No Justice saw the selectiveness of the required training as minimizing the state's assertion of need or as operating unconstitutionally in that only selected citizens—those seeking to enter the state university—were being forced to take action against their religious beliefs. It would take many years before the free exercise clause would be seen as presenting a constitutional obstacle to the placing of otherwise reasonable conditions on benefits granted by the state. See Sherbert v. Verner, 374 U.S. 398 (1963) and Torcaso v. Watkins, 367 U.S. 488 (1961). Cf. West Virginia State Bd. of Education v. Barnette, 319 U.S. 624 (1943).

10. Letter from Cardozo to Harlan Fiske Stone, Nov. 20, 1934, Stone Papers, LC.

11. 293 U.S. at 266.

12. 293 U.S. at 266, 268.

13. Letter from Cardozo to Stephen Wise, Dec. 8, 1934, SSW.

14. 10 F. Supp. 161 (E.D. La. 1935).

15. Cardozo draft opinion in Grosjean v. American Press Co., 297 U.S. 233 (1936), 2, 11–12, copy in KCC. This draft was made available to the author by Percy Russell, Cardozo's secretary–law clerk at the time.

16. Id. at 7. The reference was to John Marshall's language in McCulloch v. Maryland, 4 Wheat. 316 (1819), referring to Maryland's tax on bank notes issued by the Bank of the United States.

17. 297 U.S. at 9.

18. Justice Stone, in agreeing with Sutherland's redrafted opinion, suggested successfully that sentences that clearly indicated reliance on bad motives of the legislature as a ground for decision should be eliminated. Letter from Harlan F. Stone to George Sutherland, Feb. 5, 1936, Stone Papers, LC, Container 76.

19. John Ely, *Democracy and Distrust: A Theory of Judicial Review,* 143, 244–245, note 31 (1980).

20. Schenck v. United States, 249 U.S. 47, 52 (1919).

21. Compare Gitlow v. New York, 268 U.S. 652 (1925) with Dennis v. United States, 341 U.S. 494 (1951), rehearings denied, 342 U.S. 842 (1951), 355 U.S. 936 (1958).

22. 274 U.S. 380 (1927). A good summary of the debate within the Court is contained in Gerald Gunther, *Constitutional Law,* 1008–1039 (12th ed. 1991). See also Gerald Gunther, *Learned Hand,* 151–170, 280–281 (1994).

23. People v. Gitlow, 234 N.Y. 132, 154, 539 (1922), aff'd, 268 U.S. 652 (1925) (Holmes and Brandeis dissenting). See also Zechariah Chafee, Jr., *Free Speech in the United States,* 318–325 (1954).

24. 295 U.S. 441, rehearing denied, 296 U.S. 661 (1935).

25. 295 U.S. at 453. A full treatment of the Herndon trial is contained in Kendall Thomas, *"Rouge et Noir* Reread: A Popular Constitutional History of the Angelo Herndon Case," 65 *Southern California Law Review* 2599 (1992).

26. Cardozo had earlier been quite rigid in confining habeas corpus to testing jurisdiction and not permitting its use to test unconstitutional application of a valid statute. People ex rel. Doyle v. Atwell, 232 N.Y. 96, 103 (1921) (Cardozo, concurring). The Supreme Court had plainly held the ordinance in that case unconstitutional as applied.

27. 299 U.S. 353 (1937).

28. 301 U.S. 242 (1937).

29. See author interview with Joseph Rauh, 12–13 (July 2, 1958), KCC. Mr. Rauh was Cardozo's law clerk during the 1936 and 1937 terms.

30. Chafee, *Free Speech,* 393.

31. 301 U.S. 103 (1937).

32. Semler v. Oregon State Board of Dental Examiners, 294 U.S. 608 (1935).

33. See Bates v. State Bar of Arizona, 433 U.S. 350, rehearing denied, 434 U.S. 881 (1977), effectively overruling *Semler.*

34. 287 U.S. 45 (1932).

35. Butler and McReynolds dissented on this point and did not reach the due process issue.

36. 294 U.S. 587 (1935). But subsequently five of the nine defendants were retried and convicted, and four were released.

37. 291 U.S. 97 (1934).

38. Another case in which Cardozo first voted (and wrote) one way and then wrote the opposite way was United States v. Swift & Co., 286 U.S. 106 (1932), an important antitrust case in which Cardozo's opinion set a very high standard for modifying a consent decree at the request of the defendant. There must be "a clear showing of grievous wrong evoked by new and unforeseen conditions." Id. at 119. See Phillip Areeda and Herbert Hovenkamp, *Antitrust Law,* II, 172

(Rev. ed. 1995) for discussion of the case and its aftermath. Excerpts from Cardozo's original draft opinion are printed in Milton Handler and Michael Ruby, "Justice Cardozo: One-Ninth of the Supreme Court," 10 *Cardozo Law Review* 235, 252–258 (1988).

39. 291 U.S. at 105–106.

40. Id. at 108.

41. Id. at 113.

42. Id. at 114.

43. Id. at 116, 122.

44. While Cardozo used the prejudice analysis to determine whether there was a constitutional right in the first place, the Supreme Court in modern times has dealt with a similar problem of prejudice and reversing convictions for constitutional violation in the context of its "harmless error" decisions. Compare Chapman v. California, 386 U.S. 18, rehearing denied, 386 U.S. 987 (1967) with Sullivan v. Louisiana, 113 S. Ct. 2078 (1993).

45. This opinion in *Snyder* provoked a heated disagreement between Felix Frankfurter and Edmund M. Morgan of the Harvard Law School, the former agreeing with the dissent and the latter with the majority. Frankfurter wrote Cardozo about his disagreement and sent Morgan a copy of his letter, but his letter to Cardozo and any response have disappeared. See letter from Felix Frankfurter to Edmund M. Morgan, Feb. 23, 1934, and letters from Morgan to Frankfurter, Mar. 5 and 30, 1934. A subsequent letter from Frankfurter to Morgan, Apr. 23, 1934, states that he probably would have voted with the majority. All the extant letters are in the Edmund M. Morgan Papers, HLS.

46. Author interview with Rauh, 30–31, KCC.

47. 302 U.S. 319 (1937).

48. See John T. Noonan, Jr., "Ordered Liberty: Cardozo and the Constitution," 1 *Cardozo Law Review* 257 (1979) for a detailed analysis of the case.

49. 302 U.S. at 325.

50. Ibid.

51. Id. at 326–327.

52. Kepner v. United States, 195 U.S. 100 (1904).

53. 302 U.S. at 323.

54. Id. at 328. An illuminating discussion of the relation of Cardozo's philosophy to his opinion in *Palko* is contained in Noonan, "Ordered Liberty." Noonan contended that Cardozo found most affinity with Spinoza's view of life. Perhaps, but after reading Spinoza's *Ethics,* Cardozo commented, "I am not satisfied I should know how great they are if the commentary did not assure me." Letter from Cardozo to Felix Frankfurter, Aug. 23, 1926, FF.

55. Benton v. Maryland, 395 U.S. 784 (1969).

56. 410 U.S. 113 (1973).

57. 286 U.S. 73 (1932).

58. 273 U.S. 536 (1927).

59. Milton Handler reported that Stone told him that justices had the right to select their first assignment. Handler believes that Cardozo selected Nixon v. Condon on the basis that it was the earliest case argued of the first six majority opinions that Cardozo delivered, all on May 2. Handler and Ruby, "Justice Cardozo," 238–239. But United States v. Swift & Co. was argued the same week as Nixon v. Condon, albeit two days later. Assignments were made at the end of a whole week of argument, and so it is entirely possible that Cardozo picked *Swift* and not *Condon,* if indeed there was such a practice. Paul Freund, who worked on the history of the Hughes era in the *History of the Supreme Court of the United States* project and knew as much as anyone about the workings of the Court at that time, told the author that he had never heard of such a practice.

60. 295 U.S. 45 (1935).

61. Compare the expansion of responsibility decreed in Smith v. Allwright, 321 U.S. 649, rehearing denied, 322 U.S. 769 (1944) and Terry v. Adams, 345 U.S. 461, rehearing denied, 345 U.S. 1003 (1953) with the retrenchment of doctrine in the public utilities case, Jackson v. Metropolitan Edison Co., 419 U.S. 345 (1974), and followed in subsequent cases. None of the participants in the *Grovey* case suggested that the Thirteenth Amendment reached this discrimination. See Jones v. Alfred H. Mayer Co., 392 U.S. 409 (1968).

62. Morrison v. California, 288 U.S. 591 (1933).

63. 291 U.S. 82 (1934).

64. Id. at 94.

65. Id. at 95.

66. Id. at 116, 122.

67. Edmund M. Morgan, "Federal Constitutional Limitations upon Presumptions Created by State Legislation," in *Harvard Legal Essays,* 323, 346–351 (1934).

68. Letter from Edmund Morgan to Felix Frankfurter, Mar. 5, 1934, Edmund Morgan Papers, HLS. In Frankfurter's view, "for once" Cardozo was "fair sport," but in Frankfurter's view this was not because of his *Morrison* opinion but because of his *Snyder* opinion. Letter from Felix Frankfurter to Edmund Morgan, Feb. 23, 1934, ibid.

69. See chap. 13, text at note 22.

70. 290 U.S. 111 (1933). See chap. 3, text at note 3.

71. 290 U.S. at 115.

72. See Bernard Wolfman, "Professors and the 'Ordinary and Necessary' Business Expense," 112 *University of Pennsylvania Law Review* 1089 (1964); letter from Professor Calvin Johnson to author, Apr. 20, 1993, KCC; telephone interview with Professor Wayne Barnett, May 9, 1993. Justice Kennedy has sought to reduce the mischief-making capacity of the phrase, noting that it

"must not deter us from deciding upon some rules for the fair and consistent interpretation of a statute that speaks in the most general of terms." But he saw a kernel of wisdom in the phrase as well: "Yet we accept [Cardozo's] implicit assertion that there are limits to the guidance from appellate courts in these cases. The consequent necessity to give considerable deference to the trier of fact is but the law's recognition that the statute is designed to accommodate myriad and ever changing forms of business enterprise." Commissioner of Internal Revenue v. Soliman, 113 S. Ct. 701, 708 (1993).

73. 287 U.S. 358 (1932).

74. Cardozo's handwritten comment on the petition for certiorari in *Sunburst*, JP. Joseph Paley, who was still Cardozo's law clerk in the summer of 1932, kept all Cardozo's notes on the petitions for certiorari filed that summer. After Paley died, the material surfaced and was acquired jointly by Harvard Law School, Columbia University, and Cardozo Law School. The originals are at Cardozo Law School, with photocopies in CCC and JP.

75. 287 U.S. at 365.

76. See Walter V. Schaefer, *The Control of "Sunbursts": Techniques of Prospective Overruling* (1967).

77. 298 U.S. 1 (1936).

78. Id. at 32.

79. Id. at 33.

80. *Chicago Tribune*, 12 (Apr. 18, 1936).

81. Author interview with Felix Frankfurter, 13 (Aug. 21, 1960), KCC.

82. George Hellman interview with Alan Stroock (Apr. 19, 1961), CCC, Box 8.

83. See Richard Friedman, "On Cardozo and Reputation: Legendary Judge, Underrated Justice?" 12 *Cardozo Law Review* 1923, 1932 (1991): "Cardozo's was one of the greatest short tenures on the Court in its history."

28. Legacy

1. Author interview with Joseph L. Rauh, Jr., 47 (July 2, 1958), KCC.

2. Roger K. Newman, *Hugo Black*, 268 (1994).

3. Author interview with Joseph L. Rauh, Jr., 26–29 (July 2, 1958), KCC. *Smyth* is discussed in chap. 26, note 26.

4. Author interview with Rauh, 31, 36–38 (July 2, 1958), KCC; letter from Joseph Rauh to Felix Frankfurter, Feb. 15, 1938, KCC; 26 letters from Joseph Rauh to Jane Perry Clark between Dec. 15, 1937, and July 9, 1938, CCC, Box 8; letter from Michael H. Cardozo IV to author, April 8, 1988, KCC; and *New York Times*, 17 (July 12, 1938).

5. Author interview with Learned Hand, 19 (Nov. 12, 1957), KCC.

6. Felix Frankfurter, "Benjamin Nathan Cardozo," *Dictionary of American Biography,* 94 (Supp. 2, 1958).

7. The more thoughtful were Bernard Shientag, "The Opinions and Writings of Judge Benjamin N. Cardozo," 30 *Columbia Law Review* 597 (1930); Beryl Levy, *Cardozo and Frontiers of Legal Thinking,* 83–111 (1938); Walton Hamilton, "Cardozo the Craftsman," 6 *The University of Chicago Law Review* 1 (1938); and Edwin Patterson, "Cardozo's Philosophy of Law," 88 *University of Pennsylvania Law Review* 71, 156 (1939).

8. 39 *Columbia Law Review* 1 (1939); 52 *Harvard Law Review* 353 (1939); and 48 *Yale Law Journal* 371 (1939).

9. Compared with his colleagues, he cited three times as many secondary sources and twice as many cases. He was also notable on his court for his regular citation of federal and British cases. See William Manz, "The Citation Practices of the New York Court of Appeals," 43 *Buffalo Law Review* 139, 147 (1995).

10. 71 *Yale Law Journal* 195 (1961).

11. John T. Noonan, Jr., *Persons and Masks of the Law,* 111–151 (1976); 1 *Cardozo Law Review* 1–342 (1979).

12. For example, Thomas G. Barnes, introduction to Cardozo, *Cardozo on the Law* (1982); Paul Brickner, "Justice Benjamin N. Cardozo: A Fresh Look at a Great Judge," 11 *Ohio Northern University Law Review* 1 (1984); Alfred Konefsky, "How to Read, Or at Least Not Misread, Cardozo in the *Allegheny College* Case," 36 *Buffalo Law Review* 645 (1987); Edgar Bodenheimer, "Cardozo's Views on Law and Adjudication Revisited," 22 *University of California at Davis Law Review* 1095 (1989); Benjamin A. Zelermyer, "Benjamin N. Cardozo: A Directive Force in Legal Science," 69 *Boston University Law Review* 213 (1989); John C. P. Goldberg, "Community and the Common Law Judge: Reconstructing Cardozo's Theoretical Writings," 65 *New York University Law Review* 1324 (1990); Joshua Davis, "Cardozo's Judicial Craft and What Cases Come to Mean," 68 *New York University Law Review* 777 (1993); Joseph W. Bellacosa, "Benjamin Nathan Cardozo: The Teacher," 50 *Record of the Association of the Bar of the City of New York* 4 (1995); and Lawrence Cunningham, "Cardozo and Posner: A Study in Contracts," 36 *William and Mary Law Review* 1379 (1995).

13. "You don't have to be Justice Cardozo to arrive at these conclusions," *New York Times,* 22 (Nov. 15, 1994) (a lawyer commenting on certain trial rulings in the O. J. Simpson murder case); a description of a current judge as "no Cardozo," *New York Times,* B4 (Feb. 1, 1991); "We can't have all Brandeises, Frankfurters, and Cardozos," *New York Times,* 21 (Mar. 17, 1970) (Senator Roman Hruska, defending the appointment of mediocre judges to the Supreme Court of the United States); and *New York Times,* 1 (May 14, 1994), and 17 (Oct. 6, 1991) (testing the merits of a Supreme Court nominee by comparison with Cardozo).

14. See Richard A. Posner, *Cardozo: A Study in Reputation,* 19, note 38 (1990).

15. Thomas Reed Powell, "The Behavior of Judges," 114 *The Nation* 347 (Mar. 22, 1922) (reviewing *The Nature of the Judicial Process*).

16. See chap. 22, text at note 3.

17. The transformation in the relation between equitable and common law doctrines after the two systems were merged in the nineteenth century is a subject that requires more extended discussion than I have space for in this book. It was a major legal development that has been substantially ignored.

18. Cardozo, *The Nature of the Judicial Process,* 113–114 (1921).

19. See chap. 13, text preceding note 16.

20. Morton J. Horwitz, *The Transformation of American Law, 1870–1960,* 189 (1992).

21. William W. Fisher, Morton J. Horwitz, and Thomas A. Reed, eds., *American Legal Realism,* 3 (1993).

22. Posner, *Cardozo,* 104, 118.

23. *New York Times,* section 4, 17 (July 25, 1993), quoting from Cardozo, *The Growth of the Law,* 133 (1924).

24. Will of Benjamin N. Cardozo, KCC; Probate of the will of Benjamin N. Cardozo, File No. 1372–1938, Surrogate's Office, Westchester County, White Plains, N.Y.

25. *New York Times,* 19 (July 12, 1938). A copy of the funeral service program is in KCC.

26. Letter from Michael Cardozo IV to author, June 14, 1988, KCC; *New York Times,* 17 (July 12, 1938).

Index of Cases

General Index